AFRICA YEARBOOK

AFRICA YEARBOOK

Volume 10

Politics, Economy and Society South of the Sahara in 2013

EDITED BY

ANDREAS MEHLER
HENNING MELBER
KLAAS VAN WALRAVEN

SUB-EDITOR

ROLF HOFMEIER

BRILL

LEIDEN • BOSTON
2014

ISSN 1871-2525
ISBN 978-90-04-27477-8 (paperback)
ISBN 978-90-04-28264-3 (e-book)

This book is printed on acid-free paper.

Contents

Preface

In May 2003, the Africa-Europe Group of Interdisciplinary Studies (AEGIS) encouraged some of its member institutions to publish an *Africa Yearbook* with a wider international appeal. The African Studies Centre in Leiden (ASC), the Institute of African Affairs in Hamburg (IAA) and the Nordic Africa Institute in Uppsala (NAI) – all very active AEGIS centres sharing similar profiles – accepted this challenge and their joint efforts first bore fruit in the initial volume of the series in 2004. In 2007, the Dag Hammarskjöld Foundation in Uppsala (DHF) joined this international project, while the NAI ended its involvement with the fifth volume, published in 2009. For this current volume, Rolf Hofmeier once again joined us as sub-editor for the Eastern Africa section. We have always valued his solid input and remain grateful for his reliable services.

The country-specific articles cover domestic politics, foreign affairs and socioeconomic developments in the states of sub-Saharan Africa during the calendar year under review. While we recognise the impossibility of finding fully objective indicators for the relative importance of each of the states covered by the *Yearbook*, the length of the country-specific articles aims to reflect the approximate weight of each country. The four sub-regions are also introduced by means of an overview article. Further overviews summarise general continental developments, European-African relations and the United Nations and Africa.

The *Yearbook* is based on scholarly work, but is oriented towards a wider target readership, including students, politicians, diplomats, administrators, journalists, teachers, practitioners in the sphere of development cooperation and business people. Without forcing the individual contributions too much into a straitjacket, the volume is primarily concerned with providing factual (though not necessarily neutral) information. Each issue, in focusing almost exclusively on developments during a particular calendar year, provides a completely fresh annual overview of events and thereby adds to the cumulative record of ongoing developments

In November 2012, the *Yearbook* received the prestigious biennial Conover-Porter Award for outstanding Africa-related reference works from the African Studies Association and the Africana Librarians Council in the United States. This was an encouraging sign that the *Yearbook* has become a permanent and appreciated feature in Africanist publishing. The same year, thanks to a generous arrangement by Brill, the Africa Institute of South Africa joined as an African co-publisher, thereby greatly enhancing local distribution on the continent.

This is the tenth volume, and we are proud to have covered one decade of African affairs in what we believe is a solid scholarly contribution towards a better understanding of and more knowledge about sub-Saharan African countries. We wish to express our gratitude to all the contributors for their collaboration in this endeavour; to the partner institutions in AEGIS for encouraging us to embark on this ambitious project; to Carol Rowe for her meticulous language editing; to Bas van der Mije for his unfailing coordinating assistance; and to Brill Publishers for their continued commitment. Last but not least, we once again wish to thank our three institutions for their ongoing support.

John Daniel had been among the contributors to all ten volumes published so far. Gero Erdmann contributed to the first eight volumes. Both passed away in July. We dedicate this volume to their memory.

The Editors
(Hamburg, Leiden and Uppsala, September 2014)

List of Abbreviations

ABN	Autorité du Bassin du Niger (Niamey)
ACP	African, Caribbean, and Pacific Group of Countries (Lomé/Cotonou Agreement)
ADF	African Development Fund (Tunis)
AfDB	African Development Bank (Tunis)
AFD	Agence Française de Développement (Paris)
AGOA	African Growth and Opportunity Act
AI	Amnesty International
APRM	African Peer Review Mechanism
AU	African Union (Addis Ababa)
BCEAO	Banque Centrale des Etats de l'Afrique de l'Ouest (Dakar)
BEAC	Banque des Etats de l'Afrique Centrale (Yaoundé)
CAR	Central African Republic
CBLT	Commission du Bassin du Lac Tchad (N'Djaména)
CEEAC	Communauté Economique des Etats de l'Afrique Centrale (Libreville) = ECCAS
CEMAC	Communauté Economique et Monétaire de l'Afrique Centrale
CEN-SAD	Community of Sahel-Saharan States (Tripoli)
CEPGL	Communauté Economique des Pays des Grands Lacs (Gisenyi/Rwanda)
CFAfr	Franc de la Communauté Financière Africaine (BCEAO; BEAC)
COMESA	Common Market for Eastern and Southern Africa (Lusaka)
CPLP	Comunidade dos Países de Língua Portuguesa
DAC	Development Assistance Committee (Paris)
DDR	Disarmament, Demobilisation and Reintegration
DFID	Department for International Development (London)
DRC	Democratic Republic of the Congo
EAC	East African Community (Arusha)
ECA	Economic Commission for Africa (United Nations; Addis Ababa)
ECCAS	Economic Community of Central African States (Libreville)
ECF	Extended Credit Facility (IMF)
ECOWAS	Economic Community of West African States (Abuja)
ECOMOG	ECOWAS Ceasefire Monitoring Group

EDF	European Development Fund (Brussels)
EIB	European Investment Bank (Luxemburg)
EPA	Economic Partnership Agreement
ESAF	Enhanced Structural Adjustment Facility (IMF)
EU	European Union (Brussels)
FAO	Food and Agricultural Organisation (Rome)
FDI	Foreign Direct Investment
FTA	Free Trade Area
GDP	Gross Domestic Product
HDI	Human Development Index (UNDP)
HIPC	Heavily Indebted Poor Countries
HRW	Human Rights Watch
ICC	International Criminal Court (The Hague)
ICG	International Crisis Group
ICGLR	International Conference on the Great Lakes Region
IDA	International Development Association (Washington)
IDP	Internally Displaced Person
IFAD	International Fund for Agricultural Development (Rome)
IFC	International Finance Corporation (Washington)
IGAD	Intergovernmental Authority on Development (Djibouti)
ILO	International Labour Organisation (Geneva)
IMF	International Monetary Fund (Washington)
IOC	Indian Ocean Commission (Ebène/Mauritius)
IOR-ARC	Indian Ocean Rim Association for Regional Cooperation (Ebène/Mauritius)
MDGs	Millennium Development Goals
MDRI	Multilateral Debt Relief Initiative
MRU	Mano River Union (Freetown)
NEPAD	New Partnership for Africa's Development
NGO	Non-Governmental Organisation
OAU	Organization of African Unity
ODA	Official Development Assistance
OECD	Organisation for Economic Cooperation and Development (Paris)
OIC	Organisation of the Islamic Conference (Jeddah)
OIF	Organisation Internationale de la Francophonie (Paris)
OPEC	Organisation of Petroleum Exporting Countries (Vienna)
PALOP	Países Africanos de Lingua Oficial Portugesa
PPP	Purchasing Power Parity
PRGF	Poverty Reduction and Growth Facility
PRSC	Poverty Reduction Support Credit

PRSP	Poverty Reduction Strategy Paper
PTA	Preferential Trade for Eastern and Southern African States (now COMESA)
SACU	Southern African Customs Union (Pretoria)
SADC	Southern African Development Community (Gaborone)
SAF	Structural Adjustment Facility (IMF)
SDR	Special Drawing Right (IMF)
SSA	Sub-Saharan Africa
TI	Transparency International
UAE	United Arab Emirates
UEMOA	Union Économique et Monétaire Ouest-Africaine (Ouagadougou)
UMA	Union du Maghreb Arabe
UN	United Nations (New York)
UNCTAD	United Nations Conference on Trade and Development (Geneva)
UNDP	United Nations Development Programme (New York)
UNEP	United Nations Environment Programme (Nairobi)
UNECA	United Nations Economic Commission for Africa (Addis Ababa)
UNESCO	United Nations Educational, Scientific and Cultural Organisation (Paris)
UNHCR	United Nations High Commissioner for Refugees (Geneva)
UNICEF	United Nations Children's Fund (New York)
UNSC	United Nations Security Council
USAID	United States Agency for International Development (Washington)
WFP	World Food Programme (Rome)
WHO	World Health Organisation (Geneva)
WTO	World Trade Organisation (Geneva)

Factual Overview (as of 31 December 2013)

West Africa

Country	*Area (in sq km)*	*Population (in m)*[1]	*Currency*	*HDI (2012)*	*Head of State*	*Prime Minister*
Benin	112,622	9.6	CFA Franc	0.436	Boni Yayi	
Burkina Faso	274,122	18.0	CFA Franc	0.343	Blaise Compaoré	Luc-Adolphe Tiao
Cape Verde	4,033	0.5	Cape Verdean Escudo	0.586	Jorge Carlos Fonseca	José Maria Pereira Neves
Côte d'Ivoire	322,462	21.1	CFA Franc	0.432	Alassane Ouattara	Daniel Kablan Duncan
Gambia	11,295	1.9	Dalasi	0.439	Yahya Jammeh	
Ghana	238,500	26.1	Cedi	0.558	John Dramani Mahama	
Guinea	245,857	11.8	Guinean Franc	0.355	Alpha Condé	Mohamed Said Fofana
Guinea-Bissau	36,125	1.7	CFA Franc	0.364	Manuel Serifo Nhamadjo	Rui Duarte Barros
Liberia	111,370	4.4	Liberian Dollar	0.388	Ellen Johnson-Sirleaf	
Mali	1,240,000	15.5	CFA Franc	0.344	Ibrahim Boubacar Keita	Oumar Tatam Ly
Mauritania	1,030,700	3.7	Ouguiya	0.467	Mohamed Ould Abdel Aziz	Moulaye Ould Mohamed Laghdaf
Niger	1,267,000	16.9	CFA Franc	0.304	Mahamadou Issoufou	Brigi Rafini
Nigeria	923,768	173.6	Naira	0.471	Goodluck Jonathan	
Senegal	197,162	13.5	CFA Franc	0.470	Macky Sall	Aminata Toure
Sierra Leone	71,740	6.2	Leone	0.359	Ernest Bai Koroma	
Togo	56,785	6.2	CFA Franc	0.459	Faure Gnassingbé	Kwesi Ahoomey-Zunu

Central Africa

Country	*Area (in sq km)*	*Population (in m)*	*Currency*	*HDI*	*Head of State*	*Prime Minister*
Cameroon	475,442	21.5	CFA Franc	0.495	Paul Biya	Philemon Yang
Central African Republic	622,984	4.7	CFA Franc	0.352	Michel Djotodia	Nicolas Tiangaye
Chad	1,284,000	12.2	CFA Franc	0.340	Idriss Déby	Kalzeubet Pahimi Deubet
Congo	342,000	4.4	CFA Franc	0.534	Denis Sassou-Nguesso	
DR Congo	2,344,855	71.1	Congolese Franc	0.304	Joseph Kabila	Augustin Matata Ponyo Mapon
Equatorial Guinea	28,051	0.8	CFA Franc	0.554	Teodoro Obiang Nguema Mbasogo	Vicente Ehate Tomi
Gabon	267,667	1.6	CFA Franc	0.683	Ali Bongo Ondimba	Raymond Ndong Sima
São Tomé and Príncipe	1,001	0.2	Dobra	0.525	Manuel Pinto da Costa	Gabriel Arcanjo Ferreira da Costa

Eastern Africa

Country	*Area (in sq km)*	*Population (in m)*	*Currency*	*HDI*	*Head of State*	*Prime Minister*
Burundi	26,338	10.9	Burundi Franc	0.355	Pierre Nkurunziza	
Comoros	1.862	0.8	Comorian Franc	0.429	Ikililou Dhoinine	
Djibouti	23,200	0.9	Djibouti Franc	0.445	Ismail Omar Guelleh	Abdoulkader Mohamed Kamil
Eritrea	124,320	5.8	Nakfa	0.351	Isaias Afewerki	
Ethiopia	1,121,900	89.2	Birr	0.396	Mulatu Teshome	Hailemariam Desalegn
Kenya	569,259	44.2	Kenya Shilling	0.519	Uhuru Kenyatta	
Rwanda	26,338	11.1	Rwanda Franc	0.434	Paul Kagame	Pierre-Damien Habumuremyi
Seychelles	455	0.1	Seychelles Rupee	0.806.	James Michel	
Somalia	637,600	10.4	Somali Shilling	n.a.	Hassan Sheikh Mohamud	Abdiweli Sheikh Ahmed
(Somaliland)	137,600	3.6	Somaliland Shilling	n.a.	Ahmed Mohamed Mahamoud 'Silanyo'	
Sudan	2,505,805	34.2	Sudanese Pound	0.414	Omar Hassan Ahmad al-Bashir	
South Sudan	619,745	9.8	South Suda-nese Pound	n.a.	Salva Kiir Mayardit	
Tanzania	945,087	49.1	Tanzania Shilling	0.476	Jakaya Kikwete	Mizengo Pinda
Uganda	197.000	36.9	Uganda Shilling	0.456	Yoweri Kaguta Museveni	Amama Mbabazi

Southern Africa

Country	*Area (in sq km)*	*Population (in m)*	*Currency*	*HDI*	*Head of State*	*Prime Minister*
Angola	1,246,700	21.6	Kwanza	0.508	José Eduardo dos Santos	
Botswana	581,730	1.9	Pula	0.634	Seretse Khama Ian Khama	
Lesotho	30,344	2.2	Loti	0.461	King Letsie III	Thomas Motsoahae Thabane
Madagascar	592,000	22.5	Ariary	0.483	Andry Rajoelina (contested)	Jean Omer Beriziky
Malawi	118,484	16.3	Kwacha	0.418	Joyce Hilda Banda	
Mauritius	2,040	1.3	Mauritius Rupee	0.737	Rajkeswur Kailash Purryag	Navinchandra Ramgoolam
Mozambique	799,380	24.3	Métical	0.327	Armando Emilio Guebuza	Alberto Clementino Vaquina
Namibia	824,269	2.4	Namibian Dollar	0.608	Hifikepunye Lucas Pohamba	Hage Geingob
South Africa	1,219,090	53.0	Rand	0.629	Jacob Zuma	
Swaziland	17,364	1.2	Lilangeni	0.536	King Mswati III.	Sibusiso Dlamini
Zambia	752,614	14.2	Kwacha	0.448	Michael Chilufya Sata	
Zimbabwe	390,580	13.0	Zimbabwe Dollar	0.397	Robert Gabriel Mugabe	

(Population figures are for mid-2013 according to Stiftung Weltbevölkerung, www.weltbevölkerung.de)

List of Authors

Jon Abbink, Senior Researcher, African Studies Centre, Leiden, and Professor of African Studies at the VU University of Amsterdam, The Netherlands, abbink@ascleiden.nl

Kwesi Aning, Director, Faculty of Academic Affairs and Research (FAAR), Kofi Annan International Peacekeeping Training Centre, Accra, Ghana, Kwesi.Aning@kaiptc.org

Nancy Annan, Researcher, Faculty of Academic Affairs and Research (FAAR), Kofi Annan International Peacekeeping Training Centre, Ghana, Nancy.Annan@kaiptc.org

Alice Bellagamba, Associate Professor, Cultural and Social Anthropology, Department of Human Sciences for Education "Riccardo Massa", University of Milan-Bicocca, alice.bellagamba@unimib.it

Heinrich Bergstresser, Media Consultant, Freelance Research Associate of the Institute of African Affairs in Hamburg and Freelance Tutor of Deutsche Gesellschaft für Internationale Zusammenarbeit GIZ, Germany, heinrich.bergstresser@web.de

Keratilwe Bodilenyane, Lecturer, Department of Political & Administrative Studies, Keratilwe.Bodilenyane@mopipi.ub.bw

Valerio Bosco, PhD, Governance Officer, African Minerals Development Centre (AMDC), United Nations Economic Commission for Africa, valerio.bosco@yahoo.com

Emmanuelle Bouilly, PhD student, CESSP, Department of Political Science, Université Paris 1 Panthéon Sorbonne, Paris, France, emmanuelle.bouilly@yahoo.fr

Marie Brossier, Assistant Professor of Political Science, Departement of Political science, Université Laval, Québec, Canada, marie.brossier@pol.ulaval.ca

Brett Logan Carter, PhD, Post-doctoral Research Fellow, Center for Democracy, Development, and the Rule of Law, Stanford University, blcarter@post.harvard.edu

Nic Cheeseman, Director of the African Studies Centre and Hugh Price Fellow of Jesus College, University of Oxford, UK, niccheeseman@gmail.com

Tiyesere Mercy Chikapa-Jamali, Lecturer at the Department of Political and Administrative Studies, University of Malawi, tiyeserec@yahoo.com

John Daniel was Academic Director of the School for International Training's programme in Social and Political Transformation in Durban, South Africa.

Lewis B. Dzimbiri, Professor of Public Administration, Chancellor College, University of Malawi, proflewisdzimbiri@gmail.com

Mark Furness, Senior Researcher, Deutsches Institut für Entwicklungspolitik / German Development Institute (DIE), Bonn, Germany, mark.furness@die-gdi.de

Lansana Gberie, Academic and Writer, Ottawa, Canada, lagberie@yahoo.com

Eric Komlavi Hahonou, Associate Professor of International Development Studies, Department of Society & Globalisation, Roskilde University, Denmark, komlavi@ruc.dk

Joseph Hanlon, Visiting Senior Fellow, Department of International Development, London School of Economics, UK; Honorary Research Fellow, School of Environment and Development, University of Manchester, and Visiting Senior Research Fellow at the Development Policy and Practice Centre of the Open University, UK, j.hanlon@open.ac.uk

Ketil Fred Hansen, Associate Professor in Modern African History, University of Stavanger, Norway. ketil.f.hansen@uis.no

Kurt Hirschler, Freelance Political Scientist, Hamburg, Germany, kurt_hirschler@web.de

Nicole Hirt, Freelance Research Associate, Institute of African Affairs, GIGA German Institute of Global and Area Studies and Senior Consultant at HACOS – "Horn of Africa Consultancy Service", Hamburg, Germany, nicolehi2001@yahoo.de

Rolf Hofmeier, Former Director, Institute of African Affairs, GIGA German Institute of Global and Area Studies, Hamburg, Germany, rolf.hofmeier@giga-hamburg.de

Amin Kamete, Senior Lecturer, University of Glasgow, Scotland, UK, amini.kamete@glasgow.ac.uk

Christoph Kohl, Researcher, Peace Research Institute Frankfurt, Frankfurt am Main, Germany, kohl@hsfk.de

Dirk Kohnert, Retired Deputy Director, Institute of African Affairs, GIGA German Institute of Global and Area Studies, Hamburg, Germany, Kohnert@giga-hamburg.de

Bruno Losch, Research director, Centre de Coopération Internationale en Recherche Agronomique pour le Développement, Montpellier, France, bruno.losch@cirad.fr

Joseph N. Mangarella, PhD Candidate, African Studies Centre, Leiden, Netherlands. joseph.mangarella@gmail.com

Richard R. Marcus, Professor and Director, The Global Studies Institute and the International Studies Program, California State University, Long Beach, USA, richard.marcus@csulb.edu

Andreas Mehler, Director, Institute of African Affairs, GIGA German Institute of Global and Area Studies, Hamburg, Germany, mehler@giga-hamburg.de

Henning Melber, Senior Adviser/Director emeritus, Dag Hammarskjöld Foundation, Uppsala, Sweden, henning.melber@dhf.uu.se

Sanusha Naidu, Research Associate, Department of Political Science, University of Pretoria, South Africa, sanushanaidu72@gmail.com

Claes Olsson, Political Scientist and Editor at Global Publications Foundation, Uppsala, Sweden, claes.olsson@globalpublications.org

Helena Olsson, Political Sciencist and Staff Member at the Department of Sociology, Uppsala University, Sweden, helena.olsson@soc.uu.se

Krijn Peters, Associate Professor in Armed Conflict & Post-war Reconstruction, Department of Political & Cultural Studies, Swansea University, UK, k.peters@swansea.ac.uk

Fanny Pigeaud, Journalist, France, Fanny.pigeaud@gmail.com

Marisha Ramdeen, Programme Officer at the African Centre for the Constructive Resolution of Disputes (ACCORD) in Durban, South Africa. Marisha@accord.org.za

Edalina Rodrigues Sanches, PhD, Institute of Social Sciences, University of Lisbon, Lisbon, Portugal, ersanches@ics.ul.pt

Anita Schroven, Anthropologist, researcher at the Center for Interdisciplinary Research, Bielefeld, anita.schroven@gmx.net

Jon Schubert, Senior Africa Analyst, Lusophone and Central Africa, IHS Country Risk, London; currently teaching a course in political anthropology at Martin Luther-Universität Halle-Wittenberg, jonschubert@gmx.net

David Sebudubudu, Professor of Political Studies and Head of the Department of Political and Administrative Studies, University of Botswana, Sebudubu@mopipi.ub.bw

Gerhard Seibert, Associate professor at the Universidade da Integração Internacional da Lusofonia Afro-Brasileira (UNILAB), São Francisco do Conde, Bahia, Brazil, mailseibert@yahoo.com

Claudia Simons, Researcher at German Institute for International and Security Affairs, Berlin, Germany, Claudia.Simons@swp-berlin.org

Roger Southall, Professor Emeritus, Department of Sociology, University of the Witwatersrand, South Africa, Roger.Southall@wits.ac.za

Alexander Stroh, Research Fellow, Institute of African Affairs, GIGA German Institute of Global and Area Studies, Hamburg, Germany, stroh@giga-hamburg.de

Susan Thomson, Assistant Professor of Peace and Conflict Studies, Colgate University, Hamilton, USA, sthomson@colgate.edu

Klaus-Peter Treydte, Economist, Former country representative Friedrich-Ebert-Foundation Madagascar and Mauritius, kp3t@gmx.net

Stef Vandeginste, Lecturer, Institute of Development Policy and Management, University of Antwerp, Belgium, stef.vandeginste@uantwerpen.be

Klaas van Walraven, Researcher, African Studies Centre, Leiden, The Netherlands, walraven@ascleiden.nl

Volker Weyel, Consultant, Former Editor-in-chief 'Vereinte Nationen' (1977–2004), Bonn, Germany, weyel@o2online.de

Bruce Whitehouse, Director, Global Studies Program, Associate Professor of Anthropology, Lehigh University, USA, bruce.whitehouse@lehigh.edu

Peter Woodward, Emeritus professor, School of Politics and International Relation, University of Reading, UK, p.r.woodward@reading.ac.uk

Douglas A. Yates, Professor of Political Science at the American Graduate School in Paris, France, douglas.yates@ags.edu

I. Sub-Saharan Africa

Despite continued positive economic growth rates for most economies, capital flight, poverty and inequality remained serious problems. The despair of ordinary people was evident in the growing number of migrants seeking to enter Europe at the risk of their lives. Although the AU celebrated the 50th anniversary of its founding, the continental body remained unable to solve regional violent conflicts. The most serious military confrontations occurred in Mali, the CAR, the DRC and South Sudan, while other conflict zones – mainly in West and Central Africa – remained volatile. Elections in Kenya, Zimbabwe and Mali reduced the risk that ongoing conflicts would escalate further and in Madagascar paved the way back to legitimate governance. Elections in Equatorial Guinea, Mauritania and Swaziland hardly deserved to be called democratic. Boko Haram increased its terrorist activities, but piracy along the coasts in the West and the East declined. Natural disasters and diseases affected fewer people than in previous years; in particular, there was a decline in new HIV/AIDS infections, and mortality rates signalled a positive trend.

Africa in the Global Economy

Against the background of tottering Asian economies and slow European recovery, it was predicted that **growth** rates would fall slightly. In the second half of the year, the IMF forecast 6.1% growth for oil exporting countries and 4.4% for importers. The SSA average was predicted to be around 5%. These figures concealed considerable variations between countries and sub-regions. Mining countries such as Niger and Sierra Leone would obviously end up above average, whereas countries torn apart by political instability (Mali, the CAR) would achieve lower growth or even experience contraction.

With a third of Africa's countries said to be growing by a good 6% (according to the World Bank), economists worried that this success was too dependent on **extractive industries**. This endangered sustainable growth whilst also limiting employment opportunities. UNECA reported that, while the resources sector had grown by a quarter over the previous decade, manufacturing was in decline – its share in national GDPs having contracted to 10%. Just how problematic that might be in the medium term was shown by the fact that mineral prices began or continued to fall. Since the financial crisis of 2008, Africa's share in the global production of ten of its 12 most important minerals, including uranium, diamond, iron ore, bauxite and copper, had decreased. In 2011, the continent produced around 10% of the world's metals. However, mineral output increased in 2013 in countries such as Mozambique (bauxite, coal) and Namibia (diamonds).

FDI, although undoubtedly focused on the exploitation of natural resources, rose in 2012 by 5.5% to $ 37.7 bn, partly reflecting improved business environments, but this still only amounted to 5.6% of global FDI. **Capital flight** constituted a related problem that again captured international attention. Oxfam, which tried to interest the G 20 summit in St Petersburg (5–6 September) in the issue, claimed that lost income through tax evasion was equivalent to more than 50% of sub-Saharan health spending.

Against this background, **illegal migration** by people seeking to enter the EU via the Mediterranean reached new levels and was marked by tragic incidents. The UN estimated that during the first half of the year more than 8,000 migrants landed in Italy (especially the island of Lampedusa, close to Tunisia) and Malta, i.e., double the number in 2012. By late 2013, the figure for Italy stood at over 30,000, i.e., triple the 2012 total (including refugees from Syria). According to UNHCR, by November more than 62,000 people had arrived in Yemen from the Horn of Africa. More than 350 African asylum seekers drowned on 3 October near Lampedusa. Ten days later, over 30 more people drowned. It was estimated that, over the previous 20 years, 17,000–19,000 migrants had died at sea trying to reach Europe. At least a dozen youths from Somaliland died in the Sudanese-Libyan Sahara in May, and some 90 migrants perished in Niger, close to the border with Algeria, in October. Thousands of migrants were still being held by smugglers in desert camps in Libya, where they were subjected to extortion and maltreatment. They allegedly had to pay up to € 2,000 for the sea passage to Europe. The cash turnover from human trafficking from Libya to Europe was estimated at $ 3 m–$ 4 m.

Poverty thus remained a serious problem. Although growth rates had helped reduce poverty by a couple of percentage points since 1996, halving extreme poverty as required by the MDGs was still far off. Moreover, **inequality** had risen, at least in several oil-producing countries. An Afrobarometer survey of 16 countries suggested that improvements in the standard of living had been marginal: half of respondents claimed that they were sometimes without food or basic amenities, while people suffered greater poverty in areas where spending on infrastructure lagged behind (electricity, piped water, sewage). More than one-third of the world's extremely poor were still in SSA. **Food prices**, although they fell somewhat, were still a cause for concern. A global campaign was started by Oxfam to dissuade Western banks from speculating in food commodities. Several banks discontinued speculative trading; exceptions were Allianz and Deutsche Bank.

An AfDB seminar in Tunis on 21 February on the upcoming renewal of AGOA showed that **US**-Africa trade was still dominated by a few countries: Nigeria, Angola and South Africa. It was argued that African countries should make their trade-related positions clear before the US Congress, which would have to decide on AGOA's renewal in 2015. Poor utilisation of preferences was said to be responsible, amongst other reasons, for the limited number of countries benefiting from AGOA preferences. Nevertheless, African trade with the US in the decade 2001–11 grew by more than 500%. President Obama made a three-nation tour of the continent on 27 June–2 July, visiting Senegal, South Africa and Tanzania.

In late March, **China**'s new President Xi Jinping also made a three-nation tour, taking in Tanzania, South Africa and the Republic of Congo. Numerous trade and aid agreements were signed. The 5th Tokyo International Conference on African development took place on 1–3 June. **Japan** announced a $ 32 bn plan to improve infrastructure development and economic growth. The new aid initiative was seen as an attempt to catch up with China. The summit of the **BRICS** countries (Brazil, Russia, India, China and South Africa) took place in Durban on 26–27 March. The establishment of a development bank had been planned, but no firm decisions were taken.

On 30 April, the **AfDB** launched its new ten-year strategy for the continent's economic transformation. Infrastuctural development was one of the five key priorities. This issue was also discussed during the AfDB's annual meeting in Marrakesh (Morocco) on 31 May, where it was also resolved to move the bank's headquarters from Tunis back to Abidjan in formerly war-torn Côte d'Ivoire. On 24 July, the bank approved an ADF grant of $ 45 m to help establish the Pan-African University, which would consist of five institutes based in the various sub-regions and focus on science and technology.

As the AfDB's policies showed, **infrastructure** continued to be one of the continent's most important economic issues. The bank estimated that $ 90 bn was required to finance much-needed improvements in this area – financial pledges had halved over the previous three years as a result of the global economic crisis. Telecommunications remained a target for investment. The continental mobile phone market was predicted to grow by 6.3% a year and to be worth $ 100 bn in 2015, a world record. In the preceding six years, the number of SIM cards had tripled to over 800 m, and mobile network coverage in rural areas had grown from 65% in 2007 to almost 100%. In a related development, the Africa Coast to Europe (ACE) submarine cable reached Senegal in January, thereby boosting Internet connectivity. The continent now had around 116 m mobile broadband subscribers, i.e. some 11%, compared with less than 1% in 2007. However, while Internet penetration had more than doubled since 2007, some 80% of Africa's population remained unconnected. Finally, a WHO report concluded that Africa had the highest road traffic fatality rate in the world. Lack of awareness, speeding and lack of enforcement were said to be major causes.

African Union

In the year of its 50th anniversary as a continental organisation, the AU was immediately confronted by its inability to deal effectively with large-scale conflicts. The steadily growing rebellion in northern **Mali** was stopped in its tracks by a French intervention force, which was backed up by Chadian troops and temporarily sidelined an ECOWAS plan that had gained AU approval but had still not left the drawing board. In typical confusion, outgoing Assembly chair, President Boni Yayi of Benin, had called on NATO countries to step in while the AU Commission chairperson, former South African foreign minister Dlamini-Zuma, kept quiet until the moment that French troops arrived on the scene. At the AU's first biannual summit held in Addis Ababa (Ethiopia) on 27–28 January, Yayi could do little more than thank the French for taking the lead. The Assembly set aside $ 50 m to contribute to the ECOWAS force – which cost some $ 460 m – to be sent in the aftermath. The somewhat token AU contribution was seen as a means to mend fences with the ECOWAS members that were going to bear the brunt of the peacekeeping duties. A special donor conference held immediately after the summit raised the remainder of the required funds. At the anniversary summit on 25–27 May, held in Addis Ababa under the theme 'Pan-Africanism and African Rebirth', French President Hollande was a guest of honour.

Other conflicts that made their way onto the AU's agenda (at least formally) included the tensions between Sudan and South Sudan, the instability in Egypt and the CAR, and the situation in Madagascar. After a meeting of the Peace and Security Council (PSC), Egypt's membership was suspended on 5 July because of the army's overthrow of President Morsi two days before, which violated article 30 of the AU's Constitutive Act against unconstitutional takeovers. Dlamini-Zuma appointed a high-level committee to discuss the situation. The Assembly also condemned the "illegal seizure of power" in the CAR by the Séléka rebels, and by year's end the AU had decided to nearly double the number of troops in its peacekeeping mission there to 6,000. On 5 December, the UNSC formally established this mission as the AU-led 'Mission Internationale de Soutien à la Centrafrique sous Conduite Africaine' (MISCA). By contrast, sanctions against presidential usurper Andry Rajoelina in Madagascar were lifted on 5 September ahead of presidential elections there. The AU's long-established intervention force in Somalia (African Union Mission in Somalia – AMISOM) continued its protracted mission.

At the first annual summit, Ethiopia's Prime Minister Hailemariam Desalegn took over the Assembly presidency. Ahead of the summit, AU foreign ministers elected new members of the PSC. Other **institutional issues** included the takeover by Commission Chairperson Dlamini-Zuma of the peace and security portfolio after the Commissioner previously responsible was appointed the new foreign minister of Algeria. This clearly boosted her and South Africa's influence on AU affairs, and some observers stressed the political risks involved, as the change came in the wake of the struggle over the Commission chair in 2012, when South Africa stood accused of unprecedented muscle flexing. However, Dlamini-Zuma went out of her way to appoint numerous officials from francophone countries (which had come out as the main losers in the battle for the chair) as her special envoys to various conflict-ridden countries.

Dlamini-Zuma was also said to have brought new dynamism to the Commission's proceedings, with a more down-to-earth approach to **financial problems**. She made it clear that, with 97% of AU operational programmes and 56% of the administrative budget provided by donors, funding was unsustainable. At the anniversary summit in May, the Assembly adopted a high-level panel report from former Nigerian president Obasanjo proposing a $ 10 levy on airline tickets to and from Africa, in addition to a $ 2 'hospitality tax' per hotel stay. It was estimated that this would yield more than $ 700 m (more than twice the cost of AU programmes). However, while many members supported the proposal, countries with a more developed tourist sector such as Egypt, Seychelles and Cape Verde, resisted the plans. New talks on the panel recommendations took place later in the year but were not expected to lead to immediate results, given member states' lack of budgetary discipline: in the seven preceding years, arrears in contribution had risen from $ 43 m to $ 72 m.

South Africa continued its assertive role in AU affairs. President Zuma went on record complimenting France on its intervention in Mali (in contrast to South African opposition to earlier French interventions in Libya and Côte d'Ivoire), but he also pushed for a stop-gap measure to kick-start the long-awaited African Standby Force (ASF). Its formation had been on the books since 2004. Thus, on 29–30 April, member states discussed the **Rapid Deployment Capability**, a key component of the ASF. Spurred on by the AU's impotence in the Malian crisis, the May summit formally decided to establish the reaction force, which was set – rather improbably – to become operational later in the year. Funding and troop contributions were to come from member states on a voluntary basis. Relevant pledges were made by South Africa, Chad, Uganda and Ethiopia. Called the African Capacity for Immediate Response to Crises (ACIRC), the force was to carry out operations of limited duration. It would be drawn from a reserve of 5,000 troops, with an integrated combat unit of 1,500 troops who could be deployed at ten days' notice and be self-sustaining for a minimum period of one month. The force would also comprise an artillery support group, light armoured units and an air wing of 400 men, equipped with helicopters and strike aircraft. ACIRC's strategic command would come under the AU Commission. On 6 November a summit meeting in Pretoria (South Africa) pushed ahead, with Zuma explaining that an "independent and swift African response to crises" could not wait till the formation of the ASF. No money would be diverted for ACIRC from the AU budget and no foreign government would be asked to contribute – the force's independence was a sensitive issue, especially for South Africa. However, not all member states favoured the ACIRC plan. Concerns were voiced over the political control of the force, the growing power of the AU Commission and ACIRC's potential abuse in the form of deployment in situations deemed by some as politically undesirable. The lack of airlift capabilities necessary for deployment had not been resolved by year's end.

By contrast, the AU became even more hostile to the **ICC** and its perceived bias against African perpetrators of human rights violations. Ethiopia, as the new Assembly chair, accused the court of 'race hunting' and demanded that the cases being brought against the president and deputy president of Kenya for their alleged responsibility for the 2007 electoral violence be heard in their home country. Pressed by the Kenyans, the AU held an extraordinary summit in Addis Ababa on 12 October, where a mass African withdrawal from the Rome Statute was discussed. Things did not go that far, but Commission Chairperson Dlamini-Zuma supported deferral of the cases against the presidents of Kenya and Sudan.

Governance

The AU created the African Governance Architecture (AGA) in 2011 on the basis of a 'shared values' agenda. The essentials included the right to life, participation in governance, equality, justice, rule of law, sovereignty and independence of states. The AGA coined the term 'architecture' to signal the will to create a coherent framework of well-functioning, coordinated institutions. The **APRM**, originally created by NEPAD, was considered a relevant building bloc for achieving the AGA goals. It celebrated its tenth anniversary, including presentations at the UN in October, and claimed to have proved to be an effective platform for African peer learning and sharing of experience and best practice in the field of governance. Since its establishment, 33 countries had voluntarily acceded to the mechanism, with Tunisia and Chad joining at the beginning of the year. This tool, based on the individual decision of AU member states to join, remained only to some degree inclusive and cannot be considered an official diagnostic instrument with which all AU states need to comply. It therefore lacked continental legitimacy.

The 18th **APRM** Forum met on 26 January in Addis Ababa, coinciding with the celebrations for the AU's 50th anniversary. Twelve heads of government attended the Summit of the Committee of Heads of State and Government participating in the APRM, while the other member states had delegated other representatives of their governments. As the official communiqué stated, the chairperson of the AU Commission, Dlamini-Zuma, in her welcoming remarks expressed "concern over the inadequate implementation of the recommendations of the APRM Country Review Reports". The peer reviews on Tanzania and Zambia were discussed during the Summit, increasing the number of countries reviewed to 17. President Boni Yayi also presented a progress report on the implementation of the National Programme of Action for Benin.

However, the general mood seemed not very celebratory. The chairperson of the African Peer Review (APR) Panel, the Liberian Amos Sawyer, expressed concerns in his progress report over the slow pace at which the review process was being implemented in some member states. Observers noted that heads of state displayed an increasing **lack of enthusiasm** to expose their governance to these review exercises and to provide the necessary resources. An evident loss of momentum over the years could be observed, with little to no attendance by heads of state at the deliberations. The original architects of NEPAD and the APRM (the previous presidents Obasanjo from Nigeria and Mbeki from South Africa) had long left office and the strongest supporter as head of state (Zenawi from Ethiopia) had died in 2012. The APRM therefore lacked strong advocacy in the ranks of African governments and was weakened accordingly. Civil society members as much as donors had also increasingly lost faith and interest in the undertaking.

On 26 May, Liberian President Ellen Johnson Sirleaf was installed as the head of the APRM Forum at its 19th meeting in Addis Ababa, but made no visible impact during the rest of the year. It was decided to hire more staff to enhance the capacity of the APRM's administrative body, but none were recruited. At the same meeting, Barrister Akere Muna from Cameroon, a vice-chair of the TI board, replaced the former Liberian president Amos Sawyer as the chairperson of the APR Panel, but by year's end both eminent representatives had left the Panel for different reasons; developments suggested that something was rotten in the state of APRM, with scandals denting its image. The APR Panel of Eminent Persons was tasked to exercise oversight over the APRM process to ensure its independence, professionalism and credibility. It also oversees the selection of the APR Mission Teams and appoints them to conduct country reviews. After Muna's exit, allegations emerged that he had been prevented from criticising **dubious practices** by his predecessor and the head of the APR secretariat, violating both the ethics and principles underlying the good practice the APRM was meant to promote. After that, reports of nepotism and mismanagement, including the misappropriation of funds, made news.

The tenth anniversary year of the APRM was clearly not a good one for the body entrusted with promoting better governance across a continent, being home to six out of the top ten so-called failed states in the world and with ten heads of state who had been in power for over 20 years. A study by the South African Institute for International Affairs, in the past very supportive of and positive about the APRM, concluded its critical appraisal after ten years of the mechanism's being in place with the sceptical note that "there [was] a concrete risk that the AGA [would] slowly inch towards irrelevance".

Democracy and Elections

Some national elections were clearly meant to end fluid or interim situations. In both Kenya and Zimbabwe, transitional power-sharing arrangements ended with presidential and legislative elections. **Kenya**'s elections were held under a new constitution that also provided for a strengthened local government. The open competition, which was marked by relatively little violence, stood in positive contrast to many other elections, both in general and in comparison with past Kenyan polls. The elections were won by the somewhat unexpected 'Jubilee' coalition of parties linked to senior politicians Uhuru Kenyatta and William Ruto, both charged with crimes against humanity by the ICC in connection with election-related violence in the aftermath of the 2007.elections (when they had been positioned in different camps). Kenyatta won the presidential contest with 50.5% of the votes, while his main rival, Raila Odinga, was credited with 43.4%. It was not entirely clear what this meant for the ICC investigation. The Kenyatta-led coalition also won a relative majority of seats in parliament. **Zimbabwe** also operated under a new constitution, adopted by referendum. An unprepared opposition was confronted with an early election date, and President Robert Mugabe received around 61% of the votes; his party took 197 out of 270 seats in parliament. Mugabe, at 90 the oldest African head of state, and in power since 1980, was back in full gear, after a four-year period in which he had had to involve his rival, Morgan Tsvangirai, in government affairs. In **Madagascar** too, a very difficult transition was ended by elections. Under tight international supervision, reasonably fair elections were held after all the major politicians of the preceding era were excluded from running as candidates. In the second round, Hery Rajaonarimampianina, a former finance minister in André Rajoelina's government, emerged as the winner with 54% of the votes, but the parties of the two most recent presidents gained most votes in the legislative polls, keeping fears of a new stalemate on the agenda. In **Mali**, elections ended the somewhat chaotic interim period following the coup in 2012. Ibrahim Boubacar Keita, a well-known personality, won the presidential elections (in the second round with over 77% of the vote), and in the legislative elections his supporters also gained a solid majority in the National Assembly.

More 'business as usual' elections were held in Togo, Cameroon, Djibouti and Rwanda. In **Togo**, termed "partly free" in the Freedom House index, legislative elections produced landslide gains for the party of President Gnassingbe. The three other states, Djibouti, Cameroon and Rwanda, were rated "not free": campaigning there was strongly focused on the ruling parties and the outcome was roughly foreseeable in advance, though in **Djibouti** an opposition alliance fared better than expected. **Cameroon**'s ruling party lost a few seats to the opposition in National Assembly elections, but managed to uphold a comfortable four-fifths majority. **Rwanda**'s legislative elections saw the ruling party win 41 seats out of 80. The two other parties that won seats (12 in total) were not necessarily opposition parties, and most of the 27 indirectly elected members were believed to be in the presidential camp.

The least open electoral contests were held elsewhere: In **Equatorial Guinea** and **Swaziland**, a mixture of repression and manipulation prevented almost all competition and produced (legislative) election results that may have been prefabricated. In **Mauritania**, most opposition parties (save one Islamist one) boycotted the legislative polls, leaving the door wide open for the government party.

Coups and Unconstitutional Rule

In the **CAR**, the successful military take-over by the Séléka rebellion brought Michel Djotodia to power. As noted by many observers, he was the country's first Muslim president, but he was also another politico-military entrepreneur seeking supreme authority, and thus not much different from his predecessor and many other aspirants in the country. After the familiar suspension of major institutions and the constitution, some interim institutions were set up. The international reaction to this violent overthrow was on the one hand strong and unequivocal but, on the other, it was clear that ousted president Bozizé did not have much external support. Under strong pressure, Djotodia quickly had to scale down his ambitions, but he was at least able to travel to most countries of the subregion despite the existence of a travel ban.

In **South Sudan**, the president's camp blamed the start of a new bloody civil war on an alleged coup attempt by its opponents. In **Chad**, authorities claimed to have foiled a putsch, which served as a pretext to arrest several opponents. Less drastic were the consequences of an alleged coup plot in **Benin**, where an army colonel together with two accomplices tried, according to the authorities, to prevent the return of President Yayi Boni from a trip abroad. Ten people were detained in the **Comoros** for an alleged coup plot, amongst them the son of a former president and a former government minister. A series of mysterious attacks on government installations in several cities in the **DRC** unfolded on 30 December; the attackers were defeated and about 50 of them were killed.

The successful elections in **Madagascar** fulfilled the conditions for its readmission to SADC.

Peace and War

In the three major conflict countries of the continent (Mali, the DRC and the CAR), decisive military actions were undertaken, but only in Mali and the DRC were government troops, supported by intervening contingents from other countries, successful in combating rebel forces. A new serious armed confrontation unfolded at year's end in South Sudan. Mostly low-scale armed confrontations continued to destabilise a couple of other countries (various provinces in Sudan, and some areas of Guinea). The government of Somalia gained some control over territory and crucial road connections, but the Al-Shabaab movement was not yet defeated.

In **Mali**, a desert war between government forces – critically supported by troops from other countries – and various rebel groups ended with a quick and clear military victory for the government side, but guerrilla activities continued. French troops and fighter jets under the French-led 'Opération Serval' starting operations in early January with airstrikes against rebel positions; a substantial Chadian contingent participated in the operations, and played a significant part in achieving the result (in early February). However, the situation in the Kidal area remained volatile. In early April, the Chadian government announced the end of its operation after a suicide bomber attacked its forces in Kidal, killing four soldiers. The Malian government concluded a peace agreement with the Tuareg 'Mouvement National pour la Libération de l'Azawad' (MNLA), but not with the active Islamist groups. After the break-up of their alliance, Tuareg separatists fought Islamist groups, although at least some MNLA groups continued to attack Malian troops. On 26 September, the MNLA officially opted out of the peace agreement, claiming that the government would not respect its commitments. However, no large-scale confrontations took place thereafter. Human rights organisations accused the Malian army of involvement in revenge killings during the reconquest of the north; there were also reports from the capital Bamako of Tuaregs being targeted by security forces and having their homes raided. These were all signs of continued tensions between the Tuareg minority and the state apparatus.

DRC government troops, critically supported by a new UN-sponsored 'Force Intervention Brigade' achieved a major military breakthrough in the east of the country, almost defeating the M23 rebels, although peace negotiations were later held to stabilise the situation. About 350 rebel fighters were killed during the offensive. This military success could not conceal the fact that many more armed movements were still operational in eastern DRC; the offensive also created hundreds of thousands of new refugees and IDPs.

In the **CAR**, by contrast, the Séléka rebellion managed to take the capital Bangui without much opposition by government forces and peacekeepers; only some South African troops put up fierce resistance. The take-over did not bring any stabilisation, however. Locally, and not least in Bangui, the Bozizé regime versus Séléka conflict transformed into confrontations between rebel commandos and armed vigilante groups, which took on religious overtones of Christian-Muslim conflict. By the end of the year, the transitional institutions looked completely overburdened in managing state affairs.

In both Mali and the CAR, sub-regional peacekeeping efforts became either UN or AU missions, but only in Mali did they have an immediate stabilising effect. Various UN missions were active in the DRC, Somalia, Sudan and **South Sudan**. In the last case, the mission was unable to stop the frantic efforts of both major political contenders to control oil-producing areas: both President Salva Kiir and his former vice-president Riek Machar tried to prevail by the use of violence.

Somalia continued to be the battleground for a dirty war between government forces and AU peacekeepers plus some Western special forces on the one hand, and, on the other, the Al-Shabaab movement.

Terrorism and Piracy

The most constant terrorist threat came from the **Boko Haram** group in Nigeria. Throughout the year, the group managed to stage attacks on government institutions (particularly police stations), schools, student hostels, bus stations and villages. In six of the reported events, more than 50 people were killed. The group was also responsible for the targeted assassination of a Muslim cleric. The Nigerian army responded forcefully and killed many Boko Haram members, but this did not prevent the movement from spreading. On 3 June, the US State Department announced a reward of up to $ 7 m for information on the whereabouts of Boko Haram leader Abubakar Shekau. This was followed by a statement by Nigerian President Goodluck Jonathan classifying Boko Haram as a terrorist organisation and making membership a crime that would be severely punished. On 13 November, the

US authorities also officially declared the group a terrorist association. Clearly, the Nigerian authorities were unable to decisively weaken the organisation. The threat spread to neighbouring countries, most strongly to Cameroon, where a French family was abducted from a national park and liberated after two months of negotiations, most probably after payment of a ransom.

While Al-Shabaab continued to lose influence in **Somalia**, it proved to be still capable of acts of terror, both in Mogadishu and in neighbouring Kenya: The most spectacular attack was on the Westgate shopping mall in Nairobi in September, with 68 people killed and more than 100 injured. Al-Shabaab claimed responsibility for the attack and cited Kenya's military presence in Somalia as a justification. In September, some 160 religious leaders in Somalia issued a 'fatwa' against Al-Shabaab, condemning its activities. The Islamist group continued to control some territory within Somalia, despite the somewhat stabilised authority of the new government.

The heavy military blow against Islamist groupings in Mali temporarily reduced their activities, but individual acts of terrorism still took place.

On a continental level, **piracy** was significantly reduced (making South East Asia now the strongest affected sub-continent), but on closer inspection this trend was limited to the eastern coast, ranging from the Red Sea to the Indian Ocean, with Somalian pirates attacking only 19 ships. The number of attacks in the Gulf of Aden alone gradually fell to just six attacks, from 117 in 2009. A number of reasons may be behind this trend, but most probably the massive presence of warships as part of various maritime operations had a strong deterrent effect. Nevertheless, at one point, Somali pirates were holding two vessels to ransom with 15 crewmembers on board, while 49 crewmembers were being held on land, some of them having been prisoners for over two years. The number of attacks was more or less unchanged in the **Gulf of Guinea**, with Nigeria now reporting the highest number of attacks in Africa (31) and individual incidents recorded in Togo (7), Côte d'Ivoire (4), Congo (3), Sierra Leone and Gabon (2 each), Ghana, Guinea and Mauritania (1 each); 132 crewmembers were taken hostage and seven vessels hijacked. ECOWAS, CEEAC and the Gulf of Guinea Commission held a meeting in Yaoundé, the capital of Cameroon, which was chosen to host the headquarters of an interregional coordination centre to fight piracy in the Gulf of Guinea.

Epidemics and Disasters

HIV/AIDS figures showed that concerted efforts had produced positive results. New infection rates dropped considerably in most countries, in seven by more than 50% and in another seven by 30% to 49%, as figures for 2009 to 2012 presented by UNAIDS to an AU special conference in August showed. In Eastern and Southern Africa, the annual number of new infections fell by 30% from 1.7 m in 2001 to 1.2 m in 2011, and among children the rate of new infections fell by half. Better access to antiretroviral medication – which was received by less than 1 m people in 2005, but by more than 6 m in 2012 – was a major contributing factor.

Similarly, cases of **malaria** in Africa fell by over 30% compared with 2012, according to the World Malaria Report released on 31 December by WHO. The decisive contributing factor had been the increased delivery of bed nets as a prevention measure; a record 136 m were distributed during the year. Malaria diagnostic testing also increased considerably, but weak health systems and lack of delivery still had a negative impact. Thirty-four countries on the continent remained at risk of **yellow fever**. During the year 90% out of the 200,000 cases worldwide, causing 30,000 deaths, were registered in Africa.

By mid-May, almost 10,000 cases of **meningitis** with a fatality rate of close to 10% had been reported to WHO from 18 out of the 19 countries in West and Central Africa under enhanced surveillance for meningococcal diseases. This was the lowest number of cases reported during the epidemic season for ten years. More than 300 cases of **cholera** were reported from the north-western Kunene region of Namibia towards the end of the year. By mid-year, over 25,000 cases, with close to 500 deaths, had been reported to WHO from 18 countries, with the DRC the most affected, followed by Mozambique and Angola. **Unidentified diseases** were reported to WHO in October from Niger and in November from Tanzania. Uganda reported the outbreak of Crimean-Congo haemorrhagic fever in mid-August.

A new study released in June stated that the increasing number of **droughts**, with the subsequent devastating impacts on the lives of millions of people, was among the results of human-made **climate change**. One of the authors maintained that greenhouse gases and other emissions contributing to air pollution in Europe and the USA negatively affected rainfall in Africa. During the year, parts of **Southern Africa**, particularly Namibia, suffered from an ongoing lack of rain, which threatened close to 1 m of the country's 2.3 m inhabitants with malnutrition and hunger. The government was forced to declare a drought emergency and mobilised both internal and external resources to avoid the worst for the most vulnerable people. In October, international and local civil society and humanitarian agencies accused the Angolan government of downplaying the severe effects of drought on its people in the southern regions. In **West Africa**, erratic rainfall reduced harvests, especially in Niger, Burkina Faso, Mali and Mauritania.

Similar climate-change-related causes again led to heavy rains and **flooding** in the north-eastern parts of South Africa in January and February. The people of Malawi were similarly hit by flooding at the beginning of the year, destroying large parts of the harvest and numbers of livestock, thereby causing huge risks to food security for 2 m households. A flood at the end of August in parts of Nigeria tested the new emergency measures introduced by the Nigerian government since the biggest floods in 40 years at the end of 2012, and the early warning system in place prevented the worst. Floods and locust swarms threatened the harvests for many people in Madagascar during October, following an already poor agricultural season.

The **World Risk Report** 2013, presented on 4 September, emphasised lack of preparedness for crisis management and disaster relief as a major contributory factor to the scale of the effects of disasters on human life and security. African countries were among the most vulnerable as a result of either lack of political will or the absence of funds needed to take precautions and establish a functioning healthcare system and material infrastructure, which would make it possible to take immediate measures to combat catastrophic consequences, such as the spread of cholera.

Due to the increased risk from the combined effects of climate change and natural disasters, the High Level Panel of the UN Secretary-General on Post-2015 Development Goals suggested adding as a target to the poverty-related development goals "to build resilience and reduce the number of deaths caused by disasters". A report by the Overseas Development Institute released in October on "The geography of poverty, disasters and climate extremes in 2030" included among the 11 countries most at risk of **disaster-induced poverty** eight in SSA: the DRC, Ethiopia, Kenya, Madagascar, Nigeria, South Sudan, Sudan and Uganda.

Andreas Mehler, Henning Melber & Klaas van Walraven

II. United Nations and Sub-Saharan Africa

The 50th anniversary of the OAU took on a very symbolic connotation as the AU tried to reshape its vision and priorities for the coming decades. While the AU Agenda 2063, and the African Common Position for post-2015 articulated the continent's strategic priorities from a longer-term perspective, the AU Commission (AUC) Strategic Plan for 2014–17, along with attempts to review sources of AU financing and the creation of the African Capacity for Immediate Response to Crises influenced in the shorter term the AU's stance in the international arena and its relations with the UN.

The year witnessed important developments with regard to the renewed UN presence and engagement in Africa. The further upgrading of the UN Office to the AU, with the appointment of a Special Representative of the UN Secretary-General (UNSG) to the AU and the restructuring of UNECA, strengthened the profile of Addis Ababa (Ethiopia) as the crucial continental hub for UN-AU relations. Unfortunately, relations between the ICC and the AU worsened considerably.

Peace and security issues were dominated by the crises in Mali and the CAR. Both conflicts triggered major humanitarian emergencies but also encouraged enhanced cooperation between the UN, the AU and Regional Economic Communities (ECOWAS, ECCAS). The finalisation of the UN Strategy for the Sahel Region represented an important attempt to increase cooperation between member states, regional and sub-regional organisations, and the UN in promoting peace, security and stability. 2013 was also a crucial year for the AU and the continent in general in reshaping development priorities.

Africa in the UN

2013 marked the 50th anniversary of the OAU. The AUC Chairperson, Mrs Nkosazana Dlamini Zuma, and the Chairperson of the AU, Prime Minister Hailemariam Dessalegn of the Federal Democratic Republic of Ethiopia, emphasised at the celebrations the need for Africa to focus on structural economic transformation, accelerated industrialisation and more inclusive growth, with a view to tackling the socio-economic causes of conflict on the continent (the so called 'Addis doctrine'). The 20th and 21st ordinary sessions of the AU Summit took place in Addis Ababa in January and May. The celebration of the Golden Jubilee of the OAU/AU culminated in the adoption of the **50th Anniversary Solemn Declaration** as well as the launch of continental consultations aimed at drafting a continental development agenda for the next 50 years. While the declaration reiterated

AU member states' engagement in promoting socio-economic development, regional economic integration, peace and security, as well as democratic governance, the African leaders asked the AUC to work in close cooperation with the other two pan-African institutions, the AfDB and UNECA, to prepare and finalise, through inclusive and continent-wide consultations, an **AU Agenda 2063**. Agenda 2063 is conceived as a "shared strategic framework for inclusive growth and sustainable development" over a symbolic period of 50 years.

The 20th AU Summit, held in January, expressed AU member states' support for the **restructuring of UNECA**, which was launched by UN Under-Secretary-General (USG) and Executive Secretary of the ECA Carlos Lopes. The repositioning of the ECA launched by USG Lopes aimed at promoting and strengthening the role of the UN regional commission as the leading think-tank in Africa engaged in facilitating and supporting the continent's transformative agenda through research, data collection and statistics, technical support and advocacy.

The 21st AU Summit adopted a broad range of important decisions that were expected to reshape current and future forms of interaction and cooperation with the UN. The adoption of the report of the **High Level Panel on Alternative Sources of Financing the African Union** committed AU member states to a further review the option of designing a new financial burden-sharing pact that could help the AU to reduce its "unsustainable dependence on donor funding". In another significant move, the summit decided to establish an emergency force – the **African Capacity for Immediate Response to Crises** (ACIRC) – pending the full operationalisation of the African Standby Force currently supported by the UN and other AU partners. In addition to the above, the AUC's **Strategic Plan for 2014–17** identified the following AUC priorities: human capacity development (focusing on health, education, science, research, technology and innovation); agriculture and agro processing; inclusive economic development through industrialisation, infrastructure development, agriculture and trade and investment; peace, stability and good governance; mainstreaming of women and youth issues into all AUC activities; resource mobilisation; communication of AU actions and initiatives; strengthening the institutional capacity of the Union and all its organs. The need for the UN to better align its initiatives and programmes to AU priorities and objectives as outlined by Agenda 2063 and the AUC's Strategic Plan 2014–17 was clearly recognised by the 17th session of the Regional Coordination Mechanism-Africa, the forum that gathers UN offices and agencies operating on the continent in support of the implementation of the UN 10-Years Capacity Building Programme for the AU.

In May, Special Envoy for Sudan and South Sudan Haile Menkerios was appointed as the UNSG's Special Representative to the AU and **Head of the UN Office to the AU**, the integrated UN Department of Peacekeeping Operations, Department of Political Affairs and Department of Field Support DPKO-DPA-DFS) presence in Addis Ababa that had been established in 2010. The upgrade of the mission's head to the status of Special

Representative sent a clear signal from the UN of the importance given to peace and security cooperation with the AU. Menkerios was also expected to serve as a "trouble-shooting special envoy" for tensions and conflicts that emerged in Eastern and Southern Africa, which were not covered by a (political) UN regional office. Furthermore, the presence in Addis Ababa of two high-level officials with Under-Secretary-General status underlined the increasing relevance of Addis Ababa as the crucial continental hub for the UN.

UNSG Ban Ki-moon made **further important UN appointments** at the level of Special Representative. Former ECOWAS president Mohamed Ibn Chambas from Ghana was appointed as Joint AU-UN Special Representative for Darfur and Head of the AU-UN Hybrid Operation in Darfur. Other appointments included Nicholas Kay from the UK as Head of the UN Assistance Mission in Somalia (UNSOM), and Mary Robinson from Ireland as Special Envoy of the UNSG to the Great Lakes Region.

The UNSG's annual report on "Causes of conflict and the promotion of durable peace and sustainable development in Africa" presented recommendations aimed at the **strengthening of the Office of the Special Adviser** in Africa (OSAA). The report suggested the need to enhance the OSAA's mandate in order to enable it to effectively fulfil its brief and ensure that the link between peace, security and sustainable development was the basis for the ongoing engagement of the UN in support of Africa's priorities. On 13 September, UN General Assembly (UNGA) resolution 67/994 approved the UNSG's recommendations and invited him to keep working on the strengthening of the OSAA and its coordinating role as the leading actor in the UN Secretariat's interdepartmental task force on African affairs.

Despite the appointment of Mrs Faotu Bensouda in 2012 as Chief Prosecutor of the **ICC**, expectations of a possible improvement in relations between the ICC and African countries were dramatically frustrated. African countries consistently lobbied the UNSC in New York for the suspension of charges against African serving heads of state. In October, an extraordinary session of the AU Summit was convened in Addis Ababa to discuss the issue, focusing in particular on the Kenyan case. While AU member states were divided on the proposal for a withdrawal from the ICC en masse by the 34 African State Parties, the Summit adopted a resolution that "no charges shall be commenced or continued before an international criminal court or tribunal against a serving president of senior member of a government in power". On 15 November, the UNSC rejected the AU demand for the suspension of the ICC trial of Kenyan President Uhuru Kenyatta and Deputy President William Ruto for 12 months, in accordance with Article 16 of the Rome Statute. Seven Council members voted in favour of the resolution (Azerbaijan, China, Morocco, Pakistan, Russian Federation, Rwanda, and Togo), none voted against, and eight abstained (Argentina, Australia, France, Guatemala, Luxembourg, Republic of Korea, United Kingdom, United States). It was the first time in decades that a UNSC resolution had not been adopted even though none of its permanent members exercised their power of veto.

Peace and Security

In January, Nigeria and Chad joined Rwanda as new elected **members of the UNSC** for the biennium 2013–15. For Nigeria, which prevailed over the Gambia, this was its fifth term. In April, the Rwandan delegation at the UN held the rotating presidency of the UNSC and convened a meeting on "Prevention of conflicts in Africa: addressing root causes". The UNSC adopted a presidential statement that acknowledged the efforts of the AU. Whilst expressing deep appreciation for the valuable contribution to mediation made by regional and sub-regional bodies such as the ECOWAS Council of Elders and the AU Panel of the Wise, the UNSC asked African member states to ensure that these efforts were carried out in an effective and coordinated manner.

On 13 May, the UNSC debated the challenges of the **fight against terrorism** in Africa in the context of maintaining international peace and security. Representatives of the AU, ECOWAS and IGAD participated in the meeting and expressed their concern over the development of an arc of instability that stretched across the Sahel region up to the Horn of Africa. In a presidential statement, the Council expressed its deep concern over the increasing level of violence perpetrated by armed groups on the continent and recalled that terrorism could not be defeated by military force or intelligence operations alone. The Council also underlined the need to take a comprehensive approach that dealt with the challenges of increasing economic growth, the promotion of good governance, poverty reduction, state capacity and the fight against corruption.

The 7th joint consultation of the **UNSC and the AU Peace and Security Council** (AUPSC) took place in Addis Ababa on 8 October. The meeting discussed the situation in the Great Lakes Region, the Horn of Africa (Sudan/South Sudan and Somalia), the CAR and the Sahel Region. The AUPSC and the members of the UNSC welcomed the progress made so far in forging a more coherent and effective partnership between the AU and the UN consistent with Chapter VIII of the UN Charter. The joint communiqué stressed the need for continued efforts to enhance the existing partnership at both strategic and operational levels, in order to ensure greater synergy and coherence and a more effective response to the evolving peace and security challenges facing the African continent.

In response to the **situation in Mali**, and in line with the process that had led the UNSC to the adoption of resolution 2085(2012), which authorised the deployment of the African-led International Stabilization Mission (AFISMA), an enhanced coordinated approach was taken by the UN, the AU and ECOWAS. French intervention in Mali in January was supported by both the UNSC and the AUPSC. A Donors Conference on Mali was convened in Addis Ababa in January at the margins of the AU Summit. Over $ 453 m was pledged to bridge the funding gap, expedite the deployment of AFISMA, and enhance the capacities and training of the Malian defence and security forces. The conference was followed by an AU-UN-ECOWAS High-Level Summit on Mali, which marked the official launch of the Mali Integrated Task Force (MITF) to be based in Addis Ababa.

The MITF, which included UN, AU and ECOWAS representatives, was mandated to provide strategic guidance for the conduct and coordination of the AFISMA operation, as well as on issues related to the political process and the human rights and humanitarian situation in Mali.

In March, the UNSG, after intense consultations with the AU, ECOWAS and international partners, presented a report outlining two options for a possible **UN engagement** in Mali (S/2013/189). The first option envisaged the strengthening of African-led multidimensional presence in Bamako and transforming it into an integrated political presence with a better-resourced AFISMA, transitioning to a UN stabilisation mission. The second option proposed an integrated stabilisation mission with a military strength of 11,200 under Chapter VII alongside a parallel force to conduct counterterrorism operations that were beyond the scope of the UN's mandate. On 25 April, UNSC resolution 2100(2013) established the UN Multidimensional Integrated Stabilization Mission in Mali (MINUSMA). The mission was given the task of supporting the Malian authorities and northern groups in the implementation of the transitional road map, which included the holding of elections, the restoration of state authority to the north of the country and the facilitation of national dialogue and reconciliation at national and local levels. It decided that authority should be transferred from AFISMA to MINUSMA on 1 July and authorised a force structure of 11,200 military personnel and 1,440 police personnel. On 16 August, Council members noted the provisional results of the presidential runoff elections, which declared Ibrahim Boubacar Keita the elected president. Council members commended the Malian people for their peaceful participation in the electoral process and the transitional authorities for the successful preparation, organisation and management of the elections.

The situation in Mali was addressed by the UNSC within the broader context of the crisis in the Sahel region. On 26 June, former Italian prime minister Romano Prodi, the UNSG Special Envoy for the Sahel region, briefed the UNSC on the finalisation of the **UN integrated strategy on Sahel**. The strategy focussed on three strategic goals: strengthening national and regional security mechanisms; ensuring inclusive and effective governance; and bolstering humanitarian and development plans in Mali, Burkina Faso, Mauritania, Niger and Chad in order to build long-term resilience. The strategy was developed through consultations with regional government leaders, UN officials and key international partners, as well as religious, tribal and womens' leaders. The UNSC welcomed the finalisation of the strategy and issued a presidential statement highlighting the need for a coordinated approach by all concerned UN entities in its implementation.

A political and humanitarian crisis erupted in the **CAR**, as Séléka rebels started advancing toward the capital Bangui and threatened to overthrow President Francois Bozizé. On 3 January, the UNSC convened a meeting on the CAR and underlined the need for the political resolution of the crisis. The parties were urged to engage in peace negotiations in Libreville (Gabon) under the auspices of ECCAS. The UN, in cooperation with the AU, supported the deployment of a peace support operation by ECCAS. At the end of January, the mandate of BINUCA (the UN Integrated Peacebuilding Office, based in Bangui) was renewed until January 2014. As Séléka rebels took control of Bangui and overthrew Bozizé, the AUPSC suspended the CAR's participation in all AU activities and decided to impose sanctions, including travel bans and assets freezes, on leaders of the group. Following the recommendations for an increased role for the AU and the international community in the CAR, the AUPSC authorised on 19 July the deployment of the African-led mission to the CAR (AFISM-CAR), the concept of whose operation was officially communicated to the UNSC in early August. The mission, with its authorised strength of 3,500 uniformed personnel, was mandated to protect civilians, restore public order, stabilise the security situation and assist the reform of the security sector.

The AU and ECCAS, in cooperation with the UN, facilitated the creation of the **International Contact Group on the CAR** with a view to mobilising international support and action. On 7 October, the chairperson of the AUC, the UNSG's special representative and the head of BINUCA launched a joint appeal to the international community to provide the necessary support for the rapid operationalisation of AFISM-CAR. On 10 October, the UNSC unanimously adopted resolution 2121, updating the BINUCA mandate in five areas: implementation of the transition process; conflict prevention and humanitarian assistance; stabilisation of the security situation; human rights; and coordination of international actors. Finally, on 8 December, the UNSC adopted resolution 2127, authorising the deployment of an AU International Support Mission to the CAR (MISCA), with a mandate to protect civilians, support reform efforts and create conditions for humanitarian assistance. The resolution further authorised the French forces in the CAR – which were deployed in the country from late November – to take all necessary measures to assist MISCA. The resolution also requested the UNSG to set up an international commission of inquiry, and establish an arms embargo, sanctions committee and panel of experts.

The civil war that erupted in **eastern DRC** in 2012 following the launch of an armed rebellion by the M23 rebels continued to affect the country and the wider region. Renewed cooperation among countries of the region, the AU, UN, ICGLR and SADC led to the adoption of a more comprehensive approach in order to address the root causes of the conflict. The good offices of the UNSG played a crucial in role in brokering a Peace, Security, and Cooperation Framework for the DRC and the region, which was signed in Addis Ababa on 24 February. The UNSC endorsed this approach with resolution 2098(2013), which authorised the strengthening of the political and military role of MONUSCO and the deployment of an intervention brigade within the UN peacekeeping mission in order to address the threats posed by armed groups operating in the eastern part of the country. In August, UN-AU-ICGRL and SADC joint mediation efforts were instrumental in de-escalating the rising tensions between the DRC and Rwanda. In early October, UNSC members visited the Great Lakes Region. During high-level meetings with the DRC president, prime minister and foreign minister in Kinshasa, the DRC authorities confirmed their commitment to the implementation of the Addis Ababa Framework and to engage in peace talks with the M23 in Kampala (Uganda).

Despite the progress achieved in 2012, the situation in **Somalia** continued to face very delicate policy, stabilisation and security challenges. The establishment of regional administrations, conceived as building blocks of the federal state, proved to be difficult and required intense mediation efforts by IGAD, Ethiopia, Kenya and the UN. On 6 March, the UNSC adopted resolution 2093, extending the authorisation of the AU Mission in Somalia (AMISOM) until 28 February 2014 and authorising a partial lifting of the arms embargo for a period of 12 months to give access to weapons and training, restricted to the Somali National Security Force alone. In May, UNSC resolution 2102 created UNSOM, to be deployed for an initial period of one year. UNSOM was mandated to carry out "good offices" functions; provide advice to the government and AMISOM on peacebuilding and statebuilding; assist the government with donor coordination; and provide capacity-building support in the areas of human rights and protection of civilians. On 12 November, the UNSC unanimously adopted resolution 2124, which extended the AMISOM mandate to 31 October 2014 and increased the ceiling for troop numbers. On 18 November, the Council also unanimously adopted resolution 2125, which re-authorised anti-piracy measures in Somalia and its territorial waters for another year. In his last briefing to the UNSC for the year, UNSG Special Representative Nicholas Kay noted that reconciliation, the creation of a system of federal states, the revision of the constitution and the holding of national elections were the most relevant long-term challenges for the country.

The situation in Abyei continued to be a source of deep disagreement between **Sudan and South Sudan**. UN Special Envoy for Sudan/South Sudan Haile Menkerios was engaged in facilitating further improvements in relations between Khartoum and Juba. Nevertheless, in light of the increasing tensions between the Misseriya and Ngok-Dinka groups based in Abyei, with the former wanting the town to become part of Sudan, the UN interim security force tried to establish buffer zones in order to neutralise risks of a wider conflict. Despite calls from the UNSC and the AUPSC to refrain from unilateral actions, the Ngok-Dinka community organised a unilateral referendum in late October, which had no official support from Sudan or South Sudan. While the vote was primarily symbolic and not legally binding, the Abyei Referendum High Committee, which organised the referendum, stated that 99.9% of the more than 63,000 voters had opted to become part of South Sudan.

A sudden deterioration in the situation in **South Sudan** occurred in early December, following an increase in tensions between political factions in Juba. On 16 December, South Sudanese President Salva Kiir alleged that a coup had been attempted by forces loyal to former vice president Riek Machar. The UNSC held intense consultations for several days in order to assess the rapid escalation of the crisis. On 24 December, resolution 2132 authorised the military and police capacity of a UN Mission in South Sudan.

With regard to **Darfur**, the peace process made limited progress. In October, UNSG Special Representative and joint UN-AU mediator Mohamed Ibn Chambas briefed the UNSC on his meetings with key figures from rebel groups and reported their ongoing commitment to a negotiated political settlement. Under-Secretary-General for Peacekeeping Hervé Ladsous reported on the difficult security environment and the challenges to humanitarian assistance. On 20 November, Ambassador María Cristina Perceval (Argentina), chair of the Sudan Sanctions Committee, provided the quarterly briefing. Concern was expressed over the violations of the arms embargo and the ongoing inter-communal violence in Darfur.

Governance and Human Rights

The situation in Egypt challenged AU policies and instruments concerning the issue of **unconstitutional change of government**. While the UNSG expressed general concern over the forced removal of elected President Mohammed Morsi, the AU responded by upholding its zero tolerance of coups d'état. On 5 July, the AUPS stated that "the overthrow of the democratically elected President does not conform to the relevant provisions of the Egyptian Constitution and, therefore, falls under the definition of an unconstitutional change of Government". The AUPSC decided "to suspend the participation of Egypt in the AU's activities until the restoration of constitutional order". Despite the above, as the applicability of the norm on unconstitutional changes of government was uncertain when a popular uprising was instrumental in ousting a government, the AU decision raised deep controversies.

The issue of elections in Africa was the theme of the third edition of the **African Governance Report**, jointly produced by UNECA and UNDP. The report, entitled 'Elections and Management of Diversity in Africa', monitored governance trends and progress on the continent and recommended major electoral, institutional, political and constitutional reforms to improve the quality and credibility of elections and ensure their contribution to the democratic management of diversity.

The UNSG's annual report on **children and armed conflicts** presented detailed information about grave violations committed against children in Côte d'Ivoire, the CAR, Sudan, South Sudan, Somalia, the DRC and Mali. The report noted that, despite some improvements, notably the adoption by the DRC and Somalia of action plans to end the recruitment and use of child soldiers and sexual violence against children, the practices continued to plague the continent. On 17 September, the AU and UNICEF signed an agreement aimed at strengthening their cooperation in protecting conflict-affected children in Africa. The agreement called for the development of a joint programme of work to align domestic legislation with regional and international child rights, as well as to develop guidelines on protection of children.

In October, during his briefing at the UNSC, UN Special Advisor on the Prevention of Genocide Adam Dieng warned of **genocidal acts in the CAR**. He reported widespread acts of sexual violence committed against women and children; extrajudicial killing of civilians; enforced disappearances; arbitrary arrests, detention and torture; and the destruction and looting of property, including in hospitals, schools and churches. Incitement by Christians and Muslims to commit violence against each other was indicated as a clear manifestation of the risk of genocide.

Humanitarian Assistance

The numbers of victims exposed to a humanitarian crisis in the **Sahel region** – 20.2 m people estimated to be living in food insecurity; 11.8 m people targeted for food assistance in 2014; and 5 m children under five acutely malnourished – remained a source of concern. Nearly 200,000 Malian refugees in neighbouring countries remained in their camps, while IDPs in Mali began to return to the north in significant numbers. The launch of counter-terrorist operations in three federal states in the north of Nigeria in May was associated with increased violence and displacement. Funding of the 2013 appeal reached 63%, or about $ 1.1 bn, of the $ 1.7 bn requested. Humanitarian efforts across the region supported over 700,000 refugees. Over 1 m acutely malnourished children were treated. Agricultural assistance reached over 3.3 m farmers and agro-pastoralists. Across the nine Sahel countries, 7.4 m infants were vaccinated against measles and 1,787 nutritional centres delivered the WASH (water, sanitation and hygiene) minimum package. Despite this progress, an estimated 11.3 m people remained at risk of food insecurity, although these numbers indicated a sharp reduction from the 18 m reported in 2012.

The conflict in the **CAR** created a major humanitarian crisis. The entire population, estimated at 4.6 m, was directly or indirectly affected and almost half were in need of humanitarian assistance. UNHCR reported that the overall number displaced was 872,000, which included 639,000 registered IDPs and 233,000 refugees. Half of the IDPs were assessed as moderately or severely food insecure. In total, 20,366 refugees from the DRC and Sudan residing in the CAR also became much more vulnerable due to the deterioration in the situation. In early November, as a consequence of sectarian fighting that emerged between Christian militia groups and fighters of the former Séléka rebel movement (mainly Muslims), 215,000 people had been internally displaced. According to UNHCR, as of 20 December about 639,000 people (14% of the CAR population) had been internally displaced. In early December, the UN Office for the Coordination of Humanitarian Affairs (UNOCHA) presented a 100-day plan and requested the disbursement of $ 152.2 m to scale-up operations and increase the provision of protection and life-saving assistance to people in need of urgent care over the next 100 days. The crisis in the CAR also negatively affected food security. As of 25 December, the WFP had provided over 1,400 tonnes of food to more than 196,000 people. It also provided general food distributions in over 30 sites scattered around the country.

With regard to the continuing humanitarian crisis in **Darfur**, UNOCHA, in cooperation with humanitarian partners, launched the Humanitarian Hotline (or camp referral system). The initiative specifically targeted West Darfur and aimed at ensuring that the basic needs of an estimated 265,000 people living in IDP camps were adequately met. Out of the $ 980 m requested by UNOCHA for humanitarian assistance, only $ 546 m (54%) was received. UNOCHA also reported that, according to the Government's Humanitarian Aid Commission and community leaders in South Darfur, between March and November an estimated 55,000 people fled their homes following inter-tribal fighting in the state.

A sudden humanitarian crisis erupted in **South Sudan** following tensions between government forces and opposition groups. On 26 December, UNOCHA announced that, of the more than 121,000 people displaced in fighting that had spread to five of South Sudan's ten states, about 63,000 had sought protection at UN bases across the country. As of 25 December, UNOCHA ensured that 2,875 families were provided with food and primary assistance in Juba and its surroundings.

Modest gains were made in food security in **Somalia**. Data indicated that the number of Somalis in crisis was reduced to 870,000, but at year's end there were still 2.3 m people in "stress" who were barely able to meet their food needs and relied on livelihood support. In addition, about 206,000 children under five (i.e., one in seven) were reported to be suffering from acute malnutrition. This remained among the highest rations for child malnutrition in the world. The UNOCHA Consolidated Appeal for humanitarian assistance in Somalia received only $ 558 m out of the $ 1.14 bn requested for the first year of the triennium 2013–15. Consequently, fewer people were reached than planned and the implementation of longer-term programmes to shore up resilience was limited. In light of the on-going insecurity, humanitarian workers ability to plan and carry out aid work was negatively affected.

In the **DRC**, the estimated number of IDPs reached 2.7 m. While the numbers increased in North Kivu, Maniema and Orientale provinces, they fell somewhat in South Kivu and Katanga. Fighting between the Congolese armed forces and the M23 in North Kivu forced thousands more Congolese to seek refuge across the border in neighbouring Uganda and Rwanda. The humanitarian appeal for the DRC, estimated at $ 892 m, was only partly covered, with $ 563 m (63%) funded as of 2 December. Due to the lack of funding, some organisations were compelled to drastically restructure their presence and downsize some field offices, thus reducing the scope of humanitarian assistance they could provide.

Sustainable Development and Environment

The 21st AU Summit adopted crucial decisions on the post-2015 development agenda. Member states and Regional Economic Communities were called upon to promote, support and build alliances for an African Common Position (ACP) on the **post-2015 development agenda** with a view to ensuring Africa's ability to speak with one voice during discussion of the issue that would take place at the 69th session of the UNGA. A High-Level Committee of Heads of State and Government on the post-2015 agenda, chaired by Liberia's President Ellen Johnson Sirleaf, was also established. A Secretariat composed of UNECA, UNDP and the AfDB supported the work of the AUC in preparing the ACP, which was submitted for further discussion and approval at the 22nd Ordinary Summit of the AU. The ACP identified structural economic transformation and inclusive growth; peace and security; innovation and technology transfer; human development; and financing and partnership, as the key continental priorities. The ACP was expected to serve as platform for the African continent to engage in negotiation with international partners on the designing of a new internationally agreed development framework tasked to succeed the MDGs.

The first **Africa Food Security and Adaptation Conference** on 'Harnessing Ecosystem-based Approaches for Food Security and Adaptation to Climate Change in Africa' was held on 20–21 August at the UN headquarters in Nairobi (Kenya). Convened by UNEP, in collaboration with FAO, other UN agencies, governments and stakeholders, the conference explored ecosystem-based approaches to enhance food security, ecosystem productivity and climate change adaptation in Africa. The conference adopted a declaration on 'Ecosystem-based Approaches for Food Security and Climate Change Adaptation', which recognised ecosystem-based adaptation approaches as the first step towards building resilient food systems and adapting to climate change in Africa.

The African Climate Policy Centre (ACPC), a joint UNECA-AUC initiative, organised the Third Annual **Conference on Climate Change and Development in Africa** (CCDA-III) in Addis Ababa on 21–23 October. The conference provided a forum for sharing experience, disseminating research results and assessing how Africa was coping with the impacts of climate change. Recommendations on how to facilitate Africa's transition to a green economy, especially clean energy access, low carbon development options, and climate finance were agreed. The **Africa Climate Conference** 2013 took place in Arusha (Tanzania). The conference, organised under the auspices of ACPC and the World Climate Research Programme gathered decision-makers and climate researchers, scientists and practitioners from Africa and around the world, to identify the state of knowledge on the African climate system and define an African agenda for future climate research that would inform adaptation decisions for the 21st century. The conference identified a set of concrete research proposals aimed at addressing the critical gaps in continental knowledge of the African climate system, and providing science-based climate knowledge that would inform regional and international decision-making on the issue.

A major development in the field of natural resource management was the launch of the **African Mineral Development Centre** (AMDC) in December in Maputo (Mozambique) at the margins of the AU Conference of Ministers Responsible for Mineral Resources

Development. The AMDC – a joint initiative of UNECA, the UNDP-Bureau for Africa, the AU and the AfDB – was expected to support African countries' efforts to maximise the use of natural resources and facilitate the establishment of responsible extractive governance and regulatory frameworks that could more effectively contribute to economic transformation and national development plans.

Valerio Bosco

III. African-European Relations

Africa-Europe relations revolved around several major issues during the year. African crises once again drew a lot of attention in European media and political circles, especially with regard to France's intervention in Mali and its aftermath and the end-of-year escalation of violence in the CAR and South Sudan. The fate of African migrants to Europe made headlines but did not result in much political action. The future of relations between Africa and Europe was a recurring theme during the year, highlighted by the AU's 50th birthday celebrations and apparent in several discussions at the continent-continent level and between the EU and African Regional Economic Communities (RECs). African politics also came into focus, particularly the elections in Kenya, Mali and Zimbabwe. Nelson Mandela's passing was widely mourned throughout Europe. Security cooperation continued to be a major area of focus, particularly in the Horn of Africa and the Sahel regions. The evolution of mutual interests in sustainable economic development resulted in significant progress in tortuous EPA negotiations.

European Reactions to Crises in Mali, the CAR and South Sudan

French attacks on **Malian rebels** who had taken control of the north of the country began on 11 January, following an appeal for help from the Malian government to the former colonial power after rebel forces advanced on the important regional town of Mopti. French fighter jets and helicopters stopped the rebel advance and attacked bases behind the front line in Aghabo, Douentza, Gao, Kidal and Lere. France also deployed around 500 troops in the capital city, Bamako, to protect the 6,000 French citizens living there. One French helicopter pilot died in the operation, codenamed **'Serval'**, the name of a sub-Saharan wildcat. Other EU member states provided logistical support to the French intervention. The UK lent two cargo planes to fly armoured vehicles from France to Mali, but the British government was quick to announce that its soldiers would not take part in the fighting.

While generally recognising the need to intervene, the European press was wary of the risks of such a military operation. French Defence Minister Jean-Yves Le Drian said that France had been forced to take action by the prospect that a terrorist state would be created near Europe and France, but several commentators pointed out that the intervention might actually increase the terrorist threat if radical Islamists could successfully spin the narrative as an attack on Islam. A rebel commander in Gao told US news agency Associated Press that "no French person can feel safe anywhere in the world" following the attacks. Later in the year, two journalists from Radio France Internationale were kidnapped and murdered in Kidal, northern Mali. French newspapers warned that, although Malians, exhausted by the rebel conflict, may have been glad of France's intervention, their welcome would quickly wear thin if France's behaviour in any way resembled neo-colonialism. Some commentators pointed out that France's reasons for intervening were unlikely to have been purely altruistic. France's interests in stability in Mali and the rest of the Sahel region were linked to its own interests in securing resources, especially oil and uranium, which French energy company Areva was mining in neighbouring Niger. One UK newspaper found it disturbing that **UK Prime Minister David Cameron** involved Britain in Mali's conflict without consultation, and warned of the possibility of 'mission creep', which might trigger deeper British involvement. Another widely discussed reaction was that, although the Islamist rebels were clearly the bad guys, the Malian government in Bamako was not exactly known for its human-rights-loving democratic credentials.

In part to downplay accusations of neo-colonialism, France did not want to be seen to be acting alone in Mali. The **UNSC** approved the military intervention, and the EU promised to train Malian soldiers through its European Union Training Mission (EUTM) to Mali. France also called for a multilateral intervention from African countries, involving African troops. These signals of support from Brussels, other European capitals, and from African countries, were very important for legitimising France's intervention. Not all French voices agreed: a senior French military officer said France was better off without NATO or EU help to "reconquer" northern Mali, because cumbersome decision-making procedures, half-hearted commitment and incompetence would limit France's freedom of action and the efficiency of the military operations. But he recommended that French soldiers pull back after prevailing in the initial assault and let African soldiers, especially desert specialists from **Chad**, take over the long-term campaign to drive jihadists out of the **Sahel region**'s vast deserts.

The sudden escalation of the Malian crisis caught many Europeans by surprise. Former European Commission president, Romano Prodi, was in Bamako on 10 January when rebel forces surged towards the capital. He recalled that he had been at a meeting at 1pm to discuss the country's future, upcoming elections and governance and that, shortly afterwards, he was told that the Malian army had fallen into disarray and the government had asked France to intervene. "Three hours later," he told an interviewer, "the [French] decision was taken and I don't think anybody [at UN-level or EU-level] was consulted." The crisis kick-started regional and EU-level plans to build and train an international force to recapture rebel-held areas. **Burkina Faso, Niger, Nigeria** and **Togo** quickly pledged to send 500 troops each to help Mali's war effort and **Algeria** allowed French jets to use its airspace. **EU High Representative for Foreign and Security Policy Catherine Ashton** announced that the EU would accelerate preparations for the deployment of a military training mission to Mali. On 17 January, the **EU Foreign Affairs Council** met in an extraordinary session to discuss events in Mali. It announced that it had decided to allocate € 50 m from the **African Peace Facility** to support the deployment of the African-led International Support Mission to Mali. The Council's extraordinary session also resulted in the establishment of the already-planned EUTM to Mali. The mission, commanded by French General François Lecointre, was launched on 18 February, with a commitment to provide around 500 European military personnel.

On 15 May, the EU hosted the 'Together for a New Mali' international donor conference in **Brussels**. Participants included 13 heads of state and government, delegations from 108 countries and international institutions, and several ministers of foreign affairs, together with representatives of local authorities, civil society, the Malian diaspora and the private sector. The Malian government presented its Sustainable Recovery Plan for 2013–2014 and requested the support of the international community in financing it. Donors duly pledged € 3.25 bn for Mali over the following two years for priority areas including governance, regional cooperation, the private sector (which was expected to take on the burden of developing infrastructure and the agricultural sector), social sectors and inclusivity. The EU institutions pledged € 520 m, which **Commission President Jose Manuel Barroso** said would help Mali become "stable, democratic and prosperous" and would benefit Europe as well as Africa. The **German government** promised a further € 100 m on condition that Mali's political leaders continue on the way to the return of credible democracy. The EU council also stressed the importance of re-starting political dialogue with the Malian government under Article 8 of the **Cotonou Agreement**.

Central African Republic

Europeans kept a close watch on the **turmoil in the CAR** throughout the year following the overthrow of President François Bozizé in March. The EU expressed its deep concern at the turn of events on 5 December, when widespread violence caused heavy civilian casualties and a dramatic worsening of the humanitarian situation. EU leaders noted the risk posed by the CAR conflict to neighbouring countries and commended the rapid deployment by the AU of the International Support Mission in the CAR (MISCA), supported by France's Operation Sangaris in accordance with UNSC Resolution 2127. France stepped up its troop deployment to 1,600 in a bid to disarm the rival Christian and Muslim militias. French Foreign Minister Laurent Fabius said that Europe should pay more of the costs related to the military mission. **EU development Commissioner Andris Piebalgs** responded by allocating € 50 m from the African Peace Facility to support the African-led International MISCA mission, a force of about 4,800 soldiers. EU emergency relief aid also increased to € 76 m over the year, € 39 m of which was humanitarian aid. € 23 m was mobilised in December in response to the crisis and the EU organised several airlifts of relief material and personnel into the country.

In announcing the French troop increase, **French President François Hollande** said that the CAR operation did not "have the vocation to last long" and that it would be smaller than the one in Mali in January. As in the case of in Mali, Hollande was quick to reject suggestions that French-owned uranium mines in the resource-rich country had anything to do with his decision, insisting that he had "no other objective than to save human lives" and to "show solidarity with a small country, a friendly country, the poorest in the world, who is asking for our help". The US State Department welcomed France's decision amid reports of the murder of civilians throughout the country.

South Sudan

From an outside perspective it appeared that South Sudan's year followed a similar pattern to the CAR's, in that simmering tension boiled over into widespread violence in December. European concerns were, however, focused more on South Sudan's international relations than on its domestic travails. In June, High Representative Ashton expressed the EU's concerns at the Sudanese government's announcement that it would shut down oil exports from South Sudan through Port Sudan, and freeze the nine cooperation agreements with the government of South Sudan signed in Addis Ababa in September 2012. The oil shutdown was seen as resulting from a spat between elites in the two countries' ruling parties, and Ashton urged both sides to prioritise the interests of their citizens by pursuing mutually beneficial relations between the two states.

In December, it became clear that some senior figures in the South Sudan government were more concerned with internal politicking than with the country's development. The violence that started on 15 December received extensive media coverage in Europe, but muted official reaction from Europe's political leadership, despite concerns that it could lead to a full-scale civil war. Germany's new Foreign Minister Frank Walter Steinmeier warned that the conflict must not spread to the rest of the country. On 20 December, the **EU Delegation in Juba** issued a statement together with the heads of mission of the EU member state embassies and of Switzerland and Norway. The Delegation condemned the violence and appealed to all parties to use the good offices of IGAD and the AU to resolve the conflict. It called on the South Sudan government to release arrested politicians so that they could participate in a peaceful settlement.

The EU Commission's focus turned from long-term development programming to providing short-term emergency relief. It announced that it would make an extra € 50 m available for responding to the unfolding humanitarian crisis, bringing total EU aid for South Sudan in 2013–14 to € 259 m. The extra emergency aid included assistance for IDPs, refugees, local host communities and returnees. Many aid workers were evacuated during the Christmas period, but the Commission's Humanitarian Aid and Civil Protection Department, **DG ECHO**, sent humanitarian experts to liaise with partner organisations in

South Sudan on how best to contribute. At the diplomatic level, special envoys from the EU supported IGAD in attempting to broker talks between key leaders in the crisis.

A 'Joined up' European Crisis Response?

Cracks in the EU's unanimity with regard to African crises had started to appear by year's end. In mid-December, **German Chancellor Angela Merkel** told the European Council that the EU would not provide funding for French military missions in Africa. French President Hollande's request for a joint fund to support military operations conducted by individual states was declined by the other 27 EU members, who decided only to "rapidly examine" the ways in which European-led military operations were financed. Merkel's statement implied that the decision was based on France's propensity to launch interventions without consulting other EU members.

The Lampedusa Tragedy

The number of sub-Saharan Africans attempting to cross the Mediterranean continued to grow. Every week, hundreds of people risked their lives to try to enter the EU in unseaworthy boats. July saw 1,500 arrivals in **Malta**, a new monthly record. For those who reached Europe, life was extremely precarious – most boat people ended up being deported back to their country of origin, while those who escaped from detention centres and refugee camps condemned themselves to a life of homelessness and vulnerability on the edges of society.

Many did not make it safely across the sea. On 3 October, 359 people – mostly citizens of **Somalia** and **Eritrea** – died when a migrant ship caught fire and sank off the coast of the Italian island of **Lampedusa**. Europe's political leadership equivocated on the issue. **Pope Francis** prayed for the victims of the latest tragedy and paid homage to the desperate people who risked their lives by leaving Africa for Europe. **European Parliament President Martin Schulz** called for more channels of legal immigration to be opened. The Italian and Maltese governments called for the rest of Europe to step up and help them process migrants. The EU Commission pointed out how complicated it would be to decide which country migrants should go to and how the numbers should be fairly allocated.

The disinterested response to the tragedy by African leaders attracted criticism from some African news sites. Jean-Baptiste Natama, a senior AUC official, expressed the AU's sincere condolences to victims' families on 7 October and stressed the AU's intention to work with international partners on solutions to prevent such tragedies. He called on AU member states to create opportunities for young people to find decent jobs in their home countries. African heads of state and government eventually declared 3 November a continent-wide day of mourning and the AU advised member states to fly their flags at half mast.

In the wake of the Lampedusa tragedy, some EU leaders reacted by calling for aid to be targeted at African countries that were major sources of illegal immigration. French President Hollande said in October that he would propose a policy based on "prevention, solidarity and protection", better cooperation with countries of origin and a more active Euro-Mediterranean policy. **Italian Prime Minister Enrico Letta** said the EU response should include a re-launch of development cooperation, with more attention given to countries such as Ethiopia and Somalia. UK Prime Minister Cameron spoke of the need to "invest" in countries "before they get broken" instead of dealing with immigration problems later. The EU Commission agreed that there was a link between giving aid and containing migratory flows but insisted that the two policy areas had different rationales, especially as the MDGs did not mention migration.

AU-EU Relations and the Future of the Joint Africa-Europe Strategy

In May, EU Commission President Barroso congratulated the AU on its 50th anniversary at the celebrations held in Addis Ababa, Ethiopia. Barroso reaffirmed the EU's support for the intercontinental partnership under the **Joint Africa-Europe Strategy (JAES)**. For the rest of the year EU-AU relations were dominated by discussions over the future of the partnership amid questionable commitment on both sides. In April, the AU and the EU jointly published a statement reaffirming their vows, entitled '2 Unions, 1 Vision'. The document outlined some of the challenges facing the relationship in a rapidly changing global geopolitical setting, and called on member governments on both sides to commit fully to the partnership. Readers were reminded of successes in all of the eight JAES partnerships and called for the JAES to become more visible and better at outreach. The document also contained more information about the Commission's proposal for the **'pan-African Programme'** for financing the JAES under the next EU budget for 2014–20. It was noted that the AU had embarked upon the definition of its own policy agenda and the reappraisal of its relationships with strategic partners, including the EU. Significantly for the future of the JAES, the statement pointed out that these crucial processes would call for a "refocusing" of the Africa-EU Partnership in the coming years.

The **European External Action Service** and EU member state governments discussed reducing the number of partnerships in the JAES from eight to three, focusing on peace and democracy, sustainable growth and 'global issues'. The proposal was discussed on the African side at a brainstorming meeting held in Zanzibar, Tanzania, in June. Participants included representatives from 15 AU member states, the chefs de file for each thematic partnership, representatives from the various AU organs (the Panafrican Parliament, the African Commission of Human and People's Rights, NEPAD and the AU's Brussels office), the RECs and other stakeholders including UNECA and the AfDB. The meeting helped prepare African positions ahead of a joint brainstorming in mid-September and the

AU-EU Joint Task Force meeting in late October, both held in Brussels. The AU Commission for its part proposed five priorities: peace and security, democracy and governance, regional integration, sustainable and inclusive development, and the development of human capital.

The end results of these meetings were inconclusive, with both sides reaffirming the value and potential of the JEAS for structuring inter-continental relations, but at the same time noting that they were not very happy with how things had worked out thus far. Some key weaknesses of the partnership were not addressed head on, most notably the lack of member state political will to make it work. Participants agreed that future cooperation should focus on results in areas such as continued security cooperation (including surveillance of criminal and terrorist groups in the Sahel region), economic partnership, investment aimed at easing Africa's youth unemployment crisis, and the development of markets. It was agreed that work would continue on defining exactly what these results might be, and how they might benefit the lives of ordinary citizens of both continents, in the run-up to the **AU-EU Summit** scheduled for April 2014.

Death of Nelson Mandela

The news of Nelson Mandela's death was received in Europe with the dignity befitting a man of his stature. European leaders universally praised his leadership, vision, humility and determination to live up to the values he espoused. EU institutions flew their flags at half mast, and European leaders hurried to **South Africa** to attend Mandela's funeral. EU High Representative Ashton said in a statement that Mandela had provided an inspiration for democrats on all continents, including Europe, by showing that the moral force of democracy could triumph even in the face of the most brutal opposition. Nevertheless, a tinge of hypocrisy that was evident in some statements did not go unnoticed: upon Mandela's death, UK Prime Minister Cameron tweeted: "A great light has gone out in the world. Nelson Mandela was a hero of our time." This was somewhat different from the position taken in the 1980s by Cameron's predecessor, Margaret Thatcher, who once described the ANC "as a typical terrorist organisation".

European Reactions to African Elections

Following the **Kenyan** elections held on 4 March, European governments were silent on how they would work with the new government headed by **President Uhuru Kenyatta**. Britain and the EU praised Kenyans for holding peaceful elections but avoided naming Kenyatta and only offered blanket congratulations to all those elected. The head of the EU observer mission, Alojz Peterle, said Kenya had demonstrated "impressive commitment to democratic elections". When **Prime Minister Raila Odinga** contested the results at the Kenyan Supreme Court, High Representative Ashton cautiously called upon Kenyans to respect the rule of law. Kenyatta's Jubilee Coalition accused the British high commissioner in Kenya of "canvassing to have rejected votes tallied", an accusation the UK Foreign Office described as "entirely false and misleading". Other partners were less reluctant to accept the outcome. The **Chinese government** extended its congratulations to Kenyatta for winning the elections and praised Kenyans for voting peacefully, as did **South African President Jacob Zuma**. **The ICC in The Hague** postponed Kenyatta's trial on charges of crimes against humanity.

The European Union "took note" of the results of **Zimbabwe**'s elections, held on 31 July, but did not congratulate **Robert Mugabe** on his election victory. High Representative Ashton expressed the EU's concern about alleged irregularities, but the EU nevertheless decided to respect the assessments of the SADC and AU observers. The EU congratulated the people of Zimbabwe on a peaceful poll and for turning out in high numbers. German Foreign Minister Guido Westerwelle was very critical of the lack of transparency in Zimbabwe's presidential elections, which he predicted would cast a long shadow over the country's political and economic future. Germany joined **UN Secretary-General Ban Ki-moon** in calling for a comprehensive investigation into allegations of manipulation and voter exclusion.

The heavy European investment in stabilising **Mali** extended to the troubled country's democratic process. Former EU Development Commissioner Louis Michel headed the EU's observer mission for Mali's presidential election in August and parliamentary elections held on 24 November and 15 December. He said that all of the polls had met international standards for democratic elections. High Representative Ashton called on all candidates and parties involved to accept the verdict of the ballot box. **Former federal president Horst Köhler** represented Germany at **President Ibrahim Boubacar Keita**'s inauguration ceremony in September, and German Chancellor Merkel invited the new Malian president to Berlin soon afterwards. For his part, President Keïta declared Germany to be "Mali's most important partner in the world", a statement that was no doubt less than popular in Paris.

Peace and Security Cooperation

Aside from the crisis responses discussed above, peace and security cooperation revolved around instability in the **Horn of Africa**, the **Great Lakes** area and the **Sahel**, and on the threat posed by **piracy** to European and African shipping in Africa's coastal waters and sea lanes. The major continental-level peace and security meeting took place in Addis Ababa on 11 June, when the AU Peace and Security Council and the EU Political and Security Committee held their 6th Annual Joint Consultative Meeting. Discussions focused on the security situation in Mali, Guinea Bissau, Somalia, Sudan and South Sudan, the DRC and the CAR, as well as the regional implications for the Sahel, Great Lakes and Horn sub-regions. The international campaign to eliminate the **Lord's Resistance Army** was also on the agenda, as was ongoing cooperation in a number of peace-building operations, especially the AU Mission to Somalia.

Sahel

EU-Africa cooperation in addressing the regional implications of conflicts in Sahel countries was pushed to a new level by the Mali crisis. European leaders issued several statements during the year underlining the importance of stability in the Sahel and reiterating Europe's commitment to supporting Mali's neighbouring states' security and development under the aegis of the EU's Sahel Strategy. Luxembourg Foreign Minister Jean Asselborn accused the Mali rebels of atrocities against women and children, and raised the spectre of terrorists "creating hell on earth for people" in Niger and Mauritania as well. On 17 January, EU foreign ministers held a crisis meeting after 41 foreigners – mostly Europeans, Japanese and Americans – were taken hostage at the British-Norwegian **In Amenas gas plant** in Algeria. The hostage takers claimed that their attack on the gas plant was in retaliation for France's intervention in Mali. The actions of the Algerian security services in ending the bloody hostage crisis received only muted criticism in Europe, even though several hostages were killed.

The EU took several steps to strengthen its **Sahel strategy** during the year. On 18 March, the EU Council appointed former French ambassador to Mali and Chad Michel Reveyrand-de Menthon as **EU Special Representative for the Sahel**. Reveyrand-de-Menthon's mandate was to lead the EU's diplomatic contribution to regional and international efforts to achieve lasting peace in the Sahel. He was also asked to coordinate the EU's comprehensive approach to the regional implications of the Mali crisis. Also in March, the EU launched a new project to fight organised crime and money laundering in Ghana, Nigeria, Senegal and Cape Verde. The project, funded by the EU's **Instrument for Stability**, aimed to increase regional cooperation between countries on the 'Cocaine route' used by South American drug cartels to ship drugs to Europe, which runs through the Sahel. Also targeting organised crime, the EU Capacity Building (EUCAP) Sahel mission in Niger stepped up its activities during the year, especially regarding building the capacity of regional governments' security agencies to collect and share intelligence on the activities of organised criminal networks and terrorist groups. In November, the EU announced that it was reinforcing its support for the Sahel for the years to come. Development Commissioner Piebalgs visited the region as part of a delegation with UN Secretary-General Ban Ki-moon, World Bank President Jim Yong Kim, AU Commission Chair Nkosazana Dlamini-Zuma, and AfDB President Donald Kaberuka. Piebalgs offered around € 5 bn, allocated from the 11th EDF for 2014–20 to help the governments of Burkina Faso, Mali, Mauritania, Niger, Senegal and Chad tackle some of the complex challenges of the Sahel region, especially security, stability, governance and economic development.

Horn of Africa

The EU's Horn of Africa strategy received a lot of praise during the year for reflecting an approach to the regional dimensions of conflict that addressed complex issues in a sensitive way. In January, the EU Parliament passed a resolution welcoming the Horn of Africa strategy and its comprehensive approach based on tackling security and stability concerns. The UK Parliament complimented EU Special Representative for the Horn of Africa, Greek diplomat Alexander Rondos, for his "creditable performance". The implementation of the Supporting Horn of Africa Resilience initiative, aimed at improving the region's food security, was stepped up with the announcement that the EU would provide € 50 m to build resilience to drought in southern and eastern Ethiopia.

The focus of the major EU security mission in the region, EUTM Somalia, changed as its mandate was extended until March 2015. During the year, attention turned to training the trainers. Some older, more experienced Somalian soldiers returned for a second time to the training camp at Bihanga in Uganda. The Bihanga camp was handed back to the Ugandan army in December, and EUTM Somalia was transferred from Uganda to a new camp near Mogadishu, due to open in early 2014. Italian Brigadier-General Massimo Mingiardi was appointed EUTM Somalia's new mission commander.

The UK also returned to Somalia. Foreign Secretary William Hague opened a new British embassy near Mogadishu airport, restoring British diplomatic presence in Somalia for the first time since 1991. The UK was the first EU member state to reopen an embassy in the country since the **Somalian Federal Government** was established in 2012. Hague said that the embassy was testament to the close ties between the UK and the Somalian government, with which he promised to continue to work on shared priorities including conflict resolution, counter terrorism, piracy, humanitarian assistance, and promoting UK interests in Somalia.

The security of foreigners living and working in Africa came under the spotlight following the 21 September **Nairobi shopping mall gun battle**, in which 59 people were killed and another 175 wounded. Five British citizens were among the dead. European foreign ministries condemned the attack but offered only rhetorical support to the Kenyan authorities in dealing with the situation. High Representative Ashton said that the EU was "willing to do our utmost to help prevent such attacks happening in the future", but this stopped short of concrete offers to help track the perpetrators and bring them to justice. The ambiguity was not altogether surprising once Somalian opposition group **al-Shabab** claimed responsibility for the attack, making it clear that this was no isolated incident and that bringing the perpetrators to justice would not be easy.

Piracy

Piracy continued to be a key area of mutual interest for Europe and Africa. On 10 January, a new EU initiative to combat piracy in the **Gulf of Guinea** was launched. The Critical

Maritime Routes in the Gulf of Guinea Programme initiative focused on boosting the security and the safety of shipping routes among seven African countries (Benin, Cameroon, Equatorial Guinea, Gabon, Nigeria, Sâo Tomé and Príncipe and Togo) by training coastguards and establishing an information-sharing network between countries and agencies across the region. The European interest was clear: the Gulf of Guinea accounted for 13% of oil and 6% of gas imports to the EU. From the African perspective, the threats posed on several levels by piracy and related trade in drugs, guns and human beings, were also seen as strong reasons to support the EU initiative.

The EU Naval Force 'Atalanta' anti-piracy operation in the **Gulf of Aden** continued during the year. Several observers commended the operation's success after four years of naval deployment. In December, the US Office of Naval Intelligence reported that only nine vessels had been attacked by pirates during the year, with no successful hijackings. In May, the **German Bundestag** approved the government's request to extend the mission for a further 12 months.

The Atalanta mission was complemented by the EU's maritime security capacity building mission, EUCAP Nestor. Nestor was directed towards improving the capacity of the countries of the Horn region to prevent piracy in their own waters. The missions came together in an interesting way in December, when Atalanta's French flagship, FS Siroco, hosted a meeting with senior **Somaliland** officials, including **Vice President Abdirahman Abdallahi Ismail Saylici**. The representatives of a country whose sovereignty no EU member state had recognised were welcomed on board. The official EU press release commended Somaliland for its important role in countering piracy and strengthening regional maritime security by deterring pirates' activities on land. The event took place at sea off the coast of Berbera, Somaliland, and was an opportunity to highlight the complementary work of the two EU missions and how they worked together with regional actors to help strengthen security and local capacities.

Economic Development in Africa

Several high-profile events focussing on Africa's economic development took place during the year. The overarching structure for EU support for development in Africa, the financial protocol of the **Cotonou Agreement**, was adopted on 28 May by the EU Foreign Affairs Council. The protocol allocated a total of € 31.5 bn in development aid to **ACP states** for the 2014–20 period, most of which would go to bilateral programmes with sub-Saharan African countries. High Representative Ashton and Development Commissioner Piebalgs issued a joint statement following the adoption of the protocol, which re-iterated the EU's commitment to development cooperation. They pointed out that their efforts were backed by European public opinion: a Eurobarometer survey from late 2012 revealed that help for developing countries was supported by 85% of EU citizens. They also promised greater impact and better results from aid programmes through better targeting of resources at the poorest countries and at fewer sectors per country. The intention to focus on results was further confirmed by the EU Commission's adoption in July of a policy paper proposing that all types of development aid in the post-2015 period be considered as "a whole", with resources streamlined according to well-defined policy objectives.

After many years of deadlock, progress on **EPA negotiations** was finally made. The EU-West Africa EPA negotiations resumed after the **Dakar ECOWAS Summit** on 25 October. **EU Trade Commissioner Karel de Gucht** predicted that the EU would be able to finalise a trade agreement with ECOWAS in three months' time. Negotiations had previously broken down amid disagreement over the speed at which West African nations were willing to open their markets and lift tariff barriers. The EPAs required sweeping liberalisation of African markets, a stipulation that reminded many Africans of the World Bank and IMF structural adjustment programmes that had had destructive effects on African economies in the 1980s and 1990s. Nevertheless, ECOWAS heads of state agreed in October to implement a single customs tariff regime from 2015, allowing talks with the EU to restart.

Sustainable Development, Infrastructure and Energy

On 25–26 June, the Egyptian resort of **Sharm el-Sheikh** hosted the Global Monitoring for Environment and Security and Africa (GMES & Africa) workshop on Long-Term Management of Natural Resources. Under the EU-Africa Partnership, the decision was made to formulate an Action Plan for enhancing the use of earth observation. The JAES Support Mechanism had contributed to the process by facilitating the development of priority chapters decided by African and EU stakeholders. A consultation platform was launched through a series of three thematic workshops, including one on long-term natural resources management in Egypt. Marine and coastal areas and water resources management were addressed in two other workshops held in Mombasa, Kenya, and Abuja, Nigeria. In October, South Africa hosted the final discussions on the Action Plan, to draw recommendations for the future of GMES & Africa that could be presented at the Africa-EU Summit in Brussels in April 2014.

The fifth special session of the African Ministerial Conference on the Environment was held on 17–18 October in Gaborone, Botswana, under the aegis of the AU and was attended by **European Climate Action Commissioner Connie Hedegaard**. She called for strengthened cooperation between Europe and Africa to combat climate change. The ministerial session in Gaborone took stock of progress in Africa's preparations for the 19th Conference of the Parties to the UN Framework Convention on Climate Change (COP 19), held in Warsaw, Poland, in November. The EU and several member states pledged € 5.5 bn in "fast start financing" to meet the urgent needs of the most vulnerable countries in facing climate change, an increase on the previous two years. Participants agreed that, in addition to financial questions, the post-**Kyoto Protocol** agreement should impose new obligations for reducing greenhouse gas emissions.

The 5th Steering Committee of the JAES Partnership on Infrastructure took place in Brussels on 28 October with participants from the AU Commission, RECs, EU member states, the AfDB, and EU Commission services. The purpose of the meeting was to take stock of achievements in infrastructure-related areas under the various thematic partnerships and to work out ways of increasing the impact of the Partnership through better coordination mechanisms.

Strategic sector papers on transport, information and communication technology, energy and transboundary water were presented by officials of the two Commissions, highlighting the major developments and strategic issues in each area. It was noted that the rolling out of the Programme for Infrastructure for Africa had started to gather momentum, especially on engagement with private sector players, whose participation was acknowledged by all parties to be key to achieving infrastructure goals in Africa. The EU Commission reported on the progress made on the establishment of financing instruments aimed at subsidising private sector involvement in infrastructure development ventures, especially in the energy sector. The meeting concluded that interventions in the main infrastructure sectors needed to be pursued and up-scaled.

The EU-Africa Chamber of Commerce held a high level conference on sustainable energy in Africa, in the context of the JAES Africa-EU partnership on energy, in Brussels on 27 June. The conference was part of the sustainable energy week organised by the EU Commission. Development Commissioner Piebalgs – who was the EU's energy commissioner prior to taking over the EU's Development Directorate-General in 2010, pointed out some challenges related to investment in the African energy sector, notably the risk posed by political instability. A related challenge was the cost of borrowing, money, an important constraint to investment in Africa. Other observers expressed rather different concerns about European investments in the African energy sector. In August, a **World Wildlife Fund** report warned that Africa's oldest national park, the Virunga National Park in the DRC, was in danger of environmental destruction because of European oil concessions.

In February, Germany and South Africa agreed to set up an energy partnership focused on expanding **renewable energy development** and increasing energy efficiency in South Africa. They also agreed to cooperate on energy research, including research into carbon capture and storage technologies. This bilateral energy partnership built on prior agreements and placed emphasis on the promotion of private sector activity. As part of the agreement, Germany sent a delegation of representatives from German solar panel companies to Johannesburg to meet with South African partner companies.

The EU Commission also pushed harder for public-private collaboration by seeking the closer involvement of development banks in financing larger projects, especially in the capital-intensive energy and transport sectors. An example of this kind of cooperation was the EU's offer of € 100 m in regional funding for what it called a "groundbreaking" infrastructure programme at the EU-South Africa summit held in Pretoria, South Africa, in July. The EU money was parcelled in loans for technical project assistance and direct grants to co-finance infrastructure projects in the energy, transport and trade sectors. The intention of the Infrastructure Investment Programme for South Africa was to leverage investments from financial institutions including the Development Bank of Southern Africa, the European Investment Bank, Germany's 'Kreditanstalt für Wiederaufbau' finance bank, and the French development agency.

Africa's attractiveness to international investors continued to improve due to expanding consumer markets, various structural reforms and economic growth. The increased interest on the part of European companies in investment in Africa was driven by two major factors: more risks in Europe as the economy declined, and the strong interest of small and medium-sized enterprises in investing in Africa for the higher returns on offer.

Mark Furness

IV. West Africa

Mali's partial collapse reverberated across the sub-region, while the war with Boko Haram engulfed much of north-east Nigeria, with rising death tolls, atrocities and destruction. Though this did not (yet) lead to significant spill-over across national borders, neighbouring countries such as Niger and Cameroon were vulnerable to the conflict's spread. French and Chadian forces joined the war against Islamist fighters, who were defeated or pushed back into the Sahara, allowing the conflict to de-escalate at least temporarily. Sporadic attacks in northern Mali, southern Algeria and neighbouring Niger underlined the Sahel's continuing vulnerability. The arrival of ECOWAS contingents, 'rehatted' as a UN force, allowed the French to scale down their troops and elections to be held. Political stability in Ghana and Senegal contrasted with these dramatic developments, and security in Côte d'Ivoire also improved, despite some problems in the west of the country. Stability remained fragile in neighbouring Guinea and especially in Guinea-Bissau. Refugees from the conflicts in Mali and Nigeria drained resources. Migrants' attempts to reach Europe across the Sahara and the Mediterranean continued, leading to several tragic incidents. Growth generally proved fairly high. Plans for railway extensions in Benin, Niger, Burkina Faso and Côte d'Ivoire were notable infrastructural developments.

Coups and Electoral Politics

There were no coups d'état in the sub-region – only an alleged plot in Benin, which probably reflected nothing more than the tense political relations between the country's president and the opposition. **Guinea-Bissau** went through another transition phase following the 2012 putsch, with the beginning of internationally funded electoral preparations including the commencement of an electoral census. The general elections scheduled for November were postponed to 2014. The presidential and legislative elections in **Mali** were arguably the most important for the sub-region, as they were meant to normalise the country after the most serious crisis in its existence and to secure the conclusion of hostilities and a preliminary peace agreement between the central government and Tuareg separatists, the least dangerous of its adversaries. While doubts were expressed about the possibility of organising elections in these circumstances, the presidential polls, held in two rounds in July–August, were pulled off with remarkable ease. Realising how close their country had come to collapse, Malians largely accepted the outcome, with a new president and a cabinet made up of newcomers taking over from a transitional government. Parliamentary elections secured a majority for the party of new President Ibrahim Boubacar Keita.

Similarly, **Côte d'Ivoire** held municipal and regional elections in April that could be seen as wrapping up the difficult transition phase since the end of the civil war. However, the elections, after a postponement of a couple of months, were boycotted by the party of defeated former president Gbagbo, who was standing trial at the ICC in The Hague. The announcement of the results led to clashes in several cities. The majority of regional council and municipal seats went to the parties of the ruling coalition of President Ouattara. Legislative elections in **Guinea** were also meant to conclude the transition to that country's new civilian dispensation under President Alpha Condé. After several delays, the polls finally took place in September; there were few incidents and observers described them as broadly free and fair. The opposition protested against the results in the capital, Conakry, but in the end attended the opening of the new Assembly in December. The opposition in **Ghana**, too, contested the close results of the previous year's general polls, but accepted the Supreme Court's ruling in August in favour of the ruling party. **Togo**'s legislative polls in July, while peaceful, were held within an electoral system marked by biased constituency boundaries and thus secured a landslide for President Gnassingbé's followers. Local elections were again postponed, as they also were in neighbouring **Benin**.

By contrast, in **Mauritania** both parliamentary and local elections, which had been postponed several times, did take place in November–December. They were boycotted by the opposition, with predictable results in favour of the ruling party. Local elections in **Burkina Faso** were rerun during February in districts marked by irregularities during the 2012 polls (38 out of 45 provinces), but merely led to a consolidation of the position of the ruling party. Similarly, the local elections in the **Gambia** in April reinforced the dominance of President Jammeh's supporters.

Human Rights and the Rule of Law

Proposals for **constitutional change** fuelled debate and political tension in both Benin and Burkina Faso. Benin's president was widely suspected of seeking to end the constitutional two-term limit on presidential periods in office, although his constitutional amendment proposals did not specify such plans. In Burkina, proposals for the establishment of a senate provoked fears that a two-chamber Assembly could be called in joint session to amend the constitution. **Judicial independence** in Benin was called into question when a judge who, for lack of evidence, threw out a case related to the alleged poisoning of the president in 2012 felt forced to flee the country. In the Gambia, the judiciary's position was much worse, however, with judges being appointed by the head of state and three Supreme Court chief justices removed in the course of the year. A UN report called for a general reappraisal of the justice system in Togo.

Côte d'Ivoire's National Assembly adopted new **nationality laws** widening access to Ivorian citizenship, and a **land law** providing landholders greater possibilities to prove claims to property – the position of foreign-born residents had been a major bone of contention in the civil war. A Land Commission in Liberia presented a draft land rights policy with the aim of better protecting the land rights of indigenous communities, traditionally under threat from Americo-Liberian settler interests and now also from foreign 'land grabbing' companies.

The political climate in the Gambia was again marked by **regime brutalities** including disappearances and harassment of opposition figures. AI also reported disappearances in Mauritania, and found evidence of torture being used against detainees. Unlawful detentions increased in Guinea. All this paled into insignificance compared with the atrocities being committed in Northern Nigeria by both Boko Haram and the security forces, as reported by HRW and AI. A UN rapporteur criticised the Togolese government for the harassment of local human rights activists. AI reported overcrowding in prisons in Benin, which, however, ratified an international protocol as a measure towards abolishing the death penalty.

In contrast to observers' expectations, legislation in Nigeria banning same-sex marriage came one step closer to implementation, while in Sierra Leone, where **same-sex relations** are officially illegal, a gay rights activist was beaten up and a police chief issued negative statements about homosexuals. Senegal defended its record on gay rights to visiting US President Barack Obama by pointing out that it did not prosecute gay people but was not ready to de-criminalise homosexuality (the country being one of the rare francophone states to have such legislation). A rape trial in Sierra Leone drew attention to domestic and **gender-based violence** – in the first eight months of the year almost 7,000 cases were reported of which only 6% ended in convictions. Lack of competent personnel prevented the police from more adequately enforcing the new sexual offences law, enacted the previous year. The high incidence of such violence should also be set against the background of the earlier civil war and its effects. Liberia, with Africa's first female president, saw the submission of legislation demanding 30% female representation on parliamentary nomination lists. Finally, a UN expert urged Benin to give more priority to **child protection** – violence against and exploitation of children was reported to be a serious issue.

Corruption scandals erupted in a number of countries. Reports revealed financial malpractices in Ghana's youth employment agency, while hospital officials in the country were accused of taking bribes from patients. In Niger, health officials were arrested on charges of embezzling funds from vaccination campaigns, and a former head of the state electricity company was likewise charged with fraud; the country's position on TI's corruption perception index nevertheless improved somewhat. The anti-corruption campaign in Nigeria slowed down, however, partly because of lack of funds – the body tasked with prosecuting suspects was unable to pay lawyers handling its prosecutions and the courts acquitted several people charged with corruption. Former ministers and associates of current cabinet members were arrested and charged with graft in Benin, but a newly established body meant to lead the struggle against corruption was said to be paralysed by lack of resources. In Senegal, the battle against graft seemed set in a politicised context, as the government of new President Macky Sall put Karim Wade, the son of the former head of state, in detention on charges of embezzlement (Karim Wade had been a powerful figure in the previous administration): a saga of numerous legal proceedings began including before the ECOWAS Court of Justice.

In Guinea-Bissau, violations of **press freedom** increased through the harassment of journalists and the government put a stop to broadcasting on one occasion. A report on Togo listed the forcible closure of private radio stations and the country's National Assembly also adopted new laws granting sweeping powers to the media watchdog. In Benin, where press freedom on the whole improved, the government interfered with the broadcast of a private television channel.

The appeals court upheld Charles Taylor's conviction for war crimes and crimes against humanity, and the former Liberian president began serving his 50-year sentence in Britain. The **Special Court for Sierra Leone** formally ended, bringing to a close a special phase in the sub-region's legal history (although a residual court was put in place).

Conflict, Instability and Violence

As in 2012, Boko Haram's forces in Northern **Nigeria** acted with total lack of restraint, while half-hearted attempts at dialogue by the government, atrocities committed by the security forces and the detention of more than 1,000 civilians in terrible conditions fuelled what by now had become an all-out war. States of emergency were imposed in three federal states, vigilante groups were formed in desperate attempts to protect the citizenry, and Boko Haram and government forces engaged each other in pitched battles that even saw the deployment of jet fighters. In December, the militants attacked Maiduguri air force base, destroying several aircraft. More often than not, however, it was unarmed civilians who were attacked by both Boko Haram and government forces. The latter, in conjunction with government forces from Niger and Chad, in April attacked the town of Baga, an assumed Boko Haram hideout, reportedly leading to the deaths of over 200 people. Though this figure was disputed by the government, HRW largely confirmed it and satellite images revealed the destruction of more than 2,000 homes. In Borno state alone, more than 500 civilians were killed during the year, as well as more than 400 Boko Haram militants. In September, alleged members of Boko Haram murdered more than 140 civilians travelling on the Maiduguri-Damaturu road. Bomb attacks in Kano targeting car parks and bars added their share to the casualties. In the face of the unprecedented escalation of violence, it was difficult to keep track of the political-religious or ideological motivations, if any, underlying the conflict. Nigeria's Middle Belt states, where numerous ethnic communities and Muslims and Christians live closely together, were again the scene of communal conflicts pitting different ethnic groups, as well as peasants and pastoralists, against each other and leaving hundreds of people dead.

The violence in **Mali** did not lead to anything like comparable levels of bloodshed, but its implications for the sub-region's stability were potentially much more serious. More than 4,000 French troops, assisted by Chadian fighters, managed to defeat or drive off Islamist fighters, pushing them back into the desert and beyond, to hideouts in south-western Libya. Figures for casualties among the rebel forces were hard to come by. The new Malian government found it hard to establish a real presence on the ground, and periodic acts of violence in the form of suicide bombings, rocket attacks and shootings continued, even in areas under government control. The conflict's spill-over potential was underlined by suicide bombings by Islamist militants in neighbouring **Niger** and attacks on government facilities in the capital.

Political stability in Guinea and Guinea-Bissau remained fragile. Tense relations between the government and opposition parties in **Guinea**, which partly overlapped with inter-ethnic rivalries, led to protest marches that descended into violence on several occasions. In the run-up to the legislative elections, dozens of people lost their lives and hundreds were injured. Communal conflict unrelated to electoral politics struck the country's

Forest region, with Christian Guerzés and Muslim Koniankés engaging each other after the death of a youth; the two communities were involved in a long-standing conflict over access to local resources. Mosques, churches and homes were burnt and at least 100 people were killed. Similarly, in **Togo**, there were violent clashes between pastoralists and peasants in the far north. In **Guinea-Bissau**, security was volatile, with violence and some killings involving both police and army troops, demonstrating, amongst other things, the uncontrolled state of the country's security forces. Much the same could be said of the Gambia. Western **Côte d'Ivoire** saw an attack on an army post near the porous Liberian border; this was an outgrowth of the earlier civil war and left seven people dead. Otherwise, the country's political stability improved somewhat, with relations between the government and the opposition benefiting from the release of a dozen former Gbagbo associates. Full national reconciliation, however, was still far off. A few people died in an attack in **Senegal**'s Casamance region, which was marked by simmering separatist conflict.

Socioeconomic Developments

The average sub-regional **growth rate** hovered around the 6% mark, with underachievers such as Cape Verde (dependent on the eurozone), Niger (hit by crop failure and reduced mining revenues), and unstable Guinea being outdistanced by several countries, especially those rich in minerals. Sierra Leone achieved the highest growth rate (over 16%), followed by high achievers such as Ghana, Liberia, Burkina Faso and more peaceful Côte d'Ivoire – all boasting figures around 7% to 8%. War-stricken Mali saw its growth plummet to just over 1%, while Nigeria's solid GDP largely reflected its oil riches.

In the **agricultural sector**, Senegal boasted a good groundnut harvest, as did Burkina Faso and Benin in cotton, though the government price paid to farmers in the latter (the highest in the CFAfr zone), and the intensive use of pesticides there cast doubts on its sustainability. Despite the civil war, cereal production in Mali recovered after the difficulties of the preceding years, increasing 14% in value and pushing down prices for consumers. By contrast, cereal harvests in Niger were grossly inadequate as a result of erratic rainfall. Three million people were in need of assistance – in Burkina Faso an estimated 1.8 m, including half a million children, were said to be suffering from malnutrition. Mauritania, too, suffered from high **food insecurity**, which affected nearly a third of the population, and Oxfam reported that 800,000 Malians were still in need of assistance, despite improved harvests. Local communities in Liberia protested against the expansion of plantation agriculture.

Infrastructural developments involved numerous new projects. Among the more remarkable was the plan to link Benin, Niger, Burkina Faso and Côte d'Ivoire by the extension of existing railway lines. This had been on the drawing board since independence. Romanian mining interests, working on manganese deposits in Burkina, and

French conglomerate Bolloré became involved in what could eventually create a full West African railway loop and significantly reduce transport costs – especially for the sub-region's landlocked states. Chinese funding was said to be available for railway construction between Abidjan and San Pedro, Côte d'Ivoire's second port, and ideas were floated for railway connections between Lagos (Nigeria), Cotonou (Benin) and Abidjan (Côte d'Ivoire). **Energy** was another focus of infrastructural development, as West African economies were still suffering from chronic power shortages. Chinese and British firms began building and extending power stations in Côte d'Ivoire, which also planned to link up its power lines with the MRU states and was expected to consolidate its position as net electricity exporter in the sub-region. A new hydroelectric dam project was started in Ghana, a US company announced it would invest in a solar power plant in Guinea-Bissau (where the population protested against power failures), and Liberia benefited from President Obama's Power Africa Initiative aimed at doubling electricity access in SSA. New power plants and transmission lines were also under construction in Mauritania. Niger's capital, Niamey, suffered some of its worst blackouts (as did Senegal) when storms brought down transmission lines importing electricity from Nigeria. The huge Kandadji hydroelectric project on the River Niger was facing new delays, and the government had to initiate plans for the construction of new diesel- and coal-fired plants; China provided a loan for the building of power lines between its local oil refinery and several cities in the country. New plans to boost energy supplies in Nigeria could hardly stem the further deterioration of the country's power sector – the victim of wilful neglect. A report on a bioenergy project in Sierra Leone cast doubt on the impact of ethanol production on food security.

Oil production in Niger picked up after the difficulties in 2012, and Nigeria's high quality crude continued to fill the state's coffers, now also to be buttressed with a sovereign wealth fund. Burkina Faso, which became compliant with the Extractive Industries Transparency Initiative, added to the importance of its **mining sector** with the opening of a zinc mine. Plans for manganese production continued apace and were expected to increase the country's role in minerals production (which includes gold, nickel and phosphates). Guinea and Sierra Leone still topped the list as the sub-region's principal mineral producers. The former saw the passing of a new mining code and the AfDB provided loans to help in the renegotiation of 18 important mining contracts, which the previous military regime had signed in opaque deals with some of the world's most powerful mining conglomerates. Development of the huge Simandou iron ore project continued to stagnate, owing to legal and financial difficulties and faltering demand for iron and aluminium. (RusAl's bauxite complex was also at a standstill as a result of a labour dispute that began in 2012.) By contrast, Sierra Leone reported a 43% increase in diamond production in the first half of the year. Mining firms swapped shares in the country's magnatite production, and the government's National Minerals Agency was now fully functioning. Niger, finally, suffered from a suicide attack on one of its three uranium mines in May, in which a grinding machine was targeted. It took until August for the Somaïr mine to return to operation.

As a result, the year's total output suffered, while protracted negotiations between the government and French nuclear conglomerate Areva on a new mining contract soured relations and by year's end had not yet led to a deal. There were even rumours that Areva would close down its two old mines and that the start-up of the new vast Imouraren open pit complex could be delayed further. An Australian firm discontinued prospecting after the suicide attack and Western concern over nuclear safety after the Fukushima disaster continued to keep down the spot market price for yellow cake.

The sub-region's **humanitarian situation** improved marginally as the number of IDPs in Mali began to decline in the wake of French military intervention. However, some 170,000 Malian refugees were still living in Mauritania, Burkina Faso and Niger, which also had to cope with Nigerians fleeing the war with Boko Haram and Nigérien migrants deported from Libya. In October, Niger's government found the bodies of nearly 100 migrants near the border with Algeria; they had been on their way to Algeria when their vehicles had broken down and they died of thirst. Benin, Burkina Faso and parts of Mali had to cope with floods. Social protests rocked the body politic in several countries, including Senegal, where graduate **unemployment** led to protest action. The educational sectors in Togo and Liberia were also marked by unrest. In Sierra Leone, a study reported a youth unemployment rate of 60% – the highest in the sub-region. In Niger, there were violent protests over the limited employment opportunities in the oil industry.

Against this background, **drug trafficking** continued apace, including in Sierra Leone, where a marijuana smuggling ring with connections in the police force was uncovered. The produce had been destined for Liberia, which reported a growth in cocaine and heroin trafficking (besides cannabis). Drug enforcement operations there revealed that traffickers had infiltrated the local police force. Ghana took new initiatives to fight trafficking and, amongst other things, seized a ship from Guyana carrying large quantities of cocaine. There were reports that traffickers had also infiltrated the government of the Gambia, which dismissed the attorney general and destroyed two tonnes of cocaine with the help of an incinerator provided by Britain. In Benin, police seized a drugs consignment from Pakistan in the port of Cotonou, one of the sub-region's most important harbours. Piracy continued to jeopardise security along the West African coast, notably off Nigeria and Togo.

Sub-regional Organisations: Cooperation and Conflict

Having worked in 2012 on preparing for its **peacekeeping mission to Mali**, ECOWAS sent member state contingents to the crisis-stricken country early in the year. Its 'African-led International Support Mission to Mali' (AFISMA) constituted one of the most tangible efforts in the organisation's peacekeeping record. AFISMA, authorised by the UNSC and partly funded by the EU to the tune of $ 50 m, totalled some 7,000 troops and included contingents from non-West African states, such as Chad. ECOWAS members that contributed were Benin, Côte d'Ivoire, Ghana, Guinea, Niger, Nigeria, Togo, Senegal and Liberia. The Nigerian contingent was the largest from the ECOWAS member states, but its combat unit was withdrawn in July (when the ECOWAS force was transformed into a UN mission), ostensibly as the troops were needed for the fight against Boko Haram. Burkina's President Compaoré continued his work as ECOWAS mediator in Mali, but with diminishing effectiveness owing to his close relations with Tuareg separatists and the consequent cooling of ties with newly elected Malian President Keita. Compaoré held several talks with ECOWAS officials and others, including Commission President and fellow Burkinabè, Kadré Ouadréogo and President Ouattara of Côte d'Ivoire, who at the 42nd ECOWAS summit in Yamoussoukro on 28 February was given another one-year mandate as ECOWAS chair. The ECOWAS Commission also provided $ 500,000 in food aid to Mali through WFP.

The sub-regional body continued to be concerned with the transition phase in **Guinea-Bissau**. In April and July, new negotiations took place with the country's authorities on elections, reforms and the establishment of an inclusive government. ECOWAS, in contrast to other international organisations, had recognised the post-2012 coup regime. The 600-strong ECOWAS Mission to Guinea-Bissau (ECOMIB), deployed in 2012, stayed on to facilitate the transition arrangements. Early in the year, its mandate was renewed. The chiefs of defence staff of troop-contributing countries called for the strengthening of the force, including with maritime and air units.

More broadly, ECOWAS chiefs of defence staff met on 26 June in Accra (Ghana), to discuss sub-regional security issues. These involved, amongst other things, the growing problem of **piracy**. Defence and foreign ministers of the organisation met with their counterparts from ECCAS in Cotonou on 20 March to discuss cooperation, including the establishment of a regional base to help combat the scourge (joint efforts to this effect had begun in 2011). A summit meeting of both organisations held in Yaoundé (Cameroon) on 24 June called for the deployment of an international naval force to protect the Gulf of Guinea. They met again in Dakar (Senegal) on 26 October and, after a meeting in Banjul (Gambia) on 1 November, West African maritime experts called on the ECOWAS Commission to help develop a detailed ECOWAS Integrated Maritime Strategy. (It was said that Nigerian naval forces would assist Guinea Bissau's fragile regime in this field.)

The 43rd summit of the ECOWAS Authority of Heads of State and Government took place in Abuja (Nigeria) on 17–18 July. The conference was understandably dominated by the security problems in Mali and Guinea Bissau. Host President Jonathan of Nigeria called on his fellow leaders to put pressure on both the AU and the EU to recognise Guinea Bissau's transitional government (an issue on which ECOWAS and the international community differed), whilst he also called for the organisation of a donor conference to fund the country's next elections. The chairman of the ECOWAS Authority, President Ouattara of Côte d'Ivoire, called for the consolidation of the results achieved by the sub-regional peacekeepers in Mali, recently reconstituted as a UN force. President Compaoré of

Burkina Faso, the official ECOWAS mediator, and his co-mediator President Jonathan, were thanked for their efforts in brokering the preliminary peace agreement between the Malian government and the Tuareg separatists.

Issues of **institutional reform** played a less prevalent role in 2013, although in March the Speaker of the ECOWAS parliament called for extended powers; a draft Supplementary Act provided for direct election of the body, oversight of sectoral policies and confirmation of statutory appointees, establishment of the office of a Parliamentary Ombudsman, and the integration of the parliament into regional conflict resolution and management architecture. The Commission's membership was meanwhile enlarged to ensure equity among member states.

Finally, **economic issues** dominated an extraordinary summit in Dakar on 25–26 October. These included the negotiations of an EPA with the EU and the perennial issue of the Common External Tariff (CET), which, however, appeared to make some progress this year. Modelled on the UEMOA tariff regime, the five-band CET was endorsed by ECOWAS ministers at a meeting in Praia (Cape Verde) on 21 March. The CET had been under negotiation for years. Nearly 6,000 tariffs would fall under the scheme, with rates ranging from zero to 35%. Generally, imported basic raw materials and capital goods would be duty-free, intermediate products would be subject to a 10% tariff charge and final consumer goods would be charged at 20%. Ministers also agreed on a 1.5% Community Integration Levy, which would replace separate measures by ECOWAS and UEMOA and constitute a step towards uniform port charges, as required by the WTO. In addition, ministers reaffirmed the belief in sub-regional monetary integration, including the future introduction of a common currency. Member states, especially those outside the CFAfr currency zone, were encouraged to take measures to boost the convergence of macroeconomic policies in the secondary – non-CFAfr – zone, as an intermediate step in the process.

A meeting in Banjul on 19-20 November discussed measures for ECOWAS's fast-track regional electricity market programme. Member states were planning to raise more than $ 25 m for projects concerned with power generation and transmission lines as part of the West African Power Pool framework; private-public partnership funding was to be involved, besides traditional lending institutions. The Gambia, Sierra Leone and Mali obtained ECOWAS grants for their energy sectors. ECOWAS also started up an action plan for the construction of a six-lane motorway linking Lagos and Abidjan, the sub-region's most important economic cities; a supranational agency would take charge of its implementation. Finally, a sub-regional Investment Guarantee Agency with authorised capital of $ 1 bn was approved by ECOWAS ministers with a view to easing political risk insurance, facilitating export trade guarantee services and broadening the possibilities for reinsurance. It was planned that the Agency would boost FDI and make the sub-region "more attractive as an investment destination", according to the relevant press release.

Klaas van Walraven

Benin

Despite economic growth indicating nascent economic recovery, the political climate was sensitive throughout the year. President Thomas Boni Yayi's personal credibility was at risk after allegations of a murder plot against private investor Patrice Talon and when cases against certain suspects were dismissed by the judiciary in both France and Benin. Political debate was dominated by the president's proposals for a revision of the Constitution, which were widely seen as part of his alleged ambition to go for a third term (the present constitution stipulating a two-term limit). A series of cabinet reshuffles demonstrated the country's political instability.

Domestic Politics

Domestic politics were focused on three major issues: the revision of the Constitution, the audit and correction of the much-contested computerised electoral register called the 'Liste Electorale Permanente Informatisée' (LEPI), and the local and municipal elections planned for 2013, but not held due to LEPI shortcomings.

President Boni Yayi encountered serious resistance when trying to push through the revision of the Constitution. In his State of the Nation address in the National Assembly on 4 January, the president announced that, together with a number of political reforms (modification of LEPI, charter of political parties, status of opposition parties) and economic restructurings (including reduction of public expenditure and improvement in the business climate), the revision of the Constitution was one of his priorities. Although he indicated that he would not try to modify the permitted number of presidential mandates, the project of constitutional revision generated tensions among the opposition parties. On 6 June, Boni Yayi introduced his **constitutional proposal**. His plan called for, among other things, the creation of a Court of Accounts and its inscription in the Constitution. The 'Commission Nationale Electorale Approfondi' (CENA) would also be inscribed in the Constitution. This proposal fed public suspicions that the president intended to stand for a third term after the end of his mandate in 2016. On 18 June, Janvier Yahouédéou, former ally of Boni Yayi and former coordinator of the ruling party, 'Forces Cauris pour un Bénin Emergent', denounced the constitutional reform project in an open letter to the president. On 24 June, the Constitutional Court rejected the nomination of Euloge Akpo, close collaborator of Boni Yayi, as a new member of the Court. This was seen as a sign of the Court's independence and was considered a slap in the face to the head of state. On 17 July, the 'Alternative Citoyenne' movement launched the 'Mercredi Rouge' (Red Wednesday) campaign. Each Wednesday, hundreds of citizens began turning out onto the streets wearing red clothes to protest against the constitutional reforms. The proposal triggered considerable opposition in Cotonou, but Boni Yayi's supporters imitated the red campaign and on 19 July launched the 'Vendredi Blanc' (White Friday) movement. On 1 August, the home of political opponent Gaston Zossou was surrounded by police officers to prevent him from joining the 'Mercredi Rouge' campaign. Minister of the Interior Benoît Dégla called the red campaign "poison". **Street protests** continued for several weeks. On 24 August, a coalition of opposition parties met and held a peaceful march in Cotonou to protest against a draft bill to revise the Constitution. On 24 September, the National Assembly's law commission rejected the government's constitutional proposal.

On 8 April, at the end of its second extraordinary session, the Assembly finally adopted the 'Code Électoral' and created a permanent CENA. On 22 April, MPs adopted a law that extended the mandate of municipal councillors and mayors. Little progress was achieved on the revision of the LEPI, since the monitoring and supervising 'Conseil d'Orientation et de Supervision' (COS-LEPI) was unable to complete its work by the end of the year. As a result, **local elections** initially planned for March 2013 **were postponed** to 2014, regardless of protests by opposition parties. At the end of the year (27 December) in his State of the Nation address, Boni Yayi said that the government had made CFAfr 2,620 bn available to the COS-LEPI to correct and update the computerised electoral roll.

Benin was ranked 79th of 179 countries worldwide by Reporters Without Borders (compared with 91st in 2012), indicating a relative improvement in **media freedom** compared with other countries. However, on 21 November, a new report on press freedom indicated that current legislation governing the press in Benin remained outdated and different from African normative standards and protocols. The report urged the government to change the media laws. Beninese civil society organisations expressed their dissatisfaction with the situation and emphasised that Boni Yayi's administration was becoming marked by a disturbing increase in media restrictions. Another report, produced by AI, observed that the government was trying to suppress criticism of its record and the constitutional reform project. This was illustrated by the closure for a few days of a private television channel, Canal 3, after statements by Lionel Agbo, a former presidential adviser, that members of the president's entourage were guilty of corruption. State television justified this shut-down by referring to non-compliance with broadcasting rules. On 16 January, Berthe Cakpossa, director of Canal 3, was sentenced to three months' imprisonment and fined CFAfr 500,000 for having broadcast Lionel Agbo's interview. Charged with offending the head of state, Lionel Agbo was sentenced on 23 January, in his absence, to six months' imprisonment and fined CFAfr 500,000. Opposition parties and media, together with the journalists' union, expressed their concern about this judgment, which was seen as a threat to freedom of speech. On 30 January, both men were granted a presidential pardon.

On 12 July, Benin ratified the Second Optional Protocol to the International Covenant of Civil and Political Rights, aimed at the abolition of the **death penalty**. By the end of the year, however, the government had not yet adopted the implementing legislation. AI's report also confirmed the overpopulation of Beninese prisons. Cotonou prison held six times its intended capacity, resulting in harsh conditions for detainees. Official figures showed that, of the some 2,250 inmates held, 97% were in pre-trial detention. On 8 November, a UN independent expert urged the government of Benin to make child protection a priority on its agenda, confirming observations made by a number of NGOs pointing out that violence and exploitation of children was of serious concern.

In the course of the year, Boni Yayi conducted three **cabinet reshuffles** (5 February, 11 August and 7 October). The first allowed the government to alleviate the existing tensions and conflicts between the national union of judges ('Union Nationale des Magistrats du Bénin'), the union of justice workers and those in allied occupations ('Syndicat National des Travailleurs de la Justice et Assimilés du Bénin') and Justice Minister Marie-Elise Gbèdo, who was appointed minister for industry, trade, and small and medium-sized companies. While the first reshuffle was seen as marginal, the second concerned half the government: three days after the president had dismissed all his ministers, he installed a new cabinet of 26 ministers, including 13 entirely new faces. Importantly, at this second cabinet reshuffle Boni Yayi did not appoint a prime minister. This was attributed to tensions between the president and former prime minister Pascal Koupaki. Considered a close collaborator of Boni Yayi, Koupaki had been a minister since 2006. However, the head of the state suspected him of supporting Patrice Talon, a businessman and former ally of Boni Yayi accused of conspiring against the government. Together with Kogui N'Douro (member of the government since 2006), Minister of Justice Reckya Madougou was also dismissed because she was suspected of having met Patrice Talon when she was in France. Despite his promises, Boni Yayi did not appoint a gender-balanced cabinet. In the third cabinet reshuffle, he appointed Fulbert Géro Amoussouga as minister of the newly created Ministry of Millenium Development Goals.

On 22 February, Pamphile Zomahoun, an army colonel and close ally of Boni Yayi, was arrested together with Johannes Dagnon, an accounting expert and cousin of Patrice Talon. On 3 March, the government said that the authorities had thwarted an attempt to oust the president and install a military regime. In a statement read to journalists, State Prosecutor Justin Gbenameto said that a colonel and a businessman had been arrested for plotting "to block the head of state from returning to Cotonou after his trip and to institute a military regime". A new international arrest warrant was also issued against Talon. The case of the **alleged coup plot** was presided over by Judge Angelo Houssou, who was also in charge of the case concerning the alleged attempt to poison the president in 2012 (which supposedly also involved Talon). On 17 May, he ruled that there was not enough evidence for either case to proceed. Fearing for his life, the judge tried to flee the country that same day but was intercepted at the Nigerian border, having in his possession a three-year visa for the US. He was sent home by the police. In the view of many observers, the judge's treatment was an attack on the **judiciary's independence** and individual freedoms. Early in December, Houssou managed to flee the country and asked for political asylum in the US. On 1 July, the Appeals Court in Cotonou confirmed the dismissal of the case against Talon, whom Benin's government still wanted extradited from France. On 23 October, a Paris court ruled against the extradition of Talon and his right-hand man, Olivier Boko, on the grounds that Benin could not guarantee a fair trial, and the French appeals court also turned down the request for Talon's extradition on 4 December. Boni Yayi's government reacted strongly against these rulings.

Despite the priority given to the fight against **corruption** in Boni Yayi's new-year speech, the year was marked by a number of cases involving graft. On 3 January, François Noudégbessi, former minister of urban development, was arrested and brought to the 'Brigade Economique et Financière' in relation to a case of mismanagement of public funds to the tune of CFAfr 14 bn allocated to the construction of a new building for the National Assembly. Due to his special status as a former minister, he was freed on 9 January while eight other suspects were kept in jail. On 11 January, six close associates of the new minister of urban development were also arrested, and the president addressed a letter to the National Assembly on 16 January, asking members to vote in favour of the prosecution of François Noudégbessi and Mathurin Soulé Mana Lawani, former minister of economy and finance, in the High Court of Justice. At a press conference on 25 January, the 'Observatoire de Lutte contre la Corruption' (OLC) denounced several irregularities in the conduct of the national competitive recruitment examination for tax inspectors and recommended the annulment of the test. A series of marches in protest against the results of the test were planned by the 'Union des Scolaires et des Etudiants du Bénin', but were banned by the prefectoral authorities. On 25 March, 'Alternative Citoyenne' lodged a complaint with the attorney-general alleging massive fraud during the test. The government also established an 'Autorité Nationale de Lutte contre la Corruption' (ANLC), whose 13 members were appointed on 11 February and officially sworn in on 15 May. Placed under presidential supervision, the ANLC office began operating on 22 May (initially for a period of three years). However, on 17 November Guy Ogoubiyi, head of the ANLC, declared that his office was paralysed by a lack of resources (no budget had been allocated to it). According to TI's Corruption Perception Index 2013, Benin was ranked 94th (the same as in 2012).

Foreign Affairs

Given its long-term reliance on development aid and trade relations with neighbouring countries, Benin's foreign affairs were oriented towards the strengthening of existing partnerships. This included relations with donors and issues such as the security situation in the sub-region. Benin intensified its relations with **Nigeria**, very important for its supply of fuel and re-exports. President Goodluck Jonathan was the guest of honour at the 1 August independence celebrations and Boni Yayi reciprocated with a visit to Abuja on 1 September.

On 18 January, Benin sent 300 soldiers to assist the ECOWAS African-led International Support Mission to **Mali**. An additional contingent of 350 military personnel was sent on 23 January. Boni Yayi, as chairperson of the AU, visited Canada on 7–12 January to discuss bilateral ties, as well as the Malian crisis, and also visited a dozen central, eastern and southern African countries on 14–19 January to discuss peace issues and to prepare for the 20th **AU summit** in Ethiopia. Boni Yayi also visited Germany on 22–25 January, before being replaced as AU chair by Ethiopia's prime minister on 27 January.

Boni Yayi met French President François Hollande in Paris on 5–8 February to discuss security issues in the Sahel as well as bilateral cooperation (including in the cotton sector and regarding the extension of the railway that would connect Cotonou with Niamey, the capital of Niger). On 16 February, he attended the CEN-SAD summit in N'Djamena (Chad), and he also attended the summit of heads of state and government of the South America-Africa Cooperation Forum in Malabo (Equatorial Guinea) on 19 February. The president visited Japan on 28 February–2 March and Turkey on 13–14 March. Maritime security in the Gulf of Guinea was at the core of debates at an inter-ministerial conference of ECOWAS and ECCAS held in Cotonou on 19 March.

Benin received a number of **foreign dignitaries** including Côte d'Ivoire's President Alassane Ouattara on 8–9 March, Iran's President Mahmoud Ahmadinejad on 14–15 April, the interim presidents of the CAR, Michel Djotodia on 16 July, and of Mali, Dioncounda Traoré on 15–16 August, and Liberia's President Ellen Johnson-Sirleaf on 21–22 August.

Socioeconomic Developments

Overall macroeconomic performance was positive. According to government statistics, GDP **growth** reached 5.6 %, largely driven by reforms in customs collection, a favourable cotton harvest and improvements in the activities of the port of Cotonou. In spite of a significant increase in public investment (about 1.5% of GDP), the budget deficit remained at a manageable level, while debt continued to be below 30% of GDP (compared with an average of nearly 40% in SSA). At CFAfr 1,044 bn, the 2013 budget increased by 2.7%. Consumer prices rose by 3.1% (compared with a rise of 6.8% in 2012).

Customs reforms – one of the key aspects of the strategy undertaken by the government to strengthen public financial management – proceeded at a satisfactory pace, according to an IMF review. An **IMF** mission visited Cotonou on 1–12 July to conduct discussions on the fifth review of the programme supported by the Fund's ECF. On 23 August, the IMF decided to allocate 10.61 m in SDR (some $ 16.1 m) and approved a request for an extension of the arrangement, which was set to expire in September, through to April 2014 to allow for a rephasing of the final disbursement and especially the implementation of the new customs reform agenda. The World Bank Doing Business Index put Benin at 174, indicating no significant improvement in the regulatory environment for private enterprise.

The West African Development Bank allocated about CFAfr 140 bn in **development aid**. Cotonou held 'Islamic Development Bank days' on 8–9 April to strengthen cooperation between the bank and the Beninese public and private stakeholders. On 9 April, the World Bank approved the eighth PRSC in the sum of $ 30 m (about CFAfr 15 bn) to support economic and structural reforms. On 13 May, the Netherlands announced it would increase the volume of its aid from € 16 m (about CFAfr 10 bn) in 2012 to € 29.5 m (CFAfr 18 bn).

On 14 January, MPs unanimously adopted a law establishing the 'Code Foncier et Domanial', which guarantees equal access to land and secures investments in this sector. On 15 January, the National Assembly also unanimously approved three important **loans** between Benin and financial partners. A CFAfr 23 bn loan from the ADF was aimed at implementing a programme of economic and financial reforms framed by the 'Stratégie de Croissance et de Réduction de la Pauvreté' 2011–15. The second loan, for CFAfr 6 bn, signed with the ECOWAS Bank for Investment and Development was for health facility equipment and renovation. The third loan, provided by the 'Association Internationale de Développement', for CFAfr 17.5 bn, concerned the implementation of a regional programme for infrastructure and communication in West Africa. Benin signed an agreement with the Islamic Development Bank for CFAfr 225 bn worth of investments in the cotton industry and the energy sector, to be disbursed from 2013 to 2016).

The government resumed control of the **cotton industry** after sidelining Patrice Talon, a key commercial figure in the sector, and the country produced 240,000 tonnes of raw cotton in the 2012–13 season. Cotton constituted a major cash crop for farmers and an important source of income for the country's economy (CFAfr 110 bn), and the sector benefited from a high degree of government attention in terms of monitoring, input, equipment, subsidies, training and extension services. The increase in output led to larger-than-expected growth (5.4% during the first quarter, beating a 4.5% World Bank forecast). On 17 April, the government raised the price paid to domestic producers of high-grade cotton to CFAfr 265/kg (up from CFAfr 260/kg in 2012/13) and to CFAfr 215/kg for second-grade cotton (up from CFAfr 210/kg). In addition, the government decided to maintain the price of fertilizer at CFAfr 200/kg. Although the price paid to farmers was the highest in the CFAfr zone (standing at 44% above the international price), it remained unclear whether this strategy was sustainable. Furthermore, observers were concerned that the government would continue to focus more on the industry's income-generating capacity, to the detriment of its long-term sustainability (cotton cultivation being marked by intensive use of pesticides and fertilizer, as well as the expansion of cultivation into forest zones).

In spite of erratic rainfall in some parts of the country, preliminary estimates indicated that **cereal production** expanded by 13%, as compared with the previous year, to 1.7 m tonnes. Production of maize, the country's main staple, was estimated at a record 1.4 m tonnes. On 1 March, the government declared the reinforcement of controls on the export of cashew nuts, which was becoming an important cash crop for farmers and a source of foreign exchange.

Benin's total energy need in 2013 was 200 MW while the **energy** supplied was only 70 MW. The gap resulted in frequent power cuts, which the minister of energy deplored in an interview broadcast on national television on 20 March. In spite of government initiatives to get funding for energy supply (from Turkey, Brazil and Japan), the problem remained serious at the end of the year. The country's consumption depends entirely on imports from Nigeria and, to a lesser extent, Ghana and Côte d'Ivoire. 'Kpayo' dealers (importers of illegal fuel from Nigeria) got into violent confrontations with the military (resulting in two fatalities) when they tried to prevent the confiscation of fuel on 21–22 January. Despite the fact that President Boni met with 'kpayo' traders on 27 June, the problems caused by their activities remained unresolved by year's end. On 22 March, the union of workers in the national company for trade in petroleum products, 'Société Nationale de Commercialisation des Produits Pétroliers', asked for the dismissal of the company's director, who was accused of bad management.

Strikes crippled the health sector. On 1 October, hospital workers embarked on strike action. As talks ended in deadlock, the strike was extended without even minimal services to patients being maintained. At year's end, other health workers such as students of medicine and pharmacy workers joined the action, which led to a critical situation. Strike action also affected the education sector. On 27 December, the police violently suppressed a peaceful march by education trade unions in Cotonou. In reaction, workers launched a nationwide strike.

In August, severe **floods** hit the northern municipalities of Karimama and Malanville along the River Niger, resulting in the loss of crops and livestock and the destruction of homes. FAO launched an emergency response programme on 5 November.

On 30 January, police seized 127 kg of drugs shipped from Pakistan to Cotonou, an important access point for drug trafficking in the sub-region, according to a report by the US Drug Enforcement Administration issued on 23 April. Criminal networks in Lebanon and Africa were using the country's important second-hand car business ('Tokunbo') for money laundering. An International Narcotics Control Board mission visiting Benin on 9–12 July confirmed the increasing role of the port of Cotonou as a transit point for drugs consignments. The report expressed appreciation for the government's commitment to fighting drug trafficking in accordance with international treaties, although it argued that the country's capacities in this regard needed strengthening. Nevertheless, law enforcement authorities, in cooperation with their counterparts in neighbouring countries, boasted some successful operations and drugs seizures.

Eric Komlavi Hahonou

Burkina Faso

President Compaoré's political standing diminished in both domestic and international affairs. Preparations for the introduction of a second parliamentary chamber mobilised the opposition and significant parts of civil society to protest against the government. Critics described the senate as a costly instrument that would protect the regime's power. The reversal of the leadership in 2012 had created internal tensions in the ruling party, the 'Congrès pour la Démocratie et le Progrès' (CDP), but in rural areas the party proved its dominance in a partial municipal elections rerun and in many mayoral elections. Internationally, Compaoré continued to act as the official ECOWAS mediator for Mali and his country made a strong contribution to the UN military mission in that country, but he gradually lost political influence because he had a difficult relationship with Mali's newly elected President Ibrahim Boubacar Keita. Burkina's economic development remained largely dependent on industrial mining, while the biggest employer – the cotton industry – achieved a good harvest, encouraging optimistic forecasts for this volatile and vulnerable production sector.

Domestic Politics

Besides the municipal elections rerun in February, the domestic political scene was substantially shaped by plans for the introduction of a **second parliamentary chamber**, the senate. The constitution had been amended in 2012, following the recommendations of a 'Conseil Consultatif sur les Réformes Politiques' (CCRP) and the establishment of the senate was one of the major CCRP reform proposals. In 2013, government officials – including President Blaise Compaoré and Minister of State for Institutional Reforms Bongnessan Arsène Yé – often defended the proposal on the basis that the CCRP had based all its decisions on a consensus. This was true from the internal perspective of the CCRP, but many opposition groups had boycotted the Council, alleging government dominance. As a result, appraisal of the reforms had been ambivalent.

Critics put the senate issue at the top of their list of grievances against the government. As public anger over the cost of living and inadequate government services had persisted for years, organisations such as the 'Coalition contre la Vie Chère' (CCVC) were easily able to mobilise tens of thousands across the country. The largest **protest marches** took place in Ouagadougou on 29 June and 20 and 28 July. The first march was dispersed by police using tear gas and batons. Police officials denied allegations that live ammunition was used, explaining that protesters had claimed that the remains of rubber projectiles were lethal bullets in order to accuse the authorities. There were no reports of casualties, but the heated debate exemplified the level of polarisation. The next day (30 June), opposition leader Zéphirin Diabré complained about police excesses at a press conference, although he did not mention live ammunition.

Opposition parties such as Diabré's 'Union pour le Progrès et le Changement' (UPC) supported the protests, but the CCVC was mainly driven by trade unions and political **civil society organisations**. Former union leader Tolé Sognon headed the movement and became one of the front men of the protest movement. He argued that the introduction of a costly senate would be another example of dissipation of money for the benefit of Compaoré's political friends while ordinary people suffered from shortfalls in multiple sectors, such as health, education, housing and energy. The important news platform lefaso.net, quoting allegedly well-informed sources, reported that the senators' planned salaries would be at least CFAfr 1.75 m (€ 2.668) per month. Visual media reports showed that many protesters agreed with Sognon's argument. In his speech in Ouagadougou's Nation Square on 20 July, Sognon also urged the crowds not to march on Kosyam Palace, synonymous with the presidential office, but to focus on the political struggle against the country's social inequalities. The authorities had declared the presidential palace area to be a 'red zone' where demonstrations would not be permitted. Earlier, on 29 June, police had forcibly dispersed protesters who had allegedly entered such a 'red zone'.

As the **demonstrations peaked** in mid-year, two popular musicians, Smockey and Sams K Le Jah, joined forces with the protesters and founded the 'Le Balai Citoyen' ('The Citizen Broom') movement. It became very active in online social media, mostly using brief expressions, such as "sweeping away the incumbent ruling class" or the revolutionary slogan "la patrie ou la mort, nous vaincrons" ("fatherland or death, we shall win"). The latter had been introduced to Burkina Faso by the charismatic leftist coup leader and later president Thomas Sankara, widely revered by many protesters. However provocative the slogans were, the artists urged the protesters to act peacefully.

Those who opposed the establishment of a senate complained of more than the alleged waste of money. Opponents of Compaoré – who had been in office for 26 years – feared that his rule would continue. In their view, the senate might be exploited to amend Article 37 of the Constitution, which prescribed a limit of two presidential terms. Compaoré was currently in his second term under this rule, and so was set to leave office in 2015. CDP politicians argued that the term limit was undemocratic because it restricted the people's choice. They continued to call for the elimination of Article 37 but lacked the necessary majority in the National Assembly to bring it about. The opposition feared that both chambers of parliament, once established, would be called into session as a joint congress in which the government might find the majority required to amend the Constitution. Senior cabinet ministers, as well as the president himself, kept arguing that the **constitutional amendment** was not motivated by a hidden agenda. At the same time, the government attempted to calm protests by introducing economic concessions, including higher housing bonuses, reduced income taxes, moderate increases in student loans, and food subsidies. The same pacification strategy had been used after the 2011 riots without a sustainable impact on the expression of popular grievances.

According to the Organic Law No. 018-2013, passed by the National Assembly on 21 May, the senate would have 89 seats. An electoral college of local government councillors quickly headed to elect their share of 39 members on 28 July. The CDP won 36 of these seats while the remaining three went to minor pro-government parties. This outcome was facilitated by two factors. First, local councillors were overrepresented in rural areas, which were CDP strongholds. Second, opposition parties and even the CDP's most important ally at the national level, the 'Alliance pour la Démocratie et la Fédération/Rassemblement Démocratique Africain' (ADF/RDA), chose to boycott the senate elections. (In November, however, ADF/RDA joined the 'Republican Front' to support the creation of a revised senate, although speaking openly against dropping the two-term limit.) In addition, the head of state was empowered to appoint a further 29 senators. These two groups alone would already provide a pro-government majority of at least 76%. The law stipulated that unions, employers, traditional chiefs, religious groups and the diaspora should select the remaining 21 senators. Each group was to choose four senators, except for the diaspora, which was entitled to select five. This third batch of senators were elected in August, producing the awkward situation of 44 elected senators waiting for the creation of a body that was being rejected in heavy street protests.

As far as the groups entitled to choose senators were concerned, the traditional chiefs were considered to be largely supportive of the government while the trade unions were likely to join the boycott. However, the traditional chiefs and the representatives of the evangelical **churches** refrained from openly supporting the senate. In September, both groups emphasised that they favoured social peace over institutional reforms. The

Catholic bishops criticised the second chamber plans more openly for the same reason. In a pastoral letter circulated on 15 July and confirmed by a public statement published on 13 September, the episcopal conference of Burkina Faso and Niger – headed by Paul Ouédraogo, Archbishop of Bobo-Dioulasso – said it considered the creation of a senate as a danger to social peace. Moreover, Archbishop Ouédraogo made clear that no Catholic clergy would join the senate because of Rome's general policy of refraining from involvement in political decision-making processes. Only the secretary general of the Muslim umbrella organisation 'Fédération des Associations Islamiques du Burkina' (FAIB), Souleymane Compaoré, explicitly supported the creation of a senate, hoping this would bring advantages for the country's **Muslim community**. However, two individual FAIB member organisations distanced themselves from Compaoré, suggesting that he had not spoken on behalf of all FAIB members. According to media reports, the government sponsored FAIB's Hadj to the tune of some CFAfr 500 m (roughly € 0.75 m).

On 13–16 September, President Compaoré held meetings with all four religious and traditional groups. This was two weeks after he had received a report from the 'Comité de Suivi et d'Évaluation', created at his request earlier in August. The committee, headed by Minister of State Yé, went into session on 16 August and on 29 August handed over its report, which made the following proposals: to reduce the number of senatorial seats from 89 to 71; to lower the minimum age of appointees from 45 to 30 or 35; to make a transitional arrangement providing for the participation of all political groups that would be prepared to participate in the senate; to establish and fix in the Constitution a **conciliation committee** between the two chambers; and to reduce the number of senators appointed by the president. Shortly after, the opposition issued a declaration deploring the fact that the committee had made no effort to consult the major critics of the proposed senate. On 26 October, the national ombudsman ('médiateur du Faso'), General Tiémoko Marc Garango, supported the assertion that the senate should not be created in the present circumstances.

The **municipal elections** originally held in December 2012 had to be repeated at 680 polling stations owing to irregularities. This affected 38 out of 45 provinces but made no significant difference to the overall results. The ruling CDP added a further 23 seats, making a new total of 12,363. The UPC, the leading opposition party in the National Assembly, increased its number of council seats by 15 to 1,630, while the ADF/RDA lost 13 seats, ending with a total of 1,733. With two-thirds of all local councillors being from the CDP, President Compaoré confirmed his dominance of the country's local government.

As a consequence of the elections, two notable changes took place in some of the country's more important **mayoral positions**. First, Gilbert Noël Ouédraogo took office in his north-western hometown Ouahigouya, one of Burkina's secondary centres and known as the ancient capital of the Yatenga Kingdom. Ouédraogo is the son of former prime minister Gérard Kango Ouédraogo, also known as the Duke of Yatenga, from whom he inherited the ADF/RDA presidency. The Ouédraogo family's traditional ties to the region explain why the party managed to win back the municipality in spite of the CDP's overall dominance. Gilbert Ouédraogo also retained his post as vice president of the National Assembly, just as his fellow party member and new deputy mayor Sidiki Belem kept his post as one of the Assembly's secretaries. The number of political offices that Burkina Faso inherited from France was part of the criticism levelled by civil society groups against the political class, although it remained a minor issue.

Second, Simon Compaoré – not related to the president – stepped down as mayor of the capital Ouagadougou after serving for 17 years. He was succeeded by Marin Casimir Ilboudou, the former district mayor of Baskuy – essentially Ouagadougou's city centre. Ilboudou might best be described as a longstanding party stalwart who presumably harboured fewer political ambitions than his predecessor. Simon Compaoré and other formerly influential CDP barons had been sidelined in party elections in 2012. By the end of 2013, rumours intensified that he, together with former CDP president Roch Marie Christian Kaboré and former longstanding minister of state Salif Diallo, might break away from the CDP and create a new party. It remained unclear whether this was linked to the rumour that anonymous CDP members from Ouagadougou had called for the resignation of party chairman Assimi Kouanda and an extraordinary party convention to elect a new leadership. It seemed that the CDP's **internal power struggle** improved the position of François Compaoré, the president's younger brother, as a potential presidential successor.

On the night of 30–31 August, the Presidential Security Regiment killed the former soldier Romuald Tuina, who was said to have made an attempt on the president's life. The assailant was shot close to Kosyam Palace but the president had not been at serious risk. The **assassination attempt** was apparently not linked to the military riots of previous years or to the current political situation. The culprit had a criminal record and was wanted by the police for armed robbery.

Foreign Affairs

Political instability in neighbouring **Mali** remained the top foreign policy concern. The situation there escalated to war in January with military intervention by French troops. As a result, Compaoré's strategy to resolve the crisis in northern Mali became obsolete. He had preferred negotiations and dialogue with Tuareg rebel groups such as 'Ansar Dine' and the 'Mouvement National pour la Libération de l'Azawad' (MNLA).

President Compaoré continued to act as the **ECOWAS mediator**. In this capacity, he still held numerous talks with ECOWAS officials (e.g. commission president Kadré Ouadréogo on 26 January; acting ECOWAS chair President Alassane Ouattara of Côte d'Ivoire on 27 January) and received Malian politicians in Ouagadougou, including the president of the 'Commission du Dialogue et de la Réconciliation', Mohamed Salia

Sokona (30 April), the special presidential advisor for northern Mali, Tiébilé Dramé (20 May), and the newly elected Malian head of state President Ibrahim Boubacar Keita (31 August). Although the agreement for an inter-Malian dialogue signed on 4 December 2012 in Ouagadougou had failed to prevent the escalation of the conflict, Burkina's capital remained the major location for contacts between the Malian government and the non-Islamist Tuareg rebels of the MNLA. It was thus in Ouagadougou that the MNLA announced both the suspension (26 September) and resumption (5 October) of further negotiations with Bamako, and held its top level meeting there, on 10–12 October. According to some observers, the close relationship between the MNLA and Compaoré led to a cooling of relations between the latter and President Keita towards year's end.

In addition, Burkina Faso contributed to the international **peacekeeping** mission to Mali, now led by the UN. By the end of 2013, the country had sent 872 troops and police into Mali, the third largest contingent in the 'Mission Multidimensionnelle Intégrée des Nations Unies pour la Stabilisation au Mali' (MINUSMA). With another 1,000 personnel in the AU-UN Mission in Darfur, usually referred to as UNAMID, Burkina was also among the top contributors to this international mission in Sudan.

Burkina Faso maintained its official ties with Taiwan rather than recognising the government of the People's Republic of China. It was the only mainland African country to do so. When Ambassador Zhang Ming-Zhong bade farewell at the end of his tenure on 25 March, he asked President Compaoré to support Taiwan's cause in international organisations.

Socioeconomic Developments

The **cotton industry** remained the biggest employer, although the natural fibre was only the second most important export commodity, accounting for about 14% of export value, far behind gold (73% in 2012, the most recent available data). Production surged to 630,000 tonnes in the season 2012/13, exceeding several poorer harvests in previous years. Since this output topped the target by more than 100,000 tonnes, the 'Union Nationale des Producteurs de Coton du Burkina' published in October a more optimistic target for the 2013/14 season (730,000 tonnes). At the same time, the union demanded technological improvements for rural cotton producers in order to help increase production.

The economy continued to experience high rates of growth, largely driven by the mining industry. However, the 7% **growth** estimate by 'The Economist' and IMF represented a moderate slowdown as compared with the previous year's 9% (itself originally estimated at 7%–8%). The reason for this lay mainly in developments in the gold market and illustrated the vulnerability of Burkina's economic growth. Since 2010, **gold** had been the major source of export revenues – and national income in general – despite the fact that large-scale industrial production had begun only a few years earlier. On the one hand, there were natural limits to growth, implying a slowdown in the opening of new mines.

On the other, the world market price for gold dropped by almost a third over the course of 2013, from more than € 1,250 to less than € 900 an ounce. Thus, gold revenues could not grow by the same margins as in previous years, even though the Danish company Nordgold started production at Bissa gold mine, 100 km north of Ouagadougou, with the extraction of 7.2 tonnes of gold in 2013.

In February, Burkina was recognised as meeting all the requirements of the Extractive Industries Transparency Initiative (EITI) and became an EITI Compliant Country, with the expectation that this would attract further investment in the **mining sector**. Alongside phosphates production in Kodjari and nickel prospected at Boromo, Burkina's first zinc mine at Perkoa was inaugurated by the prime minister on 19 January. Plans for manganese mining at Tambao in the far north-east also advanced in the course of the year after a long process, and it was estimated that production would start in 2014. However, the turbulent licensing process led two companies to file complaints against the government at the International Commercial Chamber in Paris. In April, the government agreed to pay $ 2 m to the Emirati company Wadi Al Rawda Industrial Investments for unilaterally breaking an agreement on Tambao in 2008. At that time, the government had decided to cooperate with General Nice Resources (GNR) from India instead. However, in early 2013, GNR also went to the International Commercial Chamber for breach of contract since the government had decided in January 2012 to change partners again and award the mining rights at Tambao to Pan African Minerals (PAM).

In August, PAM, owned by Romanian investor Frank Timiş, was awarded the contract for a huge **railway project**: the renovation and construction of the Abidjan-Tambao line. The Canadian consultancy firm Hatch, commissioned by PAM, estimated the cost of the project at about CFAfr 500 bn (about € 762 m). While PAM had a purely logistical interest in facilitating the transportation of ore from Tambao to the coast, politicians and residents hoped the railway would also bring substantial improvements in passenger transport. It was envisaged that the line would be extended from Burkina's north-eastern town of Dori to Niamey in Niger and further south to the port of Cotonou in Benin. Together with Nigerian plans to support the construction of a railway line from Lagos via Cotonou to Abidjan (Côte d'Ivoire), this could represent the first step towards the establishment of a full West African railway loop in the distant future.

While export figures made a positive contribution to economic statistics, the country continued to have serious problems with reaching the MDGs. New studies showed, for instance, that community-based **healthcare** schemes, which had been introduced to improve sanitary conditions, tended to exclude poor people. Another study found that similar social barriers affected maternal healthcare. The 'Conseil National de la Sécurité Alimentaire' reported that 1.8 m people were suffering from **malnutrition**, including more than half-a-million children under the age of five. The UN reported that less than half of the affected population received assistance. In August, four regions across the country were also struck by **flooding**. The 'Conseil National de Sécours d'Urgence et de

Réhabilitation' reported that the floods affected at least 6,712 people, leaving one person dead and 602 homes destroyed. The number of Malian refugees fell slightly over the year, with about 45,000 remaining on Burkinabè territory. All the refugees received assistance from qualified international organisations.

The 23rd **film festival**, FESPACO ('Festival Panafricain du Cinéma et de la Télévision de Ouagadougou') took place from 23 February to 2 March. The main jury prize, the 'Étalon d'Or' (Golden Stallion), was awarded to Alain Gomis from Senegal for his movie 'Tey (Today)'. A visit by UNESCO's director-general Irina Bokova was an indication of FESPACO's international significance.

Alexander Stroh

Cape Verde

In March, Prime Minister José Maria Neves was reconfirmed as leader of the ruling 'Partido Africano da Independência de Cabo Verde' (PAICV). However, he had already announced that he would step down from the party leadership in 2015, one year before the next general elections. In June, Ulisses Correia e Silva, the mayor of the capital, Praia, was elected unopposed as the new leader of the opposition 'Movimento para a Democracia' (MpD). While the overall domestic economy was increasingly affected by the economic crisis in the eurozone, the tourism sector continued to resist its impact and registered a 3.4% increase in visitors.

Domestic Politics

On 10 March, Prime Minister José Maria Neves was re-elected unopposed in **direct party elections** as leader of the ruling PAICV, with 98% of the ballots and a turnout of 70% of the party membership. At the PAICV's 13th congress on 26–28 April, the 507 delegates confirmed what was his fifth consecutive victory in party leadership elections since 2000. He had announced that he would resign from the party leadership in 2015, one year before the next legislative and presidential elections, due in 2016, but refused to comment on his supposed ambitions for the country's presidency. During the congress, the delegates paid tribute to Pedro Pires, one of the party founders, prime minister (1975–91) and president (2001–11).

On 13–14 July, delegates at the 10th convention of the **opposition** 'Movimento para a Democracia' (MpD) confirmed Ulisses Correia e Silva, the mayor of Praia, as the new party leader. On 14 June, Correia e Silva, who replaced the long-standing party leader Carlos Veiga, had been elected unopposed by direct party member voting with 22,282 votes out of 32,802 registered members. In addition, the 304 delegates elected a new 15-member political commission, which included four vice presidents. The party was confident of winning the next legislative election in 2016, which would make Correia e Silva the next prime minister.

On 17 December, José Manuel Vaz, president of the 'Confederação Cabo-Verdiana dos Sindicatos Livres', the smaller of the country's two trade union federations, called for a **general strike** on 29–30 April 2014 in protest against the government's economic policies and low wages. Vaz demanded a 5% salary increase for civil servants to compensate for their loss of purchasing power in recent years, and back-dated payments for promotions, reclassifications and overtime for all civil servants in the state administration and municipalities. Finally, Vaz declared his solidarity with the call put out on 10 December by Júlio Ascenção Silva, the leader of the rival trade union federation 'União Nacional dos Trabalhadores Cabo-Verdianos – Central Sindical', for a demonstration against growing unemployment and decreasing purchasing power. This protest march was scheduled for 20 January 2014, the anniversary of the assassination in 1973 of Amílcar Cabral, Cape Verde's national hero. Neves acknowledged the increasing economic hardships suffered by the population, but blamed the domestic economic difficulties on the international crisis, asking the unions to solve the problems by dialogue.

Foreign Affairs

On 1 February, Prime Minister Neves left for an official one-week visit to **Portugal**, where he participated in a meeting of the Socialist International in Lisbon and a conference on investment opportunities in Cape Verde held in a Lisbon university. He also met with local authorities and the local Cape Verdean immigrant communities to discuss problems of the immigrants in Portugal.

On 28 March, **US President Barack Obama** received Neves, together with the presidents of Senegal, Sierra Leone and Malawi, to discuss the strengthening of democratic institutions and the increase of investment in Africa. Cape Verde was the first country to be awarded a second compact programme from the Millennium Challenge Corporation. While in Washington, Neves and his colleagues met with Secretary of Defense Chuck Hagel to discuss cooperation on regional security and peacekeeping in Africa and attended a dinner hosted by the Corporate Council on Africa to discuss trade and investment opportunities.

On 1–3 June, Neves and Foreign Minister Jorge Borges attended the 5th Tokyo International Conference on African Development in Yokohama, to strengthen development cooperation with **Japan**. Neves was received by Prime Minister Shinzo Abe, who promised bilateral development assistance of more than $ 68 m for energy, water supply and fishing projects.

On 3 June, President Fonseca paid a visit to the Vatican, where he was received by Pope Francis. On 10 June, the Vatican's Secretary for Relations with States Archbishop Dominique Mamberti signed a concordat with Cape Verde, which until 1975 had been part of the jurisdiction of the concordat with Portugal. The new treaty, the first signed with a West African country, gave the local **Catholic Church** autonomy to maintain its property and exercise its functions in the education, health and social sectors. The Concordat made provision for the possibility of the creation of a Catholic University in Cape Verde.

On 17–18 July, Neves participated in the 43rd **ECOWAS** summit in Abuja (Nigeria), where he pleaded for greater bilateral economic cooperation with other member states. At the ECOWAS extraordinary summit in Dakar (Senegal) on 25–26 October, he stressed his country's determination to join the scheduled customs union and to participate actively in the negotiations for an EPA between the EU and ECOWAS. With regard to ECOWAS's prospective common external tariff, the summit agreed that, because of its island status, Cape Verde would benefit from special rules in the area of free movement of people and subsidised air and sea transport.

On 4–5 November, President Fonseca paid a two-day visit to **Angola**, an increasingly important investor in Cape Verde, where he was received by President Eduardo dos Santos. The two heads of state stressed the historical and cultural ties between their countries and called for more bilateral cooperation. In addition, Fonseca addressed Angola's National Assembly, had lunch with businessmen, and gave a lecture on constitutionalism at Agostinho Neto University.

On 5–6 November, Cape Verde sent a delegation to the 4th ministerial conference of the Forum for Economic and Trade Cooperation between **China** and Portuguese-speaking Countries (Forum Macao). During the meeting, Minister of Tourism, Industry and Energy Humberto Brito and China's Minister of Commerce Gao Hucheng signed two cooperation agreements worth $ 25 m – $ 15 m in grants and $ 10 m in interest-free loans – to finance the renovation of the presidential palace and the construction of a hotel management school on Sal Island and of the university campus in Praia. In addition, the agreements included the financing of 20 annual scholarships for Cape Verdean students in China.

On 25 November, Prime Minister Neves visited the **European Commission** in Brussels. During a joint press conference, Commission President Durão Barroso praised Cape Verde's rule of law and good government and guaranteed the maintenance of European development assistance of € 55 m. During the talks, EU officials reportedly expressed concerns over Cape Verde's public debt sustainability.

Socioeconomic Developments

On 11 December, the National Assembly approved the **2014 annual budget** by 36 votes of the ruling PAICV against 21 opposition votes. The budget anticipated an 8.7% revenue increase from CVE (escudos) 41.1 bn (€ 372.7 m) in 2013 to CVE 44.6 bn (€ 404.5 m) in 2014, and expenditure of CVE 57.8 bn (€ 524.1 m), including CVE 22.3 bn (€ 202.2 m) in public investment and a 3% public sector wage increase. General public services accounted for 39.1% of expenditure, while education, social security, security and public order, and health represented 22.8%, 11.7%, 9.8% and 9.1%, respectively. The fiscal deficit was forecast at 7.4% of GDP, while public debt was scheduled to increase from 92% of GDP in 2013 to 98% in 2014. MpD leader Correia e Silva rejected the budget, alleging that it proposed excessive and unsustainable state expenditure and would increase public debt.

On 11 April, the government granted a 25-year **gambling concession** with a seven-year monopoly to the local gaming company Casino Royal to run the country's first casino, which was to be housed in the projected 240-room Hilton Hotel in Santa Maria (Sal), scheduled to open in 2015. The casino, which would cover an area of 1,000 m^2, represented an investment of € 3.6 m, while the country's first Hilton Hotel was budgeted at € 46 m. Under the agreement, Casino Royal, jointly owned by two resident French businessmen, would be obliged to pay a 10% gambling tax on its total revenue in addition to the usual income tax and to contribute 6% of its revenue to social and community projects as part of its corporate social responsibility. The government hoped that gambling would contribute to the growth of the tourism sector.

On 23 April, the Cape Verde Maritime Security Service (CVMSS) signed an agreement with the British private maritime security company SeaMarshals Ltd authorising the latter to carry out armed **maritime security operations** from Cape Verde's territorial waters. Director of National Defense Pedro Reis Brito stressed that the SeaMarshals' off-shore operations, which were based in São Vicente, were not primarily directed at the country's own maritime security (guaranteed by the national Coast Guard), but at the prevention of piracy and protection of shipping. Both CVMSS and SeaMarshals were reportedly interested in expanding their business activities beyond martime security, particularly into ship registration and inter-island maritime transport.

The biannual monetary policy report published by the central bank in late May confirmed the **economic slowdown** in recent years. With growth in 2012 of only 1%, the forecast for the current year was for a contraction of 1.5% or at best a growth rate of 0.5%. Unemployment had already climbed to 16.8% in 2012 and was now expected to exceed

20%. The central bank's experts forecast a continuation of the downward economic trend in 2013.

A major development in the **banking sector** was the sale by the Portuguese state of the Cape Verdean off-shore subsidiary of the Portuguese 'Banco Português de Negócios' (BPN) to the Angolan 'Banco BIC' for € 30 m. BPN had been nationalised by the Portuguese government in 2008 to prevent its collapse following losses of € 700 m largely due to fraud and other illicit financial practices. The purchase of the Cape Verdean off-shore branch was a logical step, since 'Banco BIC' had already acquired the Portuguese BPN for € 40 m in 2012. 'Banco BIC' intended to transform the Cape Verdean branch into an on-shore commercial bank. Since the arrival of 'Banco Africano de Investimento' in 2009, 'Banco BIC' had been the second Angolan Bank operating in Cape Verde. Isabel dos Santos, daughter of Angola's president and a major shareholder in 'Banco BIC', had already acquired the Cape Verdean cellphone operator T+ in 2012.

On 11 November, the ports authority 'Companhias Docas do Ceará' and the 'Trade Brasil Mix' company signed an agreement on the first direct regular shipping service between **Brazil** and Cape Verde. The new sea route between Fortaleza's Mucuripe port and the ports in Praia (Santiago) and Mindelo (São Vicente) was expected to reduce transport time between the two countries from 45 to seven days. While numerous companies considered Cape Verde an ideal location for the distribution of Brazilian exports to the countries on the African mainland, shipping did not start as scheduled due to insufficient cargoes.

In December, the government announced that it would speed up the long-scheduled **privatisation** of three major loss-making state-owned companies. Under the programme, the state-owned ports authority 'Empresa Nacional de Administração dos Portos' retained the supervision of the nine ports, but subcontracted the management of port services to private companies. On 17 July, Finance Minister Cristina Duarte announced that the three activities of the national airline 'Transportes Aéreos de Cabo Verde' (TACV) – air transport, baggage handling and maintenance services – would be sold separately to interested private investors. The Chinese-owned Okay Airways was reportedly expected to become a shareholder in the indebted TACV, while Ground Handling, a newly established private company, would take over all airport ground services and 300 employees from the state aviation agency 'Empresa Nacional de Aeroportos e Segurança Aérea'.

The **tourism industry** still registered some growth, although considerably less than in previous years. Compared with 2012, the number of hotel guests increased by 3.4% to 552,144, while overnights increased by 3.0% to 3.4 m. Boa Vista received 37.8% of the visitors, followed by Sal and Santiago with 37.6% and 12.1%, respectively. The United Kingdom accounted for 17.2% of the visitors, while Germany and France contributed 13.4% each, followed by Portugal with 10.5%. A drop in airport passenger traffic was compensated for to some extent by the increasing number of cruise ship arrivals. The overall number of airport passengers fell by 3.4% from 1,849,455 in 2012 to 1,786,702, representing a 15.2% reduction in the domestic market and a 6.2% increase in the international market. Sal airport received 612,117 passengers, followed by Praia airport with 469,473, and São Vicente with 204,037. In the same period, a total of 157 cruise ships carrying 75,643 passengers visited Cape Verde. Porto Grande in São Vicente received 57 ships with 40,273 passengers, while 39 ships with 26,585 passengers called at Praia.

Gerhard Seibert

Côte d'Ivoire

2013 was probably the most peaceful year since the beginning of the civil war in 2002. Alassane Ouattara, the winner of the 2010 presidential election, continued to lead successfully the long process of economic recovery. He received international praise for his management of reforms and continued support from his international backers. Compared with 2012, security improved, with a decrease in armed attacks by fighters backing the camp of defeated president Laurent Gbagbo, but the slow pace of reconciliation and the difficulties of prosecuting war criminals and those suspected of economic crimes, particularly those siding with Ouattara's camp, led to concern about the long-term prospects for stability.

Domestic Politics

After nearly two years in exile in neighbouring countries, **Charles Blé Goudé**, the leader of the pro-Gbagbo 'Young Patriots', was finally arrested by Interpol on 17 January at his home in Tema (Ghana), and then extradited to Côte d'Ivoire. Accused of war crimes for his involvement in the 2010 post-election crisis and suspected by the ICC of being "indirect co-author" of crimes against humanity, he was subject to an arrest warrant issued by the Ivorian justice department. Two other Gbagbo allies – Jean-Noel Abehi, a top gendarmerie official, and Jean-Yves Dibopieu, a leader of Côte d'Ivoire's student federation involved with the Young Patriots – were also arrested in Ghana and extradited to Abidjan on 5 February. Abehi was cited in a UN Group of Experts report issued in October 2012 as one of the leading Ghana-based pro-Gbagbo exiles and behind several armed raids in Côte d'Ivoire in August 2012.

The **municipal and regional elections** were finally scheduled for 21 April. They had been planned to take place on 24 February but were postponed due to a new attempt to improve dialogue between the opposition and the government coalition composed of the 'Rassemblement des Républicains' (RDR) and the 'Parti Démocratique de Côte d'Ivoire' (PDCI). The new date was proposed by the 'Commission Électorale Indépendante' (CEI) and approved by the Council of Ministers on 13 February. Immediately after the announcement, and in spite of government efforts to promote maximum participation by political parties, the 'Front Populaire Ivoirien' (FPI), former president Gbagbo's party, indicated that it would not contest the elections. Party spokesman Richard Kodjo argued that the date had been set without consultation and he called for CEI's restructuring and an amnesty for imprisoned supporters of the FPI. For the first time in 12 years, some 5.7 m Ivorian voters went to the polls on 21 April to elect their regional and municipal councillors in an election involving 31 regions and 197 municipalities ('communes'). Gbagbo's regime had increased the number of municipalities from 191 in 2001 to 1,323, but district reforms in 2012 had brought this back to the more realistic figure of 197. The ballot was monitored by 30,000 police, gendarmes and soldiers, supported by forces of the UN Operation in Côte d'Ivoire (UNOCI). Partial results announced by the CEI on 22 April led to incidents in Abidjan, Yamoussoukro and Ferkessedougou. Independent candidates, who had not been selected by the ruling coalition, and FPI politicians who ignored their party's boycott, were returned in 70 communes, but many of them later rallied to the RDR or PDCI. The final results gave the RDR the lead with 96 communes, followed by the PDCI (48 communes) and independents (44 communes). The ruling coalition also won the regional polls, with 11 regions going to the RDR, four to the PDCI, and nine to the 'Rassemblement des Houphouétistes pour la Démocratie et la Paix' (RHDP) – an alliance between the RDR, PDCI, the 'Union pour la Démocratie et la Paix en Côte d'Ivoire' (UPDI) and the 'Mouvement des Forces d'Avenir' (MFA). Independents took five regions.

On 16 February, police fired tear gas to disperse a **banned protest** in Abidjan. The ban had been broadcast the previous evening by Interior Minister Hamed Bakayoko. Fifty young people shouting "Free Gbagbo" were pushed back when they tried to reach Yopougon, a long-lasting pro-Gbagbo stronghold. Police received support from a UNOCI contingent, equipped with armoured vehicles.

On 14 March, a heavily armed commando group **attacked an army post** in the village of Zilebly (Bloléquin district) along the volatile and porous border with Liberia. The assailants came from Liberia and were led by a former Gbagbo warlord named "Colombo", based in Touzon, the village of former Liberian president Samuel Doe. The attackers' claimed objective was to free the western region of foreigners. To create confusion, the commandos were dressed like Dozo fighters (traditional hunters from northern Côte d'Ivoire who fought on Ouattara's side during the 2011 conflict). Seven people were killed during the clashes, including four civilians.

The release of the UN Group of Experts report on 28 April fuelled the long-lasting polemic about the impunity granted to former rebel leaders and militias who had taken Ouattara's side in his 2011 showdown with Laurent Gbagbo. The report accused these leaders, who had been integrated into the national army or given high-level positions in the new Ouattara administration such as district or regional prefectures, of being part of a **smuggling network** active in the export of goods such as cocoa, gold, diamonds, cotton and timber. Justice and Human Rights Minister Gnenema Coulibaly told a news conference that the government would not protect anyone involved in theft or smuggling, and asked for evidence in order to make further investigations. In November, the **cocoa trial** began in Abidjan, involving people formerly on the side of the Gbagbo regime. In this case, the former bosses of cocoa management boards were prosecuted for allegedly embezzling hundreds of millions of euros between 2002 and 2008. The inquiry had been opened in October 2007 at the request of then-president Gbagbo and led to the arrest of almost all the managers in the sector, including some close allies of the former head of state. On 6 November, 14 managers were sentenced to 20 years, while 13 were acquitted. However, the prosecutor did not insist that those convicted be put in detention, and it remained unclear when they would begin serving their sentence. Lawyers said it was a political trial.

Government Secretary-General Amadou Gon Coulibaly announced on 25 July that, following a decision by President Ouattara, the **cabinet mining portfolio** would be transferred to Industry Minister Jean-Claude Brou. The portfolio was taken away from Adama Toungara, who had been serving as minister of mines, oil and energy, as a consequence of a dispute with gold miners over a proposed windfall tax on profits and recurring delays in drafting a new mining code.

On 22 May, the media regulatory body 'Conseil National de la Presse' banned the opposition paper 'Bol'Kotch'. The satirical newspaper was accused of publishing misleading images and allegations about the president. In a decision on 5 August, which was presented as a **pacification measure**, the judicial authorities ordered the release of 14 top allies of ex-president Gbagbo, although their prosecutions were not suspended. Those provisionally released included Gbagbo's son, Michel, the head of the FPI, Pascal Affi N'Guessan, and the former governor of the BCEAO, Philippe Henry Dacoury-Tabley. Michel Amani N'Guessan, a senior FPI official, welcomed the move but made it clear that national reconciliation could only begin once all of the party's members had been released, including Gbagbo himself, who had been transferred to the ICC in 2011.

While the political climate between government and opposition improved, relations between the two government parties came under pressure. The PDCI, in a communiqué issued in Yamoussoukro on 17 August, accused the RDR of unfairness and complained that the PDCI's senior people were being marginalised in the management of the administration. These complaints were reiterated during the **PDCI congress** on 6 October. Henri Konan Bédié, the 79-year-old former head of state, accepted the party's ticket to run in the 2015 presidential elections. The congress gave Bédié overwhelming support, even though he was technically too old to run under existing party rules; the rules were modified accordingly. Bédié was challenged by two other contenders, including the president of the party's youth branch, Kouadio Konan Bertin, whose supporters stressed that it was time for change. Nevertheless, Bédié got 93% of the vote.

The fourth extraordinary session of the National Assembly opened on 12 August. It was set to discuss new legislation to facilitate access to citizenship for millions of foreigners and improve state regulation of land ownership, the two issues at the heart of a decade of political crisis and violence. Two **nationality laws** were passed on 23 August: one allowing foreigners to acquire Ivorian citizenship upon marriage, the other enabling foreign-born residents living in Côte d'Ivoire since before independence and foreign nationals born in Côte d'Ivoire between 1961 and 1973, and their children, to become citizens. The Assembly also voted to extend a grace period for the implementation of the 1998 **rural land law**, giving landholders ten years to prove legal claims to their property.

On 3 July, during a visit to the northern town of M'Bengue, President Ouattara acknowledged for the first time in comments broadcast on state television that he would seek re-election following the end of his term. The president's office announced on 2 December that the **2015 presidential elections** would be held in October. A presidential spokesperson said that Ouattara was not interested in recovering the time lost in the wake of the 2011 polls, when his assumption of office was delayed by more than five months as a result of Gbagbo's refusal to admit defeat.

Political dialogue between the RDR and Gbagbo's FPI finally resumed, following an offer by Ouattara to the FPI, during a visit to Didiévi in December, that they might possibly participate in the government. The two parties met on 9 December at the RDR's headquarters to discuss the organisation of a national conference proposed by the FPI. Pascal Affi N'Guessan, FPI president, and RDR interim secretary-general Amadou Soumahoro said that discussion, exchange and dialogue were the necessary steps to resolve the issues faced by the nation.

On 16 December, the ICC decided to uphold its decision not to hear charges against Laurent Gbagbo concerning crimes against humanity. As in June, it requested more evidence to confirm these charges.

Foreign Affairs

Only two resolutions (out of 46) were passed by the **UNSC** on Côte d'Ivoire. On 17 January, Bert Koenders, the UN secretary-general's special representative for Côte d'Ivoire (and soon to be appointed UN special representative in Mali), reminded the Council that the stability and economic success of the country were critical to the stability of West Africa. Setting out the context of growing Islamism in the sub-region, he urged continued support for Côte d'Ivoire to address the remaining challenges and root causes of its earlier crisis. On 15 February, the Ivorian ambassador to the UN, Youssoufou Bamba, confirmed the accession of Côte d'Ivoire to the ICC with the ratification of the Treaty of Rome. Ahead of a planned downsizing of **UNOCI**, he told the UNSC on 16 April that surveillance drones should be deployed to offset any planned cuts. Bamba was following a report by the UN secretary-general about deployment of drones in the DRC and possibly in Côte d'Ivoire. Resolution 2101, passed on 25 April, extended until 30 April 2014 the mandate of the UN Group of Experts in charge of the monitoring progress and enforcement of sanctions, as well as measures to prevent the supply of arms to the country and the trade in rough diamonds. The Council reiterated its concern about the unresolved challenges of DDR and security sector reform. International support was confirmed on 30 July by Resolution 2112, which extended the mandate of UNOCI and French troops (a small remaining contingent of 450) until 30 June 2014. This extension, however, confirmed the objective of reducing UN military personnel. The number of UNOCI troops fell from 9,583 in January to 8,837 in July (with a target of 7,137 in July 2014). Their stationing in high-risk areas in western Côte d'Ivoire was also requested.

The **new UN top envoy** in Côte d'Ivoire, Ms Aïchatou Souleymane (who took over as the head of UNOCI in place of Bert Koenders on 6 July) met with the National Assembly Speaker Guillaume Soro on 12 August. She confirmed the UN's full support and expressed her wish to work with all stakeholders in the national reconciliation and peace process, and to facilitate reforms ahead of upcoming elections in 2015.

Following a first attack in October 2012 against a Greek vessel, pirates seized a Panama-flagged oil tanker on 16 January. It was anchored in Abidjan and unable to put out a distress call in time to be rescued. Another vessel – a French tanker – was hijacked in international waters off Abidjan on 3 February. The increase in piracy in the western part of the **Gulf of Guinea** was presented as a consequence of reinforced patrols by Nigeria and Benin. Regional cooperation was improved and resulted in a heads of state conference on maritime security in the Gulf of Guinea in Yaoundé on 24 June, with President Ouattara attending.

On 22 November in Johannesburg (South Africa), the annual assembly of the Kimberley Process – the world's diamond watchdog – gave its backing to the **lifting** of the 2005 **UN embargo** (Resolution 1643) on the sale of diamonds from Côte d'Ivoire. The assembly, with delegates attending from 81 countries, acknowledged that the country had fulfilled the minimum requirements under the group's certification system. The decision cleared a major hurdle for Côte d'Ivoire to resume trading its diamonds on the international market.

All year long, tensions with neighbouring countries were a major concern. On 25 January, a long-standing dispute with **Guinea** about border demarcation was revived when around 40 Guinean troops entered a border village and removed the Ivorian flag. The issue was discussed by the two foreign ministers in the margins of an ECOWAS summit in Yamoussoukro on 28 February. The two states committed themselves to resolving the dispute peacefully and decided to withdraw their respective armies from the area. A joint commission to delineate the border was re-established.

The recurring tension and sporadic violence in the border area with **Liberia** and a deadly raid in March near Bloléquin led to a meeting in Monrovia (Liberia) on 5 April that brought together the Ivorian and Liberian governments and the two UN peacekeeping missions in their countries (UNOCI and the UN Mission in Liberia). The meeting's objectives were to discuss security issues, to deal with the recent attack in the border region, to explore ways in which the UN missions could support the security of the region, and to address the sources of conflict, including the return of refugees, reconciliation, and distribution of humanitarian aid. The participants agreed to strengthen collaboration and coordination between the security forces through exchange of intelligence information, to mutually reinforce security along the border, and to conduct joint riverine and land border patrols. Cooperation between the two countries was consolidated with the participation of Ouattara and Liberian President Ellen Johnson-Sirleaf in the Joint Council of Chiefs and Elders of frontier communities on 19 October in Zwedru, on the Liberian side of the border.

Relations with **Ghana**, where approximately 8,600 refugees remained, including a group of high-profile **Gbagbo associates**, were a recurring concern. After previously claiming that it considered Gbagbo's exiled supporters to be 'refugees', the Ghanaian authorities progressively amended their position, as shown by the extradition of Charles Blé Goudé in January. However, bilateral ties worsened again in the course of the Justin Kone Katinan case. Katinan, a budget minister in the Gbagbo government and exiled in Ghana, had been acting as Gbagbo's spokesman since the former president's arrest. Extradition proceedings against him had been under way since August 2012, when he was arrested but then released by a Ghanaian court, which considered the Ivorian justice department's charges to be insufficient. Katinan was charged by prosecutors in Côte d'Ivoire with 20 counts of conspiracy to rob. Notably, it was alleged that he had robbed a series of banks in the commercial capital Abidjan to keep afloat the Gbagbo government, crippled by sanctions after Gbagbo's refusal to cede power in the wake of the 2010 election. Ahead of a new hearing on 11 June, Katinan called the charges politically motivated. The court deferred its decision to 5 August. On 29 August, it finally decided to reject the extradition request by dismissing the robbery charges, saying the evidence was not credible. It also said the allegations were not devoid of suspicion of being politically motivated.

The construction and near completion by Ghana of a dam and reservoir on the Black Volta was another source of tension. The Ivorian authorities expressed concern about the possible environmental and social impact on the Boundoukou region of the **Bui**

Hydroelectric Dam – a 400 MW Chinese-built dam located 50 km from the border. In a letter dated 17 June, Côte d'Ivoire said the Ghanaian government had failed to consult it, thus violating international regulations about cross-border projects.

Côte d'Ivoire and Ghana decided to recommence talks to settle a dispute over their **maritime boundary**. (Ghana had awarded licences for exploration of oil and gas reserves in a disputed off-shore area.) Government spokesman Bruno Kone said on 26 November that the two heads of state had formally decided to work towards a peaceful resolution of the dispute and a mutually agreeable solution. Ghana's giant Jubilee oil and gas field had been discovered in 2007 and production had begun in 2010. Côte d'Ivoire was concerned by its partial access to the field's reserves.

President Ouattara, who was also ECOWAS chair, was actively **engaged in diplomacy**. He started with a three-day visit to Germany aimed at developing economic partnerships. He met Chancellor Merkel and spoke at the Parliament in Berlin. Mali was high on his agenda, and the Ivorian president attended the AU donor conference in Addis Ababa (Ethiopia) on 29 January and another in Paris on 15 May. Ouattara met the president of the EU Commission in Brussels the following day, and made a state visit to Benin on 8 March. Accompanied by several ministers and businessmen, he was in Doha (Qatar) for a state visit on 12–14 May, and it was resolved that Côte d'Ivoire would open a new embassy there. Ouattara attended the AU's 50th anniversary in Addis Ababa on 25 May and then visited Japan for the Tokyo International Conference for African Development in Yokohama (2 June). He continued to Paris on 5 June, where French President François Hollande received the UNESCO Felix Houphouet-Boigny Prize for Peace for his involvement in the resolution of the Malian crisis. Successive visits to Brazzaville, Libreville and Yaoundé kept Ouattara away from Abidjan for almost the whole month and this long **absence triggered criticism** from the opposition and media. Ouattara attended the inauguration of Mali's new head of state, Ibrahim Boubacar Keita, on 19 September and also participated in the UN General Assembly in New York on 25 September, and in the Africa-France Conference in Paris on 4 December.

Nigeria's President Goodluck Jonathan paid a state visit on 1–2 March and President Ouattara also hosted President Michel Sleiman of **Lebanon** for a three-day official visit on 15–18 March. Abidjan announced the re-opening of its embassy in Beirut, closed since 1988. Several economic agreements were signed and a joint commission was reactivated. The Lebanese community, numbering around 100,000 persons, is the largest non-African community in Côte d'Ivoire.

Prime Minister Duncan travelled to Canada on 25–29 September where he participated in the Forum Africa 2013 Conference in Montreal. A bilateral agreement on promotion and protection of foreign investments was signed. When touring several West African capitals, French Interior Minister Manuel Valls visited Côte d'Ivoire on 15–16 November. He met his counterpart Hamed Bakayoko and signed a convention on security issues.

Socioeconomic Developments

The year started with three days of mourning for the 64 people killed during a stampede on New Year's Eve. President Ouattara visited injured people in hospital and offered his condolences.

IMF Managing Director Christine Lagarde spent three days in the country in January and called for "a second Ivorian economic miracle", referring to the first miracle in the golden 1970s. She met President Ouattara, Prime Minister Duncan, Parliamentary Speaker Guillaume Soro, and MPs, private sector representatives and civil society groups. The president confirmed Côte d'Ivoire's ambition to become an emerging country by 2020 and Lagarde welcomed the ambitious National Development Plan for 2012–15. The IMF was helping the country with a three-year ECF of $ 615.9 m. Lagarde announced the reopening of the IMF West African Regional Technical Assistance Centre (AFRITAC) in Abidjan, which was presented as another sign of the new climate of trust.

FDI in the **energy sector** increased. Chinese state-owned hydropower engineering firm Sinohydro started to build a 275 MW hydroelectric power station near the western town of Soubre, benefiting from a $ 500 m low-interest loan from China's Export-Import Bank signed on 9 January by the Chinese ambassador. The extension of the gas-fired Azito plant outside Abidjan by UK-based Globeleq and Hyundai Engineering and Construction began on 21 March with the objective of increasing power production by 50%. The expansion was expected to cost $ 414 m and would be supported by the IFC and European development institutions. Following President Ouattara's state visit to Doha in May, the Qatari and Ivorian governments agreed on conditions for the supply of liquefied natural gas from Qatar to Côte d'Ivoire in 2015 and on the development of oil exploration and production. With these major investments, Côte d'Ivoire, which already exported electricity to Ghana, Burkina Faso, Benin, Togo and Mali, consolidated its position as a major power supplier in West Africa. This position was confirmed in August by the decision to develop a power line connecting the country with the MRU states. A bill adopted by the Ivorian parliament on 19 August authorised Ouattara to ratify a treaty for the construction, operation and development of 1,400 km of high voltage transmission lines connecting Côte d'Ivoire, Guinea, Liberia and Sierra Leone.

Among other major investments, a preliminary deal for a new **container port** in Abidjan was agreed with a consortium led by French conglomerate Bollore, which also included France's Bouygues and a subsidiary of Danish shipping giant Maersk. Additional Chinese funding of $ 2 bn was announced on 15 July for the construction of a **railway line** between San Pedro, the country's second port, and the city of Man near the Guinean border. This project, together with the new Soubre hydropower plant, was aimed at boosting regional development and facilitating the exploitation of mineral resources in the west of the country.

Bargaining started as usual ahead of the opening of the **cocoa** selling season between the sector regulator – the 'Conseil du Café Cacao' (CCC) – and the cocoa exporters, and on 30 August they rejected the price structure produced by the 2012 reforms. Exporters demanded an increase to take into account additional costs, especially those of transport and taxation. They were followed by farmers, who said the government had failed to guarantee a minimum price and pointed to a lack of enforcement, which allowed merchants to undercut the price. Consequently, the guaranteed minimum price for cocoa was raised for the new 2013/14 main crop from CFAfr 725 to CFAfr 750 ($ 1.55) per kg. The new price, slightly above the CCC recommendation, was decided at a cabinet meeting chaired by Ouattara on 2 October. The decision was largely welcomed by farmers, and exporters said the price increase would probably discourage smuggling to neighbouring Ghana. In the following weeks, concern that a significant drop in the cocoa might lead to a supply crunch fuelled strong competition among grinders, pushing up prices at port and to farmers. Exporters with local processing facilities (including Cargill, Barry Callebaut, CEMOI and ADM – among the industry's biggest players) said on 17 October that they were already paying CFAfr 845/kg in order to secure volumes.

At the end of the year, estimated GDP growth was at 8.2%, a slight decrease from the 9.5% real **growth** of 2012. Despite these encouraging results, **living conditions** for most people remained difficult as a result of poverty. GDP per capita (measured in the 2005 $ value) remained below the level reached in 2000, and 60% of the population were under 25 years of age.

Bruno Losch

Gambia

The Gambia's unexpected withdrawal from the Commonwealth on 2 October and its breaking of diplomatic ties with Taiwan on 12 November after 18 years of collaboration indicated the country's growing isolation on the international scene. However, it still benefited from the support of international donors such as the EU and the World Bank, and hope was expressed about the potential for new cooperation with the People's Republic of China. President Yaya Jammeh, re-elected in 2011 for a fourth term, came under close international scrutiny for serious human rights violations. Revelations by exiled members of the army, who had been personally involved in regime atrocities, shocked public opinion, both in the Gambia and in the diaspora.

Domestic Politics

President Jammeh and the ruling Alliance for Patriotic Reorientation and Construction Party (APRC) continued to hold a firm grip on the citizenry by using a mixture of patronage and brutal repression. There were no signs of domestic revolt as all potential opponents were either in jail or in exile, and Jammeh skilfully kept a controlling eye on the army by removing any potential rivals.

On 4 April, **local elections** confirmed the APRC's dominance with 69 councillors' seats won uncontested and another 35 taken in sweeping victories. Independent candidates took the remaining ten seats. The city of Banjul was a remarkable case. Here, the independent candidate Abdoulie Bah defeated the incumbent mayor, Samba Faal of the APRC. Of the six opposition parties, only the National Reconciliation Party stood, unsuccessfully, in ten wards. The Gambia Moral Congress, the Gambia Party for Development and Progress, the National Alliance for Democracy and Develop ment, the People's Democratic Organisation for Independence and Socialism, the People's Progressive Party, and the country's principal opposition party, the United Democratic Party (UDP) boycotted the polls, a tactic also adopted in the 2012 legislative elections. One of the issues in dispute was the heavy involvement of district and village chiefs in the APRC's propaganda efforts. Post-electoral violence, arrests and detentions were reported in the parts of the country where independent candidates defeated the incumbent.

Imam Baba Leigh, who had been arrested on 3 December 2012 after raising his voice against the executions that took place in that year, was released from detention on 10 May after an intense national and international campaign. After leaving the Gambia, Imam Leigh reported on the mistreatment he had suffered at the hands of state officials. Shocking revelations on the inner workings of the regime also came from members of the army and close collaborators of Jammeh who had fled abroad after falling out of favour with the president. In February, former warrant officer Bai Lowe in a long interview on Freedom Radio, an opposition station based in the United States, confessed to having been involved in **regime brutality**. Lowe denounced the presence of Casamance rebels in the president's home village of Kanillai, and gave details about the illicit trade in timber and cannabis trafficking with the Senegalese Casamance region, torture by the regime's secret services and extra-judicial executions by army personnel and the infamous National Intelligence Agency. Numerous well-known victims included Daba Marena (2006), the journalists Deyda Hydra (2004) and Ebrima Manneh (2006), President Jammeh's blood brother Haruna Jammeh, his sister Marcie Jammeh and a distant relative, Jasaja Kujabi. Apparently, Haruna and Jasaja had been found guilty of trying to harm the president spiritually. Marcie had made critical comments about the government after the attempted coup on 21 March 2006.

Several Gambians went missing. In May, dissidents Mahawa Cham and Saul Ndow, the former living in Accra and the latter in Dakar, disappeared after a short visit to the Casamance, where they were presumably kidnapped by Casamance rebels and handed over to Gambian security forces. Ndow was a businessman and collaborator of Jammeh in the early days of his regime. He had been on a government 'black' list since the 2006 coup attempt. Both the Gambian and the Senegalese authorities kept silent over these **disappareances**. In June, Alhagie Mamut Ceesay and Ebou Jobe – two Gambian-born US citizens – were detained in Banjul while on vacation. At year's end, they were still missing. The two had reportedly been trying to start a business venture in the country. On 9 August, former colonel Ndure Cham was arrested during a visit to his home village of Numukunda. The government considered Cham one of the leaders of the 21 March 2006 coup attempt. (He had since been living in Senegal.)

On 4 March, using an incinerator provided by the British High Commissioner, the government destroyed two tonnes of cocaine seized by the National Drug Enforcement Agency (NDEA) in 2010. Government officials, foreign diplomats and the press witnessed the event, which publicised the country's commitment to fight **drug trafficking**. The destruction had been delayed for almost two years as the NDEA lacked the proper equipment. Benedict Jammeh, head of the NDEA and the president's uncle, was dismissed and arrested at the beginning of the year together with several other members of the agency. On 12 March, the Banjul Magistrates Court charged him and Abdoulie Ceesay, a former NDEA public relations officer, with having intentionally acted against the Gambia's economic interest during the last three years. Rumours circulated that drug traffickers had co-opted state officials, border police and army personnel to facilitate the transit of drugs through the country. Whether or not President Jammeh was aware of these actions, Benedict's and similar cases testified to his government's dysfunction. In May, Benedict fled the country, joining hundreds of exiled compatriots in Senegal. On 20–21 May, President Jammeh dismissed Attorney General and Minister of Justice Lamin Jobarteh, and Solicitor General Pa Harry Jammeh. On 16 June, another of Jammeh's right-hand men, former secretary of state and head of the civil service Njogou Bah, was arrested. He was held without charge until 15 July, when together with Jobarteh and Pa Harry, he appeared in court for abuse of office and conspiracy to commit a felony.

Amadou Sanneh (UDP national treasurer), Malang Fatty and his brother Alhagie Sambou Fatty, also of the UDP, were arrested on 23 September on suspicion of fraud, together with commissioner of oaths Bakary Baldeh. Border police detained Malang Fatty on 19 September during a routine check of passengers boarding a vehicle for Senegal. He had with him a letter, written on UDP letterhead and signed by Sanneh, stating that Jammeh's regime was guilty of daily **harassment of UDP members**. On 3 October, Sanneh, Fatty and Sambou Fatty 'confessed' to their crime on national television and appealed for the president's clemency. In the wake of this arrest, intelligence officers discovered another UDP application for asylum by one Binta Sanneh, who was already living abroad. All these UDP members belonged to the Mandinka, the country's major ethnic group, to which former president Dawda Jawara also belonged. In his 'Tobaski' (Eid al-Adha) message on 14 October, the president argued that Mandinkas were free to oppose the government but that it would not tolerate those who did not love their country: "tarnishing the image of this country is treasonable and all those engaged in this would pay a high price". The Special Criminal Court sentenced Sanneh and the other two men to five years' imprisonment on 18 December. AI and human rights activists repeatedly reported on the

judiciary's lack of independence, with judges being appointed by the president and chosen from other African countries, no stability in senior judicial positions, and the removal of three Supreme Court chief judges during the year.

Foreign Affairs

The year opened with the **EU** inviting the Gambian government to a dialogue on 17 crucial issues, starting with the execution on 23 August 2012 of nine detainees on death row in the notorious Miles Two Prison in Banjul. The regime's long record of arbitrary arrests and detentions were other points of discussion. Jammeh reacted immediately, calling the EU's economic support "chicken change" and inviting Gambians to demonstrate against EU "neo-colonialism". Dialogue resumed in July. Discussions touched on regional security issues, the consequences of the introduction of biometric data for Schengen visas, and (marginally) on human and civil rights. The EU was a major donor, contributing € 10 m to a governance support programme inaugurated in 2012 and several other initiatives.

In September, while in New York to attend the UN General Assembly, Jammeh and his delegation were confronted with demonstrations by members of the **diaspora** and human rights activists. Throughout the year, the Dakar community of Gambian exiles was active. Press conferences and workshops were organised in collaboration with international organisations such as AI.

Accusations of neo-colonialism also accompanied the Gambia's abrupt withdrawal from the **Commonwealth**, announced on national television on 2 October. Two days later, a government statement accused the UK and the US of lending credibility to Gambians using the UDP as a platform for their activities. For the first time, the Gambia was included as a case-study in the UK Foreign and Commonwealth Office's Annual Report on Human Rights and Democracy, published on 15 April. The British High Commissioner urged the Gambian government "to engage constructively with the international community on these issues".

On 2 November, Jammeh cut his long-standing ties with **Taiwan**. The government hoped that this action would pave the way for future cooperation with the People's Republic of China. On 4 June, one of the biggest importers of rice, flour and chickens, **Lebanese businessman** Hussayn Tajideen of Tajco, was given 72 hours to leave the country. The government claimed Tajideen was selling food products that had passed their expiry date at his grocery stores, with serious health consequences for the citizenry. In 2009, the US Treasury Department had targeted Tajideen, his two brothers and two other business associates as global terrorists for their financial links with Hezbollah. In late October, the government pardoned Tajideen and allowed his return to the Gambia in spite of US protests. This action risked increasing the country's international isolation.

Relations with **Senegal** were tense throughout the year. Jammeh was suspected of supporting Casamance rebels, while Senegal was accused of giving sanctuary to Gambian dissidents. On 18 June, Kukoi Sanyang, leader of the attempted coup against former president Dawda Jawara's government in 1981, died in Bamako (Mali), to where the Senegalese government had deported him in April because of alleged violations of the terms of his refugee status. Jammeh's government had made several attempts to have Sanyang returned to the Gambia: he held Senegalese citizenship and was a fierce critic of the Gambian regime.

Socioeconomic Developments

On 25 January, in the framework of the Programme for Accelerated Growth and Employment launched in 2011, a presidential decree cut the working week for civil servants to four days so that they would use Fridays for prayers and engaging in **agriculture**. However, it was unlikely that urban-based civil servants without access to land could help increase the country's agricultural output. On 22 September, the agricultural sector received a World Bank grant of $ 55 m.

An IMF review in November signalled high levels of public debt in spite of optimistic government forecasts for 2013. Welfare payments to households suffering from poor harvests, lower exports, and the 10% fall in the **exchange rate** of the national currency (dalasi; D), in addition to lower donor inflows and migrant remittances, led to an increase in the government deficit. On 29 July, Jammeh announced that the exchange rage would be fixed at D 35 to $ 1 and that foreign currency could be exchanged only through authorised banks. Exchange operators' licences were revoked, and the central bank refused to issue new licences to companies such as Ria, Money Express and Wari. The new exchange rate led to increases in the prices of imported goods and many businessmen considered moving their activities to Sierra Leone.

Although the Gambia remained competitive in terms of taxation, inflation and the introduction of VAT reduced profit margins. The announcement that the government would take action against semi-legal or **illegal constructions** in Tourist Development Areas led to unrest among businessmen and diaspora Gambians. In May, bars, lodges, small restaurants and even family compounds received notice that their infrastructure was to be demolished. It became clear that the government meant business at the beginning of September, when private buildings and the premises of the 'Mama Africa – Women's Museum and Arts Centre' in the village of Batokunku in the Kombo South District were demolished by agents of the Department of Physical Planning on the grounds that they were located on reserved or private land. There were no court orders and the demolition order came directly from the president's office. Home owners showed property certificates and lease documents to the reporters who witnessed the event.

Alice Bellagamba

Ghana

The principal political issue in 2013 was the challenge brought by the New Patriotic Party (NPP) against the Electoral Commission (EC) in the Supreme Court and the way this impacted on the country's democracy and security. Economic growth was affected by rising inflation, which resulted in popular dissatisfaction with President Mahama's economic policies. Throughout the year, the government of the ruling National Democratic Congress (NDC) was confronted with allegations of corruption, including the infamous "Victoria Hammah saga"; a leaked recording of a telephone conversation revealed that a deputy minister of the ruling party was hoping to receive $ 1 m before leaving office. The country continued to consolidate its bilateral ties and abide by its bilateral and multilateral obligations, both in Africa and across the world.

Domestic Politics

An **electoral petition** filed by the NPP against the EC at the Supreme Court on 28 December 2012 took centre stage in many of the country's political debates during 2013. In the petition, the NPP, led by its presidential candidate, Nana Addo Danquah Akuffo-Addo, alleged that irregularities had been found in 24,000 electoral results sheets (known as the pink sheets), which skewed the outcome in favour of the NDC. On 3 January, the NDC was joined in the court action as the matter also involved them.

Despite the inevitable political tensions, the Office of the Chief Justice, in accordance with the provisions of the 1992 Constitution, proceeded with preparations for the **investiture** of President John Dramani Mahama and he was sworn in on 7 January. The ceremony was attended by numerous foreign dignitaries, former president and NPP leader John Agyekum Kufuor, and representatives of various political parties. However, the NPP decided to boycott the ceremony, labelling it an "illegal swearing in". On 9 January, NPP members said Kufuor's attendance had betrayed the party.

Immediately after his inauguration, Mahama began the process of selecting his cabinet. In accordance with Article 78 of the Constitution, Mahama submitted his first batch of ministerial nominees to parliament on 12 January. By 14 February, a total of 28 ministers had been appointed, which rose to 85 ministers and deputy ministers by 28 March. As a result, Mahama was accused of breaking his promise to run a lean government and of appointing numerous people of questionable competence. Assibey Yeboah, MP for New Juaben South, remarked on 28 March: "The **size of government** is just too big . . . almost every major Ministry has two Deputies; Finance, Lands and Forestry, Agriculture . . . just jobs for the boys." He further accused the president of vacillating throughout the selection process. A political scientist at the University of Ghana argued that the cabinet should not number more than 40 ministers. However, the Constitution's silence on the issue made it difficult to control appointments.

On 16 April, Mahama marked his **first 100 days** in office. Political parties, think tanks, civil society organisations and the media differed on his achievements. On 15 and 18 April, NGOs such as the policy thinktank IMANI and the Ghana Centre for Democratic Development gave the president approval rates of 47% and 67% respectively. However, on 20 April, the editor-in-chief of the 'New Crusading Guide' wrote: "There is nothing to write home about in the 100 days, and it is even in the interest of government that we don't do an assessment." Members of the NDC and other parties were also against an assessment, arguing that an evaluation after 100 days in office, a practice that had begun during the Kufuor presidency in 2001, represented an **unfair benchmark**. Thus, on 18 April, members of the People's National Convention questioned the fairness of the practice.

While the president marked his 100 days in office, the Supreme Court commenced the hearing of the NPP's **election petition** against the EC (16 April). The case attracted a lot of attention, as it was believed that the ruling would reflect the degree of Ghana's democratic maturity. To ensure transparency, the hearing was broadcast throughout the country from the day it began until the pronouncement of the verdict. Interestingly, the petition hearing revealed inefficiencies and bottlenecks in the electoral system. The petitioners accused the EC of several discrepancies, including duplication of serial numbers in 8,987 out of the 10,119 polling stations, lack of biometric verification during voting, and absence of signatures of the EC's presiding officers on some of the pink sheets. Some of these allegations were admitted by the EC. The admission on 4 June by Afari Gyan, the EC chair, of 50 cases of double registration in records of 705 Ghanaians in the diaspora was a case in point. Perhaps the advantage of such revelations was the fact that they could serve as lessons learnt for future elections. The non-partisanship, unbiased attitude and professionalism demonstrated in the **Court hearing** also proved a formative experience. Thus, on 2 July, the president of the panel of judges, Justice William A. Atuguba, sentenced Ken Kuranchie a journalist and alleged NPP supporter, and Stephen Atugiba, member of the NDC, to ten- and three-day jail terms, respectively, for contempt of court. This ruling to some extent transformed citizens' perception of the Court and reinforced their trust in the judiciary, which prior to the case had been widely seen as corrupt and unfair.

The **Court's verdict**, eight months after the closely contested election, constituted a test for the country's democracy. Political tension increased as the date of the verdict drew near. Civil society organisations, traditional rulers, the clergy, government and security officials and political parties all campaigned for peace to be maintained. On 23 August, the Ghana Police Service deployed 32,000 personnel across the country to curb any violent clashes and prevent the eruption of potential conflict. On 29 August, the Supreme Court issued a verdict in favour of the EC and NDC. The Court indicated that the petitioners had not shown adequate evidence to substantiate their case and argued that the inaccuracies in the electoral system were not sufficient to "discredit" the final results. Nana Addo Danquah Akuffo-Addo demonstrated political maturity by gracefully accepting defeat, despite disagreeing with the Court's ruling. The demonstration of national loyalty by the various stakeholders during the judicial process confirmed Ghana's political development, potentially further consolidating the democratic system. While the Supreme Court ruling led to celebrations in the NDC camp, it sparked an **intra-party backlash** within the NPP. Members blamed each other for the 2012 election defeat and the failure of the subsequent court case. Noting the simmering tensions within the party, Nana Addo Danquah Akuffo-Addo and his vice-presidential candidate, Mahamudu Bawumia, implored party loyalists during their country-wide 'Thank You Tour' on 14–22 September to "never speak ill of any fellow party member as that would only lead to cracks in the party". Nevertheless, party members and the leadership continued to trade accusations. On 24 September, the former NPP MP for Mfantseman West, Stephen Asamoah Boateng, criticised his party's general secretary, Kwadwo Owusu Afriyie, for causing divisions in the party and for mocking him for his defeat in the 2012 elections. Subsequently, on 25 September, the NPP national chairman, Jake Obetsebi Lamptey, in a letter to the party entitled 'An Open Letter to the NPP Members and Supporters: New Patriotic Party, Thoughts on the Way Forward', accused party followers of being their "own worst enemies". In addition, on 2 October, an NPP youth faction called Patriotic Future of NPP launched an attack on the party's executives, accusing them of thievery and calling them "self-seeking individuals" who caused the party's defeat. Nana Addo Danquah Akuffo-Addo's candidature as the party's standard-bearer for the 2016 election also became a dividing factor. Members who did not support Akuffo-Addo's candidature felt sidelined and pressured to accept him. On 16 October, Stephen Asamoah Boateng alleged that some party leaders were cajoling him and other members into accepting Nana Akuffo Addo as the 2016 presidential candidate.

The **NDC** was also **hit by feuds**. On 30 April, a conflict between NDC members in the Sissala East Constituency of the Upper West Region, which had begun in 2009, resurfaced. Clashes between the former NDC MP, Rafatu Alhassan Dubie, and his successor, Alijata Sulemana Gbentie (who was then also the district chief executive), escalated, with the latter setting up her own executives, so that the party's executive body in the region was divided into two. On 4 September, loyalists of late president John Atta-Mills expressed their discontent by reportedly accusing Mahama of "destroying the party", and plotting to challenge his 2016 candidature.

Corruption allegations levelled against the NDC by the general public and the opposition over its misappropriation of state funds increased party discontent. For example, on 1 November, verbal clashes within the NDC reached a crescendo when longstanding party member and MP for Nadowli-Kaleo Constituency in the Upper West Region, Alban Bagbin, accused the president of not dealing effectively with corruption and not making himself accessible for advice on the issue. This led to a violent backlash from other members of the party, who called Bagbin a "liar" and an "enemy within". These clashes abated when the party's general secretary, Johnson Asiedu Nketia, called for a truce on 5 November and established a committee to investigate Bagbin's claim.

Against this background, it is significant that NPP-NDC clashes were few. Despite its internal controversies, the NPP began preparations for the 2016 general elections by conducting country-wide **party elections** for its polling station, constituency and regional executives. Elections for polling station and constituency executives were held from 1 to 30 November and 14 November to 28 December, respectively. Regional and national executive elections were scheduled for early 2014. Generally, the elections were conducted peacefully and smoothly, with the exception of some constituencies in the Volta and Northern regions where polls had to be rescheduled due to misunderstandings and voting irregularities.

Foreign Affairs

On 19 September President Mahama took part in the investiture of Ibrahim Boubacar Keïta as Mali's newly-elected president. He also attended the 21st AU summit in Addis Ababa (Ethiopia) on 24 May, which also commemorated the 50th anniversary of the establishment of the (O)AU. On 17–18 July, he attended the 43rd ECOWAS summit in Abuja (Nigeria). Ghana's commitments to **UN peacekeeping operations** received new recognition when on 14 June 700 Ghanaian peacekeepers were awarded medals by Special Representative of the UN Secretary-General Karin Landgren for their exceptional services to the UN Mission in Liberia since the beginning of the mission in 2003.

The Mahama administration intensified its bilateral engagements. On 6 May, Ghana and **Japan** signed a $ 14 m funding agreement for the advancement of the Power Distribution System project in Brong Ahafo and the three Northern regions. This was followed by the president's participation, with the First Lady Lordina Mahama, in the 5th Tokyo International Conference on African Development in Yokohama (1–3 June). During the conference, Lordina Mahama attended, with other First Ladies, the International Symposium on HIV and AIDS. On 21 June, Ghana and the **US** signed a $ 1.4 m project agreement towards the advancement of research in agriculture and agribusiness. US Secretary of State John Kerry and Mahama had a bilateral discussion on 26 September at Kerry's official residence in New York on the progress of the Millennium Challenge Account (MCA) and future American energy support to Ghana. This meeting followed the signing of an $ 8 m Memorandum of Understanding between Ghana and the Millennium Challenge Corporation on 23 July with a view to undertaking feasibility studies for the second compact of the US-funded MCA.

The president also engaged in **sub-regional collaboration**, particularly with regard to maritime piracy and energy. On 9 August, Mahama attended a meeting of heads of state and government in Malabo (Equatorial Guinea) concerning maritime security along the Gulf of Guinea. The meeting was convened by President Teodoro Obiang Nguema Mbasogo of Equatorial Guinea in the wake of rising piracy activities along the Gulf. Participating countries discussed collaborative efforts to strengthen security in their territorial waters and curb piracy. In view of the energy deficit affecting most African countries, states along the Gulf of Guinea organised the 16th Gulf of Guinea Gas Conference in Abidjan (Côte d'Ivoire) on 6–8 November. The president was represented by Minister of Energy and Petroleum Emmanuel Armah-Kofi Buah, who encouraged delegates to pool their energy resources. The meeting also called for exchange of knowledge and experience and the formulating of strategies regarding gas production for industrial development.

On 20 September, Mahama departed for the 68th Session of the **UN General Assembly** in New York, which ran from 23 September to 3 October. It took place under the theme 'Post-2015 Development Agenda: Setting the Stage'. Mahama addressed the Assembly, calling on the international community to understand the uniqueness of African culture and values with regard to democracy. The Assembly was also attended by former president Kufuor. During the same trip, Mahama attended the 60th anniversary celebration on 25 September of the Africa-America Institute, an institution dedicated to promoting education and professional training for many African countries including Ghana. Furthermore, the president used his visit to the US to deliver a lecture on 'Ghana's Evolution as a Democracy and its Growing Economic and International Influence' at Kennesaw State

University, Atlanta, Georgia, on 1 October, as part of efforts to establish more academic relationships with foreign educational institutions.

Relations with **South Africa** were strengthened. On 5 November, Mahama dispatched Minister for Foreign Affairs Madam Hannah Tetteh to the 3rd South Africa-Ghana Permanent Joint Commission for Cooperation meeting in Pretoria. The meeting resulted in bilateral talks between Hannah Tetteh and South Africa's Minister of International Relations and Cooperation Maite Nkoana-Mashabane on on-going partnerships and future collaboration. The Permanent Joint Commission meeting was followed by a three-day state visit to Ghana by President Jacob Zuma on 25–27 November to strengthen the bilateral relationship. South Africa is the 14th largest investor in Ghana with investments between 2003 and 2013 totalling some 64 m South African rand. The main highlight of the visit was the signing of a Memorandum of Understanding on 26 November, affirming cooperation in air services, transport, electricity and energy.

The death of former South African president **Nelson Mandela**, on 5 December 2013 marked a sad end to the year. Ghana mourned the death of this iconic leader. In an interview with the 'New York Times' on 6 December, Mahama expressed his sorrow over Mandela's death, recognising his great leadership on Africa's journey towards democracy and good governance. He reportedly remarked: "His utilisation of peace as a vehicle of liberation showed Africa that if we were to move beyond the divisiveness caused by colonisation, and the pain of our self-inflicted wounds, compassion and forgiveness must play a role in governance."

Mahama concluded the year's diplomatic engagements by attending the Elysée summit on peace and security in Paris (France) on 6–7 December, an initiative of President François Hollande to consolidate Franco-African relations, especially with regard to their joint commitment to peace and security. In his speech, Mahama called for collective efforts to address security on the continent as development cannot be achieved in "an environment of maritime piracy, terrorism, rebel activities, drug and human trafficking". Almost 40 African leaders attended the two-day summit.

Socioeconomic Developments

On 21 February, Mahama delivered his state of the nation address and, like his predecessor, promised to tackle corruption across all sectors of the economy, stating "our commitment to the fight against corruption remains unshakeable". Despite these promises, corruption within state institutions increased. On 16 July, an investigative report was submitted by a five-member ministerial committee set up on 12 April by Minister of Youth and Sports Elvis Afriyie-Ankrah to assess allegations of **financial malpractices** at the Ghana Youth Employment and Entrepreneurial Agency (GYEEDA), known under the Kufuor administration as the National Youth Employment Programme. It proved the first of many tests of Mahama's anti-corruption campaign. The report, which was initially alleged to have been suppressed until it was leaked to the public, accused two NDC cronies, Abuga Pele, former GYEEDA national coordinator, and Clement Kofi Humado, MP, of involvement in a multi-million dollar scheme affecting the administration of the agency. They were said to have made payments of over $ 2 m to local companies whose work could not be accounted for. The report also revealed that several officials and companies working for the government were engaged in "bribery, corruption and circumvention of due processes". It added that the government was paying these companies over 1,200% interest a year without regard to national bidding procedures. The report also disclosed that interest-free loans of Ghana cedi (GH¢) 50 m (over $ 19 m) had been given by the Mahama government to Roland Agambire, a close ally of the president and CEO of RLG (a computer assembling company that served as one of GYEEDA's service providers). While many people expected the president to demonstrate leadership by prosecuting the offenders, they were disappointed when on 30 July Mahama announced the formation of another committee to review the initial findings. On 20 December the deputy attorney general indicated that RLG would be sued if it did not refund the loan within a year.

On 28 October, the private radio station 'Joy News', after nine months of investigation, exposed corrupt practices in one of Ghana's leading public hospitals, Korle-Bu. Its broadcast accused hospital officials of taking "**bribes from patients** to reduce their bills significantly and divert the money into their private pockets". Such protracted corrupt practices had for decades impeded the effective services provision to the general public.

Another corruption scandal that hit the headlines was a leaked telephone conversation that took place on 7 November, in which Mahama's Deputy Minister of Communications Victoria Hammah indicated that she had been granted her position on a silver platter as a result of her contacts in the NDC's inner circles. She also revealed her aspiration to use her position to make at least $ 1 m before leaving office. After the tape's release, the president was accused of selecting incompetent officials and dealing ineffectively with corruption within his government. On 8 November, Hammah was relieved of her duties.

GDP did not reach the expected 8% growth but stopped at 6.7% in the first quarter of 2013 (compared with 10.3% in the same period of 2012). By June, GDP had fallen to 6.4% before ending the year at 7.4%, according to Price Waterhouse Coopers' report on Ghana's 2014 Budget. The service sector reported a higher growth rate (12%), followed by 1.1% in agriculture and a reduced **growth** rate of 0.8% in industry. According to the Ghana Statistical Services third quarter report, production of oil, gold and diamonds plummeted by 16.0%, 29.7% and 2.9%, respectively. The 2014 budget published by the Ministry of Finance and Economic Planning on 19 November highlighted the steady rise in **inflation** from 10.1% in January to 13.1% in October. Another worrying trend, which was to be underscored by the president's 2014 state of the nation address, was the excess in commodities **imports**. Mahama noted that the country spent "almost $ 1.5 bn in foreign currency on importing rice, sugar, wheat, tomato products, frozen fish, poultry and vegetable cooking oils. Rice accounted for $ 374 m, fish $ 283.3 m, wheat $ 226.7 m, poultry $ 169.2 m, cooking oils $ 127 m, and tomato products $ 112.1 m."

As a result, public concern over the government's economic management ability increased. The ruling party quickly responded to public disaffection by blaming the reduced economic growth on the election petition case. On 7 September, for example, Deputy Minister of Information and Media Relations Ibrahim Murtala Mohammed stated that productivity had declined over the period of the petition case because many citizens were watching the live broadcast. He also indicated that the live screening of the hearing cost the Ghana Broadcasting Corporation over GH¢ 3.5 m ($ 1,341,900), which had affected the state's finances. In fact, however, the fall in economic growth was the result of a combination of factors, including inflation and the fall in value of the cedi.

On 27 November, the Bank of Ghana Monetary Policy Committee report indicated that **revenue** and grants for the year totalled GH¢ 13.9 bn ($ 5.3 bn). No breakdown of revenues per sector and commodity was provided.

With the country's increasing **agricultural and energy** challenges, the government intensified initiatives to improve these two sectors. On 3 January, it inaugurated an 80-tonnes capacity warehouse for food storage in Bazua, a community in the Upper East region, funded by the Alliance for Green Revolution in Africa as part of the Ghana Arzakinmu Programme, to provide training and storage facilities for communities in the Volta, Northern, Upper East and Upper West regions. The programme had so far led to the construction of warehouses in 18 communities and the training of 12,327 small-scale farmers across the four regions. Similarly, on 19 December, the president inaugurated the multi-million dollar Bui Hydro Power Project, which was anticipated to produce 400 MW of power to help resolve chronic energy problems. The project, which began in 2008, was funded with a concessionary loan ($ 263.5 m) from China and buyer's credit ($ 298.5 m) from EXIM Bank, with an additional contribution of $ 60 m by the government. The dam would also make possible the irrigation of 30,000 ha of farm land.

In December, the National Disaster Management Organization reported that there had been 478 incidents of fire across the country, affecting 11,766 people, most of whom were market women. It also recorded floods, which displaced over 6,000 people in 44 communities in the northern part of the country.

The government increased initiatives to fight **drug trafficking**. On 31 January, the former UN Secretary-General, Kofi Annan, launched the West Africa Commission on Drugs in Accra. Despite these efforts, there were reports of large amounts of cocaine being shipped into the country. On 19 November, a ship from Guyana was seized, which was reportedly carrying 414 kg of cocaine, worth over $ 50 m worth.

Illegal artisanal mining by foreigners, especially Chinese immigrants, led to violent clashes with locals: on 9 May, two Ghanaians were killed by Chinese miners over a contested plot of land in Obuasi, Ashanti Region. On 14 May, President Mahama established an inter-ministerial taskforce to address the issue, and on 20 June the government arrested and deported 269 foreigners (218 Chinese and 51 Nigerians). At year's end the number of **Chinese deportees** had risen to 4,500.

Kwesi Aning & Nancy Annan

Guinea

After years of political turbulence and a presidential election in 2010 that had promised a return to democracy and socioeconomic development, 2013 brought a deepening political stalemate. Despite the long-awaited legislative elections, which finally took place in September, frustration about the lack of economic revival, public insecurity and growing accusations of nepotism in the government of President Condé, along with rising ethnic violence, dominated the political landscape. The apparent stalemate not only frustrated Guineans' waning hopes for political stability and economic development, but also the expectations of the international community and investors in Guinea's vast mineral resources, whose exploitation slowed down despite the government's diplomatic efforts to attract investment.

Domestic Politics

The rainbow coalition of President Alpha Condé's 'Rassemblement du Peuple de Guinée' (RPG) and smaller parties came under pressure as a result of defections and dismissals. Key supporters including Finance Minister Ibrahima Kassory Fofana and former prime minister Lansana Kouyaté left the president's side, while others, such as regional strongman Jean-Marc Telliano, were sent off following allegations of corruption. Condé therefore had to rely more on his own party and faithful independent politicians such as Prime Minister Mohamed Said Fofana than on ministers of coalition parties, many of whom had since the inception of the government joined the opposition camp. While Prime Minister Fofana managed to keep the government on course amidst these **cabinet changes**, violent protests surrounding the legislative elections in the first months of the year led the president to transfer the security ministry from Maramany Cissé to Madifing Dianè, previously ambassador to Senegal. On 16 May, Condé decreed the replacement of various officials in the security sector and people responsible for the ongoing security sector reform, financed by the UN Peace Building Commission. Further changes in the government's composition were expected once the newly elected National Assembly began its term in 2014.

The death of Armed Forces Chief of Staff General Souleymane Kelefa Diallo in a plane crash on 11 February further helped to isolate Condé from the wider governing elite in the capital, Conakry. General Diallo had been a supporter of the president's sensitive security sector reforms, which had stirred unrest within the **army** and police. Tensions increased when former president and maverick leader Captain Moussa Dadis Camara, who still commanded a lot of respect within the army, visited his home area in the Forest Region in April to attend his mother's funeral, leaving his home in exile in Burkina Faso for the first time. On 14 April, he publicly called on Guineans to maintain calm, but internal army concerns remained over the militia forces he had recruited during his brief term in office.

The 'Commission Électorale Nationale Indépendante' (CENI), newly constituted under its chairman Bokari Fofana in 2012 and made up of members jointly selected by government and opposition, scheduled the legislative elections for 12 May. A symbol of the government's will to complete the country's transition towards civilian rule, these polls had already suffered numerous delays as a result of political and technical issues, but now opposition parties claimed that the election date had been decided without any consultations within the CENI. They also demanded that the diaspora be allowed to take part – a controversial issue that had already plagued the presidential elections – and threatened to boycott the polls. **Demonstrations** on 27 and 28 February descended into **violence**. Government troops responded with excessive force, leaving at least three dead and 200 wounded. Violence, including shooting by police, recurred in Conakry on 4 March, accompanied by looting and unrest during the funerals held for some of the earlier casualties. However, on 7 March, the prime minister began talks to end the political deadlock. It was feared that ethnic violence, which had already pitted Malinkés (Condé's ethnic group) against Peul (the ethnic group of major opposition leader and presidential runner-up Cellou Dalein Diallo) in previous years, might resurface and become more extensive than ever. The unrest spread from the capital to major cities such as Labé and Mamou.

At another **opposition rally** on 21 May, Diallo repeated his demand for the replacement of the election operator Waymark/Sabari Technology, threatening to withdraw his party, the 'Union des Forces Démocratiques de Guinée' (UFDG), from the elections, by then rescheduled for 30 June. The rally was followed by **more violent clashes** on 23–24 May, claiming at least 12 lives and 89 injured and raising the election death toll to over 50. Parts of Conakry's Cosa Market, a predominantly Peul-inhabited neighbourhood, were set alight – allegedly by gendarmerie taking revenge for the violence of the previous days. Prominent politicians Jean-Marc Telliano and Faya Millimono were injured in related incidents. Rumours of ethnic attacks followed and led to large groups of Peul leaving the capital at the beginning of June. Diallo and his entourage were attacked in his home on 19 June in what his party described as an assassination attempt masterminded at "the highest level". After this, security teams were permanently stationed at Diallo's house.

In June, with ethnic tensions rising, the international community offered **mediation** between the government and opposition. UN Special Representative Said Djinnit urged all political parties to cooperate, calling on both sides to be realistic and pragmatic. On 11 July, after the government and opposition agreed on a review of the election preparations undertaken by the South African firm Waymark, President Condé announced a new date for the elections, now set for 24 September. The CENI claimed that its $ 12 m budget was insufficient to ensure the proper conduct of the polls and asked for more international funding. The Election Monitoring Committee was made up of representatives of the civil service, political parties and international observers from the EU, AU, UN, ECOWAS and the OIF. It elected Yaya Boiro, former president of the Conakry appeals court, as chair. Election **campaigning** in August was also marred by violence. Condé's visit to his home region of Kankan led to unrest in which media representatives were also assaulted by military personnel.

After an additional delay of four days, the **legislative elections** finally took place on 28 September, without any major incidents or unrest. International observers declared that the polls had been "held in acceptable conditions of freedom and transparency" and were "broadly free and fair". Results of the elections to the 114 parliamentary seats were to be published on 2 October but only became public gradually. Upon considering their own tally, opposition leaders claimed they had won Conakry's five districts, rejecting any other outcome, and the following day they withdrew their representatives from the CENI. These claims led to a recount of ballots in Matoto and some other districts outside the capital, further delaying the publication of results. The opposition parties lodged complaints with the Supreme Court. President Condé's RPG secured 53 seats, the UFDG 37, and Sidya Touré's 'Union des Forces Républicaines' ten, with the rest taken by smaller parties. CENI's announcement of these results and their confirmation by the Supreme Court sparked protests in Conakry, with opposition leaders Diallo and Touré questioning the independence of the CENI and the Court. They called for a general strike on 24 November and accused the government of violating the election agreement mediated in July. However, the opposition attended the opening of parliament on 12 December, fearing that

Condé's RPG would be unopposed in engineering his re-election in the run-up to the 2015 presidential polls. The 'Parti de l'Espoir pour le Développement National', led by Lansana Kouyaté, which had won two seats, was the only party to boycott the proceedings.

The repeated postponements of the parliamentary elections prevented the establishment of an independent **human rights body**, as required by the 2010 government act that had also announced the creation of a human rights ministry, but the associated 'Reflection Commission' nevertheless started its work. This truth and reconciliation mechanism, created in 2011 by presidential decree, limited itself to reconciliatory prayer meetings rather than addressing the political impunity that had prevailed during the era of military rule. The Ministry of Human Rights and Civil Liberties, established at the beginning of the year, was hardly able to make its mark for lack of resources, although it advocated an end to impunity and the strengthening of the national judiciary.

While security sector reform continued, there was increasing doubt about the government's control of the security apparatus. Tensions arose within the military, and the use of violence and the practice of **unlawful detention** by police and gendarmerie increased. When the opposition and government reached an agreement on parliamentary elections on 3 July, most detainees arrested at opposition rallies had been released, but on 24–25 September, 33 people with links to the opposition were rounded up in Conakry and sent to a military facility near Kankan. Some were released after allegedly being threatened and tortured and one died of his injuries.

The judicial investigation into the **2009 stadium massacre** made slow progress. On 28 June, Minister for Presidential Security Lieutenant Colonel Claude Pivi was formally charged with being implicated in the massacre, joining the other accused, the minister in charge of fighting drug trafficking and organised crime, Colonel Moussa Tiégboro Camara, and Colonel Abdoulese Chérif Diaby, who had been health minister in 2009. Another key suspect was Lieutenant Abubakar "Toumba" Diakité, who in 2009 had shot and wounded the then-president Moussa Dadis Camara, both of whom remained free. The first interrogation of Pivi, set for July 3, was cancelled amid protests by his supporters and had not been rescheduled by year's end, nor had the government suspended Pivi or Tiégboro Camara. This drew strong criticism from human rights observers, who pointed to the government's slow and very limited collaboration with the investigations in general. Representatives of the ICC visited Conakry in January and June to assess the progress made by local investigators and also condemned the fact that former president and now suspect Moussa Dadis Camara had been able to visit the country privately in April without being questioned about the 2009 massacre.

Similar criticism was heard in another case of human rights violations. In February, the governor of Conakry Commandant Sékou Resco Camara and former army chief of staff General Nouhou Thiam were charged with torturing 17 civilians in 2010. In July, Commandant Aboubakar Sidiki "De Gaulle" Camara, former head of the presidential guard, was also indicted for participation in the same incident. Despite the **indictment**, Governor Camara remained in his high-profile position, raising further concerns about the accountability of high-ranking army officers to civil authority. This question was also addressed at celebrations for the 55th anniversary of the foundation of the Guinean army on 1 November in Labé.

On 17 July, the controversial trial related to the attack on Condé's private residence in July 2011 came to a close. The court sentenced to life imprisonment the main culprits, Commandant Alpha Oumar Diallo and Officer Jean Guilavogui, as well as four others convicted *in absentia*, including UFDG vice president Oury Bah. Six others were sentenced to five or 15 years, and 17 other suspects, including members of the military, were released.

In the course of the year some **radio stations** were closed and journalists assaulted. Critical talk shows and their hosts at 'Planet FM' had already been suspended for several weeks in December 2012. On 18 July, during ethnic violence in the Forest Region, 'Zaly Liberté FM' of N'Zérékoré, the regional capital, was closed down on the orders of the minister of communications, and 'Espace FM' was warned about the content it broadcast. In August, 'Bate FM' was ransacked in Kankan by soldiers and angry mobs in the course of election violence.

A **communal conflict** unrelated to election politics flared up in the Forest Region. On 15 and 16 July, groups of Guerzé (Kpelle) and Konianké (Mandingo) youths clashed in N'Zérékoré and Beyla and the surrounding area after an atrocity in the village of Koule two days earlier in which a group of Guerzé killed a Konianké youth. Tensions and fighting quickly spread across the region, pitting predominantly Christian Guerzés against Muslim Koniankés. Mosques, churches, market stalls and homes were looted and burnt, leaving at least 100 people dead, many more wounded and some missing. Police did not intervene and the army stayed in its barracks. President Condé sent controversial ministers Pivi and Tiégboro Camara, both native to the region, to confer with the local authorities, which succeeded in calming the population. The long-standing tensions between the two ethnic groups involved land rights and access to other resources. Similar clashes had occurred in previous years in Guéckédou, Zogota and Galapaye, as well as in neighbouring Liberia.

Foreign Affairs

In January, President Condé attended the World Economic Forum at Davos, reassuring the mining industry of a swift review of the national mining code in order to ward off irritations within the industry about major investment projects in iron ore and bauxite. On 13 February, Condé received **Russia**'s Foreign Minister Lavrov and representatives of the RusAl aluminium company. Attending the **AU**'s 50th anniversary summit in Addis Ababa

(Ethiopia) in May, Condé gave a speech on the prospects for peace between Eritrea and Ethiopia that was much commented on. While in Addis Ababa, he did not meet his predecessor, the head of Guinea's transitional government General Sékouba Konaté, who now led the AU Military Standby Force.

Ahead of the G8 meeting in Northern Ireland on 17–18 June, an international **investors' conference in London** was held at which Condé and key ministers highlighted mining potential in Guinea. The instability of the political situation was also discussed and identified as a major impediment to FDI. However, the government also tried to encourage agricultural investment, assuring potential investors of legal protection against land-grabbing charges. A private investors' conference was held in Abu Dhabi on 24–25 November, in which pledges were received of more than $ 6 bn in direct investment and multilateral development finance. These included commitments to direct investment in the Sangarédi bauxite deposits and the Kamsar mining port and aid projects to combat Guinea's high infant mortality rate. The conference, presided over by Condé and attended by key ministers, increased domestic and international regard for the government's economic ambitions as much as it drew criticism that Condé wanted to sell off Guinea to international investors.

Within the MRU, tensions remained high. In February, the Guinean army occupied the long-disputed village of Kpéaba, located in a copper-rich area along the border with **Côte d'Ivoire**. The government of **Liberia** protested that Guinea was holding some of its citizens in a N'Zérékoré prison on espionage charges, amidst rumours that some Liberian politicians might be using the borderland Forest Region as a new militia recruiting ground. While on a diplomatic mission to Liberia's Armed Forces' Day on 11 February, the Guinean delegates' plane crashed, killing six high-ranking officers, including army chief of staff General Souleymane Kelefa Diallo.

Guinea's pledge of $ 1 m to support the ECOWAS-led force to Mali was taken as a positive sign of the country's commitment to **sub-regional security** – which had long been questioned due to the narco-trafficking in which Guinea's military had been heavily involved for years, according to another UN report on the subject in February.

Socioeconomic Developments

While macro-economic developments seemed to consolidate the optimism generated by the Condé government's general stabilisation policies in previous years, purchasing power and living conditions continued to decline further. As a consequence, imports decreased. The country's main source of income, mineral exports – and hence revenue – declined from an expected 19.6% to 18.4% of the revised lower GDP, with the result that, after several years of improvement, the government was confronted with a **budget deficit** of 2.6%. Consequently, the rise in real per capita GDP was estimated by the IMF at a mere

0.4%, with Gross National Income per capita at $ 410, much lower than in previous years. The overall **growth** rate of 2.5% was significantly below the 4% attained in 2012 and the ECOWAS average of 6.3% for 2013. Analysts said this was because of the falling demand for bauxite and other minerals, the virtual halt to mining-related large-scale investment and the insecure political climate. Increased spending on public sector wages resulted in budget changes and an **inflation** rate of about 10.5%, which was still a significant improvement on the previous year's 15%. The government's monetary policies helped stabilise the exchange rate of the Guinean franc (GNF), but this came at a cost: due to the lower overall economic performance, the planned recapitalisation of the Central Bank had to be postponed to 2014.

The World Bank's Doing Business Report ranked Guinea 175th, up from 179th in 2012, reflecting general appreciation of the government's efforts in facilitating FDI. In TI's **corruption** perception index Guinea scored 24, and held the same position as in 2012, at 150th (out of 175 countries). The HDI of 0.355 ranked Guinea 178th.

In May, the IMF provided an ECF **loan** of $ 27 m and in June announced a $ 10 m programme to support micro, small and medium-size enterprises, especially targeting women. In June, France cancelled bilateral debts totalling € 74 m and, after the legislative elections of September, the EU released the last tranche of the 10th EDF to the tune of € 140 m, earmarked for five major infrastructural projects. With this move, development cooperation with the EU was finally back on track.

In October, the World Bank Group announced a new Country Partnership Strategy (CSP) for 2013–17, targeting governance and effective government services, tightly interlinked with the government's PRSP-III, which aims to use mining revenues to significantly reduce poverty. Included under the CSP are regional initiatives such as the Niger Basin Water Resource Development Project. In December, the World Bank launched a project to boost water management in the Senegal River basin, in which Guinea would subsequently receive its share of the total budget of $ 226.5 m.

Discontent with regard to deteriorating public service delivery rose throughout the year. On 10 May, protesters clashed with police due to repeated and increasing cuts of water and electricity in the capital, a city of about 2 m inhabitants. These were repeated at the end of July, with the government prohibiting further demonstrations on 1 August and promising an improvement in electricity services.

The modernisation of Conakry's international Gbessia **airport** now had a budget estimated at GNF 40 bn, part of which would be covered by bilateral investments, although most of the project would be funded by the government.

In June, the **mining code** was finalised and passed by the interim parliament after years of review by the Condé government. In July, the AfDB provided € 13 m to facilitate the renegotiation of 18 high-profile mining contracts. There were few developments surrounding the **Simandou project** (an iron ore mine to be connected by a trans-Guinea railway to a deep-sea port). Faltering demand for iron and aluminium were partly to blame, as were the government's difficulties in finding the funds to cover its 51% share in the railway project. Legal battles were another cause of delays. The Anglo-Australian firm Rio Tinto tried to push its agenda for Simandou Blocks 1 and 2 further, together with its Chinese partner Chinalco, including the financing of the much-coveted multi-purpose railway to Guinea's coast. However, the improvement of relations between the government and China, signalled a potential shift between the project partners, with Rio Tinto's position weakening. In July, the company rescheduled its first iron ore exports from Simandou from 2015 to 2018. Relations between the government and the Benny Steinmetz Group Resources (BSGR), which had partnered with Brazilian Vale to exploit the iron ore deposits of Simandou Blocks 3 and 4, continued to be difficult. The American FBI started investigating BSGR, alleging large-scale corruption in acquiring and later reselling parts of its concessions. So far, officials of previous governments and members of the late president Lansana Conté's family were implicated. In June–July, rumours circulated about a BSGR-sponsored coup attempt. President Condé made it clear that he welcomed investment by Vale, while threatening to take its partner BSRG to court.

RusAl's long-established Friguia **bauxite complex** in Fria, which had been at a standstill as a result of a labour dispute since April 2012, still did not reopen for business, although the government had pressed workers to drop their demands. As a consequence, infrastructure in the city and surroundings suffered, increasing local hardship. On 3 December, workers demanded that the government negotiate the re-opening of the Friguia plant, but security forces violently suppressed the protests. Over the course of the year, smaller mines were also affected by **strike action**, with workers demanding wage increases and better working conditions. In a context of few alternative sources of income, the increasing struggle over working conditions and pay highlighted people's increasing economic anxieties and mounting frustrations with their treatment by both the mining industry and the government.

Anita Schroven

Guinea-Bissau

Guinea-Bissau was still recovering from the 2012 military coup. Politically, the return to constitutional order was dragging on, and politically and militarily motivated human rights violations increased. Presidential and parliamentary elections were postponed to May 2014. However, an inclusive government – consisting of coup supporters and members of the pre-coup governing party – was formed in June. Meanwhile, ECOWAS, the only international organisation that recognised the transitional government, appeared to grow tired of Guinea-Bissau's authorities. The government was not able to compensate for the withdrawal of financial assistance as a result of sanctions imposed by the international community. Civil servants repeatedly went on strike because of unpaid salaries. Corruption increased. As a result of the political situation, illegal fishing and logging continued, while ineffective marketing of cashew nuts – the country's main cash crop – led to hunger and declining incomes among farmers.

Domestic Politics

Parliament passed a law on 29 May to form an 'inclusive government' that would include politicians from the majority 'Partido para a Independência da Guiné e Cabo Verde' (PAIGC) in the 'Partido da Renovação Social' (PRS)-led transitional government, renewing the Transitional Pact concluded in 2012. This prompted new conflict between the PRS and its extra-parliamentary partner parties, who were afraid they would be pushed out of lucrative government posts. In the **government reshuffle** that took shape during June, the army retained the interior and defence ministries. On 10 September, parliament rejected legislation that would have granted amnesty to the plotters of the 2012 coup.

On 1 October, strong-man General Chief of Staff António Indjai criticised the transitional government for corruption, saying, "We staged the coup to change and improve the situation of the country." Without any legal authorisation, the general staff sent 'executors' to almost all public institutions to collect taxes and hand them over to the treasury.

General elections originally planned for early 2013 were first postponed to 24 November and then finally set for 16 March 2014, owing to organisational and financial problems. They were a prerequisite set by the international community for the lifting of sanctions imposed after the coup. The transitional government confirmed in April that its members were not eligible to stand in the upcoming elections. The UN estimated the total costs of the electoral contest at $ 19.3 m. **Electoral preparations** were supported by, inter alia, the EU, US, ECOWAS, Portugal, China, Nigeria, Cape Verde and, notably, Timor, which dispatched an election assistance mission to Guinea-Bissau in May. Conflict arose between UNDP and the national Technical Office to Support the Electoral Process over overhead costs for the management of foreign funds. In June, Augusto Mendes was appointed as the new chairman of the 'Comissão Nacional de Eleições' (CNE). After much argument, politicians decided in favour of a costly and lengthy biometric electoral census, as demanded by the PRS and its allies before the coup. Though delayed, the census began on 1 December, but it was much criticised because of various technical, logistical and capacity problems. When the transitional government signed a contract with the Beninese enterprise Palmarès Technologies R&D on 15 September for the conduct of the biometric census, confusion arose as the government had already started the census without the help of Palmarès. Palmarès filed a lawsuit against the government and, as a result, ECOWAS imposed conditions on its funding. Further confusion arose in November, when smaller parties demanded their share of regional CNE presidencies. Chairpersons remained in office temporarily. On 20 December, about 100 census officials went on strike to press for payment of their salaries.

In April, exiled former prime minister Carlos Domingos Gomes Júnior (PAIGC) declared his intention of running for the state presidency, rejecting an "endless" transition period. Indjai said on 8 August that he could not guarantee Gomes' safety should he return. At the same time, Gomes declared that he had actually won the first round of the discontinued presidential elections in 2012, but that his vote had been forced down to 49% following military pressure. Two ministers of the pre-coup PAIGC government who returned from exile in Portugal were arrested upon arrival in Bissau, but later released. Former finance minister João Mário Vaz was detained for economic crimes on 5 February, and former cabinet minister Maria Adiatu Djaló Nandingna was illegally arrested by the intelligence service on 21 November.

Security remained volatile. In April, the police seized weapons and military uniforms near Cacheu. The unauthorised entry into the country of 300 Malians led to fears of Islamist infiltration. Most illegal migrants, however, originated from Guinea. Frontier guards estimated the total number of unauthorised residents in May at 200,000. In July, it was alleged that 19 prison guards had abused detainees in Mansôa. Months of politicised conflict at village level resulted in the death of a policeman in Nhacra, while in July ten pre-trial detainees escaped from prison in Bissau. A military training programme for members of both the police and the army started in July, but in late October it became known that some security officials had been victims of physical assault, and about four had died. The training had been organised by the military, illustrating the subordination of the police to the army and the problematic human rights situation within the security forces. On 24 September, police and army personnel murdered and robbed a Chinese citizen in Bafatá. Some of the soldiers had also been involved in an exchange of fire with the police in Bissau shortly before. A Nigerian resident was killed by a mob amid allegations of child abuse, which led to an attack on the Nigerian embassy on 8 October; vehicles were set on fire. Transport Minister Orlando Viegas (PRS) was severely beaten at his home on 5 November by men in military uniform. A nephew of PRS founder Kumba Yalá was alleged to be the instigator and was arrested. The background to the attack was the minister's attempt to privatise the Bissau port authority and dismiss its army-installed director, which had led to protests by its employees. The authority is under the de facto control of the army, which uses the port to import goods directly, bypassing customs. The army announced on 26 November that it had arrested four people, one of them a soldier, suspected of kidnapping. In November, the head of the UN Integrated Peacebuilding Office in Guinea-Bissau (UNIOGBIS), José Ramos-Horta, demanded the disarmament of the shadowy armed militias retained by some political parties, notably by Yalá.

On 25 April, a military court sentenced the alleged mastermind of the barracks raid of October 2012, Indjai's associate Captain Pansau Ntchama, and eight other suspects to five years in prison. He was also believed to be involved in the killing of state president Vieira in 2009.

Violations of **press freedom** intensified. In March, the state-run 'Televisão da Guiné-Bissau' prevented a broadcast by a PAIGC presidential candidate, apparently on the instructions of the state secretary for media relations, and the workers council of the state-run 'Radiodifusão Nacional' also accused the secretary of making threats. The journalists trade union said in March that certain political, judicial and military circles were increasingly intimidating journalists for writing on delicate issues. On 21 March, the 'Liga Guineense de Direitos Humanos' demanded that the transitional government stop giving instructions to the media, claiming that this was a form of illegal censorship. A journalist of the private radio station 'Galaxia de Pindjiguiti' was arrested in May for "perverting" facts and "disobeying" judicial orders. In the Reporters Without Borders annual press freedom index, Guinea-Bissau fell 17 places and was ranked 92nd (out of 175 countries). On 3 July, the Catholic 'Rádio Sol Mansi' and other radio stations had to close down temporarily on the orders of the regulatory authority for violating technical frequency norms. A political commentator from 'Rádio Bombolom' was interrogated by the military intelligence service on 11 September for criticising recent military promotions.

Former transitional president (2003–5) Henrique Pereira Rosa died on 15 May in Porto, aged 67.

Foreign Affairs

On 2 April, the **US** Drug Enforcement Agency (DEA) arrested Navy Commander-in-Chief José Américo Bubo NaTchuto, his confidant Papis Djeme, and three other navy officials off the Guinea-Bissau coast and took them to the US. The DEA operation had reportedly also targeted Indjai. NaTchuto was formally accused by the US of arms and drugs trafficking and destabilising the country. Prosecutors accused him of planning to smuggle Colombian cocaine to Guinea-Bissau in exchange for weapons and missiles for Colombian rebels. Transitional president Manuel Serifo Nhamadjo and transitional prime minister Rui de Barros were also believed to be involved in trafficking. The authorities reacted nervously, maintaining that NaTchuto and his allies had been detained illegally in Bissau-Guinean waters and accusing Cape Verde of assisting the US. When gunfire and troop movements in Bissau on 4 April triggered speculation that a new coup was under way, a local Dutch businessman was arrested for circulating false information. Guinea-Bissau's top intelligence official, Serifo Mané, was suspended in the aftermath of NaTchuto's arrest. The trial of NaTchuto and his two co-defendants in New York had not started by the end of the year for lack of interpreters. In the course of the year, the US appeared to move closer to the transitional authorities, reportedly in search for potential allies against Islamist threats emanating from the Sahel region.

The relationship between the transitional authorities and the **international community** remained tense. The UN, AU, CPLP (including Cape Verde) and EU (unlike ECOWAS) did not recognise the post-coup government. In April, the army refused to participate in a CPLP general staff meeting, while Bissau-Guinean police authorities were excluded from a CPLP police meeting in September. Guinea-Bissau was also banned from the AU summit in Ethiopia in May. Following a first mission in December 2012, the UN, AU, EU, ECOWAS and CPLP entered into negotiations with the transitional authorities again in April and July on an inclusive government, elections and reforms. They also attempted to resolve their internal divisions over the recognition issue.

Relations with **Cape Verde** remained difficult. The transitional government accused Cape Verde of being involved in the detention of NaTchuto, an accusation that Cape Verde rejected. As a result, Cabo Verde Airlines discontinued services to Bissau. On 12 July, two Cape Verdean police officials were detained by the intelligence service at Bissau's airport while attempting to carry out the official transfer from Cape Verde to Guinea-Bissau of a Bissau-Guinean national under arrest for drug trafficking. The head of the Bissau-Guinean judicial police tendered his resignation, apparently in protest, and the officials were freed on 30 July. The transferred prisoner, however, had disappeared upon arrival in Bissau. Army sources claimed he had died, but he resurfaced in late August. In September, an army spokesman rejected accusations made by former Cape Verdean president Pedro Pires that the army had played a negative role in Guinea-Bissau.

ECOWAS signalled its support for the transitional government by organising a general staff meeting in Bissau (28 May). On 16 April, Daniel Lopes Ferreira was elected president of the court of UEMOA. Indjai announced on 6 May that Guinea-Bissau's waters would be protected against piracy and drug-trafficking by ECOWAS, notably with the help of the Nigerian navy.

Civil society accused the **ECOWAS** mission in Guinea-Bissau (ECOMIB) of only serving the transitional government and not the population. In November, the UN proposed an increase in ECOMIB personnel, but the army hesitated. In December, the AU gave its backing to the proposal. On 22 February, the **UNSC** extended the UNIOGBIS mandate for three months until 31 May, and on 22 May the mandate was extended further to 31 May 2014. UNIOGBIS opened regional offices in Bafatá and Buba in November.

On 20 February, the authorities arrested five drug-traffickers arriving from **Brazil**. Another, coming from Brazil en route to Europe, was detained in June. In April, it was reported that drug-related investigations against former prime minister Aristides Gomes had been reopened and the immunity of former finance minister Victor Mandinga lifted.

On 10 December, 74 **Syrian refugees** arrived in Lisbon on board an aircraft coming from Bissau. They were carrying forged Turkish passports and had entered Guinea-Bissau via Morocco, where they had obtained Bissau-Guinean visas. Air Portugal suspended all flights to Bissau as the crew had allegedly been forced by the Guinea-Bissau security forces to take the Syrians on board. Airport security officials in Bissau were suspended. Foreign Minister Fernando Delfim da Silva and Interior Minister António Suca Ntchama tendered their resignations on 13 and 17 December, respectively. Da Silva had supported the issuing of visas, while Ntchama, an intimate of Indjai, had ordered that the Syrians be taken on board. On 23 December, the state attorney ordered Ntchama's detention after a commission of inquiry uncovered the existence of a human trafficking network between Bissau and Rabat (Morocco), but the head of the police refused to comply. Ntchama and the state attorney accused each other of disregarding the law. Bissau-Guinean diplomats accused transitional president Nhamadjo of assigning consular posts to his friends and associates, ignoring diplomatic hierarchy.

Socioeconomic Developments

The international sanctions imposed after the 2012 coup led to a series of **strikes** affecting schools, ministries, health care, state radio and post and telecommunications. Trade unions also declared a general strike on 16–21 December, demanding, inter alia, the payment of outstanding salaries and a price freeze on basic consumer goods. The strike ended inconclusively.

The **budget** approved on 17 July ran to $ 204 m, only half of which was covered by state revenue. The government hoped for financial support from Iran. On 1 May, trade unions accused the government of paying civil servants with drug money. In August, the government received a loan worth € 380,000 from the MTN telecommunications provider with which to pay its civil servants. Timor underwrote government debts in the health sector and in August the AfDB announced the partial resumption of its activities in the country. The Ivorian Kesnad Oil & Energy signed an exploration contract for off-shore oil resources. In May, the IMF forecast a 3.5% **growth in GDP**, while in July the AfDB forecast a rise of 4.2% (after a fall of 1.5% in 2012).

The sale of the **cashew** crop was delayed, and a reduction in international demand, heavy taxes and the 2012 coup caused prices to drop by 63% and hit rock-bottom at 50 CFAfr/kg. Cashew would normally account for 90% of exports and 45% of GDP. Up to 38% of the 2012 harvest was left unsold. As a result, people suffered food shortages and the government faced reduced tax revenues.

The EU redoubled its battle against **illegal fishing** in the region, which included assistance in the form of training, equipment and surveillance measures. In November, when the government had not taken action against illegal fishing, the EU banned fish imports. **Illegal logging** by individuals from neighbouring countries and Chinese companies intensified. Parliament reportedly confirmed the ban on timber exports.

Infrastructure remained poor. In February, the AfDB announced a grant of $ 82 m for the renovation of Bissau's roads; roads in the interior were also in a bad state. Lighthouses and other maritime nocturnal signalling systems were malfunctioning due to the theft of solar panels. The US Sunthrough Energy company said in May that it intended to invest $ 30 m in a solar panel plant. Residents in the capital protested about power shortages. The government did not have funds to purchase petrol for power generation or to pay electricity and water company employees.

Corruption worsened. In the Ibrahim Index of African Governance, Guinea-Bissau ranked 46th out of 52 countries (compared with 45th in 2012), and it fell from 154th to 163rd in TI's Corruption Perception Index. In June, the state attorney called for inquiries into alleged corruption in the roads authority. Corruption among traffic police, who set up more and more road blocks, led to growing public anger. The head of the traffic police and his deputy were dismissed in July. Following a strike in December, the government announced the introduction of a transparent traffic fine payment system. The **social situation** remained precarious, characterised by widespread poverty, malnutrition and child trafficking. A cholera outbreak in July left 18 dead.

The arrival of Shiite Muslims and their construction of a mosque in eastern Guinea-Bissau caused concern among popular Muslim leaders.

Christoph Kohl

Liberia

The political and social environment was marked by protests, a reminder of the country's continuing fragility. The UN Mission in Liberia (UNMIL) was transitioning to take a smaller political role. By year's end, UNMIL's military strength stood at 5,869, its police strength at 1,612, and its civilian personnel strength at 1,518, reflecting a slow and calibrated downsizing. The opposition called for President Ellen Johnson Sirleaf to resign or be impeached. Corruption remained a key concern. A study commissioned by UNMIL reported a 44% increase in incidents of mob violence over a five-month period in 2013 compared with the same period in 2012. The UN also recorded murders and armed robbery, more than a third of which involved the use of firearms. As a mark of its enhanced international prestige, Liberia early in the year hosted the third UN High Level Panel of Eminent Persons on the post-2015 MDGs, co-chaired by President Sirleaf, UK Prime Minister David Cameron, and Indonesia's President Susilo Bambang Yudhoyono. On the economic front, the country registered a growth rate of 8.1% – the third highest in West Africa.

Domestic Politics

Charles Taylor's legal predicaments in The Hague dominated the political climate in the first month of the year when a senator of the national legislature read a letter from the ex-president requesting that the government provide him with the financial benefits, amenities and diplomatic protections normally afforded to a former head of state. The request received the enthusiastic support of several prominent members of the legislature, including senior senator Prince Johnson, a former warlord-rival of Taylor. Sirleaf's government dithered, however, triggering criticism from the opposition and the somewhat pro-Taylor media. The tension subsided when on 22 January the Special Court for Sierra Leone began hearing an appeal submitted by Taylor, who had been sentenced by the Court to 50 years in prison after being found guilty of aiding and abetting war crimes and crimes against humanity in Sierra Leone in 2012. In September, the appeals chamber upheld the conviction, and Taylor was transferred to a prison in the UK in October. Reactions in Liberia were muted, indicating that support for the former president was largely opportunistic and not as deep-rooted as he claimed.

On 11 March, amidst widespread concern about corruption and inertia in the government, Sirleaf announced a **cabinet reshuffle** involving the ministries of commerce, labour, and youth and sports, and the civil service agency. She said her decisions were based on "competence, integrity, commitment and loyalty", but in fact she dismissed only one minister and several deputy ministers, and this limited action caused indignation. In response, between March and July, she appointed six new ministers, including one woman, and 14 deputy ministers, six of whom were women. Then on 8 July, the president announced the dismissal of four senior government officials alleged to have engaged in illegal practices. Sirleaf also dismissed the auditor general of the General Auditing Commission, Robert Kilby, on the basis that he had a conflict of interests – a decision that was enthusiastically endorsed by the House of Representatives on 10 July. Responding to charges of nepotism, in September Sirleaf also accepted the resignation of her son Robert Alvin Sirleaf as chair of the National Oil Company of Liberia and senior adviser.

Earlier, on 20 March, Sirleaf announced the replacement of three members of the Board of Commissioners of the National **Election Commission**, including the chair, Elizabeth J. Nelson, when their term expired. Nelson was replaced by Jerome G. Karkoya, a prominent lawyer. The main opposition party, the Congress for Democratic Change (CDC), alleged that Karkoya, who had contested a legislative seat as a Unity Party candidate in Bong County, was unfit to be chair for that reason, as it would jeopardise the Commission's neutrality. The CDC boycotted the Commission's activities for several weeks, including a 7 May senatorial by-election in Grand Bassa County, but Sirleaf stuck to her appointee. Shortly after his appointment, Karkoya submitted draft revisions to the electoral law, including a provision requiring at least 30% **female representation** on party nomination lists for candidates for the legislature. Gender balance in government had been an important issue for Sirleaf, Africa's first elected female president, and the issue had become especially salient with regard to the Liberian legislature after the 2011 elections. Only four women were elected to the 30-seat Senate and eight to the 73-seat House of Representatives. In other words, female representation amounted to only 7%, a drop from 13% in the previous legislature. A committee of the House of Representatives insisted that the amendment must first be approved by a nation-wide referendum. On 5 July, members of the legislature, accompanied by the chair of the Commission, began public consultations on the proposed amendments. By year's end, the amendment had not been passed and Sirleaf's Unity Party had only 25 of the 73 seats in the legislature.

Though Sirleaf's government had largely ignored the 2009 report of the Truth and Reconciliation Commission, it launched several initiatives touching on some of its recommendations, particularly relating to **reconciliation**. On 20 June, the president launched the 'National Reconciliation Road Map' at a national conference organised by Peace Ambassador George Weah. Though the framework for achieving the road map was not fully spelled out, its emphasis on economic empowerment, a shared national identity and an effective and decentralised justice sector that would advance both restorative and social justice, resonated widely in a country where the imperative of modern justice and economic development had tended to focus almost exclusively on the capital, Monrovia. Moreover, the road map did not rule out retributive justice for past crimes, particularly war crimes, and it also emphasised making an inclusive national history narrative part of academic curricula, a project spearheaded by the Governance Commission, headed by Dr Amos Sawyer. The national history project was supported by UNESCO. In May, Sirleaf's government launched a project aimed at drafting history curricula for primary and secondary schools. Liberia's history textbooks tended to emphasise a glorious period of settler (Americo-Liberian) rule. The history project argued, however, that this did not reflect the historical experience of the vast majority of the country's people, the so-called 'natives' (95% of the population), some of whose intellectuals now proposed that Liberia's national motto, "The Love of Liberty brought us here", should be changed because it referred to the tiny settler elite who formed the Americo-Liberian oligarchy that had misruled the country for over 100 years.

Related to this was the work of the Land Commission, set up in 2008. On 21 May, it presented to Sirleaf a draft national **land rights** policy, which sought to grant legally-guaranteed ownership – as opposed to mere custodianship – of land to indigenous communities. It integrated all forms of land ownership to allow communities to enjoy the benefits of natural resources. The extant 1986 Constitution – sections of which, particularly relating to human rights and elections, were now under review by a committee appointed by Sirleaf – provided that every citizen "shall have the right to own property alone as well as in association with others". However, that provision had never been effective in practice where indigenous community land ownership was concerned and had been largely hamstrung by various disabling laws, including the Liberian Code of Laws of 1956. This defines rules governing "aboriginal" land ownership: "tribal" or "aboriginal" people have the right to use land they inhabit for "farming and other necessities", but this does not guarantee ownership. Such land can only be converted to family holdings (guaranteeing ownership) when "a tribe shall become sufficiently advanced in civilisation" to petition the government to authorise that conversion. This discriminatory legislation was now under review by the constitutional review commission. However, by year's end the draft land policy had not been made into law.

Though these reform measures were commendable, the slow pace of their implementation somewhat undermined their ultimate effectiveness. A report by the UN Panel of Experts on Liberia noted in November that, even if the new land policy became law, it might not be effective in redressing the historical imbalance with respect to land ownership. The report noted that the Land Commission had estimated that over half of Liberian land had been parcelled out in various concessions and private deeds, most of which were unlikely ever to be overturned even in the event the land policy passed into law.

In the meantime, disputes relating to land and concessions granted to corporations continued to create tensions. On 7 May, some 50 people living on disputed land near Monrovia protested against a Supreme Court ruling that the land belonged to a prominent Americo-Liberian family, the Coopers, who had long left the country and had been resident in the US during Liberia's political upheaval. The protesters claimed that they had acquired the land legally, and produced documents to that effect. These protests had no apparent effect on the government, which on 21 December sent a team of law enforcement agents to demolish structures the residents had built on the land. On 23 December, 30 of the owners of the demolished structures protested before President Sirleaf's residence, demanding compensation and accusing her government of being responsive only to **Americo-Liberian interests**.

Tensions relating to huge land concessions granted to foreign interests led to **violent demonstrations**. In September, disputes between local communities in Grand Bassa County and Equatorial Palm Oil (EPO) led to violence. EPO's 34,500-acre concession area encompassed a 9,000-acre block, where palm oil production was taking place in an area that included 13 villages. When EPO commenced a re-survey of the entire 34,500 acres concession on 3 September, the exercise was disrupted by about 100 men armed with machetes protesting at the expansion of the agricultural development on what they claimed was community land. In response, the government deployed 25 armed paramilitary police officers to the area. Disputes relating to working conditions on some of the plantations also led to violence. On 15 February, community members in Bong County rioted over the death of a mining company worker, reportedly due to a workplace accident; on 19 April, workers at the Cocopa Rubber Plantation in Nimba County protested about their benefits and, from March to July, some 650 former workers at the Sime Darby Plantation, in Bomi County, protested against the non-renewal of their contracts.

These protests severely tested the capacity of the **Liberia National Police** (LNP). Its 4,864 personnel were projected to increase to 8,000 by 2016, in order to be able to properly deploy across the country, including in border areas. However, it had not received the necessary funding from the government, which actually reduced fiscal support for the LNP in its 2013/14 budget as part of a 10% cut to the overall security budget from $ 81.17 m to $ 72.9 m. Quite apart from its lack of capacity, the LNP lacked public trust, and had often been the target of violent protests by local communities. On 29 April, for example, a murder at the Bartel Jam gold mining camp in Grand Gedeh County prompted some 300 local residents to riot outside a police station, accusing the police of inefficiency and corruption. On 11 July, 400 villagers rioted outside the police station in Totota, Bong County, following a police raid, provoking the LNP to fire warning shots. One civilian was killed.

Of graver concern to security was a growth in **drugs trafficking** (cocaine, heroin and marijuana). In August, Sirleaf dismissed Albert Chelley, Deputy Director for Operations of Liberia's Drug Enforcement Agency (DEA), for "serious violations of the policies and ethics of the Government". Delley had conspired with drug traffickers to smuggle heroin through Liberia. Concern that international drugs traffickers were gaining a foothold, despite several successful drug busts, in the past turned to panic when two former soldiers, a US citizen and a German, were arrested in September in a sting operation after plotting to assassinate a local US Drugs Enforcement Administration agent and an informant. Crime statistics collated by the UN showed that 142 people were arrested for drugs possession during the year, a large number of them for attempting to traffic drugs into and out of the country. Of those arrested, 32 were found in possession of cocaine, 36 with heroin and 74 with cannabis. Moreover, evidence indicated a growing consumer market in Liberia itself, with major implications for health and security. In December, the LNP launched 'Operation Pyramid', which it claimed led to the (brief) arrest and detention of 167 drug dealers and users. There was evidence of the involvement of serving security personnel in drug trafficking. On 9 November, a joint security operation involving officials of the LNP, DEA and the Transnational Crime Unit apprehended a vehicle belonging to the police presidential escort, which contained ten bags of cannabis with an estimated street value of over $ 36,000. Again, on 10 December, a day after the deployment of DEA agents at Roberts International Airport, security officials arrested two police officers and one officer of the Bureau of Immigration and Naturalization trying to facilitate the entry through the airport of a smuggler carrying 3.5 kg of heroin.

The trial in Monrovia of 18 Liberians for their involvement in the killing of UN peacekeepers in Côte d'Ivoire in 2012 had important security and geopolitical implications. The trial became a rallying point for champions of **ethnic Krahn identity** and against President Sirleaf. The defendants were charged under Liberia's 1976 law against 'mercenarism', which carries a maximum penalty of life imprisonment. They were defended by a prominent Krahn lawyer, Tiawon Gongloe, who had been Sirleaf's solicitor-general and had now become a fierce critic. Gongloe argued that the law under which his clients were charged was meant to protect Liberia from foreign attackers, not prosecute crimes committed beyond Liberia's borders. The 18 accused had been in pre-trial detention for over a year. Key witnesses, most of them Krahn, had refused to testify or had simply disappeared. On 30 December, the trial judge once again postponed a scheduled hearing at the Monrovia City Court, but the accused protested. They removed their prison uniforms and damaged the prison bus. Police had to be supported by the UN to bring the situation under control.

On 9 October, police arrested Mulbah K. Morlu and ten other members of the opposition CDC, after he announced that he would lead a crowd calling for the president's resignation upon her arrival at the airport from a trip to the UN in New York. The police charged them with criminal conspiracy, sedition and criminal malevolence, and security forces blocked all routes to the airport. In contrast, Sirleaf's Unity Party had planned a rousing welcome of 100,000 of her supporters.

Signalling a more positive trend, on 23 December the UNSC removed a prominent Liberian businessman and politician, Benoni Urey (a close associate of former president Taylor), from the **UN's travel ban** and assets freeze list. In doing so, the UN indicated that associates of the former president no longer posed a significant threat to Liberia's stability, though 23 names were still listed. The Panel of Experts monitoring the sanctions reported that it did not have evidence of involvement by these Liberians in activities that could pose a threat to peace and security. Their report also noted that the measures had been politicised by Sirleaf's government, which had lobbied the UN to remove from the lists people who now supported her party. In its resolution 2128 (2013), adopted in December, the UNSC did not include monitoring the remaining individuals and assets as part of the Panel of Experts' mandate, indicating that they no longer posed a significant threat. Shortly after his delisting, Urey announced that he would stand as an independent in the presidential elections in 2017.

Foreign Affairs

Liberia's volatile and largely unpoliced 716-km border with **Côte d'Ivoire** was a key flashpoint in relations between the two countries. In March, armed militia elements, most of them Ivorians hiding in the Liberian forests, slipped across the border and attacked targets in Côte d'Ivoire. Scores of people, including Ivorian security personnel, were killed. A December report by the UN Panel of Experts claimed that, following the March attacks, the Ivorian government had begun paying militias and mercenaries hostile to the Liberian government. The report also observed that in May Liberian forces detained an Ivorian government delegation carrying funds to make these payments in Grand Gedeh (bordering Côte d'Ivoire's 'Grand Ouest'). Côte d'Ivoire's government denounced the report as a "fabrication", and in a speech shortly after the publication of the report, Sirleaf hailed her government's good relations with Côte d'Ivoire, claiming that her government had forged "positive cooperation to address border-line tensions". Nevertheless, the tens of thousands of Ivorian refugees in camps in Liberia continued to be the focus of security concerns. The UN accelerated the repatriation of the Ivorian refugees and by year's end had sent back 18,273, while 46,236 still remained in Liberian camps.

Liberia continued to play a **leadership role** in the MRU, ECOWAS and the AU, reflecting the high prestige of President Sirleaf, the only current African president who had been awarded a Nobel Peace Prize. Liberia chaired the MRU and the African Peer Review Mechanism. Liberia was also chair of the High-Level Panel on Fragile States, established under the aegis of the AfDB and intended to mitigate the vulnerability of fragile states to new political and economic shocks. Reflecting a new confidence in its security, in June Liberia deployed 46 soldiers to the African-led International Support Mission to **Mali**, the first time in 52 years that the country had participated in peacekeeping operations.

Memoranda of understanding and statements of intent were concluded with the US and the EU, establishing political consultation mechanisms for the promotion of bilateral cooperation. In March, Britain reopened its embassy in Monrovia, after more than 20 years of a non-resident diplomatic presence. Brazil, Sweden and Qatar followed suit and all three subsequently opened embassies at the level of resident ambassadors.

Socioeconomic Developments

The annual **budget**, signed by Sirleaf on 16 October, amounted to \$ 582.9 m, rather than the \$ 553 m proposed by the minister of finance. The legislature later claimed to have identified the additional \$ 29.9 m during a prolonged review of the budget. The final amount was less than the previous year's \$ 672 m but the 2013/14 budget did not include state borrowing (\$ 80 m the previous year), contingent revenue or cash brought forward (which was \$ 53 m in 2012/13). The government reported, however, that recurrent expenditure, especially civil servants' salaries (40% of the budget) and goods and services, continued to take the bulk of the budget, preventing investment in economic diversification and job creation. State expenditure for the year totalled \$ 593 m (an increase of 22% over expenditure in 2012), of which recurrent expenditure accounted for \$ 326 m.

Real GDP **growth** was estimated at 8.1%, mainly due to strong activity in the minerals sector. There was also marked expansion in the construction and services sector. Liberia was among six African countries included in US President Barack Obama's Power Africa initiative, aimed at doubling electricity access in SSA by building on the continent's gas and oil resources and its huge potential to develop clean **energy**. Power Africa was expected to mobilise the US private sector to add 10,000 MW of cleaner, more efficient electricity generation capacity, while also making electricity accessible to at least 20 m new households and businesses.

Average **inflation** rose to 7.8%, up from 6.8% in 2012. The Liberian dollar depreciated by 10%, after the government printed more local currency. (The US dollar continued to be legal tender, and much preferred.)

As before, Sirleaf's government identified high **youth unemployment** as a security risk. However, the state-funded Liberia Youth Empowerment Programme succeeded in employing only 3,219 young people, falling far short of its targeted 10,000 jobs. The private sector, largely dominated by Lebanese and other foreign interests, showed some promise after a group of Liberian nationals set up the TIBA Industrial Group, employing 90 Liberians, 90% of them women, to manufacture a variety of biscuit products.

Acute problems emerged in the education sector. In August, the University of Liberia, determined to apply strict academic admission criteria, rejected all 25,000 applicants for student places, leading to mass **protests by students**, who vandalised university property. The university authorities claimed that they had been under pressure from the government to relax standards and admit thousands of students to their degree programmes so as to close the education deficit caused by the prolonged civil war.

A 124-page report by Liberia's main bilateral donor, USAID, reported that Liberia had 4,100 'ghost schools' (non-existent schools funded by the government). Entitled '**Liberia Governance Stakeholders Survey**', and issued in May, the report also claimed that, just before the 2011 presidential elections, 9,000 names were mysteriously added to the Ministry of Education's payroll. The study found that the Liberian government did not know how much money it should be collecting in taxes, noting that companies in possession of logging concessions alone owed the government $ 34 m. As before, the government's proclaimed anti-**corruption** efforts were stymied by its lack of action on official graft. In October, the anti-corruption commission issued its second report on the verification of assets of presidential appointees. Of the 77 officials audited, 25 were found to have made truthful declarations, 22 were judged uncooperative and 30 (including a senior cabinet minister) were found to have misrepresented their assets or not completed the exercise. As usual, there was no word from Sirleaf's government about penalties.

Lansana Gberie

Mali

The year witnessed the dramatic consequences of Mali's ongoing political and security crisis, which had come to the world's attention through the March 2012 military coup d'état resulting in the ouster of the country's government. Among the most notable consequences of this crisis in 2013 were large-scale military intervention by French, African, and ultimately UN forces; the retreat of Islamist rebel groups from the cities and towns they had occupied since early 2012; the brokering of a preliminary peace accord between Tuareg separatist rebels and the Malian government; and the election of a new head of state. Yet despite these and other positive signs of normalisation, the rampant insecurity, political uncertainty, and economic distress generated by the crisis did not fully abate, and the Malian state remained weak in the face of multiple challenges, both internal and external.

Domestic Politics

Mali's **interim government**, led by Interim President Dioncounda Traoré and formed under international pressure in the wake of the 2012 coup, began the year in deadlock with supporters of that coup. Army officers had forced Traoré's Prime Minister Cheick Modibo Diarra to resign in December 2012. Civilian opposition to Traoré's regime coalesced around the 'Coordination des Organisations Patriotiques du Mali' (COPAM), which in early January held demonstrations in the capital Bamako and in the neighbouring town of Kati, demanding an inclusive national political dialogue to constitute a new government.

Divisions within Bamako's political class were soon overshadowed, however, by signs of an impending offensive by the Islamist rebel groups that had occupied the northern half of Malian territory for several months. As early as 6 January, unconfirmed reports circulated among social media users that fighters belonging to the militant Islamist groups 'Ansar Eddine', the 'Mouvement pour l'Unicité et le Jihad en Afrique de l'Ouest', and al-Qaida in the Islamic Maghreb (AQIM) had been massing in the north and were pushing southward. Skirmishes between Malian army troops and rebels along the line of control separating the two sides were reported on 8 January. Within days, government forces were retreating in the face of a large-scale **rebel assault** involving hundreds of vehicles pushing deep into the government-held regions of Mopti and Segou. In response, Traoré declared a **state of emergency** and called on France to intervene militarily. Longstanding hopes in Mali and abroad that armed conflict could be averted, or that a West-African-organised military response could counter or contain the Islamist threat, proved untenable.

Ordered by President François Hollande, Operation Serval, the French military mission in Mali, officially began on 11 January with the arrival of combat and support aircraft from bases in Chad and France, followed shortly by some 500 ground troops. The stated goals of the mission, which was carried out under the auspices of UNSC Resolution 2085, were to **halt** the **rebel offensive**, head off any potential push toward Bamako, and protect French and European citizens, of whom there were at least 6,000 present in Mali. The first French combat death was reported on the operation's opening day, when a helicopter pilot was killed by ground fire while attacking a rebel column in the Mopti region. Otherwise, French casualties were few, and the strikes carried out by French forces succeeded in driving back the offensive. As French aircraft began targeting personnel and facilities in the rebel-held regions of Timbuktu, Gao and Kidal, French and Malian troops drove northward overland from Bamako and Mopti, engaging in **fierce ground battles** with Islamist forces in the small towns of Konna and Diabaly. To offset their enemy's air power advantage, rebel fighters occupied private homes and prevented residents from fleeing, hoping to use the presence of civilians to prevent a counterattack. Nonetheless, these militants were gradually driven out of the towns they controlled as the French-led advance continued. French forces in Mali, eventually totalling over 4,000, were later joined by 6,000 soldiers from neighbouring ECOWAS countries and from Chad.

Public opinion throughout Mali was overwhelmingly in favour of Operation Serval. The operation's rapid progress and widespread popularity strengthened the hand of President Traoré, who had invited France's intervention. It also undermined his opponents in COPAM and in the Kati-based former army junta, who had vehemently objected to any foreign military presence on Malian soil. Even before Serval began, surveys showed that most Malians were in favour of their government receiving outside military assistance to retake the territory it had lost in 2012. In Bamako and other cities in central and southern Mali, as well as in northern towns newly freed from rebel control, ordinary people expressed appreciation for France's actions and rallied behind their president during what most perceived as a period of unprecedented threat to the existence of a united, secular Malian state.

At the end of January, forces from France, Mali, Chad and Niger retook the key northern cities of Timbuktu and Gao. Islamist fighters put up little direct resistance, opting instead to flee into remote pockets of the Sahara where French and Chadian ground troops, backed by French aircraft, continued to pursue them. Abu Zeid, a top AQIM field commander, was among 40 Islamists killed during a battle in February. Despite such successes, the French-led coalition struggled in the region's inhospitable terrain to root out enemy combatants. **Re-establishing authority in the north** proved equally challenging. Even in areas fully under state control, the presence of Malian security forces and administrators remained thin, and periodic acts of terrorism (suicide bombings, rocket and mortar attacks, and shootings) carried out by militants meant that residents continued to fear for their safety. International human rights organisations accused Malian soldiers and rebels alike of committing atrocities against northern civilians. Moreover, government troops never managed to take control of the sparsely populated region of Kidal, where support for the Tuareg separatist 'Mouvement National pour la Libération de l'Azawad' (MNLA) has been strongest. MNLA fighters took over the town of Kidal after it was abandoned by its Islamist occupiers in late January, and although French and Chadian troops quickly arrived to patrol the town and search the surrounding region for Islamists, they were not joined by Malian soldiers as they had been elsewhere. Many Malians loyal to the central government accused the MNLA of negotiating a secret pact with the French to keep the Malian army out of Kidal, in exchange for MNLA support in finding Islamist fighters and the six French hostages they held.

On 18 June, representatives of the Malian government, the MNLA and other Tuareg armed factions signed a preliminary peace agreement in Ouagadougou (Burkina Faso), committing both sides to a cessation of hostilities. The **Ouagadougou Accord**, brokered by the governments of France and Burkina Faso, called for Tuareg rebel fighters to be confined to barracks in the areas under their control, thus paving the way for the organisation of presidential elections throughout Malian territory. The winner of those elections would be required, under the terms of the agreement, to enter into comprehensive negotiations with rebel representatives, while the rebel fighters would eventually be disarmed. Although accepted by the leaders of both sides, the Ouagadougou Accord was deeply unpopular within many segments of the public, in both loyalist and separatist camps. Hardline loyalists opposed granting any concession to the rebels, whom they held responsible for unleashing the crisis that had engulfed Mali for nearly 18 months, and feared that the agreement granted rebels undue political legitimacy. Hardline separatists, for their part, opposed on principle any deal with the Malian government, and felt that the agreement jeopardised their goal of establishing a sovereign, Tuareg-dominated state. Nonetheless, the Ouagadougou Accord was hailed abroad as a significant step towards resolving the conflict in northern Mali. On 6 July, Traoré lifted the state of emergency to permit electoral campaigning to begin.

The first round of the **presidential elections**, involving 27 candidates, was held on 28 July. Despite numerous logistical problems, including confused voter rolls and the incomplete distribution of voter identification cards, the poll was widely seen as a great success. With more than 3.5 m ballots cast, turnout among registered voters reached an unprecedented 51%. Ibrahim Boubacar Keita, a 68-year-old elder statesman who had previously served as prime minister and parliamentary speaker, emerged from that round of balloting with nearly 40% of the vote, giving him a commanding lead over his nearest rival, 63-year-old ex-finance minister Soumaila Cissé, who took just under 20%. In the 11 August second round of voting, Keita was Malians' clear favourite, winning 77% of the vote. The electoral process was by no means trouble-free: Cissé accused Keita's camp of ballot stuffing, while poll workers and voters in Kidal (where the MNLA remained the most powerful political force on the ground) encountered intimidation. Yet, amid perceptions that their nation's very future was on the line, Malians largely supported the process and respected its outcome. Cissé, for his part, became the first losing presidential candidate in Malian history to congratulate his opponent on his victory.

On 14 August, the outgoing interim government announced the promotion of Captain Amadou Haya Sanogo, the **2012 putsch leader**, to the rank of four-star general. Six months earlier, Traoré had named Sanogo to head a military reform commission, and the captain had remained in the public eye. His promotion rankled many observers, since he and his junta stood accused of involvement in the detention and alleged disappearance of several members of Mali's elite parachute regiment, the so-called 'red berets'. Several weeks after the coup, the red berets had risen up against the junta's authority and were subsequently disbanded.

Keita was sworn in as president on 4 September and inaugurated on 19 September, and set to work forming his **new government**. He designated 39-year-old banker Oumar Tatam Ly as his prime minister. The cabinet Ly formed was a blend of newcomers (such as Moussa Mara, a parliamentarian and presidential candidate, who became minister of urban affairs), veterans of past governments (such as former foreign minister Soumeylou Boubèye Maiga, named to head the ministry of defence), and members of the interim government (such as Moussa Sinko Coulibaly, who retained his powerful post as minister of territorial administration). **Parliamentary elections** were conducted on 24 November and 15 December. President Keita's party, the 'Rassemblement Pour le Mali' won 60 out of 147 seats in the National Assembly, and established a ruling coalition with smaller parties to control 55 more seats, leaving Keita's political opponents just 32 seats in all.

Even as the process of political normalisation continued in Bamako, the **north remained unstable** amid sporadic terrorist attacks in Timbuktu, Gao and Kidal. The most high-profile such attack was the abduction and execution of two French journalists from Kidal by unknown assailants on 2 November. Timbuktu and Gao were also the scene of demonstrations by residents frustrated with inadequate public services and with graft and abuse of power by members of the Malian security forces.

On 27 November, General Sanogo was arrested by gendarmes and charged with conspiracy to commit kidnapping. The charge was linked to the disappearance of red berets detained by Sanogo's troops in May 2012. On 4 December, Prosecutor Daniel Tessogué confirmed the discovery of a mass grave near Kati believed to contain the bodies of 21 red beret soldiers executed while in junta custody. After coming to office, President Keita **purged** many of **Sanogo's loyalists** from top government posts, and with Sanogo's arrest he made it clear that he would not tolerate multiple centres of power, and that Mali's restive military must answer to civilian authorities.

Foreign Affairs

At the beginning of 2013, Mali's foreign partners sought to **forestall armed conflict**, and hoped to weaken the rebel coalition occupying the northern region by persuading certain powerful leaders (most notably Iyad Ag Ghali, head of Ansar Eddine) to break away from it. France, the USA and the UN also backed an effort by ECOWAS to send a military force to Mali by September. As fighting broke out in early January, however, these plans became moot. The deployment of Operation Serval, France's largest military operation abroad since the end of the Algerian war of independence, forced the Malian government and all its partners to adapt to new, uncertain circumstances.

The international response to Operation Serval was generally positive. **Algeria**'s government, concerned about ramifications for its own Islamist insurgency, was guarded in its endorsement of the mission but allowed French aircraft taking part in Serval to fly over its territory. **Morocco** also expressed its support, and took advantage of the crisis to begin building a closer working relationship with Mali. Numerous Western governments backed President Hollande's military response to the emerging situation. Canada, the UK and the US all contributed transport and refuelling aircraft to help ferry French personnel and equipment into the region. In late January, the US signed an agreement with the government of **Niger** to base unarmed aerial surveillance drones on Niger's territory; these drones became operational in March, providing intelligence support to French forces. The **EU**, for its part, funded a multinational mission to provide military training to Malian army units. Backed by 23 member states, the EU Training Mission in Mali (EUTM) was launched in February with the goal of building discipline, unit cohesion and combat capacity, all of which the Malian armed forces had been sorely lacking. The decision to target entire units, rather than selected personnel, for training was a response to the failure of extensive US training programmes with the Malian armed forces since the 1990s. As events in 2012 made clear, the American focus on individual skills transfer did not build the operational strength necessary for the Malian army units to prevail on the battlefield. Over the course of the year, the EUTM programme graduated three newly formed battalions, with a fourth slated for graduation in early 2014. Yet this mission also exposed longstanding fault lines in Mali's military: in June, members of the inaugural training battalion boycotted their graduation ceremony, accusing their commanders of embezzling EU funds intended for their upkeep. Isolated mutinies and disputes over leadership, pay and promotions broke out among soldiers both in Bamako and in the north. Reluctant to re-engage with what it saw as a fractured and dysfunctional army, the US did not resume the bilateral military cooperation it had suspended after the coup.

Operation Serval unquestionably strengthened Mali's relations with **France**. President Hollande received a hero's welcome in Timbuktu on 2 February, shortly after French troops had secured the city. His government pushed for rapid elections following the end of Islamist control over the north, a move many in Mali and abroad considered risky, and helped broker the Ouagadougou Accord between the Malian government and Tuareg rebel groups. Despite its military and diplomatic successes, however, French policy toward Mali continued to be regarded with suspicion by many Malians, who criticised what they perceived as France's neo-colonial motives, its implicit support for Tuareg rebels, its alleged payment of exorbitant ransoms to free French hostages from Islamist captors, and its pursuit of French economic interests in the Sahel.

In May, foreign governments pledged € 3.25 bn at a Mali **donor conference** in Brussels. In addition to the contributions of Western donors and China, other governments including Kuwait, Morocco, Nigeria and Senegal made significant pledges through the AfDB and the Islamic Development Bank. Yet the promised aid flows were slow in coming, as donors sought assurances of improved accountability and transparency in Malian public spending. Some governments were wary of renewed instability or political crisis. All military and civilian aid from Canada, formerly a major donor to Mali, remained suspended throughout 2013. As the year neared its end, a UN official observed that less than 10% of the funds pledged in Brussels had actually been disbursed.

The country's West African neighbours contributed significant military assistance to re-stabilise Mali. In January, **ECOWAS** set up the 'African-Led International Support Mission to Mali' (AFISMA), authorised by UNSC Resolution 2085. Nine ECOWAS members – Benin, Côte d'Ivoire, Ghana, Guinea, Liberia, Niger, Nigeria, Senegal and Togo – contributed troops for the mission. Non-ECOWAS member **Chad** sent another 2,000 troops, who saw heavy fighting alongside French forces in the Gao and Kidal regions and who suffered dozens of casualties. Nigeria additionally deployed two fighter jets (one of which crashed on 7 May) and two combat helicopters to support the international forces. Following the presidential elections, the Nigerian government withdrew its combat battalion of 850 men from AFISMA, leaving behind some 200 Nigerian police and support personnel. It was said the troops were needed to fight the Boko Haram insurgency in Nigeria's Northeast.

On 1 July, AFISMA troops were 're-hatted' and officially joined a new **UN peacekeeping operation**, the 'Mission Multidimensionnelle Intégrée des Nations Unies pour la Stabilisation au Mali' (MINUSMA). This mission, authorised by UNSC Resolution 2100 of 25 April, was led by Dutch diplomat Bert Koenders. MINUSMA was projected to reach a full strength of 12,000 by the end of 2013, but its total personnel remained at roughly half that number due to a lack of follow-through on pledges by member states. Some accounts in the Malian media alleged that Koenders had a difficult relationship with President Keita, and that Malian officials were reluctant to engage with the UN mission, which they saw as violating their nation's sovereignty. UN Secretary-General Ban Ki-moon visited Mali in November to hold talks with Keita and to announce new regional investments in the Sahel. Despite MINUSMA being undermanned and underfunded, the French government withdrew many of its troops from Mali in the last months of the year, anticipating a standing force of approximately 1,000 in Operation Serval by early 2014.

Socioeconomic Developments

The macroeconomic outlook rebounded somewhat from its desperate state following the previous year's political and security crisis. Mali's economy remained frail due to a lifeless tourism sector and other disruptions caused by violence in the north, where economic activity was at a standstill in many communities. Real GDP **growth** was a barely perceptible 1.6%, compared with a 1.5% contraction in 2012, and inflation dropped to near zero. Revenue from the country's gold mines grew by 9% despite a 30% drop in gold prices over the year; gold accounted for over two-thirds of export revenues. As the conflict in the north wound down, public spending increased to pre-crisis levels and the government sought to maintain existing social expenditures while also investing in new development projects. The IMF called on Malian officials to shore up the country's fiscal health by increasing tax revenues, improving treasury management, and cutting subsidies for electricity and petrol, which had long been popular with ordinary Malians. Nation-wide surveys carried out at the end of 2013 showed widespread public optimism that economic conditions in Mali would continue to improve.

In the **agricultural sector**, production recovered considerably after droughts and poor harvests in 2012, and the value of agricultural production increased by 14%. Rainfall during the growing season was regular throughout much of the country, though pockets of both drought and flooding, especially in the northern region, affected some farmers.

Cereal prices, which had risen significantly following poor harvests in 2012, declined overall, despite temporary increases in towns such as Gao and Timbuktu in the wake of international military intervention. Livestock prices remained high nationwide due to the continuing impact of insecurity on the north's pastoral economy.

The **humanitarian situation** throughout the country also improved marginally over the course of the year. The number of IDPs, which was estimated to have peaked at over 330,000 after the start of Operation Serval, dropped to below 283,000 by the end of the year, according to the International Organisation for Migration. Nearly 80,000 IDPs returned north, citing improved security in the region. Another 170,000 Malians lived as refugees in neighbouring Burkina Faso, Mauritania and Niger. Food insecurity also persisted within the country despite improved harvests. Oxfam estimated that 800,000 Malians were in need of food assistance.

Bruce Whitehouse

Mauritania

Parliamentary and municipal elections, which had been postponed several times, finally took place in November–December. The polls were boycotted by the opposition, which resulted in an absolute majority for the ruling 'Union pour la République' (UPR) and made the Islamist party 'Tewassoul' the second largest parliamentary group. Threats by al-Qaida in the Islamic Maghreb (AQIM) and the fragile situation in Mali continued to feed security concerns. The country intensified its regional and international security cooperation, including by joining the 'Mission Multidimensionnelle Intégrée des Nations Unies pour la Stabilisation au Mali' (MINUSMA). The government recognised the risks of social unrest, and several measures were taken to tackle the high level of unemployment, particularly youth unemployment. Food security improved but dependence on food imports and tens of thousands of refugees from Mali made the situation fragile.

Domestic Politics

Efforts to monitor potential extremists were intensified after the appointment in December 2012 of a Mauritanian national, Mohamed Lemine Ould Hacen, alias Abdallah al-Chinguetti, as AQIM's second-in-command and spokesman in the Sahel region. On 28

January, three alleged Salafists were arrested in Chegar and on 12 February two Mauritanian nationals were charged at a court in Nouakchott with trying to join AQIM and fight in Mali. One of the suspects was also accused of involvement in the murder of a French family in 2007. Five armed jihadists were arrested on 17 March while attempting to enter Mauritania from **northern Mali**. There were also reports of members of "armed Islamist groups active in northern Mali" having been arrested "while posing as refugees". In June, there were reports that a group with connections to Ansar al-Sharia, the political arm of AQIM, had been established at the Dar Naim central prison in Nouakchott, where many of the detainees had been jailed for membership of **radical Islamist groups**. Imams from extremist mosques and a few politicians were also reported to have joined the group.

The government remained concerned about the possibility of large-scale protests and introduced improvements in the provision of basic public services, such as healthcare, water distribution and education. It also launched several employment programmes. **Moderate religious leaders**, too, tried to initiate ways to curb extremism. The Ministry of Islamic Affairs, together with the 'Ligue des Oulémas Mauritaniens' organised a three-day gathering in Nouadhibou on 20–22 February, which produced a number of recommendations, including proposals to establish charity foundations. Earlier that month, several human rights organisations distributed a declaration stating that Salafism was fundamentally alien to the country's "social and cultural structure". The declaration was signed by various NGO leaders including the 'Initiative de Résurgence du Mouvement Abolitionniste en Mauritanie', 'SOS Esclaves', the 'Association Mauritanienne des Droits de l'Homme', the 'Association des Femmes Chefs de Famille' (AFCF), 'Conscience et Résistance', the 'Ligue Mauritanienne des Droits de l'Homme' and the 'Forum National des Droits de l'Homme'.

At the beginning of the year there were several indications that President Mohamed Ould Abdel Aziz's popularity was under pressure. Parties within the 'Coordination de l'Opposition Démocratique' (COD) questioned his credibility. In September, mediation efforts by the parliamentary speaker, Messaoud Ould Boulkheir, opened up the prospect of a breakthrough dialogue between Aziz and COD leader Ahmed Ould Daddah. In an attempt to reach out to the COD, on 17 September Aziz decided on a **cabinet reshuffle**. Altogether 12 ministries were involved, including some of the key portfolios: Mohamed Ould Abdel Salem Ould Mohamed Rare replaced Mohamed Ould Boilil as minister for the interior and decentralisation; Ahmed Ould Teguedi replaced Hamadi Ould Hamadi as minister for foreign affairs and cooperation; and Sidi Ould Zein replaced Abidine Ould el Kheir as minister for justice. However, those appointed were all regarded as close allies of the president. A government-opposition dialogue was launched on 1 October. The COD demanded a postponement of the parliamentary and municipal elections in order to allow more time for campaigning and to enable the 'Commission Électorale Nationale Indépendante' (CENI), whose credibility the opposition doubted, to complete the administrative preparations, including compiling a valid electoral register. The government rejected this and after just two days the talks with the opposition were discontinued.

Preparations for the **legislative and local elections** began early in the year. On 13 February, the CENI concluded a four-day training programme for 30 of its officials, which was organised in partnership with the International Foundation of Electoral Systems. The COD was divided over the issue of participation. Despite the efforts of COD chair Ahmed Ould Daddah to maintain the unity of the alliance, the COD finally decided to boycott the polls, apart from the Islamist party 'Tewassoul', which probably saw an opportunity to emerge as a future leader of the parliamentary opposition. The first round of elections took place on 23 November, the second on 21 December (for those constituencies where no candidate had received more than 50% of the votes in the first round). The ruling UPR won 74 of the 147 Assembly seats and, with a dozen smaller parties, the ruling coalition gained 108 seats. The opposition took 37 seats in all: the Islamist 'Tewassoul', led by Mohamed Jemil Ould Mansour, 16 seats; 'El-Wiam', a group led by former president Maaouiya Ould Taya (1984–2005), ten seats; the 'Alliance Populaire Progressiste', led by outgoing Assembly chair Messaoud Ould Boulkheir, seven seats, and the 'Alliance pour la Justice et la Démocratie/Mouvement pour le Renouveau' led by Ibrahima Sarr, one of the presidential candidates in 2009, two. Two parliamentary seats would be filled later.

Women occupied 37 of the 147 Assembly's seats; there were only four female cabinet ministers out of 28. On 21 April, Irabiha Mint Abdel Weddoud became the first woman to head the 'Commission Nationale des Droits de l'Homme de Mauritanie', an official government organ. At the same time, several civil society organisations protested against increased violence against women. AFCF reported that 4,732 cases of rape had been recorded in 2012.

The political map was redrawn by the opposition's boycott, as the COD risked losing any opportunity of exercising influence over the political agenda – where there were a host of challenges, such as shortcomings in the struggle against corruption and slavery, the rights of black citizens, the response to worker protests and Mauritania's contested fisheries agreements. Despite long-term attempts to eradicate **slavery**, the government was faced with the fact that the country was placed at the top of the 2013 Global Slavery Index, compiled by the Walk Free Foundation, a global anti-slavery charity. No reliable official data were available and human rights activists accused the government of failing to acknowledge the extent of the phenomenon. On 24–27 February, Gulnara Shahinian, the UN's special rapporteur on contemporary slavery, visited the country and on 6 March a roadmap for the eradication of slavery, prepared with the Office of the UN High Commissioner for Human Rights, was adopted.

In late June, AI conducted a ten-day research mission during which it interviewed around 60 detainees, including women and children, held in three prisons in Nouakchott. It found evidence of the use of **torture**. AI also outlined cases of **disappearances** and lack of access to legal counsel and medical assistance. On 23 February, journalists launched a new organisation, 'Le Club des Jeunes Journalistes'. On the Press Freedom Index of Reporters Without Borders, Mauritania was placed at 67th out of 179 countries, i.e. ahead of all Arab countries. While this suggested progress was being made with regard to **press freedom**, civil society activists pointed out that the coverage of community issues and human rights violations was still uneven.

Foreign Affairs

Mauritania's relations with its West African neighbours continued to be dominated by the issue of AQIM and the fragile security situation in **Mali**. Malian Prime Minister Diango Cissoko visited Nouakchott on 5–6 January. The talks focused on how to reclaim Mali's northern region, lost to Islamist and separatist fighters. Tunisian President Moncef Marzouki met President Aziz on 14 January for discussions on strengthening bilateral relations and the revitalisation of the Arab Maghreb Union. At the Arab Economic Summit in Riyadh on 21–22 January, Aziz assured delegates that Mauritania would "act to defend" its territorial integrity and its citizens against attacks by extremist groups in Mali, but he repeatedly stated that Mauritania would not send troops over the border. In February–March, Mauritania hosted international military exercises with participants from 20 African, European and North American countries. However, at a joint press conference on 11 March with his counterpart from Niger, Mahamadou Issoufou, Aziz declared that Mauritania might send troops to join a UN force in northern Mali "if the situation changes". This statement marked a change from the government's previous position of only offering indirect support by monitoring the border with Mali and blocking Islamist fighters' supply lines and escape routes.

Foreign ministers from Algeria, Mauritania and several other West African states met in Nouakchott on 17 March at a summit conference organised by the AU's Peace and Security Council. Together with representatives from the EU and the UN, they examined ways of boosting **security cooperation**, as well as the implementation of the African plan for peace in the Sahel-Sahara region and ways to assist the African-Led International Support Mission to Mali (AFISMA). Longer-term security challenges, including terrorism, arms proliferation, drugs and other forms of trafficking and improved border security, were also discussed. The EU provided support to the West Sahel Project, launched in January as part of efforts to secure Mauritania's land borders, including the 2,200-km frontier with Mali.

French Foreign Minister Laurent Fabius visited Nouakchott on 15–16 April to discuss the security situation, signing partnership documents on multiple projects, including vocational training and infrastructure. A meeting of the Economic Forum of the Western Mediterranean (5+5 group) took place in Nouakchott on 15–16 April, bringing together five European Mediterranean states (France, Italy, Malta, Portugal and Spain), and five

North African countries (Algeria, Libya, Mauritania, Morocco and Tunisia). At the meeting it was announced that Mauritania had agreed to contribute to the MINUSMA force in Mali, which was planned to replace AFISMA from 1 July. This position was not without its risks as there was considerable opposition among domestic political parties to closer cooperation with **Western intelligence and security services**. At the same time, active participation in MINUSMA contributed to the country's reputation as an active player in the war against terrorism in the Maghreb, and UN special envoy to Mali Bert Koenders visited Mauritania on 5 August, praising the county's efforts to strengthen stability in the region.

In the course of the year, the government signed several bilateral security accords. Mauritania and **Niger**, both participants in MINUSMA, signed a military cooperation agreement on 20 August. On 17 November, Mauritania and **France** signed a counter-terrorism agreement that promoted cooperation programmes in security training, new technologies and other areas such as improving governance and police training. On 14 November, Mauritania held talks with **China** on enhanced military ties, especially partnership in personnel training, equipment and technology. **Morocco**'s Foreign Minister Saad Eddine El Othmani visited Nouakchott on 11–13 March for talks on security, the situation in Mali and a stronger Maghreb Union. In April, Morocco and Mauritania agreed to start more than a dozen new social and economic projects, including in energy, transportation, construction, education, training, scientific research, water, agriculture, fishing and marine resources, housing and sanitation. Morocco also proposed an end to visa requirements between the two countries. At the same time, a number of politically sensitive issues remained, especially the case of Western Sahara, which was occupied by Morocco, a conflict in which Morocco and **Algeria** continued to take opposite sides. However, Mauritania's relations with Algeria remained stable, and on 21 March a number of new cooperation accords were signed in the fields of employment, fishing, energy and agriculture.

Iran's President Hassan Rouhani announced in July his intention of fostering a new series of bilateral relationships, including with Mauritania. Some analysts pointed out that this might be directly connected to a new and growing Shia movement in Mauritania.

Socioeconomic Developments

On 2 January, Mauritania and France signed a € 6.4 m grant agreement to benefit health-care centres and staff training, and strategic regional food stocks. On 8 January, China announced financial support to the tune of over $ 260 m for various **development projects**. On 18 February, an agreement estimated to be worth $ 1 bn was signed with two Saudi companies, the National Prawn Company and Al Rajhi International for Investment, to develop a number of agricultural projects, with a particular focus on livestock and aquaculture.

In January, the fisheries committee of the European Parliament said that the provisional **fishing agreement** between the EU and Mauritania, signed on 3 December 2012, was "not economically advantageous for the EU, and not beneficial to Mauritania either". It concluded that it should therefore not be approved. However, after several amendments, the Parliament approved the agreement on 8 October. It allowed EU fishing vessels to catch various species of fish and shellfish (octopus excluded) in Mauritanian waters in exchange for an EU payment of € 70 m a year, of which € 3 m would be development aid for the local fisheries sector.

According to WFP, 20%–30% of the country's population continued to suffer from high **food insecurity**. In April, the government presented a new two-year agriculture programme, which projected a 110% increase in arable land to enable the country to produce 37% of its total cereal needs. More than 70,000 Malians **refugees**, chiefly in the Mbera camp about 60 km from the Malian border, made the food situation more precarious, and there was a risk that the presence of refugees could lead to social tensions, especially in regions severely hit by food shortages in 2011. In June, UNHCR reported a small number of refugees returning, but as the security situation was still fragile it was not expected that many more would follow.

Africa's largest solar power plant was inaugurated in Nouakchott on 22 April, and was expected to meet the energy demands of around 10,000 households. Several large **infrastructure projects** were in progress, including a power plant north of Nouakchott and transmission lines from Nouakchott to Nouadhibou, the Tasiast mine and the capital's new international airport.

Growth was estimated at 6.4%. Consumer price inflation was around 4.2 % and the exchange rate was regarded as modestly overvalued. The IMF estimated that the overall fiscal balance, including grants, fell to a deficit of 4.1% of non-oil GDP. The main causes for this were lower fishing revenues, higher public investment and the additional spending for the legislative elections, as well as higher hydrocarbon imports. At the same time, reserves were boosted by increased FDI and the repatriation of mining revenues (i.e., their conversion into the national currency), especially by the state-owned 'Société Nationale Industrielle et Minière'.

TI's **corruption** perception index ranked Mauritania 119th out of 177 countries, compared with 122nd out of 174 countries in 2012, and the fragile security situation also affected the business environment. The World Bank's 'Doing Business Report' ranked Mauritania's business environment at 167th out of 185 countries, three places lower than in 2012. In October, Canada-based Kinross announced the downsizing of its operations in Mauritania, largely owing to a drop in the price of gold to a three-year low in June. Kinross delayed the expansion of its Tasiast gold mine until at least 2015.

Mauritania's second national employment expo was organised on 20 February in Nouakchott, with a focus on private sector job opportunities. On 2 January, the 'Agence Nationale de Promotion de l'Emploi des Jeunes' launched a programme covering all urban local authorities to get more young people into work and to support those completing technical and professional training courses. The initiative was aimed at ensuring permanent jobs for the participants.

Claes Olsson & Helena Olsson

Niger

The government charted its way through the minefield of challenges posed by the war between Islamist groups and French-led forces in neighbouring Mali and Boko Haram's revolt in Nigeria. Although Niger was seen by the outside world as a beacon of relative stability, the country's vulnerability showed itself in attacks on a military base and uranium mine by Islamists driven out of Malian territory, as well as in a jail-break in the capital, Niamey, involving Boko Haram fighters. A boost in defence spending was followed by massive troop deployment along the Malian border, the dispatch of soldiers to assist in the French- and Chadian-led reconquest of north-east Mali, and the closure of the border with Nigeria. The attacks in Niger heightened popular anxiety and led to new security measures. In August, the appointment of a government of national unity led to the first political crisis since President Mahamadou Issoufou had taken office in 2011. Defended as a security measure, the reshuffle was part of the manoeuvring between Issoufou and his main coalition partner, National Assembly chair Hama Amadou, ahead of the 2016 presidential polls. Insufficient rainfall further compounded the fragile food supply. Uranium output suffered from the attack on mining installations. With its contract set to expire on 31 December, French nuclear energy group Areva got involved in tense negotiations with the government over the renewal of the agreement. Talks had not been concluded by year's end. Fresh delays in the completion of the hydro-electric Kandadji dam, in addition to the worst power failures in years, exposed the country's rickety infrastructure.

Domestic Politics

While President Issoufou enjoyed a comfortable majority with the backing of five of the Assembly's eight political parties united in the 'Mouvance pour la Renaissance du Niger' (MRN), he repeatedly expressed his desire for a **government of national unity**. Now presented in the context of national security, the idea was linked to manoeuvres ahead of the presidential elections due in 2016. A national government might be able to discourage the defection from the MRN by the second largest party, the 'Mouvement Démocratique Nigérien' (Moden-Lumana) led by Issoufou's main rival for the presidency, Hama Amadou (also National Assembly chair), and prevent the development of an opposition block from which Amadou could make his bid. The urgency of the need for action imposed itself on Issoufou as Amadou-oriented newspapers began to criticise Issoufou's government, triggering fears that Amadou was preparing a censure motion, the dissolution of the Assembly and early elections. Members of the largest opposition party, the 'Mouvement National pour la Société du Développement' (MNSD), were interested in Issoufou's overtures, but an initial attempt to lure them to the government side came to nothing.

In the end, the **cabinet reshuffle** announced on 13 August led to internal divisions in both the MNSD and Moden. While the Tuareg Prime Minister Brigi Rafini was reappointed and key portfolios remained in the hands of presidential loyalists, six MNSD members entered the cabinet – without their party's permission. On 17 August, Hama Amadou announced the withdrawal of seven of his cabinet ministers, but three of them, including Minister of Mining and Moden Secretary-General Omar Hamidou Tchiana, refused to leave. The country's first government of national unity included no fewer than 35 ministers (of whom only five were women). Of the major departments, only the interior ministry changed hands, but it remained under the control of a presidential loyalist, Massoudou Hassoumi.

If in consequence the presidential majority in the Assembly fell to three, the result for the opposition was worse. While Hama Amadou retained control of the influential Assembly presidency, he had no choice but to join a **reduced opposition block** renamed 'Alliance pour la République, la Démocratie et la Réconciliation'. While Amadou's departure from the governing coalition was not unexpected, observers surmised that he might have moved too soon. With 12 opposition MPs disobeying their party leaderships and supporting the new cabinet, Prime Minister Rafini easily won a vote of confidence on 9–10 November. The reconfigurations did little to change the overall picture of Nigérien politics, which ever since the early 1990s had been marked by poor party discipline and constantly shifting alignments between the same political tycoons.

President Issoufou continued his crusade against **corruption**: 21 health officials accused of stealing some $ 2 m from funds meant for vaccination campaigns were arrested early in the year (and another five followed in May). On 6 May, Foukory Ibrahim, an associate of former president Tandja and an MP for the MNSD, was charged with embezzling more than $ 40 m as head of Nigelec, the state electricity company. Nevertheless, on TI's corruption perception index, Niger jumped from 134th to 113th place, signifying some gains in the battle against corruption.

With the onset of foreign military intervention to fight off Islamist fighters in **northern Mali**, the government resolved to dispatch troops in support of the operations spearheaded by French and Chadian forces. On 16 January, the National Assembly overwhelmingly approved the deployment, which involved some 700 men. In addition, more than 5,000 military personnel were deployed to patrol the porous borders, of whom 500 were stationed at Arlit, the northern town that was the site of several uranium mines. However, even with the army's expansion (to a projected 20,000 in 2014), patrolling the borders proved daunting, especially on the frontier with Libya, to where many of the defeated Islamist forces in Mali escaped. The government increased the salaries paid to key military units, hired new staff for the intelligence services, placed informers in strategic villages and tried to seal the eastern two-thirds of the frontier with Nigeria in an attempt to prevent a spill over of violence by Boko Haram. **Security expenditure** now totalled 10% of the national budget, for which some $ 80 m was diverted from spending on education and health.

With resources stretched, foreign partners provided **substantial military aid**. Dozens of French special forces personnel were sent to protect uranium mines in Arlit, some 100 French troops were stationed in the capital, and the government signed an agreement with the US for the establishment of an American base near the northern desert town of Agadez to accommodate a maximum of 300 men. In addition to providing training, the French donated three Gazelle helicopters with 20 mm cannon. In April, the government purchased two Sukhoi jet fighters manned by Ukrainians, a huge expense but the pride of the armed forces. In February, four drones were stationed at a base near Niamey, manned by American and French personnel, for surveillance of the war zones in Mali. The government had wanted them to be armed but the US feared that this could create a backlash. Indeed, civil society groups aired criticism about the stationing of French troops in Arlit and the ICG warned that the government was involving itself in security strategies over which it exercised little influence.

Thus, while the war in Mali posed an extreme danger to national security, the government took some risk with regard to the **popular response**. With many Tuareg youths distrustful of uniformed officials, some might be susceptible to recruitment by Islamist groups. Despite the involvement of Tuareg dignitaries at the highest level of the political system, overall Tuaregs enjoyed little real representation in the capital. Prime Minister

Rafini nevertheless assured journalists that Niger's peoples were cooperating with the authorities. Indeed, well-informed observers thought that neither the Islamist 'Mouvement pour l'Unicité et le Jihad en Afrique de l'Ouest' (MUJAO) nor al-Qaida in the Islamic Maghreb (AQIM) had much support among communities in northern Niger, for which the ill-fated Tuareg rebellion of 2007–9 could be partly blamed.

On 23 May, Niger experienced the first **suicide attacks** in its history. In a coordinated twin operation, cars packed with explosives drove into the Somaïr uranium mine in Arlit and a military barracks in Agadez, killing one person at the mine and 24 or 25 on the base. At least a dozen people were wounded and the blast caused extensive damage to the uranium grinding machine – which halted the production of yellow cake. Ten attackers died and French and Nigérien forces needed 24 hours to neutralise the remaining assailants. Responsibility was claimed by both MUJAO and the Algerian leader of Islamist fighters, Mokhtar Belmokhtar, who had distanced himself from the AQIM leadership to form his own jihadist outfit. In fact, he seemed to work closely with MUJAO, with which he formed a new group a couple of months later. Following these attacks, the bloodiest on Niger to date, Issoufou decreed three days of mourning, and in an act of national solidarity visited Agadez and Arlit in the company of the leader of the opposition and Assembly chair Hama Amadou. The attackers seemed to have come from southern Libya (from where it would have been one night's ride to the targets).

In June, **new attacks** took place – this time right in the capital. On 1 June, assailants attacked the prison in Niamey to free 22 Islamists, including Cheibane Ould Hama, a Malian who was serving a jail term for the murder of several Saudi citizens in 2009 (in 2000 he had murdered a US diplomat in Niamey). The attack was probably undertaken by North African MUJAO fighters after three Boko Haram inmates killed several guards with pistols smuggled into the facility; just two months previously Nigérien forces had participated in a raid with Nigerian troops on a Boko Haram hideout in north-eastern Nigeria. The prison governor and another official were arrested and the three Boko Haram fighters recaptured (with the death of one of them), while French forces, tipped off by Nigérien intelligence, re-arrested Cheibane in north-eastern Mali on 26 November. On 11 June, assailants attacked a gendarmerie base on the outskirts of the capital but were driven away. These attacks, coupled with power failures that plunged Niamey into darkness for several weeks, created general anxiety. With increased security measures in place, which seriously affected traffic, the capital seemed in a state of siege. In early September, army troops clashed with drugs traffickers in the Manguéni-Djado region. Though they may have been simply Tubus going about their business, this zone was also frequented by Islamist fighters on their way to and from their Libyan sanctuary.

29 October saw the release of the 'Arlit four' – French workers kidnapped from a uranium mine at Arlit three years earlier and held by men loyal to Abou Zeid, the Algerian AQIM leader killed in Mali by French and Chadian forces on 25 February. Since the

kidnappers' political demands had not been met, nor any detained fighters released, rumours of payment of a ransom to the tune of € 20–25 m quickly hit the headlines. The French military were said to be furious, as any such payments would allow Islamist groups to replenish their resources. An American report on the Sahel's **kidnapping industry** had it that AQIM had acquired more than $ 100 m since 2003 (special bank accounts having been opened in Mauritania for the purpose). The money for the Arlit hostages may have come from secret French state funds or from Areva, in which the French state holds an 80% stake. The French government, which had been under constant pressure to help in the liberation of the hostages, denied paying any money, but the defence minister was known to have made several trips to Niamey. Issoufou was said to have played a key role in the process, appointing Mohamed Akotey, chairman of Areva's new uranium mine at Imouraren, as mediator: a Tuareg with family connections in north-eastern Mali, he made contact with the kidnappers. The Islamists' partial dislocation in the war against French and Chadian forces undoubtedly facilitated the deal. Observers also speculated that Issoufou's role could become a quid pro quo in the negotiations on the renewal of Areva's mining contract.

Foreign Affairs

Ties with **France** received a boost as a result of Niger's key geostrategic role in the war in Mali, its perceived relative stability in the troubled Sahelian region and the threats posed by Islamist fighters to the country's security. Issoufou visited French President François Hollande four times – his last visit on 5–7 December being in the context of a summit conference on peace and security in Africa. The meeting was partly overshadowed by the difficult negotiations with Areva. Issoufou, a mining engineer himself, went on record pleading for greater equilibrium in relations with the French nuclear consortium. French Foreign Minister Laurent Fabius visited Niger in the wake of the double suicide mission on 23 May.

By contrast, these attacks led to a worsening of relations with **Libya** – already poor since the fall of Kadhafi – because of strong suspicions that the attackers had staged their operations from south-west Libya. This suspicion was also voiced by France's foreign minister, who urged cooperation between Libya and the Sahelian countries. Issoufou's statement that the attackers had come from the Fezzan drew an angry if unpersuasive denial from the Libyans, who still had an axe to grind with Niger over its refusal to extradite one of Kadhafi's sons, former football star Saadi (because of fear that he might not get a fair trial). Libya reiterated its call for Saadi's extradition and towards the end of May expelled more than 1,000 West African workers, the majority of whom were Nigériens. Suffering hunger and thirst in the course of their summary deportation, two deportees were alleged to have died. Most lost all their savings. Niger refused to budge and actually became convinced that the suicide attacks had been planned in Derna, in north-east Libya (and also outside the control of the 'central government' in Tripoli). The Nigériens aspired to discuss joint border patrols, but the messy post-Kadhafi situation obstructed normal diplomatic contacts.

Relations with Niger's Sahelian neighbours remained good, buttressed by the shared Islamist challenges to their security (in the case of Chad, Mali and Nigeria) and the signing of a new military cooperation agreement with Mauritania on 20 August. Ties with **Burkina Faso** received a boost when the International Court of Justice in The Hague issued its ruling on a simmering border conflict. The disputed territory involved was more or less carved in two, the northern half going to Niger, with the proviso that both countries should take into account the needs of their nomadic populations when arranging the details of border control. Both countries expressed satisfaction with the ruling, which would end confusion about border patrols and tax collection. (This state of affairs dated back to colonial times, when the territory of Burkina Faso, formerly Upper Volta, had been temporarily suppressed by the French and shared out between neighbouring colonies.) Gold reserves in the border zone made the need for a settlement more urgent.

Socioeconomic Developments

The rainy season ended prematurely, impeding the ripening of cereal crops. This, combined with attacks by locusts and caterpillars, led to **seriously deficient harvests**, and the government soon had to subsidise food. As early as February, well before the annual harvest, the government launched the so-called 2013 Global Call for humanitarian aid to the tune of CFAfr 177 bn. While the 2012 harvest had been 27% above average, the country was still recovering from the catastrophic 2011 crop and destructive floods the following year. Thus, an estimated 3 m people were in need of assistance. The regions of Zinder, Tahoua and Tillabéri were worst affected. In the province of Diffa, food production suffered as farmers fled the Nigerian part of the Lake Chad area, which was engulfed in the war against Boko Haram. The hostilities negatively impacted on this source of additional food imports and also led to the influx of some 6,000 Nigerian refugees, which put further pressure on resources. In the first quarter, cereal prices rose by a third to their highest level in five years.

While the two **uranium** mines, Somaïr and the smaller Cominak, run by Areva at Arlit, had registered record output the previous year (together accounting for one-third of Areva's global yellow cake production), it took the company two months to get production back to normal after the destruction of its grinder at Somaïr. In March, the French consortium announced a contribution of € 35 m to help the government protect its industrial operations. Some observers suggested that this was meant as compensation for the delays in starting up Areva's open pit mine at Imouraren, which would become Africa's largest (producing 5,000 tonnes a year), but whose completion kept being pushed forward. Insecurity was likely to lead to new delays. An Australian uranium company discontinued operations after the attack on Somaïr. Moreover, Western concern over nuclear safety since the Fukushima disaster was still reducing global demand, with spot market prices having plummeted from € 187 to around € 50 a kilo.

Negotiations on the renewal of **Areva's contract** were a protracted balancing act. Fenced in between security threats, an uncertain market and the need to protect export value, the government had to tread carefully. In order to put pressure on the consortium, it mobilised popular support. On 5 April, around 2,000 students marched through the capital denouncing Areva's 'neo-colonialism' and demanding a bigger slice of the revenues from the mines (the government holds 36% and 31% in Somaïr and Cominak, respectively). A bigger demonstration was held in Arlit on 12 October, with allegations being aired about radioactive pollution, and this was followed on 21 December by another march in the capital. Areva threatened to discontinue its operations and the French media reported that it had decided to stop work at the mines owing to diminishing profitability. This was disputed by the government, which on 20 September had announced an independent audit of the mines. Issoufou's administration, which had to make sure that it was seen to fight for a better deal, demanded a more balanced partnership and Areva investment in the country's wider infrastructure. Uranium-derived income represented only 5% of the government budget. Niger argued that this should be raised to at least 20%. On its part, Areva claimed that its two mines could not afford to lose their fiscal privileges. A war of statistics was unleashed in which Areva asserted that 70%–80 % of direct mining revenues (taxes, royalties, dividends and licence fees) landed in state coffers. These figures were difficult to verify. A report by Oxfam claiming that only 13% of direct revenues went to Niger was grossly distorted – it arrived at that figure by ignoring the company's exploitation costs. Set against the background of a 40-year relationship, the bitterness created by this discussion was unprecedented. Both sides refused to budge and at year's end no deal had been struck.

After the logistical difficulties of the previous year, **oil** production picked up. In the first half of the year, output rose by roughly a third compared with 2012 (16,500 b/d). However, construction of the pipeline to link the Agadem production field in the east with the Chadian-Cameroonian pipeline had not started. Although there were concerns over the impact of the May suicide attacks on investment, Niger was still considered an attractive investment target owing to its mineral resources (uranium, oil, coal and gold). In recent years, capital inflows accounted for 30% of all **FDI** in UEMOA.

However, building on the Kandadji hydro-electric dam ran into difficulties, despite the fact that the World Bank had arranged a $ 203 m loan to start up the second phase of construction. The project, totalling around $ 750 m, would increase **power generation** capacity to 130 MW (from the current 105 MW) and irrigated agriculture to around 55,000 ha.

Completion was said to be delayed till 2017, and in July the government terminated its contract with a Russian company active on the site, citing the delays already incurred. Not all the problems were the company's fault, however, as issues such as compensation for the affected population, financial constraints and red tape all played a part. The consequences were immediately made clear when the capital was plunged into darkness for weeks in May, after storms had brought down pylons supporting a power line importing electricity from Nigeria – a considerable part of the power needs of the cities of Dosso, Tillabéri and Niamey depended on these imports. Turbines at a power plant in Niamey broke down under the pressure of demand. The government initiated plans for the building of new plants in Niamey and Tahoua, to be fired by diesel and Nigérien coal, but these would not start operating before 2015 and 2017, respectively. China provided a $ 56 m loan for the construction of two new power lines connecting the oil refinery of Zinder to cities in the eastern and central regions.

Various infrastructural development projects began to take shape, including ambitious plans for **railways** to connect landlocked Niger with Benin and Côte d'Ivoire. For the first railway project, which had been on the books since independence, Niger, Benin and French commercial conglomerate Bolloré established a joint stock company in November with a capital outlay of € 650 m. Upon completion of the section of the railway between Parakou in Benin and Niamey, officially planned for 2015, uranium could be transported from Niger by train to the sea port of Cotonou. The other project was for a railway line to Ouagadougou, Burkina Faso, and Abidjan, Côte d'Ivoire, with completion set for 2021. In both cases, the effect would be a significant reduction in transport costs.

Social tension in the Diffa region led to clashes with security forces on 27 April, in which three protesters sustained bullet wounds. The protests were against limited recruitment in the oil industry and low salaries. Prime Minister Rafini hurried to the region to calm tempers. In February and late March, workers had laid down their tools at the Chinese-run uranium mine near Azélik and had managed to secure a 15% pay increase (which was unlikely to significantly address the wide salary gap between Chinese and local workers – the cause of considerable tension). **Refugees**, as well as **deportees** from Libya, put further pressure on local resources. The number of refugees from Mali rose to at least 60,000. Shockingly, in October the bodies of around 90 people were found in the Sahara near the Algerian border. They had died of thirst after their vehicles had broken down. They appeared to be illegal **migrants** on their way to Algeria, many of them Nigerians and Nigériens from the Magaria region; according to the UN, some 80,000 migrants cross Niger through the desert every year. On 17 November, the government announced that it had broken up the trafficking ring responsible.

It was reported that the mortality rate for **children** under five had been reduced from 326 per 1,000 in 1990 to 114 in 2012. UNICEF, however, reported on 16 October that in the past year alone around 2,500 children had died of malnutrition. Other grim statistics concerned the position of **girls**. Population Minister Maikibi Kadidiatou reported on 11 July that around 75% of girls got married before the age of 18. The government therefore continued to pursue its policy of widening access to reproductive health facilities. One specific bottleneck involved **education**. In 2011, the primary enrolment rate for boys was 84.9% and for girls 67.3%.

Guitarist 'Bombino' (Omara Moctar), a Nigérien Tuareg and a star in his own country, gave a concert for peace called 'Le chant des dunes' on 5 April in Niamey. Two members of his band had died in the repression of the last Tuareg rebellion in 2007, and so his message of peace and solidarity was a rare glimmer of hope.

Klaas van Walraven

Nigeria

The precarious security situation in the northern regions deteriorated. Clashes between the security forces – particularly the army – and the Islamist sect Boko Haram and splinter groups such as Ansaru, took place almost every day, with hundreds of people killed. Over much of the year, sectarian violence with a noticeable ethnic undercurrent spread into states in the eastern and south-eastern Middle Belt. The sheer number of attacks, counter attacks and sectarian clashes rendered an adequate account of these events all but impossible. In contrast, the security situation in the southern parts of the country improved; this was due to the fact that several gangs involved in kidnapping, robbery and murder were captured or broken up. On the political front, the leadership of President Goodluck Jonathan was directly challenged by some state governors who were members of the ruling party, party members in the National Assembly, erstwhile party strongmen such as Olusegun Obasanjo and, last but not least, a potentially new political force that resulted from the merger of some smaller parties. These developments notwithstanding, Nigeria experienced another year of remarkable economic growth, financial stability and a building boom, particularly in the prosperous south, with the government finally breathing new life into the ailing power sector.

Domestic Politics

On 5 February, ten state governors met in Lagos to endorse a plan of the main opposition parties – the Action Congress of Nigeria, the Congress for Progressive Change, a faction of the All Progressives Grand Alliance (APGA) and the All Nigerian People's Party – to merge into a **new political party**, the All Progressives Congress (APC). Behind this move were well-known politicians such as Bola Ahmed Tinubu, former governor of Lagos state, and Muhammadu Buhari, a former presidential candidate, defeated in three elections. An obvious threat to the ruling People's Democratic Party (PDP) in the 2015 elections, the creation of the new party prompted a power struggle within the PDP, with President Goodluck Jonathan and his inner circle facing a faction of powerful governors (all but one from the North) and partially backed by former president Olusegun Obasanjo. The fact that the president had quietly replaced key party figures appointed by his predecessors and unsuccessfully interfered in the leadership tussle within the 'Nigeria Governors' Forum' did not help his popularity. More important, however, was the deep-rooted desire, particularly within the northern power block, to prevent Jonathan from seeking re-election and, if at all possible, to ensure the success of a northern candidate in the presidential elections. At the end of January, it became obvious that the long-standing dispute between the federal government and the governors over the respective allocations of the lucrative Excess Crude Account and the Sovereign Wealth Fund could not be resolved out of court. The governors went to the Supreme Court, which, on 2 December, set a hearing for March 2014.

On 20 June, the PDP national executive committee retained septuagenarian Bamanga Tukur, the controversial party leader from Adamawa state, as the PDP's national chairman. Some weeks later, on 31 July, the newly founded APC was registered by the Independent National Electoral Commission (INEC) after the merger parties had their certificates of registration withdrawn, thus changing the composition of the National Assembly.

However, the APC failed its first test in the **disputed gubernatorial election** in Anambra state on 16 November. The election was poorly implemented by the state branch of the INEC and even partly cancelled. The APC candidate, Chris Ngige, polled badly; a close runner-up to the PDP candidate, he was far behind Willie Obiano of the APGA. Obiano was duly declared elected after additional by-elections in 210 polling units on 1 December, succeeding his party's twice-elected governor Peter Obi. The supplementary elections were boycotted by the APC and PDP, and the APC announced on 8 December that it would challenge the result in court.

On 18 December, 37 PDP members in the House of Representatives defected to the APC, giving the APC a majority in the house, with 174 members. Prior to that, on 31 August, seven PDP governors and several senators and members of the House of Representatives had announced the **formation of a splinter group**, New PDP (nPDP), a move that seemed to further undermine the PDP's once dominant position. Following the failure of yet another conciliatory meeting with President Jonathan, who had removed nine ministers (most of them, thanks to the political quota system, nominated by dissenting governors or by his former 'godfather' Olusegun Obasanjo), the seven PDP governors held talks with the APC in late September. Among the ministers sacked on 11 September were Olugbenga Ashiru (foreign affairs), Ms Ruqquayatu Rufa'i (education), Ms Amal Pepple (land and urban development) and Shamsudeen Usman (national planning). On 27 November, five PDP governors, Chibuike Amaechi (Rivers state), Ahmed Abdulfatah (Kwara state), Rabiu Musa Kwankwaso (Kano state), Murtala Nyako (Adamawa state) and Aliyu Wamakko (Sokoto state), together with 49 nPDP members of the House of Representatives, eventually defected to the APC, while only Mu'azu Babangida Aliyu (Niger state) and Sule Lamido (Jigawa state) reaffirmed their loyalty to the PDP.

The **power struggle** reached its climax on 2 December, when Obasanjo wrote the president an 18-page open letter entitled 'Before It Is Too late'. The letter was published shortly afterwards by the online platform 'Premium Times'. Such a direct attack was bound to be controversial but, according to the author, it was meant to draw the president's attention to a myriad of issues, which, if not addressed, could jeopardise Nigeria's survival. Jonathan finally replied on 20 December, denouncing Obasanjo's letter as a threat to national security. Towards year's end, the president fell out with the governor of the Central Bank, Sanusi Lamido Sanusi, when it transpired that the latter had allegedly leaked to Obasanjo a letter that had been written to the president, claiming that the state petroleum corporation had retained billions of dollars of oil proceeds that should have been remitted to the Central Bank. Moreover, towards year's end, the nPDP faction in the National Assembly showed no sign of backing down, thus keeping up political pressure on the PDP leadership and the president.

The **cabinet reshuffle** on 11 September saw almost all vacant post taken over by their respective minister of state, with, for instance, Ms Viola Onwuliri taking over the ministry of foreign affairs portfolio. Early in the year, on 4 February, the president had sworn in Chinedu Nebo as minister for the still ailing power sector, a post which had been vacant for over half a year, and Kabiru Tanimu Turaki as minister for special duties. The Ministry of Defence, also vacant for months, had been overseen by the then minister of state, Ms Erelu Olusola Obada. Since she was among those sacked 13 September, Labaran Maku was temporarily put in charge of defence alongside his responsibilities as minister of information. During August, September and October, Jonathan used his executive powers to appoint new board members and chairmen of the more than 40 state agencies and federal parastatals. As a constitutive part of the Nigerian political system, these short-term lucrative positions serve first and foremost to redistribute huge financial resources to a considerable number of the elite. One such appointment was that of Abisola Clark, a medical doctor turned businesswoman, who had just married the still influential octogenarian Ijaw leader, Chief Edwin Clark; she was appointed chairperson of the national ear centre in Kaduna. Earlier in the year, on 5 July, Justice Ms Kudirat Kekere-Ekun was elevated to the Supreme Court, which brought the number of female judges to four out of 17 currently on the bench.

The military promoted and redeployed their upper echelons more often than had previously been the case, an indication that all was not well in the military, particularly with respect to the ongoing insurgency in the Northeast and the widespread corruption throughout the security forces. According to local insiders, at least 80% of the annual budget of some $ 6 bn assigned to security had for years been pocketed by the upper ranks of the military and police, by top politicians dealing with security issues and by hundreds of self-proclaimed security advisers, such as retired officers, former politicians, businessmen and academics. Thus, it is not surprising that the insurgency in the North and Northwest had turned into a lucrative business, a situation whose significance was augmented by the fact that the political leadership had more or less put the destiny of the country into the hands of the security forces, particularly the military, which had not enjoyed such influence since the era of military rule. On 1 July, however, 18 soldiers including a lieutenant were court-martialled in Jos for alleged links to Boko Haram, and it was reported that more offenders were awaiting trial. In September, the media reported that the 18 had been sentenced to death, but government officials denied these reports and told reporters that the court-martial was on-going. The proceedings were not open to the public or the press.

At the start of the year, on 7 January, 14 officers were given the rank of one-star general; on 28 January, more than 300 officers as well as the strategically important **General Officers Commanding** (GOC) were redeployed. Major General Ahmed Tijani Jibrin took over the GOC 2 Mechanized Division based at Ibadan and Ebiobowei Awala of the same rank the GOC 3 Armoured Division in Jos. The latter, however, was replaced by Major General John Nwaoga at year's end. Major General Obi Umahi emerged as commander of the GOC 81 Amphibious Division, garrisoned in Lagos, and Major General Adebayo Olaniyi as new GOC 82 Airborne Division commander in Enugu. Furthermore, Brigadier Ibrahim Attahiru was appointed the new director of army public relations, and Major General Kenneth Minimah replaced Mohammed Isah as commander of the Infantry Corps and Centre, Jaji, in Kaduna state. Soon afterwards, on 19 March, Brigadier Chris Olukolade was named as new director of defence information, succeeding Colonel Mohammed Yerima, who had served in that capacity for quite some time.

On 1 July, a federal high court in the capital Abuja had nullified the appointment of all service chiefs. The court argued that the appointments had contravened the constitution because the president had failed to secure the senate's approval. However, this had been common practice ever since the redemocratisation of the political system at the end of the 1990s, and the verdict was ignored by the government and the military. A lawsuit against this practice had already been filed in 2008 by Festus Keyamo, a well-known lawyer and human rights activist. On 17 August, a **new army division**, tagged GOC 7 Infantry Division, to be garrisoned in Maiduguri with some 8,000 troops, was created against the backdrop of the Boko Haram insurgency in the Northeast. However, its first commander, Major General Obidah Ethan, was replaced unexpectedly soon, at the end of the year, by his colleague of the same rank, Junaid Bindawa. In September and at year's end, more than a dozen generals from the three arms of the military had to retire and another batch of top-ranking officers was redeployed. Another wave of promotions came at the end of November, when more than 300 high-ranking officers moved up a rank, followed by a further round of redeployment of no fewer than 30 generals on 27 December.

The **police forces** underwent similar changes. On 1 January, the promotion of more than 1,900 staff with the rank of constable or sergeant came into effect, obviously aimed at appeasing the middle ranks, who for years had suffered from poor equipment, housing and pay. A documentary on local Channels TV in mid-January, part of which was kept on the station's website, revealed the dilapidated condition of the foremost police institute, the police training college in Lagos, and confirmed the generally poor state of this security service. Nevertheless, in September and December, 47 senior officers, ranking from assistant commissioner to deputy inspector general, were given promotion. The redeployment of dozens of police commissioners and assistant inspector generals became a permanent feature, aimed at fighting the police's poor reputation for **corruption and brutality**. However, this did not prevent the police force losing dozens of staff on active duty over the course of the year.

In the course of the year, the already precarious security situation deteriorated further, particularly in the Northeast, where it reached another nadir. Half-hearted efforts by members of the northern establishment to initiate some form of dialogue with sections of the Islamist sect **Boko Haram** did not last long; this was due to the government's right of veto, the security services' own agenda and the lack of restraint on the part of the sect's leadership. Despite the state of emergency imposed by the president on 14 May in Borno and neighbouring Yobe and Adamawa states, extended for another six months in November, attacks and counter-attacks went on unabated. The formation in May–June of vigilante groups made up of youths and condoned by the military, the existence of safe havens, and the tacit approval of the Islamists by local politicians, added fuel to the flames. In the course of the year, more than 500 civilians (a conservative estimate), at least 450 suspected members of the sect and more than 50 members of the security forces lost their lives in Borno state alone. In addition, well over 1,000 people were held in military camps in inhumane conditions, which, according to a statement by AI on 14 October, had caused a number of deaths. In early December, the Nigerian Human Rights Commission (NHRC) was planning to investigate arbitrary detention centres, especially those used to incarcerate Boko Haram suspects.

One of the worst incidents took place on 19–21 April in the remote town of Baga near the Chad border, an assumed Boko Haram hide-out. Rocket-propelled grenades and heavy gunfire from a Multinational Joint Task Force, made up of Nigerian troops and reinforcements from neighbouring Niger and Chad, killed scores of people and destroyed large parts of the town. It was reported that close to 200 people fell victim to the attack, a figure vehemently disputed by the military, which put the number at 37. The NHRC, however, in an interim assessment at mid-year, found evidence of **atrocities** committed by both the security forces and Boko Haram. A report by HRW, published in May, maintained that its investigations showed 183 people had been killed; analysis of satellite images of Baga showed that more than 2,200 houses had been destroyed.

On 12 September, a confrontation took place at Kafiya Forest, which cost the lives of some **150 insurgents** and 16 soldiers with nine others missing. Immediately after the gun battle the military rejected claims that up to 100 security personnel had been killed. On 17 September, in another serious incident near Benisheik, in Kaga local government area, alleged members of Boko Haram killed more than 140 travellers on the Maiduguri-Damaturu road. In the early morning of 2 December, Islamist militants struck the **air force base** in Maiduguri, destroying five aircraft and killing two military personnel. Over 20 insurgents lost their lives, and the federal airports authority was forced to close the international airport. More was to come when, on 20 December, insurgents raided the barracks in the town of Bama in the local government area of the same name. The military repelled the attack, even using fighter jets, killing some 50 assailants. More than a dozen soldiers and an uncounted number of civilians living on the premises lost their lives during a **fierce battle** that lasted for hours. Soon afterwards, on 28 December, in a gun battle near the village of Alafa, not far from Bama, more than 50 suspected members of Boko Haram were killed during a military raid. Earlier in the year, however, during his two-day working visit to Borno and Yobe states on 7–8 March, President Jonathan had spent a night in Maduguri, which was seen in some quarters as an act of bravado.

Neighbouring Adamawa, Bauchi and Kano states were also seriously hit by the insurgents, though not on the scale seen in Borno and Yobe. At times, **foreigners** were **deliberately targeted**. Thus, three North Korean medical practitioners working in a state-run hospital in Potiskum in Yobe state, had their throats slit or were beheaded during the night of 9–10 February. Shortly after, on 17 February, a splinter group of Boko Haram called Jama'atu Ansarul Muslimina Fi Biladis Sudan, better known as Ansaru, stormed a Lebanese road construction company in Jama'are local government area in Bauchi state, killing a security guard and kidnapping and eventually killing seven expatriate workers, a Briton, a Greek, an Italian and four Lebanese. Moreover, it was suggested that, on the same day, Ansaru was also responsible for the kidnap of a French family of seven in neighbouring Cameroon, very close to the Nigerian border, thereby substantiating suspicions concerning Boko Haram's wider regional agenda. On 19 April, the family, who had probably spent some time in captivity in Nigeria, were released unharmed in Cameroon. It was reported that a ransom of between $ 3 m and $ 27 m was paid, but the French government denied making any such payment. The French engineer Francis Collomp, who had been taken hostage in December the previous year, was also fortunate to escape from his kidnappers' hide-out in Zaria on 17 November.

Kano city, capital of the state of the same name and one-time hub of the North, experienced several grisly incidents. On 19 January, gunmen opened fire on the convoy of the Emir, Alhaji Ado Bayero. The Emir survived the attack unharmed but four others died. Barely three weeks later, seven suspects were arrested, among them one Adamu Sani, who allegedly revealed that he had been recruited by two local Muslim clerics. In addition, on 18 March, a series of explosions rocked a car park in Sabon Gari, a Kano district traditionally frequented by immigrants and quite a number of Christians. More than 20 people died, scores were injured and several luxury buses went up in flames. At the end of March, men belonging to the Joint Military Task Force were shot at by gunmen during a routine patrol in Unguwa Uku, another city district. The immediate retaliation led to the death of 14 suspects. On 1 April, a police patrol vehicle was ambushed at Yan Kaba market and three policemen were gunned down. On 29 July, Sabon Gari, an urban quarter where bars and beer gardens can be found, was again hit by serial explosions, leading to **dozens of fatalities**.

A more isolated incident took place on 19 January in Kogi state, south of the Federal Capital Territory (FCT) Abuja. A Mali-bound military detachment was attacked, with two soldiers killed and five others seriously injured.

In addition to the almost daily attacks and counter-attacks, the **media campaign** between Boko Haram and the security services reached new heights during the second half of the year. In early June, the US government offered a bounty of $ 7 m for the self-proclaimed Boko Haram leader, Abubakar Shekau; this coincided with the government's decision to declare the sect a 'terrorist organisation'. On 19 August, military sources suggested that the sect's leader had been wounded in a military raid at Sambisa Forest on 30 June, and had died a few weeks later in a hide-out in nearby Cameroon. They also suggested that the second-in-command, Momodu Bama, alias Abu Saad, had been killed, too. Despite the fact that the military authorities dismissed as a fake a video showing Shekau alive, their claims were not verified. On 25 September, to the surprise of all, Shekau or his double again appeared in a video, dressed in military camouflage battledress, claiming to be alive and well. This encouraged increasing scepticism with regard to intelligence reports and the military's capacity to handle the crisis.

Despite the fact that hundreds of suspected terrorists had been detained and scores had been killed, only a small number were eventually charged and sentenced, among them four alleged members of Boko Haram who were sentenced on 9 July to **life imprisonment** for masterminding and carrying out a deadly attack on an INEC office in Suleja before polls in 2011, and for bombing a church in the same vicinity three months later. On 15 November, Mustapha Umar was given the same sentence for bombing the Kaduna office of the national daily newspaper 'This Day' in April of the previous year, a sentence that was also handed down to Kabiru Umar alias Kabiru Sokoto on 20 December for his role in terrorist activities, including the bombing of St Theresa's Catholic Church in Madalla, Niger state, in December 2011.

In the Middle Belt, particularly in Plateau, Benue, Nasarawa and Taraba states – for years a centre of **sectarian clashes** – conflicts continued unabated, leaving hundreds of people dead. One of the worst incidents took place in Nasarawa in early May, when the 'Ombatse Cult', made up of ethnic Eggons, killed more than 60 policemen and several members of the State Security Service (SSS). This brutal act eventually revealed a long-standing, deep-rooted and violent power struggle in several local communities, mainly involving Eggons, but also ethnic Idomas and Fulani herdsmen. In mid-September, for example, hundreds of soldiers had to be deployed to end **days of violence**, blamed on militias of the 'Ombatse Cult'. The other states mentioned fared no better.

In August, the Miyetti Allah Cattle Breeder Association disclosed that, over a five-year period, more than 10,000 herdsmen had been killed nationwide and some 12 m cattle rustled. These estimates could not be verified but they were an indication of the state of **rural insecurity**.

The continuing deep crisis in the Northeast and the aforementioned Middle Belt states somewhat overshadowed the **volatile Niger Delta** and the other parts of the economically booming South. Although lucrative piracy along the coast increased slightly, the security services exposed and arrested a number of notorious criminal gangs in the southern parts of the country. In January, a South African court found Henry Okah, an alleged militant leader of the Movement for the Emancipation of the Niger Delta (MEND), guilty of masterminding a car bombing during celebrations of the 50th anniversary of Nigeria's independence on 1 October 2010. He was given a 24-year prison sentence. A co-perpetrator, Edmund Ebiware, was sentenced to life imprisonment by a Nigerian court on 25 January.

The vast majority of those kidnapped off the **Nigerian coast** were released unharmed: three Italians regained their freedom on 8 January, after being held captive for more than two weeks; five Indians, who had spent more than a month in captivity, were set free on 26 January. Another group of expatriates from Russia, the Ukraine and India, kidnapped on 17 February, were released nine days later, and, on 18 June, a French national, who had been taken hostage off the coast of Togo a week earlier, was rescued by security forces in Bayelsa state. On 23 October, two US citizens, a captain and a chief engineer, were taken hostage by armed men who had entered their US-registered oil supply ship; they were freed on 12 November. On 5 February in Bayelsa state, during a gun battle involving men of the Joint Task Force and pirates, two soldiers, a retired naval officer and the pilot of a tugboat were killed. Another deadly attack took place in Delta state in early March, when militants attacked an oil barge, killing four soldiers, a former naval officer and two civilians. In another ambush on a vessel on 22 October, two soldiers lost their lives; the coxswain and three staff of a construction company were wounded. On 17 August, during a rescue operation on a hijacked vessel, the Nigerian navy killed a dozen pirates and captured four. This was one of the rare cases in which pirates were arrested. The list was in fact longer, the International Maritime Bureau claiming to have recorded more than 40 attacks in the area with some 132 crew taken hostage in the course of the year. Shortly before year's end, a spokesman claimed that what had been dubbed 'operation pulo shield' had killed 40 pirates and lost six active staff. On 23 December, Vice-Admiral Dele Ezeoba, the chief of naval staff, had informed the public that, in the course of the year, more than 1,500 illegal oil refineries, over 100 barges, some 1,400 large wooden boats and a huge quantity of equipment had been destroyed, with more than 1,600 suspects arrested.

Kidnappings and killings in the Niger Delta also continued. In early March, Chika Richard Nwabiarijie, a notorious gang leader from Rivers state, and members of his gang were arrested. They had kidnapped a hotel manager in Oguta in Imo state on 24 February, then collected a ransom and finally killed the hostage. On 21 March, Ms Olubunmi Oke, broadcaster with the Nigerian Television Authority in Odo state and married to a banker, was kidnapped. Two days later, after the family had paid a NGN (naira) 1 m ransom, she was re-united with her loved ones. Probably the ugliest incident took place in Southern Ijaw local government area in Bayelsa state when, on 5 April, 12 policemen were gunned down by remnants of the ethnic Ijaw militia group, MEND. The brutality of this attack suggested that it was related to the conviction of Henry Okah. The policemen had been deployed to provide security at the burial of the mother of a repentant warlord, Kile Selky Torughedi, alias General Young Shall Grow. Jackson Fabouwei, alias General Jasper, alleged to have masterminded the killing, was arrested on 3 June after a manhunt. On 24 August, the senior advocate of Nigeria and human rights activist Mike Ozekhome was abducted by armed men and the four policemen guarding him were killed, but he was released by his kidnappers on 12 September. An Anglican archbishop, the Most Reverend Ignatius Kattey, the church's number two, and his wife Beatrice, were abducted in Eleme in Rivers state on 6 September. He regained his freedom a week later, the captors having already released his wife. Ms Bridget Osawaru, taken hostage on 10 December in Benin City, the capital of Edo state, was killed by her captors after they collected NGN 1.5 m. The scale of hostage taking and the killing of an abducted businessman, Emmanuel Obiyan, on 17 October finally prompted Edo state governor Adams Oshiomhole to sign an amended bill into law the following day, making kidnapping a capital offence. Neighbouring Ondo state had passed a similar law in 2010, almost unnoticed.

Persistent crime in almost all federal states cost the lives of countless policemen, bank officials, politicians, traditional rulers – in fact, people from all walks of life. The combined security services broke up several gangs, particularly in the South and Southwest. On 29 January, the SSS in Abuja paraded a gang of six that had carried out several kidnapping operations, allegedly led by the dismissed police officer Ndidi Cletus. The Nollywood actress Nkiru Sylvanus was one of the gang's victims, taken hostage in December of the previous year. She was released after payment of NGN 8 m. Soon afterwards, on 4 February, police in Oyo state paraded another gang that had acquired some notoriety after taking hostage the wife of former military governor Oluwole Rotimi in neighbouring Ogun state; Rotimi paid a ransom of NGN 13 m for her release. In early August, the notorious gang leader Abiodun Ogunjobi, alias Gododogo, who had ruled the underworld of Lagos and the Southwest for some 14 years and had left many policemen and civilians dead, was finally apprehended. The dreaded gang leader Kelvin Ibruvwe Oniarah, who had carried out a number of kidnappings and killings in the greater Niger Delta area, was arrested on 25 September. Among other things, he was believed to have abducted Mike Ozekhome, the human rights activist, as well as a judge of the Edo state judiciary, Daniel Okungbowa, and to have killed the hostage Chudi Nwike, a former deputy governor of Anambra state.

Last but not least, Ondo state police announced that, in the course of the year, they had arrested 105 suspected robbers and 26 suspected kidnappers, while the authorities in Akwa Ibom state claimed to have arrested more than 1,400. Lagos and Ogun states claimed to have arrested almost 800 suspected armed robbers and 76 alleged kidnappers, numbers that had an impact on the security situation in the South as a whole.

The **anti-corruption campaign** slowed down, due in part to lack of funds. Mainly sponsored by donors such as the EU, the Economic and Financial Crime Commission (EFCC) admitted on 16 December that it was insolvent and unable to pay the lawyers handling its prosecution cases. Earlier in the year, on 4 July, the federal high court in Abuja discharged and acquitted a former minister of works, Hassan Lawal, and an erstwhile bank official, Adesanya Adewale, on charges of laundering several million naira. And, on 19 September, Ms Bridget Omotunde Sokan, executive secretary of the Universal Basic Education Commission, was acquitted by the court, along with six others, five years after being charged with defrauding her Commission to the tune of almost NGN 800 m. The EFCC suffered a further setback on 13 December when the Supreme Court overturned a guilty verdict reached in 2009, when Olabode George, then chairman of the board of directors of the Nigerian Port Authority, and five board members, had been sentenced to 30 months imprisonment for financial crimes, a sentence they had already served. On the same day, an Abuja high court discharged and acquitted the former minister of the FCT, Nasir el-Rufai, and two staff of the Abuja Geographic Information System, who had been charged with abuse of office and corruption. In October, the controversial purchase of two bullet-proof BMWs by Aviation Minister Stella Oduah on behalf of her ministry at an inflated price of $ 1.6 m instead of the market price of some $ 267,000 each, brought the ministry under public scrutiny. The cars were never delivered and some newspapers speculated that she had shared the purchase price with a Lagos car dealer. This allegation notwithstanding, she was still in office at year's end. Interestingly, in December, the German firm Bilfinger was fined $ 32 m by a US court for violating the Foreign Corrupt Practices Act, having bribed Nigerian government officials some ten years earlier. Bilfinger was closely connected with Nigeria's biggest construction company, Julius Berger.

Nevertheless, there were some minor successes, including the fact that, on 18 October, the international Financial Action Task Force removed Nigeria from the list of countries with significant deficiencies in their policies regarding money laundering and the financing of terrorism.

The precarious security situation in most parts of the country had grave effects on **human rights**. On 20 September, the military killed eight squatters in a building in the Apo area of Abuja, claiming that it was a Boko Haram hide-out. The claims could not be substantiated and, with the investigation continuing at year's end, the NHRC had started to attend the proceedings. Nevertheless, at least nine governors used their executive powers to free several hundred prison inmates, most of them common criminals. A number of them were awaiting trial, while others were granted amnesty or unconditionally pardoned.

Nigeria's longest-running court case was about to come to an end, when, on 12 July, the Court of Appeal quashed the death sentence and acquitted Hamza Al-Mustapha and Lateef Shofolahan. The court held that the prosecution had completely failed to prove a charge of conspiracy and murder. The accused had been sentenced by a Lagos high court in January 2012 for the murder of Ms Kudirat Abiola in 1996. Lagos state government, which had originally sought to appeal against the verdict, withdrew the application on 29 November and quietly withdrew its appeal to the Supreme Court.

Contrary to reports from the National Assembly in 2012, the controversial legislation banning **same sex-marriage** had been passed but not signed by the president and had allegedly been quietly set aside. On 10 December, almost unnoticed, a committee adopted a revised version which was passed on 17 December and awaited the president's assent sometime in early 2014.

Foreign Affairs

Foreign policy focused on cultivating good relations with the US, the most important customer for Nigeria's crude oil and liquefied gas and its main supplier of wheat. It increased cooperation with Britain and consolidated its relations with China, while expanding its activities in other Asian countries.

At the start of the year, President Jonathan attended the World Economic Forum in Switzerland where, on 23 January, he was interviewed by CNN's Christiane Amanpour on such crucial issues as combating Boko Haram, improving the ailing power sector and preventing oil theft. Most Nigerians watching the interview were embarrassed by the president's poor performance and weak arguments, but it had no particular impact on relations with the **US**. On 23 September, Jonathan paid a visit to the White House and, on 26 November, received the new US ambassador, James Entwistle. Earlier, on 15 August, under the umbrella of the US-Nigeria Binational Commission, Under Secretary of State for Political Affairs Wendy Sherman underlined security cooperation and the intention of the US to invest in Nigeria's institutions, people and businesses. To that end, on 29 August,

USAID disclosed that it would invest $ 100 m in the education sector in five northern states. Earlier in the year, General Electric sealed a $ 1 bn deal with the Nigerian government to boost the ailing power sector, and, in April, the Maryland-based firm Grip2Grip opened an office in Lagos, its first foreign trade office in Africa, overseeing its business activities in four other African countries.

On 13 November, the US formally designated Boko Haram and Ansaru as foreign terrorist organisations and global terrorists. Canada followed suit at year's end.

On 17 April, the US Supreme Court, in a unanimous decision, rejected the complaint brought by the relatives of the Ogoni executed in 1995 after a show-trial in Port Harcourt. The plaintiffs had accused the Anglo-Dutch company **Shell** of complicity in human rights violations in the Niger Delta. The court held that the US justice system had no jurisdiction over the issue. However, concern was growing over the fate of the charitable trust (Kiisi) set up with $ 5 m of the $ 15.5 m out-of-court settlement between Shell and the relatives in 2009. Since then, no activities had been recorded and, after alleged problems amongst the trustees, the death of one and the resignation of another, the trust lay idle in a New York bank account.

After legal wrangling in Nigerian courts, Lawal Olanyi Babafemi, alias Ayatollah Mustapha, was extradited to the US on 28 August, where he had been indicted by a federal court in Brooklyn for providing material support to al-Qaeda in the Arabian Peninsula and recruiting prospective members to Yemen. He had lived in the US but had fled the country the previous year after the FBI put him under surveillance; he was eventually arrested in Nigeria.

Legal issues also shaped relationships with **Britain**. Several hundred Nigerians were serving various jail terms in UK prisons. For years, both governments had tried to reach agreement and, eventually, on 24 April, President Jonathan signed the **prisoners' transfer deal** into law, thereby paving the way for a legally binding treaty that would empower both countries to repatriate eligible prisoners without their consent.

On 12 June, the UK Supreme Court ruled in favour of Yasmin Prest, the English ex-wife of the Nigerian oil tycoon Michael Prest, in a divorce settlement and ordered him to transfer part of his properties in Nigeria and the Caribbean, worth several hundred million pounds, to his ex-wife. The extraordinary case was carefully watched by wealthy couples, particularly from outside Britain. The lower court had passed a contrary verdict.

There was a new twist in the James Ibori saga, when, on 17 December, Southwark Crown Court postponed the former Delta state governor's complicated confiscation of assets hearing to 2014. The accused had already served a sentence for money laundering. A week earlier, on 9 December, a former Goldman Sachs banker, Elias Preko, a Ghanaian national, was sentenced to four-and-a-half years in prison by the same court for laundering $ 5 m on Ibori's behalf.

On 19 December, the Old Bailey convicted Michael Adebolajo and Michael Adebowale, two young British nationals of Nigerian ancestry, of the murder of Lee Rigby, a British soldier out of uniform. Both were Muslim converts and, on 22 May, claiming they were acting in the name of Allah, they hacked the soldier to death with a meat cleaver in broad daylight in south London. Sentence was pending at year's end. Adebolajo was not an unknown quantity. He had appeared in court in Mombasa in 2010 and was deported from Kenya for having contacts with al-Shabaab. On his return to Britain, he had to some extent been under MI5 surveillance.

Early in the year, on 6–11 February, Nigeria's president paid a six-day visit to the UK and met Prime Minister David Cameron on 10 February. In November, Jonathan, accompanied by top-ranking politicians, attended a three-day meeting of Nigeria's Honorary International Investor's Council in London, coordinated by Baroness Lynda Chalker. At the same time, the Archbishop of Canterbury, Justin Welby, held talks in London with the Emir of Kano, Alhaji Ado Bayero. The British government had declared Boko Haram a terrorist organisation in July.

At the beginning of the year, Sino Arab Energy, SAE, a Chinese company in partnership with the local firm Osabo Refining and Petrochemical Industry Limited, concluded plans to build a refinery in Cross River state valued at some $ 7.5 bn, despite the fact that all previous attempts to set up privately run refineries had failed. The new dynamics of economic **cooperation with China** was fostered by Jonathan's five-day state visit on 9–13 July, when several agreements were signed, covering the construction of power plants, defence cooperation and trade and investment. Trade between the two countries already exceeded $ 13 bn per annum. In the run-up to the state visit, the Nigerian ambassador to China, Aminu Bashir Wali acknowledged that 300 of some 400 Nigerians incarcerated in China were being held for drugs-related offences.

On 2 February, **Indonesia**'s President Susilo Bambang Yudhoyono met his counterpart in Abuja, where they discussed, *inter alia*, options relating to the exchange of prisoners as well as mutual legal assistance; finally, they signed a memo to combat drug abuse and trafficking in narcotics. The meeting was overshadowed by the fact that 14 Nigerians were awaiting execution and some 30 others were serving various jail terms in Indonesian prisons.

India was an important customer for Nigeria's crude oil and the volume of trade had risen to some $ 16 bn. In addition, there were some 100 Indian companies in Lagos alone. The growing economic cooperation notwithstanding, the killing of a Nigerian, Simeon Obodo, in Goa on 31 October, revealed the existence of a considerable Nigerian diaspora of as many as 40,000 in India, many of them living there illegally. The killing was said to be related to drug gang rivalry, and the police started cracking down on illegal immigrants, including Nigerians, and deporting them.

In October, Jonathan went on a three-day pilgrimage to **Israel**, being the first Nigerian president to do so. Interestingly, in April, the government had awarded the Israeli company Elbit Systems a contract worth some $ 40 m to monitor Internet communication in Nigeria.

Relationships between the AU and African countries were largely shaped by the **Mali crisis**. On 18 January, Jonathan attended an extraordinary meeting of ECOWAS and raised the contingent of Nigerian troops from close to 800 to 1,200. He joined the 20th AU meeting in Addis Ababa (Ethiopia) towards the end of the month, held talks in France with President François Hollande on 11 February, and, on 9 April, attended the signing of two agreements by ECOWAS and the EU worth € 76 m to support the African-led mission to Mali and the free movement of persons in the sub-region. To the consternation of the member countries of the UN stabilisation mission in Mali, Nigeria withdrew most of its troops in July, with the justification that they were needed to tackle the growing insurgency in Nigeria's Northeast.

On 9 April, Jonathan joined other African leaders in Nairobi for the inauguration of President Uhuru Kenyatta, whom he met again on 5–7 September on a three-day state visit to Kenya. On 16 April, he received South African President Jacob Zuma in Abuja. In mid-July, he had hosted the AU's special summit on HIV/AIDS, tuberculosis and malaria together with UN Secretary General Ban Ki-moon and Sudanese President Omar al-Bashir. Some hours after his arrival, al-Bashir quietly slipped out of the country and returned home to avoid possible arrest by the ICC. On 1 September, Jonathan welcomed his counterpart from neighbouring Benin, Boni Yayi. On 12 October, the president attended the AU's extraordinary session in Addis Ababa on Africa's relationship with the ICC and, on 9 November, Jonathan met Gambia's controversial president, Yahya Jammeh, in Banjul. In December, dozens of Nigerians were killed in the CAR capital, Bangui, in a wave of sectarian violence, triggering the flight of hundreds of Nigerians in the weeks that followed.

On 24 February, Jonathan received Brazil's President Dilma Rouseff; on 24 September he addressed the 68th UN General Assembly in New York and, on 5 November, at a meeting in Abuja, he assured the president of the ICC, Sang-Hyun Song, that Nigeria would not withdraw from the court's jurisdiction. He travelled to France in early December for a two-day summit on peace and security in Africa hosted by President Hollande, and attended the funeral of Nelson Mandela shortly thereafter. On 17 October, Nigeria was elected as a non-permanent member of the **UNSC** for the two-year period 2014–15 in recognition of its role in peacekeeping operations.

Socioeconomic Developments

Nigeria enjoyed high oil and gas prices the whole year round and benefited strongly from its high quality crude, which was sold at well above the $ 100 per barrel mark. Foreign reserves were kept stable at more than $ 43 bn throughout the year. External debt stood at $ 6.5 bn and domestic debt amounted to $ 41.5 bn. The external **debt stock** of the 36 federal states and the FCT stood at $ 2,384 bn, in which Lagos state led the debtors list with more than $ 600 m of debt, while Borno state had the lowest debt stock at $ 14 m. The 2013 budget, totalling NGN 4.987 trillion ($ 31.6 bn) was transmitted to the president on 15 January and he signed the appropriation act into law on 26 February, albeit reluctantly. By signing it at the eleventh hour, he forestalled the likely passing of the budget without his agreement by a two-thirds majority of both chambers of the National Assembly. Though he had identified some grey areas in the document, these were eventually dealt with by the passing of an amendment bill on 25 July, ending months of disagreement. The budget was based on an average oil price of $ 79 a barrel, against the president's original proposal of $ 75, and an assumed production level of 2.5 m b/d. This was a rather over-optimistic figure, given the welter of political and production problems in the Niger Delta, an average exchange rate of NGN 160 to $ 1 and **GDP growth** of 6.75%.

The frequent disputes over the **annual budget** even led to the cancelling of the president's 2014 budget speech just before it was due to be given on 19 November. The budget framework was aimed at reducing the budget by some 6% to NGN 4.6 trillion and set the oil bench mark price at $ 74 a barrel, well below the $ 77.5 eventually proposed by the National Assembly and eventually agreed upon by the executive. Finally, on 19 December, Ms Ngozi Okonjo-Iweala, coordinating minister for economy and finance, presented the federal budget for the 2014 fiscal year separately before the two chambers of the National Assembly.

On 21 February, ahead of the formal launch of the $ 1 bn **Sovereign Wealth Fund** (SWF) on 1 March, to be composed of the stabilisation, infrastructure and future generation funds and managed by the internationally known investment banker Uche Orji, the federal government appointed leading international financial services firm JP Morgan as the fund's custodian. On 19 September, the president inaugurated the SWF council with himself as chairman. Other members were the 36 state governors, the minister of the FCT, the attorney general and the top federal representatives dealing with fiscal matters. On 2 July, the Nigerian government issued a € 1 bn Eurobond, half in five-year and half in ten-year **bonds** with yields of 5.3% and 6.6%, respectively. The issue was four times over-subscribed. Barely two months later, on 27 August, the International Islamic Liquidity Management Cooperation (IILM), a Malaysian-based consortium of central banks including Nigeria's, issued a $ 490 m Sukuk, the Islamic equivalent of bonds. IILM was founded in 2010 to develop a cross-border market in Islamic financial instruments.

After a cautious start in 2012, the government made concrete efforts to halt further deterioration in the **power sector**. Long-standing wilful neglect had led to an annual import of generators worth some $ 160 m, which made Nigeria one of the leading importers worldwide. A new round of privatisation efforts took off in March and prospective investors started bidding for power assets. In early September, United Bank for Africa announced that, in the current year, it had already invested $ 700 m in power assets in Nigeria alone, claiming that a further $ 1.2 bn would be earmarked within the next three years. In addition to these investments, on 17 October, the Lagos state government inaugurated the 10.4 MW Alausa power project, run on natural gas and intended to supply power to the state secretariat in Alausa and its environs. It was set up as a public-private partnership and developed by the well-known local company Oando and Fidelity Bank. One way or another, the privatisation exercise was completed by the end of October, and the federal government had collected some $ 2.7 bn from successful bidders. Soon afterwards, core investors began to complain about the operational challenges facing them, but the federal government nevertheless went ahead in October with plans to establish a solar energy sector in nine northern states, to be implemented within five years by the Nigerian-German Energy Partnership, Renewable Energy and Efficient Energy Projects. This scheme was expected to have a capacity of 500 MW.

On 4 September, the Nigerian tycoon Aliko Dangote and his Dangote Group signed an agreement worth $ 9 bn with a consortium of local banks and foreign investors, to build a refinery and a petrochemical complex in the Southwest. The long-awaited privatisation of Nigeria's four **refineries**, allegedly directed by the president, was eventually announced by the Bureau of Public Enterprises on 24 December, but took a new twist at year's end. After it became known that the two trade unions involved in the oil and gas sector were threatening industrial action over the planned privatisation exercise, the government back-pedalled. Towards the end of the year, for the umpteenth time, the start of work on the Mambilla **hydroelectric power plant** in the mountainous area of Taraba state, close to the Cameroon border, was once again delayed.

The **road safety situation** went from bad to worse. According to the Federal Road Safety Commission, more than 1,900 lives were lost on Nigeria's trunk roads between January and June. During the festive period in December alone, 252 people died in traffic accidents. The worst accident happened at Ugbogui Village in Edo state, when, on 5 April, 70 people were burned to death following the collision of a luxury coach, a tanker and a van. In addition, the aviation sector suffered another setback on 3 October, when an aircraft carrying the body of the late governor of Ondo state, Olusegun Agagu, crashed on take-off at Lagos airport. Most of the 13 passengers died.

On 16 December, the Academic Staff Union of Universities suspended its five-month strike after the federal government backed down and disbursed NGN 200 m to revitalise the **university** infrastructure. The government also promised to progressively increase the education sector's budgetary allocation.

On 10 February, the Nigerian national football team, the Super Eagles, won the **Africa Cup of Nations** in South Africa, defeating Burkina Faso 1–0, 19 years after their previous win; they also qualified to compete in the FIFA World Cup in Brazil in 2014. In addition, on 8 November, the Nigerian under-17 team sealed its fourth World Cup title by beating

Mexico 3-0. Last but not least, on 11 August at the International Association of Athletics Federations World Championships in Moscow (Russia), Blessing Okagbare won the silver medal in the women's long jump, becoming the first African woman to win a World Championship medal in this event.

On 21 March, the world-famous writer **Chinua Achebe**, passed away at the age of 83 in Boston in the US. Achebe, the most widely read African author on the continent, who was seriously disabled following a car accident in 1990, first gained international attention for his novel 'Things Fall Apart', published in 1958. He was buried on 23 May in Ogidi, his birthplace, now in Anambra state.

Heinrich Bergstresser

Senegal

The first year of Macky Sall's presidency, which began in March 2012, was widely scrutinised. Following the euphoria of his triumphant election, the Senegalese population attributed great importance to the improvement of their living conditions. After his electoral promises to instil a new morality in the political arena and adopt social reforms, Sall was challenged to prove that he could break out of the controversial mode of government of his predecessor, Abdoulaye Wade. The international community warmly welcomed his commitment to 'good governance' and Senegal's restored international image allowed Sall to engage in active diplomacy at the sub-regional and international levels. However, his ambitious economic policies met with uneven success, and the government struggled with the improvement of living conditions and unemployment issues.

Domestic Politics

Having shored up the relevant administrative apparatus, the government went full-swing into an **anti-corruption drive**. A public audit in the course of the year resulted in the identification of 121,754 civil servants, 12,221 cases in which the status of public employees was unclear, and 1,017 cases of non-employed civil servants who were in fact not working. By 21 December, the government had recuperated CFAfr 48 bn in wrongly paid salaries, while it also sought to discontinue paying civil servants' housing expenses. The 'Office National de Lutte contre les Fraudes et la Corruption' was provided with a CFAfr 500 bn budget and extended powers, although its director Nafi Ngom Keïta, a former inspector-general, was only appointed on 27 July.

While President Sall gave assurances that he would not engage in a witch-hunt against officials in Wade's administration, the 'Cour pour la Répression de l'Enrichissement Illicite' (CREI) began proceedings against Karim Wade, **son of the former president** and powerful minister of energy, as well as against seven other senior officials, businessmen and journalists. Karim Wade and his alleged accomplices were charged with the embezzlement of state funds during his father's presidency. They were all extensively questioned and, although Minister of Justice Aminata Touré said they were "simple witnesses", they were not allowed to leave the country. (The ECOWAS Court of Justice ruled on 22 February that this decision was illegal.) On 15 March, Karim Wade was ordered to account for the source of his assets, property (cars, real estate) and bank accounts, valued at CFAfr 694 bn. On 15 April, he was charged with having 'biens mal acquis' (illicit assets) and two days later was placed in detention in the Rebeuss prison in Dakar. His co-accused included Aboukhalil Bourgi, Mbaye Ndiaye, Alioune Samba Diassé, Alioune Konaré, Pape Mamadou Pouye, Pierre Agboba and Cheikh Diallo, but most of them were discharged or temporarily released on health grounds. CREI officials seized Karim Wade's bank accounts in Senegal on 27 May and in Monaco on 24 June, and Dubai Ports World Dakar, SHS Senegal, ABS Senegal and Blackpearl were placed under administrative supervision as fictitious companies on 5 June and 21 September. On 10 June, the CREI launched major investigations in France, Morocco and Luxemburg, and, on 30 October, in Lebanon, which, however, refused to cooperate. On 3 September French NGO Sherpa filed a complaint against Karim Wade and his sister Sindiely at the 'Tribunal de Grande Instance' in Paris alleging ill-gotten gains. Karim Wade's lawyers filed a second complaint with the ECOWAS Court concerning his arrest, arguing that the CREI had no valid status. Dismissing their demand on 19 July, the Court declared that it did not have the jurisdiction to examine the conformity of Senegalese law with the country's international obligations. On 17 October, at the end of the legal period of six months permitted to run the investigation, the CREI issued a controversial second indictment against Karim Wade, while continuing extensive interviews of former officials. On 25 October, Wade's lawyers filed a third complaint with the Dakar Court of Appeals to invalidate the judicial proceedings against their client, and the hearing took place on 17 December. As he was receiving an increasing number of visits by political, religious and other dignitaries, Wade's visiting rights were restricted on 2 July.

On 24 April and again on 9 October, the opposition 'Parti Démocratique Sénégalais (PDS, Wade's party) and support groups including the 'Mouvement Libérez Karim' and 'Ass-Kaw' organised mass demonstrations in Dakar, presenting Wade as a credible candidate for the 2017 presidential elections. All the way through this judicial and political turmoil, the PDS continued to be subject to internal divisions, with party members criticising Oumar Sarr for taking over the PDS leadership. In the aftermath of the 2012 election defeat, former president Wade had appointed him 'national coordinator' to act as his deputy during his stay in France. As a result of the **PDS leadership struggle**, a few more officials left the party, often to join the ruling 'Alliance pour la République' (APR). Though his son had been in jail since April, former president Wade did not return to Senegal during the year but sent his wife instead, and travelled himself to Arab countries in the Gulf region (September) and the West African sub-region (December).

On 26 May, Sall initiated a 'Consultation Nationale sur la Réforme des Institutions' headed by Makhtar Mbow (the emblematic figurehead of the 'Assises Nationales' in 2008–9) to gather opinions and proposals on possible constitutional reforms. MPs adopted an amendment to the nationality code on 28 June, which was seen as a step towards gender equality. The new law allowed Senegalese women with foreign husbands to pass their nationality to their husband and children, as long as the marriage had lasted for five years.

However, several **political scandals** spoiled the image of good governance that President Sall was trying to establish. Abdoulaye Niang, director of the national police and former head of the police narcotics unit, was accused of selling drugs to a mafia network and was relieved of his duties on 25 July. In addition, from April, the media began to accuse the president and his wife of nepotism after members of their families were appointed to powerful executive, administrative and diplomatic posts. The chief of the media group Walfadjri, Sidy Lamine Niasse, went even further, asserting that the president possessed illegal assets. As a result, Niasse was taken into custody on 31 December.

Despite his political determination in fighting corruption and pursuing a new model of government, Sall was criticised for his inability to see through in-depth reform. The energy crisis remained unresolved and lasted throughout the year. **Major blackouts** occurred in January, April and August. The Chinese company Citic/Te offered on 29 May to work with the 'Société Nationale d'Electricité au Sénégal' to improve the situation. Both the centre and suburbs of Dakar suffered from **water shortages** in September, leading to serious problems for residents and institutions such as health centres. As several city districts, including Niarry Tally, Keur Massar, Parcelles Assainies and Grand-Yoff, were hit by vandalism and looting at this time, Sall, who was in New York for the UN General Assembly, hurried back home. Although the situation was described by Energy Minister Pape Diouf as a "simple incident", it took at least a month before the water supply returned to normal.

Unrest spread and hardened, affecting various social sectors. On 9 April, the 'Concertation Nationale de l'Enseignement Supérieur' – a meeting of MPs, teachers' unions and parents' associations headed by Souleymane Bachir Diagne, a renowned scholar – published a list of proposed reforms to the **educational sector**, including the development of public/private partnerships, the rationalisation of grant allocations and an increase in tuition fees. The following day, students went on strike to protest against what they called the privatisation of universities. A new 'Conseil Présidentiel sur l'Enseignement Supérieur et la Recherche' decided on 14 August to increase tuition fees to amounts ranging from CFAfr 25,000 for the first year of undergraduate study to CFAfr 75,000 a year for postgraduate doctoral programmes. In response, on 22 November students ransacked the office of the university chancellor and, on 17 December, students prevented the holding of the first forum between Dakar University and private companies, which was to have been attended by Minister of Higher Education and Research Mary Teuw Niane.

Because of these social and political tensions, Sall went for several **cabinet reshuffles**. On 14 February, Minister of Commerce, Industry and the Informal Sector El Malick Gackou (the number two in Moustapha Niasse's 'Alliance des Forces du Progrès') was replaced by Alioune Sarr of the same party. On 1 September, Prime Minister Abdoul Mbaye was succeeded by Aminata Touré, until then justice minister. Mbaye had come under attack for his past defence of the interests of the former Chadian dictator, Hissène Habré, who was in exile in Senegal. Moreover, Mbaye was considered a potential rival for the presidency in the 2017 elections. Sall's appointment of Touré, described as an 'iron lady' with a Trotskyist past, was an astute political choice. She had headed the UN Population Fund (2003–10), and as justice minister had shown her ability to take charge of the CREI ill-gotten gains proceedings, returning CFAfr 30 bn to the treasury. The second female prime minister since independence, Touré expanded her cabinet from 25 to 32 ministers, appointing, amongst others, Sidiki Kaba, a human rights activist, as the new minister of justice. Her policy speech in the National Assembly on 29 October was in line with Sall's programme 'Yoonu Yokkute' (Path of True Development). She called for national cohesion and stressed the need for the government to respond to social demands, boost the economy and reinforce the rule of law. She underlined the need to focus especially on agriculture and youth.

On 4 December at a government seminar, Sall presented his 'Plan Sénégal Emergent' (PSE), designed as a major economic roadmap intended to raise the growth rate to 7% and achieve sustainable development. Several cabinet ministers expressed strong reservations about the PSE, calling it unrealistic and unfeasible.

Relations within the **government coalition** were difficult. Ibrahima Sall, minister of education under ex-prime minister Mbaye, strongly criticised the president for excluding from government the 'Macky2012' party leaders (who had helped win his election victory). In July, he urged the president to break with the majority coalition 'Benno Bokk Yakaar' (BBY), including Moustapha Niasse of the APR and Ousmane Tanor Dieng of the 'Parti Socialiste', which had supported him during the second round of the presidential election. In turn, the BBY leaders criticised the president's record and his inability to achieve meaningful political results. Some important figures left the BBY coalition: Cheikh Tidiane Gadio on 8 April, Idrissa Seck on 12 September, Ibrahima Fall on 14 September and Youssou Ndour on 16 November. Gadio, Seck and Fall decided to run in the 2014 local elections on their own ticket. Although Sall and his ruling APR reiterated on 24

November their commitment to both coalitions – BBY and 'Macky2012' – Seydou Guèye, the APR spokesman and the government secretary-general, announced on 27 November the creation of a new 'Alliance pour la Majorité Présidentielle', supposedly to resolve the conflicts between the majority coalitions. At the same time, ahead of the 2014 local elections, relations between APR leaders such as Cissé Lô, Mor Ngom, Mahmout Saleh and Alioune Badara Cissé were marred by growing disagreement. On 5 December, members of 'Y'en a marre', a civil society movement that had helped Sall to his election victory in 2012, issued a statement criticising the lack of change since the advent of the new government and, on 23 December, civil society groups such as the 'Forum Civil' and the 'Mouvement du 23 Juin' called attention to issues of corruption.

Sall's decision on 10 October to **postpone** the **local elections** originally scheduled for 16 March 2014 also drew strong criticism. According to Prime Minister Touré, a delay of a few months would help the implementation of 'Acte 3' of the decentralisation reform programme. On 3 December, the government adopted a decree extending the mandate of the counsellors elected in 2009 at the municipal and regional level and rescheduled the elections for 29 June 2014. The distribution of voter registration cards began on 16 December. The PDS and Idrissa Seck's party, 'Rewmi', called for respect for the electoral schedule and accused the president of political manipulation.

Sall continued to maintain good relations with the main **marabouts leaders**. He paid homage on January 16 to the Sufi brotherhood, warning citizens against the dangers of extremism. Although Sall seemed to keep his distance with regard to marabouts more than Wade had, the Murid brotherhood, during the Magal public holiday (23 December), called on people to support the president in his endeavours. Pro-Wade Murid leader Cheikh Béthio Thioune, in prison since April 2012 on suspicion of complicity in the killing of two disciples, was temporarily released for health reasons and sent on 6 February to France for hospital treatment. Three of his co-accused were set free on 11 September, and although he returned to Senegal on 4 November to await trial, he was not sent back to jail. On 3 March, nine children died in a fire started in a Qur'an school, or 'daara', in Dakar city, alerting the public once more to the precarious conditions endured by young students in such places.

Regarding the continuing **separatist conflict** in the south-western **Casamance** region, Sall announced his determination to continue the dialogue with the rebels of the 'Mouvement des Forces Démocratiques de Casamance' (MFDC). Five people, including three civilians, died in an attack by unidentified rebels in Kafoutine on 2 February. The mediator from the Catholic organisation Sant'Egidio claimed on 13 April that there was no international arrest warrant against Salif Sadio, the most radical leader in the multi-factioned MFDC. As a result, on 16 April Ousmane Niantang Diatta called on his movement to introduce a third cease-fire and lay down their arms. Though the situation seemed to be improving, 12 hostages held by the MFDC remained a problematic issue. The MFDC conditions for negotiations included a demand that the government stop demining in areas occupied by the separatist movement. On 28 May, three female hostages were released and negotiations started on 11 November between the government and the MFDC in Rome, mediated by Sant'Egidio.

Foreign Affairs

After the electoral turmoil of 2012, President Sall aspired to restore Senegal's international image. He launched 20 joint commissions to improve relationships with foreign partners. The international community responded positively to the opening of the long-awaited trial of Chad's ex-president Habré, as well as to the anti-corruption drive. Numerous official visits and Senegal's participation in the G8 and G20 summits demonstrated that the country's **foreign ties** were being **normalised** and that it was once again regarded as a valid partner in international affairs. Sall focused his high-profile diplomacy on neighbouring countries and economic cooperation.

In January, 500 troops were dispatched to **Mali**, and at the AU summit Sall announced that Senegal would contribute CFAfr 1 bn for the upkeep of the UN peacekeeping force, the 'Mission Multidimensionnelle Intégrée des Nations Unies pour la Stabilisation au Mali'. Sall attended the inauguration of Mali's new President Keita on 19 September, and Senegal also contributed to the election budget of Guinea-Bissau.

Elsewhere in the sub-region, Sall tried to normalise relations with neighbours. He was the guest of honour at **Gambia**'s national holiday celebrations on 18 February, and the two countries signed a memorandum of understanding on 9 September for the building of a bridge over the Gambia River. The project, funded with CFAfr 50 bn by the AfDB, was intended to boost trade and improve connections with the Casamance region. **Mauritania**'s President Ould Abdel Aziz visited Dakar on 10 September. One of the issues dividing the two countries involved fishing rights. On 26 February, a treaty was concluded granting a fishing quota of 40,000 tonnes of fish per year to Senegalese boats fishing in Mauritanian waters. On 10 May, Mauritania issued 300 three-month fishing licences, and on 11 December returned 150 boats seized earlier from Senegalese fishermen. Senegal also concluded an agreement with Mauritania for the construction of a bridge over the Senegal River in Rosso. **Morocco** agreed to fund it. Morocco's King Mohammed VI and President Sall met twice in March and July and established several cooperation agreements on issues such as mining, energy, shipping and trade.

Sall visited Burkina Faso and Namibia in July and August, respectively, and opened new embassies in Togo and Equatorial Guinea. During a visit to Dakar on 1 October, **South Africa**'s President Zuma signed cooperation agreements on agriculture, energy, environmental issues and military cooperation. The two countries also discussed a twinning arrangement between Gorée and Robben Island. As a mark of his active sub-regional diplomacy, Sall was appointed coordinator of the ECOWAS Peace and Security Project and chairman of the policy committee of NEPAD heads of state and government. He also took charge of supervising EPA negotiations with the EU, in the framework of ECOWAS.

Sall tried to broaden his diplomacy towards **emerging countries**, especially with regard to economic issues. Talks with Turkey's Prime Minister Erdoğan, who visited Dakar in January, bore on the question of external debt, the abolition of Turkish visas for Senegalese citizens, and the boosting of trade exchanges, which were expected to reach CFAfr 125 bn by 2015. On the occasion of the Doha Forum in May, Senegal and Qatar signed an agreement against double taxation and tax evasion, and debated quotas for Senegalese skilled workers and opportunities for Qatari private investment. On 6 November, China and Senegal signed a CFAfr 8.8 bn economic and technical agreement, including an interest-free loan of CFAfr 3.2 bn.

Invited to the White House in March with three other African leaders, Sall had a private meeting with **President Obama**. A few months later, Obama chose Senegal as one of his African tour destinations. During his visit on 26–28 June, Obama acknowledged Senegal's democratic track record and its on-going struggle to increase transparency and crack down on corruption. He called Senegal "one of the strongest partners in the region", which is plagued by terrorism, military coups and transnational crime. Accompanied by a 600-member delegation, Obama pleaded for boosting economic ties between the US and Africa. He expressed concern over development issues and guaranteed that USAID would invest CFAfr 400 bn in the country by 2015. The controversial issue of gay rights came up during the press conference. While Obama reminded people of the principles of equality under the law and human rights, Sall replied that "Senegal is a very tolerant country" where "homosexuals are not being prosecuted, persecuted", but that its society was "not ready to decriminalise homosexuality". He very subtly explained that countries may have different views as a result of their differences in culture and religion, and he pointedly reminded Obama that Senegal had ten years earlier abolished the death penalty while in other countries capital punishment was "still the order of the day", a statement warmly welcomed by public opinion.

France and Senegal confirmed their close relationship. On 17 July, Jean Félix Paganon, formerly French special envoy in the Sahel, took over as the new French ambassador to Senegal, his predecessor Nicolas Normand being considered too close to former president Wade. In return, Senegal appointed Paul Badji as ambassador in Paris. Sall was hosted twice by President Hollande, in March and December. He secured special assistance for decentralisation to the tune of CFAfr 1.5 and € 60 m as budget support over a 25-year period. He secured special assistance for decentralisation to the tune of CFAfr 1.5 bn and budget support of € 60 m over a 25-year period. On the occasion of the French home secretary's visit to Dakar on 15 November, the two countries signed a funding convention for a new plan against terrorism (PACT) to the tune of about € 700,000. Sall took part in the Elysée summit on peace and security in Africa held in Paris on 6–7 December, in the course of which he pleaded for the establishment of an African Rapid Reaction Force.

Socioeconomic Developments

Overall macroeconomic performance was judged satisfactory. **Growth** reached 4%, compared with 3.5% in 2012. Inflation fell from 1.4% to 0.7%. The deficit decreased, reaching an estimated CFAfr 408.3 bn (according to the Ministry of Economy and Finance). The country improved its budgetary balance as public expenditure fell faster (– 0.9%) than public revenue (– 0.4%). Expenditure decreased from CFAfr 2,090 bn in 2012 to CFAfr 2,072.1 bn, mainly thanks to reductions in running costs. Despite recurrent announcements by the Treasury about the refunding of internal and external **debt**, the outstanding discounted debt remained high: 46.7% of GDP, compared with 42.9% in 2012. Public revenue decreased slightly because grants were lower than the exceptionally high amounts received in 2012. In fact, excluding the 'Fonds de Soutien au secteur de l'Energie' and grants, revenues increased. The reduction in income tax introduced in 2012 was balanced by growing customs duties and corporate taxes. The revised Finance Act even showed a growth in non-tax revenues, thanks to royalties paid by Dubai Port World (CFAfr 24 bn) and Millicom (CFAfr 11 bn). By year's end, the introduction of visas for foreigners on 1 July had yielded CFAfr 1.4 bn.

The budget was mainly devoted to fostering agricultural production, developing transport and telecommunications **infrastructure**, improving energy management and reinforcing decentralisation and local governance. Year-end resources were allocated to education, health and the civil service. The government carried on its provision of farming supplies in the form of subsidies for seeds (CFAfr 5 bn) and fertilizers (CFAfr 13.8 bn). The budget of the Ministry of Agriculture and Rural Planning rose by 45%. February saw the launch of a CFAfr 14 bn programme to build 1,000 km of roads and trails and 29 bridges. Other projects involved the extension of the VDN ring road in Dakar and of the inner-city highway as far as the new international airport in Diamniadio. In order to speed up these projects, the government signed several procurement contracts through over-the-counter market agreements ('marché de gré à gré'), by-passing the 'Code des Marchés Publics'. This practice was firmly criticised by the 'Syndicat National du Bâtiment et des Travaux Publics', as well as by the IMF. In contrast, normal procedures for the construction of two piers in Dakar harbour were respected. In November, the authorities awarded the contract to French conglomerate Bolloré.

The primary sector maintained itself thanks to a good **groundnut harvest**, livestock development, and growth in cotton, fruit and vegetables, and industrial fisheries. Local **fishermen** were protected by a freeze on licences for foreign industrial trawlers, which compensated for the difficulties faced by the artisanal sector in its conflict with the Mauritanian authorities. The tertiary sector picked up, thanks to telecommunications (+7.9%), transport (+10%) and services (+4.5%), although **tourism** still suffered from the effects of the global recession, despite a huge investment to the tune of CFAfr 200 bn made through the 'Société d'Aménagement et de Promotion des Côtes et Zones Touristiques'.

The secondary sector performed poorly: **industrial production** fell by 4.7%. Only the building materials industry was booming (+11.5%) and, more modestly, the power sector (+2%). Mining, chemicals and industrial food production plummeted (down by 19.6%, 16.7%, and 7.1%, respectively). Industrial breakdowns, the rising cost of raw materials and uncontrolled food imports were partly to blame. The government reacted by freezing sugar and onion imports and imposing a ban on scrap iron imports. In July, it also created a CFAfr 20 bn 'Fonds de Restructuration'. Subsidies to the energy sector still represented 2% of GDP.

These measures did not settle the structural trade deficit, estimated at CFAfr 1,791.7 bn, but contributed to efforts to reduce the **cost of living**. The authorities decided to impose a ceiling on the price of key consumer goods such as rice, sugar, cooking oil and vegetable milk. A dispute between millers and bakers over the price of bread led to a strike-call by bakers in February. The government intervened and set the price of flour and standards for the weight of bread. Prices for other staple products such as onions, tomatoes, meat, cooking gas and energy increased.

With 80% of the population having no access to **healthcare**, President Sall launched on 20 September a programme called 'Couverture Maladie Universelle'. On 1 October, Minister of Health and Social Action Awa Marie Coll Seck announced the introduction of free healthcare for children under five. In December, the special commission on **rents** issued its report, which recommended state regulation of rents. **Unemployment** remained the most sensitive and challenging issue. In February, three ministers visiting the president's electoral heartland, Kaolack, were pelted with stones by young people claiming jobs that had been pledged during the 2012 election campaign. Unemployed graduates organised sit-ins and marches all year round. Peddlers and squatters were evicted from the main commercial roads of Dakar and the area of the airport, causing unrest. Sall renewed his commitment to create 30,000 jobs for young people and 5,500 jobs in the civil service by the end of the year. On 20 February, thousands of candidates gathered at the 'Building Administratif' to apply for a civil service job, causing chaos. The Ministry of Youth launched two programmes, 'kiosque emploi' (February) and 'accueil emploi' (December), in order to assist job seekers.

Emmanuelle Bouilly & Marie Brossier

Sierra Leone

Following victory in the previous year's elections, incumbent President Koroma started the year with the inauguration of his new cabinet. The first year of his second term brought some exceptional GDP growth figures – among the highest in Africa – which were expected to remain so for the rest of his five-year term. This was mainly due to the ever expanding mineral extraction industry, which saw large injections of FDI. However, the challenge to turn this into poverty alleviation for the broad population remained. In September, the Appeals Chamber of the Special Court for Sierra Leone upheld the 50-year prison sentence imposed on Charles Taylor. The following month, he started serving his sentence in the UK. This brought to an end – after 11 years – one of the central elements of Sierra Leone's post-war transitional justice process.

Domestic Politics

Following the November 2012 elections, which brought victory to incumbent President Ernest Bai Koroma, he appointed the first 16 ministers of his **new cabinet** on 5 January. Sahr Sam-Sumana became vice-president. Other key positions were taken by Samura Kamara (foreign affairs) and Kaifala Marah (finance and economic development), while Momodu Kargbo and Alhaji F.B.L. Mansaray were both appointed ministers of state.

In Sierra Leone, the president is commander in chief of the armed forces, but the position of minister of defence was allocated to Alfred Paolo Conteh. J.B. Dauda became minister of internal affairs and Frank Kargbo the new justice minister and attorney-general. The challenge of achieving balanced and sustainable economic development – a significant one given that per capita GDP remained one of the lowest in the world although GDP growth was at the same time projected to remain in double figures in the coming years – was the responsibility of a number of ministries. New appointments (or in some cases re-appointments) were as follows: Alhaji Osman Boie Kamara was appointed minister of trade and industry, Oluniyi Robbin-Coker became the new minister of energy and Momodu Maligi was made responsible for water resources. A.P. Koroma took up the works, housing and infrastructural development post (but was sacked on 19 October) and Diana Konomanyi became responsible for local government and rural development.

The new minister for transport and aviation was V.C. Minah, but he was appointed Sierra Leone's permanent representative to the UN on 7 June and was replaced in the cabinet by Balogun Koroma. Captain M.A. Pat-Sowe, the new minister of marine resources and fisheries, faced the challenge of fighting illegal trawler fishing by foreign countries in Sierra Leone's waters. The two pillars of economic development in Sierra Leone remained agriculture, which employed the majority of the working population, and mining, which made by far the largest contribution to GDP. These pivotal ministries were allocated to Alhaji Minkailu Mansaray (mines and mineral resources) and J. Sam Sesay (agriculture, food security and forestry). The more social-development-oriented posts were taken by Alhaji A.B.S. Kanu (information and communications), Miatta Kargbo (health and sanitation), Moijueh Kaikai (social welfare, gender and children's affairs), Minkailu Bah (education, science and technology) and Musa Tarawally (lands, country planning and the environment).

In addition, three resident ministers were appointed to cover provincial affairs: William Juana Smith (East), Muctarr Conteh (South) and Alie D. Kamara (North). The following month, Koroma completed his cabinet with the announcement of ministers for the remaining posts. **Koroma was inaugurated** during a ceremony held at the national stadium on 22 February.

The **Special Court for Sierra Leone**, established by the government of Sierra Leone and the UN in 2002 with the task of trying persons charged with bearing the greatest responsibility for serious human rights violations during the civil war, entered its final year of operation. For the previous four years, the only significant case on its books was that of the Liberian warlord-turned-president, Charles Taylor. The year started with an incident concerning one of the Court's investigators. On 25 January, Prince Taylor (no relative), a former Special Court defence investigator, was found guilty on five counts of interfering with Special Court witnesses. Four of the charges were that he had "otherwise interfered" with prosecution witnesses who had testified against Charles Taylor. It was alleged that, through former Revolutionary United Front (RUF) member Eric Koi

Senessie, he had attempted to induce the four witnesses to recant their testimony. The fifth charge was that Prince Taylor had interfered with Eric Koi Senessie at a time when he was a potential witness in contempt proceedings before the Chamber. On 8 February, he was sentenced to two-and-a-half years in prison, but he appealed on 4 June and on 30 October his contempt conviction was overturned by a majority of the three-judge panel of the Appeals Chamber.

On 22 January, lawyers for the prosecution and defence presented their final arguments in **Charles Taylor's case** before the Appeals Chamber, and on 26 September the Appeals Chamber unanimously upheld both his conviction and his sentence. On 15 October, Taylor was transferred from the Netherlands and the custody of the Special Court to the UK, where he started to serve the remainder of his 50-year sentence for war crimes and crimes against humanity. Britain was the only country that had offered and accepted to enforce the remainder of Taylor's sentence.

On 2 December, the government and the UN formally **closed the Special Court** at a ceremony hosted by the president at State House in Freetown. Under-Secretary-General for Legal Affairs and UN Legal Counsel Miguel de Serpa Soares, representing the UN secretary-general, praised the historic day as "very much a landmark, not only for the Special Court, but also for international criminal justice in general". On the same day, 16 judges of the Residual Special Court for Sierra Leone were elected, including the new president of the Court, Justice Philip Waki of Kenya. Justice Waki took over from Justice George Gelaga King of Sierra Leone, who had been elected on 4 June to succeed Justice Shireen Avis Fisher of the USA.

On 27 July, Ibrahim Bah, a.k.a. Ibrahim Baldeh, from Senegal was **deported from Sierra Leone** to his home country. Bah was a former ally of Charles Taylor. Earlier, on 31 May, a UN panel of experts report had found that he had supplied arms to the RUF. Justice Minster Frank Kargbo – formerly the executive secretary of Sierra Leone's Truth and Reconciliation Commission – stated that the government preferred deportation because there was insufficient evidence for a successful prosecution. However, a local human rights group, the Centre for Accountability and Rule of Law, acting on behalf of a group of civil war victims, expressed surprise and dismay with regard to the deportation, having expected Bah to be in court on 5 August to answer charges.

The trial of former deputy education minister Mahmoud Tarawally, accused of raping a 24 year old university student, was ongoing. This high-profile case underlined the omnipresence of sexual violence. In the first eight months of the year nearly 7,000 incidents of domestic and **gender-based violence** were reported. However, only 6% resulted in a conviction, although this was a significant improvement compared with 2012. According to Charles Vandi, director of gender affairs at the Ministry of Social Welfare, difficulties in enforcing the 2012 sexual offences law were related to inadequate staffing and training of the relevant police body, the Family Support Unit. High costs associated with court cases and the overstretched state of the court system also contributed to the low conviction rate.

In October, Jonathan Leigh, editor of the newspaper 'Independent Observer', and Bai Bai Sesay, a journalist, were arrested following publication of an article in which President Koroma was compared to a rat. Until then, Koroma's government had been marked by considerable **press freedom**, but in response to these arrests Kelvin Lewis, president of the Sierra Leone Association of Journalists, stated that the government's human right record was beginning to deteriorate.

Endemic **corruption** remained a key concern. TI's Global Corruption Barometer 2013 showed that Sierra Leone was the country where the highest number of respondents (84%) admitted to having paid a bribe. Together with Liberia (75%), Sierra Leone was one of only two out of 95 countries surveyed that scored above 75%. The world average was 27%.

Foreign Affairs

On 25 March Koroma, as commander in chief of the armed forces, gave a farewell statement to an infantry battalion of 850 soldiers who were about to be sent to Somalia as part of the African Union Mission in Somalia. He then left for the USA for talks with President Barack Obama at the White House on 28 March, which focused on ways to strengthen African economies and promote democratic values. Also at the meeting were the leaders of Senegal, Malawi and Cape Verde. In early June, Koroma attended the Tokyo International Conference on African development in Yokohama, **Japan**.

In October, Koroma met with the British Minister for Africa Mark Simmonds, at State House in Freetown. The **British government** had been the country's single largest bilateral donor since the end of the war and provided support for the building up of governance institutions, the police and the military. On 7 November, a high-powered delegation from **China**'s Communist Party visited the offices of the ruling All People's Congress and met President Koroma, who expressed continued support for the 'One China' policy (meaning recognition of mainland China, not Taiwan). China remained the country's single largest foreign investor.

On 6 December, the president attended the **Peace and Security Summit** hosted by French President François Hollande in Paris, which brought together more than 40 African leaders. Topics discussed included tackling youth unemployment and combating growing transnational crimes and piracy in the Horn of Africa and the Gulf of Guinea. The president concluded a year of foreign trips when he and a high-profile entourage attended the memorial service for the late Nelson Mandela in South Africa, on 10 December.

Socioeconomic Developments

The number of **cholera** victims was significantly lower than in 2012 – not uncommon for an infectious disease that usually follows a two-year cycle. Less than 400 cases were reported during the rainy season, as compared with 20,000 cases the previous year. Nevertheless, access to improved **sanitation** was still a luxury enjoyed by less than 13% of the population. Freetown in particular continued to be a high risk area according to the National Cholera Taskforce, with the capital's main water supplier, the Guma Valley Water Company, serving more than double the population their reservoirs were originally built to supply. Following heavy rains, a colonial-era bridge in Freetown collapsed on 9 August, killing a number of people. The Jimmy Bridge was used heavily by both vehicles and pedestrians, including homeless people who frequently slept under it.

The slowly emerging tourism sector – heavily dependent on the pristine beaches of the Freetown peninsula – was increasingly suffering from illegal **sand-mining**, caused by the country's construction boom. According to Kolleh Bangura, the director of Sierra Leone's Environmental Protection Agency, "The police work[ed] 9am–5pm, so most of the mining now happen[ed] at night."

In the first half of 2013, a 43% increase was reported in diamond exports, up to $ 102 m, which provided the government more than $ 5 m in taxes. Just over 60% of the 331,471 carats exported in the first six months of the year was by Koidu Holdings, the only commercial pit miner in the country. To assure investors in the **mining industry** in the Mano River region, Sierra Leonean officials met with their Guinean, Liberian and Ivorian counterparts in London in June to discuss the alignment of their mining codes, tariffs and tax laws. Furthermore, to regulate the industry and make sure that at least $ 1.5 bn of the total revenue generated through mining was allocated to poverty reduction, Sierra Leone now had a fully functioning National Minerals Agency. In September, African Minerals (AM) received a $ 990 m cash injection from Chinese Tianjin Minerals and Equipment Group, in exchange for a 16.5% stake in AM's magnetite deposits in the Tonkolili district, which started production in late 2011. This was on top of the $ 1.5 bn investment in AM in 2012 by the Chinese Shandong Iron & Steel Group.

In November, six people, including policeman Perry Dolo, were arrested, for allegedly smuggling 297 kg of **marijuana** into Liberia. According to Liberia's Drug Enforcement Agency, Dolo had been caught with three others while heading the presidential motorcade 'Escort 1'. The other people arrested were a Liberian policeman, a Sierra Leonean officer, a businessman, a taxi driver and a former member of the armed forces.

Also in November, the EU's Court of Justice ruled that **homosexuals** from Sierra Leone, Uganda and Senegal who feared imprisonment in their home country had grounds for asylum in EU member states, Sierra Leone being among those African countries where consensual same-sex relations are illegal. In May, gay activist George Freeman, organiser of the Pride Equality group, was beaten up by two motorcyclists in Freetown, after a local newspaper printed his photograph and an article he had written about his sexuality for a foreign magazine in 2012. Inspector General of Police Munu said, "These [gays and lesbians] are very strange phenomena in our society and we do not have any special protection for them because they are not recognised by the laws of Sierra Leone." **Female genital mutilation** (FGM) was another taboo that could not be discussed openly. In June, the

International Development Committee published a report that showed that the FGM prevalence rate in women aged 15–19 was 75.5% and as high as 96.4% in women aged 35–39.

In September the NGO ActionAid released a damning report concerning the activities of the Addax **Bioenergy** project, approved in 2008 and expected to start exporting in 2014. About 14,300 ha were currently planted with sugar-cane in Bombali district, with the total lease covering 57,000 ha. When it reaches full capacity, the project should produce 85 m litres of ethanol a year, enough to meet 12% of Britain's ethanol consumption. But despite the fact that the project was promoted as socially and environmentally responsible, ActionAid found reasons for concern. Based on interviews with local community members in the areas affected by the Addax plantation, ActionAid concluded that the majority of respondents stated that: "hunger was prevalent in the Addax project area" (99%); "hunger was due to the loss of land to Addax" (90%) and "food production had declined in their communities" (99%). There was also dissatisfaction regarding Addax communication, with 78% stating that they had never seen the land lease agreement and 85% saying that the information on the advantages and disadvantages of Addax's investment was inadequate. The Addax project received significant funding from the Emerging Africa Infrastructure Fund.

Following a visit to China to attend the World Peace Forum, President Koroma announced on 5 July a series of **infrastructural works** to take place in the next few years at a total cost of $ 8 bn. The Chinese-funded projects included a $ 300 m deal with the Chinese Railway International Company to construct a new international airport, so that international visitors would no longer have to undertake the cumbersome journey from Lungi airport across the Sierra Leone River estuary to reach Freetown. A $ 1.7 bn deal was signed with Kingho Energy Group to build 250 km of railway track from Tonkolili to Sulima, a power plant, a mine and a port. In September, the Russian oil company LUKOIL started drilling 50 miles offshore. Expectations were high that they would strike oil in commercially viable quantities.

In July, Deputy Minister of Transport and Aviation Ibrahim Pat-Sowe visited the Isle of Man to thank the population for donating a fishing patrol vessel the previous year. It was the government's only patrol ship and was of key importance in the fight against **unauthorised trawler fishing** by foreign vessels. At the time of the visit, eight arrests had already been made and $ 400,000 worth of fines imposed. In October, the Environmental Justice Foundation claimed to have uncovered a case of illegal shipping of fish to Asia. A Korean-flagged vessel was detected fishing close to Sherbro Island and allegedly had 4,000 boxes of illegally caught fish on board.

GDP as forecast by the World Bank put Sierra Leone at the top of the list of African countries. **Growth** was about 17%, i.e., just 1% below the 2012 level, and with forecasts for 2014 and 2015 put at about 14% and 12%, respectively, GDP remained well into double figures. A booming mining industry, associated with multi-billion dollar foreign investments, was overwhelmingly responsible for the sound growth rate, but the majority of Sierra Leoneans had still not experienced anything of the trickle-down effect.

On 12 August, Sierra Leone launched its first ever UNDP-financed "Status of the Youth" report, providing a comprehensive overview of education, well-being, **youth employment**, and participation in the development process. Some of its key findings were that 60% of young women and men between the ages of 15 to 35 were unemployed, among the highest rates in West Africa, and 80% of youths were unable to earn enough to lift themselves and their families above the $ 2 per day poverty level. Because of the significant role of youth in the decade-long conflict, President Koroma identified youth unemployment as a security and development challenge.

Krijn Peters

Togo

Peaceful but undemocratic legislative elections consolidated the power of the Gnassingbé regime. In view of the absolute majority gained by the ruling party, its inclination to implement meaningful reforms, as demanded by the opposition and the donor community, was reduced further. The growing Islamist threats in neighbouring countries meant that the donor community condoned the delays in democratic reforms including the conduct of local elections, which were pushed back several times. Promising growth prospects were overshadowed by increasing poverty and inequality.

Domestic Politics

The new year was heralded by **two large fires**, which ravaged the central markets of Lomé and Kara on the night of 10–11 January. The famous Adawlato market halls in Lomé, a hub of local and international traders, were completely destroyed. No loss of life was reported but merchants and the population suspected politically motivated arson, in view of the coincidence of the two simultaneous fires and other circumstances. The government was quick to promise an impartial investigation, assisted by two French police experts who arrived on the spot soon afterwards. However, before the experts concluded their probe, the public prosecutor accused leaders of the opposition alliance 'Collectif Sauvons le Togo' (CST) of masterminding the blaze. Almost all the CST leaders were charged, most notably Zeus Ajavon, the CST co-ordinator, and 23 people were temporarily detained, including Agbéyomé Kodjo, former prime minister and leader of the opposition 'Organisation pour Bâtir dans l'Union un Togo Solidaire' (he was released on bail on 25 February), and CST vice-president Gérard Adja. Thus, the fires fanned political flames at the start of the campaign for the postponed legislative elections, originally due in October 2012. In early March, two more opposition leaders were charged, Jean Pierre Fabre, leader of the CST's principal component group 'Alliance Nationale pour le Changement' (ANC), and Frédéric Abass Kaboua, president of the 'Mouvement des Républicains Centristes'. They were questioned at length and banned from leaving Lomé, while their party headquarters and homes were searched.

The arrests triggered outrage, and the opposition organised **demonstrations** to protest against what it saw as a government attempt to discredit it ahead of the elections and to divert attention from the real political issues. As the much-awaited evaluation report of the French expert mission, promised for the end of February, was kept secret, the CST started its own investigations, but its final 19-page evaluation report arrived late, coming four months after the elections on 11 November; in its report, the opposition alliance accused eight regime officials of being the instigators of the fires. They included Ingrid Awadé, director general of customs and taxes, financial adviser to the cabinet and close intimate of President Faure Gnasingbé, and Colonel Félix Kadanga, then head of the army's Rapid Intervention Force (who in 2005 had been accused of the arson attack on the Goethe Institute in Lomé).

On 19–20 February, a meeting of government and opposition representatives took place in an attempt to overcome persistent differences over the technicalities concerning the conduct of the local and parliamentary elections, as had been originally agreed in the 2006 'Accord Politique Global' (APG). The meeting, in which all major donors took part, was facilitated by Archbishop Nicodème Barrigah, former president of the 'Commission Vérité, Justice et Réconciliation', and was organised by the US ambassador, Robert Whitehead. It focused on **electoral reforms**, and five major issues were discussed. First, the biased composition of the 'Commission Electorale Nationale Indépendante', whose 17 members included only three who belonged to the opposition. Second, electoral boundaries: a decree of 10 April on the division of parliamentary seats by constituency increased the number of National Assembly seats from 81 to 91, but this still ignored the imbalance between distribution of seats and population density in the northern constituencies – stronghold of the ruling 'Union pour la République' (UNIR). Third, the voting system, which since the 2002 constitutional coup had provided for a single-ballot in presidential elections, and which favoured the incumbent. Fourth, a limit to presidential terms: the APG provided for a return to the 1992 limitation of two consecutive terms, which had been cancelled in 2002. While the government agreed, it demanded that this rule be applied only from 2015 onwards. The opposition objected because this would allow Faure Gnassingbé to stand for a third and a fourth term. Fifth and finally, equitable access to the media for political parties. The debate on these issues did not lead to agreement, as the opposition saw consensus on these points as a precondition for the elections, while the government first wanted to await the outcome of the parliamentary polls.

Strikes during subsequent months by health workers and teachers demanding substantial pay increases led to school closures and developed political undercurrents as demonstrations by pupils met with violent suppression by the authorities. This escalated on 15 April with the shooting of a 12-year-old schoolboy in Dapaong, the northernmost prefectural capital, when the police tried to stop a crowd from storming a government building. The **unrest** spread to several areas.

Nevertheless, the government continued with preparations for the polls. Voter registration, completed in April, totalled 3.1 m voters out of a population of 6.6 m. The **legislative elections**, rescheduled for 24 March and then 21 July, finally took place on 25 July, although the electoral reforms had not been implemented. All in all 1,174 candidates, including 159 women, stood for 91 seats by means of a party list, with the seats to be allocated on the basis of proportional representation. The opposition, which had threatened a boycott up to 8 July, was again outwitted by the president and confronted with a Hobson's choice. Although it was always likely to be defeated in view of the biased electoral system, it had to participate if it wanted to retain some influence on future constitutional reforms, notably any extension of President Gnassingbé's mandate in the 2015 polls. As expected, the elections resulted in a landslide for UNIR, which won 62 out of 91 seats, a two-thirds majority. The CST came second with 19 seats and the moderate opposition coalition 'Arc-en-Ciel' was third with six. The 'Union des Forces de Changement' (UFC) of Gilchrist Olympio, the main opposition party until its 2010 coalition with the RPT ('Rassemblement du Peuple Togolais')/UNIR, was crushed, retaining just three of its 27 seats.

The results, contested by the opposition, were confirmed by the constitutional court on 12 August, although UNIR had won an absolute majority with fewer votes than the opposition; with 46.7% of the votes, they took 68.1% of Assembly seats. The CST became the only opposition party with the status of a parliamentary group (for which 10% of seats is the required minimum), and Fabre became **formal leader of the opposition**, providing him with greater prerogatives and benefits.

Local elections, scheduled to run concurrently with the parliamentary polls, were postponed *sine die*. On 4 November, the ANC accused the government of violating the constitution by continuing to appoint its favourites to the posts of municipal and prefectoral councillors. (They should have been elected, but the last local elections took place in 1987.) The ongoing postponement could be interpreted as another indication of the refusal of the ruling class to honour the obligations of the APG and the 22 commitments vis-à-vis the EU, entered into in 2004, towards democratising and decentralising political power.

On balance, the elections were not free and fair but were largely peaceful, which was hailed by leaders of the churches, Togolese Muslims and the international community. However, the decline in **voter turnout** from 85% in the previous legislative elections (2007) to 65.8% pointed to increasing dissatisfaction on the part of the electorate, as also exemplified by various evaluations of human development and happiness research.

On 2 September, UNIR's MPs unanimously elected one of their members, Dama Dramani, as **National Assembly chair**. An old regime stalwart who had served as minister and chief of protocol during the late General Eyadéma's presidency, Dramani succeeded Abass Bonfoh, who had occupied the Assembly office for the previous 11 years. The opposition boycotted his election. A **cabinet reshuffle** on 17 September reduced the number of ministers from 31 to 26, including six women. Kwesi-Ahoomey Zunu remained prime minister. The all but annihilated UFC, which had joined the cabinet of national unity in 2010, held on to only three of its former seven ministries. The rest of the opposition refused to join the government. Robert Dussey, political scientist and theologian, became foreign minister, replacing Elliot Ohin of the UFC. The Reverend Kofi Essaw replaced Tchitchao Tchalim, the conservative lawyer from Pya (home of the Gnassingbé family) as minister of justice. The security portfolio remained with Colonel Damehane Yark, and the defence ministry continued as a de facto branch of the presidency to prevent potential coup attempts.

In a reshuffle exercise in the **armed forces**, the chief of defence staff, Major General Atcha Titikpina, was replaced by Félix Abalo Kadanga (brother-in-law of Kpatcha Gnassingbé, the imprisoned former minister of defence), who had been promoted one year earlier to chief of staff of the army's land forces, which post was taken by Colonel M'Ba Koffi Batanda, former head of the Presidential Guard. Rumours had it that Titikpina had been accused of secretly amassing weapons, possibly to stage a coup d'état; arms trafficking could have been another possibility, although not mentioned in the sources. The navy was entrusted to Captain Adjo Vignon Kwassiv and Captain Takougnadi Nayo was appointed chief of military staff of the president.

The informal group of **presidential advisers** changed, too, although the longstanding legal advisor, Charles Debbasch, a notorious French lawyer labelled a 'white collar mercenary' by the AU, stayed in place. However, at year's end the powerful Ingrid Awadé, a Kabyé like the Gnassingbés and confidante of the president since 2006, had to make way for her adversary, Minister for Economy and Finance Adji Otèth Ayassor, who besides his ministerial duties became a key presidential adviser. Raymond Germanos, a retired French five-star general and a freemason with a criminal record for paedophilia, became security adviser, a function he had previously exercised for the president of Cameroon.

Corruption and nepotism remained endemic. According to representative analyses by Afrobarometer published in November, Togo was ranked 4th from the bottom of the list of 16 African states investigated; 66% of respondents said the government was not making sufficient efforts to fight corruption, which was estimated to be especially rampant among custom officials (48%), judges (45%), police (43%) and central government bureaucrats

(40%). TI, which relies in its annual surveys on the perception of the business community, ranked Togo in the lower third of the countries surveyed (123rd out of 177).

On 19 February, parliament approved more rigid media controls, including granting sweeping powers of censorship to the government-dominated media watchdog, 'Haute Autorité de l'Audiovisuel et de la Communication'. Although the Constitutional Court annulled some of these repressive amendments in March, the lack of press freedom remained a point of concern for national and international **human rights** bodies. On 19 December, the special rapporteurs of the UN Commission on Human Rights published a report in which they called for a general popular appraisal ('états généraux') of the justice system. The special UN rapporteur on human rights, Margaret Sekaggya, had already taken the government to task in October because of the hostile environment in which human rights activists had to carry out their work, although the situation had improved since the last evaluation in 2008. The New York-based, Committee to Protect Journalists complained on 2 October about media censorship, including the forcible closure of private radio stations. In the annual ranking of the Press Freedom Index of Reporters Without Borders, Togo fell by four places (to 83rd out of 179 countries).

As a result of increasing **piracy**, maritime insurance companies classified Togo's coast and that of neighbouring countries as high risk zones, which had the potential to negatively impact on trade for Lomé's deep-water port. On 19 September, the EU representative in Benin launched the Gulf of Guinea Maritime Route project, a pilot-project of seven African countries, including Togo, to enhance maritime security. Lomé, which had already served as a hub in West Africa's cocaine trade for several years, now also entered heroin trade networks connecting Asia with Europe. According to the UN Office on Drugs and Crime, the proceeds of trafficking were increasingly going to Islamist terrorist groups.

Foreign Affairs

On 11 February, Nicholas Westcott, director general of the **EU** Africa Department, reaffirmed the EU's demand that the government respect the APG and the relevant EU recommendations as a pre-condition for electoral support. At the end of June, the EU sent a two-man election expert mission to observe the electoral process. Just two days after the elections, EU High Representative for Foreign Affairs Catherine Ashton congratulated the country on the conduct of the polls. Overriding concerns over sub-regional security and Lomé's active role in UN peace keeping missions apparently played a role in this assessment, although it contradicted the analysis of the EU's own expert mission, which on 7 August had pointed to certain "dysfunctions" in the election process. The observation missions of the AU, ECOWAS, UEMOA and the OIF followed suit and declared the elections credible, free and transparent.

A first contingent of 100 **Togolese peacekeeping troops** arrived in Bamako on 17 January to take part in ECOWAS' African-led International Support Mission to Mali; 400 more were to follow. In April, Lomé sent its 18th contingent of 258 (of 500) troops to join the UN troops in Côte d'Ivoire. On 1 August, the US provided $ 1.5 m for the training and equipment of 150 Togolese policemen and gendarmes within the framework of the peace-keeping operation in Mali, thus honouring Togo's role as the very first African state to have mobilised its troops for the French-led intervention mission. During a state visit to Paris on 13–15 November, Faure Gnassingbé and French President Hollande confirmed their common commitment in fighting terrorism.

On 8 November, the EU announced the allocation of € 216 m in **development aid** on account of the 11th EDF, a 70% increase on the previous EDF (2008–13). It focused on governance, consolidation of the rule of law and development of regional urban centres and their surrounding river basins. At the same time, the EU insisted on binding arrangements concerning the conduct of local elections, which should be in line with the APG and include a calendar to be announced before the end of the year.

In May, Togo assumed the monthly rotating presidency of the **UNSC**. In October, Chad was elected to succeed Togo as non-permanent member as of 2014. In the same month, Gnassingbé participated in two **sub-regional summits** in Dakar: the UEMOA meeting focused on the economic situation in the CFA zone whilst that of ECOWAS centred on the controversial EPAs to be negotiated with the EU. Early in November, Gnassingbé visited the Republic of Congo, where he was apparently initiated into the freemasons on the recommendation of Congo's President Sassou-Nguesso, his godfather and reportedly a masonic grand master.

Socioeconomic Developments

The primary and secondary sectors (contributing 38% and 21% of GDP, respectively), particularly cotton and phosphates, contributed most to **growth**. Agriculture (27% of GDP) remained the backbone of the economy. Although prospects for growth had been promising in recent years (real economic growth rising from 4.5% in 2010–11 to 5.75% in 2012–13), it had not been sustainable and inclusive. The IMF staff report of 20 November therefore urged the government to work towards meeting popular expectations and address the country's development needs. This also necessitated a focus on growing inequality. According to the AfDB's economic outlook, **poverty** (afflicting 61.7% of the population) fell by 3% in the period 2006–11, partly as a result of internal migration. However, extreme poverty rose from 28.6% to 30.4%. Increasing fiscal deficits caused additional concern. At the end of the year, parliament approved the budget for 2014 (totalling CFAfr 832.2 bn), which provided for an increase of 19.5% compared with 2013. At the start of the year, the government announced its aim to reduce **unemployment** from 30% to 15% by 2017. According to the national employment agency, there were 60,000 new entrants into the labour market every year, including 10,000 young graduates. The government provided the 'Agence National de Promotion du Volontariat' with a budget of

$ 6 m to reduce unemployment by at least 0.5% – and under-employment by 1.0% – per year. On 12 March, 750 new graduates entered the 'Programme de Volontariat National au Togo', bringing the total enlisted in this kind of community service to 3,530 since its foundation in September 2011.

Togo continued to profit from substantial **donor support**. On 9 September, the IMF granted a three-year ECF of some $ 55 m in SDR, subject, however, to approval by its Executive Board. In addition, on 5 December, the World Bank endorsed an IDA credit line of $ 14 m; this represented the Bank's sixth loan to Togo since the resumption of aid in 2008. The Bank's 2013 Doing Business Report indicated an improved ranking (156th of 185 countries), five higher than in 2012.

In January, the government issued two gold exploration permits in the Dapaong area, and Togo attained Extractive Industries Transparency Initiative compliant status in April. On 28 May, the president launched the state-owned Togo Investment Corporation with an initial capital outlay of $ 40 m. Its purpose was to enhance the 750 km north-south development corridor with infrastructure projects to promote the **mining** ventures in the north and improve communications with land-locked Burkina Faso and Niger.

In December, bloody confrontations took place between Fulbe nomadic cattle **herders and peasants** in Moba (Borgou) in the far north. Five people died and numerous others sustained injuries. Minister for Territorial Administration and Decentralisation Gilbert Bawara used the occasion to warn local authorities against corruption and action privileging nomadic interests, as this could fuel the frustration of the local population and even lead to lynchings.

The OECD gender index reported nearly half of Togo's population to be practising **polygamy**. A legal social arrangement that is particularly widespread in rural areas and among the illiterate population, polygamy is a deeply rooted custom conferring social status. Even President Gnassingbé is said to have eight wives, none of whom, however, serves as official First Lady.

Dirk Kohnert

V. Central Africa

With the massive crisis in the CAR and on-going troubles in the DRC, Central Africa proved to be the least peaceful sub-region on the continent. Absorbed by crisis management, sub-regional organisations were incapable of playing a positive role in socio-economic development. However, most economies showed fairly good results in terms of GDP growth. Despite this single positive trend, the impression grew that the sub-region was falling further behind all the rest with regard to more or less all governance issues, resulting in a diminished capacity to meet future challenges.

Democracy and Elections

National elections took place in only two countries in the sub-region – **Cameroon** and **Equatorial Guinea** (in both countries legislative, senatorial and municipal elections were conducted, partly combined). Cameroon's elections had been postponed from 2012. For the first time ever, the Senate was elected (although this had been foreseen constitutionally since 1996), indirectly by members of the municipal councils. Of the 100 senators (70 elected and 30 appointed by President Biya), 82 were members of the ruling party; five other parties shared the remaining 18 seats. The opposition fared slightly better in elections to the National Assembly, when 148 of the 180 seats were won by the ruling party – five fewer than in the previous elections in 2007. The biggest opposition party was able to extend its representation slightly, from 16 to 18 seats. However, the result of the municipal elections offset this encouraging result when the ruling party took control of more municipal councils than ever before. The distinction between a firmly authoritarian and a dictatorial context still accounted for a difference in the degree of (not) respecting the will of the voters. Some elections in the sub-region were in fact a farce. This was not surprising with regard to legislative and municipal elections in Equatorial Guinea, where the ruling party together with some sympathetic minor organisations officially won 54 of the 55 seats in senatorial elections (with 15 additional members appointed by the president). In the National Assembly, the result was similar, with the ruling party taking 99 of the 100 seats, and 295 out of 300 elected municipal councillors were from the presidential camp. In these circumstances, it was clear that elections did not fulfil the role commonly attributed to them in democracies. Municipal elections were also held in **Gabon**, where the dominance of the ruling party was confirmed, quite similarly to Cameroon.

In the **CAR**, the suspension of the constitution and the dissolution of the National Assembly led to transitional institutions. Rebel leader Michel Djotodia was indirectly elected by the 'Conseil National de Transition' and by the end of the year an electoral authority began preparing for elections amidst a situation of deep crisis and with no clear potential date for such elections (though the duration of the transition phase had been fixed at 18 months from its formal inception in August). According to Freedom House, democracy levels declined throughout Africa, and with the CAR joining Equatorial Guinea in the "Worst of the worst" category, the sub-region certainly made its contribution to this development.

Instability, War and Peace

The **CAR** saw its fifth violent change of government since independence. François Bozizé fell prey to the attacks of a new coalition of rebel groups, the Séléka coalition, only formed in 2012 from four major and some smaller movements. Rebel leader Michel Djotodia copied many pages from Bozizé's book, including relying on foreign, mostly Chadian, mercenaries, organising forces on the periphery and quickly taking provincial capitals, and finally gaining the support of the Chadian regime. Other parallels were the weakness of the regional peacekeepers in the face of better equipped rebels, the demoralised state of the national army and a quick international condemnation of the coup followed by grudging acceptance of a new order. However, Djotodia did not manage to build a solid domestic and international foundation for his rule – despite being welcomed for short visits in Chad, Gabon and Equatorial Guinea in defiance of an active AU travel ban. Bozizé had clearly been losing sympathy within the sub-region for some time and neighbouring countries had become alienated: when Bozizé supported the candidacy of Dlamini Zuma (South Africa) for the role of AU Commission chairperson in 2012 against the sub-region's candidate Jean Ping, he lost Gabon's support. And when he declared former CEMAC director Antoine Ntsimi persona non grata in 2012, he also lost sympathy in Ntsimi's native Cameroon. But many heads of state in the region had good reason to suspect that another politico-military leader at the helm of a neighbouring state would impact on them negatively, so Djotodia came to power without much in his favour.

In eastern **DRC**, major military encounters between the army, helped by international peacekeepers, and the M23 movement left many people dead and many more homeless. Official casualty figures were not given, but some 350 (mostly rebel) fighters probably lost their lives during the year, and hundreds of thousands of people became refugees or IDPs. The M23 itself was shaken by internal rifts and came increasingly under attack when 3,000 soldiers from South Africa, Tanzania and Malawi joined the UN peacekeeping mission with a special fighting assignment; by October, the M23 was considered defeated. The movement belatedly agreed to peace talks and was ready to accept most of the conditions laid down by the opposing side, including the demobilisation of its fighters (though sweetened by an amnesty for the rank and file), and its transformation into a political party. In the end, however, the government declared that it would not sign a peace agreement with a rebel group that was already defeated and demobilised. On 12 December, both the government and the M23 finally signed separate declarations in Nairobi. This did not mean that peace was now at hand in the largest country of the sub-region. Many more militia and rebel groups remained operative, and not only in the Kivu provinces. On 30 December, apparently coordinated attacks were staged on government installations in Kinshasa and some provincial towns, although they were unsuccessful.

In **Chad**, the authorities claimed to have foiled a coup d'état on 1 May; later they simply spoke of "a conspiracy against the state". The event was the pretext for a series of arrests and repression of civil liberties.

Trans-border problems grew during 2013 for many countries. **Cameroon**'s security forces were preoccupied by many cross-border incursions, from both Nigeria and the CAR, with several incidents recorded at the frontier with the latter, the most severe on 31 December. Chad, though playing a dubious game in the CAR crisis, also had to bear the consequences, with many refugees now flowing in and potentially destabilising its own border region. Historical **inter-state tensions** played a minor role in 2013, with Gabon and Equatorial Guinea still looking for a solution to their **ongoing territorial dispute** over the ownership of the island of Mbañe. A UN mediator was called in and tried to channel the conflict into formal litigation at the International Court of Justice. UN

Secretary-General Ban Ki-moon met with both heads of state separately in September and also advised this procedure.

In some protracted violent conflicts, it appeared at least superficial to stress only the cross-border and national dynamics while ignoring local contexts. An ICG report ('Understanding Conflict in Eastern Congo') pointed to **local roots of violent conflict**. This perspective also offered a possible explanation for the geographical pattern of conflict escalation. An example of this was the CAR during its latest crisis, where the Mbororo minority was targeted by many village communities in the northern part of the country who held them responsible for all sorts of crimes committed in the previous decades. Weak governments and opportunities created by political entrepreneurs may be only one context condition for conflict escalation in the sub-region.

UNHCR statistics (for mid-2013) showed the uneven distribution of the **refugee** population. With an upsurge of violence in both Sudan and the CAR, Chad was hosting 418,451 refugees, more by far than the neighbouring countries; the DRC came second (183,244) and Cameroon third (105,456). Over 100,000 refugees from the DRC were assisted to return from Congo (Brazzaville), reducing the number of refugees there to 66,189. Only three countries had **IDPs**. The largest number of IDPs in Africa were again found in the DRC, where they numbered about 2.6 m, a figure that has remained quite constant for years. The number of IDPs in the CAR grew at an alarming rate, almost doubling from 206,000 to around 400,000 by year's end (with 220,000 refugees also having fled to adjacent countries). Figures for IDPs in Chad remained constant, with about 90,000 people from earlier periods of conflict still not resettled.

Human Rights

Violent conflicts were the context of the most severe human rights violations. The best-known international NGOs in the field produced substantial reports documenting some of the atrocities in the **CAR**. AI issued a report on war crimes and crimes against humanity committed during and after the 5 December attack in Bangui, entitled "None of us are safe". HRW published not only a major report on forgotten humanitarian crises ("I can still smell the dead"), but also an additional document entitled "They came to kill", describing the acts of vengeance carried out by anti-balaka militias against Muslim communities near Bossangoa in September.

The alleged coup plot in Chad was the pretext for the temporary arrest of most of the country's main opposition figures in early May. Independent **media** had a rough year, with many arrests and sanctions, mostly in this same conspiracy context. In the DRC, a community radio journalist was murdered; not only state representatives, but also rebel commanders exercised censorship and issued threats, as did the M23 in Goma. Reporters Without Borders noted a toughening stance on the part of Cameroon's media regulatory body against the private press and radio stations, with harsh sanctions being imposed on several journalists on 5 September. Congo's media regulator suspended three newspapers for four months after they allegedly published "seditious articles". Leaders of a teachers' trade union were arrested without warrant in Brazzaville (Congo) after they had initiated a strike, and held in detention for one week; they were also denied access to their lawyers.

The Lord's Resistance Army (LRA) continued to cause trouble in the region, particularly in the CAR – helped by the additional chaos created during the new civil war. In January, the Ugandan Army announced that its troops in the CAR had killed the chief bodyguard of LRA leader Joseph Kony. Uganda was the most active member of a Regional Task Force consisting of troops from the four affected countries (the CAR, DRC, South Sudan and Uganda), who had pledged in 2012 that they would provide a total of 5,000 troops to hunt down the LRA and its leaders. On 3 April, the US government offered a reward of up to $ 5 m for information leading to the arrest of Kony and some of his top aides. The LRA was under strong pressure, but new militias entered the scene, forcing the Regional Task Force to redeploy to safer locations. CAR President Djotodia, desperately searching for outside legitimacy, stated in December that he was in contact with Kony, who was close to surrendering (and that he was encouraging him to do so). But by year's end no progress had been achieved.

The **ICC** continued to follow events in the Central African sub-region closely. In connection with the trial against former DRC vice-president Jean-Pierre Bemba (for crimes committed in the neighbouring CAR), the ICC issued a warrant in November against four of Bemba's associates (and Bemba himself, who was already in custody in The Hague) for several offences against the administration of justice, including incitement to give false testimony. Bosco Ntaganda, former military commander of the 'Forces Patriotiques pour la Libération du Congo' and founder of the M23, voluntarily surrendered to the ICC on 22 March after the split within the M23. He was charged on four counts of war crimes and three counts of crimes against humanity, but probably most specifically for enlisting child soldiers. An initial hearing took place before a pre-trial chamber on 26 March. On 9 December, ICC Prosecutor Fatou Bensouda issued a stern warning to the principal armed actors in the CAR that war crimes, crimes against humanity and genocide fell under ICC jurisdiction, and called on them to stop attacking civilians or risk being investigated and prosecuted by her office. This could not have any deterrent effect, given the amorphous structure of the groups fighting each other.

Socioeconomic Developments

There were major differences between the economic trends in the countries of Central Africa. According to the IMF's World Economic Outlook (published in April 2014), the CAR experienced a dramatic downturn following the new civil war (–36% **GDP** per capita); to a lesser degree this was also true of Equatorial Guinea (–4.9%), after the oil boom came to a provisional halt. In contrast, some substantial progress was reported in other countries, resulting in a brighter picture overall than in most preceding years. In the DRC, 8.9% growth was recorded. Gabon (5.9%), Cameroon (4.6 %), Congo (4.5 %), São Tomé and Príncipe (4.0 %) and Chad (3.6 %) followed.

Inflation was clearly **moderate** compared with 2012, and even particularly low in some places (Chad 0.2%, Gabon 0.5 %, the DRC 0.8%, and Cameroon 2.1 %). Moderate inflation was even recorded in Equatorial Guinea (3.2 %) and Congo (4.6 %). Less reassuring were the inflation rates in the CAR (6.5 %) and São Tomé and Príncipe (8.1 %).

In September, the ECA issued a report on **sustainable development goals** in Central Africa in preparation for the so-called post-MDG agenda. The report was meant to identify and analyse priority issues and classify Central Africa's key sustainable development areas. It noted important variations in some respects (not least with regard to GDP growth rates), but indicated that a very high security threat, lack of governance and weak institutions, lack of infrastructure, extremely high unemployment rates, strong population pressure, unsatisfactory living conditions and significant pressure on the environment should all be sources of serious concern. The only positives on the balance sheet were the great wealth of natural resources in the sub-region and quite satisfactory average growth rates over recent years. The report was based on the CEEAC framework, so the inclusion of economically vibrant Angola (plus Burundi) in Central Africa may have had a positive influence on the picture presented.

Interest in **large-scale land acquisitions** continued in Central Africa, but the current business climate, in addition to the widespread violence, clearly did nothing to attract foreign investors. After protests from many local and international environmental NGOs against a major investment project in south-west Cameroon, the ministry responsible issued an order to stop work and Herakles Farms, the US-based company involved, suspended its project temporarily in May.

Sub-regional Organisations

CEMAC met for its ordinary summit on 14 June in Libreville (Gabon). It mainly discussed the crisis in the CAR, which had made it impossible for the CEMAC commission to meet in Bangui. The summit was attended by the heads of state of Chad, Congo, Equatorial Guinea and Gabon, and by Cameroon's prime minister and the not yet inaugurated interim president of the CAR. Progress in sub-regional integration was again minimal, as the recurrent appearance of the issue of a sub-regional airline (Air CEMAC) on the agenda of such summits showed. With Air France only conditionally ready to serve as Air CEMAC's strategic partner, the situation appeared blocked again. On 20 November, the six ministers in charge of the internal affairs and integration within CEMAC met in Libreville to discuss again the implementation of a policy of free circulation of persons within the CEMAC community. This issue proved divisive, with four member states in favour (Cameroun, the CAR, Congo and Chad) and two against (Gabon and Equatorial Guinea – significantly, these two were the countries with the highest per capita GDP). Equatorial Guinea gave security concerns as the reason for its reservations, while Gabon listed a number of preconditions, including the setting up of centres for police cooperation, the centralisation of databanks, and a system of records on people wanted by Interpol. CEMAC headquarters in Bangui faced enormous difficulties in functioning at all in the situation on the ground there. CEMAC personnel were frequently harassed and some staff lost relatives during the 5 December attack by anti-balaka forces.

It was again **CEEAC** that appeared the more important sub-regional organisation, although it clearly had difficulties in fulfilling some promises. In accordance with the continental institutional architecture, the AU gave CEEAC the responsibility of steering the crisis in the CAR. At first, the CEEAC framework faced up to this task when mediator Denis Sassou Nguesso managed to get all the major actors to sign a peace agreement (in Libreville) at the end of an extraordinary summit on 9–11 January. This was only one of five extraordinary meetings at this level to be held on this crisis during the year and five heads of state attended; the sub-region's commitment to managing the crisis could therefore be called remarkable. However, not many observers gave CEEAC much credit as it had failed to produce stability in earlier phases of the crisis both on a political level and on the ground by (not) providing security via its peacekeepers. This scepticism was dramatically proved well-founded when the final Séléka assault toppled the regime in Bangui in March. A CEEAC summit was held on 3 April in N'Djamena (Chad) and looked into the situation only a few days after the violent take-over in Bangui; a further summit was held on 18 April, again in N'Djaména, which decided to raise the numbers of sub-regional peacekeepers from 500 to 2,000. The main message for the new self-declared President Djotodia was that he had to make serious efforts to include all major stakeholders (except Bozizé) in the institutional architecture of a transitional phase. CEEAC's follow-up committee of the (failed) Libreville agreement met with the new president on 10 June, again putting pressure on him to normalise the situation. After the authorisation of a 'Mission Internationale de Soutien à la Centrafrique' (**MISCA**) on 19 July by the AU Peace and Security Council, the MICOPAX peacekeeping mission merged into this broader African mission. A change occurred within CEEAC's governing circles on 29 July, when Chadian President Idriss Déby nominated the experienced diplomat Ahmad Allam-Mi, Chad's former foreign minister and ambassador to the UN, as the organisation's new secretary-general. He replaced Nassour Guelengdouksia Ouaidou (also from Chad), who had directed the CEEAC secretariat for only 16 months. No official reason was given for this replacement.

The **Gulf of Guinea Commission** (GGC) received new impetus after a summit on maritime security attended by 25 West and Central African heads of state and bringing together GCC, ECOWAS and CEEAC delegates in Yaoundé (Cameroon) on 24–25 June.

One of the decisions taken was that Yaoundé would host the headquarters of an inter-regional coordination centre to fight piracy. A regular GGC summit was held in Malabo (Equatorial Guinea) on 10 August (attended by five heads of state) and came to some far-reaching structural proposals. The executive secretary would come from Nigeria, the deputy executive secretary for political affairs from Angola, and the deputy executive secretary for natural resources from Cameroon. Gabon would nominate the financial director and Equatorial Guinea the administrative director of the Commission. This arrangement probably reflected dissatisfaction with the out-going secretariat under former São Tomé and Príncipe president Miguel Trovoada, although he received words of gratitude from his peers and provisionally remained in his position. One other issue on the agenda was membership fees; important arrears had still not been paid by some member states. It was decided to look for a new membership fees formula that would link the amount to be paid to each country's economic weight. The GCC presidency was transferred from Dos Santos of Angola to Obiang Nguema of Equatorial Guinea.

Andreas Mehler

Cameroon

From the institutional point of view, Cameroon made significant progress with the creation of the Senate, an event that had been awaited since 1996 and a key factor in arranging the succession to President Biya, in power since 1982. The country also faced serious security problems: for the first time, the north witnessed abductions of French citizens, officially attributed to elements of the Nigerian-based Boko Haram movement, while armed groups of Central Africans carried out several murderous raids in the east. The crisis in the CAR also precipitated the arrival and temporary stationing of the French Army on Cameroonian territory, which gave rise to tensions.

Domestic Politics

As he had already announced in a speech delivered on 31 December 2012, President Paul Biya approved the implementation of an institutional reform that had been pending for 18 years: **the creation of the Senate** – a crucial element in the arrangement of his succession if he should die in office. According to the constitution of 1996, the president of the Senate should take interim responsibility in the event that the position of head of state should fall vacant. It was presumably in order to remain in control of politics that

President Biya, who turned 80 in February, had repeatedly postponed the creation of this institution, which had been demanded with growing insistence not only by the opposition and the country's creditors, but also by members of his own party, the 'Rassemblement Démocratique du Peuple Camerounais' (RDPC).

The **first senatorial elections** were held on 14 April. As stipulated by the Constitution, the electoral college was composed of municipal councillors and had the task of electing 70 senators, 30 more being appointed by the head of state. This ballot particularly mobilised the elites of the political parties, as the prospect of securing a remunerated appointment aroused the appetite of numerous ambitious personalities, thereby provoking internal dissensions. Tensions were strongest in the RDPC, the party leadership having thrust certain candidates aside to the benefit of others. Another contentious issue was the timing of the election: opposition leaders vainly called for the municipal elections to be held before the senatorial elections on the basis that this would have been logical, the municipal councillors' mandate having expired in mid-2012 before being extended by Biya.

Not surprisingly, the RDPC emerged victorious from the electoral process: of the 100 senators, 82 (of whom 56 were elected) came from its ranks. The remaining senatorial seats were shared by five other parties, notably the Social Democratic Front (SDF), the main opposition party, which secured 14 seats. The SDF chairman, John Fru Ndi, suffered a setback, having failed to be elected in his home region in the north-west of the country. Moreover, none of the senators appointed by Biya belonged to the SDF. In June, Marcel Niat Njifenji, a member of the RDPC, was chosen to become president of the Senate, thereby assuming the status of potential constitutional successor to the president. Having served as deputy prime minister in the early 1990s, 79-year-old Niat Njifenji had been director-general of the state power utility Société Nationale d'Electricité' (SONEL) for many years.

While the creation of the Senate succeeded in filling an institutional gap, it failed to resolve all the problems pertaining to the succession of the head of state. The actual legitimacy of the election of the president of the Senate, for instance, was weak, as was that of the president of the National Assembly (Cavayé Yéguié, 73, in office since 1992): officially administered by the electoral commission, 'Elections Cameroon' (Elecam), the senatorial elections were in fact under the direct control of the presidential administration. Furthermore, a **Constitutional Council**, although required by the Constitution, had not been created. One of its functions would be to determine whether the head of state had become incapacitated. Knowing that he was expected to act on this point, Biya announced in his speech at year's end that a Constitutional Council would be created "within a reasonable period of time".

On 30 September, a few months after the senatorial elections, the **legislative and municipal elections** that should have taken place in July 2012 were finally held. They elicited very little participation and interest on the part of the majority of citizens, who, as in previous elections, doubted the impartiality of the electoral process. The opposition repeatedly criticised the authorities and the presidential party, accusing the government of – among other things – holding back the public funds necessary for financing the electoral campaign. Following the ballot, the opposition charged the RDPC with fraud, as in all preceding elections. Some 40 appeals were lodged, but they were dismissed by the Supreme Court. As a result of the vote, the RDPC won 148 of the 180 parliamentary seats (compared with 153 in the preceding elections of 2007). The SDF won 18 seats (compared with 16 in 2007). The 'Union des Populations du Cameroun' (a branch of the historical opposition party) won three seats, and the 'Mouvement pour la Renaissance du Cameroun', a party founded in 2012 by Maurice Kamto (a former minister turned oppositionist), took one.

The RDPC also obtained an overwhelming majority in the municipal elections, gaining control of 305 out of 360 municipalities (compared with 297 previously). Of the 35 political parties in the race, only ten secured municipal council seats. In the eastern and southern regions, the RDPC received the majority of votes in all municipalities and it also remained dominant in the centre of the country, where the capital Yaoundé is located. In the economic capital, Douala (Littoral Region), the RDPC carried Douala I, II, IV, V, and VI, leaving only Douala III to the SDF. In the north-west, Prime Minister Philemon Yang's home region and the stronghold of Fru Ndi, the RDPC took 19 municipalities and the SDF 15. It succeeded in ousting the SDF in Fru Ndi's native village of Santa. In the south-west, the RDPC was victorious everywhere except in Tiko, Kumba I, and Kumba II, which were won by the SDF. In the western region, traditional homeland of the opposition, the presidential party obtained a broad majority: apart from the Noun *département*, where the 'Union Démocratique du Cameroun', led by Adamou Ndam Njoya, won five municipalities, and only the town of Bafang went to an opposition party, namely the 'Union des Mouvements Socialistes', led by Pierre Kwémo. The SDF obtained only a relative majority in the municipality of Bafoussam I. The election results in the northern region brought no surprises: the RDPC and its ally, the 'Union Nationale pour la Démocratie et le Progrès' shared the seats.

Aside from these electoral events, political life saw little change: although still a taboo subject, the Biya succession remained the principal topic of concern among the political elites. A number of victims of the **anti-corruption campaign** 'Opération Épervier' (Operation Sparrowhawk) attracted attention, several of them having been presented as possible successors to Biya. Some made the headlines again on the occasion of their trials: on 2 October, the court sentenced the former prime minister, Ephraïm Inoni (imprisoned in 2012), to 20 years in prison for embezzling public funds and imposed the same sentence on his co-defendant, the former secretary-general of the Presidency, Jean-Marie Atangana Mebara (imprisoned in 2008). The former minister of basic education, Haman Adama, sparked a flood of comment upon leaving prison, having been released by the judicial authorities on 19 September after pleading guilty before the 'Tribunal Criminel Spécial'

(TCS) and reimbursing the money she had been accused of embezzling. Upon her release, she thanked President Biya and immediately began campaigning for the upcoming legislative elections on behalf of the presidential party. Her release after more than three years in detention was interpreted as a way of securing support for the RDPC in the north, i.e. in her home region. It was also the home territory of the former secretary-general of the Presidency and onetime interior minister, Marafa Hamidou Yaya, who had officially fallen from grace in 2012. He had been sentenced to 25 years in prison in September 2012 for embezzling public funds, but continued to attract attention by publishing several letters from prison in the Cameroonian and foreign press. Expressing his views on the economy, politics and justice, his letters presented him as an alternative to the Biya regime, even though he had been one of its principal collaborators for 25 years. Known to entertain close ties to French as well as American business and diplomatic circles, Marafa was visited by US Ambassador Robert P. Jackson in June on the premises of the Secretariat of State for Defence, where he was imprisoned. In November, the Supreme Court rejected his application for a provisional release from detention. At the same time, two French lawyers, Jean-Paul Benoit and Jean-Pierre Mignard, a close friend of French President François Hollande, decided to take on his defence.

Even though Biya appeared to have retained overall control of the political system in the wake of the elections, he nevertheless encountered serious difficulties on the **security front**, with several alarming incidents now posing a threat to both the country and his own authority. The first such incident took place in the north, on 19 February, with the abduction of seven French citizens: the Moulin-Fournier family of three adults and four children, who were travelling as tourists in the vicinity of the border with Nigeria. According to the official version, they were detained by the Nigerian Islamist group Boko Haram before being liberated in April. In October, a French priest, Georges Vandenbeusch, was kidnapped in the same region and regained his freedom on 31 December. Official sources had little to say about these incidents. Even though the French authorities denied it, it subsequently became apparent that substantial ransoms had been paid to the abductors by Cameroon. Domestic and international observers also determined that these abductions had been organised in order to destabilise the Biya regime. Further unofficially leaked details showed that the Cameroonian security services suspected the involvement of a fringe group of the current regime that was hostile to Biya and included members of northern political elites. These incidents had at least one negative consequence for the country and its president: having received considerable media coverage in France (French Foreign Minister Laurent Fabius came to Yaoundé three times on their account), they left Western public opinion with the impression that Cameroon was a dangerous and insecure country.

On 27 December, Biya reacted by taking extensive measures to secure the borders with Nigeria, and also those with the CAR, as elements of armed Central African groups had repeatedly made incursions into Cameroonian territory. One measure taken was the creation of command posts for motorised rapid intervention battalions ('bataillons d'intervention motorisée') in Ngaoundere, Garoua, and Maroua, as well as at other, less important locations (Kousséri, Mora, Poli, Tibati). The security forces were also reinforced with newly created units. The recruitment of 4,400 men (2,300 for the defence forces, 300 NCO students for the gendarmerie, and 1,800 gendarmerie students), scheduled to begin in March 2014, was also announced.

Foreign Affairs

Though not readily apparent in public, relations between Biya and **France** seriously deteriorated over the months. A number of events caused the Cameroonian president to become increasingly wary of French government officials. The year had actually begun rather well: on 30 January, Biya was received in Paris by his presidential counterpart François Hollande. During this official visit, Biya met with prominent French businessmen (French companies still held a monopoly over many economic sectors in Cameroon, which also remained France's foremost partner in terms of security and defence cooperation). While in France, however, Biya was also confronted with an intensely hostile campaign by the major French media. On the day of his visit to the Élysée Palace, 'Le Monde' published a column signed by Marafa and entitled "The post-Biya era must begin". Numerous media also highlighted the case of Thierry-Michel Atangana, a Franco-Cameroonian who had been detained in Cameroon since 1997 on a charge of corruption in conjunction with an affair that linked him to the former secretary-general of the Presidency, Titus Edzoa. Both had been sentenced to 15 years in prison in 1997, and were condemned to another 20 years in 2012. Siding with Atangana, the French media argued that he was being detained for political reasons and that Biya should release him.

Subsequently, the situation continued to deteriorate for the Cameroonian president. The Atangana case, which had long failed to attract the interest of the media and French officials, was mediatised several times by Paris and in May Hollande declared that the duration of Atangana's detention was "unacceptable". Biya suffered yet another indignity during the summit on Africa organised by the French presidency in December: he became the target of a verbal attack by Cameroonian citizens in the lobby of a large Parisian hotel, the 'Hôtel Meurice'. The incident was not well taken by the Cameroonian regime, which suspected the complicity of the French authorities. In spite of all appearances (Hollande publicly thanked Biya for his support on several occasions), the abductions of French citizens also placed additional strain on relations between Biya and his French dialogue partners. Yaoundé was shocked that France chose to declare the entire north of Cameroon a 'red zone' following the kidnapping of the Moulin-Fournier family and urged its citizens to leave the area immediately.

In spite of this strained situation, Biya authorised the **French Army** to land in Douala in order to proceed to the CAR within the framework of UNSC Resolution 2121: on 28 November, the French Navy's amphibious assault ship Dixmude arrived at the port of Douala with 350 soldiers and roughly 100 vehicles on board. On 5 December, the soldiers crossed the country to reach the CAR border. The French Army also established a temporary base at Ngaoundere airport (in the north). This presence gave rise to a number of problems, notably when the Cameroonian Army opposed the French Army's attempt to raise the French flag over the airport. Some Cameroonian media expressed surprise over the requisitioning and privatising of the airport by the French military. Others were alarmed at this presence, which brought back bad memories of the French colonial army's war against Cameroonian nationalists in the 1950s. The pro-presidential press, in turn, flatly accused France of planning to overthrow Biya as a follow-up to its intervention in the CAR.

Prior to the arrival of the French Army, Cameroon had already been directly affected by the crisis in the **CAR**. When the Séléka rebels seized power in Bangui, elements of the national army that remained loyal to ex-president Bozizé had indeed sought refuge in Cameroon. Bozizé himself officially went into exile in Cameroon on 25 March. Entering Cameroon from the east, he subsequently resided in Yaoundé. During the following months, after various units of the Rapid Intervention Battalion had been deployed on the border with the CAR, several clashes occurred with elements of the Séléka, including exchanges of fire with the Cameroonian Army over two days in mid-May. Another incident directly linked to the crisis in the CAR took place on 16 September, when Abdoulaye Miskine, the leader of the rebel group 'Front Démocratique du Peuple Centrafricain', was arrested in Bertoua (eastern Cameroon) and taken to prison in Yaoundé. A former ally of the Séléka, he was wanted by the new authorities in Bangui. Further outbreaks of violence occurred in November, when several other armed incursions and attacks on CAR citizens took place. In the early hours of 31 December, the Séléka also shot and killed five people, including two soldiers, in the village of Ondiki in the district of Kétté. Cameroon was also directly involved in the international reactions to the crisis in the CAR: on 10 October, following the adoption of resolution 2121, UN Secretary-General Ban Ki-moon sent his special representative in the CAR to Yaoundé. Subsequently, on 18 October, Biya took the further step of nominating General Martin Tumenta Chomu as commander of the armed forces of the AU's International Support Mission to the CAR, which, by the end of the year included 500 Cameroonian troops.

Socioeconomic Developments

The Cameroonian economy continued to fail to meet expectations due to its poor regulatory system. In his end-of-year speech, Biya himself said: "It seems that our efforts alone, no matter how laudable, will not suffice at their current pace to make Cameroon an emerging country in 2035. (…) In 2013, our growth rate stands at 4.8%, and thus below our forecast of 6.1%." At the beginning of the year, the World Bank estimated that poverty had increased in the poorest regions, situated in the north (North, Extreme North, Adamaoua) and east of the country.

The implementation of the annual **budget**, in particular, was plagued by serious delays and difficulties. Budgetary expenditures and revenues had both been fixed at CFAfr 3,236 bn, which represented an increase of 15.6% over the previous budget. Of this amount, CFAfr 2,912 bn were to come from domestic revenues and CFAfr 324 bn from external sources, as compared with CFAfr 2,280 bn and CFAfr 249 bn respectively in 2012. The government earmarked 60.7% of the total budget for direct operating costs, 29.6% for investment, and 9.7% for debt repayment. However, it was not until April that the budget began to be implemented, i.e. after a delay two months longer than in previous years. The situation did not improve thereafter: in November, implementation of the domestic budget for public expenditure in, for instance, the Ntem *département* (South) stood at only 4%. Similarly, as in previous years, there were numerous delays in the implementation of large-scale infrastructure projects due to lack of involvement by the state officials responsible, and also on account of administrative sluggishness and numerous other deficiencies. Biya himself explained at the end of 2013 that the delays in decision-making were causing "bottlenecks". He also said that it was necessary to "question the usefulness of certain project monitoring committees which are unable to take any decisions". An inquiry commissioned by the government to look into the years 2011–13 revealed that the state had signed project agreements without any reference to the state assuming responsibility for the costs of repairing access roads, compensating residents for infrastructural projects, project planning, and the like. The inquiry concluded that these omissions delayed the beginning of projects and led to disappointing results as well as additional costs.

The construction of a **bridge over the river Wouri** in Douala began after a long delay: on 14 November, during one of his rare journeys inland, Biya presided over the laying of the structure's foundation stone. The new bridge, with a projected length of 760 m, was expected to ease congestion on the only existing bridge, built in 1954, and was set to be completed by 2016. The cost of the project was estimated at CFAfr 120 bn (nearly € 180 m) and the 'Agence Française de Développement' agreed to provide finance in the amount of CFAfr 87 bn (roughly € 133 m), in the form of a sovereign loan of € 100 m and a € 33 m subsidy taken from the second Debt Reduction-Development Contract (C2D). The building contract was awarded to Sogea-Satom, a subsidiary of the French industrial group Bouygues. Various media claimed that France had pressured the Cameroonian authorities into rejecting a Chinese proposal. For some years, the government of Cameroon had been holding talks with China, which had commissioned the Gezhouba Group to look into the feasibility of the project. The latter had submitted a cost estimate of CFAfr 93 bn. China had planned to finance 85% of the costs, the Cameroonian share thus amounting to 15%.

In order to implement its infrastructural projects, the state was compelled in December to issue government bonds. This enabled it to raise CFAfr 80 bn on the Douala Stock Exchange (DSX). The funds raised from this call for capital were earmarked for construction projects, including the Memvé'élé Dam, to which CFAfr 23 bn were to be allocated. Further shares would go to the construction of the industrial port complex in Kribi

(CFAfr 9 bn), the Douala-Yaoundé motorway (CFAfr 10.5 bn) and the Ring Road (CFAfr 7 bn) that was to connect the major cities of the north-east of the country. Somewhat more than 10% of the total budget was to finance the state's participation in business ventures.

The country's electricity supply, always unreliable and provided by the US-based AES Corporation, remained a matter of concern throughout the year. In mid-December, the government announced that it had approved an agreement to sell the Cameroonian assets of the AES Corporation to the British investment fund ACTIS for CFAfr 110 bn, a decision that attracted criticism from civil society actors and experts. The latter pointed out that the AES Corporation had kept none of the promises it had made in 2001 when it acquired a share in SONEL, 44% of which continued to be owned by the state: AES Corporation had promised, among other things, to invest CFAfr 1,000 bn of its own capital and to provide 68,000 new electrical connections per year, which it had failed to do.

Mobile telephone communications were still in the hands of two network operators, the French Orange SA and the South African MTN Group. A third operator, the Vietnamese Viettel Group, was chosen by the Cameroonian government in December 2012, but was still not operational.

Shortages also plagued the mining sector, on which the country officially relied to offset the drop in oil revenues, and it practically came to a halt. Large-scale projects (mining of an iron deposit in the south by CamIron, and of a cobalt/nickel deposit in the east by GeoCam) were at a standstill due to lack of motivation on the part of the promoters, as well as poor management and funding shortages. On 23 July, the US's Geovic Mining Corporation announced that it had signed an agreement with the Chinese Jiangxi Rare Metals Tungsten Holding Group for the sale of its shares in the GeoCam project, of which the Cameroonian state held 20%, at a time when strong suspicions of embezzlement were being voiced against the American company.

Only **diamond** deposits were being industrially exploited: according to the Ministry of Industry, Mines and Technological Development, Cameroon had exported slightly more than 2,414 carats of diamond since its admission to the Kimberley Process Certification Scheme on 14 August 2012. Handled by the Korean company C&K Mining, which held the mining concession in the diamond field of Mobilong (East), these exports generated profits of slightly more than CFAfr 281 m, of which 12.5% went to the state. According to the results of a survey conducted in July, there were seven small-scale diamond production zones. The National Permanent Secretariat of the Kimberly Process estimated that their production capacity amounted to about 5,000 carats per year.

As in 2012, the country's **oil production** experienced a very slight increase, reaching 24.2 m barrels (15.2 m barrels devolving to the state and 8.9 m barrels to the partner companies of Cameroon in the oil production sector), compared with 22.6 m barrels in 2012. Oil generated revenues of slightly more than CFAfr 832 bn (on a budgetary prediction of CFAfr 708 bn), compared with CFAfr 785 bn in 2012. Of this total revenue, the 'Société Nationale des Hydrocarbures' (SNH) reported that it had transferred CFAfr 553 bn to the public treasury, compared with CFAfr 510 bn in 2012. The state expected an increase in production for 2014, now banking on 30 m barrels due to the beginning of production in the Mvia oil field (in the Douala-Kribi-Campo Basin) in November 2013.

The level of **transparency in the extractive industry sector** remained low: in mid-May 2013, an American NGO, the Revenue Watch Institute (RWI), gave Cameroon a "failing" score for its governance of the oil sector. In its report, Cameroon ranked 47th out of 58 countries investigated throughout the world. It specified that the Cameroonians did not always have access to the information that was needed to ensure that the share of wealth issued from the natural resources of their country was fair. RWI also noted that the licensing process lacked transparency. It observed that there were few control mechanisms for monitoring the SNH, which collected the major part of the state's oil revenues, and estimated that only a part of the oil revenues actually found their way to the public treasury. In spite of these problems, and after several failures, Cameroon was recognised in August as a "compliant state" by the international committee of the Extractive Industries Transparency Initiative, indicating that it abided by prescribed norms of transparency.

The business climate was still poor, as Biya himself admitted in his end-of-year speech. Cameroon's ranking in the World Bank's global index "Doing Business" fell by six places, taking it down from 162nd to 168th place (out of 189 countries). The **fight against corruption** again failed to make significant advances and remained limited to a few spectacular arrests of individuals belonging to the ruling regime. In mid-January, the TCS, which came into existence in 2011, dropped a charge of embezzlement of public funds (CFAfr 230 m) against the former director of the now defunct Cameroon Airlines, businessman Yves Michel Fotso, who repaid the stolen money. For the first time since the launching of Operation Sparrowhawk, a prominent personality had officially returned the money that lay at the root of his legal troubles. Unlike Haman Adama, who went through the same process in September, Fotso did not regain his freedom: he was sentenced to 25 years in prison in relation to another matter. On 18 February, the director of the National Refining Company (SONARA), Charles Metouck, was arrested and imprisoned three days after being removed from his post. According to the Supreme State Audit, he was to pay around €41 m in compensation for his bad management from 2007 to 2010. Even more important on the symbolic level was the arrest and imprisonment, on 10 June, of Iya Mohamed, who had been director general of Sodecoton (a public enterprise for cotton manufacture in the north of the country) for 29 years, president of the Cameroon Football Federation (Fécafoot) since 1998, and an eminent member of the RDPC. Although the arrest of this prominent personality from the north of Cameroon took place shortly after a defeat of the national football team, it was officially prompted by his management of Sodecoton, after he was accused of embezzling CFAfr 113 bn.

Few activities or changes took place on the social level. Between February and June, students staged **strikes at the University of Buea**, which is accustomed to such revolts.

The students called for better studying conditions, the payment of research grants and the abolition of fees beyond the tuition fees (fixed by the state at CFAfr 50,000), etc. They also protested against the disbandment by the university's administration of the University of Buea Students Union, a powerful local student organisation. During these strikes, several outbreaks of violence occurred between the security forces and the students. In November, five students were sentenced to four years' imprisonment and fined CFAfr 800,000 for "inciting public unrest".

Several international and Cameroonian NGOs continued their protest, begun in 2012, against a **palm oil plantation** project on 73,000 ha in the south-west of the country. In June, two Cameroonian NGOs announced that they had brought a charge of corruption against Herakles Farms in the USA, the parent company of SG Sustainable Oils Cameroon Ltd, the company responsible for implementing the project. In late April, a report by the Ministry of Forestry and Wildlife accused the US company of using intimidation and corruption to acquire land. In mid-May, the Cameroonian authorities decided to suspend Herakles' activities, specifically for violations of the forest regulations, but this suspension was revoked on 29 May, without any explanation. At the same time, Greenpeace International and the Oakland Institute published a report claiming that employees of Herakles Farms had used corruption to obtain favours in Cameroon. In November, Biya finally granted the company 20,000 ha of land for a concession period of three years, at the end of which a very long-term leasehold agreement could be signed with the state.

Throughout the year, the EU urged Cameroon to ratify, before 31 October 2014, the interim **EPA** signed in January 2009, i.e. within the period stipulated by the EU. One organisation of employers, E-Cam, expressed its opposition. Its executive members explained that the Cameroonians had not had the opportunity to defend their points of view and spoke of the EPA as a "weapon of mass destruction of Cameroonian enterprises". Quoting various studies, they also emphasised that the EPA would not only threaten the nation's still nascent industrial fabric, but also cause the Cameroonian customs to lose around CFAfr 100 bn a year.

Fanny Pigeaud

Central African Republic

The year saw the rising and declining star of yet another politico-military entrepreneur at the helm of the state. Michel Djotodia declared himself president after a rebel alliance swept the Bozizé regime overboard. However, in the aftermath of the uprising, Djotodia was unable to stabilise his regime – and even less the country as a whole. In the western half of the country bloody encounters between predominantly Muslim Séléka groups and Christian militias spiralled out of control, leading to interreligious massacres. The humanitarian situation remained disastrous throughout the year.

Domestic Politics

The first days of the year saw new assaults by the Séléka alliance, moving closer to the capital, Bangui, and facing little resistance. A joint effort by the army, critically supported by peacekeepers of the 'Mission de Consolidation de la Paix en Centrafrique' (MICOPAX), provisionally halted the rebel advance. The MICOPAX commander issued a strong statement: a rebel advance to the strategic city of Damara would be considered a declaration of war on all Central African countries. He was confident that this warning would be heeded and, indeed, rebels and government were then prepared to send envoys to peace talks. A **peace accord** was concluded in Libreville, capital of Gabon, on 11 January, specifying that the president should remain in office until general elections in 2016. An inclusive government of national unity should be formed to serve for that period. President François Bozizé appointed the former human rights activist and opposition politician Nicolas Tiangaye as prime minister on 17 January. Tiangaye did not manage till 3 February to form a broad government of national unity; it included Michel Djotodia, leader of the 'Union des Forces Démocratiques pour le Rassemblement', the best-known Séléka component, as vice-prime minister and defence minister, plus four other prominent rebel representatives. The Bozizé camp retained the key ministries of foreign affairs, economy, public security and mining, while civilian opposition groups and civil society were equally represented.

It was not only the Séléka combatants outside Bangui who were unhappy with this outcome of the peace process. Mohamed Moussa Daffhane, another Séléka leader and now minister of forestry, publicly declared that the rebels had not been given enough positions. Individual acts of violence perpetrated by Séléka rebels were now constantly reported. A rebel attack on Sido in the north-west by the 'Convention des Patriotes pour la Justice et la Paix' (CPJP) caused 4,000 inhabitants to flee to neighbouring Chad and was condemned by two Séléka leaders. In mid-February, probably without the consent of the ministers representing them in government, rebels attacked a number of cities, including the centrally located Sibut, and Bangassou, Gambo and Rafai in the east. Apparently anxious not to lose their power-base, five Séléka ministers (including Djotodia) began touring the interior of the country to discuss peace options and were allegedly captured by rebels on 17 March; this was a tactical ploy. A rebel commander set a 72-hour ultimatum for a number of older demands to be met (liberation of all political prisoners, departure of Ugandan and South African troops, and the dismantling of road blocks). When the three days expired, the Séléka troops attacked again and passed the strategically located city of Damara without resistance by the peacekeepers stationed there – the earlier declarations had obviously become worthless. Entering Bangui on 23 March was more difficult as South African troops put up fierce resistance, but they were soon outnumbered. Bozizé fled Bangui in the direction of Cameroon. This marked the **fourth violent regime change** in the history of independent CAR (after 1965, 1981 and 2003). Djotodia, obviously not a prisoner of the rebels, immediately declared himself president on 24 March. He dissolved the National Assembly and the Constitutional Court, suspended the Constitution and announced on 25 March that elections would take place within three years.

In search of some **minimal legitimacy**, Djotodia had himself elected as president on 13 April by a quickly formed 'Conseil National de Transition' (CNT), a provisional legislature consisting of 105 members (among them 24 representatives of political parties and 15 members of Séléka, plus representatives of all prefectures, religions, civil society organisations, etc.; it was later enlarged to 135 members). The vote took place by acclamation. Djotodia kept Tiangaye as prime minister, a further tactical step aimed at acquiring some outside recognition, but the thin veneer of constitutionality deceived nobody. Tiangaye presented a new government on 31 March; it included some names well known on the political scene plus some rebel leaders, now in more prominent positions. Djotodia changed course over time, bowing to international pressure. First, significantly, on 13 June he added two former Bozizé supporters to an enlarged government (which also included nine ministers from Séléka, seven from the former opposition parties and 16 representatives of civil society and other political parties). On 18 July, Djotodia promulgated a transitional constitutional charter, adopted on 5 July by the CNT – again, apparently under pressure. The charter fixed the transition period at 18 months and stated the ineligibility of the transitional president and the transitional prime minister to stand in future elections. On 15 August, an interim Constitutional Court was installed. The relationship between Djotodia and Tiangaye remained tense. The interim president was inaugurated on 18 August (marking the official start of the transition).

Much more dangerous for the new regime was its inability to establish order. In April, Séléka troops raided large parts of northern CAR. HRW documented the destruction of about 1,000 houses. The Séléka fighters proved undisciplined, divided not only into their five main components, but also into smaller uncontrolled units, and did not obey orders from Djotodia. The nature of Séléka as an irregular ad hoc alliance now proved to have far-reaching consequences. In Bangui neighbourhoods, different **Séléka** units established their zones of control and started a **reign of terror**. But soon resistance grew. Serious crimes by Séléka elements, reported from all over the country, went unpunished and local self-defence groups retaliated. It was at first unclear what role the deposed president was playing in funding or arming such groups, which were summarily named **'anti-balaka'** (anti-machete). In such circumstances, it was unrealistic to believe that an orderly disarmament and demobilisation process would be possible, although some Séléka forces were officially concentrated in specific sites in preparation for such a move. Many official security forces reported back weeks or months after they had disappeared during the battle for Bangui.

Within the **Séléka leadership, major schisms** developed. Mohamed Moussa Dhaffane, senior minister of water and forests, was accused of recruiting mercenaries and buying arms; he was dismissed and arrested on 29 June. As the leader of the 'Convention des Patriotes pour le Salut du Kodro', he had headed one of the main components of the alliance that assaulted Bangui. Séléka factions had clashed with each other in the aftermath of that battle in Bangui and in Bangassou on 15 July. A further government reshuffle took place on 22 August: Nourredine Adam, one of the most prominent Séléka commanders, was replaced as minister of security and immigration by one of Bozizé's key ministers, Josué Binoua, and appointed to a secret service position. In August, more targeted attacks on the new regime were recorded, most probably master-minded by Bozizé, including attacks on villages close to Bossangoa in the west, causing 18,000 people to flee to the prefecture's capital (the number later swelled to 35,000). Many operations officially launched to disarm civilians caused serious trouble. On 28 August, one such operation in the Bangui districts of Boy Rabé and Boeing turned particularly violent. As a result, the population of those districts took refuge on the tarmac at Bangui M'Poko International Airport, bringing a halt to air traffic. On 10 September, Djotodia dismissed Chief of Staff Jean-Pierre Dollé-Waya and replaced him with the former head of the presidential guard under Ange Félix Patassé (1993–2003), Ferdinand Bombayeke. Under strong international and domestic pressure, Djotodia finally announced the dissolution of Séléka and of the CPJP as one of its components on 13 September.

However, this did not prevent the **climate of insecurity** from spreading further – with organised pro-Bozizé militias attacking Bouar in late October, and frequent attacks and acts of retaliation in Bangui, where a judge was killed on 17 November and another gravely injured shortly afterwards in a grenade attack. By that time, the on-going attacks and counter-attacks on villages and neighbourhoods were clearly following religious lines. The **interreligious violence** had spiralled out of control. Boko Haram elements from Nigeria reportedly joined Séléka fighters. However, various local roots of division were more important and were exploited. This was clear with regard to the precarious situation of minority Muslim (partly Chadian) traders in Bangui, who had already in the past made easy scapegoats in times of crisis. Previous events were also an essential element in the targeting of (Muslim) Mbororo nomads in the north-west, who had for decades been accused of being involved in highway robbery. The Catholic Sant'Egidio community invited government and religious representatives to peace talks in Rome in September and the transitional government signed the resulting "republican pact" on 7 November. The document was meant to serve as a framework to promote an inclusive national dialogue, calling *inter alia* for the disarmament of all militias, but this failed to produce tangible results on the ground. The Djotodia régime was not able to mobilise the necessary support either at home or abroad: Neither financial aid, nor the much needed military support was initially forthcoming. When French troops finally bolstered the 'Mission Internationale de Soutien à la Centrafrique' (MISCA) peacekeeping force in November, they found it more difficult than anticipated to reduce levels of violence, even in Bangui. On 5 December, anti-balaka groups launched a major attack against Muslims in the capital, killing more than 1,000 people, according to the UN, and causing the displacement of 214,000. Séléka forces were able to repel the attackers. North of Bangui, cities such as Bossangoa, Bouar, Bozoum and Paoua were the scene of continued fighting.

In these circumstances, less attention than usual was paid to the continued activities of the **Lord's Resistance Army** (LRA). However, several attacks on villages in diamond-producing areas in the east were reported in June and July, with dozens of people killed, villages burnt and about 30 people abducted (the typical LRA strategy). A hitherto unknown 'Mouvement de la Marche Populaire pour la Démocratie Centrafricaine' (MMPDC) had earlier attacked Obo in the east on 25 May. Though joint national and Ugandan forces cooperating in the framework of a Regional Task Force repelled the attack, this meant they had to redeploy to Zémio, thus making them no longer able to track LRA forces. Similarly, the little-known rebel movement 'Front pour la Restauration de l'Unité et la Démocratie en RCA' seized the diamond town of Boda in the west of the country – the movement was earlier reported to be rather active close to the Chadian border and led by the dubious businessman Sani Yalo who had been instrumental in establishing Bozizé's regime in 2003.

The CNT adopted a draft electoral code on 7 November and an 'Autorité Nationale Electorale' was appointed on 16 December to prepare for elections. However, at year's end there was **little prospect of orderly elections** being held soon. Two days later, Djotodia fired Security Minister Binoua, Finance Minister Christophe Mbrémaïdou and Rural Development Minister Joseph Bendounga, apparently without consulting the prime minister and against the stipulations of the transition arrangements.

Foreign Affairs

Peacemaking, peacekeeping and humanitarian aid were the main aspects of international involvement in the CAR. The peace agreement brokered on 11 January in Libreville by Congo's President Denis Sassou Nguesso was obviously too little, too late.

The **violent change of government** on 24 March led to immediate **international reactions**, both the UNSC and the AU issuing harsh statements. The AU suspended the CAR's membership immediately on 25 March. The AU Peace and Security Council advocated in no uncertain terms a "total isolation" of Bangui and announced sanctions including travel bans targeted at seven Séléka leaders. In accordance with Africa's inter-governmental architecture, it was, however, the CEEAC that continued to steer crisis management. Mediator Sassou Nguesso (a former coup leader) did not want to ignore the clear military victory of one party to the conflict. Djotodia ignored the travel ban and visited numerous African countries during his first months in power (Benin, Burkina Faso, Chad, Gabon, Equatorial Guinea and Sudan). However, a CEEAC summit on 3 April in N'Djamena (Chad) put pressure on the new regime. In order to normalise the institutional situation, the heads of state called for the establishment of an interim legislature in the form of the CNT. CEEAC tried to convey the impression that the Libreville peace agreement still had some validity. A follow-up committee on the Agreement met with Djotodia on 10 June and mainly discussed the political transition and the confining of Séléka fighters.

Two African countries had a particular impact on the CAR during early 2013. Some 250 **South African troops** were the only armed units putting up strong resistance to the Séléka incursion in the CAR, but they suffered heavy casualties when 13 soldiers died in the battle for Bangui (27 were wounded). News of this sent shockwaves to South Africa and also infuriated President Jacob Zuma. Zuma, accompanied by three ministers, attended the aforementioned regional summit in N'Djaména, where he agreed to the departure of the South African troops, one of Séléka's key demands. A further sub-regional summit was convened, again in N'Djamena, on 18 April, and Zuma again showed up, confirming his continued commitment. In April, Prime Minister Tiangaye, on his first long diplomatic tour, visited not only European countries but also South Africa, in search of support.

The fact that both summits were held in **Chad** was even more significant. Chad had obviously changed sides during Bozizé's last months in power, although President Idriss Déby had originally been crucial in establishing the Bozizé regime. It was an open secret that the passivity of the Chadian peacekeeping contingent facilitated the rebel advance, the fall of Damara being clear proof of this. Unknown but substantial numbers of Séléka fighters were of Chadian origin. Chad's ambassador later denied that Chadian special forces had helped to take Bangui on 24 March, as Bozizé alleged. On 9 April, Eritrea also denied having armed the rebels, another Bozizé allegation.

At the beginning of the year, the **MICOPAX force** consisted of about 500 personnel in total, with Chad deploying some 400 and Congo, Cameroon and Gabon promising to send up to 120 each. The sub-regional organisations CEEAC and CEMAC renewed their support for the peacekeeping mission several times before the AU's Peace and Security Council decided on 19 July to authorise the deployment of an African-led mission (**MISCA**) for a period of six months. Its overall strength was set at 3,652, including 2,475 military personnel and 1,025 police and it was to be mainly composed of contingents currently serving in MICOPAX – the transition was initially set for August. The AU expressed the wish to see the EU and the UN assisting MISCA. The deployment of additional troops was slow, however. By 31 October, MICOPAX had deployed 2,589 uniformed personnel (mostly military, with only a few police); more than 60% were operating in the capital. An assessment of the mission by the AU and CEEAC found that many basic requirements were lacking, including maintenance and engineering capabilities, air support, command and control communication systems and ammunition. The transfer of authority from MICOPAX to MISCA was rescheduled to 19 December. A joint AU-CEEAC delegation (ministers from Congo and Chad plus the AU commissioner for peace and security) visited Bangui on 28 December.

The bloody anti-balaka attack on Bangui and retaliation by Séléka fighters on 5 December triggered the next level of international engagement. French President Hollande had made it clear in late 2012 that France would not intervene to save Bozizé's regime from attack, but he was unable to avoid getting dragged into the crisis. On 13 October, French Foreign Minister Laurent Fabius visited Bangui and expressed France's willingness to help the country, and on 9 December Paris launched the so-called **Operation Sangaris**, deploying 1,600 troops in support of MICOPAX. Sangaris and MICOPAX started immediately by disarming Séléka fighters, some of whom were now helpless against attacks by Christian militias. The AU Peace and Security Council increased the authorised strength of MISCA to 6,000 troops on 13 December; 850 additional troops from Burundi were quickly deployed until 20 December.

The UN apparatus was again strongly involved in managing the crisis when a **UNSC** resolution on 10 October reinforced the mandate of the 'Bureau Integré de l'Organisation des Nations Unies en Centrafrique', asking for a stronger presence on the ground. On 5 December, the UNSC adopted a further resolution, not only authorising MISCA and Sangaris, but also imposing a one-year arms embargo and urging the UN secretary-general to prepare and plan the possible transformation of MISCA into a full UN peacekeeping operation. Donors tried to coordinate themselves better. A newly formed International Contact Group held a first meeting in Brazzaville (Congo) on 3 May, establishing a trust fund to support the transition, and met again in November. On the ground, the UN, AU, EU, France and the United States established a "group of five" to coordinate their actions.

The involvement of countries of the **sub-region** in the CAR crisis, and the repercussions of the crisis on the region, were a source of concern. Besides the Chadian influence, there was some speculation that South Sudan was involved (along with Séléka) in the MMPDC, although the South Sudan authorities denied this. One of the main demands by Séléka had been the withdrawal of Ugandan troops from CAR territory. After pressure from the AU and the UN, Djotodia issued a statement on 18 June giving assurances that he would support the AU Regional Task Force set up to fight the LRA. Cameroon faced repeated cross-border incursions from armed CAR combatants.

Socioeconomic Developments

The sequence of events – with the renewed outbreak of the civil war, chaos in Bangui and the inability of the new state leadership to establish order – had widespread catastrophic consequences. Real **GDP** was estimated by the IMF to have contracted by about 36%. On 15 November, the transitional government provided a new revenue target of CFAfr 86 bn, only about one-third of the figure in the initial budget. Finance Minister Mbrémaïdou reported that domestic revenue would have fallen by 45% since the coup in March. The decision by the Kimberley process in mid-May to suspend diamond trading with the CAR with immediate effect was also set to have negative effects on **government revenues**, although it was clear that 'blood diamonds' did in fact help to fund the various armed groups operating in the country; the ban was meant to curtail this illegal trade. According to the IMF, the external current account deficit nearly doubled (to 10.4 % of GDP).

The decline in food production as a result of insecurity in the countryside plus supply disruptions produced important shortages, and also resulted in the acceleration of inflation from 5.9% in 2012 to an official 6.6%. The crisis in the CAR developed, in the UN terminology, into a **'complex emergency'**. UN Emergency Relief Coordinator Valerie Amos and the European Commissioner for International Cooperation, Humanitarian Aid and Crisis Response Kristalina Georgieva visited the country on 11 and 12 July. Amos declared that all 4.6 m CAR residents were affected by the conflict. About 1.6 m people were considered at that stage to be in need of assistance, including protection, food, healthcare, water and sanitation and shelter. By November, the civil war had produced 400,000 IDPs and 66,000 refugees in neighbouring countries. In November, 1.1 m people were still rated 'food insecure'. The ongoing civil war also caused widespread material damage. Looting and rape were reported from several scenes of violence, and other atrocities, including cannibalism, were reported by the international media. Establishing an exact figure for people killed proved difficult.

Women and children were strongly affected by the violence. Sexual abuse was widely reported. The Séléka alliance had many child-soldiers in their ranks (reportedly 3,500), and the anti-balaka recruited mostly children and adolescents. Many schools were attacked and looted or served as shelter. According to an international report, 70% of the schools in Bangui, 48% in Ouaka, and 44% in Ombella-Mpoko had been attacked; in some prefectures not a single school was operating. This meant that the **education** system entirely collapsed. The state-sponsored **health** system broke down entirely and only international NGOs maintained some services in some parts of the country. Of particular concern were HIV-infected people on retroviral treatment, who could no longer be treated (with a risk of further deaths and the development of resistance against some drugs). Despite increased international attention, the disaster was listed as one of the world's "forgotten crises". By mid-December, the country had received a total of $ 136 m in humanitarian assistance, representing 47% of the UN appeal launched in December 2012, with the European Commission the most important provider. The full impact of the crisis on socioeconomic development was not yet evident at year's end, but there was no doubt that recent events had taken place at enormous cost and annihilated many years of effort in several key sectors.

Andreas Mehler

Chad

President Déby re-affirmed his control of the Chadian regime during the year. Internationally, he was acclaimed as a saviour when Chad responded quickly to the UN-backed French call for troops to fight Islamist insurgents in northern Mali in January. Regionally, Déby took advantage of the end of the Kadhafi regime and the chaotic situation in Libya to raise the profile of his own role as regional benefactor and power broker. This was most evident in the CAR, where Déby was a key player in the calamitous situation. At home, he easily averted an attempted coup d'état in early May and used the opportunity to put numerous politico-military adversaries out of play.

Domestic Politics

President Idriss Déby Itno continued to run his government by totally imposing his own will. Like many previous years, 2013 saw **multiple changes in the government**. By the end of the year, Chad had witnessed two major ministerial reshuffles and four other government adjustments. On 21 January, Déby appointed Joseph Djimrangar Dadnadji as Chad's new prime minister, replacing Emmanuel Nadingar. Having spent 34 months in office, Nadingar was the longest serving prime minister under Déby when he was forced to leave. Just five days after his appointment, Prime Minister Djimrangar Dadnadji announced a new government, composed of 42 members (34 ministers and eight state secretaries), of whom 26 had been members of the former government but now had different posts. Women were appointed to five posts, representing a mere 12% in the government, so Chad was far from attaining its official goal of a 30% share in government for women. A limited adjustment occurred as early as 19 February, when six members of government were dismissed or changed portfolios. Another adjustment was announced on 23 July, when two ministers were dismissed and others changed functions. On 17 October, another important reshuffle took place when 11 ministers and state secretaries had to go. One of the newly appointed ministers, Daoussa Déby Itno, was the brother of President Idriss Déby and Chad's former ambassador to Libya. This was not the first time Déby had appointed members of his family to important positions, but history has demonstrated that they were not automatically secure. The president's son, Brahim Déby, was murdered in 2007, a year after being sacked by his father from his post as presidential adviser, and Timan Erdimi, a nephew of the president, from being a trusted administrator within the presidential palace had become a leading military rebel sentenced to death in absentia by his uncle after the attempted coup d'état in 2008.

After exactly ten months in office, on 21 November, Prime Minister Djimrangar Dadnadji, was forced to resign. A petition signed by 74 parliamentarians accused him of causing chronic instability in the government and of failing to tackle Chad's high cost of living. In addition, he was accused of making arbitrary arrests in the wake of the attempted coup d'état against Déby in May (see below). He was replaced by Kalzeubet Pahimi Deubet, who had held various ministerial posts in various Déby governments and was, at the time of his appointment, CEO of the important parastatal cotton company CotonTchad. A final adjustment of government occurred on the last day of the year when the young, unknown newcomer Doumagoum Ousman Adda was appointed vice-minister for urbanisation.

By replacing ministers suddenly and without advance notice, often after only short periods in office, Déby made sure that no potential rival could develop a strong power base. As a side effect of this practice, many ministers took advantage of their position to enrich themselves quickly before they were removed. The standard reason given for dismissals was **corruption** in office, but it was common knowledge that one of the surest ways of becoming rich was to become a minister. Accordingly, Chad had for years figured among the most corrupt countries in the world. TI ranked Chad 163rd (out of 177 countries) on its Corruption Perception Index. However, on 26 June, Déby for the first time stated explicitly, in a presidential decree, that a member of government was being dismissed "for embezzlement of funds designated for a development project", showing clearly what most people already thought – that the judicial system was not independent of the will of the president and that many people were judged before a court had considered their case. In fact, many observers argued that the judicial system in Chad was very weak and arbitrary, which was confirmed by other rankings: the Mo Ibrahim 'Index of African Governance' ranked Chad 48th out of 52 countries, taking safety and rule of law, participation and human rights, sustainable economic opportunity, and human development as indicators.

The Legatum Insitute, a think tank that advocates for freedom and prosperity in the world, ranked Chad 142nd (out of 142 countries) on their 'prosperity index' for 2013.

Sacking and replacing top personnel was equally frequent in various state controlled businesses and organisations. For example, in July, Rector Mahamat Ali Moustapha dismissed ten professors at the **University of Abeche** without prior notice. Most commentators ascertained that they were sacked not on the basis of any job-related issue, but for supporting the political opposition.

An indication of the low status of the **rule of law** was the number of presidential decrees issued. The issuing of an occasional presidential decree was regarded by some as a sign of presidential vigour and initiative, but issuing large numbers of them was probably more a way to avoid democratic procedures – and in 2013 Déby issued a record 1,168 decrees. Presidential decrees were thus instruments for achieving his own goals and allowed him to make laws quickly and without challenge. There is no doubt that this practice effectively undermined parliament, and the principle of accountability and democracy more generally.

On 1 May, the regime announced that its defence and security forces had foiled an attempted coup d'état, later reduced to "a conspiracy against the state". In fighting against a small group of "ill-intentioned individuals", three members of the security forces were killed before Déby's forces managed to "neutralize" the conspiracy. The number of conspirators killed was not announced, but two generals (Weiding Assi Assoue and David Gomine) and two members of parliament (Mahamat Kadre and Saleh Makki) were arrested on the same day for attempts at "destabilizing constitutional order and the security of the state". On 7 May, the Department of Justice gave orders for the arrest of Saleh Kebzabo, Ngarlejy Yorongar, Routaouang Yoma Golom and Gali Gata Ngoté, **prominent political opposition figures** and/or members of parliament. Accused of complicity with the conspirators, Ngoté and Golom were imprisoned for a few days, while Yorongar was immediately released. Kebzabo was out of the country but returned for the hearings on the conspiracy in the capital, Ndjamena on 21–22 May. According to official sources, a total of 21 persons were detained by the police following the attempted coup on charges of "conspiracy, endangering the constitutional order and complicity in assassination". Independent newspapers and human rights activists in Chad argued that the real number of detainees was much higher and included two who had died.

Arbitrary arrest and unlawful detention continued to be a serious threat to the population. Freedom House classified Chad amongst the most repressive societies in its world report, stating that it was among the countries that "severely suppress opposition political activity, impede independent organisations, and censor or punish criticism of the State". During the year, AI revealed several instances of political persecution, arbitrary arrest and detention, often without trial, of the regime's perceived political opponents.

The year was particularly perilous for the **media** and opposition forces. Journalists, bloggers and pro-democracy activists were targets of arbitrary arrest and detention.

Many were arrested in May following the attempted coup. Press freedom and freedom of speech were becoming more restricted: Chad was ranked 139th out of 167 countries in the Reporters Without Borders Press Freedom Index, falling 36 places in only two years. A renowned anti-regime blogger known as Vourboubé Pierre was identified as Jean Laokolé by the secret service and arrested on 22 March. Accused of defamation in various weblogs on corruption and bad governance, he was detained at an unknown location for close to five months. Various international and national human rights and freedom of expression organisations campaigned on his behalf. On 19 August, he was sentenced to three years in prison, but was subsequently released.

In May, Makaila Ngeubla, an anti-government blogger from Chad living in Dakar, was threatened by the police and expelled from Senegal. He gained political asylum in France, where he continued his acclaimed regime-critical blog. On 6 May, Eric Topona, the general secretary of the 'Union des Journalistes Tchadiens' (UJT) and freelance journalist for various international news agencies, was arrested and accused of defamation and "abortive conspiracy against public order". Topona was held in detention for more than 100 days without trial before being sentenced to three years in prison, although he was subsequently released. Topona was later granted a residence permit in Germany. On 7 May, the treasurer of the UJT and publisher of the 'Abba Garde' newspaper, Moussaye Avenir de la Tchiré, was arrested and held in detention for four months without trial, accused of inciting a popular uprising. In August, he was sentenced to two years in prison and fined CFAfr 1 m. The sentence passed on 18 September 2012 on the editor of the newspaper 'Ndjamena Hebdo', Jean-Claude Nékim, was upheld on appeal on 4 June. Nékim was given a one-year suspended jail sentence for defamation and his newspaper was banned from publication for three months.

A different type of **politically motivated trial** also took place. On 15 May, the police arrested Mahamat Djibrine, alias El Djonto, on accusations of torturing political enemies of former president Hissène Habré (1982–90). On 17 May, the authorities issued international arrest warrents for four of former president Habré's main collaborators: Bandoum Bandjim, Bichara Idriss Haggar, Abakar Torbo and Mahamat Nouri, all prominent politico-military opposition figures. Most commentators related the arrest orders to the attempted coup in May. Déby himself had collaborated with Habré for years and Mahamat Nouri had been both minister and ambassador under Déby before he became a politico-military opposition leader. It was thus probable that collaboration with Habré was being used tactically and as a pretext, while the main aim was to get rid of politico-military critics of the regime.

Foreign Affairs

On 16 January, Déby decided to deploy 2,000 Chadian troops to support the French-led military mission to hunt down Islamist insurgents in **Mali**. As the only African state to send troops quickly to Mali, Chad gained international renown and this firm and rapid response was probably influential when the UN General Assembly voted in October for Chad to become a non-permanent member of the UNSC for a two-year term (2014–16). In addition, by sending Chadian troops to Mali, Déby also managed to repair relations with France, on hold since Déby and President Hollande had taken opposing positions on the upheaval in Libya in 2011. While Déby supported Kadhafi to the bitter end, France had been the first country to recognise the Libyan interim government. After losing more than 20 soldiers in a desert battle in February and a few more in a suicide bomb attack in March, Déby decided to withdraw Chad's troops from Mali in April. On 2 March, he had proudly announced that Chadian soldiers had killed Abdelhamid Abou Zeid and Mokhtar Belmokhtar, two prominent insurgency leaders in Mali. While the death of Abou Zeid was confirmed by DNA tests some weeks later, the death of Mokhtar Belmokhtar has never been confirmed. He was responsible for the attack on the natural gas facility near In Amenas (Algeria) in January, and was thus very well-known to the international news-reading public.

Déby played an important role in the change of regime in the **CAR** in March. Having considered the CAR as his backyard for years, Déby was instrumental in the fall of President François Bozizé on 24 March, despite having also had a hand in the coup d'état that brought him to power in 2003. Bozizé himself was convinced that Déby's special forces had helped the Muslim dominated Séléka rebellion to oust him, but other sources had it that it was former Chadian rebels and irregular Chadian soldiers who helped overthrow the CAR president. Whatever the case, Déby's military strength and his willingness to deploy troops abroad allowed him to position himself as the Central African strongman, filling in many ways the vacuum left by the death of Kadhafi.

Chad decided to take part in the African-led International Support Mission in the CAR, known as MISCA, to protect civilians and restore state authority as soon as the UNSC authorised its deployment on 5 December. However, the Chadian troops very soon got into trouble in the CAR because many inhabitants, at least of the capital Bangui, viewed Chad as part of the problem rather than of the solution. In a rally in Bangui in December, inhabitants accused the Chadian troops of supporting the Séléka rebels. Chadian troops opened fire on the rally and one demonstrator was killed. There was apparently a discipline problem among the troops of the new regional strongman.

Relations between Chad and **Libya** were friendly and vibrant until the fall of Kadhafi in 2011, following which relations between Déby and the new Libyan regime had encountered many difficulties. Diplomatically, relations became very tense when, in April and May, Déby publically accused the new Libyan authorities of allowing Chadian rebels to arm and train in Libya. The Libyan authorities firmly rejected these accusations. On the ground, numerous conflicts between various ethnic groups living in the border zones between Chad and Libya escalated. In particular, clashes for control over smuggling routes and trafficking between Chadian Toubous and Libyan Arab Zwai intensified during the year. Libya had formally closed its border with Chad, although the more than 1,000 km of desert that makes up the border is hardly controllable. Nevertheless, supported by various donors' development aid money, Chad and Libya reached agreements and made some efforts to strengthen border security between the two countries.

Chad's relations with **China** were put severely to the test in August. Since 2006, when Chad had turned its back on Taiwan and established diplomatic relations with Beijing, China had been a firm investor in Chad. Participating in financing roads, hospitals and the new international airport near Ndjamena, it had established a rather positive image in both political and public opinion. In August, huge oil spills were discovered near Koudalwa village, within the exploration site operated by the China National Petroleum Corporation (CNPC). The oil spills were apparently not only known to the Chinese but were a deliberate act by the CNPC management as part of their strategy to reduce exploration costs. CNPC exploration in Koudalwa was suspended for a few weeks, while the authorities ordered an investigation into the oil spills and the resultant environmental damage. By year's end, the results of the investigation were not known and bilateral relations looked reasonably amicable. The regime's calculation was to make sure that both China and the US remained engaged in oil exploration in Chad in order to be able to negotiate and re-negotiate deals with both of them. The **US** continued to be by far Chad's most important commercial partner, buying more than 80% of the value of total exports from Chad. However, China had overtaken France and was now Chad's second most important buyer.

Déby continued to ignore the ICC's arrest warrant for Sudan's President Bashir (active since 2009) on charges of genocide, war crimes and crimes against humanity in Sudan's war-torn Darfur region, and Déby allowed Bashir travel to Chad to attend the Great Green Wall summit in Ndjamena on 10 May.

After 15 years of intense advocacy by Chadian and international human rights activists, Chad's former president, **Hissène Habré**, in exile in **Dakar** since 1991, was arrested by the Senegalese police in July. He was detained and accused of crimes against humanity, war crimes and torture. He was due to be tried in a Senegalese court in 2015.

Socioeconomic Developments

Concrete planning for a new 30 ha business area in Ndjamena began. It was set to include eight office buildings, a shopping centre and the headquarters of the Chadian Oil and Energy Ministry. The ambition behind the CFAfr 250 bn investment was to turn Chad into the business hub of francophone Central Africa, but the country had a long way to go to raise the interest of international businesses and investors, having one of the world's least favourable **business environments**. In the World Bank's 'Ease of Doing Business Index' issued in June, Chad ranked at the very bottom of the 189 countries classified. The World Economic Forum also ranked Chad the lowest of the 148 countries scrutinised in its 'Global Competitiveness Index', which measured a combination of access to credit, resolving insolvency, enforcement of contracts and ease of access to electricity and registration of property. Nevertheless, GDP rose by an estimated 4%. **Oil** accounted for revenues of about $ 2.1 bn, or 80% of the state budget. While oil production was around 10% lower than in 2012 due to technical problems that had disrupted drilling operations, Chad still produced close to 100,000 b/d, and prospects for 2014 were highly positive, with an estimate that oil production would double. Yet, in spite of massive economic growth during the previous ten years – all based on the exploitation and export of oil – the majority of the population continued to live in abject **poverty** and Chad ranked 183rd out of 187 countries on the HDI.

Chad faced a continued influx of **migrants** during 2013. Many of the roughly 150,000 Chadian returnees from Libya following the upheavals in 2011 continued to need support. Most IDPs in eastern Chad were in need of assistance, not least due to insecurity in the Sudanese Darfur region. Chad had for years hosted a large number of Sudanese refugees from the conflict there and their numbers increased by 30,000 during 2013, reaching close to 350,000, living in 12 camps in eastern Chad. In addition, substantial numbers of refugees from the CAR crisis arrived, leading to increasing conflicts with the local population in south-eastern Chad. By the end of the year, five camps in southern Chad were hosting roughly 75,000 refugees from the CAR, an increase of 10,000 compared with 2012, and many thousands of Chadians living in the CAR also had to return to Chad as they were targeted by the so-called anti-balaka militias. Clearly, the massive number of refugees and returnees placed a heavy burden on local societies and made serious demands on local and central administrations.

The **agricultural harvest** was particularly good, but did not prevent many people from living on the very margins of food security. Even with lower and more stable food prices than in 2012, WFP estimated that around 2 m people in Chad were food insecure. Some 240,000 Chadians were in acute need of food aid to survive, most of them living in the northern (Sahelian) regions of Chad.

WHO estimated that acute **malnutrition**, especially in children, was so significant in five regions that emergency aid was needed. Neither the government nor the international community responded to the needs adequately, however. International appeals for food and health aid were to a large degree ignored. For example, contributions to UNICEF's appeals for Chad met only 28% of the amount called for. Nevertheless, international organisations in collaboration with the government of Chad managed to support tens of thousands of children in severe need of food and water.

While cholera had hit Chad severely in 2012, malaria was the most serious **health** threat in 2013. More than 600,000 suspected cases of malaria were reported, a 50% increase from 2012. An intensive campaign during 2013 provided polio immunisation to close to 0.5 m children and, for the first time, a whole year passed with not a single case of polio registered.

The shrinking of **Lake Chad** over previous decades from 38,000 km^2 to a mere 1,300 km^2 was posing serious problems for fishermen, agriculturalists and herders who depended on water from the lake, and a heavy rural exodus from villages near the lake had already been taking place for years. A strategic plan to halt the exodus and make investments to sustain activities in and around Lake Chad was to have been discussed at a huge international donor conference. However, insecurity and conflicts with neighbouring Nigeria due to actions near the lake by Boko Haram Islamist militias made the government postpone this major event to 2014.

Ketil Fred Hansen

Congo

With President Denis Sassou Nguesso's second term set to expire in 2016, he prepared to engineer a constitutional revision to retain power with a veneer of legitimacy, however thin. Sassou Nguesso expected opposition to his plans from two main sources: his domestic opponents and the French government. Consequently, his domestic and foreign policies focused largely on inoculating himself against their eventual criticisms. At home, he reasserted control over key military and financial posts, while undermining the opposition with an uneven mix of carrots and sticks. Abroad, Sassou Nguesso sought to limit French judicial investigations into regime corruption and attract investors from China and Russia. As Congo's oil production continued to decline and the government's modest efforts to diversify the economy stalled, Congo's growth rate slowed and the unemployment rate reached unprecedented levels.

Domestic Politics

Colonel Marcel Ntsourou, once second-in-command of the 'Conseil National de Sécurité' (CNS) and key lieutenant during the 1997 civil war, had been incarcerated in April 2012, following deadly explosions at a Brazzaville munitions depot. Ntsourou was sentenced to five years' hard labour in September, but released the same month; he had reportedly been tortured in custody. Upon his release, Ntsourou began a media campaign: in a series of interviews with 'Radio France International' (RFI) and independent newspapers in Brazzaville, he accused Sassou Nguesso of gross corruption and, more notably, of ordering the Beach Massacre of 1999, when nearly 400 young men were killed in Brazzaville after repatriation by the UN. The accusation gave new life to a French judicial investigation. Ntsourou was soon visited by two prominent Sassou Nguesso emissaries – his brother Maurice, a prominent businessman, and Admiral Hilaire Moko, a nephew and leading figure in the security apparatus – who advised him to refrain from further criticism. Ntsourou refused and, on the morning of 16 December, his Brazzaville home was raided by the Republican Guard. Four hours later, nearly 40 of Ntsourou's bodyguards had been killed and 55 people arrested, including Ntsourou himself. He was still in police custody at the end of the year.

Sassou Nguesso declared 2013 the "year of education". On 25 February, however, a leading **teachers' union**, the 'Concertation pour la Revalorisation de la Profession d'Enseignant', went on **strike** to protest stagnant wages and underfunded schools. In April, four union leaders were detained for a week, without charge, by the 'Direction Générale de la Surveillance du Territoire'. Denied access to lawyers, the four were labeled "prisoners of conscience" by AI. The union ended the strike in May, after public school teachers were awarded their first pay increase in recent memory. Less than a week after the union leaders were released, the government detained without charge another prominent human rights activist, Joe Washington Ebina, who represented several thousand victims of the 4 March 2012, explosions. The arrest attracted the attention of RFI – Ebina's brother, José Cyr, was a member of parliament and a Sassou Nguesso ally – and Ebina was released a week later.

After securing an overwhelming parliamentary majority in 2012, the government was in no hurry to stage local elections, originally scheduled for June. The government had promised a new census in 2012; the last, conducted for the 2009 presidential elections, had inflated voter rolls in regime strongholds. But Sassou Nguesso ordered the new census only in May. It remained unfinished by December, and **local elections were postponed** until 2014.

The Sassou Nguesso family maintained its reputation for **corruption**. On 13 February, as part of an ongoing French judicial investigation, French police searched the Neuilly-sur-Seine mansion of Julienne Sassou Johnson, a daughter of the president, and reportedly sized $ 10 m. French police soon targeted homes owned by the president's nephews Edgard and Willy, daughters Claudia and Ninelle, son Denis Christel, brother Maurice, wife Antoinette, and Sassou Nguesso himself. In May, Antoinette celebrated her 70th birthday in St Tropez, a five day affair that reportedly cost nearly $ 1.3 m. In December, the French press reported that, between 2005 and 2011, Sassou Nguesso had spent nearly $ 70 m on various luxury goods and property, including $ 1.7 m on suits at a single Paris boutique.

Although 2013 witnessed no ministerial shuffles, Sassou Nguesso made several key **appointments** that reaffirmed his control over the financial and military bureaucracies. Albert Ngondo, director of the public treasury since 1997, announced his retirement. In December, Sassou Nguesso selected his replacement: Calixte Nganongo, his nephew and currently director of financial operations at the key national oil company 'Société Nationale des Pétroles du Congo'. With Ntsourou incarcerated, the CNS was left without a permanent second-in-command. In October, Sassou Nguesso appointed Colonel Christ Bonaventure Engobo, a retired 66-year-old from Owando, Cuvette. A longtime friend, Engobo had played a central role in the 1997 civil war effort.

Brazzaville's independent **media** grew more critical. In May, 'L'Observateur' even suggested that "Sassou Nguesso was at the epicentre of an enterprise almost criminal in its dealings". In June, the 'Conseil Supérieur de la Liberté de Communication' (CSLC), responsible for monitoring local media and presided over by Philippe Mvouou, Sassou Nguesso's former minister of mines, suspended four newspapers for several months for regime criticism. Despite widespread protest, the CSLC issued three more nine-month suspensions in November, which generated unprecedented self-censorship among the few remaining independent newspapers.

Despite widespread public frustration, the political **opposition** remained in disarray. The 'Mouvement Congolais pour la Démocratie et le Développement Intégral' (MCDDI), which dominates the Pool region surrounding Brazzaville, suffered a schism in January. The party's executive bureau removed Hellot Matson Mampouya, its former spokesman and then minister of primary education, from the party. This schism was apparently fostered by the regime itself. Party leader Guy Brice Parfait Kolélas was widely believed to harbour presidential ambitions for 2016, which would require breaking the MCDDI's electoral accords with the ruling 'Parti Congolais du Travail' (PCT). Mampouya, relatively unknown outside Pool, was less threatening to Sassou Nguesso: Mampouya's new 'Dynamique Républicaine pour le Développement' was widely believed to be funded by the regime. The other major southern opposition party, the 'Union Panafricaine pour la Démocratie Sociale' (UPADS), remained virtually irrelevant. Its June party congress elected Pascal Tsaty Mabiala first secretary; just prior to the conference, Christophe Moukouéké, a rival for the party leadership, challenged the legitimacy of the congress. With only seven seats in the National Assembly and four seats in the Senate, the UPADS increasingly lacked the organisational resources to mobilise voters.

Whereas Sassou Nguesso fomented internal divisions among the southern opposition, he simply repressed his northern rivals. The northern opposition was led by two ethnic tékés, Matthias Dzon and André Okombi Salissa, both former government ministers and 2016 presidential hopefuls. The government sought to silence Dzon, in part by depriving his 'Union Patriotique pour le Renouveau National' of elected office. In May, Dzon declared that "Sassou Nguesso's departure in 2016 is non-negotiable"; by the end of the year he was forbidden from travelling abroad and threatened with house arrest. Okombi

Salissa, for his part, was essentially robbed of his political party, the 'Comité d'Action pour la Défense de la Démocratie' (CADD-MJ). Since the CADD-MJ was technically founded by Sassou Nguesso in 1993, he was legally able to abolish it, which he did – much to Okombi Salissa's anger – in May. The government then recruited Lambert Galibali, a minister under former president Pascal Lissouba, to return from Paris and build a constituency in Lekana, Okombi Salissa's home village. In December, Okombi Salissa was "indefinitely suspended" from the PCT Central Committee.

The year witnessed the death of two prominent members of the **military establishment**. General Emmanuel Avoukou, head of Sassou Nguesso's Republican Guard, died in Brazzaville in January, aged 59. A native of Loboko, Cuvette, Avoukou was among Sassou Nguesso's most trusted military aides, having presided over the Republican Guard since 2002. Avoukou was replaced by Nianga Ngatsé Mbouala, 54, a veteran of the civil war effort against Lissouba. In April, General Blaise Adoua died in Rabat (Morocco). An Oyo native, Adoua occupied a series of high level posts following the 1997 civil war effort, and was chief of presidential security at the time of his death. Sassou Nguesso named Adoua's successor in October: Serge Oboa, an ethnic Mbochi and nephew of Jean Jacques Bouya, the minister of great projects and de facto prime minister.

Foreign Affairs

On 29 March, Sassou Nguesso welcomed President Xi Jinping of the People's Republic of **China**, to Brazzaville. The visit was widely interpreted as an indication of China's interest in the continent's natural resources, and Jinping toured a series of Chinese infrastructure projects: a new library at Marien Ngouabi University, Maya-Maya airport in Brazzaville, and a fibre-optic cable connecting Pointe-Noire and Oyo, by way of Brazzaville.

The ongoing investigations into Sassou Nguesso's Paris real estate continued to sour relations between Congo and **France**. Sassou Nguesso travelled to Paris on 7 April, accompanied by nearly 200 aides. He met with French President François Hollande, their first encounter since the latter's 2012 election. Hollande reportedly refused to halt the French judicial proceedings, much to the delight of the hundreds of Congolese nationals who surrounded the Elysée Palace in protest. In December, Sassou Nguesso's lawyer threatened France with legal action.

As tensions between Sassou Nguesso and Hollande grew, French businesses were increasingly squeezed out of the Congolese market. The China Road and Bridge Corporation (CRBC) won a contract to construct a new shipping port just outside Pointe-Noire. Covering an area of 9 km^2, the port would consist of 31 quays, a potassium factory, an oil refinery, and a power plant to serve the needs of area businesses. Despite the lobbying efforts of Jean Jacques Bouya, the CRBC lost its bid to construct an oil pipeline to connect Pointe-Noire with Brazzaville and, ultimately, Oyo, a distance of some 900 km. The contract was finally awarded to OAO Stroytransgaz, a Russian firm with close links to

Vladimir Putin and originally a subsidiary of Gazprom. The firm's principle shareholder, Gennady Timchenko, had wealth estimated at $ 14.1 bn and was subject to an asset freeze in the USA.

As part of his effort to curry international favour prior to a constitutional revision, Sassou Nguesso sought to brand himself as the region's elder statesman. Accordingly, he played a leading role in mediating in the **crisis in the CAR**. In May, Sassou Nguesso dispatched some 400 soldiers as part of the AU peacekeeping mission and, in November, General Jean Marie Michel Mokoko, a presidential counsellor, was named the AU's special representative to the CAR; the CAR's newly installed President Michel Djotodia visited Congo six times after seizing power in March. If Sassou Nguesso emerged as the chief mediator in the CAR dispute, he also became a leading African creditor. Only two years after securing debt relief from the World Bank, IMF and Paris Club, he offered generous loans to Côte d'Ivoire, Niger, Guinea and successive CAR governments. In January, Forbes announced its first French language edition, 'Forbes Afrique', with a distribution of some 25,000 across 23 francophone African countries. It was published by Lucien Ebata, a Congolese businessman born in Ollombo, some five miles from Oyo, and CEO of Orion Oil. Ebata was among Sassou Nguesso's closest confidants, although the latter charged Ebata with creating Orion Oil in 2004 to evade the vulture funds, who were seizing oil tankers operated by the state oil company. The new magazine became a central component of Sassou Nguesso's **public relations offensive**. In July Sassou Nguesso both financed and hosted the first Forbes Africa Forum, a day-long event that welcomed more than 200 guests from Europe and North America. All the guests' expenses were paid by the government; Jean-François Copé, president of the French 'Union pour un Mouvement Populaire', was reportedly paid some $ 30,000 to attend. More generally, this appeared to be part of Sassou Nguesso's effort to shift the economic centre of Central Africa from Libreville (Gabon) – which hosts the New York Africa Forum each August – to Brazzaville.

Socioeconomic Developments

Congo's real GDP grew by 3.6%, reaching $ 12.5 bn. Though Congo's **oil production** dropped slightly, to 290,000 b/d, global crude prices were high enough to offset this fall. Congo remained Africa's third leading oil producer – behind only Nigeria and Angola – but most analysts expected production to continue to decline, and with it the economic growth rate. The Sassou Nguesso government failed to replicate the 8.8% **growth** rate it achieved in 2010. As in previous years, the oil sector accounted for roughly 90% of Congolese exports, with timber and cement responsible for the balance. Although Congo's total exports fell to $ 10.5 bn, the government managed to diversify its trading partners. Whereas China and the USA accounted for nearly 60% of Congolese exports in 2012, in 2013 their share fell to 52%, although China alone accounted for 43% of Congo's crude oil exports. Congo's current account balance rose to $ 638.2 m, and its foreign exchange position remained strong at $ 5.2 bn. After reaching the HIPC completion point in 2010, Congo's external debt was largely forgiven by bilateral and multilateral creditors. External debt totalled $3.3 bn, or roughly 32.1% of GDP and inflation remained low, at 1.7%.

Notwithstanding the government's ongoing infrastructure investments, Congo's **business climate** remained unattractive. The World Bank's Doing Business report judged Congo the fifth worst business climate in the world, ahead only of countries wracked by civil war: Chad, the CAR, Libya and South Sudan. Aspiring entrepreneurs required, according to the World Bank, more than 100 calendar days to start a business; another 135 days to acquire electricity from the 'Société Nationale d'Électricité'; more than 50 days to import or export goods across national borders; and ultimately paid an effective total tax rate of nearly 65% of total profits. Congo's **unemployment** rate, consequently, stood at 53%, placing it 196th of 203 countries ranked by the US Government's World Factbook.

As in previous years, oil revenues had little effect on the living standards of the general population. The country's HDI score remained at 0.53, as it had every year since 2011; 54% of Congolese were living on less than $ 1 per day, a figure unchanged since 2005. Life expectancy inched up to 58 years from 56.3. Clean drinking water and sanitation facilities remained scarce; nearly 30% of the population lacked reliable access to clean drinking water, and nearly 85% of the population were without access to clean sanitation facilities. The US Government World Factbook ranked Congo 186th out of 190 countries for government spending on healthcare as a percentage of GDP (2.5%). Congolese citizens continued to seek a better life elsewhere, leading to a net migration rate of –7 per 1,000 migrants. According to the US Government Factbook, this placed Congo 204th out of 222 countries, just above Somalia. Citizens unable to leave the country continued to migrate to urban areas, leading to an urbanisation rate of nearly 65%, and Brazzaville, the capital, continued to grow steadily.

Brett Logan Carter

Democratic Republic of the Congo

The year was marked by the continuation of the M23 rebellion and their eventual defeat in late October by the Congolese army with the support of a newly established UN Intervention Brigade – the first ever victory of the national army over a Rwandan-backed rebellion in North Kivu. Furthermore, the notorious rebel leader Bosco Ntaganda, who was the key figure in founding the M23 in 2012 and had been wanted by the ICC since 2006, surprisingly turned himself in to face charges in The Hague. Various parallel attempts to end the war with the M23 were ongoing throughout the year. On a national level, the Kampala peace talks finally concluded in December after more than a year of foot-dragging. Controversial national consultations were held about reforming state institutions and security sector reform gained momentum. Meanwhile, on the regional level a framework agreement was signed engaging regional heads of state and the UN. On the international level, a special force, consisting of 3,000 regional troops and tasked with neutralising rebels in the eastern provinces, was put under the mandate of the United Nations Organization Stabilization Mission in the Democratic Republic of the Congo (MONUSCO), and a UN special envoy for the Great Lakes Region was appointed and tasked with overseeing the implementation of the framework agreement. The World Bank granted special funds for fostering peace on a regional level and some donor countries, notably the US, began to take a more offensive position towards the M23. It was the first time in recent history that the crisis in the east was tackled comprehensively on all three levels. However, apart from the M23, a plethora of other armed groups remained active in the eastern provinces and at times benefited from the ongoing war between the 'Forces Armées de la République Démocratique du Congo' (FARDC) and the M23. Due to the continued fighting, the humanitarian situation deteriorated further.

Domestic Politics

Fighting with the M23 rebel group in the eastern province of North Kivu continued until October, when it was eventually defeated by the FARDC and the newly established UN Intervention Brigade (see below). The M23 had been formed and started fighting in March 2012 as a splinter group of the 'Congrès National pour la Défense du Peuple' (CNDP), which had signed a peace deal with the Kinshasa government in 2009. It had been backed by Rwanda from the beginning, had quickly gained ground and made international headlines by occupying and looting Goma, the provincial capital of North Kivu, for a few days in November 2012 under the eyes of the MONUSCO troops stationed there. The mission had come under fierce criticism for its inability to address the crisis. The first initiative of the newly formed MONUSCO brigade was to set up a security zone in and around Goma on 30 July, after heavy fighting broke out between the M23 and the Congolese army close to the city. Expectations of the Intervention Brigade were high in Goma, and local civil society groups engaged in protests in early August to push MONUSCO to finally work together with the new brigade. Protests resumed in late August, when bombs landed on Goma, killing seven civilians. Two protesters lost their lives in unclear circumstances.

Meanwhile, the **M23 suffered from internal friction**. In late February, fighting between factions of the M23 associated with its founder, Bosco Ntaganda, on the one hand and its military leader, Sultani Makenga, on the other caused at least ten deaths. Disputes around the withdrawal from Goma in early December 2012 and what to do with looted goods were at the root of the conflict between Ntaganda and Makenga. On 27 February, Makenga sacked M23 president Jean-Marie Runiga, a close ally of Ntaganda. Heavy fighting between the factions ensued and lasted several weeks, increasingly isolating the faction around Ntaganda and Runiga. Makenga appointed a new M23 president, Bertrand Bisimwa, and continued the peace talks in Kampala. By mid-March, the Makenga faction had gained so much ground in the internal struggle that several high-ranking figures around Runiga went into hiding in Rwanda. Hundreds of soldiers loyal to Runiga crossed the borders into Rwanda and Uganda, handed themselves over to the new M23 leadership or laid down their arms with the help of MONUSCO. On 18 March, **Ntaganda** surprisingly turned himself in at the US embassy in Kigali and asked to be transferred to the **ICC**. It remains unclear whether the Rwandan government knew about his presence on Rwandan soil and why he decided to hand himself in. He was transferred to The Hague on

22 March. The ICC had renewed its arrest warrant for Ntaganda in 2012, adding several charges of war crimes to the charge of recruiting child soldiers already listed. Other sanctioned individuals close to Ntaganda, namely Runiga, Ngaruye, Zimurinda and Badege, who sought refuge in Rwanda, were allowed to stay there, despite arrest warrants issued by the DRC government.

The split seriously weakened the M23 and the new leadership around Makenga struggled to rebuild capacities with the help of Rwandan officials. For several weeks, the M23 was not able to take any ground from the FARDC and had to evacuate several positions, allowing other armed movements, such as the Rwandan Hutu militia called the 'Forces Démocratiques de Libération du Rwanda' (FDLR), to take over. **Heavy fighting between the remaining faction of M23 and the FARDC** erupted around Goma in late May (putting an end to the unilateral cease-fire the M23 had declared in December 2012), and again in mid-July and late August. Fighting between the M23 and FARDC/MONUSCO continued until early November. During a major FARDC/MONUSCO offensive in late October/early November, around 700 M23 fighters were killed in only ten days, according to the FARDC. On 30 October, the M23 lost their last remaining stronghold in the town of Buganana. On 5 November, the **M23** delegation at the Kampala peace talks issued a declaration that it had **renounced the rebellion** and called on M23 soldiers to prepare for demobilisation. It was the first ever military defeat by the government army of a Rwandan-backed rebellion in North Kivu. Hundreds of M23 soldiers, including the top leadership, crossed over into Uganda and dispersed. According to the UN Group of Experts (UNGoE), however, the M23 reassembled and continued to recruit in Rwanda, even after the formal renunciation of the rebellion, and it remains to be seen, whether the group will re-emerge at a later stage. Several factors contributed to the **defeat of the M23**: the weakening of the group due to its internal division and the defection of hundreds of rebels, the robust intervention of the UN Intervention Brigade, the improved performance of the FARDC as a result of restructuring, and increased international pressure on Rwanda, which significantly reduced its support for the rebels compared with 2012.

The **Kampala Peace Talks** between the M23 and the government, which had started in late 2012, officially continued until December. The M23 rebels travelled freely between the DRC and Uganda to participate in the peace talks despite a UNSC collective financial and travel ban from 31 December 2012. However, the talks did not lead to substantial results and were suspended several times. The Kabila government took the view that the peace talks should only deal with a revision of the 2009 agreement, which was given as the official reason for the formation of the M23, whereas the M23 called for fully-fledged peace negotiations, including proposals for a transition period and integration into the army. Both groups were often absent from meetings and only negotiated via Ugandan intermediaries. As early as March, the government drafted a peace deal and the M23 followed up with its own proposals. After these first drafts, several others were put forward by both sides, as well as by the Ugandan mediators, and every time talks were suspended due to ongoing fighting and disagreement between the government and the rebels. One critical issue was the signing of a cease-fire: the M23 first announced in January and repeated in May that they would only continue to talk if the government signed a formal cease-fire agreement, which Kinshasa refused to do. Another crucial point was the fate of the top M23 leadership. The government offered to integrate rank and file fighters into the army but not a number of high ranking officers, basically comprising the entire rebel leadership.

It was only on 4 November, after the de facto defeat of the M23, that both parties agreed on an 11-point draft, notably including the demobilisation of M23 rebels, amnesty for M23 rank and file fighters, the prosecution of war crimes, the release of prisoners of war, the transformation of the M23 into a political party, refugee return, a national reconciliation commission and a commitment to a Framework Agreement. During a joint ICGLR and SADC summit in Pretoria (South Africa), regional heads of state announced that the agreement was about to be signed but, at the last minute, the government declared that it would sign a declaration but not a peace agreement with a rebel group that was already defeated and demobilised. On 12 December, both parties finally signed **separate declarations in Nairobi**, which contained the same points as the final draft agreement, accompanied by a declaration by the ICGLR and SADC.

Following the defeat of the M23, MONUSCO turned their attention to **other rebel groups** operating in the DRC, as foreseen in UNSC resolution 2098. On 14 November, the UNSC issued a statement stressing the need to neutralise remaining armed groups, specifically mentioning the FDLR, the Ugandan militia Allied Democratic Front (ADF), the Lord's Resistance Army (LRA) and "various Mayi Mayi groups". In fact, a number of armed groups operating in North Kivu announced their willingness to disarm and disperse. By late November, around 2,230 rebels had surrendered to the FARDC in North and South Kivu, notably from Nduma Defence of Congo, the 'Alliance pour un Congo Libre et Souverain' (APCLS), the 'Coalition des Patriotes Résistants Congolais', Mai Mai Hilaire, Raia Mutomboki and other Mai-Mai groups.

However, other armed rebels in the eastern provinces continued their activities and benefited from the sometimes chaotic situation in the Kivu provinces and support from the FARDC. In January, the creation of an alliance of various Mai-Mai groups in South Kivu, the 'Union des Forces Révolutionnaires du Congo' under the leadership of a notorious South-Kivu military man, Gustave Bagayamukwe, caused a furore. Bagayumukwe was arrested on 10 February. On 15 May, the 'Mouvement pour la Restauration de la Démocratie au Congo' carried out a brief attack on the important North Kivu city of Beni. Throughout the year, the ADF extended its reach in the province of North Kivu and in early July captured several towns in the area, causing over 66,000 people to flee across the border into Uganda. The Burundian rebel militia 'Forces Nationales de Libération' (FNL) managed to recruit in Burundi and remained active in South Kivu with around 300 fighters, despite some 70 surrendering to or being captured by the FARDC during the year.

Their leader, Agathon Rwasa, reappeared in Burundi in September after being in exile – presumably in South Kivu – since the Burundian elections in 2010. Despite the official determination that the FARDC should fight rebel groups in the east, several local militias in North Kivu received financial and material support from the FARDC, including the APCLS in Masisi, who benefited from fighting between M23 factions and raided the town of Kitchanga in February, causing 5,000 people to flee. The FDLR also benefited from the chaotic situation in the Kivus and support from the FARDC, notably in the form of ammunition supply and joint operations. The FDLR suffered some serious setbacks during the year, including ongoing investigations in Germany and before the ICC as well as the loss of some high ranking officers: the deputy commander of the FDLR, General Stanislas Nzeyimana, disappeared in Tanzania; in September; Ferdinand Nsengiyumva, in charge of operations in South Kivu, was arrested by the FARDC; South Kivu sector commander Hamada Habimana deserted in November; and the FNL killed the FDLR liaison officer in the Ruzizi plain, a sign of increasing conflict between the two former allies. Renewing ties with the FARDC was thus crucial to the survival of the group. However, after the defeat of the M23, MONUSCO underlined its determination to end the FDLR rebellion, and the FARDC started to attack the FDLR. In a communiqué on 12 November, the FDLR asked MONUSCO to refrain from military action and called for negotiations with the Rwandan government. In addition to the armed groups referred to above, a number of Mai-Mai militias were active in South Kivu, partly negotiating integration into the FARDC while continuing to recruit and arm themselves.

Apart from the Kivu Region, **other provinces were also affected by armed violence**. In Ituri/Orientale Province, the 'Force de Résistance Patriotique de l'Ituri', under the leadership of dissident FARDC Colonel Justin Banaloki, alias Cobra Matata, continued to control large areas where there was no authoritative government presence – despite their brief formal integration into the FARDC in 2012. During a major attack on the rebels by the FARDC in August, which displaced more than 30,000 civilians, the army was able to win back a number of villages. In Maniema, heavy fighting around the cities of Kasese and Punia erupted in January between the FARDC and the Mai Mai militia group Raia Mutomboki, causing the displacement of tens of thousands of people. Soon afterwards, Raia Mutomboki attacked Shabunda in South Kivu. The Raia Mutomboki had become increasingly important in South Kivu since the 2011 elections but had only recently started to expand their activity into bordering provinces. In Katanga, the Kata Katanga militia, fighting for the province's independence, attacked civilians in and around Lumbumbashi, the provincial capital, in January, February and July, creating some 45,000 new IDPs. The growing number of attacks showed the government's increasing inability to secure this rich mining area, as most efforts to contain militias were concentrated in the Kivu provinces. In June, the governor of Katanga called for UN reinforcements in the area to address the worsening security situation. Since 2011, the fighting in Katanga had displaced around 400,000 people.

The **LRA**'s operations in Orientale Province continued to decrease during the year and, according to the UNGoE, only about 50 armed LRA fighters remained in the DRC. On 27 July, the LRA commander in the DRC was killed in Garamba National Park in unclear circumstances. Despite the decline in operations, LRA brutality continued to terrorise local populations and caused widespread displacement. In February, the government assigned 500 soldiers to the **joint military task force** deployed by the DRC, South Sudan, the CAR and Uganda, which was launched in March 2012 with the aim of hunting down LRA fighters in the region. Between September and November, the FARDC launched operations against the LRA with assistance from the US Africa Command (AFRICOM).

With the deepening of the crisis in the East, **pressure on Prime Minister Matata Ponyo increased** significantly. An MP for the opposition 'Union pour la Nation Congolaise' (UNC), Baudouin Mayo, initiated a vote of no confidence, stating that Ponyo was unable to handle the crisis in the Kivu provinces. Mayo was able to collect 137 signatures from both the opposition and the presidential majority, which would have sufficed for the censure motion to be passed in parliament. However, on 17 April, 41 MPs withdrew their support, leading to the cancellation of the vote. Ponyo had a good reputation both within the DRC and in donor circles for his economic reforms, although his measures had also touched on the interests of powerful officials, drawing criticism even from within government ranks.

Security Sector reform gathered pace. In January, over 100 high-ranking FARDC officers who had been unable to defend Goma in November 2012 and were said to be involved in the embezzlement of funds and internal competition, were removed from the Kivu provinces. Some had obviously developed close links with local rebel groups. In a further move, thousands of new troops were sent to Goma. In February, Kabila increased the defence budget by $ 91.5 m, arguing that Parliament's original budget proposal was insufficient to deal with the crisis in North Kivu. The government also drafted plans to reform the army, focusing mainly on new structures, equipment and training, and sidelining the pressing question of human rights abuses, impunity and parallel command chains. Supply chains, salaries and the management of elite troops were improved, leading to better performance by the army, notably in North Kivu, and contributing to the later military success against the M23. Rumours of mutilation of corpses and mistreatment of prisoners by the FARDC attracted international attention in July. UN Secretary-General Ban Ki-moon declared that the UN would rethink their support for the FARDC if such infractions continued. The US-trained battalion that was involved had already been accused of mass rape in the town of Minova in 2012. However, after some arrests, including that of the battalion's deputy chief of staff, the issue disappeared from the agenda.

The government also continued its **reform of the Commission Électorale Nationale Indépendante** (CENI). At the end of April, Kabila signed a new law governing the CENI. Its main innovation was the inclusion of three civil society representatives as members of the Commission as a third component besides representatives of the government (six members) and the opposition parties (four members). On 12 June, the new CENI board took office. The controversial head of the Commission, Daniel Ngoy Mulunda, was replaced by his predecessor, Apollinaire Malu-Malu, a Catholic priest. Mulunda had been accused of massive election fraud in 2011. Malu-Malu had a substantially sound reputation, although he faced some criticism, mostly for being close to the government and for his role in the 2006 elections, which had been generally considered free and fair.

On 7 September, **national consultations** ('concertations nationales') started in Kinshasa. Kabila had announced in December 2012 that inclusive talks would be held to end the crisis in the east and reform government institutions, but it was not till 26 June that he finally issued a decree for talks to be convened. They started with a controversial speech in which Kabila compared the talks to the National Conference of the early 1990s and the Inter-Congolese Dialogue of the early 2000 – two landmarks in Congolese history. The two weeks of talks, which gathered together hundreds of participants from the government, opposition parties, civil society and the churches, dealt with five main topics: governance and state institutions; the economy and public finances; demobilisation and reintegration of armed groups; communal conflicts; and peace and reconciliation, as well as decentralisation and reinforcement of state authority. From the start, the talks took a polemical tone. All the important opposition parties criticised the government for taking exclusive control of the talks and announced a boycott, but they then participated (with the notable exception of the 'Union pour la Démocratie et le Progrès Social' [UDPS] and the UNC). The president of the Senate and the president of the National Assembly, who chaired the 'concertations nationales', were initially unable to decide on the form and scope of the talks and issued statements about their aims that did not correspond with the content of the presidential decree. The talks lasted until 5 October, but it was only on 23 October that Kabila addressed the public to give his view on their results. He announced the formation of a government of "national cohesion", without specifying the composition or leadership of such a government. Among more minor decisions, Kabila also announced the holding of a general census before the next elections and the reconsideration of proportional representation for legislative elections. He did not, however, refer to the potential extension of his mandate – which loomed large throughout the year, and was silent about whether Ponyo would remain as prime minister in a new government. The recommendations that came out of the talks were non-binding, but some were acted upon, including the promulgation on 22 October of a law, passed by Parliament three years before but never promulgated, on the establishment of a Constitutional Court. The Court, prescribed by the Constitution, would be the only court able to hold the president to account.

Despite these reform efforts, **conflicts between the government and the opposition**, particularly the most important opposition party, the UDPS, continued throughout the year. The UDPS had not recognised the 2011 election results and its leader, Etienne Thisekedi, continued to claim that he was the legitimate state president. On 25 April, the government arrested 13 UDPS followers on allegations of involvement in a planned coup against the president. Thisekedi himself complained that he was under house arrest in Kinshasa, although the government said it was only protecting the opposition leader – from what exactly they did not mention. The UDPS fiercely criticised the reform of the CENI and boycotted the national consultations.

On 30 December, **fighting** broke out in several strategic places **in Kinshasa**. A group of around 30 armed people attacked the national radio station and announced the "liberation" of the Congo. At the same time, around 20 armed people attacked Ndjili international airport, and another 20 people attacked the Thsathi military base and the presidential residence 'Marble Palace'. In key cities in Maniema and Katanga provinces, shooting erupted between Mai-Mai militias and the army, and the militias briefly occupied the airport at Maniema's capital, Kindu. By the evening, many attackers had been arrested and some 50 people had died. It remained unclear who was behind the attacks and whether they were a concerted action by the same group or the result of different groups jumping on the band wagon. Rumour had it that the group(s) behind the attacks were followers of the influential self-proclaimed Katangan prophet Joseph Mukungubila Mutombo, who supported violent anti-Rwandan action.

Foreign Affairs

On 24 February, 11 countries in the region, including Rwanda and Uganda, signed the **Peace, Security and Cooperation Framework Agreement** (PSCF) in Addis Ababa (Ethiopia). The short agreement addressed two main points: the non-involvement of neighbouring countries in Congo's internal affairs and the reform of Congolese institutions, notably the security and justice system and local administration. The agreement also foresaw improved donor coordination and established a regional oversight mechanism involving all the signatories to the PSCF. On 23 September, the oversight mechanism adopted a number of measurable benchmarks for the implementation of the PSCF, focusing on peace and security, impunity, refugee return, cooperation in resource exploitation and economic cooperation. The benchmarks were developed with the support of a newly established **UN special envoy for the Great Lakes Region**. Mary Robinson, the former Irish prime minister, was appointed to this position by the UNSC on 17 March and tasked with overseeing the implementation of the PSCF. On 13 May, Kinshasa further adopted a three-tier oversight mechanism for the implementation and monitoring of national reforms committed to in the PSCF. However, the three committees of the mechanism remained largely dominated by the presidency.

Proposals to send a special force to hunt down the M23 had emerged as early as August 2012 but had not been pursued. The ICGLR sought to establish an intervention force of 4,000 troops, but lacked funding and logistics. In January, Foreign Minister Raymond Tshibanda held talks with the AU about the deployment of a neutral African force to

Goma, but this did not produce results either. The UN proposed the incorporation of a special intervention force into the existing MONUSCO structure, intending that this would be part of a regional peace agreement to be signed in January, but the proposal failed owing to disagreement between the regional heads of states over the force's exact mandate. On 28 March, UNSC Resolution 2098, spear-headed by France, extended **MONUSCO**'s mandate by a year and finally established an **Intervention Brigade** consisting of three infantry battalions, artillery, special forces and intelligence services to be deployed in and around Goma. The Intervention Brigade was put under Tanzanian command and integrated into MONUSCO. The brigade's task was to carry out targeted offensive operations to neutralise and disarm all rebel groups operating in the DRC. By July, 3,000 soldiers from South Africa, Tanzania and Malawi had gradually been deployed. The decision to establish the brigade marked a shift in UN policy towards the DRC from a largely reactive position focussing on the protection of civilians, to a preventative military stance, and strongly contributed to the weakening of the M23. On 17 May, the Brazilian General Carlos Alberto Dos Santos Cruz was appointed military chief of MONUSCO, replacing the Indian Chander Prakash. On 1 July, the German diplomat Martin Kobler became new Special Representative of the Secretary-General and head of MONUSCO, replacing the USA's Roger Meece. In his first days in office, Kobler repeatedly visited Goma and frontlines in North Kivu. His rather clear and straightforward vision to finally end the war in the Kivus – by military means if necessary – and the fact that he openly took sides with the FARDC surprised many analysts and politicians in the region and marked the beginning of a new robust UN strategy on the diplomatic level, too. This was further reflected in the deployment of **surveillance drones** from December on to monitor the border between the DRC and Rwanda and gather intelligence about rebel groups operating in the area. This move was contested from the beginning, particularly because it was unclear who would have access to the information gathered. Rwanda had been especially opposed to the UN proposal presented in January, arguing that the drones would not help foster the peace process and stating that the region was not to become a laboratory for foreign intelligence devices.

The **ICGLR** held a series of extraordinary summits on the situation in the DRC. During a meeting in Kampala (Uganda), in early September, the ICGLR granted MONUSCO permanent representation in the Expanded Joint Verification Mechanism (EJVM) established in August 2012, which comprised senior military officers from the member states and was tasked with controlling the border between the DRC and Rwanda.

Relations with Rwanda worsened through the year, with their governments accusing each other of shelling their respective territories. After a total of 34 bombs landed on Rwandan soil in the last week of August, the Rwandan army deployed tanks along the border and issued threats that they would invade the DRC if the government was not able to bring the situation under control. However, an EJVM report dated 1 October suggested that most of the shells originated from M23-held territory. Kigali furthermore accused the UN Intervention Brigade and Tanzania of supporting FDLR militias in North Kivu, while Kinshasa continued to accuse Rwanda of backing the M23. According to the UNGoE's interim report in July, Rwanda's support for the M23 had decreased in the first half of the year compared with 2012, although the M23 continued to recruit fighters on Rwandan soil and in phases of combat the M23 received ammunition and arms, as well as direct military support from the Rwandan Defence Forces. Despite Congolese arrest warrants for a number of M23 leaders who had crossed the border into Rwanda after the split between Ntaganda and Makenga, Rwanda did not extradite them. In August, the UNSC was unable, due to Rwanda's opposition, to agree on a French-backed declaration on the situation in the DRC which called on the M23 – but not on the FARDC, as Rwanda demanded – to end hostilities. A week later, on 28 August, Rwanda effectively prevented the UN from imposing sanctions on two M23 leaders.

South Africa strengthened its alliance with the DRC. The reason behind the rapprochement was twofold. First, relations between South Africa and Rwanda soured due to an ongoing struggle for regional influence and diplomatic problems between Pretoria and Kigali. By taking sides with the DRC in the Kivu crisis, South Africa hoped to curtail Rwandan influence in the region. Second, South Africa's ANC government had a growing economic interest in the DRC. Besides the oil sector, its biggest investments were flowing into energy provision for electricity from the Inga Dam. On 29 October, an agreement was signed on the development of the Grand Inga project, granting South Africa 2,500 MW of power from the dam and thereby significantly easing South Africa's power shortage. In February, the South African authorities arrested 20 members of the Congolese rebel group 'Union des Nationalistes pour le Renouveau' (UNR), including Etienne Kabila, who claimed to be President Kabila's half-brother – a claim repeatedly denied by Kinshasa. The group was allegedly involved in a coup plot against the Congolese government. The presidents of the DRC, South Africa and Angola met on 12 March and 23 August in Luanda (Angola), to launch a "tripartite mechanism" that foresaw widespread cooperation between the countries. In August, the defence ministers of the three countries signed a memorandum of understanding on cooperation in training the DRC army and police. The appointment of Carlos Dos Santos Cruz as force commander of MONUSCO caused a serious dispute with South Africa, which had hoped to gain more control over the mission to balance the appointment of a Tanzanian commander of the Intervention Brigade.

On 23 April, **Angola** and the DRC decided to jointly develop a portion of an offshore oil block situated in the 10 km-wide Common Interest Zone (CIZ) off the DRC coast. It had been established by Angola and the DRC in 2004 and was operated by the US oil company Chevron. This marked a new direction in a dispute over maritime borders and offshore oil located in the CIZ between the DRC and Angola that had been simmering since 2003. In addition to the "tripartite mechanism" launched in March and the memorandum of understanding signed in August, this was a further sign of improved relations between Kinshasa and Luanda.

Relations with **Uganda** revolved around the M23 rebellion and the Kampala peace talks, facilitated by Ugandan Defence Minister Crispus Kiyonga. According to the UNGoE, although the M23 maintained recruitment networks in Uganda, there was no evidence of widespread support for the rebels by the Ugandan government or army. After the defeat of the M23, its top leadership, including Makenga, crossed the border into Uganda and had not been extradited by the end of the year.

On 15 February, **US** President Barack Obama signed a law allowing the US government to offer financial rewards for information leading to the arrest of war criminals. In his press statement, he did not name individuals but specifically mentioned the M23 and the FDLR as affected by this new legislation. The year thus marked a slight change in US policy towards the region. Hitherto, the US had strongly supported the Rwandan government, but as increasing evidence of Rwandan support for the M23 was published by the UN, the US became increasingly reluctant to back Kigali unconditionally and took a more offensive stance towards the M23 rebels. AFRICOM continued to assist the anti-LRA joint task force by, inter alia, training FARDC units. Under the presidency of the US and chaired by Secretary of State John Kerry, the UNSC debated the situation in the Great Lakes during an extraordinary meeting on 25 July.

Relations with **China** were dominated by the mining industry. A mines-for-infrastructure deal between the Chinese consortium Sicomines and the Congolese government, signed in 2009, included Katangan mines that were to start operating in 2013 – which did not happen until the end of the year. On 19 June, AI published a report on conditions in artisanal mining in the DRC, accusing Chinese operators of the worst human rights violations in the industry. In an effort not to endanger the DRC's relations with China, Communication Minister Lambert Mende called the report unfair, stating that working conditions were the same in other mines.

Investigations into the **FDLR leadership in exile** took place during the year. The trial of former FDLR president Ignace Murwanashyaka and vice president Straton Musoni, begun in 2011 in Germany, made some progress, as Musoni finally decided to testify in August, although he denied any knowledge of war crimes or crimes against humanity committed by the FDLR.

Socioeconomic Developments

The **humanitarian situation** continued to deteriorate, especially in North Kivu. Violence against civilians increased, including sexual violence and recruitment of child soldiers by the M23. Due to the volatile security situation in North Kivu, humanitarian aid also faced serious challenges in reaching affected populations, which left hundreds of thousands without proper assistance. The M23's main source of finance was by looting and levying taxes on the population in the area they occupied, which further affected the living conditions of people living in M23-held territory.

According to the UN, the number of IDPs increased to 2.9 m by December, with more than 50% of them coming from North Kivu (over 1.1 m) and South Kivu (580,000). **Numbers of refugees** rose to 430,000 in December, hosted mainly in Uganda (150,000), Rwanda (72,000), Burundi (43,000), and Tanzania (64,000), but with a significant number also residing in the Republic of Congo, South Sudan, Zambia, the CAR, and Angola. In October, the alleged arrival north of Goma of thousands of Kinyarwanda-speaking returnees caused controversy, as various local authorities and organisations accused Rwanda of infiltrating Rwandan citizens among them.

A cholera epidemic struck the province of Katanga and, according to the UN, more than 11,000 cases and 257 deaths were reported between January and July. Other provinces affected by outbreaks of cholera during the year included South Kivu and Orientale Province.

During a three-day visit to the region in May, **World Bank** President Jim Yong Kim, announced a $ 1 bn aid package of interest-free loans for development projects in the region – including the DRC, Rwanda, Burundi and Tanzania – to foster regional economic cooperation and thereby the peace process. The World Bank said the package was conditional on the implementation of the PSCF, but gave no further details. Nearly half of the funds were assigned to hydropower projects in the three countries, $ 165 m to road construction projects in the DRC's eastern provinces and a further $ 180 m to infrastructure and border management between the DRC and Rwanda.

Transparency in the mining sector continued to pose serious challenges. On 15 January, the government presented the latest Extractive Industries Transparency Initiative (**EITI**) report, covering revenues for 2010. Reporting had been much improved since the previous report but serious flaws remained. On 18 April, the EITI board suspended the DRC's candidate status for a year, offering the government an opportunity to address the flaws by March 2014. EITI certification is usually refused if all requirements are not met at once and, with the DRC failing to meet two requirements, this decision was thus rather mild. On 29 May, the Africa Progress Panel, headed by Kofi Annan, issued a report underlining the vast negative impact on DRC government revenues of the lack of transparency in mining deals concerning state-owned assets.

The **revision of the mining code**, which had been scheduled for 2012, dragged on throughout the year, having been delayed several times by resistance on the part of mining companies and some politicians. The government's aim was to increase the state share in mining from 5% to 35%, raise royalties on cobalt and copper from 2% to 6% and raise tax on profits from 30% to 35%. Another proposed change was to lower the stability clause from three to ten years. The clause protects companies from legislative changes. Mining companies fiercely criticised the government's plan to ban exports of cobalt and copper concentrates in order to boost local processing. The companies claimed that the electricity supply was insufficient to process ore in the DRC, although important producers such as the Swiss company Glencore and the US company FreeportMcMoRan, responsible for over 50% of the DRC's copper output, were already processing on site. In addition, the state-owned Gecamines announced in January that it would invest $ 1.5 bn in a copper processing plant in Katanga with an annual capacity of 200,000 tonnes, although it was unclear how construction would be financed. The export ban was announced in April but was delayed several times.

After talks with the government in February, the **IMF** decided to withdraw its offer of a $ 225 m, part of a three-year loan agreement worth $ 532 m. The agreement had been suspended in late 2012 after the government failed to provide details of the 2011 sale of 25% of the Gecamines Comide Sprl copper project to Straker International Corporation, which is owned by Dan Gertler, an Israeli businessman and close ally of Kabila. The government had hoped that the IMF would revisit its decision but failed again in February to provide the missing information.

Gold production continued to increase. Kibali mine in Orientale province, the largest gold mine in the DRC, and one of the largest in Africa, started production in September. According to the US-based operator Rangold Ressouces, the mine had reserves of over 10 m oz of gold. Rangold held a 45% share, the South African AngloGold Ashanti 45% and the state-owned Sokimo 10%. The $ 1.7 bn investment project required the resettlement of some 4,000 families. The mine was expected to provide a significant boost both to local income and to the country's economy as a whole. Despite the increase in gold mining in peaceful parts of the country, the UNGoE stated in their end-of-the-year report (issued on 23 January 2014) that most of the officially exported gold was in fact blended with gold produced in conflict areas. The report estimated that 98% of gold produced in the DRC, with a value of between $ 383 m and $ 409 m, was smuggled out of the country.

In an attempt to spur lending, the **Central Bank** cut its benchmark lending rate from 20% in late 2011 to 2% in November 2013. On 15 May, Mwana Nyembo was appointed governor of the Central Bank following the retirement of Jean-Claude Masangu after 16 years in post. Nyembo largely continued to follow Masangu's policy of focusing on maintaining low inflation and stabilising the local currency. Consumer price **inflation** continued to fall from over 50% in 2009 to under 10 % 2012 and finally to 1.3% in 2013. **GDP** continued to grow at a rate of 7.9%, mainly due to increased mining activity. Despite infrastructural shortcomings, such as the inadequacy of the road network and shortage of electricity, investment in the mining sector continued to flow and multilateral and bilateral public infrastructure programmes, as well as private investment mainly in Kinshasa, boosted the construction sector.

Claudia Simons

Equatorial Guinea

The year was characterised by the consolidation of both the ruling clan's power and its long-term strategic positioning. The sweeping victory of President Teodoro Obiang Mbasogo and the Partido Democrático de Guinea Ecuatorial (PDGE) in the legislative elections in May, which were accompanied by allegations of foul play by both opposition parties and human rights advocates, led to the entrenchment of the elite establishment for the foreseeable future. The president's son, Second Vice President Teodoro Nguema Obiang Mangué (Teodorín), narrowly escaped embezzlement charges in US courts but remained wanted for money-laundering in France. Following Western pressure for transparency in the hydrocarbons sector and continued criticism of the regime's human rights record, the president and his inner circle of ministers took more steps to end the country's perceived over-dependence on Western FDI and aid by inviting the further engagement of regional and Chinese business interests. At the same time, consistent forecasts of a decline in oil production and pressure to meet goals outlined by the country's National Development Plan, Horizon 2020 (NDP), led the government to continue to diversify its revenue base away from oil and towards natural gas and non-hydrocarbon sectors that predated the extractive era.

Domestic Politics

The constitutional reforms approved by a highly criticised referendum in November 2011 formally aimed to improve democratic governance by creating a separation of powers, with planned **senatorial, parliamentary, and municipal elections**. Although the elections were originally set for the beginning of the year, the government postponed them to May, purportedly so as not to conflict with the Africa-South America Summit held February in the capital, Malabo.

Despite government rhetoric to the contrary, the process leading up to the May elections was criticised as being neither free nor fair, while the election results, an unqualified victory for the ruling PDGE, were highly disputed. The **Convergencia Para la Democracia Social (CPDS)**, the most critical opposition party, publicly questioned the validity of the voter registration process as only 291,713 nationals had been registered by late February, while as many as 330,000 had been registered for the 2011 constitutional referendum. It was claimed that the names of deceased persons and children appeared on the register, and **intimidation of the opposition** was allegedly widespread. In January, a member of the CPDS was detained for possession of campaign material outside the official campaign period, which began in late March, and several reporters and human rights advocates were arrested after that, leading up to election.

The campaign itself was also deemed to be fraught with intimidation, not only of parties opposed to the ruling PDGE but also of voters themselves. The CPDS lodged further complaints that the PDGE had threatened sanctions against those who voted for the CPDS, as the PDGE continued its public denigration of the opposition party as "bandits" and enemies of the country. Furthermore, the regime had managed to consolidate support for the PDGE by co-opting all ten pro-presidential opposition parties, including the 'Union Popular' (UP), a move that superficially cast the elections as open and legitimate while effectively strengthening the president's base. In addition, the president reportedly had Facebook and opposition websites blocked in May following an announcement of anti-Obiang protests by students and opponents.

The 26 May elections produced a **lopsided victory for the PDGE**, which, along with its ten coalition partners, captured all but one seat in each house of Parliament. The official results gave the PDGE and its coalition 54 of the 55 seats in the 70-member Senate (the remaining 15 members being constitutionally appointed by the president). In the lower house, the ruling party captured 99 of the 100 seats, while it took 295 of 300 municipal posts. Although the CPDS published its own results, which gave them 17 seats in Parliament, ten in the Senate, and 46 in the municipalities, the regime's tight grip on the electoral process and the president's de facto control of the judiciary precluded any serious appeals.

Despite **international criticism of a flawed election**, the regime continued to stifle dissent by dispersing an unauthorised CPDS protest against the election results on 25 June in Malabo. It went even further by briefly detaining nine CPDS leaders. Furthermore, increased spending on security, arbitrary arrests and torture were deployed to silence continued internal criticism. Outside the country, civil rights groups such as HRW, AI, and EG Justice issued damning statements.

Following the elections, the president, pursuant to his constitutional powers, appointed a new cabinet in September, though it differed little from previous governments. The ministers of justice (Francisco Javier Ngomo Mbengono) and agriculture and forestry (Miguel Oyono Ndong Mifumu) were removed, the latter being replaced by UP leader Alfredo Mitogo Mitogo, who had given the president his support.

Foreign Affairs

Much of the regime's diplomatic activity was driven by the continued need to reduce dependence on traditional Western donors and financiers sensitive to accusations of graft by international civil society, while the government also sought to promote external and internal legitimacy and commerce through summits and state visits.

Continuing court actions against Teodorín further soured relations with the West. An attempt by the US Justice Department to seize Teodorín's property fell flat as the federal judge dismissed a complaint under the Federal Corrupt Practices Act alleging that a $ 38.5 m jet had been procured through the private use of public funds. The judge first ruled that the prosecution had failed to provide enough evidence but then granted the Justice Department more time to collect the necessary proof, holding out the probability of future proceedings. As a result of the previous decision, however, **an international arrest warrant issued by Interpol was withdrawn**.

In contrast to the setback for US prosecutors, the French authorities moved to liquidate Teodorín's multimillion-dollar property in Paris. In another blow to Teodorín, an arrest warrant issued by a French judge in July 2012 for a money-laundering conviction was upheld. His appeal, which argued that the villa in question was used for diplomatic purposes, was dismissed and his request that the International Court of Justice (ICJ) annul the warrant failed to gain traction since neither France nor Equatorial Guinea had consented to relevant portions of the Vienna Convention that would have granted compulsory jurisdiction. It came as little surprise, then, that the president accused France and Total in mid-summer of orchestrating fuel shortages in order to "provoke social unrest in Equatorial Guinea."

A series of high-profile summits held in Malabo served to legitimise the regime amid a torrent of bad publicity, as well as to address other pressing concerns: UK Prime Minister David Cameron publicly denounced the country's human rights record at the June G8 Summit and US President Barack Obama further indicated a **diminished need for Equatoguinean oil exports** in the US. These statements followed a harsh critique by the State Department of the regime's stewardship of the legislative elections, despite the pomp on the occasion of the opening of the new American embassy in the capital. In February, the Equatoguinean authorities played host to the Third Summit of Heads of State and Government of Africa and South America, an event the president used to delay legislative elections, while in August the Third Summit of Heads of State of the Gulf of Guinea Commission (GGC) was held in the Sipopo Conference Centre in Malabo. At the GGC, President Obiang presided and focused on security within the oil-rich Gulf region, an urgent topic due to the **heightened incidence of pirate attacks and the implications for regional maritime security and investment.** In February, a UK-flagged ship sailing in international waters between Equatorial Guinea and Cameroon with a cargo of wood was attacked; its crew were taken hostage and the cargo was paid as ransom. In March, a large wooden boat capsized off the shores of Malabo, killing 166 passengers believed to be Igbo traders heading to Gabon, and in April, a further example of **insufficient maritime security** occurred when a German cargo ship was attacked nearer the Equatoguinean island of Bioko. In August, the authorities enjoyed a brief respite from security shortcomings when Egypt handed over to Equatorial Guinea the Chair of the UN Africa States Group, a symbolic post but one that nonetheless entailed the first visit to the country by a president of the UN General Assembly.

Largely ceremonial events were interspersed by bilateral state visits aimed at shoring up FDI in the hydrocarbons sector and **realigning the country towards regional and Eastern donors and investors.** Coinciding with the awarding of several oil blocks to Nigerian companies, President Obiang received Nigeria's President Goodluck Jonathan in both February and March, officially to discuss both maritime security and economic links between the two countries. For officially similar reasons, Obiang visited Luanda to meet with his Angolan counterpart Jose Eduardo Dos Santos. One topic of discussion was Equatorial Guinea's unlikely inclusion into the CPLP, to which it had been repeatedly denied entry. Lastly, Second Vice President Teodorín met with Chinese Vice President Li Yuanchao in Beijing during Teodorín's lengthy tour of China in November. The visit was aimed at building on increasing Chinese investment and cooperation in the oil and gas sectors, in which China, Nigeria and Angola already had significant links or investments.

Frustrating the regime's efforts to secure future revenue, however, was an **ongoing territorial dispute with Gabon** over the ownership of the potentially oil-rich islet of Mbañe. The two sides did not reach a settlement but, at the prodding of a UN mediator who arrived in April, agreed to consider having the border dispute adjudicated by the ICJ. UN Secretary-General Ban Ki-moon also argued for a resolution to be sought at the ICJ in separate meetings with each head of state in September.

In regional politics, the government eschewed the pressing need to diversify its oil-driven economy, as well as to build international support for the regime, by stating in November that **it would not implement the CEMAC accords** necessary to advance regional integration. The accords would have increased the free regional movement of people and goods – a potential boon to the private sector – but they failed due to formidable opposition in Equatorial Guinea and elsewhere in the oil bloc. Not only did the regime view such integrative steps as threats to its sovereignty, but the country's influx of foreign workers had also traditionally been a source of tension thanks to stark inequalities in pay between employees in the oil industry and those in other private enterprises. In December, however, the authorities revealed their pragmatic stance towards regional politics in an image-conscious show of commitment to the AU's objectives when the government committed 200 troops to peacekeeping efforts in the CAR.

Socioeconomic Developments

As a result of having a tiny population of roughly 700,000 and an estimated GDP of $ 17 bn, Equatorial Guinea again registered the highest per capita income in SSA. Even so, extreme levels of **income inequality** meant that, according to the IMF, around 75% of Equatoguineans were living below the national poverty line. This situation was probably only tenable thanks to a stabilising mix of oil-financed repression and clientelism. Reporters Without Borders ranked Equatorial Guinea 166th out of 179 surveyed states in its Press Freedom Index, a drop of five places from 2012. On TI's Corruption Perception Index 2013, the country ranked 163rd out of 177 states, another slight dip from the previous year. The UN Africa Progress Panel, in its annual Africa Progress Report published in May, noted that "Equatorial Guinea is richer than Poland but has a child death rate 20 times higher."

Equatorial Guinea is the fourth largest producer of oil in Africa, and crude oil remained its most important extractive industry, accounting for 90% of government revenue, while hydrocarbons production contributed around 90% of GDP. Nevertheless, **real GDP contracted by an estimated 1.5%**, most probably due to a parallel **drop in oil production** from an estimated 313,000 b/d in 2012, according to the 'Business Monitor International', to roughly 276,000 b/d in 2013, according to the Economist Intelligence Unit. Furthermore, the country again faced a negative current account balance of $ 2.6 bn (nearly 16 % of GDP) and external debt of $ 2.2 bn. Projections of economic decline led the BEAC to cut its lending rate twice during the year in order to spur growth. Maturing oilfields such as Zafiro, Ceiba, and Okumé, operated by ExxonMobil, Amerada Hess and Hess, respectively, continued to face declining output. The coming on stream of the Noble-operated Alen gas field later in the year somewhat offset the decline, and the state-run Sonagas, with its 3% share in the field, contributed a little to government revenue.

As a result of **dim longer-term prospects in the oil sector** and the implications of that for growth, the government's response was twofold. First it looked to increase hydrocarbons production and the revenue therefrom, though expectations of major discoveries remained low except with regard to natural gas. The year's initiative began with the awarding by February of eight new production-sharing contracts (PSCs), to which the signatories included many junior oil companies from China, Nigeria and Ghana. In January, for example, RoyalGate, the international arm of Nigeria's Atlantic Energy, won operating rights in block Z and a minority stake in block Y off of Bata, the largest mainland city.

In spite of these efforts, the government and its state-owned oil firm, GEPetrol, still continued to demand 35% of all oil revenues, and the government's desire to increase the capital gains tax on multinationals may have contributed to the relative absence of oil majors in the new PSCs. In June, **civil proceedings between the government, Hess and Tullow Oil** were yet again postponed for failure to reach an agreement on the payment of tax on the 2001 acquisition of the large Ceiba offshore field. In October, however, another dispute involving the government's desire to tax the sale of CMS Energy's share in the Alba licence and block D to Marathon Oil in 2001 looked on the cusp of resolution as both sides submitted pledges before the International Centre for the Settlement of Investment Disputes, an outcome that might inform the tussle with Hess and Tullow. The **unlikelihood of huge discoveries being made** in these blocks may have also been a factor in the absence of resident perennial giants like Noble, Marathon, and Amerada Hess from the list of signatories. Lastly, the process of awarding the PSCs was relatively opaque, and larger Western majors were more susceptible to civil society criticism at home than many of their East-Asian and African counterparts.

The regime's second response to projections of long-term contraction was to diversify its economy and attempt to reduce poverty in accordance with the NDP, though progress towards both these ends was minimal. In April, the IMF published its Article IV Consultation report, which revealed excessive public spending on prestige projects in recent years, minimal investment in health and education, weak oversight and waste, scant provision of public services, and a dangerous overdependence on volatile oil markets, a combustible mix considering the mounting government and current account deficits. Despite its acknowledgement of improvements in infrastructure, the IMF urged the government to **expand the non-hydrocarbons sector and shift spending to the poor**.

In view of these assessments, the government implemented **several initiatives, with questionable results**. In June, it announced a plan to reinvest in two sectors predating the extractive era, namely agriculture and fisheries, and also to invest in eco-tourism, by issuing loans through the private National Bank of Equatorial Guinea. The first loans, guaranteed by the Ministry of Economy, Commerce, and Business Promotion and totalling $ 740,000, were disbursed in August to 22 unidentified small and medium-sized enterprises. The anticipation of a potential boost to local private-sector development was tempered by suspicions that nepotism and corruption would derail such efforts. In September, as part of another NDP initiative, an American company began construction of a solar power plant on the remote island of Annobón whose miniscule population of 5,000 would enjoy cheaper electricity and reinvigorated local commerce. Lastly, yet another NDP initiative to relieve dependence on expensive diesel generators saw a $ 1 bn deal reached with the China Machinery Engineering Corporation to begin a four-year electrification project, further details of which remained unknown.

Joseph N. Mangarella

Gabon

Municipal and cantonal elections were held in December, resulting in another victory for the ruling 'Parti Democratique Gabonais' (PDG). President Ali Bongo, travelling around the world to attract foreign investors, continued pursuing his development programme 'Gabon Emergent'.

Domestic Politics

The big news politically in 2013 was **local elections**. By 30 March, 14 parties had formed an opposition coalition called 'Union des Forces du Changement' (UFC). The government's failure to submit new biometric electoral lists one month before the vote scheduled to take place on 23 November led opposition parties to cry foul and demand a postponement. Prime Minister Raymond Ndong Sima filed a request with the Constitutional Court on 23 October, which granted a postponement until 14 December. This was the first time that elections had ever been postponed in response to opposition demands.

In total, **54 communes** around the country were up for grabs, in addition to **48 departments**. The ruling PDG had traditionally done well in the vast and sparsely populated interior of the country but had less solid results in the densely populated cities. The last local elections, in 2008, gave the PDG 1,154 out of 1,990 municipal seats (58%), but in the capital, Libreville, the country's most populous city, with 700,000 inhabitants out of a total population of 1.5 m, opposition parties managed to take control of three of its six *arrondissements*.

In particular, the concentration of ethnic Fang in the capital had long been the base for a number of powerful opposition parties, including 'Rassemblement Pour le Gabon', the now-dissolved 'Union National' (UN) in the 2nd district, and 'Cercle des Libéraux Réformateurs' in the 3rd district. On the other hand, the ruling PDG had managed to take control of the southern oil capital, Port-Gentil, away from its ethnic Punu-Eshira opposition party, 'Union du Peuple Gabonais' (UPG), after the death in 2011 of its long-time leader Pierre Mamboundou. Of course, the ruling party had always managed to hold onto eastern Franceville, hometown of the Bongo clan, and the third largest city in the country, but not the fourth largest city, Oyem, a bastion of the rebellious northern Fang, where independent candidates had traditionally prevailed.

On 14 November, the Constitutional Court declared Casimir Oyé Mba, a Fang and former prime minister who had joined the opposition, ineligible to put himself forward as 'head of list' in the commune of Ntoum, 40 km south of the capital, because he was registered to vote in a village located outside the municipality's territorial boundaries. Mba had been a head of list for the ruling PDG in the local elections of 1996, 2002 and 2008, despite voting in his village of birth. But when Ali Bongo succeeded his father to the presidency in 2009, Mba made the fatal error of joining other former PDG barons in the losing opposition party, UN, later dissolved when its candidate, André Mba Obame, declared the ballot count fraudulent and proclaimed himself the winner. From then on, both he and other Fang former barons who had defied the Bongo dynasty found it impossible to re-launch their political careers.

The election was held on 14 December. This was the first time a ballot had been conducted on the basis of 'biometric' electoral lists. This is important because the failure to provide **biometric voting** was the main reason for the opposition boycott in the 2011 legislative elections, which had resulted in the PDG taking 114 out of 120 seats in the National Assembly. The opposition observed that, despite using new lists, the PDG had failed to provide them with biometric voting cards, and so election officers were still permitted to identify voters visually. Opposition members were angry about the difference between words and deeds when voting cards were delivered without electronic chips and nothing more than a photo and personal identification number – in fact nothing qualifying as 'biometric'.

On 20 December, the national electoral commission published provisional results showing that the **ruling party had taken**, "without surprise", **1,517 out of 2,404 seats**, and had kept its overall majority in Libreville (winning in three of its six districts). Elsewhere, the ruling party continued to dominate all the large cities with the notable exception of Oyem, in the north, and Mouila, in the south. But despite losing the city of Oyem, the PDG did take the northern department in which it is located, with a list headed by Prime Minister

Raymond Ndong Sima. In Port-Gentil, the PDG took four districts, winning 36 out of 73 council seats, after a tight race against two opposition formations, including the UPG. “The turnout largely exceeded 55–60%,” said PDG spokesman Alain-Claude Bilié Bi Nzé, recalling the 70% abstention rate in the 2008 municipals.

Foreign Affairs

On 11 January, a peace agreement was signed in Libreville between President Bozizé of the **CAR** and CAR rebels. On 24 March, France sent 350 troops through Libreville to secure the airport in Bangui, CAR, when armed rebels entered the capital to overthrow Bozizé. The French army had 900 troops already stationed in Gabon, at Camp Charles de Gaulle outside Libreville, the oldest permanent base still maintained by the former colonial power. In addition, France had a dominant role in the Gabonese economy, accounting for 35% of imports in 2013, and receiving over 50% of all Gabonese exports. As the year progressed, and sectarian violence exploded, France increased its military presence in the CAR, using Gabon as a launch pad for military intervention.

On 28 March, King Mohammed VI of **Morocco** paid an official visit to Gabon to sign five cooperation agreements and a memorandum of understanding for a framework of strategic partnership in the domains of technology and information systems, agriculture, fisheries, health and communication. This was a continuation of cooperation between the two countries over many decades, based upon the close personal relationship between the former king of Morocco and the former president of Gabon.

On 11 April, the Gabonese former Chairperson of the AU Commission, Jean Ping, was promoted to membership of the board of directors of the West Africa Emerging Markets Growth Fund, having evolved from being a government functionary working on international peace to become an investment portfolio manager of Côte d'Ivoire-based Phoenix Capital Management. His role was to manage a package of $ 50 m provided by private investors, the African Development Bank, and the ECOWAS 'Banque d'Investissement et de Développement de la Cedeao'. Ping's absence from the foreign policy establishment in Libreville marked a departure of one of the most influential diplomats from the previous Omar Bongo era.

On 30 June, a high-level forum of 40 African Capacity Building Foundation governors was held in Libreville to strengthen bonds with Gabon, which was selected to host the 22nd annual session of the foundation in June 2014. On 17 July, the **2nd New York Forum Africa** ended in Libreville with the successful signing of agreements for the development and distribution of refined petroleum products from Port-Gentil, the creation of a new hotel district in Libreville, and another deal with the Chinese Harbour Association.

On 24 September, President Bongo addressed the UN General Assembly, where he condemned the use of chemical weapons by the Assad regime in Syria. He announced the creation of a $ 200 m “Train My Generation” fund to create several learning centres for

100,000 young people in his country's CEMAC sub-region, and he reiterated his strong commitment to fighting against poachers and transnational criminal networks dealing in endangered species. On 26 September, Germany and Gabon held an event at UN headquarters to mobilise international opinion on this last matter.

On 18 November, Bongo travelled to Kuwait to participate in the Arab-African Summit of Heads of State. This summit, the third of his kind, was intended to review the progress made in partnerships between the two regional groups, and to define ways and means of reinforcing them. A 'Kuwait Declaration' was adopted calling for an increase in commercial and financial exchanges in the Afro-Arab world, with the aim of creating an 'Arab-African Plan of Action 2011–2016'. In particular, Gabon declared its hope of creating a business centre for telecommunications.

Bongo participated in the French Summit for Peace and Security in Africa on 6–7 December, presided over by French President François Hollande at the Elysée Palace in Paris. The goal of the summit was to discuss regional security issues, conflict prevention, and reinforcement of peacekeeping missions in Africa, as well as piracy, terrorism, and reinforcement of African troops. On 9 December, an accord was reached during a high-level meeting on the margins of the Elysée summit dedicated to the **protection of endangered species**. France pledged to provide € 10 m for the fight against the trade in illegal ivory. According to leading conservationists, Gabon had lost 19,000 elephants to poaching over the previous ten years. In order to deal with this crisis, the government deployed armed forces personnel to help secure border zones, and even the gendarmerie was called on to provide officers.

On 16 December, Gabon was invested as head of the UN Human Rights Council at its headquarters in Geneva, Switzerland.

Socioeconomic Developments

Gabon's real growth rate was 5.5% in 2013, amid continued stagnation in oil production and total exports. Declining oil reserves weakened income and fiscal revenues, despite the regime's attempts to pursue policies of diversification away from oil and trying to create a business-friendly environment. Adoption of an ambitious public investment programme – **'Gabon Emergent'** – constrained the government's ability to implement the kind of austere fiscal policies that were encouraged by international financial institutions but, on 28 February, the IMF nevertheless concluded its Article IV agreement with Gabon.

On 31 January, the government formalised its budget at $ 6.35 bn, a 14% increase in expenditure over the previous year. Less than half was dedicated to operating expenses (42%). More than one-third was allocated to public investment (34%) and around one-fifth to debt servicing (16.2%). Standard & Poor reappraised Gabon's sovereign debt rating from 'stable' to 'negative' (BB-/B) in April, a judgment later confirmed in September when the Fitch rating agency downgraded the country's financial position from 'positive' to 'stable'. Both ratings agencies recognised that Gabon was in a difficult position, because it had been conducting a **major programme of infrastructural development** at a time when the long-term trend of declining oil production was reaching a critical point.

On 13 February, France's financial crime unit searched two villas in southern France owned by the Bongo family. This was part of a long investigation into the ruling dynasty's corrupt practices, known in the French press as the "biens mal acquis" (ill-gotten gains) affair. On 27 February, the Extractive Industries Transparency Initiative de-listed Gabon, publishing a scathing report that highlighted serious shortcomings in the way oil and other mining activities were reported in the country.

The government was also slow to enact significant **public-sector reform**. On 21 October, Prime Minister Raymond Ndong Sima launched a programme for the voluntary redundancy and anticipated retirement of public sector workers. It was announced that civil servants between the ages of 41 and 55 with at least 15 years of service would qualify for early retirement. Military personnel over 36 years of age with at least 20 years of service also qualified. With around 70,000 full-time public servants for a population of 1.5 m, the civil service was by far the **largest employer** in Gabon, but many were not productive because they lacked either the facilities or the will to work. The government also identified some 26,000 fictional civil servants on the payroll. Public spending continued to crowd out private investment opportunities and kept fiscal deficits at about 12% of GDP. Despite inadequate efforts to cut spending, Gabon continued to run overall fiscal surpluses, which enabled it to reduce its debt to 47% of GDP.

On 30 August, the French subsidiary Total Gabon, despite some minor difficulties, presented somewhat satisfactory results for the year, but its net profits had fallen by 5%, from $ 236 m in the previous year to $ 225 m, due to a decrease in its business and an increase in its exploration costs. Total reported that it had invested $ 1.2 bn in making improvements to the Anguille and Mboukou oil fields. Because it had long been accused of exploiting the country's non-renewable resources without providing any jobs, Total Gabon collaborated with the French embassy in Libreville to hold a job fair on 29–30 November in order to expose Gabonese youth to employment opportunities in the oil sector.

On 28–29 October, a **round of bidding for offshore oil fields** was held in Libreville, with 18 foreign companies from around the world participating. The last time a round of bidding for offshore blocks had been attempted was in 2010, but it had been a failure because the deepwater offshore fields were not well-known to the region's operators. Then Total Gabon, the historical French actor in the country, made a major discovery in a deepwater concession, and other operators were encouraged to try drilling there. The government wanted to open bidding on 42 offshore blocks, but only 13 were of any interest to the participants. Neither Shell Gabon, the largest oil producer in the country, nor Total Gabon acquired any new permits. Petroleum Minister Etienne Dieudonné Ngoubou, however, announced that Ophir had acquired four blocks, and three other companies –

Impact, Marathon and the Chinese firm Perenco – had each acquired single blocks. Several foreign joint-ventures – (Spanish)Repsol/ExxonMobil, Elenit/(Malaysian)Petronas, ExxonMobil/Noble, Petronas/Perenco, and Marathon/Cobalt – also acquired offshore blocks. He announced that these oil blocks represented "a new start for the Gabonese oil sector", while recognising that it would take a minimum of seven years to bring them into production.

On 20 December, presidential spokesman Alain Claude Billé By Nzé announced that the state had acquired the whole capital of the 'Compagnie des Mines de Belinga' (COMIBEL), which had been established to exploit the **Belinga iron reserves** in the north-east quarter of the country. President Bongo had instructed his government to completely rewrite the production convention that his father had signed with COMIBEL, which was 75%-owned by the Chinese company CMEC. It was agreed through an amicable settlement that the Chinese would be compensated to the tune of some $ 33.9 m for expenses the company had incurred over the past decade for geological studies and other work at Belinga, one of the world largest untapped iron ore mines.

On 28 October, the **manganese** mining company COMILOG, owned by French ERAMET, announced that it had generated $ 1.5 bn of business, an increase of 4% over the previous year. This followed a rise in the demand for steel, principally from China, and despite a fall in the price in Europe. The company's production of manganese at Moanda had increased by 27%, and by the third trimester it was breaking production records. Currently number two, Gabon aimed to become the world's number one producer of manganese ore. One of the government's ambitious projects was to have a metallurgy complex constructed by the Chinese close to the Moanda mines.

Forestry, the oldest industry in Gabon, has traditionally employed by far the largest number of workers in any industrial sector. One of Bongo's most ambitious moves had been a 2010 decree ordering foreign firms to stop exporting raw unprocessed logs, and to invest in local value-added projects, such as sawmills. By 2012, two units had been established, one to cut timber, and the other to produce plywood. On 29 November, the **'Société Nationale des Bois du Gabon'** set in motion construction on its third site, for the production of wood panelling. With this new factory, the complex should eventually produce around 250,000 m^3 of panelling, making Gabon the regional leader in lumber. This third site would create 182 new jobs and thereby attain the goal of 450 full-time posts in the sector, part of the government's effort to fight unemployment. On 25–30 November, the 'Conseil International des Bois Tropicaux' was held in Libreville to study the economic indicators and public markets relevant to the trade in tropical wood. At the meeting, the government announced that, since 2009, more than 8 m ha of Gabonese forest had been placed under sustainable management, of which 2 m ha were 'certified' (by the Forest Stewardship Council).

Douglas A. Yates

São Tomé and Príncipe

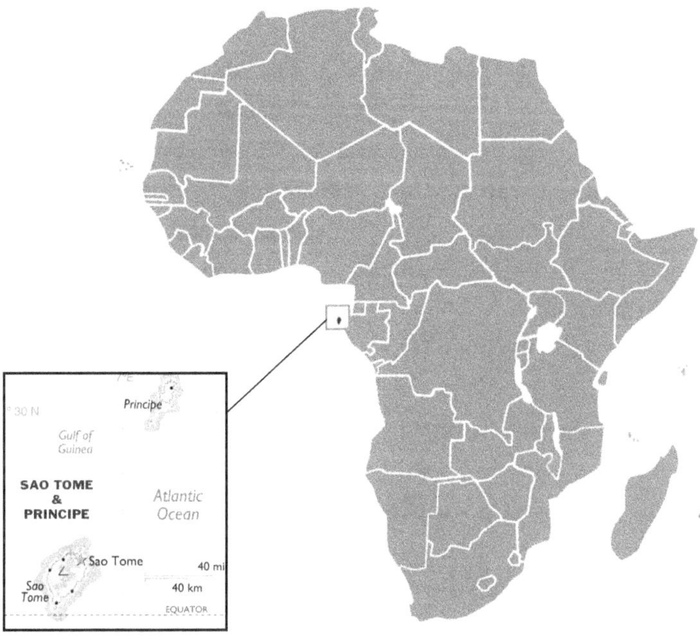

Following the controversial confiscation of two ships chartered by Stena Oil in March, the Swedish company accused São Tomé of state piracy. However, after eight months of mutual threats and tough negotiations the government emerged as the winner of the legal dispute. The country's oil hopes suffered another blow in September, when the French Total pulled out of the Joint Development Zone (JDZ) with Nigeria. At the end of the year, Angola granted São Tomé a credit line of $ 180 m for a three-year period.

Domestic Politics

On 20 February, the government was forced to **dismiss the public prosecutor** Elsa Pinto, just 15 days after her appointment. Straight after Pinto took office, opponents questioned her personal integrity since she had allegedly been under criminal investigation for making a payment with a $ 15,000 cheque that had bounced. Her appointment was also criticised because of her long career as a party politician and minister in three governments of the 'Movimento de Libertação de São Tomé e Príncipe/Partido Social Democrata' (MLSTP/PSD). The president of the local Bar Association, Celiza Deus Lima, publicly demanded Pinto's dismissal on the grounds that her past profile was incompatible with the function of public prosecutor. Elsa Pinto, wife of National Assembly President Alcino

Pinto (MLSTP/PSD), rejected all allegations, denied that her political past would affect her new function, and refused to resign. Eventually, however, the government dismissed her to safeguard its own credibility, and Frederique Samba, hitherto judge at the local court, took office on 29 March as the new public prosecutor.

On 15 March, São Tomé's coast guard captured two tankers chartered by the Swedish company Stena Oil, the Turkish-owned 'Düzgit Integrity' and the German-owned 'Marida Melissa', when they allegedly performed unauthorised transhipment operations six miles off the coast of the island. The two captains were charged with smuggling and violation of the country's territorial waters. Stena rejected these accusations as completely unfounded, arguing that the coast guard had appeared before any transfer had started. Notwithstanding, on 29 March, a local court sentenced the two captains to three years' imprisonment each and imposed a fine of $ 6.5 m to be paid by Stena and the ship-owners, while the two vessels and the cargo were declared confiscated in favour of the state. On 9 July, São Tomé's high court approved this decision. In response, **Stena accused the local authorities of de facto piracy** by staging a show trial to enrich themselves by seizing foreign property. On 26 September, President Pinto da Costa pardoned the two captains, but insisted on the payment of the fine. On 11 October, the 'Marida Melissa' left São Tomé after the shipowner had paid a fine of € 28,000. On 18 October, the government unilaterally broke off negotiations with Stena and sold the seized cargo of the 'Düzgit Integrity' – 8,000 tonnes of fuel worth $ 7.5 m – to the Danish bunker company Monjasa. The 'Düzgit Integrity' finally left the island on 25 November, after the owner had paid a fine of € 28,000.

On 28 May, Pinto da Costa **postponed the local elections** scheduled for July to July 2014 when the next legislative elections were due, justifying this by citing lack of finance and delays in the updating of voter registration, which had last been reviewed in 2010. The three coalition parties, MLSTP/PSD, 'Partido de Convergência Democrática' (PCD) and 'Movimento Democrático Força de Mudança' (MDFM), accepted the president's decision, but the 'Acção Democrática Independente' (ADI) accused Pinta da Costa of not having done everything possible to solve the technical problems, alleging that he was afraid of the outcome of the elections.

On 25 July, the 29 members of parliament of the three coalition parties, MLSTP/PSD, PCD and MDFM, unanimously **rejected a censure motion** submitted by the ADI, which alleged government responsibility for the import of 3,000 tonnes of rotten rice, instances of corruption, and civil rights violations by the executive. Prime Minister Gabriel Costa fiercely rejected the accusations in the motion, which had been preceded by weeks of continuous public criticism of the government by the ADI.

Although the intergovernmental Financial Action Task Force concluded that São Tomé's **anti-money laundering** and combating the financing of terrorism (AML/CFT) framework still contained a number of strategic deficiencies, it took São Tomé off its blacklist on 18 October, arguing that the small size of the country's financial sector had only a low impact on the international financial system. The decision was the result of the approval of revised AML/CFT legislation by the National Assembly in early August.

Foreign Affairs

On 20–23 February, President Pinto da Costa participated in the **3rd Africa-South America Summit** held in Malabo (Equatorial Guinea), where he held separate talks on bilateral cooperation with presidents Dilma Roussef of Brazil, Goodluck Jonathan of Nigeria, Jacob Zuma of South Africa, Jorge Carlos Fonseca of Cape Verde and Obiang Nguema of Equatorial Guinea, as well as with FAO Director-General José Graciano da Silva.

Angola was the principal focus of São Tomé's external relations. On 11 April, Pinto da Costa left for a three-day visit to Luanda, where he held talks with President Eduardo dos Santos. It was his third official visit to Angola. Shortly before his departure, the government abolished visa obligations for Angolan businessmen. On 8–10 June, Prime Minister Gabriel Costa led a government delegation to Luanda. He was received by Dos Santos, met with ambassadors accredited in São Tomé and resident in Luanda, and participated in a meeting with businessmen to promote investment in São Tomé. On 9 October, Pinto da Costa again met dos Santos in Luanda. Their encounter coincided with the end of a one-week visit to Luanda by Minister of Public Works Osvaldo Abreu, and Minister of Finance Hélio Almeida. On 10 December, the latter and his Angolan counterpart signed in Luanda a financial agreement on a **credit line of annually € 60 m** for 2014–16.

Western partners were involved in the archipelago's **maritime security**. On 17 June, Portuguese Defence Minister José Pedro Aguiar-Branco and his local counterpart Óscar Sousa signed in São Tomé an agreement on Portuguese military assistance to patrol the country's Exclusive Economic Zone (EEZ). On 25 October, Glyn Cartmell, consul at the British embassy in Luanda, and Anna Butchart, of the maritime security desk at the UK's Foreign Office, discussed with Prime Minister Costa British support to combat arms and drugs trafficking and piracy in the country's territorial waters.

Important foreign allies under the country's one-party socialist regime were another focus of foreign policy efforts. On 15 June, Pinto da Costa made a five-day visit to Havana **(Cuba)**, where he was received by President Raul Castro to discuss the countries' long-standing bilateral cooperation. He also visited the Museum of Command Headquarters and the Latin-American School of Medical Science and met with Sãotomean students in Cuba.

In late October, a government delegation headed by Foreign Minister Natalia Umbelina visited Beijing to discuss the re-establishment of commercial relations with China. The mission revived rumours that São Tomé might re-establish full diplomatic ties with the **People's Republic of China**. A few days later, Finance Minister Hélio Almeida participated as observer in the 4th ministerial conference of the Forum for Economic and Trade Cooperation between China and Portuguese-speaking Countries (Forum Macao) held on

5–6 November in Macao, where China promised soft loans of $ 293 m to the seven lusophone member countries. Finally, on 12 November the People's Republic of China inaugurated a **trade mission** accommodated in its former embassy in São Tomé, which had been closed in 1997, making São Tomé the first of Taiwan's three allies in Africa to host a Chinese trade mission. Trying to keep a low profile, the government only sent Minister of Natural Resources Osvaldo Abreu to the inauguration ceremony.

To appease the Taiwanese, on 14 November a government delegation headed by Prime Minister Costa and including Foreign Minister Umbelina and several other government officials left for an official four-day visit to **Taipei** to strengthen bilateral cooperation and attract private Taiwanese investments.

Socioeconomic Developments

On 12 March, the regulatory authority 'Autoridade Geral de Regulação' (AGER) admitted Unitel International Holding BV as the country's **second telecoms operator**. The Amsterdam-based company, solely owned by Isabel dos Santos, daughter of the Angolan president, offered immediate payment of $ 7.5 m for the licence, which also included capacity on the Africa Coast to Coast fibre-optic cable system. The licence for Unitel-STP marked the end of the monopoly of the 'Companhia Santomense de Telecomunicações', established in 1990 and owned by the Amsterdam-based Africatel Holding BV (51%), a 75% subsidiary of Portugal Telecom, and the state (49%). During a visit to São Tomé on 29 May, Isabel dos Santos, whose positions included being a shareholder and member of the board of Angola's telecoms company UNITEL, announced that Unitel-STP would establish a training centre for telecoms engineers in São Tomé.

On 7 May, Prime Minister Costa inaugurated two new petrol stations in Guadalupe and São Tomé town, constructed by the fuel company 'Empresa Nacional de Combustíveis e Óleos' (ENCO). In addition, ENCO, 77.6% owned by the Angolan Sonangol, established a third new filling station in Príncipe Island and announced the construction of a fourth new station in Neves. ENCO's general director, Osvaldo Vaz, stressed that the new filling stations, which represented investments of $ 1.5 m each, followed hygiene and security practices in line with modern international standards.

Animal husbandry attracted two major investments. On 20 July, 110 head of beef cattle of the Nelore breed imported by the government from Brazil arrived in São Tomé. The 20 bulls and 90 cows, purchased with $ 1.2 m in finance from the AfDB, were allocated to the renovated dairy centre in Nova Olinda (Cantagalo district) to contribute to the genetic improvement of the local herd. On 24 July, a shipment of 56 pigs from England was unloaded. The pigs were financed by Taiwan as part of a project that included technical assistance to 30 pig breeders until 2017 to cross-breed the English and local pigs in order to increase pig production to an annual average of 1,600 animals. The increased pork production was expected to help achieve a 10 kg per capita annual meat consumption, the quantity recommended by FAO.

On 12 August, a local judge approved an injunction filed by local environmentalists against the company Agripalma, owned by the Antwerp-based STP Invest NV (88%) and the state (12%), to halt the **deforestation of protected areas** in the south of São Tomé. The environmentalists declared that they were not opposed to Agripalma's $ 38.5 m investment, but only wanted to defend the country's unique flora and fauna. In fact, the decision did not impede the continuity of the company's clearing work for the establishment of large palm oil plantations, but imposed concrete conditions with the objective of effectively protecting specific environmental areas. Agripalma, which claimed that it employed 800 local workers, publicly rejected the accusations of illegal deforestation.

On 23 September, the country's oil hopes suffered another setback when the French company **Total abandoned JDZ Block 1**, where the company was operator with a 45.9% stake taken over from Chevron in 2010. Total justified the exit by citing the disappointing results from two exploration wells drilled in the first half of 2012. Total's disinvestment further increased doubts about the commercial viability of the limited deep-sea oil reserves discovered in the JDZ. However, the Joint Development Authority in Abuja (Nigeria), which had not organised a licensing round since 2004, was confident of attracting other oil companies interested in risking investments in the four blocks abandoned by large oil companies since 2012.

On 9 October, the National Oil Agency signed a **product-sharing contract** (PSC) for Block 2 of the country's EEZ with the Hong Kong-registered private oil company Sinoangol, established in 2010 by the Portugal-based Chinese businessman Zhan Yongqiao. Under the agreement, Sinoangol was expected to invest $ 154 m in seismic surveys, environmental studies and exploration drillings during an initial period of eight years. The PSC further included the payment of a signature bonus of $ 5 m, annual payments of $ 5 m for social projects, and a further $ 250,000 for training national oil personnel. Development and production were only scheduled for a second concession period of 20 years.

On 14 November, Minister of Public Works and Natural Resources Osvaldo Abreu and Enézio Alves Rosa, the Brazilian owner of the Luanda-based company Tecnic Serviços Lda., signed an agreement on the **construction of three small hydroelectric dams** with a capacity of 12 MW on the Ío Grande, São Tomé's largest river. Under the agreement, the company would invest $ 62.6 m (€ 46 m) in the construction of the dams, scheduled to be concluded in 2016. In addition, Tecnic Serviços received a 25-year concession for the project's management and electricity supply to the state-owned utility 'Empresa Nacional de Água e Electricidade' (EMAE). In the same week, 'Energias de Portugal' promised that it would help EMAE to modernise the country's outdated power line network, established in the colonial period, which was losing about 40% of the electricity produced.

On 12 December, the National Assembly initiated the debate on the **2014 national budget** of $ 159 m submitted by the government. About 90% of the budget was expected to be financed by external donors, mostly non-Western countries. Angola alone promised to contribute $ 60 m as part of the three-year credit line of $ 180 m.

By December, almost 15,000 bank account holders were using the **automatic payment system** 'Cartão Dobra24' launched by commercial banks in October 2011, an increase of about 50% compared with the 10,500 card holders in 2012. On average, about € 1 m per month was channelled through the ATM system, of which only about € 60,000 went through the more than 50 posts of sale introduced in local shops in the 2012.

Gerhard Seibert

VI. Eastern Africa

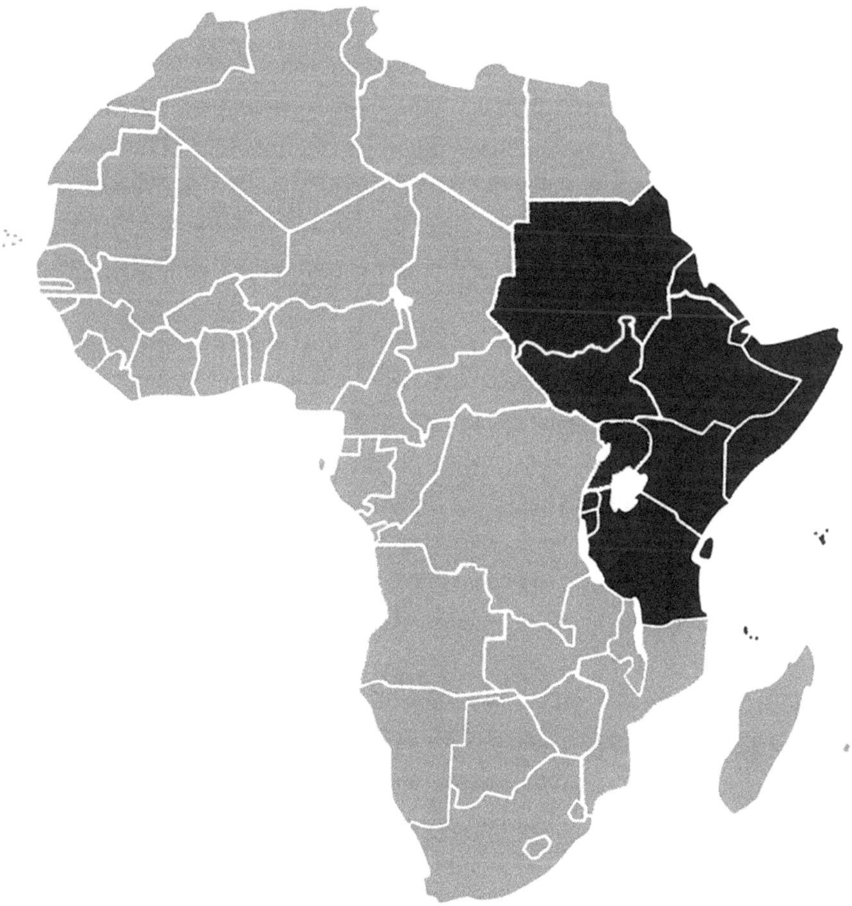

Throughout most of the year the Eastern Africa sub-region did not attract much notable international attention. It was, by and large, a fairly 'normal' year, almost without major upheavals or unexpected developments, although practically all existing conflict configurations persisted and were by no means resolved. The sudden flare-up of massive violence, with signs of a possible civil war, in mid-December in South Sudan in the wake of a simmering power struggle caught the sub-region by surprise and led to frantic conciliation attempts. There was apprehension about the conduct of a fiercely contested election battle in Kenya, but general relief when it turned out to be peaceful and largely free of violence, while shocking pictures of a subsequent terrorist attack on a shopping mall in Nairobi were widely relayed. The new federal Somali government in Mogadishu made modest further progress with the consolidation of its authority during its first full year of existence.

Somali piracy activities in the Indian Ocean were almost entirely halted, following on a sharp decline in 2012. Low-key conflicts in various parts of Sudan continued, while Uganda and Rwanda remained entangled in the on-going conflicts in the eastern DRC, where a regional peace initiative under the auspices of the ICGLR and the deployment of a robust intervention brigade brought at least some partial improvement.

The year saw practically no changes in the prevailing political situation in the sub-region. National elections were held in three countries, but in the cases of Djibouti and Rwanda did not provide any realistic chance of weakening the dominance of the ruling authoritarian regimes. In Djibouti's parliamentary elections, an opposition coalition received a surprisingly large share of the votes, but was heavily disadvantaged by the electoral system and took only a few seats. No genuine opposition parties were allowed to participate in parliamentary elections in Rwanda and the ruling party and its allies thus made a clean sweep. The elections in Kenya were an entirely different affair, however, with strong open competition between a variety of presidential candidates, parties and party coalitions. A new president and a newly-founded coalition formed the government under the provisions of a new constitution, which also introduced significant changes to the country's administrative set-up.

The sub-region's macroeconomic performance was again quite mixed and, considering persisting global financial and economic crisis conditions, moderately satisfactory. The majority of countries showed some recovery and had slightly higher GDP growth rates than in 2012; only Eritrea and Rwanda experienced a marked deceleration of economic growth. Climatic conditions were by and large relatively normal throughout the sub-region and brought regular harvests. By far the best economic performer was Ethiopia with almost 10% growth, followed by Tanzania with 7%. Most other countries only achieved relatively modest growth rates in the range between 3% and 6%. Only South Sudan was a complete exception with an upsurge of 25% growth, resulting from the resumption of oil production and a subsequent recovery from the disastrous GDP contraction of 50% in 2012. Most countries were able to substantially reduce the inflation rates that had previously been the cause for growing widespread popular dissent. Only Sudan and Eritrea were still struggling with exceptionally high inflation rates, while all other countries remained below a threshold level of 10%.

No formal institutional changes occurred with respect to the various sub-regional organisations. South Sudan's and Somalia's membership applications to the EAC were again deferred. For several months, however, sharp divergences between two camps of EAC member countries emerged and temporarily even threatened to provoke its potential split-up. The future of the EAC, hitherto widely regarded as the most advanced regional economic community in Africa, suddenly seemed to be seriously jeopardised, but the exaggerated tensions calmed down before the end of the year, and a protocol was signed for the creation of a monetary union within ten years. No visible progress was made concerning plans for an extensive envisaged tripartite FTA (made up of COMESA, the EAC and SADC), and the long-overdue conclusion of a full EPA between the EU and the EAC was once again deferred. IGAD was expected to play a mediating role in the new conflict in South Sudan. Again no progress was made on reaching a permanent new agreement on the sharing of the water resources of the River Nile between upstream and downstream riparian states. The conclusion and signing of a new treaty continued to be resisted by Egypt and Sudan, while Egypt feared the effects of the construction of Ethiopia's Renaissance dam.

Political Developments

After a very difficult 2012, the situation in both **Sudan** and **South Sudan** was markedly relieved by a compromise agreement on transmission fees for the transport of the South's oil via Sudanese pipelines to Port Sudan on the Red Sea. The resumption of South Sudan's oil production provided crucial revenues for both governments and allowed a return to the relatively normal functioning of state institutions, although widespread social unrest caused by severe economic hardships persisted. The regime in Khartoum nevertheless managed to remain on top of weak opposition forces. Again, no permanent peace solutions were in sight for the decade-old conflict in Darfur and the other more localised conflicts in areas near to the border with South Sudan in Blue Nile and South Kordofan provinces. Sudanese President al-Bashir continued to be subject to an ICC arrest warrant on charges of crimes against humanity in Darfur. In South Sudan, President Salva Kiir dissolved his entire cabinet and tried to consolidate his control over all political institutions by ejecting key former allies who had become sharp rivals, but this backfired a few months later with the outbreak of an open power struggle in December, mounted by Kiir's former deputy. The rebellion led to massive battles between government troops and rebel units and to the displacement of thousands of civilians. By the end of the year, it was unclear whether this was possibly the beginning of a new civil war with pointed ethnic connotations.

No change was discernible with respect to the domestic political situation in **Eritrea**. The authoritarian regime remained in undisputed control and showed no sign of permitting even limited public debate on political issues. A substantial refugee exodus continued unabated, but exiled opposition groups still failed to make any noticeable impact on the internal situation.

The authoritarian regime in **Ethiopia** was able to maintain full control over all public affairs both at the centre in Addis Ababa and in the provinces. The sudden mid-2012 death of Prime Minister Meles Zenawi, who had been the single dominant political figure for over two decades, had not jeopardised the stability of the political system, which continued to be characterised by constant intimidation of all kinds of political dissenters. The reign of Prime Minister Hailemariam Desalegn did not lead to any visible changes in the repressive political climate or the government's general development strategy, which was geared towards high growth and rapid modernisation.

After a decade of boycotting elections in **Djibouti**, opposition parties opted to participate in parliamentary elections and obtained a surprisingly large share of the votes, almost on a par with the long-ruling dominant party coalition, but due to a peculiar electoral system they took disproportionately few seats. All hopes for a partial liberalisation of the political situation were quashed, however, when accusations of election fraud provoked days of violent street demonstrations and led to renewed heavy-handed repression of critics by the state security services. The well entrenched political power of President Guelleh's government was not seriously challenged and remained unperturbed.

The new federal government of **Somalia**, which had been installed in Mogadishu in 2012 after two decades without a modern state structure, continued to make modest progress with the consolidation of its authority, although this still remained fairly limited and applied to only some parts of the country. The government was recognised internationally and received support from many sides; there was a noticeable upsurge in economic activity and of urban reconstruction in Mogadishu, largely undertaken by returning Somalis and financed by remittances from the large Somali diaspora. Radical Islamist groups, particularly al-Shabaab, nevertheless continued to subject considerable parts of the population to their draconian rules and regularly launched armed attacks against all representations of formal state institutions. The internal situation in **Somaliland** remained stable, allowing for the normal administrative functions of a regular state, despite continued lack of progress with respect to Somaliland's desire for full international recognition as an independent state. **Puntland** also maintained its status as a semi-autonomous state in practice; another similar entity appeared to be in the making in **Jubaland**.

Kenya experienced another turbulent political year, dominated by highly contentious elections in March, the installation of a new government and the challenges of implementing a new politico-administrative state structure (devolution) brought about by the 2010 constitution. Despite considerable anxiety, the elections were conducted without major incident. Uhuru Kenyatta was elected as the new president with just marginally more than 50% of the votes, thus avoiding a widely expected run-off. His main opponent, the outgoing Prime Minister Raila Odinga, brought charges of fraud and petitioned the Supreme Court, which, however, upheld the official result. In a familiar Kenyan pattern, Kenyatta and his running mate, William Ruto, led a coalition of several ethnically-oriented parties, and the same was true of Odinga's rival camp. Much public attention centred on the fact that Kenyatta and Ruto remained formally indicted by the ICC as primarily responsible for the 2008 post-election violence; they went to great lengths to try to prevent any progression of the ICC process. The creation of a Senate and 47 new counties enforced the devolution of a hitherto highly centralised state and led to new forms of political battles between different authorities. A high-visibility terrorist attack on a Nairobi shopping mall underscored security problems linked to Kenya's proximity to Somalia.

All political debates in **Tanzania** were focused on the on-going constitutional review process that had been initiated in 2011 to produce a new Constitution. After extensive public hearings throughout the country, the Constitutional Review Commission formulated a first draft of the expected document as a basis for further public discussion. A revised second draft was put out at the year's end. No concrete outcome was yet discernible, as final decisions were to be made by a Constituent Assembly in 2014. By far the most important and contentious issue was the future structure of the existing Union arrangement between the mainland (formerly Tanganyika) and Zanzibar. Voices in the semi-autonomous **Zanzibar** archipelago that had long demanded a revision of the current asymmetrical structure of Union and separate Zanzibar authorities increased in number. Rather surprisingly the draft constitution documents proposed a new three-tier structure, but this was strongly opposed by the long-ruling dominant party, and President Kikwete and his party remained in undisputed control of all political institutions.

President Museveni's government in **Uganda** was able to maintain full control over all public affairs, but faced considerable public discontent and sympathy for opposition protests, which continued to be harshly suppressed by the security forces. The authoritarian tendencies of the entrenched ruling system and intimidation of outspoken critics were increasingly evident. There appeared to be growing disillusion with the sheer endlessness of Museveni's rule – he had been in power since 1986. Rumours abounded about that he might possibly run again in the next election in 2016 or groom his son as his successor. Increasingly numerous critical voices were also raised from within the ruling party and groups of MPs, who were no longer willing always to follow the prescribed party line and presidential directives. Public criticism of the government was possible to some extent, but had very limited impact on the policies pursued.

The authoritarian domestic political situation in **Rwanda** remained largely unchanged. President Kagame and his ruling party exercised absolute control over all aspects of public life and firmly suppressed all potentially dissenting voices. Parliamentary elections in September brought a clean sweep for Kagame's dominant party and its two allied satellites, which generated a semblance of diversity. An opposition party was registered belatedly, but was prevented from participating in the election. Despite the outward appearance of extreme stability and unity in the political system, signs of internal dissension and cracks in the inner circles were sometimes discernible. Rising foreign criticism by hitherto supportive donors led to a reduction of aid funding and a need to pressurise the population into mobilising more local resources for the government's development ambitions.

In **Burundi**, there was still no reconciliation in sight between President Nkurunziza's ruling party and the alliance of opposition parties that had boycotted the elections in 2010. The opposition parties were left in a weak extra-parliamentary position and also without any influence on the local level. Some prominent opposition leaders returned from exile, but found almost no room for effective political activity, while the government secured its position by using strong-arm tactics of harassment and, allegedly, even the extra-judicial killing of suspected opponents. Growing tensions emerged between Nkurunziza's dominant party and its junior coalition partner and provoked internal divisions within the latter.

President Michel and his long-ruling government party remained in full control of all spheres of public life in the **Seychelles**. 2013 was a rather uneventful political year, devoid of marked controversies. Opposition groups remained weak and appeared resigned to their fate of being unable to gather more popular support.

Comoros had another (third) unusually calm and peaceful year, uncommon for a country that had for years been habitually fluid and characterised by tensions between the leaders of the three constituent islands of the Union. After lengthy discussions, a compromise was found for holding harmonised parliamentary and communal elections in November 2014. President Dhoinine was able to further consolidate his own authority, but was faced by the increasingly open political ambitions of his predecessor and earlier mentor. Not all inter-island rivalries were eliminated, but a relatively cooperative style prevailed and enabled the government to pursue long-overdue social and economic reforms.

In the entire **Eastern Africa sub-region**, there were only very minor changes in **Freedom House's** annual assessment of **political rights** and **civil liberties**: reductions by one point for political rights in Uganda and for civil liberties in South Sudan, and a one point improvement for civil liberties in Rwanda. None of the 13 sub-regional countries scored top points (on a scale of 1 at the top to 7) in the 'free' category, and seven countries were still listed in the 'not free' category (Djibouti, Eritrea, Ethiopia, Rwanda, Somalia, South Sudan, Sudan). Eritrea, Somalia and Sudan remained among the ten lowest-rated countries in the world (with scores of 7 for both political rights and civil liberties). However, Djibouti, Ethiopia, Rwanda and South Sudan were only slightly better (with scores of 6 for political rights), and in civil liberties Ethiopia and South Sudan also scored 6, and Djibouti and Rwanda 5. Six countries were categorised as 'partly free' (with both political rights and civil liberties in the 3–5 point range, except for Uganda). Among these, Seychelles and Tanzania were again judged the best (with 3 points in both categories), followed by Comoros (3 for political rights and 4 for civil liberties), Kenya (4 and 4) and Burundi (5 and 5). Uganda, despite a deterioration to 6 points for political rights, was judged to be 'partly free' on the strength of 4 points for civil liberties. Somaliland was also assessed as 'partly free' (4 points for political rights and 5 for civil liberties).

TI's Corruption Perception Index for 2013 once again revealed wide discrepancies between the countries of the sub-region. Of the 175 countries listed, Seychelles and Rwanda achieved outstanding top positions with overall rankings of 47th and 49th, respectively, and scores of 54 and 53 points (out of 100). Both countries moved up a few places compared with 2012 and were well ahead of the rest of Eastern Africa. All other countries had scores markedly below 50 points, which was the threshold indicating the incidence of serious corruption. Somalia was rated as the worst country (ranked 175th with 8 points), while Sudan (174th with 11 points) and South Sudan (173rd with 14 points) were also at the very bottom of the list. The remaining countries, like most SSA countries, ranged somewhere between 36 and 20 points in the following order: Djibouti

(94th), Ethiopia and Tanzania (111th), Comoros (127th), Kenya (136th), Uganda (140th), Burundi (157th) and Eritrea (160th).

Similar divergences between countries were discernible with regard to **press freedom**, as indicated in the 2014 Press Freedom Index by **Reporters Without Borders** (with scores ranging from 0 to 100). Of 180 listed countries, Eritrea for the seventh consecutive year ranked last in the world (scoring 85). Somalia (ranked 176th), Sudan (172nd), Djibouti (169th) and Rwanda (162th), with scores ranging from 73 to 57, were also again judged to be general offenders against the principle of freedom of the media. Practically no change had been observed in comparison with 2012. The relatively best marks for press freedom were given to Comoros (ranked 53rd, score 25) and Tanzania (69th, score 27), more or less confirming an unchanged situation. Kenya (90th, score 31) had fallen 29 places as a result of a clear hardening of the government's media policies. Some fall in the ranking was also recorded for Seychelles (103rd, score 32) and Uganda (110th, score 33), while South Sudan (119th, score 36) moved up five places. Press freedom was also judged as highly restricted in Burundi and Ethiopia (ranked 142nd and 143rd, score 41). From a global perspective, the whole sub-region was again considered to be stagnating towards the bottom of the list.

Transnational Relations and Conflict Configurations

Again, no substantial progress was made towards bringing the **Darfur** conflict in **Sudan**, on-going since 2003, closer to a sustainable solution. Limited fighting between various rebel factions and government forces continued to occur throughout the year, and over 2 m people were still forced to remain in IDP camps. Widespread lawlessness and banditry prevailed in the absence of regular state structures. The large hybrid UN-AU Mission in Sudan (**UNAMID**) remained tasked with protecting the civilian population and performing a peacekeeping role, but its effectiveness was severely restricted. After the independence of **South Sudan** in 2011, new conflict zones had emerged along the uncertain border. A promised referendum to determine the disputed status of the oil-rich **Abyei** area was again not held, and a UN Interim Security Force for Abyei (**UNISFA**) remained deployed to prevent the outbreak of full hostilities. In parts of Southern Kordofan and Blue Nile states, local population groups continued to carry out rebel activities against the Khartoum authorities.

South Sudan was in mid-December suddenly faced with the outbreak of a vicious armed conflict between government forces and rebel groups loyal to the country's former vice president, who had been dismissed a few months earlier. Heavy fighting, particularly for control of key oil-producing areas, involved large parts of the country and turned many thousands of civilians into hapless refugees. Initially a classical political power struggle, the rebellion quickly also assumed the appearance of an ethnic confrontation and had the possible makings of the beginning of a **civil war**. This worrying scenario had threatening implications for all neighbouring countries, and **IGAD** was quickly identified as a suitable body for mediating between the opponents. The Juba government obtained primary support from Khartoum and Kampala. The UN Mission in South Sudan (**UNMISS**) was completely overwhelmed by the sudden outbreak of the conflict and unable to deal with the scale of fighting.

The population in remote areas in the triangle between **South Sudan**, the **CAR** and the **DRC** still continued to be victimised by small remnant groups of the **Lord's Resistance Army** (LRA), which had until 2006 terrorised large parts of northern **Uganda**, but had since then been completely driven out from there. Although the LRA was no longer a domestic Ugandan issue, the Ugandan military was still pursuing LRA leader Joseph Kony in the CAR and DRC in the context of an AU regional task force and with logistical support from American military advisers, but Kony and his fighters remained elusive.

Eritrea remained seriously isolated in the sub-region and at loggerheads with all other governments, with the partial exception of Sudan. There was still no permanent solution in sight for the border conflicts with either **Ethiopia** or **Djibouti**. There were no open military confrontations along the disputed borders, but no agreement on mutually accepted frontiers, either.

All neighbouring countries had for many years been significantly affected by the insecurity and turmoil in **Somalia** and had been greatly relieved by the installation of an internationally recognised new president and government in Mogadishu in the latter half of 2012. But radical Islamist groups still controlled considerable parts of the countryside, imposed strict Islamic rules on the population and repeatedly launched armed attacks on installations and representatives of the government. With EU and US support, a new national police force and army continued to be trained and to expand their operational capacities, but had yet to become an effective force against al-Shabaab. Security protection by the AU peacekeeping mission (**AMISOM**) therefore remained essential. AMISOM's numerical strength was further increased to a total of about 22,000 military and police personnel. Troops from Burundi, Djibouti, Kenya and Uganda were augmented by a unit from Sierra Leone and formally joined by contingents from Ethiopia, who had already been operating on their own on Somali territory. **IGAD** repeatedly discussed the Somalia problem at ministerial and summit meetings and was fully supportive of the federal government; it also was instrumental in mediating in the hefty leadership struggle in Jubaland. **Kenya** was particularly affected by an overspill of the Somali conflict through a number of terrorist attacks by al-Shabaab adherents, most notably on a shopping mall in the centre of Nairobi. The threat by **Somali pirates** to international shipping in the Gulf of Aden and along the East African coast was further remarkably reduced in continuation of the previous year's trend. Only seven piracy incidents were recorded during the year, compared with 160 in 2011. Intensified and coordinated international anti-piracy activities had finally proved to be quite effective, although at very high cost.

The **Great Lakes Region**, with its wide-ranging significance across several national borders, continued to witness the complex interplay of many groups and interests from various countries in two sub-regions: Eastern Africa and Central Africa. 2012 had brought renewed violent confrontations, caused particularly by the emergence of the M23, a new rebel group in the **DRC** allegedly supported by **Rwanda**, and concerted multilateral efforts to contain the situation and prevent further inter-state hostilities. A series of meetings and initiatives in the context of the ICGLR and **Ugandan** mediation between the M23 and the Kinshasa government had brought no tangible results and were thus continued in 2013. On 24 February in Addis Ababa, 11 African countries (all, apart from South Africa, ICGLR members) signed a **UN Peace, Security and Cooperation Framework** for the region in the presence of the UN Secretary-General. The Framework focused mainly on reform of the DRC's state and army and the neutralisation of all perceived 'negative forces' (i.e., various rebel groups) active in the eastern DRC, and included the creation of a 3,000-strong **'Force Intervention Brigade'** (FIB) to complement the long-existing but rather ineffectual UN Stabilization Mission in the DRC (**MONUSCO**). The FIB, with troops from **South Africa, Malawi** and **Tanzania** was established in late March under a Tanzanian commander and gradually deployed over the following months. Equipped with a robust mandate, it engaged in serious combat with the M23, which admitted defeat and declared the end of its rebellion on 5 November. This was evidently also a set-back for Rwanda. Kigali insisted that the FIB also remove other rebel groups still active in eastern DRC, particularly the 'Forces Démocratiques de Libération du Rwanda' (FDLR). This was considered, but had not been achieved by year's end.

Bilateral relations between **Rwanda** and **Tanzania** deteriorated considerably after Tanzanian President Kikwete publicly suggested during an AU summit in late May that the Rwandan government should engage in a dialogue with its externally-based critics, particularly the FDLR. Rwanda's President Kagame, who viewed the FDLR as the culprits responsible for the 1994 genocide, took this as an affront and inappropriate interference. Tanzania's prominent role in the FIB further strained the relationship, as did the expulsion from Tanzania of around 8,000 Rwandans who were alleged to be illegal immigrants, although most were long-term residents in Tanzania. This bilateral aggravation also had negative implications for both countries' membership of the EAC.

UN peacekeeping activities in the sub-region continued to face severe constraints. The large **MONUSCO** contingent in the DRC had in the past only achieved limited success in containing an overspill of rebel raids (FDLR, LRA, Allied Democratic Forces) into neighbouring East African countries and in stabilising the internal Congolese situation. The **FIB**, with its unusually robust mandate, proved to be considerably more effective against the M23, and it was hoped that this could be further pursued against other rebel groups. The **UNMISS** in South Sudan was relatively ineffective and not able to cope with the sudden outbreak of an armed revolt. The large hybrid **UNAMID** continued to struggle rather ineffectually to fulfil its peacekeeping role in the embattled Sudanese Darfur region. But at least **UNISFA** was able to prevent the outbreak of open hostilities in the disputed Abyei border are between Sudan and South Sudan.

The indictment of Sudanese President al-Bashir for crimes against humanity in the Darfur conflict, issued by the **ICC** in 2009, again had few practical consequences, but partially restricted his international travel. Kenya's newly elected President Kenyatta and Vice President Ruto also remained charged by the ICC in connection with Kenya's 2008 post-election violence. Case hearings against Ruto started in September in The Hague, while the start of Kenyatta's case was postponed well into 2014. An extraordinary AU summit on 12 October decided that no serving head or deputy head of state should be charged by an international court while in office, but a subsequent motion for a deferral of the Kenyan cases did not obtain the required majority in the UNSC.

Socioeconomic Developments

The **macroeconomic performance** of countries in the sub-region was again quite diverse, but on the whole reasonably satisfactory. They continued, by and large, to weather the effects of the persisting global and financial crisis better than had initially been feared, and most countries managed to achieve a slight acceleration of economic growth. In contrast to the exceptional drought conditions in 2011, it was climatically a relatively normal year, which led to average harvests almost everywhere. Overall growth rates were in most cases somewhat higher than in 2012, with exceptionally strong recoveries in Sudan and South Sudan following the unusually severe GDP contractions in 2012 due to the politically-motivated shut-down of oil production in South Sudan.

According to preliminary IMF figures for April 2013, the **2013 GDP growth rate** for SSA was 4.9% (the same as in 2012). Of all Eastern African countries, South Sudan (24.4%) and Ethiopia (9.7%) managed to achieve particularly outstanding growth, but in the case of the former this was only a partial recovery from an almost 50% slump. For Ethiopia, by far outperforming all other sub-regional neighbours, it was the tenth consecutive year of exceptional growth. Tanzania (7.0%) maintained its relatively stable growth path. Uganda (6.0%), Kenya (5.6%) and Djibouti (5.0%) had higher growth than in 2012 and achieved somewhat better than the SSA average. Rwanda (5.0%) and Eritrea (1.3%) suffered from a noticeable decline from their previous growth rates. Somewhat lagging behind and below the African average were Burundi (4.5%), Seychelles (3.6%), Comoros (3.5%) and Sudan (3.4%), although they all achieved slightly higher rates than in 2012. The five-member EAC block as a whole was estimated to have accelerated its growth to above 6%.

Most countries officially pursued cautious monetary policies and modest **inflation** targets, and were by and large successful in markedly bringing down average consumer price increases from the high 2012 levels that had resulted from high global food prices and oil costs. The IMF's preliminary estimate of average SSA inflation for 2013 was

6.3% (compared with 9.0% in 2012). Not surprisingly, the track records of individual countries differed widely, with some far exceeding the continental average. Clearly top of the list were Sudan (36.5%) and Eritrea (12.3%) with practically the same inflation rates as in 2012. All other countries managed considerable reductions in inflation and avoided the double-digit figures that had largely prevailed in the previous year. Burundi (8.8%), Ethiopia (8.0%) and Tanzania (7.9%) still recorded significant inflation rates, while the remaining countries had moderate rates of less than 6%, below the SSA average. South Sudan experienced an astounding turn-around from 45% inflation in 2012 to zero in 2013. The EAC block practically halved inflation within a year to around 6.5%.

Practically all countries in the sub-region (except Eritrea and South Sudan) again had considerable negative **current-account** balances, in contrast to the only slightly negative SSA average of –3.6% of GDP (due to surpluses on the part of major oil and mineral exporters, which strongly skewed the average). Burundi had by far the highest current-account deficit, at 23.2% of GDP, followed by Seychelles (17.7%), Tanzania (14.3%), Djibouti (13.2%), Uganda (11.7%) and Sudan (10.6%). The remaining countries had deficits of less than 10% of GDP, with the exceptions of South Sudan and Eritrea with current-account surpluses of 2.2% and 0.3% of GDP, respectively.

A good measure of the intensity of domestic development efforts, without simply relying on the inflow of aid funds, is the volume of **government revenue** (excluding grants and expressed as percentage of GDP). Most countries in the sub-region remained somewhat below the yardstick of the projected 2013 SSA average of 25.7%. The EAC as a group was estimated to have achieved only 19.6%, which was nevertheless a continuing small improvement over previous years. Seychelles (36.4%), in line with a long-standing past record, Djibouti (28.3%) and Kenya (23.4%) were again able to demonstrate high domestic revenue generation. In contrast, exceptionally low rates were estimated for Sudan (9.9%), Burundi (13.0%), Ethiopia (13.2%), South Sudan (14.1%), Comoros and Uganda (both 14.9%), Rwanda (15.3%), Eritrea (16.8%) and Tanzania (19.1%). All these countries (except Eritrea) relied heavily on the influx of external grants (in very different forms) to meet government expenditure.

UNDP's 2013 **HDI** (with 2012 data) again clearly highlighted considerable variations in the sub-region in respect of general socioeconomic development levels. With the exception of Seychelles, all Eastern African countries (out of 187 listed) appeared in the low human development category. Seychelles, with an HDI value of 0.806 and ranked 46th, was by far the highest-ranked African country, at the bottom of the very high human development category. Kenya (HDI value 0.519, ranked 145th) and Tanzania (0.476, ranked 152nd) had a slightly higher HDI value than the SSA average of 0.475, while Uganda (161st), Djibouti (164th), Rwanda (167th), Comoros (169th), Sudan (171st), Ethiopia (173rd), Burundi (178th) and Eritrea (181st) showed a lower-than-average HDI. Somalia and South Sudan were not listed.

The World Bank's **Doing Business Report** regularly assesses the general ease of doing business in 187 surveyed countries, based on ten different categories of indicators, and thus provides a valuable overview of the prevailing business climate. As of mid-2013, Rwanda (ranked 32nd, up 20 places) and Seychelles (80th) were considered the most business-friendly economies in Eastern Africa, while Eritrea and South Sudan, near the bottom of the list, were clearly in the opposite category of countries that largely obstructed private business ventures. The remaining countries, ranging from Ethiopia (125th) to Djibouti (160th), all belonged to an intermediate group of countries that in principle wanted to foster more business activity, but were still hampered by an overly burdensome bureaucracy, legal weaknesses and other impediments. Rwanda, Djibouti and Burundi were singled out as being among the ten countries in the world that had most improved in the period 2012–13.

The World Economic Forum's **Global Competitiveness Index 2013–14** provided a somewhat similar attempt to compare the attractiveness of a total of 148 listed countries (including only seven from the sub-region). Again, Rwanda (ranked 66th) and Seychelles (80th) were considered to have the most competitive economic environment, while Kenya (96th) improved by ten places and Burundi (146th) remained near the tail of the list. Tanzania (125th), Ethiopia (127th) and Uganda (129th) were in the lowest quarter of the global ranking.

Sub-regional Cooperation and Sub-regional Organisations

The **EAC** held its 11th extraordinary **summit** on 28 April near Arusha (Tanzania). Kenya's newly-elected President Kenyatta participated for the first time, and Jackson Njoroge was appointed as new Kenyan deputy secretary-general of the EAC to replace his compatriot Julius Rotich. The presidents pledged to better coordinate national policies on the recently discovered oil and gas resources in East Africa. At the 14th ordinary **EAC summit** on 30 November in Kampala (Uganda), the rotating chairmanship rather unexpectedly passed from Uganda's President Museveni to Kenyatta, although it would normally have been Rwanda's turn. President Kagame officially surrendered the role because he had too many domestic responsibilities in 2014, but the move appeared to be connected with the internal divisions in the EAC. The summit took note of the ongoing negotiations with South Sudan regarding its application for EAC membership, but the decision was deferred to April 2014; in early November, a high-level South Sudanese delegation including ten ministers had visited the EAC secretariat to put its case. A verification committee to deal with Somalia's pending application was put in place and expected to report in November 2014. The jurisdiction of the East African Court of Justice (EACJ) was extended to cover trade, investment and monetary issues, but it was directed to work with the AU in matters of human rights and crimes against humanity. The summit noted a report on the EAC's establishment of a single customs territory which was to come into effect on 1 January 2014. By far the most important outcome of the summit, however, was the approval and signing of a protocol on an envisaged **Monetary Union**, which had been the subject of intense negotiations by a high-level task force since early 2011; a road map outlined a number of institutions to be set up and convergence measures to be taken over a ten-year period for the eventual introduction of a single currency. A cautionary attitude on this crucial integration step prevailed in view of constant criticism by the East African Business Council that there were still many obstacles blocking the smooth implementation of the requirements of the **Customs Union** and **Common Market** protocols. Many of the relevant regulations had still not been fully incorporated into national legislation, and a host of non-tariff barriers continued to hamper the formation of a genuine Common Market.

On 6 June, the **East African Legislative Assembly** (EALA) approved the **EAC budget** for 2013/14 to the tune of $ 131.8 m, down from $ 140 m in 2012/13. The budget was still heavily donor-dependent, with 65% of the total expected to come from contributions of external development partners. It allocated 53% of expenditure to the EAC secretariat in Arusha, 23% to the Lake Victoria Basin Commission, 10.5% to the EALA, 7.5% to the Inter-University Council and the rest to the EACJ and other minor institutions. On 15 February, an **EAC Peace and Security Protocol** was signed by the partner states' defence ministers. Again, no substantial progress was made on the protracted controversial issue of signing a full **EPA** with the **EU**. The final deadline for concluding this long-awaited trade pact was now set for October 2014.

Throughout the second half of the year, **major divergences between key leaders of the EAC** partner states seriously threatened to undermine the level of integration that had been achieved. It all started on 24–25 June with a meeting of the Kenyan, Rwandan and Ugandan presidents in Entebbe (Uganda), where they discussed a number of major infrastructure projects in the so-called Northern Corridor, but also spoke of fast-tracking the concept of an East African political federation and introducing a single tourist visa for their countries. This trilateral approach was further confirmed by another infrastructural summit on 28 August in Mombasa (Kenya) (also attended by ministerial delegations from Burundi and South Sudan) and a third similar meeting in Kigali (Rwanda) on 28–29 October. Tanzania had not been invited to these gatherings, which was widely interpreted as a deliberate affront in reaction to Tanzania's often expressed reservations regarding faster and more far-reaching integration measures. The trilateral group was quickly labelled the **Coalition of the Willing** (CoW) in the media and by the general public. The CoW was seen as propagating a two-speed approach to the integration process in East Africa, leaving a perceived reluctant Tanzania somewhat behind. Acrimonious statements by various politicians and in the media poisoned the climate, and some observers even feared a break-up of the EAC. Some Tanzanians ventured the idea of pushing a rival trilateral cooperation with Burundi and the DRC. One underlying cause of the rivalry was rooted in the long-existing competition between the ports of Mombasa and Dar es Salaam (Tanzania) and their respective hinterlands along the Northern and Central Corridors. After considerable public excitement, a consensus was eventually reached that partner states were free to make their own arrangements to pursue projects in which they had a shared interest as long as these did not clash with provisions of the EAC treaty. The acrimony cooled remarkably when the presidents met in Kampala for the end-November summit and confirmed the long-term ambition to establish a Monetary Union.

The regularly foreseen 17th **COMESA** summit, to be held in Kinshasa (DRC), was postponed to February 2014, so Uganda's President Museveni continued as COMESA chairman throughout the year. No noticeable new developments in the organisation were recorded. The DRC, Ethiopia and Uganda were still processing their full accession to **COMESA's FTA**. The establishment of the envisaged **COMESA Customs Union** remained uncertain since most of the 19 member states were slow to align their national tariffs with agreed common external tariffs, and the transition period had been extended several times. Little publicly visible progress was made either with regard to the ambitious plan to create a grand **Tripartite FTA** (TFTA) made up of all 26 member states of COMESA, the EAC and SADC, stretching from the Cape to Cairo. A series of technical-level meetings continued to prepare the ground, and the optimistic aim was to clinch an agreement on the TFTA by June 2014.

The previously rather inconspicuous **ICGLR** had in 2012 gained enhanced international recognition as the most appropriate sub-regional institution to deal with the renewed escalation of conflict in the eastern DRC and the deterioration of relations between the Congolese, Rwandan and Ugandan governments. This continued to be relevant throughout 2013. Most of the 12 ICGLR member states signed the UN Framework for Peace, Security and Cooperation for the DRC and the region on 24 February in Addis Ababa. A special intervention brigade was created (with troops from Tanzania, Malawi and South Africa) on the basis of UNSC resolution 2098 of 28 March, and tasked with a robust mandate to engage all belligerent groups in the eastern DRC, primarily the M23. Under the chairmanship of Uganda's President Museveni, two extraordinary ICGLR summits were held in Nairobi (31 July) and Kampala (5 September), which reaffirmed support for the Kampala dialogue between the Kinshasa government and the M23 and for the role of the intervention brigade in view of a renewed and worsening security situation. A **joint summit** of **SADC** and the **ICGLR** in Pretoria (South Africa) on 4 November outlined possibilities for more cooperation between their organisations and noted with satisfaction that all issues in the Kampala dialogue had been agreed and that the M23 had renounced rebellion.

Again, only limited progress was made towards the revitalisation of the **CEPGL**, which continued mostly with support from Belgium and the EU. The small secretariat in Gisenyi (Rwanda) had almost no funds; only Rwanda paid the agreed contributions, and the CEPGL budget was hamstrung due to Burundi's and the DRC's arrears.

Apart from pursuing its development-oriented activities with only moderate success, **IGAD** was again mostly occupied in the political field by the critical situations in Somalia, Sudan and South Sudan, as it was the only sub-regional institution that covered the entire Horn of Africa region. Two extraordinary IGAD summits on 3 and 24 May in Addis Ababa dealt with progress reports on the situation in Somalia, expressed particular concern about rising tensions in Somalia's southern Jubaland area and decided to send an IGAD confidence-building mission to Mogadishu and Kismayo with the intention of playing a mediating role. A joint ministerial meeting of the EAC and IGAD on 12 October in Addis Ababa was meant to sort out disagreements over Somalia and to generally strengthen integration efforts. After the sudden outbreak of massive violence in South Sudan, a high-level ministerial IGAD delegation was immediately dispatched and was in Juba from 19 to 21 December. On 27 December, the 23rd extraordinary IGAD summit was convened in Nairobi to consider the institution's possible mediating role in this new conflict.

The 28th ministerial council meeting of the **IOC** was held on 17 January in Victoria (Seychelles). Seychellois President Michel used the opportunity to appraise the 30-year existence of this modest grouping of five island states and territories. The rotating IOC presidency was passed on from Seychelles to Comoros, offering the prospect of convening a rare heads of state summit in 2014 in Moroni. The council approved a new Strategic Development Plan and amended the organisation's four original strategic axes. A study on an envisaged regional maritime service that would regularly connect the member states was completed in November.

The 20 member states (including eight from Africa) of the **IOR-ARC** met for their 13th ministerial council meeting on 1 November in Perth (Australia). The organisation's name was changed to **Indian Ocean Rim Association (IORA)** and Australia assumed the chairmanship, previously held for two years by India. Both countries had become the main drivers of a noticeable reinvigoration of the organisation, which had long been almost moribund. The adoption of the 'Perth Principles' document reaffirmed the IORA's founding orientation towards the productive and sustainable use of the Indian Ocean and its resources.

The water ministers of the ten **Nile Basin Initiative** member states held their 21st council meeting on 20 June in Juba. Again, no formal conclusion was reached in the protracted negotiations for a new consensus treaty on the joint equitable utilisation of the water resources of the Nile river system by all riparian states. Egypt and Sudan still vehemently opposed the text of a **Cooperative Framework Agreement** (CFA) that had been signed in 2010 and 2011 by six upstream countries as a key step towards the establishment of a fully-fledged permanent Nile River Basin Commission. Egypt rejected the CFA text in fear of losing its power of veto over any changes to the historical water rights formulated in colonial-era treaties. The DRC and South Sudan had still not signed the CFA, but promised to do so. Ethiopia and Rwanda went ahead and ratified the CFA in their parliaments in June, while this still remained to happen in the other four signatory countries. Ethiopia tried separately to pursue a trilateral dialogue with Egypt and Sudan to alleviate their fears regarding the ongoing construction of its huge **Blue Nile dam**, but Egypt remained adamantly opposed. Electricity from the dam was expected to be distributed widely throughout the ten member states of the Eastern Africa Power Pool.

Rolf Hofmeier

Burundi

The prospect of the 2015 general elections had a significant impact on the functioning and strategies of domestic political actors. 2013 was marked by increased tensions between the two main partners in the coalition government, the dominant party, President Nkurunziza's CNDD-FDD, and the smaller UPRONA. These tensions were particularly related to the activities of the National Land Commission and land law reforms, contentious amendments to the Constitution, and Nkurunziza's eligibility for a third term as president. The return to Burundi of self-proclaimed opposition leader and FNL chairperson Agathon Rwasa did not significantly affect the unity or strategy of the opposition coalition, ADC-Ikibiri. Relations between the government and various social sectors – media, bar association, trade unions, university students, etc. – were marked by animosity. Burundi stepped up its involvement in peacekeeping operations on the African continent. Early in 2013, the UN presence in Burundi was extended for another year, but the government strongly insisted that UN involvement be scaled down from early 2014 onwards. The central market in the capital city Bujumbura was destroyed by a massive accidental fire, which caused tremendous damage to the local economy. After an alarming depreciation in early 2013, the national currency stabilised later in the year.

Domestic Politics

The makeup of the **government** of **President Pierre Nkurunziza** continued to be fully in accordance with the Constitution, reflecting the country's ethnic diversity and including members of all three political parties represented in parliament. Members of the 'Conseil National pour la Défense de la Démocratie – Forces pour la Défense de la Démocratie' (**CNDD-FDD**) held 16 of the 21 cabinet positions, as well as the posts of president and second vice president, and so continued to dominate the coalition government. There were two government reshuffles during the year. In February, seven new ministers were appointed but key ministerial portfolios were not affected. Interior Minister Edouard Nduwimana, heavily criticised in the media and by civil society, retained his post and, throughout the year, became an increasingly influential cabinet member. Although he had not had a military career, he was seen as a close associate of the group of 'generals', close advisors to Nkurunziza, who were said to govern the country. This group included the president's two chiefs of cabinet (Alain-Guillaume Bunyoni and Evariste Ndayishimiye) and the head of the intelligence service (Adolphe Nshimirimana). In October, as a result of an internal power struggle within the 'Union pour le Progrès National' (**UPRONA**), First Vice-President Térence Sinunguruza, a long-standing heavyweight within the party, was replaced by Bernard Busokoza (Tutsi, Bururi province). The appointment of Busokoza came as a surprise to many, including most CNDD-FDD members of the National Assembly, who walked out of parliament in protest – but were soon called to order by Nkurunziza when asked to confirm Busokoza's appointment. Busokoza was widely seen as one of the most senior military officials responsible for the failed coup attempt against the then newly elected president Melchior Ndadaye on 2–3 July 1993. Ndadaye (Hutu) was the first democratically elected president of Burundi and was assassinated on 21 October 1993. In the early 1990s, several CNDD-FDD MP's had been members of Ndadaye's 'Front pour la Démocratie au Burundi' (FRODEBU), which explained the controversy around Busokoza's appointment. A sign of political reconciliation according to some observers, his appointment was seen by others as a victory for impunity and obscure business partnerships. **Parliament** convened in regular sessions, conducting legislative work but, in the absence of parliamentary opposition, there was little significant parliamentary control over government action.

A survey conducted by Afrobarometer and widely covered in the media in February, indicated that Burundians had high confidence in **President Nkurunziza**, more than in any other institution, which boosted his political weight within the CNDD-FDD. Nkurunziza remained a popular and charismatic leader and he and his wife were the centre of a growing personality cult with an increasingly important religious 'born again' Christian dimension. In various public addresses, Nkurunziza stressed the divine origins of political leadership. First Lady Denise Bucumi's 'Eglise du Rocher' (Rock Church) became increasingly popular among political dignitaries. In August, four national days of prayer ceremonies were held. On the occasion of the 51st anniversary of Burundi's independence, Nkurunziza granted an award to the first lady (alongside 11 other laureates) for her remarkable contribution to development and charity work. Rumour had it that Bucumi might become a candidate in the 2015 presidential elections if Nkurunziza himself, under international pressure, agreed not to stand for a third term. International awards to the president (as 'Leader of African Community Development') and his wife ('MDGs 2013 Women's Progress Award') were widely celebrated domestically.

Throughout the year, the **CNDD-FDD** youth division 'Imbonerakure' ('those who see from afar') became an increasingly active political player, accused by several observers of taking on a para-military militia character. Opposition parties frequently denounced intimidation by Imbonerakure, who sometimes paraded in the streets of small provincial towns. In May, an Imbonerakure leader who was also a member of the National Economic and Social Council, declared on radio RPA ('Radio Publique Africaine') that, in politics, "one does not kill, one simply removes obstacles". He was arrested but was released a month later. Local elections to the national Women's Forum, a consultative body on local development, were held in March and were perceived as being strongly controlled by the CNDD-FDD. Both the youth and women's divisions of the party were likely to become important mobilization tools in the 2015 electoral campaign. In November, the party celebrated the 'week of the combatant' in commemoration of the tenth anniversary of the peace agreement it had signed when it was a rebel movement. CNDD-FDD also multiplied its efforts to divide the political opposition by orchestrating the creation of 'government-friendly' wings in the opposition parties. There were many voices critical of the CNDD-FDD in the capital, Bujumbura, but the party concentrated its pre-electoral campaign on the densely populated rural areas.

In a context of ongoing internal divisions, the **UPRONA** leadership increasingly criticised government policy. This shift on the part of the pro-government wing of the party allowed for an internal rapprochement with the more radical dissident wing ('le Courant de la Réhabilitation'), but this led to a difficult situation in which UPRONA, although a party in the governing coalition, increasingly behaved like an opposition party. This repositioning of UPRONA resulted, in October, in the replacement of First Vice-President Sinunguruza referred to above, after party chairman Charles Nditije publicly withdrew his support for Sinunguruza, accusing him of no longer representing the policy and interests of UPRONA. The three main issues – developed in more detail below – that divided UPRONA and CNDD-FDD were land, the possibility of Nkurunziza's third term in office, and the amendment of the Constitution. Although disagreements around the land issue followed substantially ethnic lines, the broader division between the two parties revealed that political groupings in Burundi no longer coincided with ethnic differences. For example, the chairman of UPRONA (traditionally associated with Tutsi elites), Nditije, was a Hutu, while Interior Minister Nduwimana of the CNDD-FDD (historically a Hutu rebel movement) was a Tutsi. This made an important contribution to mitigating conflict.

Throughout the year, the most controversial political issue at the domestic level was the functioning of the national **Land Commission** ('Commission Nationale Terres et autres Biens'; **CNTB**) established to settle land-related disputes between (mainly Hutu) returning refugees and the de facto occupants of the land (many of them Tutsi). In 2013, more than 3,300 cases were settled by the **CNTB**, which also received 1,200 new files. Under the controversial leadership of its chairperson Sérapion Bambonanire, the CNTB was increasingly criticised, particularly by Tutsi civilians and political elites, for failing to settle disputes amicably and for systematically ruling against Tutsi occupants even when they had acquired houses or land in good faith. This resulted in some evictions in suburbs of Bujumbura, highly publicised in the media, with the police violently intervening to enforce CNTB decisions. From being an institution mandated to promote reconciliation, the CNTB thus became a source of division and the subject of political contestation. While the UPRONA leadership increasingly distanced itself from CNTB policy, the government as well as the CNDD-FDD repeatedly expressed support for the Land Commission. On internet fora, the debate around the CNTB was strongly ethnically loaded. Some comments condemned the CNTB policy as state-sanctioned land spoliation against Tutsi. New legislation to extend the powers of the CNTB was adopted on 31 December, in the absence of UPRONA MPs, who boycotted the parliamentary session. At cabinet level, additional legislation was drafted aimed at the establishment of a Special Court to hear appeals against CNTB rulings in place of the 'classical' judicial system.

Although he had not yet explicitly announced his candidacy for the 2015 presidential elections, leaving it to his party to select a candidate, Nkurunziza's possible **third presidential term** was the subject of considerable political controversy. In accordance with the Arusha Peace and Reconciliation Agreement of August 2000, the Burundian Constitution provided for a two-term limit for the presidency. However, a transitional arrangement (not provided for under the Arusha Agreement but included in the Constitution) was interpreted by some – notably the CNDD-FDD leadership – as allowing the incumbent president to run for an additional term. The transitional provision stipulated that, exceptionally, the first president after the completion of the peace process should be elected not directly by a popular vote but indirectly by the National Assembly and the Senate. Nkurunziza having been indirectly elected for his first term in 2005, CNDD-FDD party chairman Nyabenda stated in September that it had been only in 2010 that Burundians were able, for the first time since the start of the civil war in 1994, to elect their president by universal suffrage. This was widely perceived as an indirect announcement of Nkurunziza's intention to stand for the 2015 elections. All opposition parties – except the 'government-friendly' dissident wings crated at the instigation of the CNDD-FDD – rejected the possibility of his candidacy, referring to the clear limit laid down in the Arusha Agreement. After some initial hesitation, UPRONA chairperson Nditije also opposed a third presidential term for Nkurunziza. Relations between the two parties immediately deteriorated significantly.

In October, the cabinet – with Sinunguruza still leading the UPRONA group of ministers – adopted a draft **constitutional amendment**. Protests against a unilateral, CNDD-FDD-controlled amendment of the Constitution were overwhelming and included objections by diplomatic representatives of Burundi's partner countries. After some revisions, a new draft constitutional amendment was tabled for debate and adoption in Parliament in November. In the Senate, CNDD-FDD had the required two-thirds majority but in the National Assembly it did not have the required four-fifths majority. UPRONA, FRODEBU Nyakuri and three coopted MP's representing the Batwa minority formed a united front, thus blocking a vote in favour. The proposed constitutional amendment was controversial for a number of reasons, including the expansion of presidential powers to the detriment of parliament and some other reforms that were seen as contrary to the spirit of the Arusha Peace Agreement. In order to ease political tensions, the 'Bureau des Nations Unies au Burundi' (BNUB) convened a high-level meeting involving all political parties and civil society organisations to discuss the constitutional amendment in the context of an evaluation of the 'Kayanza roadmap', which had been agreed on by all political stakeholders in March to prepare for peaceful, free and fair elections.

The opposition coalition 'Alliance des Démocrates pour le Changement au Burundi' **ADC-Ikibiri** – which, as the government spokesperson recalled from time to time, was not formally registered and was therefore illegal – made efforts to come up with a united electoral platform and a single presidential candidate for the 2015 elections. At the same time, however, it suffered from ongoing internal divisions, some of which were clearly instigated by the CNDD-FDD. In February, the small 'Conseil des Patriotes' party withdrew from the ADC coalition. In November, CNDD-FDD encouraged the establishment of an alternative so-called opposition platform, the 'Alliance pour la Paix, la Démocratie et le Développement'.

Except for Leonard Nyangoma (CNDD), **opposition party leaders** who had left the country after the 2010 elections returned to Burundi. They included Alexis Sinduhije ('Mouvement pour la Solidarité et la Démocratie', MSD), Pascaline Kampayano ('Union pour la Paix et le Développement', UPD) and, most notably, Agathon Rwasa ('Forces Nationales de Libération', FNL), who returned in early August. Rwasa went back to Burundi despite the fact that he was not restored to the official party leadership – which in 2011, at the instigation of CNDD-FDD had been handed to the government-friendly dissident FNL wing led by Emmanuel Miburo. In February, Interior Minister Nduwimana had officially recognized Miburo as leader and official spokesperson of the opposition. Shortly after Rwasa's return, Banyamulenge survivors and relatives of victims of a massacre committed at the Gatumba refugee camp in 2004 filed a complaint against him. In the immediate aftermath of that massacre, FNL spokesperson Pasteur Habimana had claimed responsibility for the massacre, although – in line with a long-standing tradition of impunity for human rights violations in Burundi – no one had ever been brought to justice. Rwasa denied all responsibility and denounced the complaint and the subsequent judicial inquiry as politically motivated. He also claimed provisional immunity as granted to all political leaders in Burundi's series of peace agreements, although the peace accord with the FNL explicitly excluded crimes against humanity from immunity. Because Rwasa continued to present himself as the 'real' FNL chairperson, he was excluded from party membership by Miburo. In October, another former Rwasa ally, Jacques Bigirimana was elected as the new FNL chairman, replacing Miburo. In November, Rwasa's rehabilitation as party leader was requested in a petition signed by over 67,000 of his supporters, a highly unusual phenomenon in Burundian politics. Also in November, eight ADC parties (including FRODEBU, MSD, CNDD and UPD, but not FNL) signed a joint manifesto for the 2015 elections and announced they would put forward one presidential candidate. In early December, former vice president Frédéric Bamvuginyumvira – who had allegedly been on the ADC presidential candidates shortlist – was arrested on charges of adultery and corruption.

Apart from some isolated attacks on police stations, there were **no armed insurgency activities** on Burundian territory and the security forces retained full control. A midterm report by the UN Group of Experts on the DRC, published in July, pointed to some raids against civilians that were carried out by two military factions of the FNL on Congolese territory, some in conjunction with Rwandese FDLR ('Forces Démocratiques pour la Libération du Rwanda') combatants. In general, however, the UN Group reported that the FNL remnants were divided and weakened. In March, the commander-in-chief of the 'Front pour le Peuple Murundi – Alliance Divine pour la Nation' (FPM-Abatabazi) was reportedly killed during fighting with a Congolese armed group. In May, FPM leader Guillaume George Majambare announced the creation of a new armed resistance movement 'Alliance Intore', also including Richard Ciramunda's 'Mouvement National Burundais'. Alliance Intore claimed responsibility for an armed attack in Gatumba on a bus reportedly transporting Imbonerakure.

In June, new legislation was adopted to regulate the **media**. Media professionals and domestic as well as international human rights groups strongly protested against what they perceived as excessive restrictions on freedom of expression. Diplomatic representatives of Burundi's development partners also publicly expressed concern. Particularly troubling were obligations for journalists to reveal their sources in a number of vaguely worded circumstances, the prohibition on publishing information that might threaten national unity, the security of the state or morality, and high fines for journalists and media houses that violated the **new media law**. Against the background of the new legislation, action was undertaken by the High Media Council against the popular and internationally funded newspaper and website Iwacu, as a result of which Iwacu decided to suspend its activities for a month in protest. Other journalists also complained of harassment and threats to their safety. The 'Union Burundaise des Journalistes' filed a complaint against the new legislation in the Constitutional Court and, somewhat unexpectedly given the

Court's recent record, several provisions in the law were found to be incompatible with the human rights bill included in the Constitution.

Other draft legislation adopted by the cabinet and tabled for debate in parliament was also criticised from a **human rights** perspective, including draft legislation regulating NGOs and draft legislation regulating public meetings and demonstrations. Regarding the latter, the National Assembly amended several provisions taking into consideration recommendations by civil society movements, but no final vote had taken place by the end of the year.

Burundi's universal periodic review took place in January. While welcoming progress in some areas, the UN Human Rights Council expressed particular concern about impunity for extrajudicial executions and other human rights violations. Also in January, the first Burundian cases ever were brought before the UN Committee against Torture. Burundi also ratified the Protocol to the UN Torture Convention. In March, police violently broke up gatherings of a spiritual movement in Businde (Kayanza province), killing nine worshippers. The victims were followers of Zebiya Ngendakumana, who claimed to see apparitions of the Virgin Mary. Some 200 other pilgrims were arrested for disrespecting the local administrator's ban on religious gatherings. In July, the religious site was made into a military camp.

A **justice sector summit** ('Etats-Généraux de la Justice') was held in August, involving the Ministry of Justice, the judiciary, the Bar Association and civil society organisations. While the Arusha Peace and Reconciliation Agreement did not impose any ethnic quotas on the composition of the justice sector – contrary to what was provided for the legislature, the executive branch and the security forces – the summit recommended a 40% Tutsi and 60% Hutu composition of the judiciary. The summit also proposed a new composition for the High Judicial Council ('Conseil Supérieur de la Magistrature) in order to enhance its independence. These recommendations were incorporated in the draft amendment of the Constitution adopted by the cabinet in October. The summit was held in the context of longstanding disagreement between the government and a justice sector trade union. The judiciary in particular feared excessive restrictions on the sector's right to strike. Throughout the year, the Bar Association protested against the administrative and judicial harassment of its president, Isidore Rufyikiri.

Despite repeated announcements by government officials and in a long radio interview in January by Nkurunziza himself, no progress was made in the field of **transitional justice**. Draft legislation on the establishment of a truth and reconciliation commission (TRC), tabled for debate in the National Assembly in December 2012, was not adopted. Fearing that the proposed TRC would lack independence, UPRONA continued to oppose its establishment. In the government's public discourse, increasing weight was given to the need to forgive, reconcile and pardon rather than to the fight against impunity for perpetrators of human rights violations. International pressure in the area of transitional justice was scaled down. In light of the contestation around the CNTB, diplomats feared that the TRC would negatively impact on ethnic pacification and political stability, in particular in the run-up to the 2015 elections. Notwithstanding the political stalemate on the TRC, there was considerable transitional justice activism and public debate on how to deal with Burundi's violent past.

Foreign Affairs

In February, the UNSC extended the presence of the **BNUB**, led by the UN Secretary-General's Special Representative Onanga-Anyanga, for another year until 15 February 2014. The BNUB mandate included, in particular, supporting the government in the areas of political dialogue in preparation of the 2015 elections, institutional capacity building, human rights protection and the fight against impunity, regional integration, and socio-economic reintegration and development of those regions most affected by the armed conflict. For all of these areas, a number of benchmarks and indicators of progress were agreed upon between the government and the **UN** in order to enable a more structured assessment of the evolution in Burundi and to inform the future gradual evolution from BNUB to a regular UN country team presence. In August, Foreign Affairs Minister Laurent Kavakure addressed a 'note verbale' to the UN Secretary-General highlighting the progress made on several of the agreed benchmarks and requesting that the UN presence be reduced to a country team by February 2014. The UN Department of Political Affairs conducted a strategic evaluation between September and December. Despite the progress achieved, the evaluation report noted several remaining challenges in the area of democratic consolidation, rule of law and human rights and recommended an extension of the BNUB mandate until the 2015 elections, much to the dissatisfaction of the government. In response, Burundi stepped up its diplomatic activity ahead of the February 2014 UNSC debate. In December, a meeting and exchange of letters between Nkurunziza and UN Secretary-General Ban Ki-moon failed to produce a consensus solution. Nkurunziza expressed particular concern that a continued BNUB presence would create a false perception among potential investors that Burundi was still in post-conflict transition.

Nine countries established **diplomatic relations** with Burundi. For the first time ever, the Netherlands opened an embassy in Bujumbura. The USA inaugurated a new embassy compound. In April, Nkurunziza met his Iranian counterpart Ahmadinejad during a controversial visit to Iran.

Bilateral relations with neighbouring countries remained generally friendly, despite diplomatic tensions within the **EAC**. Declarations by the Tanzanian president with regard to negotiations with the FDLR were very badly taken by the Rwandan government and this had repercussions on Burundi's position within the EAC. Burundi and Tanzania, a long-standing ally of Burundi's Hutu rebel movements and therefore seen as closely associated with the current Burundian government, were on several occasions excluded from high-level EAC meetings between Rwanda, Kenya and Uganda. In September, the

Burundian government publicly protested against its "exclusion" from high-level meetings but reconfirmed its allegiance to the EAC. In May, Rwanda, Burundi and the DRC in the context of the 'Communauté Économique des Pays des Grands Lacs' (CEPGL) announced the establishment of a joint court of justice to prosecute transnational crimes. A national commission to demarcate the borders between Burundi and its neighbouring countries was established in October.

Burundi played an increasingly active role in **AU** and **UN peacekeeping** operations on the African continent. By the end of the year, around 5,000 Burundian peacekeepers were deployed as part of the AU peacekeeping operation in Somalia (AMISOM). In November, General Silas Ntigurirwa was appointed as military coordinator of the AMISOM operation. It was commonly agreed that the Burundian presence in Somalia also had an important socialisation effect at all levels within the Burundian army, which was composed of members of a former government army and former rebel movements. In addition, Burundi sent military and/or civilian police to Mali, the CAR, South Sudan and Ivory Coast in the context of multilateral peace and security interventions. After the terrorist attacks on Nairobi's West Gate shopping centre in September, there was an increased fear that Bujumbura might become the next target of the Somali al-Shabaab militia and police rounded up some 300 suspected al-Shabaab sympathisers.

Socioeconomic Developments

On 27 January, a **massive fire** destroyed Bujumbura's **central market**. This represented the heart of Burundi's local economy, with an estimated daily turnover of around $ 4 m. Although there were no casualties, the disaster destroyed or reduced the livelihoods of tens of thousands of small agricultural producers, local traders, businessmen and other actors in Burundi's informal economy. It also had important negative consequences for the state's fiscal revenues. The fire constituted another blow to an economy that was already in crisis. A judicial commission of inquiry concluded that the disaster was accidental, but it also pointed at several aspects of mismanagement (in terms of security, urban planning, corruption, etc.) of the market and its surroundings. As a result, several local administration officials were dismissed and in March the former mayor of Bujumbura, Evrard Giswaswa, who had meanwhile been appointed as CEO of Air Burundi, was arrested.

Throughout the year, several social and economic sectors were affected by **strike movements**. These were both the cause and effect of the suspension and banning of a number of trade unions, including in the trade sector (SYGECO), the justice sector (SYMABU) and the education sector (CONAPES and STEB). In addition, the main public university, 'Université du Burundi', was the scene of repeated strikes by students and staff. Political involvement in the appointment and career management of academic staff worsened relations between several faculties and departments and the university management. In his address on the occasion of the 51st anniversary of Burundi's independence, Nkurunziza warned against the abuse of the right to strike. The strikes were part of a more general protest campaign – particularly visible in Bujumbura – against sharp rises in the price of consumer goods and their impact on the already harsh living conditions. New legislation on VAT adopted in July was one of the protestors' concerns. In October, the mayor of Bujumbura prohibited a public conference organised by movements protesting against rising consumer prices.

In early 2013, the **depreciation of the Burundian currency** against the US dollar and the Euro reached alarming levels. In January and February, the Burundian franc lost around 11% against the dollar. This was largely due to Burundi's conspicuous balance of payments problems and even gave rise to a meeting and public declaration by the National Security Council, which called upon the government, the central bank and commercial banks to take all necessary measures to stop the depreciation. By the end of the year, the rate had more or less stabilised at the February level. This was in part due to new disbursements of budget support by international development partners.

In the **2013 Global Hunger Index**, Burundi was listed last of 78 ranked countries on the basis of three key indicators (calorie deficiency, underweight children under five, child mortality rate). More than 60% of the population were reported as malnourished. The northern province of Ngozi was most seriously affected with a malnutrition rate of over 71%. On UNDP's **2013 HDI**, Burundi was ranked 178th out of 185 countries.

In the World Bank's 2013 **Doing Business Report**, Burundi rose markedly to rank 140th out of 189 countries (compared with 187th in 2010) and was commended as one of the seven countries making the biggest improvements since 2005. The improvement was particularly due to the establishment in March of a one-stop shop for registering property transfers, reforms that facilitated trade with overseas business partners, and measures that protected the position of minority shareholders. The end of the Regideso monopoly of the sale of electricity transformers was also assessed positively by the World Bank. Burundi's performance was discussed and evaluated during a high-level Country Policy and Institutional Assessment in early October, organised jointly by the World Bank and the government.

As a follow-up to the October 2012 international donor conference in Geneva, two **sectoral conferences** were organised on the initiative of the second vice president. The first, in July, dealt with infrastructure, education and private sector development. The second, in October, dealt with governance, social protection, health, energy and regional integration. The aim of these conferences was to mobilise financial support for the implementation of Burundi's Second Poverty Reduction and Growth Strategy Paper (PRSP II).

In September, the government and the **Chinese** minister of commerce signed an agreement for the construction of a new hydro-power dam and a new presidential palace.

In April, contrary to the World Bank's recommendation of the privatisation of state-owned companies, the UN Special Rapporteur on the Right to Food, Olivier De Schutter, and the UN Independent Expert on the effects of foreign debt on the enjoyment of human rights, Cephas Lumina, raised alarm over the World Bank-led **privatisation of the coffee sector**. Given the fact that coffee accounted not only for 80% of the country's export earnings but also for the livelihoods of 55% of the population, mostly small-scale farmers, the two experts recommended a suspension of the privatisation programme, pending a full human rights impact assessment. In August, the National Assembly also protested against the **privatisation of the national telephone company** ONATEL.

In March, in order to combat tax evasion in the gold sector, Nkurunziza decreed the suspension of all **gold exploitation** for two months. In October, a new **Mining Code** regulating various stages of the mining process (prospecting, research, exploitation, commercialisation) was adopted in parliament as part of a wider programme of reforms in the mining sector. It was hoped that the mining sector (accounting for only 1% of GDP) could develop its significant potential more rapidly in the coming years.

Macroeconomic performance was marked by a modest acceleration in **GDP growth** compared with previous years at an estimated 4.5% (4% in 2012). The industrial sector (accounting for around 20% of GDP) was expected to expand, most notably in construction activities. In his tri-annual budget plan for 2014–16, the Finance Minister predicted a continued rise in GDP growth to 7.2% in 2016. The report of the IMF's third review under the current ECF arrangement was less optimistic and predicted a GDP growth of 4.7% in 2014, 4.8% in 2015 and 5% in 2016.

In January, a new income tax law was adopted. Prepared with IMF technical assistance, this new law had a negative short-term effect on **fiscal revenue**. The new tax law significantly narrowed the tax base, providing for partial exemptions for most agriculture-related activities, pensions and allowances for transport and housing. Because of the revenue slippages, a revised budget was adopted in parliament in July. This included a reinstatement of the previously suspended taxes on food and petroleum products.

In December, a **budget for 2014** was adopted in the National Assembly, based on a limited 1.4% increase in revenue and a 2.5% increase in expenditure. This budget anticipated a likely drop in aid disbursements. Consumer price **inflation** was expected to fall to 7% in 2014 (compared with 18% in 2012 and 8.1% in 2013).

Stef Vandeginste

Comoros

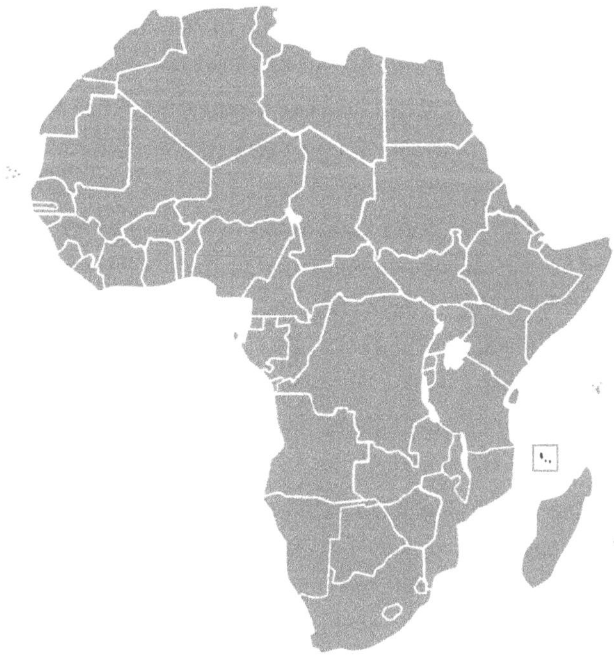

Despite some signs of a possible re-emergence of the vicious political confrontations that had long characterised the country during its often turbulent past, 2013 turned out to be another (third) year of relatively calm political normalcy without any major upheavals. A failed coup attempt had no noticeable effect on the stability of the government. President Dhoinine managed to further consolidate his leadership position despite an escalating rift with his predecessor and former mentor Sambi. The long-existing frictions between the three islands of the 'Union des Comores' and their political elites continued unchanged, but caused no immediate problems. A compromise was found on the disputed issue of a harmonised election cycle, while key political parties showed signs of internal disarray. The contentious Mayotte issue and ambivalent relations with France continued to dominate the foreign front. Further progress on debt cancellation was made and there was a moderate general improvement in the economic situation, while structural reforms of key parastatal enterprises remained stalled.

Domestic Politics

A foiled **coup attempt** in April recalled memories of Comoros' unstable past, with more than 20 coups or coup attempts since independence in 1975, but had no lasting negative effect on the prevailing political situation. On 19–20 April, a total of 16 persons (including seven foreigners, mostly Congolese) were arrested for an alleged attempt to destabilise the country. The evidence that was officially put forward remained rather opaque, and the trial process had not begun by the end of the year. The alleged plot was to assassinate **President Ikililou Dhoinine** and replace him with Mahmoud Ahmed Abdallah, a son of Comoros' first president Ahmed Abdallah, who had been murdered in 1989 by the French mercenary Bob Denard. Recruitment and preparations for the plot had allegedly been undertaken in France by Patrick Klein, a notorious mercenary formerly associated with Denard.

The sacking of the transport and communications minister in late June on account of serious corruption charges, and the subsequent public uproar about the wider implications of a financial scandal, obliged Dhoinine to carry out a **cabinet reshuffle** on 13 July. This was the first change in the government team since the government had taken office in May 2011. Six of the ten cabinet members, including two women, were new, but all three vice presidents kept their positions as representatives of their respective islands, although Vice President Fouad Mohadji (from Mohéli, like the president), lost the important production and energy portfolio and was moved to health since he had on several occasions openly sided with the positions of critics of the government.

During the year, former president **Ahmed Abdallah Sambi** expressed increasingly **sharp criticism** of the government's performance, despite having been personally instrumental in the selection of Dhoinine as his successor in the 2010 presidential election. In mid-February, having returned from a lengthy stay in Dubai after the end of his mandate, Sambi used the occasion of a religious ceremony to make his first public appearance in Moroni, criticising the government before a large audience. It became evident that he wanted to regain influence and was ambitious to return to active politics. A final rupture between the two men then occurred in mid-August when Dhoinine intervened to stop Sambi from holding a public rally on Anjouan, but he was unable to prevent him from making a scathing speech on private premises. Sambi strongly attacked Dhoinine as being responsible for an alleged general regression in the country. He announced the creation of a new party and claimed, "We are on the way to regain power." On 30 October, Sambi's party 'Juwa' (sun) was officially launched in the presence of prominent politicians such as Vice President Mohadji and Parliamentary Speaker Bourhane Hamidou. Thus it was clear that an important new political alignment was in the making. Sambi announced his intention to run for president in the 2016 elections, although it was not at all clear whether this was constitutionally possible. According to the rotation principle, the next president should come from Ngazidja island (Grande Comore), whereas Sambi originated from Anjouan.

From September onwards, much political attention centred on discussions about the **date** of the **next parliamentary elections** (as well as island council elections). According to a ruling of the Constitutional Court (on 12 September), the mandate of the Union

National Assembly was to end in April 2014, while other interpretations put the date at April 2015. Irrespective of constitutional ambiguities, the majority of politicians were in favour of extending the assembly's term from four to five years. Months of controversial discussions finally culminated on 8 November in a meeting of all 'grands élus' (top office holders from Union and the islands), where a compromise on the holding of **harmonised elections** was agreed that satisfied most members of the political class. Elections for three levels of representatives (National Assembly, island councils, local communities) were thus to be held simultaneously in November 2014. The necessary changes to Article 20 of the constitution were then passed in parliament on 20 December, while formal approval still remained to be sought from the majority of island councillors.

Parliamentary discussions about regularising the hitherto unregulated status of political parties led on 21 November to the passage of a new **law on political parties**, which stipulated clear criteria for their official recognition. This had, however, no immediately noticeable effect on the long-standing fragmentary existence of a multitude of loosely organised political parties and movements that were mostly geared to gathering the supporters of individual politicians. Not surprisingly, this political environment encouraged frequent new alignments and dissensions within the various camps. Overall more than 50 **political parties** were estimated to exist, although the vast majority were without any real significance. In March, several groups supporting the president re-formed as two new organisations, the 'Union pour le Développement des Comores' and the 'Mouvement pour la Majorité Presidentielle', while another new grouping, the 'Alliance pour la Justice et le Développement', brought together Sambi's supporters. In September, the pro-government Orange movement was established as a political party and a congress attended by over 4,000 followers elected Mohamed Daoud, aka Kiki, as its president. Subsequent to the evident schism between Dhoinine and Sambi, emerging cracks and internal divisions became apparent in all the major political camps, including the main opposition party, the 'Convention pour le Renouveau des Comores'.

The familiar **inter-island rivalry** and that between the Union and island administrations had by no means disappeared, but caused less concrete frictions than in most recent years. Internal conflicts and problems on each of the islands had only limited ramifications for the national political scene. Early in the year, the **Mohéli** governor, Mohamed Ali Said, was faced by public discontent and low-level unrest and was accused in an open letter to Dhoinine, himself from the island, of bad governance practices. Following a meeting between Dhoinine and the opposition, the situation calmed down, but some tensions remained. In late December, the governor of **Ngazidja** only narrowly survived a motion of censure in the island council, based on allegations of irregularities and non-respect of laws.

Charges of widespread **corruption** repeatedly served as a rallying point for opposition forces. In September the Franco-Comorian lawyer Said Larifou, president of the opposition party 'Rassemblement pour une Initiative de Développement avec la Jeunesse

Avertie', started a comprehensive anti-corruption campaign, detailing a number of specific cases in a complaint memorandum. Particular controversies centred on the shadowy accounting of revenues from the **Economic Citizenship Programme** (ECP) initiated by Sambi, whereby Comorian passports were offered to foreigners in return for commitments to substantial investments. (The ECP was intended to be targeted mainly at Arabs.) On 12 November, civil society organisations conducted a big public demonstration against corruption and impunity.

Foreign Affairs

The long-standing conflict with **France** over the status of **Mayotte**, the archipelago's fourth island, continued to be a national focus, but without materially jeopardising the delicate relations with Comoros' former colonial power. Mayotte had become France's 101st regular *département* in 2011 and was set to be fully recognised as a peripheral territory of the EU by January 2014. Although all Comorian governments had always insisted that Mayotte remained an integral part of the Comoros under international law, the completion of the integration of Mayotte into the French state had by now been reluctantly accepted as inevitable by most politicians and the general population. Bilateral **Comorian-French relations** thus continued to be characterised by considerable ambivalences between the Mayotte conflict and Comoros' traditional substantial dependence on France as a major economic partner and donor. During his first official visit to France, Dhoinine met French President Hollande on 21 June. While there was clearly no progress on the political disagreements, a friendship and cooperation declaration was signed, together with three bilateral agreements on aid and debt relief. The partnership framework document also included a substantial section on security and defence, thus safeguarding continued French support. A new 'Haut Conseil Paritaire' was to be established to serve at regular intervals as a dialogue platform. In a speech at the UN General Assembly on 25 September, Dhoinine once again naturally focused on the Mayotte issue, but equally stressed the good relations that existed between Comoros and France. The celebration of the annual 'Journée Nationale Maore' on 12 November served to publicly underline the claim to Mayotte, with some agitators even suggesting that someone from Mayotte should be elected as the next president in 2016 in accordance with the inter-island rotation principle.

Otherwise, the government continued to pursue an **open-door policy** within the very limited scope available to it, and attempted to maintain equally cordial relations with Western powers (particularly France and the USA) and with China, Iran and many Arab countries (particularly Kuwait, the UAE and Qatar), in the expectation of attracting aid or commercial investments from these diverse sources. Most of the quite substantial investments promised at a 2010 investment conference in Doha (Qatar) had, however, so far not materialised. Some new openings were also pursued with Southeast Asian countries. Visits to Moroni by the president of the Pan-Arab parliament in May and by the Iranian foreign minister in July underscored the **priority given to existing links** with the **Middle East**. In January, Dhoinine attended the 3rd Arab Economic Summit in Riad, and his mid-December official visit to the Sultanate of Oman also served to widen the spectrum of Comoros' friendly Arab donors. Also in December, he participated in the summit on African peace and security in Paris. In August, a trade agreement was signed with Vietnam over rice imports of 60,000 tonnes per year, which provided an assuring element of food security, rice being the second-largest import after petroleum.

In January, Comoros assumed the annually rotating chairmanship of the **IOC** from Seychelles and held a number of senior officials' meetings during the year in Moroni.

Socioeconomic Developments

The year opened with unusually **optimistic prospects** for the **economy** in the wake of the mid-December 2012 declaration of the IMF and the World Bank that Comoros had at last reached the long-awaited **completion point** under the **HIPC initiative**, making it eligible for comprehensive **debt relief** under both HIPC and the **MDRI**. This had marked the end of the country's HIPC process, which had only started in June 2010 with the attainment of the decision point. As the 35th country to have reached the completion point, Comoros was very much a latecomer compared with other countries, since necessary reforms and adjustments of economic policies had been neglected for many years as a result of recurrent political turbulence. The expected significant easing of the future debt burden offered the prospect of allowing more room for genuine development-oriented efforts and investment on the part of the government. In February, further debt cancellations were authorised by the AfDB and cancellations of debts amounting to $ 8 m were arranged with creditors of the Paris Club. The Islamic Development Bank and Kuwait also followed suit with debt cancellations in June. Despite these significant measures, the IMF still judged that the country remained vulnerable to renewed debt distress.

IMF missions in March and September performed the fifth and sixth (final) reviews of the three-year ECF ($ 13.5 m) approved in September 2009 and later extended to December 2013. It was expected that a new ECF would be arranged in 2014. Upon completion of the current ECF, the IMF commended the government for **significant progress** in **stabilising the economy** and implementing the IMF-supported adjustment programme. All but one of the agreed performance criteria and all indicative targets had been met. The main macroeconomic objectives had been achieved, growth with low inflation had been sustained, and the fiscal situation had strengthened. This positive assessment was a testimony to the Dhoinine government's generally satisfactory economic performance, in stark contrast to most of the recent past. Difficult structural reforms, particularly with respect to restructuring key public utility companies and the bloated civil service, had, however, still not brought any lasting results.

Preliminary statistical data for 2013 confirmed a stabilised moderate **macroeconomic performance**, but were still quite far from portraying a dynamic surge in the economy. The **GDP growth rate** was projected to have slightly increased to 3.5%, moderately better than in 2012 (3.0%), but noticeably higher than earlier annual averages of around only 1%. A clear, although modest, acceleration in the growth of the economy seemed to be underway. The average inflation rate for the year of under 3% (compared with 6.3% in 2012) was largely due to the restraining effect of membership of the franc zone, whereby the Franc Comorien (FrC) remained pegged to the Euro and supported by France (at FrC 492:€ 1). Substantial remittances from the large Comorian diaspora (contributing over 20% of GDP) and inflows of aid revenue remained essential to counterbalance the traditional enormous **structural trade deficit**. Estimated export revenues of around $ 20 m (practically all from cloves, vanilla and ylang-ylang) covered just one-tenth of the estimated import bill of $ 208 m, due largely to the country's heavy dependence on importing food staples. The current-account deficit was projected to widen to 8.7% of GDP, while foreign exchange reserves experienced a small drop, but continued to provide a comfortable safety cushion of over six months import coverage.

Despite progress in revenue administration and tax collection, the **fiscal performance** weakened somewhat during the latter half of the year, largely as a result of the temporary suspension of inflows from the ECP. Some public investments had been launched in anticipation of expected external funding, which did not materialise. Early in the year, some budget support funds were obtained from the AfDB and the World Bank. Public sector salaries were regularly paid, in contrast with the past, when salary arrears of several months were sometimes experienced. This improvement avoided the recurrence of frequent strikes, which had formerly been common. In late December, parliament approved the new **budget** for 2014, which envisaged a small fiscal surplus on the optimistic assumption that revenues would be obtained from the envisaged privatisation of some parastatals. An evaluation of the **PRSP** for the period 2010–14 revealed that most MDG objectives had not been achieved and that there had been no noticeable reduction in poverty. Work started on the preparation of a new poverty reduction and growth strategy document.

Demands for a fundamental reform or **privatisation** of notoriously badly managed **parastatal companies**, particularly key public utilities (electricity, water and telecoms) had for years been a prominent item on the IMF and the World Bank's agenda in debt relief discussions, but little progress had been made because of resistance from powerful local vested interests. Recurring power and water crises were a constant burden in the daily life of the population and for the economy. Again no substantial progress was made during the year towards solid improvement of the situation. In September, grants were obtained from the AfDB and the World Bank to shore up the commercial management and financial performance of **Ma-Mwe**, the ailing power and water company. An attempt in 2012 to bring in a competent foreign partner to take charge of the company had failed due to conflicts between various political interests. The external funds were now intended to restructure Ma-Mwe, which was to keep its present parastatal status. Privatisation was generally hampered by the low level of interest on the part of potential external investors, who did not see much promise in the Comorian economy. In October, in a sequence of rapid management changes, the notoriously loss-making oil importer and distributor, 'Société Comorienne des Hydrocarbures', had a retired colonel appointed as its new director, supposedly in the expectation that he would execute tough reform measures. The much delayed planned privatisation of **'Comores Télécom'** once again encountered severe resistance from politicians and trade unions, who feared the inevitable loss of up to 1,000 jobs. The government envisaged a formula of 51% of ownership going to a private investor, 34% to the government and 15% to the staff. This plan was expected to be approved by parliament in late December, but in view of persisting public anxieties MPs demanded social guarantees and refused to vote on the relevant bill. The issue thus remained in limbo, with the government now planning to license a second telecoms operator to bring in an element of competition.

Hopes for success in **oil and gas** exploration in Comoros' extensive coastal waters were also dashed. Expectations had risen following substantial recent finds along the East African coast and Sambi made unsubstantiated claims in February that Comoros' gas reserves might be bigger than Qatar's. A first exploration licence had been awarded to a Kenya-based company in 2012, but there was continued intense quarrelling between two vice presidents over the responsibility for awarding licences. A parliamentary debate in late December on production-sharing contracts with foreign companies that had been drafted was suspended because it was blocked by some MPs. In actual fact, no exploration had begun by the year's end.

Rolf Hofmeier

Djibouti

The year opened with a note of optimism regarding chances of some modest advances towards introducing limited democratic elements into a political system hitherto characterised by the authoritarian regime of President Guelleh and its undisputed full control of all aspects of public life. A hastily arranged coalition of opposition parties participated in legislative elections in February for the first time in ten years, thus ending a period of election boycotts in protest at the unfair electoral system. However, violent demonstrations against alleged election fraud quickly led to renewed sharp confrontations between government and opposition forces. Elected opposition candidates refused to take up their seats in parliament, and an attempt to conduct a dialogue between the opposing political camps broke down after initial rounds of talks. No end to the deadlock was in sight, while a climate of intimidation and repression persisted. Guelleh continued to represent his small state at many international forums and to pursue the vision of transforming Djibouti into an important commercial hub by taking advantage of its strategic geographical location. General economic performance was relatively satisfactory and a number of ambitious new infrastructural projects got underway or were planned.

Domestic Politics

Changes in the **electoral laws**, passed by parliament in November 2012, had made for a cautious opening up of more democratic space in the political system. The new laws introduced an element of proportional representation for 20% of the seats in the legislature, thus lessening the effects of the existing block-voting system in large constituencies. This had disproportionately favoured the ruling coalition to the detriment of smaller opposition parties and been the cause of election boycotts since 2003, when the opposition had received 37.3% of the votes, but not a single seat. With **parliamentary elections** scheduled for **22 February**, the various opposition groups had to quickly decide whether to stage another boycott or to participate and declare their candidates by 24 January. In December 2012, a 'Union Sacrée pour le Changement' had been created by a number of the existing opposition parties as a provisional umbrella body for the formation of a united opposition coalition.

On 17 January, agreement was reached by the leaders of five registered opposition parties to set up a new wider opposition coalition under the name **'Union pour le Salut National'** (**USN**), which was to present joint lists of candidates in all constituencies. The USN was comprised of the 'Alliance Républicaine pour le Développement' (**ARD**) under Ahmed Youssouf Houmed, the 'Mouvement pour le Renouveau Démocratique et le Développement' (**MRD**) under Daher Ahmed Farah, the 'Parti National Démocratique' (**PND**) under Aden Robleh Awaleh, the 'Parti Populaire Djiboutien' (**PPD**) under Ahmed Dini and the 'Union pour Démocratie et Justice' (**UDJ**) under Ismael Guedi Harid. After some wrangling, the head of the ARD, mainly representing Afars, was selected as USN chairman, while the MRD leader was appointed USN spokesman, having returned to Djibouti in early January from ten years in exile in Belgium. The leader of the UDJ was top of the list of candidates in the capital, Djibouti-Ville. All opposition party leaders were veterans of Djibouti's political scene; they had all at one time or another been associated with the ruling establishment, but for various reasons had fallen out of favour. Also aligned with the USN was the new and not yet legalised 'Mouvement pour le Développement et la Liberté' (**Model**), which included several Muslim sheikhs and presented itself as having a moderate Islamist orientation with links to the Muslim Brotherhood. Further USN support was also generated by the independent 'Rassemblement pour l'Action, la Démocratie et le Devéloppement', which had quite unexpectedly won the communal elections in Djibouti-Ville in March 2012.

With the creation of the USN and its participation in the electoral contest confirmed, the stage was thus set for a new competitive political experience after years of a rather lacklustre opposition. The long-ruling regime of **President Ismail Omar Guelleh**, widely dubbed IOG, was now challenged to defend its supremacy. The governing **'Union pour la Majorité Presidentielle'** (**UMP**) coalition had the president's own **'Rassemblement Populaire pour le Progrès'** (**RPP**) as its core element, supplemented by the internal wing of the 'Front pour la Restauration de l'Unitè et de la Démocratie' (FRUD) and three smaller, rather marginal parties. A third force in the election contest, besides the UMP and USN, was the 'Centre des Démocrates Unifiés' (**CDU**), which had only been founded in 2012 by a former FRUD MP and was widely perceived as being close to the ruling regime. During the generally calm campaign period, no major confrontations took place, with the USN clearly attracting more attention and larger crowds than the UMP. Election day passed peacefully, and the foreign election observer groups (from the AU, Arab League, IGAD and OIC) deemed the elections to have been conducted by and large correctly.

The official **election results** were confirmed on 12 March by the Constitutional Council: 67% of the 184,000 registered voters had actually voted; the UMP received 61.5% of the total valid votes, the USN 35.7% and the CDU 2.8%. These figures did not, however, indicate the sharp contrast between the capital city, accounting for two-thirds of the population, and the five outlying regions. In Djibouti-Ville, the competing coalitions were almost on a par, with 49.4% of votes going to the UMP and 47.6% to the USN, while in the rural regions the UMP scooped 81.2% of the votes. Due to the peculiarities of the electoral system (only 20% of seats were allocated proportionally), the UMP again formed an overwhelming majority in the legislature, with 55 seats in the new National Assembly, against 10 for the USN. The discrepancy was most glaring in the case of Djibouti-Ville with the UMP and the USN taking 28 and 7 seats, respectively, despite having received an almost equal number of individual votes.

Immediately upon the announcement of the first provisional results, the USN leaders disputed the figures and made allegations of serious **election fraud**. A petition was rejected by the Constitutional Council for having missed the deadline for submission by one day. For several days, violent **street demonstrations** broke out in Djibouti-Ville, several hundred protesters were taken into custody and a number of people were killed and injured. As part of a harsh government clampdown, most USN leaders and also a number of outspoken Muslim ulema were temporarily detained or put under house arrest. In the ensuing months, several prominent USN leaders were repeatedly arrested, released upon court orders, but then imprisoned again. After the initial post-election eruption, government security forces soon contained the situation and the rest of the year passed without further disturbances.

In the inaugural session of the new **parliament** on 18 March all ten newly-elected opposition MPs refused to take their seats, and their boycott continued thereafter. The idea that they might set up a parallel parliament was raised but not pursued. The parliament's speaker and the government over the following months repeatedly warned the USN to take up their seats, but to little avail. Only Aden Robleh Awaleh (MRD) joined parliament in mid-June, amid applause from the house. On 1 October, the speaker again threatened to exclude the remaining nine USN MPs by 31 January 2014 at the latest, if their **boycott** persisted. It was also made clear that the USN had no formal legal status, since it had only been created as an election coalition. Despite on-going post-election tensions, attempts were made to initiate a **dialogue** between the government and the opposition. In late April, the USN chairman addressed an open letter to IOG with that demand. It took until 14 August for an official dialogue between UMP and USN delegations to start, with the need for a climate of confidence and cordiality being stressed by both sides. Several rounds of discussion of most contentious issues took place, but were then bogged down in September over mutual accusations of intransigence, particularly over the question of prisoners still in detention. The UMP insisted that the cases of prisoners accused of ordinary violations of public order and inciting violence could not be part of the political dialogue. The situation thus remained stalled for the remainder of the year, with the government continuing to exercise its authoritarian control and hopes for an opening up of the regime and the building of a better government image having been dashed.

On 31 March, in a follow-up to the elections, President Guelleh announced a new **cabinet** of 17 ministers (including five newcomers). Defence Minister Abdoulkader Mohamed Kamil was promoted to the position of prime minister, a post that had been loyally held for 12 years by Dileita Mohamed Dileita. Both men were seen to represent the Afars from the north of the country, thereby signalling a counterbalancing of the general predominance of the Issa ethnic group. Foreign Minister Mahamoud Ali Youssouf was given the role of official government spokesman. The new government's focus was stated to be on the fight against poverty, reform of the public administration, the improvement of the education and health sectors and continued expansion of Djibouti's infrastructure. It was hoped that a rejuvenated government might somehow improve the critical light in which the UMP and the RPP were seen in the eyes of the population, which had become evident in the election.

A few isolated incidents in northern Djibouti involving the remaining **rebels** of the illegal armed wing of the FRUD had no noticeable impact on public life and the stability of the country. The government's legal battles to confiscate the assets of the businessman Abdoulrahman Boreh, a former close associate of the president and for some years an exiled dissident and active supporter of the opposition, continued on several international fronts (in London, Dubai and Singapore) with no end in sight.

Foreign Affairs

Most attention continued to be focussed on relations with neighbouring countries in the conflict-prone Horn of Africa region. The contentious situation on the border with **Eritrea** remained calm, but again no progress was made towards a final demarcation of the frontier, and relations remained quite frosty. Djibouti's government continued to take a close active interest in the complex political developments in **Somalia**, its ethnically closely linked and crisis-ridden neighbour. Full political support was extended throughout the year to the new Somali government, installed in Mogadishu since September 2012. Somalia's prime minister came several times to Djibouti for political consultations, and

President Guelleh personally attended the international Somalia conference in London in early May and the Brussels donor conference for Somalia in mid-September. A Djiboutian military contingent of about 1,000 soldiers continued to be stationed in the Hiiran region as part of the AU peacekeeping mission in Somalia; this was to be augmented by another battalion in early 2014. Friendly relations and close cooperation were also maintained with the self-declared Republic of **Somaliland**, for which Djibouti continued to serve as a vital link to the outside world.

Relations with **Ethiopia**, Djibouti's large neighbour and a hegemonic player in the sub-region, remained very close and cordial. Several projects were undertaken or in the planning stage to improve the infrastructural and trade links on which both countries depended, albeit in very different ways. Ethiopia was by far the most important client of Djibouti's ports, and the country benefitted generally from the sustained boom in Ethiopia's fast expanding economy. The 2011 emergence of **South Sudan** as an independent state had raised some expectations that Djibouti would potentially be able to serve as a transit centre for that country, *inter alia* for its oil exports. Some tripartite techno-political meetings between Djibouti, Ethiopia and South Sudan were held with that in mind, but in view of the prevailing uncertainties in South Sudan no concrete plans had yet materialised at year's end.

The **US** continued to attach great importance to its **military base**, due to Djibouti's strategic geopolitical location. More than 3,000 US troops, civilians and contractors worked at Camp Lemonnier, where they trained foreign forces, gathered intelligence and delivered humanitarian aid, all as part of the fight against Islamist extremism in the sub-region. Fighter jets and drones constantly operated from the base on operations over Yemen, Somalia and beyond. In January, some tensions arose between the government and the US military over anger at a drone crash on the airport runway in mid-December 2012, and drone flights were temporarily suspended. In addition, a lengthy strike in June–July by local workers over working conditions on the base did not help to improve the local perception of the isolated US base. Rents for **US, French** and **Japanese military installations** continued to provide the government with significant and stable revenue of well over $ 100 m a year.

President Guelleh again had a very full international travel schedule and continued to personally represent his tiny nation at many **international forums**, such as the AU, OIC, CEN-SAD, Arab League, two Somalia conferences, the June aid summit in Tokyo, the December African security summit in Paris, etc. In May, Guelleh briefly met French President Hollande in Addis Ababa on the margins of the AU's 50th anniversary celebrations. All this was in pursuance of Guelleh's ambition to increase Djibouti's visibility around the world. An international campaign by Djibouti's ambassador in France, Rachad Farah, to become UNESCO's director-general obtained the backing of the AU, OIC and IGAD, but was not ultimately successful. The most important visitors to Djibouti during the year were Gabon's President Ali Bongo Ondimba (January), Japan's Prime Minister

Shinzo Abe (August) and Spain's Prime Minister Mariano Rajoy (December). Both Abe's and Rajoy's visits centred mainly on an inspection of their countries' contribution to the international efforts to combat Somali piracy activities. Close links continued to be maintained with the **Arab Gulf states**, particularly the UAE and Qatar. **China** also showed strong interest in investing in infrastructural projects.

Djibouti generally continued to receive pledges of aid and to attract private foreign investments from a diverse spectrum of sources, benefitting from its valuable strategic location in an international conflict zone (allegedly threatened by Islamist extremism) and from its role as the most suitable base for coordinated international anti-piracy activities in the Indian Ocean and the Gulf of Aden. All external partners largely refrained from expressing any sharp criticism of the authoritarian regime and its civil rights violations, but rather turned a **blind eye** on Djibouti's **political deficiencies**. Protests by Western human rights organisations about the post-election persecution of the opposition did not attract any noticeable attention.

Socioeconomic Developments

Djibouti's **economy** had in less than a decade experienced a quite **substantial transformation**, driven primarily by large inflows of FDI for major infrastructural projects and by service sector earnings, mainly benefiting from the sustained economic boom in Ethiopia. Capital-intensive investments and construction activities had little impact, however, on the alleviation of the structural persistence of very high levels of poverty and unemployment among the population.

The overall **macroeconomic performance** in 2013 was again mixed, but generally satisfactory and confirming the recent trend of gradual improvement. The **GDP growth rate** was estimated at 5.5%, a further acceleration compared with 2012 (4.8%) and the highest rate for years. **Inflation** was successfully brought down to 2.2% from 7.9% in 2012. The current-account deficit was probably only slightly reduced to 8.6% of GDP as a result of continued substantial capital goods imports for infrastructure projects. Foreign exchange reserves were substantially augmented to about $ 350 m to allow a healthy import coverage of over six months. The Djibouti franc (Dfr) remained pegged to the US dollar under a currency board arrangement (at a rate of 177 Dfr:$ 1). Estimated exports (in fact mostly re-exports) of $ 114 m continued to be dwarfed by imports of $ 565 m, thus maintaining the traditional huge structural trade deficit. The **budget** outturn for 2013 was expected to show an increased deficit of 2.6% of GDP, thus clearly failing to achieve a promised surplus target. Extensive tax exemptions granted to FDI projects undermined the government's revenue mobilisation efforts. There seemed to have been some improvement in the general business environment, as Djibouti moved up by 12 places (to rank 160th of 189 listed countries) in the World Bank's 'Doing Business 2014' assessment. But almost all major commercial and business ventures still needed high-level political patronage to be successful, thus limiting prospects for a more transparent and dynamic business climate.

A four-year ECF arrangement with the **IMF** had been completed in mid-2012. Although the government had requested a follow-up arrangement, there was no indication during the year that this would happen. The IMF apparently still felt that the government's general performance was weak, although it had recognised that this had in the 2011–12 period been mainly due to exogenous factors (such as the global context and regional drought). The IMF was mainly concerned about the persistence of fiscal deficits and the need for stringent fiscal reforms, the continued high risk of debt distress, slowness of structural administrative reforms in the public sphere and, above all, failure to make noticeable progress in the fight against **poverty** and an alarming level of **unemployment**: 42% of the population were assessed to be living in extreme poverty, and the unemployment rate was estimated at around 50%. Djibouti's generally deficient socioeconomic standard was clearly reflected in its low **HDI** rank (164th out of 187 countries).

The recent ambitious expansion of Djibouti's **infrastructure** picked up more steam during the year. A completely new **mineral port** was under construction at Tadjourah and was expected to serve for the export of 4 m tonnes of Ethiopian potash per year upon completion in 2015; this was contingent on the parallel completion of a new railway connection to Mekele in Ethiopia. In April, construction started on another **new port** at Goubet, which was expected to serve for the annual export of 6 m tonnes of **salt** from Lake Assal and was largely financed through a Chinese credit. In the presence of several foreign dignitaries, foundation ceremonies took place on 8 September for both the construction of a new **livestock port** at Damerjog (for the export of up to 5 m head of livestock mainly to the Arabian Peninsula) and the expansion of the **Doraleh container port**, doubling its capacity so that it would handle 3 m standard container units a year. In September, construction began on a **water pipeline** (financed by a $ 340 m Chinese credit) to supply Djibouti-Ville with drinking water from Ethiopia. The main highway between the two countries, a vital lifeline for Ethiopia, was also to be completely upgraded and a second **electric power line** was to connect Djibouti with the Ethiopian grid in order to meet Djibouti's unsatisfied demand and bring down costs. The AfDB in July confirmed the financing of a geothermal power station, while China also intended to support the energy sector. In July, work was started on a new 756 km electrified standard-gauge **railway line** to connect Djibouti with Addis Ababa; it was to replace the long-abandoned, old and dysfunctional Ethio-Djiboutian railway built by France. Construction was undertaken by a Chinese company and financed with a Chinese credit of around $ 2 bn.

A UK-Djibouti **trade and investment forum** on 8 May in **London** was intended to attract more investors from Europe, in addition to those from Arab and Asian countries. A Chinese fund had in December 2012 acquired a 23.5% share in Djibouti's port authority for $ 185 m. Renegotiation discussions were under way about the long-term management contract with DP World from Dubai for the Doraleh container port, which had initially been arranged by the now disgraced Abdoulrahman Boreh on terms that were felt to be unfavourable to Djibouti. In October, Djibouti's state-owned oil company started a joint venture with a Kuwait-based firm; the new Djibouti Oil Supply Co. was intended to strengthen Djibouti's position as a regional hub for the distribution of oil products. The **Djibouti Free Zone** had become a success story due to its attractive incentives for investors (attracting 170 companies from 40 countries) and reached its full capacity. A new Free Zone was to be started in 2014. The **finance sector** had also seen a remarkable expansion in recent years with the presence of 11 fully-registered banks (compared with only two in 2006). Due to its liberal regulatory regime, Djibouti was also geared to become a financial centre for the wider Horn of Africa region.

Rolf Hofmeier

Eritrea

No changes were made to the political and economic system during the year, but the government's autocratic rule was increasingly challenged. In January, a group of soldiers temporarily occupied the Ministry of Information and demanded the implementation of the Constitution and the release of political prisoners. It remained unclear whether the operation was a failed coup d'état or a mutiny led by dissatisfied middle-ranking officers. The mass exodus of the younger generation to escape from the time-wise unlimited national service continued unabatedly. In October, 360 Eritrean refugees died near the Italian island of Lampedusa when their boat capsized. The government media's initial concealment of the event caused indignation among Eritreans inside the country and in the diaspora. The economy remained in very poor shape and food insecurity prevailed despite additional income being generated through the mining sector.

Domestic Politics

No changes were made to Eritrea's political system, but opposition to **President Isaias Afewerki**'s autocratic leadership increased. On 21 January, a military unit by at least 100 soldiers occupied the Ministry of Information in Asmara. They forced the director of EriTV to read a statement demanding the release of political prisoners and the implementation of principles laid down in the Constitution. The **mutiny** was led by **Colonel Said Ali Hijay ('Wedi Ali')**, a veteran of the liberation struggle, and **Colonel Saleh Osman**. There were rumours that the occupation was part of a wider **coup attempt** that failed due to organisational flaws, and that the aim had been to capture and overthrow Isaias, who was supposed to hold a meeting with regional administrators at the ministry on that day. He was, however, warned and changed the venue for the meeting. Mediators, including **Defence Minister Brigadier Sebhat Ephrem**, were sent to the mutineers and succeeded in persuading them to give up and retreat. The organisers of the operation were promised immunity, but were eventually captured and arrested. Wedi Ali shot himself to avoid imprisonment, while Saleh Osman was reportedly set free. He enjoyed a high reputation in the army for his heroic role in the battle of Assab during the 1998–2000 Eritrean-Ethiopian war, when he refused to surrender and leave the port city to the Ethiopian army; hence the regime did not dare to take rigorous measures against him. The January mutiny was dubbed **Operation Forto** by the diaspora opposition, since the Ministry of Information was situated on a hill commonly known as Forto, a name it was given during the time of Italian colonisation.

In the aftermath of Operation Forto, up to 63 persons were arrested, most of them **Muslim political figures**. Most prominent among them were the governor of the Southern Region Mustafa Nurhussein, the Director of Organisational Affairs of the ruling **People's Front for Democracy and Justice (PFDJ)** Abdella Jaber, and Minister of Energy and Mines Ahmed Haj Ali. Colonel Abdurahman Mahmoud Jaser, a prominent figure in the National Security Office, died in mysterious circumstances on 2 February. None of those arrested was accused of any offence or brought before a court of law, but the arrests could be seen as an **attempt by the ruling elite** to mark the mutiny as a **'Muslim uprising'**. Presidential adviser Yemane Gebreab arbitrarily labelled the leaders of the operation as Islamists, although they were known to be ex-combatants of the liberation struggle with absolutely no links to religious extremism. Meanwhile, representatives of the Eritrean opposition in the diaspora attributed the event to widespread dissatisfaction among lower-ranking officers and the rank and file of the Eritrean Defence Forces. **Opposition activists** described Operation Forto as an attempted coup d'état and organised demonstrations in London, Rome, Milan, Berlin, Washington DC and Tel Aviv in order to express their support for the dissident soldiers. Eritrean state media remained silent for three weeks. On 14 February, Isaias gave an interview to EriTV, in which he called the occupation of the ministry "a minor incident" carried out by a handful of disgruntled individuals.

Local Government Minister Woldenkiel Gebremariam passed away on 6 July. The **Cabinet of Ministers** met on 14 February and 1 October, to discuss working papers presented by Isaias related to various development programmes. The post of minister of information had remained vacant since the defection of Ali Abdu in late 2012, and no one was appointed to the vacant position of minister of local government. The major generals who headed Eritrea's four military command zones retained their powerful positions, which included involvement in local politics at the expense of the civilian governors of the country's six regions. However, there were reports of **rifts within the military leadership**. All of the generals remained loyal to the president, but they competed for Isaias's favour and for access to power and resources. The health of Major General Gebrezgheir Andemariam ('Wuchu') deteriorated during the year and he did not play any significant political role. Brigadier General Teklai Kifle ('Manjus') continued to be involved in illegal activities such as the smuggling of goods, weapons and people across the Eritrean-Sudanese border. Major General Haile Samuel ('China') remained commander of Zone Four and Major General Philipos Weldeyohannes, commander of Zone Two (centre), was appointed commander of military operations for Asmara. Defence Minister Sebhat Ephrem, who had been perceived as a critic of the president by various analysts, acted on behalf of Isaias during Operation Forto, when he persuaded the mutineers to surrender and to return to their camps.

The **mass exodus** of the younger generation to avoid the time-wise unlimited and largely unpaid national service continued. About 3,000 Eritreans escaped to refugee camps in eastern Sudan every month, and similar numbers headed for Ethiopia. In December, the UNHCR had registered 86,000 Eritrean refugees in Ethiopia, and 118,280 in Sudan. A further 110 Eritreans reached Djibouti every month. Many Eritrean refugees became victims of **human trafficking**. Following the closure of Israel's border with Egypt, Eritreans stopped using the escape route through the Sinai Peninsula, where thousands had previously been held captive and tortured to extract money from their relatives. Instead, hundreds of Eritreans were now kidnapped either by corrupt military personnel inside Eritrea, or by human traffickers in eastern Sudanese refugee camps. The relatives of the captives were pressured to pay ransoms of $ 7,500 to $ 10,000 and, if they failed to raise the money, the victims were forcibly transported to Sinai and sold to Bedouin traffickers, who tortured them and demanded ransoms of up to $ 50,000.

Thousands of Eritrean refugees risked their lives in attempts to reach European countries. With **access to Israel blocked** by a border fence and with the demise of the Kadhafi regime in Libya, the route across the Mediterranean from Libya to Italy or Malta once again became the most popular flight route. On 3 October, a disastrous accident occurred, when a boat bringing some 500 migrants from Libya capsized off the Italian island of Lampedusa. When a fire broke out on board, the passengers jumped from the boat in panic and 360 persons drowned, while 155 survived. Almost all of the passengers, and all of the victims, were Eritreans. The **Lampedusa tragedy**, unlike similar previous disasters, triggered huge media coverage and fuelled general discussion about **Italian and European immigration policies**. Statistics revealed that 30,100 people had crossed by sea to Italy in 2013, among them 7,500 Eritreans. The Eritrean government initially tried to cover up the fact that the victims of the tragedy had been Eritreans. On 4 October, EriTV reported that over 300 "illegal African migrants" had died in Italy without making reference to their Eritrean nationality. However, the population inside Eritrea was well aware of the event and traditional obituaries with names and pictures of victims were posted on public walls, although later removed by the regime. The **government's heartless attitude** towards its own nationals fuelled growing resentment among the population. Eventually, the intense media coverage of the accident forced government officials to issue statements. On 9 October, a government press statement related the incident to "criminal human traffickers" and alleged that "after various conspiracies against the country had ended up in utter failure, the enemy quarters resorted to the human trafficking ploy with a view to disintegrating (. . .) the indomitable people and government of Eritrea". The statement accused the US government of being behind the smuggling of Eritreans and thus of responsibility for the deaths of the Lampedusa victims.

On the weekend of 26 October, members of the **Tigray People's Democratic Movement (TPDM)** carried out a roundup ('*gffa*') in downtown Asmara to hunt for draft dodgers. The TPDM was an Eritrea-based Ethiopian opposition force that had been armed and trained by the Eritrean government. When the citizens of Asmara realised that they were being rounded up by TPDM soldiers, whom they considered to be a mercenary army, they protested by throwing stones at them, and shots were heard in the city centre. In the aftermath of the event, security officers visited schools and called meetings at local authority premises to explain that the soldiers were Eritreans and not from Tigray (the Ethiopian region bordering Eritrea). On 5 November, General Teklai 'Manjus' assembled leading commanders of the police, security and military to discuss the event. A major whose battalion was involved in the operation stated that the **national service recruits** who were supposed to carry out the roundup **refused orders** to do so, and thus TPDM forces were brought in. The event showed the growing recalcitrance among recruits and rank-and-file soldiers.

Defections of prominent personalities continued. In early April, female Eritrean Air Force pilot Rahwa Gebrekristos was sent to Saudi-Arabia to bring back the presidential jet that had remained there after the defection of two air force pilots in 2012. However, instead of returning with the aircraft, she asked for asylum. On 12 November, three more members of the air force followed her by entering Saudi airspace with their fighter jet and asking for asylum. In late December, another air force pilot escaped to Djibouti with his jet in order to request political asylum. Once again, the **national football team** absconded and asked for asylum in Kenya during a regional football tournament in mid-December. Nine players and the coach turned to the UNHCR for protection. Following the Lampedusa tragedy, one of Eritrea's most popular singers, **Yohannes Tikabo ('Wedi Tikabo')**, turned his back on the regime. He had been on a PFDJ-organised US tour to rally support and raise resources from the diaspora. With the PFDJ cadres continuing to organise parties while the nation was mourning the Lampedusa victims, he decided to defect, a symbolic act that had strong repercussions among the diaspora. Another prominent figure and former PFDJ supporter, the wealthy businessman **Tewelde Tesfamariam ('Wedi Vaccaro')**

toured US and European cities campaigning against the government. Unlike conventions of the traditional opposition parties, his meetings attracted hundreds of diaspora Eritreans.

Eritrea's **judicial system** continued in a state of disarray. The formal court system remained weak and prone to government interference. Imprisonment for political reasons as well as arrests for alleged offences mostly took place without respect for legal process, and those affected were arbitrarily kept in prison and subsequently released without having been brought before a court of law. Civil cases were mostly handled by traditional elders and mediators on the basis of customary law. The 'special courts' headed by military lay judges which had pronounced spoken verdicts in corruption cases remained largely inactive; **corruption remained common practice** among military officers, PFDJ cadres and state employees and was widely tolerated by the government. TI's Corruption Perception Index ranked Eritrea as highly corrupt (160th out of 177 countries). The arrested **members of the G15**, a group of prominent PFDJ members who had demanded political reforms and were detained in September 2001, remained in custody without charge. Apparently, only two of the 11 detained had survived the abysmal prison conditions, namely Petros Solomon (former fisheries minister) and Haile Weldetensae ('Dru'e', former foreign minister). On 28 May, the **UN Special Rapporteur on the situation of human rights in Eritrea**, Sheila Keetharuth, presented her first report to the UN Human Rights Council. The report confirmed systematic and widespread violations of human rights, including extrajudicial killings; a policy of shoot-to-kill for persons attempting to cross borders; enforced disappearances and incommunicado detention; widespread torture; inhumane prison conditions; no respect for civil liberties; sexual and gender-based violence; and violation of child rights, including conscription. **Religious freedom** remained **restricted** and Sunni Islam, and Orthodox, Catholic and Lutheran Christianity were the only permitted religions, while adherents of Pentecostal Churches, Jehovah's Witnesses and Muslims opposed to the government-appointed mufti were considered as "radicals" and faced persecution. In November, security forces raided a prayer meeting of an underground religious community known as 'Hyaw Amlak' (Living God) and arrested 185 persons, including many women and children. They were released after signing an agreement that they would refrain from meeting with other believers in future. **Freedom of the press** remained **non-existent**, and Eritrea was ranked last worldwide in the Reporters Without Borders press freedom index.

Eritrea's **diaspora-based political opposition** continued to suffer from internal splits. The **Eritrean National Conference for Democratic Change**, an umbrella organisation of various opposition parties, remained unproductive and poorly organised. On 19 March, the chairman of its executive office, Yussuf Berhanu, met representatives of the EU to discuss the situation in Eritrea in the aftermath of the Forto mutiny. The **'Arbi Harnet' (Freedom Friday)** movement remained active throughout the year. The activists made hundreds of random robo-calls to Eritrea, calling upon citizens to passively resist the regime. Internal supporters of the group secretly distributed two editions of an **underground magazine** called Meqaleh Forto. The **Eritrean Forum for National Dialogue** was founded as a new organisation to promote change in Eritrea. It was led by former PFDJ officials who had become critics of the regime: Andeberhan Welde Giorgis, a former ambassador to the EU; Asefaw Tekeste, a former College Dean in Asmara; and Abdalla Adem, a former ambassador to Sudan.

Foreign Affairs

In pursuance of the **sanctions** imposed on Eritrea by the UNSC in December 2009 (resolution 1907/2009), the **Monitoring Group on Somalia and Eritrea** (SEMG) delivered a letter to the UNSC on 25 July, which stated that the Eritrean government had realigned its policy towards Somalia for tactical reasons. According to the report, the government was courting the new Somali government of President Hassan Sheikh Mohamud, while simultaneously maintaining close relations with several war lords, including at least two al-Shabaab leaders. SEMG further claimed that Eritrea was still in breach of the arms embargo by purchasing army equipment and civilian aircraft that were used for military purposes. The report also stated that the government continued to pressure Eritreans in the diaspora to pay a tax of 2% on their income and make donations to the military. On 24 July, the UNSC decided to extend the mandate of the SEMG until November 2014 and reaffirmed the arms embargo. Eritrea also remained in breach of the UN sanctions by refusing to provide information about the number and condition of **Djiboutian prisoners of war** it had been holding since 2010. There was no progress in the peace process between the two countries, and the Qatari-led mediation remained in deadlock. In February and March, Qatari envoys visited Asmara in order to discuss the stalled mediation process. In early April, Isaias made an unannounced trip to Qatar and met with the Emir, reportedly to discuss Eritrea's conflicts with Djibouti and Ethiopia. On 23 July, the **Emir of Qatar**, Sheikh Hamad bin Khalifa al-Thani, a close friend of Isaias, handed power to his son, Sheikh Tamim bin Hamad al-Thani. The Eritrean president did not attend the coronation, and it seemed that **relations** between the two countries had **cooled** significantly.

The no-war-no-peace situation between Eritrea and **Ethiopia** prevailed, but there were no Ethiopian incursions on Eritrean territory throughout the year, and it seemed that the Ethiopian government was preventing the ethnic-based armed Eritrean opposition movements it hosted from attacking targets inside Eritrea. On 5 December, **Sudan's President Omar al-Bashir** announced that he was going to mediate in the conflict between Eritrea and Ethiopia, and that he had initiated indirect talks between the leaders of the two countries. Earlier in the year, there were indications that **Qatar** might have offered its services in mediating the stalemate. Two weeks after Isaias's visit to Qatar in April, the Emir visited Ethiopia and it was speculated that he discussed possible mediation with Ethiopian government officials. On 20 December, Ethiopia's **Prime Minister Hailemariam**

Desalgn reaffirmed his willingness to negotiate with Eritrea. However, none of these efforts brought any tangible results.

Relations between Eritrea and **Sudan** remained close, and the two presidents met several times during the year. In mid-January, Bashir travelled to Asmara for an official working visit. In early February, he made another unannounced visit to discuss the January mutiny. In mid-June, Bashir met with Isaias again and, on 23 November, the latter attended the inauguration of the Karora–Port Sudan highway and a festival in Port Sudan. On 23 June, Foreign Minister Osman Saleh visited **South Sudan**, where he met President Salva Kiir and offered Eritrea's good offices in mediating in the conflict between South Sudan and Sudan. When civil war broke out in December, the Eritrean embassy in Juba announced that it would engage in evacuating Eritreans residing in South Sudan. About 5,000 Eritreans, most of them PFDJ-loyalists, lived in Juba where they had controlled about two-thirds of all local business operations prior to the beginning of the violent conflicts. In contrast, the government had not taken any action to alleviate the plight of Eritrean refugees who were held hostage on the Egyptian Sinai Peninsula or had gotten into trouble in other countries. In mid-December, Isaias paid a visit to **Kenya** to participate in the country's 50th Independence Day anniversary along with more than 20 African heads of state.

Israel hosted about 36,000 Eritrean asylum seekers, who were treated as "illegal infiltrators" by the authorities. The 2012 amendment to the country's infiltration law allowed the imprisonment of asylum seekers for up to three years, and around 1,400 refugees, mostly from Eritrea and the Sudan, were held at the Saharonin Detention Centre. During the year, Israel had approved only four out of 2,593 requests for refugee status. In mid-September, the Supreme Court overturned the 2012 amendment as unconstitutional. In order to circumvent the court's decision, the Knesset passed a new amendment in mid-December, which required refugees to live in the Holot "open" Detention Centre in the Negev Desert. In response, thousands of refugees demonstrated in December against the restrictive asylum policy in Tel Aviv. Another strategy applied by the Israeli government was to coerce Eritrean refugees to leave the country, offering them an incentive of $ 3,500. As a consequence, 106 Eritreans left Israel during the year, some of them for Uganda. In August, the Foreign Ministry of **Uganda** denied having entered into an agreement with Israel to accept thousands of African migrants in exchange for weapons and money. In early July, 14 Eritreans were "voluntarily" repatriated to Eritrea, and the Israeli newspaper 'Haaretz' reported that at least one of them had been tortured after his arrival. The **UNHCR protested against Israel's policy** and required that Israel should treat asylum seekers in line with international refugee and human rights laws.

Eritrea continued to extort a **2% diaspora tax** from Eritrean nationals and persons of Eritrean origin residing abroad. It was thus in breach of UN resolution 2023/2011, which demanded that the government should stop coercion to collect taxes outside Eritrea. On

29 May, **Canada** expelled the Eritrean consul general. He had previously been warned to stop requesting the 2% tax from Eritreans residing in Canada, but had continued to demand payments. No other states followed the UN resolution's provision to hold responsible those individuals who were collecting the tax on behalf of the Eritrean government. The **EU** continued its approach of pursuing a policy of engagement vis-à-vis the Eritrean government, while at the same time expressing its concern about the dire human rights situation in the country. In the aftermath of the Lampedusa tragedy, Eritrean opposition parties and civil society organisations approached the EU to ask for better protection for Eritrean refugees en route to Europe and the empowerment of Eritrean non-state actors to bring about positive change in the homeland. In response to the events, the EU put a new European border surveillance system in place and announced the strengthening of efforts to counter human trafficking and smuggling. Relations between Eritrea and the **USA** remained poor, and Isaias continued to accuse the US government and the CIA of being responsible for virtually all the problems the country was facing. However, former Assistant Secretary of State for Africa Herman Cohen stated in December that "the time has come to bring Eritrea in from the cold". He expressed his hope that the conflict between Eritrea and Ethiopia could be resolved soon and called for the lifting of UN sanctions against Eritrea.

Socioeconomic Developments

There were no reforms of the ailing Eritrean economy, which remained firmly in the hands of the PFDJ and the military. Reforms announced in late 2012 to facilitate investment and to privatise parts of the economy did not materialise. However, in February the government **liberalised** the heavily restricted **foreign currency market**. Foreign visitors were no longer obliged to register the foreign currencies they were carrying upon arrival or to provide upon departure evidence of any currency exchange made during their stay. The regulations related to holding foreign currency accounts in state-controlled banks were also slightly liberalised. Yet, since the exchange rate with the US dollar remained fixed at the massively overvalued rate of 1$:15 Eritrean Nakfa, most diaspora Eritreans continued to send their remittances through informal channels, which offered a **black market rate** of about 1$:47 Nakfa. Government agents both inside and outside Eritrea were involved in black market money exchange. **Electricity** supply remained inadequate and there were regular blackouts throughout the year. In an interview with state media in early September, Isaias admitted electricity shortages and spoke vaguely of the possibility of importing electricity from Ethiopia once the Great Ethiopian Renaissance Dam was finished. With regard to the persistent water shortages in Asmara, he blamed those who complained about the lack of drinking water for being greedy and inconsiderate of the plight of those living in remote areas of the country, whose situation was far worse. Diesel fuel remained in short supply and was sold on the black market, which was largely controlled by corrupt military personnel.

Chronic food insecurity continued and UNICEF reported that, due to frequent droughts and a fall in aid, the child malnutrition situation had worsened. In the Gash-Barka Region, the wasting rate (low weight for height) in under-five children reported in July was 22.7%, compared with 14.5% a year earlier. The rate had steadily deteriorated from 13% in 2001, a year that was marked by massive internal displacement due to the Eritrean-Ethiopian war. The 2013 Global Hunger Index ranked Eritrea as one of three countries worldwide where the nutritional status was "extremely alarming". The main rainy season in summer started late and rainfall remained at 20% to 50% below average. However, the government failed to acknowledge the dire situation on the ground and continued to deny NGOs access to the country. In December, state media announced that Eritrea was on track to achieve most of the **MDGs** ahead of time. Assuming the accuracy of the data published by the health authorities, the country had in fact met the health-related goals, including the improvement of maternal health and the reduction of malaria and HIV/AIDS prevalence. However, government media were silent about the fact that the country was far from reaching MDG 1, the eradication of extreme hunger and poverty. The 2013 Africa MDG Report (AfDB, ECA, etc.) stated that Eritrea's primary school enrolment rate had been 34.9% in 2010, the lowest in Africa, and that gender disparity in primary and secondary education had regressed steadily since 1991.

The **Warsay-Yikealo Development Campaign**, which forced all Eritreans of productive age to perform national service for unlimited periods of time, remained in place. National Service conscripts were employed in infrastructure projects run by PFDJ-owned construction companies, in military-run agricultural farms, and in the public administration. The campaign was the main push-factor for the continuous mass exodus of Eritrean youth. Elderly citizens were used as armed neighbourhood militias and regularly pressured to attend military training, which forced them to neglect agricultural and other bread-winning activities.

Availability of economic and financial data remained extremely poor, and the government did not show any transparency with respect to the state budget, including the amounts received in mining revenues. There was no financial monitoring of the PFDJ's financial and economic activities. The African Economic Outlook (AfDB, OECD) estimated the 2013 **GDP growth rate** at around 7% (similar to 2012), stating that this growth was driven by gold production in the Koka and Zara gold mines, although neither of these mining projects had yet started production. **Inflation** was estimated at 13% (somewhat lower than in 2012), and the current-account balance stood at about –3% of GDP. Export receipts of about $ 500 m covered roughly half the value of imports.

According to Canadian **Nevsun Resources**, who operated the Bisha mine in a joint venture with the Eritrean National Mining Corporation (ENAMCO), the mine produced low-cost silver doré until mid-2013 and then switched to copper concentrate. Bisha remained the only operational mine in Eritrea. In early July, the Zara Mining Share Company (ZMSC) entered into a contract worth $ 53.6 m to commence construction work at the Zara Gold Project. ZMSC was a joint venture between the Chinese **SFECO Group**, which held 60% shares, and ENAMCO. It was to undertake the Koka gold mining project in the Zara area. The third company with tangible plans to commence mining activities in the near future was the Colluli Mining Share Company, a joint venture between Australian **South Boulder Mines** and ENAMCO, which both held 50% shares. The Colluli Potash Project located in the Danakil Depression was scheduled to commence production in 2016. A mining conference was held in Asmara in early October, sponsored by the Ministry of Energy and Mines. In late November, Eritrea and **Sudan** signed a **memorandum of understanding** for future cooperation in the mining sector. This would include the processing of gold in Sudan's refinery. In August, the government approved the construction of more than 1,000 apartments in Asmara. The project, managed by the Housing and Commercial Bank, aimed at attracting hard currency from diaspora Eritreans. Only persons who had fulfilled their "national duty", including the payment of the 2% diaspora tax from 1993 to the present, were eligible as buyers, and a 25% deposit payment was required. The government had announced similar projects in the past, none of which had been concluded. In October, **Lufthansa** ceased flights to Asmara, pending the signing of a new air traffic agreement with the government. Lufthansa had been the only European airline that served Asmara. Eritrean Airlines remained non-operational. The cessation of Lufthansa's operations negatively affected postal services, as the airline had been the main carrier of mail from and to Eritrea.

Nicole Hirt

Ethiopia

Ethiopia maintained strong economic growth and received increased foreign investment, but remained one of the most authoritarian and repressive regimes in Africa, with government control extended over the economy, political life and cyber-space, and the containment of private business and overall human development. Political pluralism was officially tolerated but denied in practice. Media freedom was strongly curtailed and human rights problems remained serious. A new opposition party, the Semayawi (or Blue) Party, consisting mainly of young people, was closely monitored and disrupted at strategic moments. Mass Muslim protests against "state interference in religious life" continued on a regular basis, but were repressed. Muslim grievances were not addressed and no dialogue was held.

Economic growth was evident in increased GDP, infrastructural expansion and continuing investment in the health and energy sectors, but benefits were distributed very unevenly. The construction of two large river dams (on the Blue Nile and the Gibe-Omo) went ahead despite local and international objections, lack of scientific studies and a significant rise in the national debt. More FDI, including in industrial production, was visible. Sharp nationwide inequalities became further entrenched, with a party 'nomenklatura' and a new state-supported, co-opted middle-class on the one hand, and the large mass of the population still at the margins on the other. Agrarian area extension and large-scale land leases continued, while the pastoralist sector was further discouraged and repressed to make room for commercial plantation agriculture. Some schemes did not deliver and others provoked a regular stream of criticisms from local people, NGOs and human rights organisations, whose analyses were categorically rejected by the government. No inclusive options or adequate compensations for land loss were offered. Several million people were in need of emergency (donor) food aid throughout the year. Religious communal tensions were less prominent than in previous years, but several clashes between ethnic communities still occurred. The low-key armed conflict in the Ogaden (Somali) region continued.

Ethiopia confirmed its dominant role in the Horn of Africa, IGAD and the AU. Its military and diplomatic efforts in Somalia continued, with its forces nominally placed under the AU Mission to Somalia. Rivalry between Ethiopia and Kenya persisted with regard to the future scenario for Somalia, although both countries supported the federal government in Mogadishu. Ethio-Egyptian tensions over the impact of the huge 'Renaissance' dam under construction on the Blue Nile, which was expected to severely reduce Nile water levels in Egypt, were not resolved. Neither was there progress in settling the 'border conflict' with Eritrea. Northern Ethiopia received a continuous stream of thousands of young people fleeing from Eritrea.

Domestic Politics

Political life remained fully controlled under the heavy authoritarian hand of the ruling **Ethiopian People's Revolutionary Democratic Party (EPRDF)**, the sole ruling party for 22 years. No development towards a democratic system or democratic public debate could be discerned, although new terms such as 'developmental democracy' occasionally surfaced. State and party remained closely intertwined, and all higher-ranking government personnel had to be party members or were pressurised to join. Opposition party members were not allowed to be appointed to any important positions in the politico-economic system. Party members were regularly briefed and 'educated' on party programmes and policy in training sessions and meetings. Party membership increasingly became a prerequisite on the job market, e.g., for college graduates. **Prime Minister Hailemariam Dessalegn** appeared to be unchallenged at the helm of government.

There was no scope for the **political opposition** to exert any influence. The government could not handle policy criticism and tended to react to it in bad faith. The activities of a new opposition **Semayawi Party** (Blue Party), a moderate democratic movement with broad support and a youthful constituency, built upon the experience of previous democratic parties, but it was obstructed and kept under constant surveillance. The opposition party 'Medrek' ('Forum') also complained of constant intimidation and harassment. Several opposition party leaders, among them Adualem Arage, remained in prison on a dubious charge of 'terrorism and treason'. The parliament (with only one of opposition member among the 547 MPs) showed few signs of life and was used by the executive to rubber-stamp its decisions. On 14 and 21 April, **local and city council 'elections'** were held, with the bizarre result that of the 3.6 m seats (!) only five went to opposition or independent candidates. On 7 October, the parliament elected a new president (a merely ceremonial function) for a six-year term: Mulatu Teshome, of Oromo background and educated at a Chinese university.

A tenacious feature of Ethiopia's politico-economic system was **corruption**, although it was generally felt to be less serious than the average for Africa, except at the elite level and in fast growing sectors such as mining, land acquisition, infrastructure investment, etc. During the year a number of officials were arrested on corruption charges, including, on 10 May, the head and deputy-head of the Ethiopian Revenue and Customs Authority, Melaku Fanta and Gebrewahid Woldegiorgis, together with several businessmen. High Court judge Zerihun Assefa was also detained on 21 January, accused of accepting bribes. In the course of the year, the Oromia State authorities dismissed 82 employees for corruption in connection with land management. However, the anti-corruption drive was quite selective and made no dent in the web of nepotism and bribery as a whole, and only some cases were reported. Many complaints were registered – even in a World Bank report – about the Ethiopian Telecommunications Authority as a hotbed of corruption. However, Ethiopia held a surprising 111th place (of 177) on TI's Corruption Perceptions Index. On various other indexes prepared by global institutions, Ethiopia's rankings remained roughly unchanged, with slight improvements in economic freedom. Serious deterioration was seen in Internet freedom, press freedom and human rights.

The government's **tense relationship with the Muslim community** was not resolved, although increased scrutiny and repression muted the protests. The trial of Muslim community leaders arrested in 2012 made little progress. Regular peaceful Muslim demonstrations continued, calling for the government to respect the constitutional provision of 'non-interference of the state in religious affairs' and the release of those arrested On 12 December, 12 of the 29 Muslim leaders in custody were released and their charges dropped. On 4 August, at least 14 Muslims were killed by security forces in Kofele and Totolamo villages during an attempt to arrest a 'suspected' local imam. During the 8 August 'Id al-Fitr' celebrations over 1,000 Muslims were arrested and detained. On 13 October, two Somalis were killed in Addis Ababa, apparently when they were preparing a bomb. The government kept up its rhetoric against Muslim extremism, including in the state press and through a new TV documentary on the risks from religious fanatics.

Media suppression continued, with the few remaining independent newspapers closely monitored. Two of them, 'Addis Times' and 'Le-Hilina', were closed down. Journalists Eskinder Nega, Woubshet Taye Yusuf Getachew, Solomon Kebede, Bekele Gerba, Olbana Lelisa, and Ms. Reeyot Alemu (recipient of a UNESCO 'world press freedom prize') remained in prison, often serving disproportionately heavy sentences, and with some being refused urgent medical attention. In February, the noted journalist Temesgen Dessalegn, of the closed-down weekly 'Feteh', was charged with 'defaming the government' in connection with articles about the late prime minister, Meles Zenawi. On 25 December, a court in Awassa condemned journalist Asfaw Berhanu to two years in prison for an article on dismissed government officials. The authorities also regularly took other journalists and editors in for questioning and short periods of detention.

Telephone services and the **Internet** were continuously **censored**, with most diaspora and opposition sites blocked. The state-owned Ethio-Telecom Corporation remained the sole provider. The government, with the help of Chinese technology and experts, continued to perfect Internet and e-mail surveillance with DPI ('deep packet inspection') programs and FinFisher Trojan tools, going well beyond any security concerns and with reference to the controversial 'anti-Terrorism' proclamation of 2009. This drive toward surveillance led to a lack of independent information exchange and self-censorship across the board. Throughout the year, public activism by opposition party members or civil society activists in Addis Ababa, Gondar, Dessie, Alamata, and other towns was also met with arrests and dispersal.

As in previous years, **ethnic conflict** was a source of underlying countrywide tension, which sometimes came out in the open. On 23 September, severe inter-communal clashes between Oromo and Somali communities in the Meyu and Kumbi districts in East Hararghe Zone of Oromiya Region resulted in some 90,000 people being displaced by the violence.

The armed **conflict in the Ogaden** Somali region also continued. The Ogaden National Liberation Front (ONLF), the main insurgent group fighting for justice and autonomy for the Somalis, was weakened but not defeated. The Region 5 authorities remained quite unpopular with the ethnic Somali population, as incumbent Regional president Abdi Mohammed Umar, a former security man and staunch EPRDF loyalist, ruled with a heavy hand via his 'Liyyu Police' (special forces) and was regularly accused of human rights abuses and corruption. In October, government talks with the ONLF in Nairobi (Kenya) failed because of the government's precondition that the rebels accept the Ethiopian constitution.

Religious tensions between the three main blocks of believers – Orthodox Christian, Muslim and Evangelical/Pentecostal – were limited, but caused regular problems at the local level and within communities. Traditional believers, especially in the South, were regularly targeted and ostracised, notably by Evangelical/Pentecostal believers, who rarely tolerated them. Within the Muslim community, there were ongoing tensions between so-called 'reformists' and radicals and the mainstream, more Sufi-leaning groups. On 28 February, the 71-year-old 'Abunä' Matthias, originally from Tigray, was elected by the synod of the Ethiopian Orthodox Church as the new patriarch after a six-month interregnum. In December, he was unexpectedly placed under house arrest and interrogated, after allegedly criticising the EPRDF.

Human rights concerns continued to be invoked by observers, noting illegal detention, disappearances, extra-judicial killings, and prison torture, notably of political opponents and protesters. There were also indications of substantial human trafficking. Facts were difficult to check due to the non-cooperation of the authorities.

Persistent **human rights transgressions** were also noted in the wake of the regime's frantic **developmental efforts** regarding **dam building** and **large-scale commercial agricultural ventures**. The appropriation and clearing of large tracts of land to make room for new plantations raised continuous problems, e.g., in Gambela, Afar, and the Omo Valley. No respect was given to local customary or land use rights. Reports by human rights organisations and journalists confirmed that people were often forcibly displaced, with frequent use of violence and intimidation. Cases of arbitrary arrests and killings, even by army snipers, were cited. In the case of some smaller ethnic groups, virtually all land was confiscated, endangering their livelihood system and causing food scarcity and poverty. Local inhabitants alleged that no consultations were held and no compensatory mechanisms of any substance were in place. **Evictions from the land** and **forced villagisation**, notably in Gambela, led to despair and protest, notably among Anywa (one-third of whom – about 40,000 people – were already displaced). In October, local residents set fire to an Indian-owned farm. In other places, locals threw rocks at security guards, cars and agricultural machinery. The government, instead of opening up the issues to public scrutiny or improving its procedures, denied everything. No charges were brought in cases of army or police abuse of citizens. Donor agencies such as the UK's Department for International Development (DfID) and USAID said that "no abuses" were evident, and denied the local evidence.

The **judiciary** functioned in ways that usually supported the political stance and policies of the government and could only be called independent in name, despite the professionalism and sincerity of many judges, who often had to bend to political pressure. Pro-government bias was visible in political and media freedom cases, as well as in business disputes. In the eyes of law experts, access to fair and timely justice for citizens could not be said to exist. Constitutional provisions were often 'pragmatically' interpreted and overruled by additional, restrictive laws. This was especially evident in the field of human and civil rights. The **Freedom House Index** put Ethiopia in the problematic category of **'not free' countries**, and rated the quality of its legal environment as very low. The country's Internet freedom ranking was fifth from bottom, and the worst in Africa. Several reports published during the year by international organisations, including HRW, alleged the systemic use of **torture** in Ethiopian prisons, as well as appalling prison conditions for the approximately 80,000 inmates.

Despite **donor countries** refusing to investigate or act on possible **misuse of aid money** or human rights problems, reports of rights abuse under donor-funded schemes were serious enough to urge the African Commission on Human and Peoples' Rights to call for a halt to the forced relocation of thousands of local people in the South in connection with 'resettlement' and 'villagisation'. The World Bank finally put its Inspection Panel to work to investigate some complaints, among them one of an Anywa farmer forcibly displaced from his land in the Gambela region. Evidence was available from local people that money received by the government under the 'Protection of Basic Services' (PBS) programme was used to fund forced displacements and evictions from the land. The World Bank appeared to follow up on its November 2012 statement that a "plausible link" existed between the PBS programme, partly funded by the Bank, and the (forced) resettlement process and dispossession in Gambela. But the Bank appeared slow in acting on this: by year's end no field investigation had been carried out and nothing was heard of the case. The government adamantly refused to cooperate with the investigation. On 12 October, Ethiopian-Americans held a demonstration outside the World Bank offices in Washington, DC, accusing it and the IMF of "financing tyranny in Ethiopia". The US State Department's annual report on Ethiopia was also very critical of repressive politics and human rights abuses.

Foreign Affairs

Ethiopia cultivated **good neighbourly relations** in the **Horn of Africa region** with Kenya, South Sudan, Somaliland, the Somali federal government and Puntland. Djibouti was needed for its vital port services. Ethiopia paid Djibouti an annual total of $ 722.5 m in port duties – apart from the additional costs incurred by Ethiopian traders. In December, new conditions were imposed by Djibouti regarding advance payment for goods to be transferred to Ethiopia. There were some **tensions with Kenya over Somalia**, where both countries had troops – and some differences in strategic aims and support for various parties. For instance, in the southern autonomous Jubaland region, Ethiopia and Kenya supported opposing clan-group militia leaders for the regional 'presidency'. Ethiopia remained prominent in **IGAD** and in the **AU**. From 27 January to 3 February, the 20th AU summit was held in the new AU building in Addis Ababa, during which Prime Minister Hailemariam Dessalegn was elected as AU chairman for a one-year term.

Tensions with Egypt over the **Nile issue** were not resolved. In fact, an on-going dispute was the controversy over the massive $ 4.2 bn hydro-electric 'Grand Ethiopian Renaissance Dam' on the Blue Nile, a national prestige project for Ethiopia and a bone of contention in its relations with Egypt due to the drop in the Nile water flow that was expected during and after construction. Egyptian Foreign Minister Mohamed Kamel Amr and his Ethiopian counterpart Tedros Adhanom met on 18 June in Addis Ababa to defuse tensions over the dam, which had intensified after Ethiopia began to divert the river waters to form the 70 bn m^3 reservoir in April. They reached no agreement, however, either in June or in follow-up discussions later in the year. Ethiopia denied that the construction of the dam would have any negative effect on Egypt's use of the Nile. On 20 June, the member states of the **Nile Basin Initiative** met in Juba (South Sudan), to discuss future Nile water cooperation. Ethiopia urged other riparian states to ratify a controversial water deal, the Cooperative Framework Agreement, proposing that upstream countries be allowed to implement irrigation and hydropower projects without first seeking Egypt's approval. This was opposed by Egypt and Sudan. No clear results came out of the meeting, apart from normative resolutions about the desirability of 'cooperation'. On 26 February, Saudi Arabia's Deputy Defence Minister Khalid bin Sultan spoke fiercely of the Renaissance Dam constituting a threat to Egyptian and Sudanese security, but the Saudi government later distanced itself from this statement.

In the global context, the **US** remained a **staunch ally** of Ethiopia, as did the **UK** and **China**. The country's apparent stability in the volatile and terror-prone Horn of Africa region induced these donor countries and economic partners to continue to support the regime with few questions asked and to treat reports of human rights abuses, domestic repression and displacements with benign neglect. Apart from regional security agenda priorities, the developmental discourse and economic dynamics of Ethiopia also remained unreservedly popular among donor countries, who often disregarded wider issues of local people's rights and livelihoods as well as environmental problems in the wake of rural 'development'. 'Abuse-free development' was not a donor interest.

Ethiopian leaders undertook a fair number of **international visits**, and in turn the country, as a key state hosting the AU headquarter, was visited by several world dignitaries and politicians. Hailemariam Dessalegn visited China on 14–19 June, and Sudan on 3 December, for high-level talks. As AU chairperson, he was at the Climate Change conference in Denmark on 28 October, and met with Egypt's interim president Adly Mansour during the African-Arab summit in Kuwait on 19–20 November to discuss the Nile water issue. On 15 December, the prime minister gave a speech at Nelson Mandela's funeral. Foreign Minister Teodros Adhanom paid many foreign visits, among them to the UK in January, the US in May, and South Sudan in February.

Visits to Ethiopia included one by a UK parliamentary delegation on 18–22 February to explore health policy issues. On 24–27 February, US Deputy-Assistant Secretary of State for Democracy, Human Rights and Labor Karen Hanrahan visited for talks on economic, political and human rights issues. US Secretary of State John Kerry was in Addis Ababa on 25–26 May for high-level meetings and to attend the AU 50th anniversary celebrations, while on 23–24 July US Deputy-Secretary of Defense Ashton Carter came to meet with senior government and military leaders on the "U.S.-Ethiopia security partnership" and to attend an AU meeting. Ethiopia was also visited by UK Deputy Prime Minister Nick Clegg on 15 February. During a 17 July visit, an EU parliamentary delegation urged Ethiopia to release journalists and opposition politicians jailed under the 'anti-terror' law. On 23–26 November, Chinese Vice-Premier Ms. Liu Yandong was in Addis Ababa to meet Hailemariam and other leaders for talks on bilateral relations. In November, Thailand's prime minister visited Ethiopia and, on 9 December, Queen Máxima of the Netherlands, in her capacity as the UN Secretary-General's special advisor on 'inclusive finance', was in Ethiopia to promote the UN's programme for improving financial services to the poor.

In early July, a delegation from Ethiopia's Somali Region visited the government of neighbouring **Puntland** in Garowe for political and business talks, with a return visit in late August by a delegation from Somalia's Puntland to Region 5 (Somali) of Ethiopia. On 2–3 September, the president of Puntland, Abdirahman M. 'Farole', visited Addis Ababa for talks in connection with Ethiopian mediation in the dispute between the autonomous Somali region of Jubaland and Somalia's federal government in Mogadishu. **Somaliland**'s President Ahmed Mohamud ′Silaanyo′ and several of his cabinet members were in Ethiopia on 8 December for talks and to attend the 8th Ethiopian 'Nations, Nationalities and Peoples' Day, an official state "celebration of ethnic diversity", held in Jijiga, capital of Ethiopia's Somali Region.

No rapprochement between Ethiopia and **Eritrea** over their border dispute and other bilateral tensions was achieved. On 29 April, at a meeting in New York with UN Secretary General Ban Ki-moon, Ethiopian Foreign Minister Teodros Adhanom repeated an earlier offer by his prime minister to open direct talks with Eritrea, but no response was forthcoming. A mediation effort by Qatar – aimed partly at reasserting its presence in the Horn of Africa to counteract Turkey's growing influence – did not see progress either.

Socioeconomic Developments

Ethiopia's economy, measured in GDP terms – and infrastructural investment, minerals exploitation and food production – continued to grow, although figures were approximate due to inconsistent records and exchange rate fluctuations. The country's **total GDP** was estimated at **$ 46 bn** (or ETB (birr) 877.5 bn), a **7%–8% increase** for the year. The World Bank and IMF saw the year's GDP growth rate as 7%–7.5%, while the government spoke of 11%. Some 46.5% of GDP was generated by agriculture (of which 19% by the livestock sector), 14.5% by industry, and the rest (38%) by services and donor funds and loans. **Inflation** remained high, at about 10% over the year, reflected in the commercial banks' prime lending rate of 14.5%, but was 10%–13% lower than in the previous year.

The **state budget** announced on 7 July (start of the budget year) amounted to **almost $ 8.3 bn**, 10% higher than the previous year, of which some 20% was foreign-sourced. Defence spending was increased to 15%, and agriculture took 10%. The current-account balance was $ –3.484 bn, or minus 7.5% of GDP. Government revenues, although expanding as a result of better tax collection, remained below target, reaching ca. $ 5.8 bn. These data made the financing of all developmental aims in the 2010 Growth and Transformation Plan (GTP) improbable, even with all the external funding.

Total **international aid** to the country (including loans and grants) was **more than $ 3.3 bn**, almost 40% of the national budget, meaning that the pace of growth was quite heavily dependent on external input. The UK and the USA were the largest donors. China,

India and Brazil were the fastest growing business investors, also partly providing loans (e.g., for infrastructure and new manufacturing outlays). Turkish and Saudi investments also increased. The UK's DfID again became the target of criticism due to its disregard for human rights aspects of its aid programmes, including its apparent financing of part of the training for the 'Special Forces' in Somali Region 5, and its denial of human rights abuse in developmental schemes in the South, even after sending a delegation to 'investigate' the issue. Other Western embassies rhetorically committed to respect for 'inclusive development', 'human rights' and 'rule of law promotion', were equally indifferent, primarily focusing instead on doing business in the shadow of expanding Chinese and other international competition.

FDI inflow was estimated at $ 970 m, significantly higher than in 2012. **Remittances** by Ethiopian migrant communities abroad were not all registered but again were massive, **estimated at $ 1.3 bn**; they were an essential lifeline for many families and provided start-up capital for small private businesses. The combined external financial resources (at least $ 4 bn) offset the big import-export imbalance and the relatively low domestic revenues.

The **economy** remained **heavily centralised** and **dominated by the state**, in particular by the sole ruling party, the EPRDF, which aimed for total 'institutional capture'. It owned all large corporations, e.g., building materials and transport providers, export/import businesses, the media, infrastructure projects, etc. The military nature of the development process was striking: for instance, most of the sugar plantation projects in Southern Ethiopia were run by the state-owned Metals and Engineering Corporation, led by (ex-)military personnel, all party members. Also the Gibe-3 and Blue Nile hydro-dam construction sites were run like military camps, with multiple perimeter fences and a heavy security presence. No foreign banks were allowed to operate in the country. Long on-going discussions about accession to the WTO were again not concluded.

On the **economic freedom index**, Ethiopia was ranked 151th of 178 listed countries, meaning 'mostly unfree' and showing only slight improvement. Ethiopia further solidified its typical top-down state/party economy, with all leading positions held by party members, who received regular ideological training to keep them in line with the official growth and development plans and the party management system.

Agriculture continued to be the most important economic sector, employing 70%-80% of the work force. Production output increased, notably as a result of the efforts of smallholders, and not from large-scale plantations or state farms. In a surprise move, the government revoked the land-lease allocations of around 3,000 investors for their alleged "failure of developing the land". They included the Indian entrepreneur Karuturi, who saw his allotted area of 300,000 ha. significantly reduced.

The **food security situation** generally improved during the year, as average June-to-September rains in most areas were favourable. However, the June-to-August main harvest was below average in parts of Amhara, Tigray, and Oromiya. Weather hazards, including floods, hail storms and landslides, destroyed property, damaged crops, displaced populations and resulted in the death of livestock in Amhara Region and the Southern Nations, Nationalities and Peoples Region. A major economic setback in August was caused by **flooding** in parts of the Somali Region and Amhara Region, notably North and South Wollo zones and in North and South Gondar, Oromiya, and West Gojjam zones. Nearly 40,000 households were affected and some 33,000 ha of crops were badly damaged.

Despite ongoing investment in healthcare and education, **human development**, measured on the basis of the HDI, was slow in improving and the country was still ranked 173rd (of 187 countries). The HDI differed markedly between regions and urban areas.

The **import bill** was almost $ 11 bn, while **export earnings** were estimated to total $ 2.8 bn to $ 3 bn, almost equal to the previous year. The **trade deficit** was therefore about $ 7.5 bn. The slight export growth was partly due to global market price fluctuations. The number 1 crop remained **coffee**, producing 26% or $ 747 m, down from $ 832 m the previous year (global price decline). Other exports were khat, bringing in $ 271.5 m (up 13%), leather products ($ 121.9 m, an increase of 10%), and textiles ($ 97.9 m; up 16%). This showed the same sectors predominating, as before, and also growing. Flower exports yielded ca. $ 246 m, but this sector showed signs of stagnation, if not slight decline. An underestimated currency earner, because largely unregistered, was **livestock**: much of it was traded cross-border to Sudan, Somalia, Djibouti, or Kenya, and was estimated to bring in at least $ 300 m. **Gold**, however, was the second (and growing) foreign currency earner, representing $ 570 m of a total of ca. $ 600 m revenue for minerals export. Artisanal miners produced 8.3 tonnes of placer gold, valued by the National Bank at $ 420 m. MIDROC, the only Ethiopian company involved in gold-mining, produced ca. 4 tonnes. In line with its monopolistic, state-capitalist policies, the state continued to force out local artisanal miners from their mining areas, to be transferred to companies (MIDROC, Ezana Mining). A few international companies were given prospecting rights for gold and base metals, e.g., the British firm Nyota Minerals in Wollega Zone and the Egyptian company Ascom Precious Metals Mining in western Ethiopia.

Oil and gas exploration continued, but an eagerly anticipated oil find in the South Omo block did not materialise. On 6 March, the UK-based Tullow Oil company announced that no commercial-grade oil deposits had been discovered in the area. With the aim of starting to **export hydro-electricity** to neighbouring countries, Ethiopia worked on the construction of power transmission lines, expected to be functional in 2015, from the Gibe-3 hydro-electric dam site to Djibouti and Kenya. The 2,000 MW line to Suswa in Kenya was financed with loans worth $ 1.2 bn, mainly from the World Bank and the AfDB.

There was a gradual **expansion of industrial production**, leading to an estimated 9% growth rate, as foreign partners/companies, alongside domestic investors, were allowed to set up production lines, Ethiopia being attractive as a (very) low-wage country. A new industrial zone for export-oriented manufacturers was set up in Addis Ababa. China intensified its plans for industries, and more licences were also granted to (state) companies from India, Turkey and South Korea, for leather and shoe production, textiles, car assembly, etc. Without it being admitted openly, the dogmas of "Agricultural development-led industrialisation" advocated by the late prime minister, Meles Zenawi were being abandoned or 'adjusted' in favour of a more direct, autonomous path to industrial investment.

In the course of the year, Ethiopia concluded deals on **railway construction projects** – e.g., to Awasa in the South and to the port of Djibouti – with Turkish and Chinese companies, to be financed partly with foreign investor capital. In June, China's Exim Bank announced a loan $ 475 m for the railway. As part of its extension of **urban** transport facilities, the government commenced the construction of an **Addis Ababa Light Rail Transit**, an electrified light-rail system with a total length of 34 km. It was planned to be completed in 2014 and to have capacity to transit 80,000 passengers per hour. Other state-led development projects in infrastructure (especially roads), large-scale commercial agriculture, educational and health outlets and state enterprises went ahead during the year, following an almost unchanged course since the 2012 death of Meles Zenawi and his GTP of 2010.

All this was, however, accompanied by a rapidly **growing national debt**, estimated at $ 16.11 bn, according to data from the Ministry of Finance and Economic Development. In 2008, it had been only $ 4.35 bn. The debt-to-GDP ratio reached an all-time high of 36%. There was a gradual shift from concessional loans to market-based loans. The high debt and the growing repayment burden (debt servicing cost ca. $ 440 m) made the country vulnerable to falls in the price of its export products, such as coffee. The government made no effort to establish a needed local secondary market for both government and private debt issuance, where bonds could be traded. There was only a primary bond market, specially for bonds to finance the construction of the (not yet fully cost-covered) Renaissance Dam. Of the total debt, the domestic public debt stood at $ 4.9 bn. High inflation (currently at ca. 12% and in previous years 20%–30%) reduced the attractiveness of domestic bonds.

No reliable figures were released on **unemployment**, but in view of the massive rates of outmigration of young jobless people, including college graduates, it was estimated to be very high (some 40%). Official figures indicated that ca. 29% of the population lived below the 'poverty line', especially lower-class and rural families with many children, but the real number was probably higher. There continued to be large numbers, estimated at around 150,000, of **street children**, often orphans, of whom there were about 90,000 in Addis Ababa alone. No adequate social support structure existed to alleviate this problem, although a number of foreign and local NGOs tried to address it. In urban areas, thousands of 'illegal' houses were demolished without proper replacement or compensation, victimising large numbers of the poorer urban population.

Despite the much vaunted economic growth, investment, political 'stability', etc., the Ethiopian authorities issued **two humanitarian aid appeals** to the donor community, one for January–June and one for July–December. The first cited 2.4 m people in need of food relief, with a gross emergency food and non-food requirement of $ 258.9 m. After deducting the then available resources of $ 83.2 m, a total $ 175.7 m was required for the first half of the year (including 165,751.7 tonnes of food, at an estimated cost of around $ 132.4 m). In July, the appeal for the rest of the year was made to the tune of $ 285.3 m to meet emergency requirements for ca. 2.7 m people. Thus, the situation of **constant food emergency** for millions of people continued. These figures were nevertheless considered as 'progress', because with a fast growing population (reaching about 90 m) the number of needy was not much higher than in previous years. According to several observers, the figures for food aid may have been an underestimate, because requirements for pastoral areas in the south, east and southwest were often not fully assessed. As usual, the government counted on (Western) donor countries to pay for most of the food aid. And again, they did: the US government alone had already provided more than $ 212 m. In fact, by 30 September, donor countries had committed nearly $ 484 m to humanitarian relief operations.

Ethiopia thus remained one of the **largest aid and development assistance recipients** in Africa. Most of it went straight to the central government and was spent according to its wishes. No evidence of donors seriously monitoring the conditionalities of aid was visible. Few of the funds and projects went into peripheral areas such as the Afar Region or the Ogaden, where the ONLF insurgency continued and where facilities for the civilian population remained seriously underdeveloped. Pastoralist peoples in general received little support. Only one initiative was noted: an $ 85 m loan provided by IFAD for 'pastoral community development'.

A major dramatic event was the **(forced) return of at least 140,000 Ethiopian workers** and domestic servants from **Saudi-Arabia** (ILO figures), after a number of violent incidents in which Ethiopians were humiliated or killed by Saudis in the streets. A stream of 'return migrants' started in November. This sudden exodus was the culmination of years of Saudi anti-foreigner (especially anti-Ethiopian) sentiment and abuse by the public and police. Both Muslim and Christian Ethiopians were hit by this. Most, though not all, returnees came back to Ethiopia as 'failures', with little capital and limited prospects of finding work or state support. Even their relatives in Ethiopia were ambivalent about their return, because of the extra burden of having to maintain them. The stream of out-migrants to Yemen and Saudi Arabia from Ethiopia via Somalia (Puntland's port of Bossaso), normally up to 80,000 to 90,000 per year, continued but dropped by one-third.

The number of **IDPs** within Ethiopia due to flooding, drought (as in Afar Region), or conflict was estimated at 370,000, with many being seen as 'protracted' cases with no return or resettlement in sight. The UNHCR estimated in August that Ethiopia also had 420,579 refugees from neighbouring countries, including about 240,000 from Somalia.

Jon Abbink

Kenya

Developments in 2013 were dominated by general elections in March and the proceedings against President Uhuru Kenyatta and Vice President William Ruto at the ICC. Although many elements of the electoral process failed, prompting the losing party to reject the results, the polls passed peacefully. The election of Kenyatta and Ruto, combined with their criticism of the ICC proceedings, led to deteriorating relations with key donors, but succeeded in forcing the ICC into a series of concessions throughout the year. Despite high levels of political uncertainty, the economy continued to grow, although it remained too early to assess the political and economic impact of the introduction of devolution, which came into effect following the election of 47 new county governments.

Domestic Affairs

The elections of 4 March were preceded by a complex and dramatic period of coalition building, which ultimately gave rise to three new coalitions. From mid-2012 onward, it became clear that the presidential polls would pit Luo leader (and current prime minister) **Raila Odinga** against the Kalenjin leader **William Ruto** and the Kikuyu leader **Uhuru Kenyatta**. Ruto, leader of the United Republic Party (URP), had been Odinga's most effective ally during the 2007 elections. But deteriorating personal relations between them led Ruto to abandon Odinga. When the ICC announced that it would be bringing cases against both Ruto and Kenyatta, the former rivals formed a 'marriage of convenience' designed to protect themselves against the charges. Many commentators predicted that the enmity between the Kalenjin and Kikuyu communities in the Rift Valley – a legacy of electoral violence in the 1990s and 2008 – would quickly destabilise the pact, but it proved to be far more durable.

What was not entirely clear, however, was what the broader coalitions would look like. Odinga moved first to finalise his electoral coalition, forming the **Coalition for Reform and Democracy (CORD)** with the Kamba leader Kalonzo Musyoka, vice president in President Kibaki's government (2007–13) who, despite having done what was asked of him, became marginalised as Kenyatta emerged as Kibaki's successor. CORD brought together Odinga's Orange Democratic Movement (ODM) and Musyoka's Wiper Democratic Movement, and aimed to secure support from Odinga's Luo community, Musyoka's Kamba community, and in historically marginalised parts of the country such as the former Western and Coast Provinces.

Although predictable, the deal startled Kenyatta and Ruto into approaching another former Odinga ally, the Luhya leader Musalia Mudavadi, and inviting him to become the presidential candidate of what would become the **Jubilee Alliance**. Mudavadi accepted, only to be humiliated when Kenyatta backed out of the deal, claiming that "the devil" had made him sign it. What appeared more likely was that powerful figures around Kenyatta were determined to have their man in State House, and that Kenyatta, unsure as to whether Mudavadi could be trusted to protect his interests, relented. Mudavadi went on to contest the polls for the **Amani** coalition, with a narrow support base in Western Province. Minus Mudavadi, Kenyatta took on the mantle of **Jubilee presidential candidate**, and the coalition came to rely heavily on his Kikuyu support base and his party The National Alliance (TNA), and the Kalenjin community and the URP of Ruto, who stood as his running mate.

Although there was initially speculation that Mudavadi might secure over 10% of the vote, significantly complicating the election, his campaign struggled to get off the ground. Instead, opinion polls pointed to a two horse race, and for much of the contest gave Odinga a healthy lead over Kenyatta. In November 2012, an Ipsos Synovate poll had given Odinga 33% with Kenyatta on 26% and Mudavadi on 4%. As the coalitions took shape and the number of undecided voters fell, public support began to concentrate on the two main contenders, but it was Kenyatta who benefitted most. By January 2013, Odinga's **poll rating** had grown to 46%, but his lead over Kenyatta had shrunk to just 6%. In large part, this was because Jubilee's **election campaign** was more dynamic, better organised and more effective. Able to draw on his own vast personal wealth and the resources of his family and backers, Kenyatta comprehensively outspent Odinga. He invested his resources wisely, bringing in the British consultancy firm BTP Advisors, who gave his campaign a slick and polished tone. Under its guidance, the Jubilee Alliance developed an **election strategy** that had three main strands.

First, and somewhat ironically given the nationality of its advisors, the Jubilee Alliance set out to demonise Odinga, the ICC and critical Western donors. By creating a **siege mentality** within the Kalenjin and Kikuyu communities, Ruto and Kenyatta managed to mobilise their distinctive bases while also sustaining the unity of their political machine. Second, the Jubilee Alliance emphasised the modern and transformative leadership that Kenyatta and Ruto would offer, contrasting their "digital" approach with Odinga's old fashioned "analogue" policies. Kenyatta's strong performance in Kenya's first ever televised presidential debate, promises such as one laptop for every child, and an emphasis on ambitious infrastructure projects, forced this message home. Third, by integrating a number of former Odinga allies such as Najib Balala and Charity Ngilu into their campaign, the Jubilee Alliance were able to confer on their leadership team a more national feel that was less likely to alienate Kenyans from non-Kikuyu and non-Kalenjin backgrounds.

By contrast, Odinga's campaign looked somewhat lacklustre. His performance in the **TV debates** was generally considered disappointing, and gave credence to the rumour that age and ill health had caught up with the once dynamic opposition leader. In contrast to the 2007 elections, there was no pentagon of regional leaders lining up behind Odinga to proclaim him the 'first among equals', which served to highlight the fact that most of his former allies had joined the Jubilee Alliance. CORD also struggled to develop a compelling message, and ODM came up with few ideas to match the innovative strategies deployed in 2007, such as the presentation of a tailored party manifesto for each province. By the time of the last opinion poll in February, the difference between the two campaigns was beginning to show, and Kenyatta had pushed marginally ahead (44.8% to 44.4%). This may have slightly underestimated Jubilee's advantage at this stage, as rates of voter registration were higher in Jubilee's heartlands such as Central Province and Rift Valley than in CORD's heartlands in Nyanza, Eastern, and at the coast. However, even taking this into account, the election remained too close to call, and no credible commentators predicted a first round victory for either candidate.

The **process of voting** was largely uneventful in many parts of the country. A sad exception was Mombasa, where, in an apparently coordinated series of attacks, ten police officers were killed on the eve of the election. This depressed turnout at the coast – to the likely detriment of the CORD – but elsewhere voters went to the polls in their droves, leading to a record turnout of 86.7%. This was verified by the parallel vote tabulation conducted by the Elections Observer Group (ELOG) domestic monitors, who recorded 86.4% turnout in the polling stations they visited.

As in 2007, the problems started when the votes began to be counted. Following the post-election violence of 2008, the old Electoral Commission of Kenya had been replaced by the **Independent Election and Boundaries Commission** (IEBC). In the run-up to the 2013 polls, the effective management of a number of by-elections and the introduction of a raft of new technology had built public confidence in the new institution. In the run-up to the election, however, the IEBC did not allow sufficient time for the new technology to be tested on a national scale. As a result, there were few safeguards against the total collapse of the system. The first use of technology was the deployment of biometric voter registration, using fingerprints to ensure a cleaner electoral roll. This worked well, but the corresponding process to electronically verify voters before they cast their ballot on polling day – the **electronic voter identification system** – failed comprehensively. The ELOG domestic observers found that in a majority of polling stations the kits failed at one point during the day. As a result, the IEBC fell back on the same manual voting process used in 2007 – not a sign of rigging in itself, but evidence that the electoral process was not as insulated from malpractice as Kenyans had been led to believe.

This would not have been so problematic had a system established to allow the immediate transmission of results by **mobile phone** – with a live total immediately broadcast on television and the Internet – worked. That would have conferred credibility on the counting process. As it was, most electoral officials found that the results could not be transmitted in this way. The problem appeared to be that the server did not have the capacity to deal with the volume of information it received. Again, this did not constitute rigging in and of itself, but it meant that a critical check on the process of counting and aggregating the results had fallen by the wayside.

The official results, when finally released, were something of a surprise: they gave Kenyatta not only a comfortable lead, but also a first round victory. CORD leaders cried foul, citing the opinion polls as evidence that Kenyatta could not have secured the 50% + 1 necessary to avoid a run-off. An **exit poll** conducted by American political scientists concurred, finding that Odinga and Kenyatta had both secured about 45% of the vote – a statistical tie, but strong evidence that Odinga got enough to at least earn a run-off. The domestic ELOG observers also found that Kenyatta had won less than 50% of the vote, but downplayed this and instead chose to emphasise the fact that the official figures fell within the range of results consistent with their analysis. The official IEBC results showed 50.07% for Kenyatta, 43.3% for Odinga, 3.9% for Mudavadi and marginal scores of less than 1% for five other candidates.

The multiple question marks hanging over the electoral process invited legal challenges from losing parties and civil society organisations. In the end, three **petitions** regarding the presidential election were brought before the **Supreme Court**. One wanted the court to rule on how the rejected votes should be dealt with, and the other two – brought by CORD and the Africa Centre for Open Governance – sought orders to compel the IEBC to cancel the certificate of election to Kenyatta and to hold a fresh election. However, although the petitions managed to show a series of irregularities, they struggled to find the 'smoking gun' of a clear plot to rig the polls. This was necessary, because the Supreme Court decided to impose a high burden of proof; to be successful, the petitioners were required to "clearly and decisively show the conduct of the election to have been so devoid of merits and so distorted, as not to reflect the expression of the people's electoral intent". Given the short time frame that CORD had to assemble evidence, and the late availability, or unavailability, of some key data as a result of the failings of the IEBC, this was simply unfeasible.

In a surprisingly pithy **verdict** delivered on 30 March, the Supreme Court ruled that the elections had been conducted in compliance with the Constitution and law. They further ruled that Kenyatta and Ruto had been validly elected, and that rejected votes ought not to have been included in voting calculations, which served to increase Kenyatta's margin of victory. The decision dismayed CORD supporters, who had been sure that **Chief Justice Willy Mutunga** could be relied upon to rule in their favour. Further criticism followed when the full judgment was published on 17 April, because the numerous problems recorded by the Court in that document ran counter to the more positive tone that had characterised the announcement of 30 March. Combined with the fact that the decision was unanimous, this created the impression that the Court had taken a political, rather than a juridical, decision. CORD leaders also complained that the Justices had not read all material submitted to them, and that the Court had developed an understanding of the election that was patchy at best.

As a result of the controversy of the presidential race, far less attention was paid to the **subnational elections**. These generally proved less problematic, although by March 2014 six petitions had been successful, giving Jubilee one additional parliamentary seat. The results of the elections for MPs and the newly created positions of **governors** and **senators** were interesting because, as a result of various agreements among coalition partners about where to run a common candidate and where to engage in open competition, they did not follow the national pattern. This was important, because the subnational polls gave CORD supporters a significant stake in the political system. Most notably, CORD secured the governorship in the most important county – the capital Nairobi – and at the coast. When the likely allegiance of each small party was taken into account, it was revealed that CORD had won 47% of the contests for governor, compared with Jubilee's 40%, and had captured a healthy proportion of senators (43%) and MPs (40%). The Jubilee Alliance had nevertheless obtained a strong legislative position, commanding 47% of MPs and 45% of senators. Altogether 22 different parties received mandates as MPs, senators or governors. The relative strength of the three major parties was: ODM – 78 MPs, 11 senators, 16 governors; TNA – 72, 11, 8; and URP – 62, 9, 10.

Subsequent to his inauguration on 9 April, Uhuru Kenyatta made a big play of appointing a **technocratic cabinet**. Taking advantage of a constitutional change that allowed him to select cabinet secretaries from outside parliament, he appointed what he billed as a high-quality team, with only Najib Balala and Charity Ngilu as clear concessions to political necessity. However, confidence in the capacity of the government fell sharply following the **Westgate terrorist attack** of 21 September, when unidentified gunmen took over a shopping mall in Nairobi, killing at least 67 people. The radical Somali Islamist group al-Shabaab later claimed responsibility, saying that the attack was punishment for Kenya's invasion of Somalia in 2011. The world watched as a three-day siege ensued, with first Kenyan police and then the **Kenya Defence Forces** (KDF) surrounding the building.

In the immediate aftermath of the atrocity, the government received a good deal of praise. President Kenyatta resisted the temptation to target Kenya's Somali community and Kenyans were initially told that the gunmen had all been captured or killed. But rumours and allegations quickly began to emerge: The government had been warned of the Westgate attack months before it happened; the security forces had no plans of the building and no strategy for retaking it; the police had the situation under control until they were forcibly removed by the KDF; the military then proceeded to loot the shopping centre, the siege having effectively ended on the second or third day; there may only have been four shooters, some of whom may have escaped alive; and, perhaps most shockingly, much of the damage to the building was caused by the Kenyan military in a desperate attempt to cover up their incompetence.

Instead of removing the hapless **Cabinet Secretary for Interior and Coordination of National Government** Joseph Ole Lenku, the government lashed out at media coverage of the scandal, with the police chief, David Kimaiyo, accusing the press of provoking propaganda and inciting Kenyans through hate speech. This blatant attempt to intimidate the media was only one of a number of infringements on **freedom of speech** that occurred towards the end of the year. Despite its rhetorical commitment to good governance and democracy, the Jubilee Alliance introduced a **media bill** that would see the formation of a quasi-governmental body to regulate the press, with the power to fine media groups up to KSh (shilling) 20 m should they breach a code of conduct. Although Kenyatta initially vetoed the proposals, he later signed an amended version into law on 17 December. Dashing the hopes of many commentators, the new legislation proved to be even worse than the first draft because it located the **Communications and Multimedia Appeals Tribunal** within the executive, granting the president and cabinet secretary the power to appoint and dismiss members of the board. The Committee to Protect Journalists described the bill as "draconian".

Foreign Affairs

Tensions between the government and a number of prominent donors over the prosecution of Kenyatta and Ruto at the **ICC** continued in early 2013, as President Kibaki's administration sought to clear the way for his successor. The government hoped to persuade the international community that the charges should be dropped, or at the very least postponed until after the elections. As in 2012, the strategy adopted by the Kibaki administration had two strands. On the one hand, Kenya employed 'shuttle diplomacy', sending emissaries around the continent in order to strengthen its bilateral relations. On the other, it worked through regional bodies such as the **AU** to build pressure on the ICC, successfully depicting it as a Western imperial imposition. Both strategies strengthened the government's position on the world stage and increased the pressure on the ICC to compromise.

ICC proceedings had been postponed from November 2012 to 11 April 2013 so that they would only begin after the elections on 4 March, but this was not the end of the matter because, as had often been the case over the last three years, the ICC miscalculated: 4 March was only the date of the first election round and the new Kenyan Constitution of 2010 had introduced a provision for a run-off election should no candidate secure an absolute majority in the first round. Although the date of the potential run-off went unspecified for a long time (because it depended on whether or not petitions were lodged against the first round results), the dominant interpretation of the electoral law suggested that it would need be held on or before 11 April, raising the prospect that Kenyans would be heading to the polls at exactly the same time that Kenyatta was heading to the Court. The ICC was thus forced into a second concession on 27 February, this time postponing the cases until August.

However, the decision to delay the trials did not result in an improvement in relations between the government, the ICC and Western donors. Many donor representatives recognised the danger of being seen to tell Kenyans how to vote, but despite choosing their words carefully a few prominent figures nonetheless became embroiled in controversy. This was the case for **UK High Commissioner Christian Turner**, who sought to stay on safe ground by simply outlining the official UK position: "We cannot meet ICC indictees, except for essential business." However, what appeared to Turner as a neutral statement of fact came across to many Kenyans as a threat that the UK would abandon Kenya if the Jubilee Alliance won the election.

In normal circumstances, Turner would have been backed up by the US, which was believed to have taken a firm stance in private discussions with the government in the run-up to the polls. However, **US Ambassador Scott Gration** had resigned in June 2012 citing "differences with Washington regarding my leadership style and certain priorities". Gration had left Kenya on 28 July 2012, leaving a vacuum at the US Embassy. He was replaced as Ambassador by **Robert Godek**, but it was not until 15 February that President Kibaki agreed to meet the new envoy. Prior to this, Godek lacked accreditation and did not feel empowered to speak out. As a result, Turner cut a rather isolated figure during the critical months of December 2012 and January 2013.

This turn of events, and the fact that Turner represented the former colonial power, encouraged the government to adopt an aggressive strategy. The high commissioner's relatively bland comment, and others like them, was depicted as an infringement of Kenyan sovereignty. The more Turner or his supporters protested that they were being misrepresented, the easier it became for the Jubilee Alliance to accuse the UK of interfering in the electoral process. As part of this rhetorical battle, senior Jubilee advisors came up with the concept of "**evil society**" as a way of demonising their opponents within the international community and Kenyan civil society. The claim underpinning the "evil society" campaign was that Western donors, opposition political parties and the ICC were engaged in a concerted and coordinated campaign to undermine Kenyan sovereignty. This was a clever strategy. By depicting Odinga as an agent of the West, Jubilee implied that he was a puppet of foreign powers unfit to lead an independent Kenya. By depicting the ICC as a conspiracy dreamt up by Odinga and the West, Jubilee was able to effectively make its case that the ICC was not an impartial institution and could not be trusted to dispense justice. And by claiming that key donors such as the UK government were actively supporting opposition parties, the concerns of Turner and colleagues could be explained away as the product of partisan self-interest.

The effort to demonise and intimidate international critics was aided by the campaign by veterans of the **Mau Mau** rebellion to secure compensation from the British government for abuse and torture inflicted during the state of emergency imposed in the 1950s. On 5 October 2012, the High Court in London had ruled that three Kenyan veterans could sue the British government for damages. Following the presentation of clear and compelling evidence, UK Foreign Secretary William Hague announced on 6 June 2013 that the UK would pay out £ 19.9 m in costs and compensation to more than 5,000 Kenyans. However, although the outcome of the process was widely welcomed, previous attempts by the British government to have the case thrown out – and so deny the Mau Mau veterans justice – undermined the moral credibility of the UK's Africa policy.

Britain's international reputation was further undermined when investigations surrounding the case revealed that the **Foreign and Commonwealth Office** (FCO) had "forgotten" about a secret archive of files relating to the colonial era, despite the legal team for the Mau Mau veterans having sought access to them on more than one occasion. The FCO and the records office pleaded incompetence rather than conspiracy, a position backed up by the official investigation into the fiasco. Unfortunately for Turner, the revelations further called into question the moral standing of the FCO at the precise moment when the right of the British government to comment on Kenyan affairs was being challenged in Nairobi.

All these developments meant that, by the time Ambassador Godek had officially taken up his post, the political landscape in Kenya had changed dramatically. By this point, the high number of prominent stories in Kenyan newspapers that featured Jubilee leaders condemning the "patronising" attitude of the international community had forced Western donors onto the back foot. It quickly became clear that, far from undermining Jubilee's momentum, further international intervention would play directly into Kenyatta's hands. It was therefore unsurprising when a much vaunted 'video message' from **US President Barack Obama**, which was trailed as a hard-hitting message targeted at Kenya's political and business elite, turned out to be little more than a gentle expression of hope for a peaceful, free and fair election. Jubilee leaders were so delighted that they cited it as evidence that a Kenyatta victory would not undermine the quality of the country's international relations.

However, there was one American intervention that particularly rankled with Jubilee leaders. On 7 February, **US Assistant Secretary of State for African Affairs Johnnie Carson** said that, while it was not for him to tell Kenyans who to choose in the elections, "We live in an interconnected world and people should be thoughtful about the impact that their choices have on their nation, on the region, on the economy, on the society and on the world in which they live. Choices have consequences." This simple truism became the most infamous utterance of the election campaign, and was quickly adopted as an ironic rallying cry by Jubilee activists, who saw it as another international attack on Kenyan sovereignty.

But the furore over Carson's comments overlooked the fact that he had been moved to make them by growing frustration about the mixed messages emanating from the American side. Shortly before his notorious interview, **Jendayi Frazer**, Carson's predecessor, who was said to have strong ties with the Kenyatta family, had publicly criticised the ICC, describing it as a kangaroo court. Following Carson's comments, Frazer responded by denouncing his statement as "reckless and irresponsible" and claimed that the case against Kenyatta was "a weak one based on hearsay". Following Kenyatta's victory, Frazer went on record to say how happy she was to hear the result. The international community may have become a major part of the story of the Kenyan elections, but they were far from united, either in Nairobi or back home.

Against this backdrop, tensions between the government/Jubilee Alliance and the UK/US continued to escalate, reaching their apogee when, on 6 March, Charity Ngilu expressed her concern at the "shadowy, suspicious and rather animated involvement of the British High Commissioner in Kenya's election". She went on to allege that the British High Commissioner had been canvassing to have rejected votes tallied in an attempt to deny the Jubilee Coalition outright victory and to demand that Turner explain what she described as the "alarming" and "abnormally high influx of British military personnel in the country, which began around voting day". More of the same was to follow, as figures close to Jubilee alleged that Turner was involved in a plot with **human rights campaigner Maina Kiai** to pressurise the chair of the Electoral Commission into rigging the elections in Odinga's favour.

The victory of the Jubilee Alliance did little to improve matters. Godek and Turner both encouraged Kenyans to accept the election result, but neither country was effusive in its congratulations of the new government. The election of Kenyatta and Ruto also served to return the question of the ICC to the headlines. Empowered by his electoral mandate, Kenyatta set about intensifying the pressure on the ICC to abandon its hearings. On 12 October, an **AU summit** in Ethiopia passed a resolution stating that no sitting head of state should appear before an international court and mandated Kenya to write to the UNSC to seek a deferral of the case against Kenyatta. However, an attempt to orchestrate a mass African walk-out from the ICC failed, and the AU's decision failed to persuade the **UNSC**, where a resolution to delay the trial only secured seven of the nine votes needed to succeed; eight countries abstained, including the UK and the USA.

But political pressure was not the greatest problem facing the ICC. In the absence of an effective witness protection campaign, the victory of Kenyatta and Ruto undermined the prospects for a successful prosecution for two reasons. First, it made it less likely that nervous witnesses would stay the course and testify against Kenya's new leaders. Second, it made it less likely that the Kenyan government would comply with the Court's requirements. A lawyer familiar with the investigation told the 'New York Times', "There was not a shred of cooperation; they wouldn't give you as much as a weather map." Officials close to the case also said that they believed that key witnesses against Kenyatta and Ruto had been paid off, intimidated and in some instances even killed. This significantly weakened the cases over time. Although the Ruto case began on 10 September, the trial of Kenyatta – where the evidence was believed to be considerably weaker – was yet to begin. On 19 December, **Chief Prosecutor Fatou Bensouda** was forced to admit that the withdrawal of two key witnesses had undermined the evidence base of the case against Kenyatta, and to request that proceedings be adjourned.

Despite the ongoing ICC controversy, the shock and horror of the **Westgate terrorist attack** in September inspired a period of international cooperation, at least for a short while. The mall was operated and owned by Israelis, and Israeli security officials were thought to have advised Kenyan security forces and participated directing in the counter-offensive. UN Secretary-General Ban Ki-moon expressed his solidarity with the Kenyan authorities while the ICC adjourned the trial of Ruto to allow him to deal with the crisis. Following the end of the siege, the New York Police Department was allowed to carry out an investigation into the incident to "familiarize them with what to expect" should the Big Apple face a similar attack.

The attack also served as a powerful reminder that Kenya's military engagement in **Somalia** had not served to make its citizens safer. During 2013, there were a reported 13 successful terrorist attacks on Kenyan territory, typically taking the form of a hand grenade thrown into a restaurant or a vehicle. Excluding the Westgate attack, at least 21 people died in these incidents, and scores more were injured. Kenya responded by bombing al-Shabaab strongholds in Somalia, and claimed to have destroyed a training camp that had been used during preparations for terrorist operations in Kenya. However, this military 'solution' had little discernable impact on the level of insecurity.

The government's concern over terrorism, its critical attitude towards international donors, and engagement in Somalia, made natural allies of Kenyatta and Uganda's President Museveni. During Kenyatta's inauguration on 9 April, Museveni took the opportunity to lambast the ICC. Over the next three months, Kenyatta, Museveni and Rwanda's President Kagame formed what became known as a **Coalition of the Willing** (CoW) – a group of countries determined to push forward with regional economic integration. On 26 June, a meeting of the three presidents in Kampala (Uganda) led to an agreement to construct a standard gauge railway line to connect the three countries and to build a joint oil pipeline and refinery.

But the closer ties between Kenya, Rwanda and Uganda did not mean that it was smooth sailing for the **EAC**. While the renewed enthusiasm for regional coordination was welcomed by donors, it caused consternation in Tanzania. Successive Tanzanian governments had repeatedly expressed concern that unfettered integration would lead to Kenyan economic domination. Tanzanian recalcitrance led to the emergence of a 'two track' integration process in which the leaders of Kenya, Rwanda and Uganda met on their own to discuss joint projects. But this option also proved to be unpalatable to the Tanzanians, whose minister of East African cooperation issued a statement on 21 October that was highly critical of the CoW and alleged that the trilateral talks were against EAC protocol. During the regular EAC summit on 30 November in Kampala, however, the conflicts seemed to be sorted out, when the five partner states reaffirmed their commitment to cooperate closely and signed a protocol on a future monetary union.

Tension with traditional Western donors encouraged Kenyatta to consolidate Kenya's ties with **China**, leading to a high-level delegation visiting Beijing soon after the Jubilee Alliance won power. On 20 August, Kenyatta and Chinese President Xi Jinping signed deals worth $ 5 bn to improve wildlife protection, support an energy project, and to build part of the railway line discussed by Kenya, Rwanda and Uganda. The last was undoubtedly the most significant announcement: Kenyatta saw the construction of the **standard gauge railway** – which would initially link Mombasa to Nairobi, and would later be extended to reach South Sudan, the DRC and Burundi – as the "project that will define my legacy". Of the estimated $ 5.2 bn cost of laying the track and purchasing the locomotives, 85% was to be financed by the Export-Import Bank of China.

Socioeconomic Developments

Upon coming to power, the Jubilee Alliance committed itself to a course of continuity, endorsing the **Kenya Vision 2030** strategy developed by the previous Kibaki government. In doing so, Kenyatta embraced the fiscal stimulus package put in place by Kibaki to sustain economic growth, but also committed his administration to restraining inflation and reducing the country's debt burden in the medium term. One of the key features of the Kenya Vision 2030 and of the Jubilee Alliance manifesto was a determination to embark on a series of ambitious and high-profile infrastructure projects, such as the standard gauge railway, the one laptop per child project, and the Lamu Port Southern Sudan-Ethiopia Transport Corridor. Thus, despite Kenyatta's stated preference for private enterprise and an economically less interventionist state, the government was set to remain a major player in the construction, industry and transport sectors for some time to come.

The economy performed reasonably well in 2013 – in contrast to previous years when elections had had a deleterious impact on a range of economic indicators. Despite high levels of political uncertainty surrounding the polls, the economy grew by 5.6%. Significantly, **per capita GDP** also increased to $ 1,800, up from $ 1,737 in 2012. This was not spectacular by regional standards, but represented a small increase on 2012 (4.6%) and 2011 (4.4%). This positive trend was expected to continue into 2014, with growth increasing to over 6% – although this was lower than the government's more optimistic estimate.

Most of the growth came from expansion in the **agriculture, industry and services** sectors. Partially as a result of the government's ambitious infrastructure plans, industry led the way, growing by 6.4%, 1.9% more than in 2012. The agricultural sector also accelerated, growing by 4.6%. However, while the service sector also grew, the 3.6% achieved in 2013 was lower than the expansion in 2012 (4.5%), as tourists avoided the country fearing a repeat of the electoral violence that followed the 2007 polls. By July, visitor numbers had fallen by 18.4% year-on-year to 255,500. This had a dramatic impact on hotels and restaurants, whose contribution to GDP fell by 15.8%. The tourist sector took another major hit following the Westgate terrorist attack in September and had yet to recover.

Most other economic indicators remained healthy. Central government revenue increased as a percentage of GDP from 24.7% in 2012 to 25.7% in 2013, while the **current-account balance** improved from $ –4,253 m to $ –3,879 m. Overall, Kenya's solid economic performance enabled the Kenya shilling to retain its value: the exchange rate of KSh 86 to the dollar was significantly weaker than the rate of KSh 76 in 2009, but was consistent with the rates of 85 and 86 in 2011 and 2012, respectively. Somewhat surprisingly, given the high levels of government expenditure around elections, the government exceeded its target of restraining inflation to below 7.5%, with year-on-year **inflation** averaging just 5.6%. However, it was not all good news. The national debt stock rose by $ 11.1 bn to $ 13.2 bn, and was expected to continue to rise for the next two years. As a result, the cost of debt servicing also increased from $ 569 m to $ 688 m.

Further concerns over the national finances emerged late in the year in relation to the two flagship programmes of the Jubilee Alliance, both of which became beset by **corruption allegations**. Towards the end of the year, Kenyatta was forced to defend the decision to award the contract for the standard gauge railway to the Chinese company Road and Bridge Corporation. This had been a condition of the loan from the Export-Import Bank of China, but raised serious concerns because the company was debarred by the World Bank for fraud relating to work it had carried out in the Philippines. Critics alleged that the costs of the project were too high, and they rose from $ 2.5 bn to $ 3.8 bn when it emerged that rolling stock and locomotives would be provided by the Chinese. Similar questions were asked about the procurement process for the 'one laptop per child' policy, after it emerged that Olive Telecommunications, an Indian firm, had bid KSh 23 bn but been awarded a contract for KSh 24.7 bn.

Remittances continued to play a critical role in the economy, and official transfers climbed by 10.2% to $ 1.3 bn in 2013, a record. However, the rate of growth fell to its lowest since 2010, largely as a result of the slow economic recovery in North America and Western Europe. Roughly half of all remittances originated from the US and Canada, with 27% coming from Europe and 25% arriving from the rest of the world. One reason for the increase in remittance flows over the previous five years had been the high number of Kenyans leaving the country to live abroad, most notably in the Middle East. It was estimated that 40,000 Kenyans were currently residing as 'guest workers' in the UAE. Although there was considerable controversy about whether remittances were invested in a way that contributed to sustainable development or were simply consumed by those who received them, a World Bank report concluded that "large amounts of remittances find their way into real estate, **building and construction** which has increased the demand and prices in the non-tradable sector".

Analysts believed that the investment of remittances in the **housing sector** was one of the reasons behind the sky-rocketing price of property in Kenya. House prices varied markedly across the country, but the average value of a recorded sale reached KSh 24.4 bn in December 2013, up from just KSh 7.1 bn in 2000. Unsurprisingly, the largest increases occurred in Nairobi. According to the Wealth Report 2013 produced by consultancy firm Knight Frank, average prices in the capital's high-end estates rose by 10% in 2013. This growth was in part driven by the increasing number of wealthy Africans looking to make their home in Kenya's capital. Knight Frank estimated that the number of "ultra-high net worth individuals" – people with $ 30 m or more in net assets – living in Nairobi increased to 65 in 2013, making Nairobi the fifth most popular destination for the continent's super-wealthy after Johannesburg and Cape Town (South Africa), Cairo (Egypt) and Lagos (Nigeria). **Rental prices** also increased rapidly in the final months of 2013. The annual housing report by HassConsult estimated that recorded rents in Nairobi rose by 8.5% in 2013, with the average rent for a property rising to KSh 120,372 a month in December 2013. High rental prices were underpinned by rising demand as a result of exceptionally high mortgage rates, which meant that, although members of the middle class were enjoying higher wages, many could not afford to buy a property.

One of the biggest economic stories of the year was the way that **government revenue** was **distributed within the Kenyan state**. With responsibility for the provision of key services such as health care, education and the maintenance of local roads being devolved to **47 new counties**, the distribution of government revenue had to change accordingly. The legislation establishing the devolved system of government created the **Commission on Revenue Allocation** (CRA) and tasked it with deciding how revenue should be shared between the national and county governments, and how much each county should get.

It was initially agreed that 84.5% of all revenues would go to the national government, with 15% going to the counties and the remaining 0.5% designated as an equalisation fund. However, this did not prevent a **tug of war** developing **between the governors and the central government** over exactly how much money would be transferred to the county level. Key questions that were publicly debated included whether counties' staff costs should be paid for by the county governments themselves or by central government, and whether it was prudent to transfer the full allocation in one go, given the limited capacity of many counties to absorb the funds. In the end, the central government disbursed KSh 210 bn to the counties. This was less than the KSh 258 bn demanded by the Senate, but according to external analysts still represented 20% of domestic revenue, a considerably larger share than was originally envisaged.

The upward pressure on county allocations was significant because it meant that, when the 2.5% of government revenue allocated to the **Constituency Development Fund** was taken into account, subnational actors spent almost a quarter of national revenue in 2013. The implications of this for the capacity of the government to undertake central planning and to ensure the quality of service delivery were not felt during 2013, partly because of delays in the transfer of responsibility to the new units, but devolution was likely to present the central government with real political and economic challenges from 2014 onwards.

The question about which counties would receive the highest allocations under the new economic arrangements attracted a great deal of interest from mid-year onwards. The **formula for sharing the revenue**, which was proposed by the CRA and subsequently approved by the National Assembly, set out a progressive basis for the calculation: 25% (equal share), 45% (based on population), 20% (poverty index), 8% (land area), 2% (fiscal responsibility).

The biggest winners were **Nairobi, Turkana** and **Mandera** counties, reflecting the criteria used to determine revenue allocation. Nairobi was the largest county by population, whereas Mandera and Turkana had pervasive poverty and, while less densely populated, were two of the largest counties in Kenya. The allocation of funds was also notable for favouring counties in northern Kenya, which was an important development considering the economic and political marginalisation that these parts of the country had suffered since colonial times.

However, when the county governments' budgets were reviewed in August, it was revealed that a number of counties were not prepared to operate on the basis of the share of revenue identified by the CRA. While 23% of counties submitted a surplus budget and 23% managed to balance the budget, a majority (54%) proposed a deficit. In some cases, such as Kisii, the planned deficit was modest (2%) and perfectly understandable for a new institution trying to establish new staff and facilities. But other counties clearly set out to manipulate the weak framework governing budgetary planning by proposing ridiculous and unsustainable expenditures. The most egregious culprits were **Nyamira, Mombasa** and **Vihiga** counties, which proposed deficits of 74%, 79% and 91%, respectively. They were not alone: in total, seven counties planned budget deficits in excess of 30%, and 14 approved deficits over 10%, raising the prospect that poorly managed counties would quickly find themselves bankrupt, jeopardising the success of the whole devolution project.

This danger was confirmed by a more detailed analysis of budget returns, which revealed that a number of counties had set aside vast sums for personnel and very little for public services. For example, Bomet earmarked almost as much for the office of the governor as for energy, trade, industry, tourism, lands, housing and planning combined. Some budgets were puzzling as well as troubling. In Kisumu, KSh 3 m was allocated for recurrent expenditure through the county executive (governor) compared with just KSh 1 m through the County Assembly. At the same time, KSh 2.4 m was allocated to 'others'.

Nic Cheeseman

Rwanda

The ruling RPF government continued to maintain strict controls on political and public life. The regime, led by President Paul Kagame, further consolidated its grip on power via parliamentary elections held in September. The government faced little internal political opposition. Progress slowed in public service delivery as donors cut or suspended aid as a sanction for Rwanda's alleged continued support of the M23 rebels in the DRC. The RPF continued to lose standing with its international donors, including for the first time the USA, a staunch ally of the government since it had taken power in 1994 at the end of the genocide. The government continued its vigorous denial of any military involvement in the neighbouring DRC through proxy militias. To appease donors, the government embarked on a series of peace talks hosted by the government of Uganda. Bilateral relations with the DRC remained cordial despite Congolese President Kabila's public statements that Rwanda should stop supporting rebels in its eastern provinces. Relations with Tanzania soured and remained strained at year's end. The dip in available foreign aid constrained the government's development plans as it accounted for some 40% of budgeted revenue. Foreign aid cuts combined with higher international interest rates and lower domestic public spending, along with poor tea and coffee receipts, slowed Rwanda's economic growth to slightly less than 5%.

Domestic Politics

The ruling **Rwandan Patriotic Front (RPF)** continued to dominate all levels of socio-political life, from the lowest levels of the administrative bureaucracy up to **President Paul Kagame**'s inner cabal of advisors. The government's grip on power was confirmed when the RPF secured a **landslide victory in parliamentary elections** on 16 September. For foreign and domestic observers, the RPF's win highlighted the lack of political freedoms in the country. On paper, the RPF was contending with nine other parties. In practice, Rwanda's nearly 6 m voters had little choice on the ballot. A total of **98%** of the votes went to the **RPF** and its four **coalition parties**. The RPF alone obtained 76.2% of the votes and 41 of the 53 directly elected seats in parliament, while the 'Parti Social Démocrate' got 13% and seven seats and the 'Parti Libéral' 9.3% and five seats. A further 27 MPs were indirectly elected to represent women (24), youth organisations (two) and disabled persons (one). The **Democratic Green Party of Rwanda** (DGPR), led by Frank Habineza, was after a lengthy process of almost four years officially registered as a political party in August, but only one day before the deadline for production of the list of candidates in the September elections. As a result, no DGPR candidates were able to stand. With women now holding 61 (64%) of the 80 seats in parliament, a higher share than in any other country in the world, the RPF boasted of its commitment to gender equality, but this number masked the reality. Like their male counterparts, female parliamentarians had little room to develop policy or even to debate openly; space for **free and open political expression was very limited**.

Kagame highlighted **power struggles** within the ruling RPF in two unexpected **cabinet reshuffles**. In February, he swapped the main economic portfolios. Claver Gatete was appointed finance minister while John Rwangombwa was appointed governor of the National Bank of Rwanda. Gatete was a member of the RPF and a close ally of Kagame. Analysts believed that he was awarded the finance portfolio because of his close relationship with the president, thus allowing Kagame a hand in steering the national budget. Gatete was charged with navigating the budget shortfall as a result of donor aid cuts and driving the second tranche of the Economic Development and Poverty Reduction Strategy (EDPRS II, 2013–18). Again in May, Kagame unilaterally reshuffled his cabinet, replacing the justice minister, the cabinet affairs minister and the director of the cabinet in the prime minister's office. Tharcisse Karugarama was replaced as justice minister by Johnston Busingye in a move that analysts considered punishment for Karugarama's remarks in April that Kagame should step down as president in 2017, as constitutionally mandated. The other new appointments in the cabinet, Stella Ford Mugabo and James Kimonyo, were seen as rewards for loyalty to Kagame. Both were members of Kagame's inner circle, identified as Tutsi and grew up in exile in Uganda. Analysts viewed both cabinet reshuffles as illustrative of **tensions within the political elite**, as Kagame sought to promote trusted supporters while removing critics and potential threats to his authority from government. The cabinet reshuffles followed Kagame's February request to have senior members of the RPF draft a transition plan for the end of his second and final presidential term, in 2017.

Whatever the reason, the shake-up among Kagame's aides continued a broader trend of **domestic disillusionment** with the RPF. Members of the RPF's core constituency – urban, educated and English-speaking Tutsi – felt that Kagame had lost his vision for ethnic unity and economic prosperity for all Rwandans. In addition to the continuing trend of government scapegoating of the political opposition and an increasing tolerance for nepotism and bribery among members of the ruling clique, domestic critics had also noted the selective way in which those closest to Kagame were able to benefit economically from the relationship, while those who questioned the policies or practices of the government were accused of **corruption**. In November, TI confirmed this trend while noting that the international perception was that Rwanda was not corrupt under the leadership of the RPF. In July, Global Integrity, in its Global Corruption Index, reported that Rwandans regularly paid bribes for basic service delivery, and that petty corruption among police and local-level government officials was rife. Predictably, Rwanda responded to the criticism from both organisations, highlighting that it was the least corrupt country in East Africa. The government also highlighted Rwanda's enabling business environment, citing the 2013 **World Bank's Doing Business index**, which ranked Rwanda 52nd (out of 185 countries) across ten categories that determine the ease of doing business. According to the index, Rwanda had been the top reformer in SSA and the second highest reformer in the world since 2005.

The RPF continued to **lose legitimacy** with its core constituency, individuals who identified as ethnic Tutsi. Important to note was that these former party loyalists were not clamouring for increased democracy or a more economically inclusive Rwanda. Rather, dissatisfaction with the regime was expressed in complaints about lack of access to credit and other economic benefits of RPF rule. There was thus no organised or viable opposition to Kagame's political might. The president still commanded the loyalty of much of the Rwandan Patriotic Army, so a coup remained unlikely. Political opponents of the regime, ethnic Hutu, Tutsi and Twa alike, continued to regularly accuse Kagame of **increasing authoritarianism** and of **trampling on civic and political rights** and freedoms. International and domestic human rights organisations regularly accused the RPF government of harassment and intimidation of its political opponents and of journalists. The RPF in general, and Kagame in particular, no longer denied their control of the political sphere, citing the need to give priority to state security and economic growth over political freedoms.

In the course of the year, the RPF ramped up attacks on political opponents and outspoken critics, whether of its policies or of Kagame himself. Freedom of expression and association thus remained tightly controlled. In addition to the repression of independent voices inside Rwanda, those **living in the diaspora** became targets of RPF-led attacks and threats. In October, former Kagame bodyguard **Joel Mutabazi** went missing from a safe-house where he was living in Uganda. The Rwandan police confirmed they had Mutabazi in custody a week after his disappearance, despite Mutabazi's legal status as a refugee, leading analysts to conclude that he had been kidnapped. Mutabazi's abduction followed the **loss of refugee status** by an estimated 100,000 Rwandans living outside of the country, mostly in the DRC, Burundi, Uganda, Kenya, Tanzania, Zambia and Malawi. In June, the UNHCR cessation clause came into effect. The clause caused refugees to lose their status if the country of origin had instituted fundamental and durable changes to alleviate the factors that instigated their original flight. Critics of the cessation clause noted that an influx of returning Rwandans created the potential for local-level conflict, particularly around land ownership and use.

The fear that Rwandan critics of the government felt was compounded by the continued **harassment** of key members of the **political opposition**. The president of the opposition party **PS-Imberakuri**, Bernard Ntaganda, remained in prison after the Supreme Court rejected his appeal against his conviction for endangering state security and promoting ethnic divisionism. HRW alleged that the charges against Ntaganda related solely to his public criticisms of the government's reconciliation policy. In December, the Supreme Court rejected the appeal of **Victoire Ingabire**, president of the **FDU-Inkingi** party, against her conviction for conspiracy to undermine the government and genocide denial. She was sentenced to 15 years in prison, almost double the eight years she had received at her 2012 trial. Led by HRW, international human rights groups claimed that her right to a fair trial and due process had been abused, noting in particular the interference of officials from the president's office, the Ministry of Justice and the **pro-government media** by coercing and intimidating witnesses. Ingabire's trial also confirmed the role of the RPF in co-opting the last of Rwanda's independent human rights organisations. In August, the **'Ligue Rwandaise pour la Promotion et la Défense des Droits de l'Homme'** (LIPRODHOR) was taken over by individuals believed to be loyal to the RPF. The Rwanda Governance Board then approved its new board of governors. Police threatened members of the old board with imprisonment if they failed to cooperate with the new board. The government's take-over of LIPRODHOR followed the July withdrawal of the Association for the Defence of Human Rights and Public Liberties and the 'Maison de Droit' from the 'Collectif des Ligues et Association de Défense des Droits de l'Homme au Rwanda'. For international and regional human rights advocates, the LIPRODHOR take-over marked the end of independent civil society in Rwanda.

Throughout 2013, members of the FDU-Inkingi and PS-Imberakuri parties were **arrested, threatened or detained**. In March, **Sylvain Sibomana**, secretary general of the FDU-Inkingi, and **Dominique Shyirambere** were arrested following a confrontation with police outside the courthouse where Ingabire's trial was taking place. In November, Sibomana was sentenced to two years in prison for contempt of public officials and illegal demonstration; Shyirambere was sentenced to five months on the same charges. Sibomana also faced charges stemming from a September 2012 case linked to eight other

FDU-Inkingi members. In July, seven of the eight accused were each sentenced to two years in prison on charges of holding illegal meetings and of collaborating with the Hutu-chauvinist **Forces Démocratiques de Liberation du Rwanda** (FDLR). The RPF continued to maintain that the FDLR had a destabilising effect on Rwandan peace and security as its primary goal was to finish the Tutsi genocide of 1994.

Freedom of the press remained curtailed despite the passage in February of a revised media law that enshrined the right of journalists to freedom of opinion and expression. Journalists based in Rwanda continued to practise self-censorship, mindful of the prison sentences handed down to critics of the RPF or Kagame. In June, the government released Saidati Mukakibibi, a journalist with the Kinyarwanda-language newspaper 'Umurabyo' at the end of her three-year sentence. The newspaper's editor, Agnès Uwimana, had her sentence reduced from 17 to four years, and remained in prison. In March, the sentence of Stanley Gatera, editor of the Kinyarwanda-language newspaper 'Umusingi', was upheld and he was released in July, after a year in prison. In March, the international media watchdog **Reporters Without Borders** condemned the RPF for attacks on journalists based in Rwanda and abroad for their criticism of government policy. **Freedom House** classed Rwanda as "not free" (ranking it 161th out of 174 countries) in its 2013 Press Freedom Index. Even in neighbouring Uganda, international journalists experienced harassment and intimidation. In November, a Kampala-based correspondent for an international news organisation left Uganda because he feared for his life after receiving disturbing threats from Rwandan intelligence officials. In June, Tom Malaba, a journalist working for Ugandan Radio Network claimed he had been followed repeatedly and his home had once been attacked at night after he asked a question at a press conference that upset Rwanda's Ambassador Frank Mugambage. Malaba had sought clarification of allegations that the ambassador headed a commando unit that hunted down Rwandan exiles in Uganda.

International donor representatives resident in Kigali continued to voice concern about the various restrictions on freedom of expression and lack of political openness, reminding the government that neither the FDU-Inkingi nor the PS-Imberakuri posed any real threat to its political power. Highlighting this fact was the continued muted presence in Rwandan politics of the **Rwandan National Congress** and the DRC-based **FDLR militia** throughout 2013. International and domestic political analysts believed that both groups currently posed no serious political or military threat. Kagame's strongly negative stance on the role of "foreign meddlers" in domestic politics was best exemplified in June, when he reacted angrily to the suggestion by his Tanzanian counterpart **Jakaya Kikwete** that Rwanda should hold talks with the FDLR, a group the US government had put on its terrorist watch list in 2005, and who the RPF believed still harboured an intention to continue the ethnic cleansing of Tutsi.

In February, the appeals tribunal of the **International Criminal Tribunal for Rwanda** (ICTR) in Arusha (Tanzania) acquitted two former government ministers, Justin Mugenzi and Prosper Mugiraneza. The acquittals led to renewed government accusations of the judicial incompetence of the ICTR, which resulted in a protest march outside the Tribunal's office in Kigali. The government considered the acquittal of two senior government ministers an affront following the warming of relations in 2012 as the ICTR began to transfer cases to Rwanda's domestic courts. In July, the ICTR transferred Bernard Munyagishari to face trial in Rwanda. His case was ongoing at the end of the year. The ICTR announced in December that it intended to conclude its work in July 2015.

Foreign Affairs

As in previous years, foreign affairs were dominated by Rwanda's presence (critics would say interference) in the **eastern DRC**. The UN Group of Experts (UNGoE) report, published in 2012, continued to loom large in Rwanda's foreign relations. It had accused the Rwandan government of supporting a military rebellion in neighbouring eastern DRC, led by its proxy militia known as the **M23**. In January, ahead of a second round of peace talks with the DRC government hosted by the government of Uganda in Kampala, the M23 rebels declared a ceasefire. In April, the rebels withdrew from the peace talks, noting that they resulted in little more than a lull in the fighting among the dozens of rebel movements operating in eastern DRC. The move followed the voluntary surrender in March of Bosco Ntaganda, a Congolese general wanted by the **ICC**, and formerly leader of the M23's predecessor organisation. Ntaganda walked into the US embassy in Kigali, asking to be handed over to the ICC. His voluntary surrender, the first in the ICC's history, was significant as he had been a major player in the eastern DRC in the previous decade. His grip on power had weakened in the course of 2012 and he apparently feared that the on-going **UN-mediated peace talks** would result in his capture. Ntaganda seemed to have hedged his bets, sensing that the **UN's Peace, Security and Co-operation Framework**, which focused on the reform of the Congolese state and army and on ending foreign interference in the DRC, would make it difficult for his reign of impunity to continue.

The UN's Cooperation Framework was signed by 11 African states, all except South Africa members of the **ICGLR**, on 24 February in Addis Ababa (Ethiopia). The M23 militia continued to clash with the Congolese army, the UN peacekeeping force MONUSCO and its new 3,000 strong Intervention Brigade intermittently throughout the rest of the year. In November, the **M23 declared an end to its rebellion** as its leaders sought safe haven in Rwanda and Uganda. The disbanding of the M23 followed a new **UNGoE report**, leaked to the press in October, that alleged continued troop and tank movements from Rwanda into the eastern DRC. Analysts speculated that the M23 had ended its rebellion at the behest of Kagame in advance of Rwanda's taking a seat on the UNSC on 1 January 2014. The RPF government, Kagame and **Foreign Affairs Minister Louise Mushikiwabo** continued to deny any support for the M23 rebel group, citing their support for the deployment of UN-sponsored surveillance drones along Rwanda's border with the DRC as evidence of their commitment to peace in the DRC. The government initially opposed the use of surveillance drones, but gave the green light to their use in December, presumably as a mark of good faith in advance of taking up its UNSC seat.

In October, the **US government cut some of its military aid** to Rwanda in reaction to the alleged continued forcible recruitment of men and boys to join the M23 rebels. The cut, amounting to $ 500,000, was the second such sanction imposed by the US. In 2012, it had cut $ 200,000 worth of military assistance for the same reason. While the cuts were largely symbolic as American aid to Rwanda amounted to $ 170 m per annum, they did send an important diplomatic message to the Rwandan government to reduce its presence and continued interference in the DRC. Despite the aid cuts, Rwanda's military cooperation with the **USA**, through its Africa Command (AFRICOM), remained strong. They cooperated in Ntaganda's transfer to the ICC, and the US reached out to Rwanda for intelligence following the September attacks by Somali Islamist militants at the Westgate shopping mall in Kenya.

The disbanding of the M23 did not remove the stark foreign aid choice faced by the government. Rwanda was unable to convince its traditional aid donors that it was not involved in the financing of the M23 rebellion. Rwanda's bilateral donors, including the USA, the UK, the Netherlands and Germany, continued to **withhold aid** – specifically, important budget support. Following the continued suspension of aid, the government made a commitment to increase cooperation with the Congolese armed forces as a mark of good faith to contain the rebel activity that was a source of instability for both countries.

In an unexpected twist, **Rwanda** and **Tanzania entered into a diplomatic spat** in May when Tanzanian President Jakaya Kikwete urged President Kagame to enter into talks with the FDLR. Kikwete made the suggestion on the sidelines of the 21st AU summit. The spat was best viewed as part of increasing diplomatic tension between the two countries. Tanzania had hosted Rwandan refugees since 1994, and was currently home to at least 500,000 individuals that Kigali wanted returned to Rwanda. In June, frosty relations between Rwanda and Tanzania undermined the third **EAC** Dialogue on Political Integration, raising concerns about the viability of the harmonised economic and political regimes, and underscored the challenges to crafting an effective and operational EAC among Rwanda's regional neighbours (Burundi, Kenya, Tanzania and Uganda). Despite the frosty regional relations, Kenya, Rwanda and Uganda agreed in August to introduce a **single tourist visa** as of 2014. The move signalled the potential emergence of a two-tiered EAC. Burundi and Tanzania had consistently sought to move slowly towards regional integration, and regional analysts concluded that the introduction of the single visa without the support of Burundi and Tanzania appeared to mark the end of Kenya's, Rwanda's and Uganda's patience. To add insult to injury, **Tanzania expelled 3,500 Rwandan refugees** living in north-western Tanzania, citing lack of valid residential documents. Rwanda again turned its back on Tanzania later in August, when the government announced it was entering into a **single customs agreement** with Kenya and Uganda. Analysts concluded that the announcement confirmed Rwanda's intention to push for increased regional integration with or without Tanzanian involvement. At the end of the year, bilateral relations with Tanzania remained cool as relations with Kenya and Uganda appeared much closer.

In contrast to the negative reverberations around the suspension of donor aid and chilly regional relations, the government continued to nurture its close economic relationship with **China**. In May, the two countries signed a technical and economic agreement valued at $ 5 m in interest-free loans. This was in addition to $ 9 m in loans offered to Rwanda in 2012. Relations with **France** warmed following a chilly 2012. In November, French appeals courts approved the extradition of Claude Muhayimana and Innocent Musabyimana, both wanted by Kigali. This was the first time France had taken such action. At the end of the year, their cases were pending before a higher French court for final approval. In addition, criminal trials of Rwandan genocide suspects on the basis of universal jurisdiction took place in other **European national courts** in Germany, Norway, Sweden and the Netherlands, resulting in convictions and prison sentences. In a change from the series of extradition requests by Rwanda that were blocked in 2012, Denmark, Sweden and Norway agreed to extradite genocide suspects to Rwanda.

With the reduction in donor aid, 2013 was the first year in more than a decade that **Kagame** was **not showered with international praise** and awards for his post-genocide leadership. The only award Kagame received all year was granted in May, amidst protests from Rwandans living in Britain. He received the African Growth Award for his commitment to economic growth, which was awarded by a student-led group at the Saïd Business School at Oxford University.

Socioeconomic Developments

The government continued to promote its policy of national unity and reconciliation as the basis of **economic development**. This marked a shift in the government's narrative of social harmony and political development, and was in part driven by the closure of the **gacaca courts** in 2012. The Kagame government repeatedly lauded its achievements in institutional governance, technocratic competence, and continued economic growth. As foreign aid cuts of up to 40% of Rwanda's budget threatened to derail the country's development agenda throughout the year, the government intensified its public commitment to economic growth through the crafting of a **unified Rwandan spirit** as central to Rwanda's journey to **self-reliance**. According to the government, central to an economically self-reliant Rwanda was a unified national identity built on trust and truth. In March, the government introduced the **'Ndi Umunyarwanda' (I am Rwandan)** campaign as part of its programming to mark the 20th anniversary of the genocide in April 2014. Critics accused the government of using the 'Ndi Umunyarwanda' campaign to apportion blame to ethnic Hutu for crimes committed during the 1994 genocide.

In July, the government held its annual conference to mark the 7th anniversary of the **'imhigo'** programme, which was credited with having substantially increased poverty reduction and improved service delivery in rural Rwanda. In a speech to gathered government officials, Local Government Minister James Musoni highlighted the success of the government's **imhigo contracts** programme in **improving rural service delivery**. These performance contracts required local government officials to make commitments directly to President Kagame to meet specific development goals in their bailiwicks in accordance with national policy objectives. Minister Musoni's office regularly removed from their posts government officials who failed to meet their contractual development obligations. Critics noted that, although Rwanda had an impressive service infrastructure, it lacked the necessary human resources to deliver services. For example, **WHO** reported in January that Rwanda only had two doctors per 100,000 people.

On the heels of the proclaimed poverty reduction successes in 2012, the government announced in April a **new agricultural sector strategy** to increase tea production. As part of the strategy, the government opened the Mushubi tea factory, and committed itself to improving roads and increasing electrification to enhance Rwanda's competitiveness in the crowded international tea market. In May, the government began three months of **exploratory geothermal drilling**. If successful, it was estimated that the project would provide 10 MW of clean energy to meet Rwanda's growing but still largely unmet demand for electricity. In August, the World Bank committed $ 340 m to fund a **new hydropower plant** at Rusumo Falls, located on the Rwanda-Tanzania border, to boost the supply of electricity to Rwanda, Tanzania and Burundi. In May, the cabinet endorsed the second Economic Development and Poverty Reduction Strategy (EDPRS II), expected to run from 2013 to 2018. It was centred around four thematic areas: economic transformation, rural development, private sector productivity with a focus on youth employment, and accountable governance. The EDPRS was the first occasion that the government had declared to donors its intention to **generate greater private sector investment** to reduce poverty. A major challenge was that 80% of Rwandans earned a daily average subsistence income of $ 1.50 and were not yet, according to the government, "contributing to economic growth". Analysts predicted that the EDPRS would fall short of its lofty goals for two reasons. First, to fully finance EDPRS II, private sector investment needed to increase from 21% 30% of GDP by 2017. Second, suspended donor aid was not expected to be restored to the level required for full implementation of the Strategy. Despite this lukewarm prognosis, the government had ploughed ahead with strategic economic policies and practices to meet its ambitious poverty reduction goals. In April, Rwanda issued a **$ 400 m Eurobond**, which more than replaced the $ 75 m in lost foreign aid. In July, the government passed a **Minerals Bill**, introducing a transparent legal framework for the sector. Mineral exports accounted on average for 28% of Rwanda's total export earnings (second only to tourism and well ahead of tea and coffee exports). In December, the **IMF** approved a new three-year policy support instrument to facilitate the government's implementation of its EDPRS strategy. The government took the opportunity to chastise its bilateral foreign donors for failing to fully support the EDPRS II.

In June, Finance Minister Gatete presented to parliament a **budget** to the tune of $ 2.6 bn for the **2013–14 fiscal year**. The budget was based on assumptions of increased domestic revenue, notably projected revenue of $ 1.3 bn from private sector investment. The budget also assumed that donor receipts would provide 40% of revenue, which seemed unlikely given the current aid suspensions. Analysts considered the budget to be overly ambitious and aspirational rather than rooted in strong economic fundamentals. They noted in particular the limited capacity of **Rwanda Revenue Authority** staff, and the government's imposition of a new electronic tax filing system. Low levels of technology literacy, limited computer access and sketchy Internet connectivity, particularly in rural areas, would further hamper domestic tax revenue collection. The government was in the midst of rolling out free Wi-Fi access across the country, with the first free spots made available in Kigali in October. In January, the government also instituted a freeze on the hiring of new civil servants to further rein in public spending. The overall **GDP growth rate** experienced a marked slow-down to 4.6% (down from 7.3% in 2012), mainly due to the effects of the foreign aid cuts, lower domestic public spending and poor tea and coffee receipts. The year's average **inflation** rate declined to 4.2% (down from 6.3% in 2012).

Susan Thomson

Seychelles

The domestic political scene was exceptionally calm throughout the year, with no outstanding changes or events. President Michel and his long-ruling Parti Lepep continued in undisputed control of all political affairs. The opposition parties remained weak and showed signs of resignation in view of the sustained popularity of the president and the government, which went to great lengths to maintain a remarkable level of social well-being for the population. No visible progress was achieved on the long contentious issue of electoral reform. On the international stage, Michel pursued his efforts to enhance the recognition of his tiny country and to be seen as a champion of the interests of small island developing states. Economic performance was again quite satisfactory, with another record year for the tourism industry and further moves to liberalise the economy. Five years after the initiation of drastic economic reform measures, Seychelles was praised by international organisations as a role model for successful reform-oriented policies. Despite a significant decline in the threat of Somali pirate activity, the subject continued to attract international attention to Seychelles as an important hub for concerted anti-piracy efforts.

Domestic Politics

As a result of clear victories in the 2011 presidential and parliamentary elections, **President James Michel** and his long-ruling **Parti Lepep (PL**, People's Party) continued to be comfortably in practically undisputed control of all aspects of the political scene. The next elections were not due before 2016. During the year, there were no changes in the composition of the government and no by-elections took place. In the absence of any significant political controversies and as a consequence of the rather subdued activities of opposition parties, 2013 thus turned out to be an exceptionally uneventful year. In January, Michel executed the third phase of a government restructure, which had begun in March 2012 with a reorganisation of the cabinet and government. This third phase only involved a repositioning of various government departments and the appointment of new senior civil servants and parastatal heads.

The composition of the National Assembly, with just a single opposition MP from the **Popular Democratic Movement (PDM)**, tended to give the impression of a *de facto* reversion to the former era of a one-party regime. Michel and the PL leadership were, however, quite keen to avoid this impression and to maintain a conciliatory climate with regard to other political parties and general civil society interests. PDM Chairman David Pierre was recognised as official leader of the opposition in the National Assembly. Michel and Pierre held regular monthly meetings in a cordial atmosphere without much public attention to exchange views on all current issues. Pierre generally refrained from any aggressive confrontation with the government and stressed his understanding of constructive opposition. As a consequence of their 2011 election boycott, the traditionally strongest opposition party, the **Seychelles National Party (SNP)**, and its leader Wavel Ramkalawan remained largely relegated to the role of political bystanders, with no means of exercising any substantial influence on public affairs. Compared with previous years, the SNP was thus restricted to a relatively low level of activity. Many former SNP members had in 2011 dissented over the issue of the election boycott and broken with the party to form the new PDM. In August, the small New Democratic Party (NDP) was dissolved by its leader, Ralph Volcère, simultaneously with his launch of the new **Seselwa United Party (SUP)**. The NDP had been a remnant of the earlier Democratic Party of James Mancham, the country's first president, who was deposed in 1977 by the predecessor of the PL under its leader France Albert René. After a long period in exile, Mancham had for some time assumed the role of a non-partisan elder statesman, representing Seychelles in various international forums. He supported the dissolution of the NDP, allegedly because it had become too aggressive and partisan for his liking. The SUP and SNP leaders pledged to cooperate closely as the main opposition forces. The PL held its 27th congress in May as a matter of routine, with Michel as party president and Vice President Danny Faure as secretary-general.

The controversies between government and opposition had long centred mainly around demands for an unpoliticised public service, an independent judiciary and electoral body, and the liberalisation of the media. Demands for **electoral reform** had been the core issue in the political confrontation in 2011 and failure to meet them had been the key reason for the election boycott. The long overdue report of the **Forum for Electoral Reform** was at last presented to Vice President Faure on 30 July. The Forum, made up of representatives of the five registered political parties and the NGO Citizens Democracy Watch, as well as the five members of the Electoral Commission and a representative of the Attorney General, had been established in late 2011 to consider a road map for generally agreed electoral reforms. A consensus on the desired revisions of relevant electoral laws seemed to have been reached. Only the small Seychelles Freedom Party had walked out of the Forum's deliberations at an earlier stage, making caustic criticisms of the alleged over-compliant attitude of the other parties vis-à-vis the PL. In December, although concrete reviews of election-related laws still remained to be carried out, the National Assembly approved without debate a new **Public Order Act** to replace the highly contentious previous legislation, which had prohibited the holding of any public meetings without explicit police permission. The SNP and SUP leaders were, however, quick to voice their objections to the new Act, claiming that, without any consultation with them, all the recommendations of the Forum for Electoral Reform had been rejected. They intended to challenge the Act in the Constitutional Court.

The year thus ended with renewed disagreement between the PL and key opposition elements over the creation of an enabling fully democratic environment. Political and social life nevertheless remained generally quite harmonious in this tiny island community of barely 90,000 people. On several public occasions, President Michel stressed the sense of unity, patriotism and social cohesion among the population and tried to convey a feeling of pride in the successful execution of the programme of reform and the economic stabilisation of the country.

Foreign Affairs

The Seychellois government continued to pursue the promotion of **active public diplomacy** to raise the visibility of its mini-state on the international stage. Various international forums were used to underline the specific problems of small island states and to raise concern about the inherent dangers of climate change. Seychelles remained an active member, and saw itself as a natural leader, of the group of small developing island states within the UN. The government continued its campaign for Seychelles to be a candidate for a non-permanent seat on the UNSC in 2017, subject to support by the AU.

President **Michel**'s foreign travel activities once again focused on **Asia**. In June, he was in Japan to attend the 5th Tokyo International Conference for African Development, in August he undertook an official state visit to Vietnam, and in November he attended the Commonwealth summit in Sri Lanka. An official visit to Réunion in July was intended to intensify the cooperation with this French territory in the sub-regional neighbourhood. Vice President **Faure** represented the country at a number of high-level international meetings, such as the UN General Assembly, AU summits, the 3rd African-Arab summit in Kuwait (November) and the Paris conference on African peace and security

(December). The most important visitors to Seychelles during the year were Nkosazana Dlamini-Zuma, the chairperson of the AU Commission, in June, and Sri Lanka's President Mahinda Rajapaksa, who made a state visit in July that focused on enhanced cooperation in the Indian Ocean area. A colourful India Week in October, with several Indian stars of show business as high-profile guests, underscored the importance of close political and economic relations with this major regional power. A reciprocal visa waiver agreement with China became effective in June, which was indicative for the fast-growing importance of Chinese tourists and business interests.

A minor **diplomatic problem** arose when Sakhr el-Materi, the convicted son-in-law of Tunisia's deposed former dictator, Ben Ali, asked for political asylum in February and **Tunisia** subsequently demanded his extradition. After some hesitation, he was granted a one-year residence permit, but not asylum. In July, the government vehemently rejected as inaccurate an official US report that placed Seychelles on a watch list in connection with suspicions of being implicated in people trafficking.

In mid-January, the 28th ministerial council meeting of the **IOC** was held in Victoria, opened with a speech by Michel that commemorated the 30th anniversary of the founding of this sub-regional institution. Seychelles had held the rotating presidency since October 2011 and now handed it over to Comoros.

Despite a significant further general decline of **Somali pirate activity** in the Indian Ocean, this problem remained at the centre of Seychelles' most pertinent foreign policy concerns. The country's geographic location had made it a strategic hub for many international anti-piracy operations, whose participants used Victoria as a convenient port of call and supply base between their periods of patrol at sea. Global concern about the dangers of Somali piracy had led to far more international focus on Seychelles than was commensurate with its size. On 25 February, a new UK-funded regional anti-piracy coordination centre was opened by Michel and the British junior minister for maritime security. Seychelles continued to be praised internationally for its role in prosecuting apprehended pirates, since other countries in the sub-region were not willing or able to undertake this important task. This had become a heavy burden for the small country, stretching its prison capacity to the limit. In October, a further eleven Somali pirates were convicted by the Seychelles Supreme Court and sentenced to prison terms of up to 16 years. At the same time, six previously convicted pirates were repatriated to Puntland to serve their prison terms there. This was a welcome relief for the Seychelles and also reflected growing confidence in the improving situation in Somalia.

Socioeconomic Developments

The Seychellois economy continued to show remarkable resilience in the face of prolonged global uncertainties. The general **macroeconomic performance** again turned out to be quite satisfactory with a small acceleration in the growth rate and a deceleration of inflation. The government proudly celebrated five years of its successful programme of reform, which had been introduced in late 2008 as a kind of shock treatment to ward off the near-collapse of the unsustainably indebted and heavily welfare-oriented economy. This change of policy orientation towards a liberal market outlook and an investor-friendly climate had since then stabilised the situation to a remarkable extent, while safeguards for the social sectors continued to be maintained. The adjustment process had thus been socially less painful than had originally been anticipated. In the 2013 **HDI**, Seychelles was ranked 46th in the very high human development category, by far the highest of any African country. This also reflected the well-balanced attainment of both economic and social goals. In the World Economic Forum's Global Competiveness Index for 2013–14 Seychelles was ranked 80th (out of 148) and fifth among SSA countries. The World Bank's Doing Business Report 2014 showed the country in 80th position (down six places), and sixth in SSA. With an annual per capita income of about $ 25,000 (PPP), Seychelles was clearly in a different league from most of the rest of Africa. All MDGs were largely achieved.

Recovering from the previous year's slump, the **GDP growth rate** accelerated somewhat to an estimated 3.5% (compared with 2.9% in 2012 and 5% in 2011). Consumer price **inflation** was brought down to an annual average of 4.5%, compared with 7.1% in 2012. On 1 January, a new 15% VAT (replacing the goods and services tax) was introduced, which had been postponed in 2012 for fear of further fuelling the then prevailing inflationary trend. The Seychelles rupee (SR) strengthened considerably during the year, largely as a result of further increased receipts from tourism. The average annual exchange rate was calculated at about SR 12.1 per $ (compared with 13.7 in 2012); during the first half of the year it had even been below SR 12 per $. Foreign exchange reserves continued to grow considerably to $ 425 m in December, equivalent to a comfortable 4.3 months' import coverage (compared with just two weeks' in late 2008). The structural deficit of the tiny import-dependent island's **balance of trade** hardly changed, however, with imports amounting to almost double the value of exports; about half the latter was accounted for by tuna fish and most of the rest by oil re-exports. The (provisional) **current-account deficit** was lowered from a revised 27% of GDP in 2012 to about 22.6%, with good prospects for further improvements in the coming years, mainly due to growing service sector receipts. The key **tourism sector** had another excellent year and had a major impact on the stabilisation of the economy, contributing more than a quarter of GDP. Visitor numbers increased by 10.6% to a new record of 230,000; while the traditional European markets showed a good recovery, new markets (China, Russia, Arab countries) also continued to provide growing tourist numbers. Total tourism earnings were projected to have risen by 11%. With FDI inflows also remaining buoyant (mainly for tourism projects), closing the current-account deficit was thus easily achieved. Despite a remarkable unemployment rate of less than 4%, fears were occasionally expressed of alleged competition from growing numbers of Asian workers for local jobs (mainly on construction sites). This was largely the result of a mismatch between locally available skills and unreasonable expectations. Some rise of xenophobic sentiments also stemmed from the many land and luxury real estate purchases by Arab and Russian investors.

The government successfully continued a policy of **strict fiscal discipline** in pursuance of its goal to gradually redress the huge debt that had been accumulated during the René era of welfare-oriented socialist policies. For the sixth consecutive year, an overall **budget surplus** of an estimated 1% of GDP was achieved. The primary fiscal surplus (excluding interest payments) was equivalent to 5.2% of GDP, about 1% lower than in 2012. The total **public debt** was further reduced to 71.6% of GDP (compared with 124% at end-2009), consistent with the strictly pursued target for 2018 set at a sustainable 50%. External debt was down to 43% of GDP, a strong decline from 90% in 2008. The restructuring of past external debts had largely been completed. In recognition of the government's remarkable efforts, Fitch again maintained its three-year-old good B **credit rating** for Seychelles, with a positive outlook.

IMF missions in February and October conducted the seventh and eight reviews of the government performance under the $ 31 m three-year Extended Fund Facility (EFF) arranged in December 2009 and extended in 2012 by $ 10 m and one year to December 2013. All performance criteria were found to have been met, while items on the broader reform agenda, such as tax reforms and further privatisations of parastatal enterprises, were also considered to be well underway. The EFF-supported economic programme had clearly met its goals of placing the economy firmly on the path to external and fiscal sustainability. Structural reforms had helped to raise the economic performance and address important macroeconomic risks.

Both the AfDB and the World Bank provided new loans for modernising the business environment and promoting **private-sector development**. A local stock exchange was opened in August, with initially only one listing by the State Assurance Corporation. This was another small step with respect to the intended **privatisation** or successful commercialisation of publicly-owned enterprises, whose realisation had remained slow. The creation of a new Public Enterprise Monitoring Commission was expected to increase attention to this issue. The national airline, **Air Seychelles**, after concluding a strategic partnership with Etihad Airways in early 2012, managed to nearly double its passenger numbers and to end years of loss-making. It stopped all flights to Europe and concentrated on regional destinations. The Seychelles Petroleum Company continued to incur heavy losses in the operation of its fleet of five tankers, and the conversion of the Public Utilities Company into a commercially viable enterprise also remained problematic. The mid-2012 arrival of a submarine **fibre-optic cable** had provided a boost for services of the financial and IT sectors. The government pledged to contribute actively to transparency on matters of international financial services and taxation, but it remained under the suspicious scrutiny of the OECD. Although not blacklisted, Seychelles was found still not to be in full compliance with all OECD demands. About 30 companies were offering services to the **offshore financial sector**, where an estimated total 120,000 companies were registered. With the conclusion of several bilateral trade agreements, further progress was made in respect of the long-awaited accession to the **WTO**, now expected to be achievable in 2014.

Prospects for possible **oil** or **gas** finds in the Seychelles' extensive maritime zone suffered a temporary setback when expected exploration activities were delayed due to the withdrawal of a potential partner company. New relevant legislation was completed by the government to create a situation where it was feasible to invite foreign companies to undertake oil exploration. Seychelles and Mauritius planned to establish an authority for joint hydrocarbon exploration in their 396,000 km^2 area of the continental shelf. A new **fisheries agreement** with the EU was signed in November, which would bring in € 30 m over a period of six years. The local **fishery sector**, the second pillar of the economy after tourism, experienced substantial improvement with the almost complete disappearance of threats by Somali pirates. The government repeatedly promoted its concept of the specific values of a 'blue economy' and regarded this as a fundamental characteristic of an island state.

Rolf Hofmeier

Somalia

Somalia continued to struggle with two main problems: the violent Islamist insurgent movement al-Shabaab, still in control of large chunks of the interior and destabilising the country, and the task of establishing a credible national administration with a nationwide programme for economic and social recovery. In both fields, results were mixed and precarious. African peacekeeping troops remained essential in assisting the new Somali Federal Government (SFG) in Mogadishu to reclaim south-central Somalia from al-Shabaab and helped the government to gradually expand its territory. The overall security situation, especially in the south, only improved marginally. Al-Shabaab still held on to the coastal town of Baraawe and some other minor towns in the interior, and its terror attacks created numerous victims. US special forces kept up operations to neutralise the al-Shabaab leadership, but its main leader, Ahmed Abdi Godane, was not caught. With regard to political and institutional developments, the SFG could not assert its own authority and was heavily dependent on donor countries and the various specialist organisations and agencies of the UN. They were deeply involved in providing the SFG with logistical, financial and political support and training in all fields. Economically, Somalia showed some recovery across the board, with more Somali diaspora investment, remittances and returnees. Donor support for the government remained strong, but problems of maladministration and corruption were a continuing hindrance.

The distinct parts of Somalia, apart from south-central, which was divided between the federal government and al-Shabaab, were Puntland, Somaliland and Jubaland, which reaffirmed their autonomous status. Centrifugal tendencies towards additional autonomous regions were strong (e.g., Galmudug, Himan-Heeb, and Southwest State in the Rahanweyn area). Jubaland installed a new president, supported by Kenya. No tangible progress was thus made in 'restoring' a unified Somalia.

The international engagement of donor countries and the UN with Somalia, while strong and confirmed during several international donor conferences, could not decisively impact on the formation of an effective and credible federal government The SFG was hampered by factional interest struggles, shaky legitimacy, military weakness and lack of capacity and political unity.

Domestic Politics

Somalia, with some 10.4 m inhabitants, remained a volatile and insecure environment, both politically and economically, divided between various regional governments, a fledgling federal army, clan and local militias, and insurgent groups, but it saw a gradual movement toward more stability in comparison with previous years.

The new **Somali Federal Government (SFG)** in Mogadishu, installed in 2012, **slowly expanded its power** and made some modest headway with policy-making and institution-building. Among its tasks was to develop the provisional constitutional order and organise the first nation-wide elections in 2016. The Upper House of the bicameral federal parliament, as foreseen in the 2012 Provisional Constitution, was not yet formed. Despite political progress and a new spirit of hope, the expectations of the international community were over-extended, as the **SFG did not deliver decisive breakthroughs** and remained caught in webs of clan politics, economic favouritism and administrative ineffectiveness that hindered the solid extension of its writ across south-central Somalia. **SFG President Hassan Sheikh Mohamud** (from the Hawiye/Abgal/Wa'eysle subclan) emphasised his 'Six Pillar' strategy (stability, economic recovery, peace building, service delivery, international relations, and national unity), but results were not too impressive. Not all targets cold be pursued simultaneously and some contradicted each other. The mere fact that the SFG was dependent on the more than 17,700 troops of the AU Mission in Somalia (AMISOM) was enough indication of its political-military weakness. SFG and AMISOM forces together greatly outnumbered the al-Shabaab militants, but still could not recover all of Somali territory. Donor countries recognised the new SFG and very much wanted it to succeed, but they kept expressing *sub voce* **complaints about disappearing funds, corruption, political divisions, and slow progress with building effective and reliable army and police forces.** Observers also saw too much influence on the SFG leadership from the 'Damul Jadid' ('New Blood') faction of the al-Islah movement, a non-elected interest group.

Despite progress, the political order thus remained insecure due to the provisional nature of the 2012 constitution, weak party formation, clientelism, and the divisiveness of clan politics. A bad sign was the **resignation of Yussur Abrar as Central Bank Governor after only seven weeks** in the job, due to what she called "the government's double-dealing behaviour", which had damaged the international community's trust in the SFG and put the 'Six Pillar' new deal in jeopardy. The judgement of the EU's Catherine Ashton on 11 February that Somalia "was no longer a failed state" was premature, as indicated by a UN report that accused the new Central Bank governor, Abdisalam Omer, of being at the centre of misappropriating state assets.

Mohamud followed several of his predecessors in frequently **disagreeing over policy with his prime minister**. On 12 December, Prime Minister Abdi Farah Shirdoon was voted out of office because of alleged corruption, personal loyalties and 'clan politics', but more likely because of constitutional disagreements with the president, i.e. the latter perceiving that he was losing power to the prime minister. But Shirdoon could point to achievements, e.g., a growth in monthly government revenues (from $ 2.5 m to $ 10 m over the year up to December), new laws on foreign investment, advances in education, civil aviation and counter-terrorism, and the appointment of a human rights task force. Shirdoon was replaced by Abdiweli Sheikh Ahmed (also from the Marehan-Darod clan).

A persistent SFG problem was the lack of unity and professionalism in the **Somali federal army**, which was being trained with the help of foreign funds and programmes but continued to show internal divisions based on clan identity, opportunism and a high rate of attrition (due to low pay, for example). Some soldiers left after training, or even joined the **al-Shabaab insurgents** and sold equipment to them. The federal army was also regularly accused of abuse and extrajudicial killings.

Two detailed reports by the **UN Monitoring Group on Somalia and Eritrea** further showed that the SFG remained divided by clan loyalties and interest groups, some of which were connected to several **'spoiler networks'** extending to al-Shabaab and former warlord businessmen. The report also gave evidence of Eritrea trying to obtain control of political agents close to the Somali presidency. One "Eritrean agent of influence" was Abdi Nur Siad Abdi Wal, a 'warlord' also reported to have a close relationship with a senior al-Shabaab commander. Another was Mohamed Wali Sheikh Ahmed Nuur, a political coordinator for al-Shabaab and recipient of funds from Eritrea. These spoiler networks and their activities, including the re-emergence of some former warlords, endangered the legitimacy and effectiveness of the SFG. This revealed the perennial challenge to establish effective governance and rule of law in a country where any state authority was inherently distrusted and conflicts were deep-rooted.

Press and media freedoms were precarious throughout Somalia, and deteriorated in Puntland and Somaliland, where some backlash against independent journalists was seen. New private radio stations were not allowed a license. South-central Somalia retained its reputation as one of the most dangerous places for media people to work. Despite vibrant and dynamic journalistic activity in Somalia, with journalists showing remarkable courage, the Reporters Without Borders 2013 report named Somalia as one of the five worst countries in the world for press freedom.

The challenge from the **'Harakat al-Shabaab al-Mujhahideen' (al-Shabaab)**, the uncompromising violent Islamist movement seeking to establish a Muslim state in Somalia and beyond, remained the country's key problem. Although their political 'ideals' were not shared by many Somalis, they still had some adherents – forced or voluntary – in several areas, especially where they had inserted themselves in the structure of clan relations and mediated in local resource conflicts. The movement was weakened, however, with respect to its hold on territory. During the year, the towns of Aw-Dheegle, Jannale, Barrire, Dardan, Jirada-Kullow, Mahadeey, Biyo Adde, Mubarak, Ugunji, Nuun and Furuqley and several rural areas were captured by the SFG and AMISOM troops. On 22 February, government forces also captured the airfield of Jowhar. Al-Shabaab held on to the port city of Baraawe.

Apart from the loss of local support, there were also continued **internal disagreements among the al-Shabaab leadership**. This internal dissent led its main leader, Ahmed Abdi Godane, to try to monopolise control and further push his violent Islamist agenda. In June, he used al-Shabaab's internal 'security' unit (the 'Amniyat') to kill his rivals Ibrahim H. Jama 'al Afghani', leading commander Abdihamid H. Olhaye, and al-Shabaab's chief youth recruiter, Moallim Burhaan. On 12 September, the notorious American-born jihadist Omar Hammani was reported killed by al-Shabaab members, apparently on Godane's orders.

The long-time Hizbul Islam and al-Shabaab member Hassan Dahir 'Aweys', a veteran hard-core Islamist, also began to oppose Godane, and he escaped assassination when he surrendered on 25 June to the authorities in Himan-Heeb Region in north-central Somalia. He was later transferred to Mogadishu, where he became somewhat of an embarrassment to the SFG authorities because he was no longer seen as having anything to offer. Aweys, however, still had some followers among militias in the capital dominated by members of his sub-clan (Hawiye/Habr Gidir/Ayr). This may have been one reason why the government – surprisingly – did not start legal action against him, despite his record of sabotage and violence warranting immediate prosecution. The last important opponent of Godane within al-Shabaab, Mukhtar Robow (Rahanweyn/Leysan clan), retreated to his clan's home area in southern Bay-Bakool and resisted an attack by Godane's forces on 3 August.

Al-Shabaab's weakening, however, did not mean that it was a spent force. In the interior it continued to 'rule', using intimidation and draconian measures to subdue the population, despite people showing mounting resentment against the movement. It still had some support in various rural areas that opposed the federal government and were without a social and educational infrastructure. Al-Shabaab cadres arbitrated in local conflicts on the basis of their version of Sharia law, but the constant harassing of youths and others with strict Islamic rules and regulations led to unrest and flight on a regular basis. Al-Shabaab members roamed the streets to round up anyone not abiding by the group's strict dress code, harassing people using cell phones or television sets, playing football and listening to or playing music. The movement also abducted children for recruitment as fighters, arbitrarily confiscated livestock and arrested or kidnapped local elders of communities when people refused to cooperate in "helping the Muslim troops engaged in jihad". This happened for instance in November, in the El Bur area. Al-Shabaab also maintained its propaganda on Internet sites and Facebook and Twitter accounts.

In its terrorist-military actions, **al-Shabaab** continued to rely on **hit-and-run attacks throughout southern Somalia**, targeting opponents ranging from SFG soldiers and employees to teachers, aid and NGO personnel, journalists, students and women's groups. The movement carried out such attacks almost weekly, thus steadily extending its appalling criminal record and undermining its appeal among the Somali populace. On 14 April, its militants targeted Mogadishu's main courthouse, using multiple suicide bombings, and killing at least 29 people. On May 5, al-Shabaab militants bombed the Maka al-Mukarama hotel in Mogadishu, popular with government officials and businessmen, and several people were seriously wounded. The same hotel was attacked again on 8 November, this time resulting in six people killed and 20 injured. Al-Shabaab gunmen also made an assault on the UNDP office in Mogadishu on 19 June, when a suicide bomber detonated a car bomb at the gate. On 19 November, an al-Shabaab attack on a Beledweyn police station killed 18 people (officers and civilians) and injured at least 11. Ten militants were also killed. The attack drew widespread condemnation, including from UN Secretary-General Ban Ki-moon. On 24 and 30 November, they assassinated judges, and on 6 December a federal MP was killed. On 27 December, in a grenade attack on a teashop in Mogadishu's Daynile district, at least 11 people were killed and 15 wounded.

The **worst Islamist terror attack**, however, was on 21 September in the **Westgate shopping mall in Nairobi** (Kenya), an action well-prepared and carried out by young Islamists from the US and European Somali diasporas, orchestrated by al-Shabaab but coordinated by the radical al- Hijra Islamists from Kenya. It lasted four days. The attack, allegedly 'in response' to the Kenyan army presence in Somalia, was horrific in the number of killed (at least 68) and wounded (more than 100) and the ruthlessness of the attack, with the torture and summary execution of mall visitors carried out without hesitation. Al-Shabaab and al-Hijra here made use of the weak local surveillance and organisational structure of Kenya's security and police forces. The attack drew global condemnation but al-Shabaab boasted of the attack in its online magazine 'Gaidi Mtaani' on 12 November. On 31 October, Kenyan Defence Forces destroyed an al-Shabaab camp in Hurguun (Dinsoor District), a location where some of the Westgate mall attackers had been trained. Vehicles and a weapons store were destroyed and an estimated 300 al-Shabaab recruits present were killed or injured.

The USA kept a covert presence in Somalia, as evident in a 28 October drone strike on a vehicle near Jilib in Lower Shabelle, which killed two senior al-Shabaab members: Warsame Balle and Ibrahim Ali Abdi, the latter an explosives specialist. More foreign presence in Somalia was evident from a botched French covert mission on 11 January to liberate French hostage Denis Allex (an intelligence officer held since 2009) in Bulo Marer. The mission by French forces failed and al-Shabaab fighters reportedly killed Allex and two French soldiers.

Apart from al-Shabaab terror, there were also **other security problems**, including regular conflicts between (sub-)clan groups about boundaries and land and water issues. Federal and regional authorities regularly tried to mediate in these conflicts to avert or end 'blood feuds', as, for example, on 2 December in Lamaweyn village (Galgudud region), and on 11 November in Ba'adweyne and Amara villages (Muduug region). One of the basic unresolved problems facing the federal government was how to create credible and working administrative, fiscal and judicial structures in the areas that it took over from al-Shabaab, where it showed lack of capacity and policy consistency.

While the **three Somali territories continued their autonomous existence** (and were even joined by a fourth – Jubaland in the South), there were talks in Ankara (Turkey) on 13 April between Somaliland and the SFG on security cooperation, bilateral relations and possible options for the future. They signed a seven-point agreement. Mohamud mentioned 'national unity' as one of his priorities, but the chances of this remained slim. In view of its relatively good record of autonomous development, Somaliland was not inclined to make any haste with this option. Political life in the separate Somali territories proceeded along the lines of local autonomy, with **Somaliland** (ca. 3.5 m inhabitants) being most independent of any developments elsewhere. No progress was made in its gaining international recognition.

Local elections in **Puntland** (3 m inhabitants) scheduled for July were cancelled and delayed until 2014 due to disagreements over the constitutional process and party registration and doubts about a fair and transparent electoral process. President Abdirahman Mohamed 'Farole' (Darod/Majerten/Isse Mohamud clan), in his fourth year in power and pointing to his relatively good record in office, announced his intention to extend his presidential term by one year until new presidential elections scheduled for January 2014. Within Puntland, the **Khatumo** region (predominantly a Dhulbahante-clan area) asserted its autonomous status, but there were armed clashes between Puntland forces and residents of Khatumo in Taleh (capital of Khatumo), in which between ten and 13 people were reported killed. Also in Puntland, al-Shabaab loyalists led by Mohamed Said Atom and Abduqadir Mumin remained in place in the Galgala and Golis mountains, from where the state's military could not dislodge them. On 5 June, however, the head of al-Shabaab in Puntland, Abdikafi Mohamed Ali, was captured in Bossaso. The general security situation in Puntland deteriorated somewhat, despite the further build-up of the Puntland army, a ban on carrying arms in public, and institution building. There were several terror attacks: on 5 December a suicide car bomber targeted Puntland government forces near a busy intersection at a densely populated market place in Bossaso, killing seven and injuring 37. On 28 November, there was a militia attack on Vice President Abdisamad Ali Shire's security escort in Taleh District (Khatumo), and eight people were killed and several wounded. The dispute between Somaliland and Puntland on the contested **Sanaag-Sool-Ayn region** was not resolved. On 5 August, Puntland cut all relations with the SFG, accusing it of undermining the federal constitution, ignoring 'national reconciliation' efforts and not fairly sharing international aid money.

On 15 May, the autonomous southern region of '**Jubaland**', during a conference in Kismayo of about 500 (male) elders and local leaders, elected as its first 'president' Ahmed Mohammed 'Madobe' (Darod/Ogadeni clan), a former Islamist warlord, who since 2012 had been a key ally of the Kenyan military. He was supported by his Ras Kamboni militia. The autonomy of Jubaland was not recognised by the SFG. On the same day, the former Somali defence minister and ex-warlord Barre Adan Shire 'Hirale' (from a rivalling Marehan-Darod clan), at a separate conference also declared himself president of Jubaland. He was supported by Ethiopia. On 4 July, armed clashes between the forces of these two rivals erupted in the Kismayo area, resulting in 70 dead and over 300 injured. Both the SFG and even IGAD subsequently tried to mediate between the competing groups, but the underlying conflicts remained, with Madobe apparently getting the upper hand.

Foreign Affairs

Somalia's problems engaged a large range of **international actors** interested in securing stability and growth as well as regional peace: the UN, international donors, Turkey, IGAD and others were involved. **Troops** from **Kenya, Djibouti and Ethiopia** stayed on in the country and were brought under the nominal command of AMISOM. Kenya favoured the establishment of a pro-Kenyan local government in Kismayo, the 'Jubaland' capital, while Ethiopia kept its control of the border areas north of Baidoa. On 23 April, Kenya announced that it would gradually withdraw from Somalia, to be replaced by SFG and AMISOM troops, but revised this decision on 4 October after the Westgate Mall attack in Nairobi.

The SFG worked hard to improve its international profile and firmed up links with the donor community (organised in the Somalia Donor Group). Mohamud made a large number of foreign trips to showcase the 'new Somalia' and garner economic and financial support for his government and also visited Puntland on 28–29 April. The **foreign diplomatic presence** in Somalia itself was very **limited** (only seven embassies), but Iran and the UK opened embassies in Mogadishu during the year. Italy maintained a special diplomatic delegation and a Technical Mission to Mogadishu and announced that it would re-open its embassy, as did Egypt.

A second **London conference** (after one in 2012) on Somalia was organised on 7 May, and led to pledges of $ 300 m in expertise and funding support for the SFG, notably for its plans for security, justice and public financial management. Somaliland and Puntland leaders were not present at this event, however. Another **international donor conference on Somalia** was held in **Brussels** under EU auspices on 16 September, with the aim of establishing a 'new deal', with aid pledges of some $ 1.8 bn over three years and support for the SFG's political and administrative reforms. But perceptions were that the results of this latest effort at helping the failed state of Somalia would not be guaranteed.

On 12 November, the **UNSC extended the AMISOM mandate** to 31 October 2014 and authorised a **force increase from 17,731 to 22,126 troops**. AMISOM consisted of troops from Burundi, Djibouti, Ethiopia, Kenya and Uganda and was early in the year augmented by a contingent from Sierra Leone that had been expected for some time. However, this force was not without its problems, as evidence was produced of corruption within the Ugandan contingent and even of the sale of weapons to Somali arms traders on the Bakaraaha market and thereby indirectly to al-Shabaab. Following revelations, 24 officers were recalled or suspended, including Uganda's contingent commander Brig. Michael Ondoga.

Somali leaders made several **foreign visits**, Mohamud topping the list with numerous trips abroad, e.g., to Uganda, Kenya, London, Brussels, Ankara and the US. In Washington on 16–18 January, the Obama administration announced its recognition of the new Somali federal government, a prelude to restoring diplomatic relations. The president also attended the AU summit in Addis Ababa on 26 May, and met with Kenyan President Uhuru Kenyatta on 27 April for talks facilitated by IGAD.

Somaliland continued to be stonewalled by the international community in its quest for full international recognition, despite its relatively good record – certainly compared with the rest of Somalia – of (self-generated) political and economic development. But its 'limbo' status endangered stability and economic progress. Somaliland President Ahmed Mahamud 'Silanyo' visited Abu Dhabi, UAE, in March for business talks, and met the British government in London on 11 February. He was in the US (State Department and USAID) in April and met Ethiopian leaders in Addis Ababa and Jijiga on 3–4 May. He also met with Mohamud on 13 April in Ankara for talks on the future of Somalia.

Puntland's President Abdirahman Farole visited Djibouti in January, made a month-long trip to Kenya, Australia, and the UAE in June–July, and attended the 3rd International Counter-Piracy Conference held on 11–12 September in Dubai.

Socioeconomic Developments

Under conditions of insecurity and lack of regulations, the **Somali economy expanded slowly**, driven primarily by private informal activities and growing investments from both diaspora Somalis and a substantial influx of donor funding. Donor support was confirmed at two major conferences in May in London and Brussels in September. Economic data and statistics were poor in quality, showed discrepancies, and had a serious time lag, making estimates inevitable.

Somalia experienced an estimated **GDP growth rate** of 2.5%, with an annual per capita income of about $ 600, giving a total aggregate GDP of some $ 2.5 bn. Somaliland's GDP was estimated at $ 1.5 bn and per capita income at some $ 360. One third of GDP was derived from the livestock industry, 20% from wholesale and retail trade, 8% from crops and 6% from real estate activities. Somaliland's trade deficit was ca. $ 500 m, financed through a combination of remittances and external aid. Levels of investment were low, as was the employment-to-population ratio (est. 30% for males and 17% for females). For Puntland, no GDP figures were available.

The **SFG budget** was $ 151 m, including $ 31 m specially earmarked for social services and $ 11 m for the security forces. **Puntland's budget** was $ 41.1 m, of which 70% was procured from taxes on import-export business. **Somaliland's budget** reached $ 125 m, a 17% increase compared with 2012, with priority focus given to security services, the health and education sectors, and road-building.

Somalia earned about $ 520 m from **exports**, consisting of agrarian products such as bananas and sesame seeds, livestock sales (cattle, sheep, goats), and hides. The fishing industry also brought in revenue. Charcoal, mostly produced in an unregulated manner and depleting the remaining forest/bush areas, also brought in foreign currency, although trade in charcoal was officially banned by a UNSC resolution. Exports, e.g. from Kismayo, went predominantly (83%) to the Gulf States, Yemen and Oman. Contraband trade was rampant, including that of wildlife products such as ivory, most of it poached by al-Shabaab, bringing an estimated yearly revenue of $ 5 m.

The **service sectors**, especially privately owned **mobile telecom and ICT companies**, continued to expand. Urban renewal and economic investment was again visible, notably in Mogadishu, where Mayor Mohamud Ahmed Nur 'Tarsan' led an ambitious programme of socio-economic and infrastructural improvement.

Somalia was known to have oil deposits, as well as a demonstrated reserve of 5.6 bn m^3 of **natural gas**, all of which remained **unexploited**. The country thus depended on the import of virtually all of its fuel (oil). In April, Somaliland issued **oil exploration rights** to Norway's DNO International, a company allied to RAK Petroleum of the UAE. The SFG also gave new exploration concessions to foreign oil companies (the UK's Soma Oil & Gas) and Puntland, in sometimes disputed border areas.

Somalia received a total **international aid package** of about $ 850 m. Some $ 120 m of FDI was also registered. But topping all was income to the tune of $ 1.3 bn, equal to the 2012 volume, from overseas **remittances** sent by the estimated **1.2 million overseas Somalis**. The Dahabshiil money transfer company was the main channel, with nearly 300 branches across the Somali territories. A crucial setback for Dahabshiil, and for three other Somali money transfer companies, was the closure as of 10 July of its bank accounts for remittances hosted by the UK's Barclays Bank, under pressure to monitor money laundering and criminal financing of Somali cash flows, e.g. via Dubai. While the closure deadlines were extended several times, at year's end no solution was yet in sight. Within Somalia, these money transfer companies remained essential as an economic lifeline for at least 40% of the population. They had also started to offer new services such as debit cards (initially only in Hargeisa), deposit accounts, and loans to small businesses.

Piracy in Somali waters declined dramatically during the year, with only seven incidents recorded, down from 160 attacks in 2011. However, 77 vessels and seven hostages were still being held for ransom by pirates. The reduced number of incidents reflected the success of naval forces using new spotting techniques and preventive action by commercial ship-owners, but also domestic Somali and Puntland actions against pirate vessels and on-land pirate bases. A growing social rejection of piracy, increased domestic stability and some alternative economic avenues for male youths probably also had an effect. For example, Puntland invested in several new economic facilities, among them a new fish market, built with funds from the UK and the UNDP, in Garowe. It opened on 22 April. Similar marketplaces were to be launched in Galkayo and Qardho. But some pirate networks remained active and moved into other businesses.

On 10 November, a **tropical cyclone** hit Puntland's coast. It killed more than 100 people and devastated livestock and the livelihoods of hundreds of families. President Farole visited the area and promised aid to the victims.

Social conditions were marked by insecurity and violence, with everyday problems of crime, most prominently including theft, extortion, robbery, assault, and sexual violence against women, the latter described in an Amnesty International report as an "ongoing epidemic". Government authorities were not seen to be developing policies to tackle it. Social security networks (family and clan-based) were under great stress due to poverty, conflict and internal upheaval and migration. Thousands of Somalis (and Ethiopians) traversing Puntland again tried to cross the Red Sea to reach Yemen, Saudi Arabia or the Gulf States, despite high risks and a policy of discouragement by the authorities.

The overall **literacy rate** was estimated to be 38% and, while the **educational system** was in the process of being expanded, it was not able to reach all children. In Somaliland about 50% of 6–13-years-olds attended primary school, the highest rate in Somalia. Overall secondary school attendance was no more than 12%–13%. Private universities continued to expand, however, including in Somaliland, Puntland and Mogadishu, and led to unemployment problems among graduates in a non-absorptive job market.

Health indicators remained among the worst in Africa, with life expectancy estimated at 49.7 years. Infant and child mortality rates stood at 108.4 and 178 per 1,000 live births, respectively (against the Africa average of 84 and 135). The maternal mortality rate was 1,400 per 100,000 live births (compared with 683 for Africa), but the population growth rate was 2.8% per annum.

Environmental concerns or consciousness had little priority, as evident in the deleterious effects of charcoal burning, wildlife poaching, pollution, and depletion of natural species, but, on 23 October, Puntland launched a three-year 'Environmental Protection Campaign', funded by the EU, to be assisted by local aid agencies and civil society groups.

In the wake of armed conflicts, clan-group tensions, and the famines of recent years, about 900,000 to 1.13 m Somalis were still **IDPs**. The Consolidated Appeal by the UN Office for the Coordination of Humanitarian Affairs for humanitarian aid to Somalia in 2013 reached a staggering $ 1.33 bn, showing that a solution to Somalia's problems was not in sight.

Jon Abbink

South Sudan

The year proved something of a roller coaster. There were initial hopes for an economic recovery when agreement with Sudan allowed the re-opening of the vital oil pipelines to the Red Sea, which South Sudan had closed in 2012. However, simultaneously there was a political deterioration at the top of the ruling Sudan People's Liberation Movement (SPLM), which led to the year ending in confusion and conflict, with hundreds killed in a wave of ethnic violence that threatened the survival of the state just two years after its independence from Sudan. And with the violence came uncertainty about the security of existing and future oil exports, on which the economy was almost entirely dependent.

Domestic Politics

The **major political crisis** that hit the country in **December** was brewing over the course of the year. Relations between **President Salva Kiir** and **Vice President Riek Machar** had always been central to the newly independent state established in 2011, and were known to have potential problems. Kiir had been a Sudan People's Liberation Army (SPLA) loyalist from the early days of the liberation war back in 1983: he had been number two to its leader John Garang, and he was his undisputed successor when the latter was killed in a helicopter crash in 2005. In contrast, Machar had led a breakaway group in the SPLA in 1991, going against Garang's allegedly autocratic leadership, and in 1997 had tried to make his own peace deal with the Sudan government known as the Khartoum Peace Agreement. By early 2013, it was clear that Machar had retained both his criticism of autocratic tendencies in the SPLM government under Kiir and his own personal ambitions. Nor was he alone, for other leading SPLM figures, including Secretary General Pagun Amum, were showing growing discontent with Kiir's leadership. Clearly there was a potential split in the ruling party, which was to emerge and widen as the year went on. The first major public sign came in April, when Kiir restricted Machar's role as vice president, while the latter began to talk openly of challenging Kiir in the presidential election scheduled for 2015. Two months later, Kiir sacked Machar and then went on to replace him as vice president with James Wani Igga. Machar outwardly took his sacking very calmly, but he also made it clear that his ambitions were not diminished.

In July, **Kiir** summarily **dismissed his cabinet**, and then went on to announce further sweeping changes to the structure of the government, including cutting the number of ministries. But at the same time there was also something of a clear out of those whose loyalty he suspected, including Pagan Amum. There were also promotions for more trusted figures, including Kuol Manyang, who was made minister of defence, Aleu Ayieny Aleu, appointed as minister of interior, and Barnaba Marial as minister of foreign affairs. In November, it was the turn of the **SPLM leadership** itself to be **dissolved**, except for the secretariat at national and state levels, amidst speculation that Machar and his supporters were seeking to stir up the local membership throughout the country. The delayed National Liberation Council of the newly purged SPLM was just beginning in December when the crisis erupted, with some reports suggesting that the ousted Machar had tried unsuccessfully to gatecrash its opening. At the same time, there were reports of growing ethnic tensions in a number of areas, with some seeing the Dinka as threatening to take over the country and referring to a growing 'Dinkaocracy' (a charge earlier levelled against the first South Sudan government in the 1970s). In particular, while Kiir came from the Dinka, the largest ethnic group in South Sudan, Machar was the leading figure of the Nuer, often seen traditional rivals.

Matters came to a head on **15 December**, when **fierce fighting broke out** apparently amongst the presidential guard in the capital, Juba. There was an irony here, for, in an effort to reduce the risk of ethnic conflict within the SPLA, the guard had been trying to integrate different groups as part of the strengthening of a national army. But when fighting broke out it appeared to be started by clashes between Dinka and Nuer in the guard. Kiir himself swiftly claimed that it was an attempted coup, blaming Machar and others and arresting 11 prominent figures, including Pagun Amum, whilst Machar disappeared from Juba.

Whether it was a **spontaneous outbreak of violence** amongst the presidential guard or a **failed coup** attempt, as Kiir asserted, was not immediately clear, but whatever its origins the country appeared to erupt, with **ethnic conflict** spreading across at least five of its ten states. Much attention focussed on killings carried out between the Dinka and Nuer, but in the past ethnic violence in South Sudan has extended beyond these two communities, and as the conflicts spread it was largely unclear exactly who was fighting whom, or the levels of killing. After a week the UN estimated around 1,000 deaths, but many feared the total could be much higher with little reliable information available from many areas.

Machar may or may not have planned a coup attempt, but it was soon clear that he was taking a very political role in events, in opposition to Kiir. Having escaped the round-up in Juba, Machar was soon taking to the air waves, while his supporters were **seizing the key town of Bor**, capital of Jonglei state, just north of Juba, where the local SPLA commander, Peter Gadet, controlled his own militia and, having once allied with the SPLM, now defected again. As the SPLA struggled to retake it, Bor had changed hands three times by the end of the year with heavy civilian casualties. At the same time, the key oil-producing areas and the Nuer homelands in the north of Unity and Upper Nile states were also seized by local forces supporting Machar, adding weight to his position in his verbal exchanges with Kiir. The oil flowed north to Sudan and the Red Sea out of Kiir's reach, and Machar called for the payments for the continuing flow to be paid to his group rather than to the government. Kiir's response was to try and reverse the situation militarily, and he soon claimed that Bor had been retaken.

The **international community**, especially the UN, was swiftly involved in the situation. The **UN** already had one of its largest operations, the **UN Mission in South Sudan (UNMISS)**, in the country and with seemingly random killings underway the UN estimated that 180,000 displaced civilians from various ethnic groups were seeking shelter in UN compounds across the country. The UN was rapidly overwhelmed and called for more supplies of basics such as food and water. A UNSC resolution recognised the severity of the situation and called on the warring parties to agree a ceasefire, as well as committing a further 5,500 peacekeepers.

In addition to the UN, the leading international group to respond to the crisis was the regional **IGAD**. The leaders of Ethiopia and Kenya, Prime Minister Hailemariam Desalegn and President Uhuru Kenyatta, soon arrived in Juba and called for a ceasefire. Kiir responded positively, but Machar set conditions: first, he demanded the release of the politicians seized at the start of the crisis – to which Kiir responded by releasing eight of the 11 – and he then objected to Uganda's involvement in view of the latter's alleged partisan support and military aid to Kiir in his attempts to retake rebellious areas. In spite of these comments, however, as the year ended both Kiir and Machar had agreed to send delegations to Addis Ababa for talks, though, in the light of the scale of the crisis, it was clear that, even if agreement of some kind proved possible, peace in the country as a whole remained a long way off.

The crisis was in many ways a reflection of the **problems of governance** in South Sudan, which had become increasingly clear since independence, threatening the country's very survival. At the core was the extent of SPLM/SPLA domination. As noted above, the **SPLM** itself was an **increasingly unstable** institution, with the top men divided, while Kiir's handling of the party served only to heighten tension within it. At the same time, the **SPLA** was both the **major structure of the state**, consuming by far the largest part of the budget, and unreliable, with splits and uncertain loyalties within it. International training and talk of reform – the total number of people in the SPLA was uncertain – had had only a limited impact, as the events at the end of the year were to show. This weakness also had an impact on the **police**, many of whom were former SPLA soldiers, often hurriedly trained and of limited value in their new roles. The situation worsened in August, when it was discovered that there were 11,000 'ghost' policemen on the national payroll. Like the president, many ministers were SPLA veterans, and increasingly accused of ineffectiveness in government, as well as corruption. There were signs that Kiir was becoming aware of both the domestic and international criticism of his government and, in **July**, he made apparently major changes by **sacking his cabinet** and reducing the number of ministries from 32 to 19 in an effort to reduce what had become a burgeoning and inefficient bureaucracy. Nevertheless, a number of old faces regarded as the president's loyalists were simply moved to new positions, and criticism continued.

Service provision remained **very weak**, with the primary concern of the government appearing to be focussed on the distribution of jobs and resources, often in efforts to satisfy regional and ethnic demands, as well as the dangers of possible revolt, with incidents of violence occurring in the majority of the country's ten states. There was also continuing concern about high levels of corruption: TI listed South Sudan as one of the three most corrupt countries in the world. Kiir suffered considerable personal embarrassment in March, when it was revealed that $ 6 m in cash had gone missing from his own office. Kiir recognised the need for action and his legal advisor, Telar Ring Deng, was tasked with fresh investigations. One of the ministers sacked in July, Deng Alor, was investigated in connection with a corrupt transfer of SSP (South Sudanese pounds) 23.6 m, but that and other cases remained unresolved. One problem was the slow progress by the National Audit Office in getting up to date with national accounts, which would be relevant to the prosecution of suspects.

There were also continuing **problems at state and local government levels**. SPLM governors dominated the state leadership positions, with most of the revenues available to the states coming from the central government in Juba, driven by oil revenues. The decline in these revenues following South Sudan's closure of the oil pipelines in 2012 resulted in a fall in funding for the states, even though the oil flow resumed in 2013. There were also allegations of nepotism and corruption in some state and local governments. Thus, in spite of pledges to fund development, development activity took place primarily in and around Juba, rather than being driven by sub-national levels of government in the various states.

At all levels, the power of the SPLM remained such that the various legislatures, from the bi-cameral National Legislative Assembly and Council of States down to state and local councils, had little critical impact on government. In spite of growing general discontent with the lack of progress in social and economic development, **opposition parties** remained **very weak**. Some of the most pertinent criticism came from the **media**, especially the press. However, as the year went on a growing number of measures were introduced to limit the freedom of the press, a development highlighted by a number of human rights organisations, which were themselves subject to denunciation. This decline in effective scrutiny of the government at all levels contributed to charges that the government was becoming increasingly autocratic, and thus to the political crisis that exploded at the end of the year.

Foreign Affairs

Relations with **Sudan** continued to be at the centre of foreign policy making for the government in Juba. The 2012 decision of South Sudan to cut the **flow of oil through the pipelines via Sudan** to the Red Sea, which had hurt both countries economically, was finally reversed by agreement in March, though there was a flurry of threats by both governments to cut it once more during the summer. There was also agreement, under international pressure, that the troops of both sides would be pulled back from border areas to limit the risk of direct clashes between them, which could endanger the security of both countries. However, other **outstanding issues remained**, including a final agreement on border demarcation, the longstanding debts of the former Sudan, the future of the disputed border area of Abyei, and citizenship. Nevertheless, in April, in order to underline the improvement in working relations between the two countries, Sudan's President Bashir made his first visit to Juba since South Sudan's independence, and shortly afterwards the two presidents met again on the fringes of the AU's 50th anniversary meeting in Addis Ababa, while Kiir also visited Khartoum in September. It was notable that, when the crisis in South Sudan erupted in December, Bashir expressed support for Kiir – even though Machar had once been an ally of the Khartoum government.

At the same time, it was clear during the course of the year that South Sudan was endeavouring to move closer to its main **East African neighbours**. Ethiopia remained concerned for reasons of regional security and especially the possible impact of instability on south-west Ethiopia. Conflict in Jonglei state, which was quite fierce in April, led to an influx of refugees, stretching the capacities of the relief agencies in that area. **Ethiopia** also had economic interests, with significant amounts of its oil having come from

South Sudan via Sudan, while it also sought Juba's support on the contentious issue of the Nile waters, especially Ethiopia's large planned Grand Renaissance Dam on the Blue Nile. Economic relations were also of growing importance for South Sudan with regard to **Kenya** and **Uganda**. Ever since independence, the South Sudanese government had wanted an alternative outlet for its oil via East Africa, and in 2013 progress was made with plans for a pipeline down to a new Kenyan port at Lamu. The importance of such a pipeline was increased by the development of oil fields in north-west Kenya around Lake Turkana, which attracted fresh international interest to the region. Uganda also had strong commercial ties to South Sudan, with many Ugandan businessmen in Juba in particular. It was then hardly surprising that the crisis in December was of great importance to these African neighbours and they took the lead in convening special meetings of IGAD in Addis Ababa, where talks between the two main sides in the South Sudan conflicts were being sought as the year came to an end. Indeed, Uganda went further and sent planes and troops to assist Kiir.

Relations with **Asia** were also important, especially with **Japan** and **China**. In April, Kiir visited Japan and shortly afterwards it was announced that Toyota would be supporting the building of the proposed pipeline to Lamu. Another related sign of involvement came from China later in the year, when it announced a $ 5.2 bn. investment in a rail network for East Africa that would link South Sudan, Uganda and Rwanda to the Kenyan coast. It was also hoped that China's plans for a new dam, delayed when oil flows stopped in 2012, would re-start. In addition, a large delegation of South Sudanese businessmen went to China in October for a conference on trade and investment. However, China, which was heavily involved in South Sudan's oilfields, was very concerned when the crisis erupted in December and broke its normal silence on political developments by calling for a ceasefire and peace talks.

Elsewhere in the world there was less direct involvement in South Sudan. The **Arab states** remained concerned about the Nile waters, but problems in Sudan and the wider Arab world were of greater significance. In **Europe**, there was concern over the humanitarian problems facing South Sudan, especially with the continuing need for food aid. In the **USA**, there was some disappointment that a new state in whose creation it had been heavily involved had turned out to have so many continuing problems and generally failed to live up to the hopes for it at independence.

As far as international organisations were concerned, the international community in general left the lead to Africa, especially the **AU** High Level Implementation Panel led by Thabo Mbeki, based in Addis Ababa for much of the year, and during the December crisis to **IGAD**. On the ground, the **UN** found itself close to feeling overwhelmed, especially with regard to security. UNMISS, one of its largest peacekeeping operations in the world (10,000 troops), could do little in the face of conflict in various areas for much of the year, so much so that there was talk of surveillance drones and even gunships to help protect civilians in the most troubled areas, especially Jonglei state. At one point, the UN special representative in South Sudan, Hilde Johnson, sounded almost despairing when she said that the UN could not be the police force for the new state. In the December crisis, UN bases found themselves almost overwhelmed by thousands of civilians seeking refuge from the fierce fighting and, while the UNSC was swift to pass a resolution calling for a ceasefire, it had little effect.

Socioeconomic Developments

The **oil export** situation remained central to social and economic developments. South Sudan had been heavily reliant on oil, which had been the source of 98% of government revenues and accounted for an estimated 70% of GDP. The government's shutdown of exports over its dispute with Sudan in 2012 was thus a major blow, and left the issue in need of early resolution for both countries. In March, agreement was reached and soon afterwards the oil was flowing once more. Production figures soon rose to some 250,000 b/d, though this was still 100,000 b/d less than before the shutdown and the issue remained for South Sudan of trying to find other export routes to overcome dependence on relations with Sudan in the future. Various options were considered, with the frontrunner always being the southern route to Lamu (Kenya) on the Indian Ocean. However, the fresh optimism was to be dashed by the worsening political crisis. As soon as the fighting exploded in December, the mainly Asian oil companies – China's Greater Pioneer Operating Company (GPOC), Malaysia's Petronas, and ONGC Videsh of India – pulled their staff out. Meanwhile, Machar said that he would export oil from the fields his supporters had seized. All this put the oil sector at the heart of the crisis and, by the end of the year, it appeared that fighting over **control of the oil fields** was more important to both the main parties to the conflict than negotiating seriously as the international community encouraged. The situation could hardly be more crucial for the new state: in the short term, the on-going fighting cut the government's revenues drastically, while in the longer term the lack of political stability might well deter the foreign investment on which oil exploitation overwhelmingly rested. This would affect not only the oil sector, but also the uncertain future of foreign investment in agriculture.

In the wake of the re-opening of oil exports in April, there was optimism around the **budget** presented by Finance Minister Agrey Tisa Sambuni to the National Assembly in September. It envisaged overall spending of SSP 17.3 bn ($ 5.9 bn), with expected revenues of SSP 12.1 bn. The planned deficit was to be financed from international sources, and the governor of the central bank, Komello Koriom, announced a $ 20 m loan from the AfDB for budgetary support and the reform of public financial management. Talks were also on-going with the IMF for a loan of $ 50 m. Financial difficulties also led to the official devaluation of the SSP from 3:$ to 4.5:$, closer to the black market rate.

There was concern that **half the budget** was for **'security and law enforcement'**, which appeared to indicate that spending on the army, police, justice and prisons could rise from SSP 3.8 bn in 2012–13 to nearly SSP 9 bn for 2013–14. This level of spending on security would do little to attract donors and lenders, though there could be no doubt of its importance by the end of the year. Other heads of expenditure included infrastructure, particularly roads and bridges, which were very poor outside Juba (which has the country's only bridge over the White Nile), and there were also plans for a new road link to Ethiopia to carry oil by truck. Members of parliament were also to have a special fund to spend on development projects required in their constituencies. However, funds to improve the very poor provision of social services remained limited: in practice much of this provision came from international NGOs and aid funding of $ 1.3 bn from the USA and Europe, in addition to the food aid on which many people were still dependent.

Peter Woodward

Sudan

The year started with the country in a difficult situation. South Sudan had closed its oilfields early in 2012 and so Sudan was receiving no revenue from the transit fees of South Sudan's oil across Sudan's territory. Government finances were badly affected since the bulk of its oil revenue had come from South Sudan's oil prior to that country's secession in 2011. As a result, Sudan had had to introduce an austerity programme which was already deeply unpopular, and discontent only increased with time as inflation escalated. Meanwhile, in the areas of conflict – in Darfur, Blue Nile and South Kordofan – there were few signs of peace being any nearer, while the future of the dispute with South Sudan over the Abyei border also remained unresolved. The government's response was twofold: throughout the year it was seeking to divide the opposition, especially by preventing a linking of the political parties and the fighters in the conflict areas, while also trying to give the impression of being willing to reform, but – as became ever clearer – on its own terms. Relations with South Sudan were a major feature of these problems, especially the restoration of rents from the oil pipelines, but it was far from clear whether these could be resolved before the situation in Sudan worsened still further. Other foreign relations were less urgent, but Sudan still found that it made little headway with its attempts at reconciliation with the West, leaving it largely dependent on Asia, especially China, and the Gulf.

Domestic Politics

During the year, the government experienced growing internal tensions along familiar lines. Central to this was the position of **President Omar Hassan al-Bashir** himself. He had seized power as a military ruler in 1989 with the backing of the National Islamic Front and the aim of creating an Islamic state. Since that time, there had been a number of shifts and growing speculation about Bashir himself, especially after more than two decades in power. With elections due in 2015, there were questions about whether he would stand again or announce his retirement as he sometimes suggested. The central question for Bashir and his closest supporters was what their collective future would be if he were to stand aside, and for others in his ruling National Congress Party (NCP), whether in 2015 he would be an asset to the party or a liability.

After a **self-proclaimed Islamic revolution**, and in the context of a broader Islamic Movement, there had long been tensions concerning not only Bashir, but also the Islamic legitimacy still claimed by the government, especially since the break between the NCP and its former leading ideologist, Hasan al-Turabi, in 1999. The growing challenge within the party in 2013 came from Ghazi Salah al-Deen al-Atabani, who had for several years aspired to the intellectual leadership of the NCP, and who repeatedly expressed concern for its reform to give it new appeal in the face of worsening conditions in the country as a whole. To Bashir and his tight inner circle dominated by security figures, Ghazi was less a threat than an annoying gadfly, and in April he was dismissed from his positions as a Presidential Advisor and as the leader of the NCP block that dominated the National Assembly. Ghazi, however, was not to be so easily discarded, especially when the deteriorating economic conditions produced in September the largest **popular demonstrations** against the government since 1989. Such was readiness of the government's counter-insurgency strategy that it survived, but only after shooting scores of protestors and thus deepening resentment, especially in the towns and cities where the confrontations occurred. Following this, Ghazi appeared again in November, leading a group of NCP critics, but now saying that the NCP was beyond the reforms he had sought previously and that he would now try to register a new political party in opposition to it.

The government's response to the **growing opposition** was to try to present a **reformist image** of its own. In December, a number of leading figures announced their withdrawal from front-line politics, where they had been active since 1989. Amongst them were the First Vice President, Mohammed Osman Taha, often seen as the brains of the government and its chief negotiator with the South in the deliberations that had led to the Comprehensive Peace Agreement (CPA) of 2005; Awad al-Jaz, who had been the leading figure in Sudan's oil policy for many years; and Nafie Ali Nafie, the presidential adviser who had long been regarded as the hard man of the regime. Taha was replaced as First Vice President by Bakri Hassan Salih, who with Bashir was the only officer surviving in the government from the 1989 coup. Nafie's place was taken by the more diplomatic Ibrahim Ahmed Ghandour, but the former was still concerned with security matters. It was hoped that the **departure** of such high profile members **of the old guard** would appear to freshen up the government with younger NCP figures (in contrast to the elderly leaders of the leading opposition parties, Sadiq al-Mahdi of the National Umma Party and Mohammed Osman al-Mirghani of the Democratic Unionist Party [DUP]), but there were many who doubted that it heralded a significant change. Some of the new appointees were little known outside NCP circles, though they appeared to include some from more outlying parts of the country, probably in an effort to offset accusations of the limited regional and ethnic base of the old leadership. However, the group of Islamist rulers had been somewhat opaque ever since they seized power in 1989, and it was likely that those who had officially retired would still wield influence at least within the NCP. In reality, the security chiefs were still at the heart of the regime. There had been surprise in 2012 when Salah Gosh, the former head of the National Intelligence and Security Service was arrested, but in June he was released, presumably no longer regarded as a threat.

The **traditional political party** closest to the government remained the **DUP**, still under the patronage of the leader of the Khatmiyya Islamic sect, Mohammed Osman al-Mirghani. The DUP already had representatives of the party serving in the government, but as protests grew during the course of the year Mirghani came under increased pressure from within the always highly factionalised DUP leadership to pull the ministers out. After some prevarication, he refused, but by November had been driven to talk more of the need for some kind of national conference, though with little response from the NCP.

The DUP's great traditional rival, the **Umma Party**, under the leadership of former Prime Minister and head of the Ansar Islamic sect, Sadiq al-Mahdi, was more critical of the government, with Mahdi repeatedly calling for a national conference. However, he also made clear his opposition to any kind of use of force, even during the big September demonstrations when many were shot on the streets by the security forces. The reluctance of both Mahdi and Mirghani to side with the growing general opposition led some sceptics to wonder whether they were influenced by the roles of their sons, Abdal-Rahman al-Mahdi and Ja'afar al-Mirghani, who continued as official presidential advisors with offices in the Republican Palace.

A number of smaller national parties that had set up a joint front known as the **National Consensus Forces (NCF)** in 2012 became increasingly critical of the deteriorating situation and called for stronger links with the Sudan Peoples' Liberation Army-North (SPLA-N) fighting in Blue Nile and South Kordofan. These new links led to the signing of the **New Dawn Charter**, but its significance remained in question. A number of those involved were arrested, though some were later released. Overall, the strength of the NCF remained limited, while its composition ranged over a variety of groups from Islamists, such as the Popular Congress Party, led by the controversial Hasan al-Turabi, to the Sudan Communist Party. The government's response was to welcome the splintering of the opposition while playing cat and mouse with arrests and releases: Turabi in particular had been in and out of prison since 1999.

Overall, the **splintering of the opposition** made it easier for the government to deal with the **widespread demonstrations** that broke out in response to a sharp rise in the cost of living brought about by cuts in subsidies in September. At the same time, the demonstrators used slogans reminiscent of those of the Arab Spring, including "The people want the regime to fall", while some NCP offices were attacked. In the face of demonstrations on a scale with the legendary protests that brought down military regimes in Sudan in 1964 and 1985, the government turned to its well-trained security forces, claiming that the SPLM-N and other "traitors" were behind the demonstrations as it used unprecedented levels of force, including the employment of tear gas and live ammunition, the closure of the Internet to prevent the use of social media, and sweeping arrests. It later admitted that 74 had been shot dead, while the opposition claimed the figure was over 200. In addition, many more were wounded, hundreds were detained, and measures to crack down on the media were intensified. After the demonstrations were finally over, the government rubbed salt into the protestors' wounds by staging an intimidating triumphal march around the capital by the security forces.

Beyond the central areas of the country, the **conflicts** in **Darfur, South Kordofan** and **Blue Nile**, which amounted to a belt of conflict across the southern areas of the country, remained unresolved. All three regions included predominantly rain-watered agricultural areas with a relatively large population, and with both traditional agriculture and a record of growing commercial agricultural schemes, which had often contributed to local land tensions and exploitative working practices. In addition to local issues, the conflicts have reflected national developments. The fighting in Darfur had continued in various parts of the region and at changing levels of intensity since it erupted in 2003, attracting considerable international outcry. Conflict in the other two areas had grown since the signing of the CPA in 2005 and the independence of South Sudan in 2011.

In **Darfur**, 2013 was another indecisive year: though the government endeavoured to depict the situation as improving, this was offset by the UN reporting continuing fighting and 150,000 more people displaced. In 2011, the government had backed the formation of a new faction, the Liberty and Justice Movement, under the leadership of Tijani Sessi, a former governor of Darfur. However, other groups had not joined the **new Doha Agreement** and continued fighting, while talks in Doha dragged on, making little headway, though in April the government announced that another small faction had decided to join the talks. The Justice and Equality Movement (JEM)-Bashar faction – a breakaway from the main JEM – signed the Doha Agreement, for which it was granted a pardon. At the same time, there was an international donors' conference in Doha, at which Qatar in particular pledged additional humanitarian aid to the region. Other rebels, notably the JEM and the Sudan Liberation Movement/Army (SLM/A), more emboldened since the secession of South Sudan, called for a new peace process, even mentioning possible self-determination for the region, but the government rejected this, saying that the Doha process would continue. Nevertheless, a UN-sponsored meeting took place in Arusha (Tanzania) in August aimed at trying to broaden the Darfur groups' involvement in peace talks, but without achieving significant progress. The need for aid could hardly be greater, with hundreds of thousands still displaced, many in IDP camps in very poor conditions. **Fighting continued** in various areas, particularly in east Darfur on the border with west Kordofan – which also saw some fighting – though it was often less than clear who exactly the combatants were. While the government and the 20,000-strong hybrid UN-AU Mission in Darfur (UNAMID) reported that the overall level of conflict was down, opposition groups and some humanitarian organisations disputed this. A UN report in March also claimed that some of the rebels belonging to the mainstream JEM, one of the largest groups, had a base in South Sudan near Bentiu. UNAMID also suffered a major blow in July when seven peacekeepers were killed in an ambush.

The other area of significant challenge from rebel forces was in **South Kordofan**, to the west of the White Nile. A core area of conflict in South Kordofan had long been the **Nuba Mountains**, where the SPLA had been well established for much of the long civil war in the South. With the local problems of the Nuba people unaddressed, it was a natural area for continuing violence after the separation of South Sudan. In 2013, this continued with the locally based SPLA-N, under the leadership of the experienced Abdel Aziz Adam al-Hilu, deciding on a new tactic of flying attacks on towns in North Kordofan. In April, the important town of Umm Ruwaba on the railway line running west from the White Nile to Darfur was briefly held; and shortly afterwards rebels also occupied the town of Abu Kershola. Though the SPLA-N was forced to pull back in both cases, this was an embarrassment to the Sudan army, and provoked the government to try and crush the rebels with fresh attacks in the eastern Nuba Mountains area. It also sought to avoid the establishment of local camps for the displaced in an endeavour to prevent North Kordofan turning into another Darfur, especially since some Darfur groups, including elements from the JEM, were fighting with the SPLA-N.

In **Blue Nile**, conflict continued to be driven primarily by local factors, especially access to resources including land. The SPLA-N fighting there remained under the command of the respected former state governor, Malik Agar, and in the early part of the year had some successes. However, they were later pinned down in the southern part of the state by the Sudan army, which held most of the key strategic points. While the SPLM-N was hard pressed for weapons, with declining cross border support from South Sudan, the government forces were better supplied and had air control as well as being able to recruit local militias (as in other regions). The conflict brought continuing civilian victims, with 154,000 refugees in Ethiopia and South Sudan, as well as over 80,000 IDPs in SPLM-N-held areas, many in appalling conditions.

Abyei was the border area with South Sudan that had remained unresolved after the signing of the CPA in 2005. It had been the focus of substantial international efforts, including a referral to the Permanent Court of Arbitration in The Hague, but with little effect on the ground. Following border clashes between government forces and SPLA forces from South Sudan, there had been a period of reduced conflict, with the UN introducing a successful peace keeping Interim Security Force of 4,200 mainly Ethiopian troops. However, the issue of its future – whether Abyei should join South Sudan or Sudan – remained undecided. The on-going problem was discussed in September, when the two presidents met in Khartoum, but there was no agreement on the formation of a UN-proposed joint administration pending the referendum promised in the CPA in 2005. Following that, the Ngok Dinka people of Abyei, who clearly wanted to join South Sudan, decided that, if the two governments could not agree, they would conduct the long promised **referendum** on their own, and they duly went ahead with that in November with an overwhelming and predictable result. However, in the northern part of Abyei, the Messeriya Arab tribe, which wished to stay in Sudan and spoke of a referendum of its own, rejected the Ngok Dinka process, as did the two governments.

Foreign Affairs

Relations with **South Sudan** remained central to Sudan's external relations. Following South Sudan's closure of its oilfields in 2012, there had been speculation that the two governments were trying to break each other, but when that failed to happen, and as the cost to both countries of the continued closure of the pipelines was becoming ever clearer, they reached an agreement in March on the rent to be paid for the oil flowing through Sudan to the Red Sea. However, although oil flowed again, there were further exchanges of threats to cut the oil by both governments before international pressure from the AU and China, followed by meetings between the two presidents, improved relations somewhat. Both men visited each other's capitals for the first time since South Sudan's independence, as well as meeting during an AU meeting in Addis Ababa to celebrate the founding of the OAU in 1963. In addition, international pressure contributed to an agreement to pull their respective troops back from the border in the Abyei area. However, progress was slow in the negotiations on the demarcation of the whole border between the two countries, which were still not completed as the year ended. Other issues, such as citizenship and the division of the pre-2011 national debt of Sudan, also remained unresolved. Following the crisis in South Sudan in December and the swift spread of the fighting from Juba to key towns in the oil-producing states, there was fresh concern about the continuing flow of oil. South Sudan's former vice president, Riek Machar, who soon emerged as the voice of the new rebels, claimed to have taken control of the oil fields and called for new accounts to be set up by Sudan for the opposition to receive the payments that would keep oil flowing through the pipelines across the country. However, Khartoum did not respond to this, but instead indicated its support for President Salva Kiir in his efforts to crush the rebels and regain control, apparently fearing that any other outcome would result in insecurity of oil flows and hence of Sudan's revenues.

In the **Arab world**, Sudan continued to look towards **Qatar**, where the Doha talks on Darfur dragged on. It also looked towards Qatar for financial help, especially as its financial and economic problems worsened with the loss of oil revenue. Qatar also agreed to fund a new road from Darfur to Chad, though with insecurity still present it may take time to accomplish, and in any case there was as yet no paved road from central Sudan to Darfur itself. In April, Qatar put up $ 500 m for investment in real estate, banking and agriculture; while in October it offered $ 1 bn to help with the deficit. Sudan also followed developments in **Egypt** closely, especially the deposing of President Mursi and the subsequent banning of the Muslim Brotherhood, with which Sudan's Islamists had once had close links. At the same time, there had long been intelligence and security cooperation with Egypt's military, so Sudan had to tread carefully. Sudan was also involved in the disagreement between Egypt and **Ethiopia** over the latter's building of the Grand Renaissance Dam on the Blue Nile, all of whose waters flow down through Sudan to Egypt. In the summer, a panel of international experts had approved Ethiopia's plans, but Egypt called for a delay for further study before any agreement on its part. Sudan was caught in the middle and tried to reconcile the two countries, but to little effect. **Saudi Arabia** caused concern when it decided to expel thousands of migrant workers. There were an estimated 500,000 Sudanese working there, making significant remittances to their families. By November, 11,000 had returned to Sudan but there were worries that this figure could rise significantly. Further east, links with **Iran**, a close ally in the early 1990s, also improved, though this brought the displeasure of Saudi Arabia, which refused permission for Bashir to overfly its territory en route to Tehran for the inauguration of Iran's new president.

Sudan's relations with **African states** saw little change. To the immediate east, **Ethiopia** remained an important country and the arrival of its new prime minister, Hailemariam Desalegn, did not result in any significant change in relations. Trade relations between the two countries continued to develop, with much of Ethiopia's oil coming from Sudan, while Sudan looked to the development of Ethiopia's hydroelectric capabilities, especially as work on the new Grand Renaissance Dam proceeded. At the same time, Sudan retained good relations with **Eritrea**, which was an important player in the maintenance of a mainly peaceful environment across its border with eastern Sudan. Thousands of Eritrean refugees fleeing the harsh conditions of life in their own country arrived in eastern Sudan, where many stayed in refugee camps. However, Sudan did not allow this to damage relations between the two governments. Bashir met President Isayas Afwerki in Port Sudan in the summer and they spoke of cross-border economic cooperation. In December, Bashir offered to mediate between Eritrea and Ethiopia, though there were few signs of a response from two governments, which had held fast to entrenched positions for several years. To the west, **Chad** remained important in efforts to contain the rebels in Darfur (and for Chad to do likewise for its rebels in eastern Chad) and the two countries continued to cooperate on border security.

With regard to **East Africa**, the most difficult relations were with **Uganda**. For several years before the secession of South Sudan, Uganda and Sudan had accused each other of supporting each other's rebels: Uganda supporting the SPLA in South Sudan, and Sudan assisting the Lord's Resistance Army (LRA) in Uganda. During 2013, Bashir found it necessary to warn Uganda not to help rebel groups fighting in southern Darfur. However, when trouble broke out in December in South Sudan, Uganda and Sudan found themselves on the same side, both supporting President Kiir. Relations with **Kenya** remained stable: with the secession of South Sudan and its moves to closer relations with Kenya, Sudan's own connections were not as close as when Kenya was one of its neighbours.

Relations with the **West**, particularly the **USA**, remained cooler than Sudan wished. Sudan had long hoped for at least an easing of US sanctions, which had had the effect of deterring Western companies from doing business in Sudan if they were in any way connected to companies listed on the New York stock exchange. There were hopes in Khartoum that, following South Sudan's secession, things would improve, and again in 2013 that the resumption of oil flows from South Sudan and the improved relations with President Kiir would lead to a change of mind in Washington. But once more it failed to happen. The USA felt that, with the continuing conflicts in Darfur, South Kordofan and Blue Nile, sanctions should remain in place. Nevertheless, the USA signalled its continuing concern by appointing in September a new special envoy for Sudan and South Sudan, Don Booth, an experienced diplomat. **European** involvement was also limited by the US sanctions, although a number of countries were involved in humanitarian aid, especially following severe floods in the summer.

China remained an important ally in Sudan's economic relations. There was relief in Beijing when Sudan and South Sudan agreed to re-open the oil pipelines, since China was a major purchaser of the oil. At the same time, China continued both mineral exploration and building infrastructure projects, mainly roads and bridges. Importantly, in July it pledged $ 700 m for the long-discussed new international airport for Khartoum; and there was also talk of funding for canal development for agricultural irrigation. A number of other Asian countries also continued to be involved, especially in the hunt for minerals.

Sudan's relations with **international organisations** remained difficult. The hybrid UNAMID continued, though it often felt harassed by the government as fighting persisted. In March, it was Thabo Mbeki, as leader of the AU High-Level Implementation Panel, who negotiated the removal from the immediate border areas of both Sudan's and South Sudan's armed forces. Sudan also hoped that the AU summit in Addis Ababa would turn the growing criticism of the ICC's apparent concentration on charging figures in Africa into an official AU rejection of that body, which was still charging President

Bashir with war crimes and crimes against humanity over Darfur. In addition to damaging his reputation, this also restricted his movements internationally to only those countries where he could be sure there was no risk of arrest. However, the AU did not adopt any such a move, leaving some to speculate that, if the charges were still in place in 2015, it might make it harder for Bashir to retire. Sudan welcomed the concern of IGAD with the December crisis in South Sudan, in which it quickly sought to mediate.

Socioeconomic Developments

The major problem at the start of the year was the continuing **impact** of South Sudan's decision a year earlier to **close the oil pipeline**. At the height of Sudan's economic growth in the mid-2000s, it had enjoyed revenues from oil exports approaching 500,000 b/d. Following South Sudan's secession and the loss of the majority of Sudan's oil fields, the failure to replace the loss of income by agreement on rents for South Sudan's oil being piped to the Red Sea left a major shortfall in government revenues. When **agreement to reopen the flow of oil** was eventually reached in March, the rent fixed was approximately $ 10 per barrel, which still left much reduced revenues, even though Sudan was continuing to produce its own oil at a rate of approximately 150,000 b/d. But much of Sudan's oil went for local consumption or regional export, especially to Ethiopia, rather than reaching world markets. At the same time, new exploration in some areas failed, including the offshore work by China in the Red Sea.

Growth in **mineral exports**, however, still remained a central aim of policy. China in particular continued to seek **new oilfields**, including in Darfur, and the government was hoping that output might soon be increased to 260,000 b/d. It also announced that new companies from Canada and Brazil were interested in exploration. The government also hoped for an increase in gold production. There had been something of a gold rush in recent years, much of it focussed on the Red Sea Hills and the northern deserts, and its importance was reflected in the fact that gold had risen to constitute over 30% of the value of exports. Commercial companies had been involved, notably a Canadian company at the Hassai mine, as had many local artisanal diggers hoping to make their own finds. However, with international gold prices fluctuating and the amounts found limited, it proved difficult to attract new investment and it remained unlikely that gold would fill the gap created by the fall in oil income. It might also encourage local conflicts, as was reported from northern Darfur in January, when conflict erupted in the Jebel Amir artisanal gold mining area between two tribes, the Beni Hussein and the Aballa Rizeigat, which led to reports of thousands being displaced and 800 killed.

The other great hope for Sudan had long lain in the growth of **commercial agriculture**. Land had been acquired by **Gulf states** including Saudi Arabia, the UAE and Qatar, and the government announced that substantial areas would be used to grow wheat in order to cut imports. However, only a minority of the land taken up by the Gulf states had in fact been utilised and, where developments had taken place, there had been some clashes with indigenous farmers. In reality, many of the country's rural inhabitants still relied heavily on subsistence agriculture for their livelihood. Some optimism remained with work starting during the year on dams funded by China at Setit and on the Upper Atbara River in eastern Sudan, which could lead to an increase in both electricity production and irrigated agriculture after their scheduled completion in 2015.

Crops along the fertile Blue Nile in south-east Sudan were hard hit by **floods** in August. It was customary for the river to rise following the summer rains at its sources in Ethiopia, but floods on the scale of those in 2013 had not been seen for decades. In addition to destroying crops, an estimated 500,000 people had their homes inundated, including around the capital, Khartoum, and a number of fatalities were also reported. Unusually high rainfall also contributed to flooding reported in other parts of the country, including parts of Darfur, Red Sea state and along the White Nile. Government calls for assistance met with some response in the international community. Concern was also expressed that crop losses could add to inflationary pressures.

The hardship caused by the floods was compounded by the government's decision the following month to **remove** the **subsidies** on **petroleum products and wheat**. It appeared to be responding to international pressures, especially by the IMF, with which it had been negotiating to raise further loans. The IMF took the view that lifting subsidies would not have a major impact on inflation, and in any case poorer people would be less affected than the better off, who consumed more of both commodities. It was also thought that, by pursuing its austerity programme, the government hoped to appear in a better light with the Paris Club as it sought to have its $ 40 bn **debt re-scheduled**. However, for many people, especially in urban areas, the floods were simply an additional burden at a time when the impact on the economy of the loss of revenue from South Sudan was being widely felt. In addition, the **lack of foreign exchange to buy wheat** was blamed for shortages of bread, though the government moved swiftly to alleviate the situation. On 23 September, **large-scale demonstrations** broke out, with thousands protesting in several towns and cities. The government was able to ride out the largest demonstrations since the coup of 1989 brought Bashir to power, but it was left in a weaker position at home, with widespread anger persisting.

The financial position also continued to look weak during a year of such wide-ranging domestic problems. **Inflation** fluctuated, but the average figure was around 35% over the year as a whole, reaching 43% in November, and this contributed significantly to the widespread demonstrations when the government lifted the subsidies on basic consumer necessities in September. The restoration of oil rents from the pipeline was helpful to the government, but the losses since early 2012 had been severe, while world oil prices for Sudan's own output were on a downward trend. More exploration licences were granted across the mineral sector, but no major developments were reported, while the social and political instability made some international firms wary, even without the threat from US sanctions. High inflation and uncertainties on so many fronts also had the effect of driving down the value of the **currency**. By November, the official dollar rate was lowered from Sudanese pounds (£S) 4.4 to £S 5.7 to the dollar; while the black market rate was between £S 7 and £S 8 to the dollar.

These weaknesses were reflected in the outline of the 2014 **budget** presented by Finance Minister Badr al-Deen Mahmoud in December. The budget was set at £S 46.2 bn (which involved a deficit for which help was being sought from the IMF and Gulf donors). It included promises of no new taxes, a rise in government salaries, and higher spending on health and education. However, detailed figures were yet to follow, while few expected the high spending on security and the armed forces to fall. Overall, there was little good news for a population that had for a number of years before the secession of South Sudan seen rapid rises in GDP of 8%–10%. This trend had been harshly reversed as, according to IMF estimates, **GDP** had in 2011 and 2012 effectively **contracted** by about 2% and 3%, respectively. Preliminary estimates now showed a **GDP growth rate** of 3.9% for 2013, while many thought even the 2.6% prediction for 2014 was optimistic. At the same time, the mood was not helped by TI's assertion that Sudan remained one of the three most **corrupt** countries in the world.

Peter Woodward

Tanzania

Throughout the year, most political attention was absorbed by discussions over the progress of the constitutional review process that had been initiated in 2012. A first draft of an envisaged new constitution was published in June and served as a reference point for all ensuing debates. Most contentious was the delicate issue of the future structure of the Union between Zanzibar and the Mainland. The draft somewhat surprisingly proposed a new three-tier set-up in contradiction to the position of the ruling Revolutionary Party ('Chama Cha Mapinduzi'; CCM), which favoured the continuation of the current system. Final decisions on the constitution were left for a Constitutional Assembly, to be convened in early 2014. Internal power struggles between various CCM factions continued as the party tried to regain some of its lost credibility and was already gearing up towards the next elections in 2015. In reaction to revelations of massive human rights violations during an anti-poaching campaign, four ministers were sacked. Continuing social and religious tensions led to unrest and demonstrations and raised fears about a possible end to Tanzania's hitherto typically stable and peaceful political climate. Two newspapers were temporarily suspended, indicative of government nervousness.

State visits by the Chinese and US presidents underscored Tanzania's enhanced international recognition as both an influential political actor in Africa and a resource-rich country with a projected positive economic future. As part of a new UN peace enforcement operation in the DRC, a military battalion was deployed and engaged in battles. Relations with Rwanda deteriorated markedly, while there was also a noticeably increased crisis of confidence between Tanzania and its EAC partners. Macroeconomic performance remained quite satisfactory and continued to be commended by the IMF, the World Bank and donors, but the majority of the population still saw little concrete progress despite a moderate decline in the measured poverty incidence. Many large infrastructural investments were underway or planned, and high expectations centred on prospects for Tanzania becoming a major gas producer.

Domestic Politics

In continuation from 2012, much of the year's political attention centred on the **constitution review process**. In early January the **Constitutional Review Commission** (CRC) completed the first phase of collecting views of citizens regarding a new or revised constitution. According to CRC chairman Joseph Warioba, the commission had conducted more than 1,700 public hearings all over the country in which over 1.3 m people had participated. More than 300,000 written or oral contributions were made, including statements made by mobile phone, and via the CRC website or Facebook. In a second phase in January/February, representatives from more than 160 societal groups (civil society organisations [CSOs], political parties, governmental and non-governmental institutions, etc.) were heard by the CRC. Numerous CSOs had conducted workshops with stakeholders to analyse the current constitution and to formulate their demands for a new mother law. Despite generally positive attitudes towards the process, CSOs as well as opposition parties followed the CRC's activities with great suspicion. It was widely feared that the **long-ruling Revolutionary Party** ('Chama cha Mapinduzi'; **CCM**) would not allow the CRC to operate independently, and would at some point or another 'hijack' the process, trying to use its power to manipulate the process to meet the party's (or some influential individual's) interests, regardless of the benefits for the country or the will of the people.

In May, the debate gained momentum when CSOs and opposition parties demanded new regulations concerning the composition of envisaged **district constitutional forums**. These forums were designated by law to discuss and amend the CRC'S first draft of a new constitution, again involving the opinion of the populace. Critics, however, voiced concern that the forums were to be assembled by district authorities, most of which were controlled by CCM members. CSOs and opposition parties criticised the process for forming the district forums as marred by irregularities, alleged favouritism and corruption, upon which the CRC reacted by publishing guidelines for the forums that explicitly allowed CSOs and others to independently convene their own forums and come up with their own recommendations for a second draft.

The detailed **first draft** of a new **constitution**, formulated by the CRC and published on **3 June**, was received with surprise and mixed feelings by the general public. Whereas most CSOs, opposition parties and academics welcomed the proposal, it was strongly rejected by the CCM. The draft text, consisting of 240 sections, proposed a **fundamental change in the country's polity** towards a federal system by introducing a separate government for the Tanzanian mainland in addition to the already existing Zanzibar government, and a reshaped union government ("three tier government"). Matters to be dealt with by the union government were to be reduced from the present 22 to only seven. Changes were also proposed with regard to the union cabinet and parliament. The number of ministries was to be reduced from about 30 to 15, and ministers should no longer be selected from among MPs. By reducing the number of constituencies, the number of MPs was also to be drastically reduced to 75 (from about 360), and the allocation of special seats for women was to be discontinued; instead, each new constituency would be represented in parliament by one man and one women. Tenure for MPs was limited to three terms, and voters would have the right to re-call their MP at any time. With a view to increasing the political impartiality of the office, the speaker of the National Assembly would no longer be an MP.

Although the draft only made provisions for a new constitution for the United Republic, it implicitly proposed the creation a **new entity of Tanzania Mainland** (or **Tanganyika**), with responsibilities formerly vested in the union being split between the union and that new entity (and its counterpart Zanzibar). Whereas Zanzibar already had existing institutions, such as a parliament, a president and a constitution (although they would also have to be adjusted to the new set-up), such institutions needed to be established for the new entity on the mainland. The proposals concerning the new union structure naturally attracted most attention. However, the draft included numerous other changes, many of which had long been demanded by CSOs and opposition parties. Most importantly, the draft reduced the powers of the president, allowed for independent candidates in elections, introduced a modern bill of rights, and removed many restrictive regulations.

Although CSOs, academics and opposition parties criticised some aspects (such as keeping the death penalty, removal of land ownership from the matters under union jurisdiction, the doubtful independence of the Electoral Commission and the inconsistencies and vagueness of some clauses), the **draft was widely welcomed** by representatives of **civil society** as a progressive and people-centred foundation for the country. The **CCM** turned out to be the only relevant force that **rejected the draft**, primarily because of the proposed new government structure. CCM strongly favoured the existing asymmetrical set-up with two governments. However, the party's official position was challenged by some prominent CCM members who were willing to accept the CRC's proposal as an expression of the people's will. CCM's Zanzibar wing even actively supported the proposed structure as the best setting for Zanzibar. Since the ruling party's stance on the union question had long been known, it came as a surprise to many observers that the CRC proposed a draft that was evidently against the CCM's will. The CRC explained that in designing the draft it had been strongly influenced by the statements citizens had made in the hearings. According to CRC chairman Warioba, the proposals in the draft reflected citizens' wishes and were assented to unanimously by all 30 CRC members, despite and regardless of their differing political backgrounds and preferences.

The CRC's draft changed the interactions between all main actors significantly. Opposition parties and CSOs (especially the very outspoken Constitutional Forum) no longer regarded the CRC with suspicion, but perceived it as their ally and shifted their attempts to influence the CRC's second draft (due in December) from the district forums (which were conducted without much attention) towards the decisive **Constituent Assembly (CA)**. The CA was to debate and improve the second, revised draft in early 2014 and come up with a final proposal that would be put to all eligible Tanzanians in a referendum. However, the envisaged **composition of the CA** raised concerns that it could conceivably reject the CRC's draft for "egoistic reasons". After a heated debate, amendments to the **Constitution Review Bill** were endorsed by parliament on 6 September. However, opposition MPs protested against the bill and walked out of the house. According to the bill, the CA should be composed of all members of the National Assembly, all members of the Zanzibar House of Representatives and 166 members of societal groups, appointed by the president. Since the CRC draft had proposed regulations that would directly affect MPs (drastic reduction in the number of seats, limitation of tenure, threat of recall by voters, no appointments of MPs to ministerial posts), it was feared that the CA, being made up overwhelmingly of MPs, would reject these provisions. Furthermore, it was feared that the CCM would use its majority to block the proposed three-tier government structure. Although the inclusion of 166 civil society representatives was welcomed, there was vehement criticism that they were too few and that they were to be hand-picked by the president. On 21 September, the main opposition parties CHADEMA (Party of Democracy and Progress), CUF (Civic United Front) and NCCR-Mageuzi (National Convention for Construction and Reform – Change) staged a joint rally against the bill in Dar es Salaam and announced plans to hold country-wide demonstrations. They demanded an equal representation of Zanzibar in the CA and clear rules for the appointment of the additional 166 CA members. To reduce tension, **President Jakaya Kikwete** met representatives of six opposition parties on 15 October and agreed on a compromise. Consequently, parliament **amended the bill** again in early November, increasing the number of civil society delegates to 201 and stipulating clear rules on how and from which sectors of society they should be selected. Despite this compromise, MPs and CCM members would still constitute the clear majority in the CA.

After the CRC's deadline to complete its work and submit a second draft had been twice extended by the president, the Commission unveiled its **second draft on 30 December**. Despite attempts from the CCM to influence the CRC to change the contentious crucial provisions, the second draft did not differ much from the earlier version. However, it added some 31 further clauses (and increased the matters under union jurisdiction to eight), not all of which were welcomed by CSOs and opposition parties. Among other points, some of the newly introduced provisions were criticised as restricting the freedom of independent candidates.

During the entire process, the **CCM** never managed to control the developments or set the agenda. Its refusal to support changes that were supported by majority public opinion made the party appear a destructive force, more guided by egoistic motives than by public interest. Corruption allegations, theft of public funds and various scandals, the beginnings of infighting for positions in the run-up to the 2015 presidential elections, and what was widely perceived as an unsatisfactory government performance, further **tarnished CCM's reputation**. Its preparations for the next general elections had begun in 2012 with changes in the party constitution, the formation of a full-time secretariat and elections to the National Executive Committee (NEC). In June, the NEC finally elected the remaining 14 members of the influential Central Committee (CC); this step had been deferred since the National Congress in November 2012, while only the ex-officio members occupied their posts. The CC was expected to play the important role of choosing the party's presidential candidate for the next elections in late 2015. Given that President Kikwete was not allowed to stand again after two terms, the selection of his successor was expected to become an extremely sensitive issue, especially in a situation in which the opposition was vigorously gaining ground and the splits between various feuding CCM factions were threatening the party's dominance. However, the leadership's modest attempts to reform the party appeared not to be very successful. In his opening remarks at a party workshop in late October, Kikwete accused party leaders of being "agents of fuelling corruption" and warned that the party could lose the forthcoming elections if it continued its corrupt practices. In early June, a joint workshop of UNDP and the National Assembly revealed that **20% of the government's budget** was eaten-up by **corruption**. In TI's corruption assessment, Tanzania dropped slightly from 102nd in 2012 to 111th in 2013.

In a seeming repetition of a cabinet reshuffle that had become necessary in May 2012 due to allegations of ministerial corruption, misuse of funds and incompetence, the **government again came under parliamentary fire** towards the end of the year. In reaction to national and international pressure to deal with the increasing problem of **elephant and rhino poaching**, the government had in early September started **'Operesheni Tokomeza' (Operation Wipe-Out)** to contain this evil. The operation was a joint effort by four ministries and involved soldiers, policemen, game rangers and forestry officers. However, after only two months 'Tokomeza' was called off by the National Assembly, following reports of **rampant human rights violations** in the course of its operation. A parliamentary inquiry uncovered the murder of 13 civilians, arrests of over 1,000 people, torture, rape, sexual harassment, seizure of property and other abuses by agents of the operation. Upon the presentation of the report in parliament on 20 December, MPs demanded the **resignation** of **Prime Minister Mizengo Pinda** and the **four ministers** of the ministries involved in the operation.

Only a few days earlier, MPs had already demanded that the Prime Minister and the Minister of State for Regional Administration and Local Government step down for allegedly not reacting to the **misuse and theft of public funds in local authorities**, which were revealed by three parliamentary oversight committees. On 14 December, even the CCM's CC and secretariat presented a list of seven ministers and deputy ministers to Kikwete and recommended that they should be taken to task for underperformance. On 20 December, Kikwete **dismissed the four ministers** whose ministries were involved in 'Operesheni Tokomeza' (Defence, Home Affairs, Tourism and Natural Resources, and Livestock Development). Pinda and the other ministers who were criticised by the CCM organs remained untouched, but Kikwete announced a cabinet reshuffle for early 2014.

Apart from the challenges caused by its internal problems, CCM's position was also threatened by the activities of the **main opposition party CHADEMA**. Buoyed by growing popularity, the party continued with its efforts to win more public support – but at the risk of confrontation with the security agencies. In the struggle for a revised constitution, CHADEMA emerged as a driving force that was able to pressurise the government to give in to popular demands. Long-smouldering leadership conflicts erupted rather surprisingly on 22 November, when the party's CC announced that it had **deposed** the party's **deputy secretary-general Zitto Kabwe** and two other prominent leaders. Kabwe, CC member Kitila Mkumbo and former Arusha regional party chairman Samson Mwigamba were accused of planning a plot against the current party leadership to be enacted at the next internal party elections and were stripped of all their leadership positions, except their party membership. On the same day, CHADEMA's vice-chairman for the mainland, Said Amour Arfi, resigned. The three ousted leaders were given two weeks to explain why they should not be expelled from the party. Kabwe declared the accusations baseless and appealed against his deposition to the party's Executive Council (the highest party organ). The young and charismatic Kabwe, an MP for Kigoma North, deputy leader of the opposition in the National Assembly, shadow finance minister and chairman of the influential Public Accounts Committee, had for many years been one of the party's most prominent and popular figures, and CHADEMA owed much of its success to his activities. However, his personal ambitions had long been a source of contention and had led to leadership struggles in previous years. A lengthy internal conflict was likely to weaken the party's prospects in the forthcoming elections of 2014 and 2015.

As in previous years, **political, religious and socio-economic conflicts** posed a **threat to security**. On 17 February, a Catholic priest was shot dead in **Zanzibar**; two days later, a church was burnt down. On 7 August, two young female British volunteers were attacked with acid by two men on a motorcycle, and on 13 September, acid was thrown on a Catholic priest. Several people were arrested, but the culprits were not found. It remained unclear whether there was a connection to suspected al-Shabaab activities in the region or whether these attacks were a result of growing religious intolerance or anti-

Union and anti-Mainland sentiments, since the growth of Christianity in Zanzibar was perceived to be the result of the influx of Mainlanders. On the **Mainland**, in Geita Region, a pastor of the Assemblies of God church was beheaded on 11 February. In early April, riots between Christians and Muslims in Tunduma, on the Zambia border, about slaughtering rituals prompted the authorities to temporarily close the border. At least two people were severely injured and a mosque under construction was destroyed. A bomb attack on a Catholic church in Arusha killed at least three people and injured 60 on 5 May, during a visit by the Vatican ambassador to Tanzania and the Archbishop of Arusha. Media reports that nationals from Tanzania and Saudi Arabia had been arrested raised concern about a possibly growing Wahhabi influence in Tanzania. However, the Arabs were soon released when it became clear that they were just tourists. Arusha was again shocked by a bomb blast on 15 June during a CHADEMA rally. The bomb, thrown at CHADEMA chairman Freeman Mbowe and the local MP, killed two people and injured several others. Both politicians were unhurt. A few days later, CHADEMA supporters clashed with the police. Arusha, having emerged as a CHADEMA stronghold in the 2010 elections, had since then witnessed several violent incidents involving security forces and party supporters. Politicians, religious leaders and members of CSOs expressed their deep concern at the alarming increase in violence between members of different religions and called for mutual tolerance and respect.

The conflict over government plans to construct a **gas pipeline** from the natural gas fields near the southern town of **Mtwara** to Dar es Salaam resulted in **violent clashes** between protesters and security forces on 26 January, which left four people dead and a dozen injured. The government arrested more than 50 people and put Mtwara under tight security control. Protests had started in late December 2012 with peaceful demonstrations jointly organised by several opposition political parties, followed by further demonstrations in January. Demonstrators protested against the planned pipeline and demanded to see local benefits from the natural resources found in their region. On 1 February, Kikwete announced plans for several **development projects in the region**, including a power station, expanded ports, factories and others. According to him, there were plans to pipe only 16% of the Mtwara gas to Dar es Salaam, with the remainder staying in the region. Prime Minister Pinda and five ministers visited Mtwara to hold discussions with residents and political and religious leaders and called for calm. Despite these efforts, the situation escalated again on 22 May, when protesters demolished a bridge, attacked several government and party offices and set some on fire. At least one person died and several were injured, most likely as a result of a heavy-handed response by the police. More than 90 people were arrested, and the government deployed the army to Mtwara to restore calm. Pinda visited Mtwara again and promised that several factories would be built and 1,000 jobs created in the region. The protests were an immediate reaction to a televised parliamentary statement by the energy and minerals minister that the pipeline would be built as planned.

The annual **human rights report** of the Legal and Human Rights Centre and the Zanzibar Legal Service Centre, published in April, indicated an increase in human rights violations in 2012. Mob justice and gender-based violence, including female genital mutilation, were among the major human rights problems. **Restrictive actions against the press** continued to occur during the year. On 8 January, community radio journalist Issa Ngumba was found murdered in a forest in Kigoma Region. Ngumba had been working on an investigation into the murder of a local shepherd. It was unclear whether he was killed because of his reporting or for other reasons. Two local radio stations in Morogoro and Mwanza, run by religious institutions (one Christian and one Muslim), were banned by the Tanzania Communications Regulatory Authority for six months for broadcasting statements that allegedly violated the law and broadcasting ethics, and a programme by the popular Clouds FM radio station was banned for allegedly promoting homosexual marriage. On 27 September, the government announced a 14-day ban on 'Mwananchi' newspaper and a 90-day ban on 'Mtanzania' newspaper. The **bans** on these two reputable **newspapers** were criticised by national and international media stakeholders and human rights activists as a restriction of the right of press freedom.

Foreign Affairs

Tanzania's growing importance as an emerging economy with vast natural resources, especially gas and uranium, an entry point to Eastern and Central Africa and the most peaceful and stable country in the region was reflected in two high-ranking state visits that seemed to be an expression of global competition and were regarded with envy by Tanzania's neighbours. For newly-appointed **Chinese President Xi Jinping**, Tanzania was only the second country he had visited, after Russia, and the first on his three-country Africa tour. During his visit (24–25 March), he signed a number of agreements on new development projects and on economic, trade and cultural cooperation. Among them was the planned construction of an entirely new port near Bagamoyo with an envisaged capacity 20 times that of the chronically congested Dar es Salaam port. A high-ranking delegation of ministers, regional commissioners, senior government officials and businesspeople, led by Prime Minister Pinda, participated in the **first Tanzania-China Business Forum** in Guangzhou in early November as part of a nine-day tour of China to bolster trade and investment links between the two countries.

During his visit to Tanzania (1–2 July) as part of an Africa tour, **US President Barack Obama** announced the launch of two new initiatives aimed at bolstering trade and increasing access to electricity. 'Trade Africa' was intended to increase internal and regional trade within Africa, with an initial focus on the EAC member states, and to expand trade and economic ties between Africa, the USA and other global markets, and the 'Power Africa Initiative' aimed at doubling electrical power generation and supply. Obama was accompanied by a 700-member delegation, mostly business people. He and his predecessor, George W. Bush, who was attending a conference in Dar es Salaam, laid a wreath to commemorate the victims of the al-Qaeda attack on the US embassy in 1998.

Generally good relations with the **donor community** were overshadowed by continuing misuse of donor funds and corruption. In late November, the Netherlands, Sweden, Finland, Ireland, Japan and Germany suspended their support to the Local Government Reform Programme and demanded a refund of more than $ 370,000. The six donors accused government officials of stealing the money. In early December, the government closed the programme's secretariat and dismissed several officials who were accused of embezzling the funds. Relations with Germany were temporarily shaken after Tanzania in mid-September rejected the back-to-back posting of the German ambassador to Kenya to the same position in Dar es Salaam. Although no reason was given by the Tanzanian authorities, it was widely believed that the unprecedented move was caused by the former envoy's close relations with the political opposition in Kenya.

Tanzania continued to play an active role in the search for a solution to the armed **conflicts in eastern DRC**. On 24 February, together with ten other African countries (all except South Africa ICGLR members), it signed a UN-sponsored agreement in Addis Ababa (Ethiopia) to bring peace to the region, which paved the way for the deployment of a regional military brigade to eastern DRC to complement the long-installed UN Stabilization Mission in DRC peacekeepers. Between May and June, Tanzania deployed at least 1,300 soldiers to the **UN Force Intervention Brigade (FIB) in the DRC**, which was established on 28 March and tasked with a robust mandate to carry out offensive operations against armed rebel groups in eastern DRC, mainly targeting the M23 rebel group, but also other so-called "negative forces". Tanzania, South Africa and Malawi contributed to the 3,069 strong force, commanded by the Tanzanian General James Aloisi Mwakibolwa. Tanzanian troops were involved in direct combat with the M23, which finally surrendered on 5 November. In another international mission, seven Tanzanian peacekeepers of the **UN-AU mission in Darfur** (UNAMID) were killed and 17 others injured while on patrol on 13 July. Tanzania had contributed more than 1,000 soldiers, police personnel and experts to the mission in February 2012. On 4 June, the Tanzanian Lieutenant General Paul Ignace Mella was appointed UNAMID Force Commander.

Relations with **Rwanda** worsened considerably in late May in reaction to Kikwete's suggestion during the AU summit in Addis Ababa that the DRC, Rwanda and Uganda should initiate direct talks with their respective rebel groups in the Great Lakes region. This was most strongly rejected by Rwanda, which accused Tanzania of thus implicitly recognising and backing the DRC-based FDLR rebels, held responsible for the 1994 genocide in Rwanda. Kikwete was viciously attacked in Kigali's state-controlled media. Although Rwanda had signed the February UN peace framework for the DRC, Tanzania's leading role in the FIB was hardly conducive to reducing the tension. The FIB fought against the M23 rebels, which Rwanda was supposedly supporting. The war of words between the two countries accelerated further, when Tanzania expelled thousands of Rwandans in late July and August. While Rwanda interpreted this as an unfriendly action, Tanzania justified it as an effort to cleanse the country of "illegal immigrants". On 25 July, Kikwete issued an order that "**illegal immigrants**" and "criminals" should leave the country by 11 August. The authorities forcibly expelled 7,000–8,000 Rwandans and at least 15,000 Burundians, many of whom had been living in Tanzania for decades. Malawians living in Tanzania reported xenophobic attacks against them, presumably due to the border dispute between the two countries. About 1,000 'illegal' Malawians were temporarily arrested, but also offered the opportunity to regularise their status in Tanzania by applying for residence permits. In October, Tanzania was still hosting 102,000 officially registered refugees.

This crackdown on residents from neighbouring countries contributed to long-standing irritations about Tanzania's apparent reluctance towards a deeper and faster **EAC integration** process. Tanzania felt side-lined when a so-called **Coalition of the Willing (CoW)**, comprising the presidents of Kenya, Rwanda and Uganda, met in June, August and October to discuss several joint infrastructural projects in the so-called 'Northern Corridor'. Burundi, initially excluded, was invited to join the CoW, but decided to remain aloof, while a delegation from the EAC-aspirant South Sudan did participate in the meetings. Tanzania strongly ruled out joining the CoW, and insisted that the trilateral talks contravened EAC protocols and were a threat to EAC integration. On 30 October, Minister for East African Co-operation Samwel Sitta told parliament that Tanzania was considering leaving the EAC and initiating a closer alliance with the DRC and Burundi. In an eagerly awaited televised speech, Kikwete declared on 7 November that Tanzania was clearly determined to stay in the EAC; however, he sharply criticised the CoW and insisted that all EAC member states should follow the agreed regulations. This self-assured statement, two days after the defeat of the M23, was interpreted by some observers as an expression of Tanzania's 'victory' over Rwanda. On 10 November, Kenya's foreign minister paid a visit and promised that Kenya would work closely with Tanzania. During the regular EAC summit on 30 November in Kampala (Uganda), the conflicts appeared to have been sorted out; the five partner states reaffirmed their commitment to close cooperation and signed a protocol on a future Monetary Union. According to observers, the apparent split between the diverging EAC groups was rooted in three issues: first, the CoW's impatience for further and faster integration, which was perceived to be blocked by Tanzania; second, the conflict between Rwanda and Tanzania about their respective roles in the DRC and their alleged support for rebel groups; and third, economic competition between Kenya and Tanzania over control of the transport routes from the Indian Ocean to the landlocked countries and attracting (Chinese) investments.

There were no decisive developments in the **Lake Nyasa border dispute** with **Malawi**. In January, both sides presented their legal positions to the SADC Forum of Former Heads of State and Government, which had been addressed by both sides for a ruling in December 2012. In April, Malawi withdrew from the process, claiming bias by one of the officials involved, but returned in early May. In June, Malawi complained about Tanzania's plans to start operating passenger ships on the lake. Malawi's President Joyce Banda set a 30 September deadline for the Forum to come up with a resolution, failing which she would take the case to the International Court of Justice. However, at year's end the SADC mediation process was still on-going.

As chairman of the **SADC** Organ on Politics, Defence and Security Cooperation (**SADC Troika**), Kikwete played a crucial role in negotiating a way out of the political crisis in **Madagascar**. During the regular SADC summit on 17 August in Malawi, Kikwete handed over the rotational Troika chair to Namibia's President Pohamba. Kikwete's tenure also witnessed the peaceful but controversial re-election of President Mugabe in Zimbabwe.

Socioeconomic Developments

The overall **macroeconomic performance** again continued to be quite robust and in line with the strong continuous growth trend over more than a decade since the early 2000s. In this period, Tanzania had become one of the fastest growing and most consistently performing economies in Africa, albeit still characterised by a very low absolute level of material wealth. In the 2013 **HDI** (data for 2012), Tanzania was ranked 152nd (out of 185 countries), in the low human development category. **Per capita income** was estimated to have reached about $ 625 in 2013 ($ 1,615 in PPP terms). In the face of the continuing global economic and financial crisis, Tanzania's economy again proved to be remarkably resilient. The **GDP growth rate** for 2013 was estimated at 7.1%, slightly above the 6.9% in 2012 and on the high side of the growth trend of most preceding years (range of 6%–7%). Climatically, it was a fairly average year with good harvests, which allowed the agricultural sector to grow by about 4.6%. Expectations of a faster and more fundamental transformation of the economy were increasingly linked with the prospect of becoming a significant producer of natural gas, although full commercial exploitation was still a number of years away. In the World Economic Forum's Global Competitiveness Index 2013–14 Tanzania was ranked 125th (out of 148 countries), five places lower than before.

High **inflation** rates in previous years (12.7% in 2011 and 16% in 2012) had been a major cause of growing popular discontent. Inflation was successfully and steadily brought down during the year from 10.9% (January) to 5.6% (December). The year's average inflation rate of 7.9% was largely attributed to a noticeable fall in food prices and the pursuit of a tight monetary policy. This also contributed to the stabilisation of the **exchange rate**; with some minor fluctuations during the year, it was in December (TSh 1,617 : $ 1), just 2% lower than in January. This stability was a clear sign of widely prevailing confidence in the economy's prospects. The **structural trade deficit** grew substantially by almost 20% to $ 5,258 m, principally as a result of unchanged export earnings. While imports grew normally by about 8% to $ 11,159 m (with oil alone accounting for one third), exports practically stagnated at a value of $ 5,901 m. This was partly explained by lower world prices for some commodities, particularly gold, the main export item (accounting for roughly one-third of total exports). On balance, only 53% of Tanzania's import needs were covered by its own export revenues. The (preliminary) **current-account deficit** was thus estimated to have remained at the 2012 level of about 15% of GDP, the highest for several years. Gross **foreign reserves** were further strengthened at $ 4.5 bn (compared with $ 4.0 bn in 2012) by the year's end, sufficient for a comfortable import coverage of over four months. While the **external debt** had previously been substantially reduced to a low of $ 4.2 bn in 2006 as a result of concerted debt cancellations under the HIPC initiative, it had lately been creeping up again rather fast, reaching $ 13.6 bn at year's end (compared with $ 11.6 bn at end-2012). Linked with the many on-going large investment projects, **FDI** inflows remained very substantial at an estimated $ 1,790 m ($ 1,632 m in 2012). Likewise, **tourism earnings** of $ 1,472 m ($ 1,563 m in 2012) remained Tanzania's most important foreign exchange earner, even topping gold.

On 3 June, the **IMF** completed its sixth and final review under the **Policy Support Instrument (PSI)**, an unfunded IMF instrument designed for countries that do not need balance of payments financial support. The Tanzanian PSI had been operative since June 2010. The IMF commended the Tanzanian authorities "for their commitment to policies aimed at containing demand pressures, strengthening macroeconomic stability, and preserving a sound fiscal position". Simultaneously, a second review was conducted under the 18-month **Standby Credit Facility (SCF)** that had been approved in July 2012 for about $ 228 m as a precautionary measure against the potential downside risks of a global slowdown; in February the government had drawn $ 114 m under this SCF to support the currency. An IMF mission in early November conducted the biennial Article IV discussions, discussed a possible new PSI and assessed the performance under the SCF. Again, the economy was judged to be performing well and the economic outlook was seen as promising, but some concern was expressed about the appearance of fiscal pressures in excess of agreed targets.

On 13 June, Finance Minister William Mgimwa submitted the 2013–14 **budget** to parliament. Contrary to previous practice, the individual ministerial votes had already been discussed since April. A review of the previous financial year's outturn revealed that the overall **fiscal deficit** for **2012–13** had markedly increased to 6.2% of GDP (from 5.0%), mainly the result of the government's overestimation of revenues and underestimation of expenditure. Contrary to ambitious targets, domestic revenues had only increased marginally and foreign aid inflows had also been below initial projections. Significant adjustments to the financing side of the budget had to be made by way of higher than targeted public (domestic and external) borrowing. A seven-year bond for over $ 600 m was issued in March by private placement with banks, but the contemplated issue of a sovereign bond was postponed to 2014 and still needed an official credit rating. The observable finance tendencies seemed to reflect a remarkable recent government policy shift. While the pursuance of a relatively tight monetary policy had successfully controlled the inflation rate, a more relaxed fiscal stance was seen as an appropriate instrument to promote economic growth. An accelerated drive for the development of social and physical infrastructure was clearly intended under the **"Big Results Now" (BRN)** initiative launched by Kikwete on 22 February. This was a copy of a similar successful programme in Malaysia; 300 Malaysians had been invited to coach Tanzanian top civil servants on the approach. BRN was expected to accelerate the transformation of the economy towards the goal of becoming a middle-income country, as envisaged in the Tanzania Development Vision 2025. BRN covered six priority areas, namely energy and gas, agriculture, water, education, transport and resource mobilisation.

The **2013–14 budget** clearly reflected an expansionary intention, with a more than 20% higher volume than the previous budget. Domestic revenue was optimistically expected to increase to a 20.2% share of GDP (compared with 17.6% achieved in 2012–13), and the expected fiscal deficit was set at a reduced 4.4% of GDP. Efforts were to be made to scrap many of the tax exemptions that had in 2011–12 been estimated to have cost 4.3% of GDP. Total expenditure was budgeted at TSh 18,250 bn (about $ 11.4 bn), with 69% foreseen for recurrent expenditure and 31% for development programmes, whereby almost half of the development budget was expected to come from external sources. The breakdown of the total budget funding was as follows: domestic revenue 63%, general budget support (external) 6.4%, foreign loans and grants 14.8%, domestic borrowing 9.3%, non-concessional foreign borrowing 6.9%. In the mid-year budget review, it became evident that revenue was falling short of assumptions and that considerable expenditure arrears had been built up. The IMF expressed concern about the need to attain a fiscal deficit close to the target of 5% of GDP.

In mid-November, new official **poverty** data were released, based on the 2011–12 Household Budget Survey (HBS); 28.2% of the population were assessed to be living below the **absolute income poverty line** of TSh 36,482 ($ 22.7) per month. This seemed to indicate some reduction of poverty from the 33.6% measured in the 2007 HBS, but the methodologies of the surveys had not been strictly comparable. The absolute number of about 12.3 m poor people was, however, roughly the same as in 2001. The incidence of poverty was very unevenly distributed and affected 33.3% of the rural population, but only 4.2% of Dar es Salaam residents and 21.7% of other urban dwellers. Around 10%

of the total population did not even reach the **extreme food poverty line** of TSh 26,085 ($ 16.3) per month; this was the case for 11.3% of rural people, but for only 1% in Dar es Salaam. Income inequality was measured as relatively moderate with a Gini coefficient of 0.34 (in Dar es Salaam 0.35, in rural areas 0.29).

Optimistic expectations of a general upturn in the economy centred strongly on increasingly promising prospects for the exploitation of Tanzania's substantial **natural gas** resources, although full commercial benefits were only expected to build up in about seven to ten years. According to some forecasts, the gas sector might then potentially contribute about one-third of GDP. With on-going exploration activities, proven gas reserves had been rapidly updated to around 43 trillion cubic feet, but more seemed very probable. In October, the postponed fourth gas and oil licensing round for seven offshore blocks and the Lake Tanganyika area was launched, to run until May 2014. Production-sharing agreements with 18 international exploration companies were already in existence. The decision of the energy and mining ministry to exclude private Tanzanian business interests from the gas block auctions, with the assertion that capital-intensive exploration activities were beyond their means, provoked strong protests. During the second oil and gas conference in October, the government floated the intention of creating a special "gas revenue fund" to manage all future proceeds. In May, the ministry presented a second draft of a national **natural gas policy**, which outlined a comprehensive framework for the gas sector, but left many concrete specifications open (such as the exact mandate of a regulatory body and the future role of the parastatal Tanzania Petroleum Development Company). The passage of specific legislation to adapt outdated old mining laws was expected in 2014. The gas policy stated clearly that priority should be given to developing the gas sector in order to bring major benefits to the domestic economy, but plans for a liquefied natural gas plant for export were also envisaged. The on-going construction of a Chinese-financed gas pipeline from Mtwara to Dar es Salaam was poised to be completed in late 2014. This would allow a dramatic increase in **electricity** generation and hopefully end the recurring problems of long-endured **power failures**. The heavily loss-making power utility TANESCO continued to be a major financial burden for the government; average tariff increases of about 40% as of January 2014 were deemed to be no more than a partial solution.

Gold production continued to contribute significantly to overall growth and exports, despite some setbacks and gold's relative loss of importance. New **mining** ventures were about to start production of nickel and uranium and were faced with protests from environmentalists. Chinese investors proceeded with an ambitious $ 3 bn project for the exploitation of coal reserves and iron-ore deposits in the south-west. The improvement of the country's physical **infrastructure** (roads, railways, ports, power installations) was a major focus of the government's development strategy, although the implementation of announced projects often remained uncertain. Strenuous efforts to attract more **foreign**

investors were somewhat dashed by continued weaknesses in the domestic business climate. In the World Bank's 'Doing Business 2014' report, Tanzania slipped down to 145th place (from 136th). A December announcement raised the prospect of the removal of restrictions on capital flows within the EAC, bringing opportunities for improved integration of regional capital markets. Long-known weaknesses in Tanzania's **education** system were shockingly exposed in February, when two-thirds of students failed the O-level exams. This confirmed a widely-held consensus that the level of education had deteriorated considerably, with drastic consequences for the country's future prospects.

Kurt Hirschler & Rolf Hofmeier

Uganda

Although somewhat prematurely, Ugandans were already considerably preoccupied with the 2016 presidential (and parliamentary) elections. Internal cleavages in the ruling party became increasingly evident and the president appeared to have embarked on his re-election campaign without openly saying so. Uganda's standing in international affairs remained high, as it continued to play an important role in peacekeeping efforts in Somalia and mediated in the crisis besetting the Great Lakes region. It faced untoward events in neighbouring areas, however. The calamitous situation in the DRC had a spill-over effect, and the sudden turmoil in South Sudan was followed by an influx of refugees. The collapse of public order in the CAR led to a temporary setback in the pursuit of the remnants of the Lord's Resistance Army (LRA) there. The economic situation continued to improve and the promise of confirmed oil reserves remained the subject of much interest, though production remained far from imminent.

Domestic Politics

Whilst **President Yoweri Kaguta Museveni** kept firm overall control of the state apparatus, the Uganda People's Defence Forces (UPDF) and the ruling party, the National Resistance Movement (NRM), internal cracks became even more visible than before.

Disrespect for parliamentary proceedings was demonstrated in January by thinly-veiled threats of a military takeover by some army commanders and the president himself.

Some **NRM** MPs, appalled by corruption and other undesirable developments, took an independent stance. Museveni threatened the introduction of "legal" measures to rein in critical MPs. Disciplinary measures taken by the NRM against four of them, dubbed as 'rebels', led to their expulsion from the parliamentary party. This led to a constitutional legal battle over whether they should lose their seats in parliament since they no longer represented the party. Parliament Speaker Rebecca Kadaga proved that she was not working in a rubber-stamp fashion and safeguarded the rights of these MPs despite pressure.

A battle of wills developed between the president and Parliament over the death of an outspoken young NRM MP, Cerinah Nebanda Arioru, in mid-December 2012. Some politicians suspected deliberate poisoning and government involvement. Attempts to recall Parliament to discuss the issue as requested by more than 100 MPs were foiled. In a February by-election, the NRM candidate, Cerinah Nebanda's sister Florence Andiru Nebanda, was elected as the new woman MP for Butaleja. Cerinah Nebanda's boyfriend was arrested in Kenya, extradited and charged with manslaughter.

Prime Minister Amama Mbabazi clung to his function as NRM secretary-general though he should have vacated it due to his government position. Relations between him and the president were believed to remain strained, since Mbabazi considered himself fit for the presidency. An open though hardly impressive challenge to Museveni came in May from former vice-president Gilbert Bukenya, who had been dropped in the 2011 cabinet reshuffle. He declared his intention to stand as a candidate in the party primaries ahead of the **2016 presidential election**. Museveni remained vague about his plans for 2016, usually asserting that it was party members who were the ones to choose the flag bearer, but he nevertheless made extensive tours of all parts of the country. Among his attempts to fortify his support base was the stronger involvement of army personnel in local development endeavours. The 'envelope culture' – the distribution of cash handouts to various recipients – flourished. A gift of money in a large bag, said to contain the equivalent of $ 100,000, handed to the Busoga Youth Forum in April, aroused international curiosity.

The coordinator of intelligence services General David Sejusa aka Tinyefuza, also a member of the UPDF High Command and an army MP, came forward with a claim that the president was pursuing a hidden agenda, the **'Muhoozi project'** – a scheme aimed at secretly and through assassination of senior government and army leaders paving the way for Museveni's son Muhoozi Kainerugaba to succeed his father. Sejusa absconded to London in May; his defection received a guarded response in the ranks of the opposition, some suspecting him of being a government mole. He teamed up with moderately prominent exile figures Amii Omara-Otunnu, brother of Uganda People's Congress (UPC) leader Olara Otunnu, and Henry Gombya to launch the manifesto of the 'Freedom and Unity Front' in December in London.

On 20 May, coverage of Sejusa's claims culminated in a partial **media shutdown** by the government: the quality paper 'Daily Monitor', part of the East African Nation Media Group owned by the Aga Khan, the tabloid 'Red Pepper' and two FM broadcast stations were closed for ten days, with the police trying to compel the journalists to disclose their sources of information.

Also in May, Museveni carried out a minor **cabinet reshuffle**. General Aronda Nyakairima was nominated as minister of internal affairs in place of Hilary Onek, who took over relief and disaster preparedness. Ruhakana Rugunda was (once again) appointed minister of health replacing the unsuccessful Christine Ondoa. Rugunda's job as communication and ICT minister was given to General Duties Minister John Nasasira. Minister of Information and National Guidance Mary Karooro Okurut became minister of gender, labour and social affairs.

The **protest campaign** led by veteran oppositionist Kizza Besigye continued to some extent, starting with a planned clean-the-city exercise, which police regarded as an illegal political rally. On 26 January, the police arrested Besigye, along with Kampala Lord Mayor Erias Lukwago. This was Besigye's first arrest in 2013; in July, a count by the Ugandan paper 'Observer' revealed that, over a five year period, Besigye had been arrested at least 28 times, put on trial six times and detained once in Luzira prison.

Lukwago, who had been elected Lord Mayor as an independent in 2011, faced conflict with the central government. Tensions prevailed with the minister responsible for the affairs of the capital and with the government-appointed executive officer of the city authority, Jennifer Musisi. In June, the minister set up a tribunal, which found Lukwago incompetent and guilty of abuse of office. On 25 November, Lukwago was impeached by **Kampala** city councillors in a vote of 29 to three at a special meeting chaired by the minister. The news of the impeachment sparked protests in the city and Lukwago successfully appealed against the decision in the High Court.

The leader of the main opposition party **Forum for Democratic Change (FDC)**, Major General (retired) Mugisha Muntu, was at loggerheads with his rival for the FDC top office, Nathan Nandala-Mafabi, who disputed the result of the 2012 party convention; a reconciliation commission and later another committee to look into the matter were created. Muntu eventually kept his post. Uganda's oldest party, the **Democratic Party (DP)**, under the leadership of Norbert Mao, also had its internal wrangles. Mao found it difficult to control the Uganda Young Democrats (UYD) faction, which disputed his leadership. In May, the DP started a "revival crusade". The **UPC**, headed by Olara Otunnu, remained in limbo between him and his critics, including Lira MP Jimmy Akena, son of the late Milton Obote.

The Appointments Committee of **Parliament**, tasked with vetting presidential nominations for top positions, arrived at two widely-criticised decisions. It approved the appointment of General Nyakairima, hitherto chief of the UPDF, as minister of internal affairs, even though he did not resign from the army before taking up his new post, and it also agreed to Chief Justice Benjamin Odoki's term in office being extended by two years, despite his having reached the 70-year age limit.

Important legislation was introduced, including the **Anti-Money Laundering** Bill, 2009, passed on 10 July as a measure to combat corruption. The **Public Order Management Bill**, 2011, which had caused serious concern with regard to freedom of assembly, was passed with a few improvements on 6 August and was signed into law by the president on 2 October. It gave the police "the power to regulate the conduct of all public meetings in accordance with the law". The **Oil Bill**, passed in December 2012, was signed into law by the president in March. Before that, a second bill on the subject, aimed at regulating various related activities and ensuring a transparent process of licensing by the minister responsible, was approved by Parliament on 21 February and came into force as the Petroleum (Refining, Conversion, Transmission and Midstream Storage) Act on 26 July. The **Anti-Pornography Bill**, 2011, was passed on 19 December; it sought to prohibit pornography, which was believed to pose dangers to individuals, families and communities. A day later, the **Anti-Homosexuality Bill**, 2009, was approved. It was based on a private member's bill, proposed by NRM MP David Bahati, which had for some time caused much debate but had remained shelved. Events took an unexpected turn when on 20 December the bill was put on the parliamentary agenda by Speaker Rebecca Kadaga, with no prior notice being given. Government had continuously blocked the bill, but was outmanoeuvred. Prime Minister Mbabazi rushed to Parliament, pointing out that there had been no consultation with government beforehand and that there was no quorum for passing the bill, but his arguments were ignored and the bill was passed without a vote, the opposition parties concurring with NRM members. The bill's main provisions were life imprisonment for people convicted of homosexual acts – including lesbian acts – and seven years' imprisonment for people found guilty of "aiding and abetting homosexuality". The president, who must sign any act for it to become law, reacted reluctantly, referring to the prime minister's point concerning the quorum.

In a prominent **corruption** case that had dragged on for years, MP and NRM national vice chairman for the eastern region Michael Mukula, who had been state minister for health from 2001 to 2006, was found guilty in January of embezzling Global Alliance for Vaccines and Immunization (GAVI) funds and jailed for four years by a magistrate's court. Immediately, cultural leaders and elders from Teso, led by a retired Anglican bishop, visited Museveni at his Rwakitura country home and requested him to pardon Mukula. The president instead pointed to the appeal process and took on Mukula's legal fees, believed to be close to $ 40,000. On appeal, the Anti-Corruption Court found Mukula innocent and he was released after serving less than two months of his sentence. The solidarity shown by local leaders in the cases of former minister of health Jim Muhwezi and his minister of state Mukula illustrated that attitudes towards corruption constituted a societal problem.

Fraud in the **office of the prime minister** uncovered in 2012 led to the conviction of the principal accountant, and he was sentenced to five years in prison. Others who the police alleged had been implicated in the scam were transferred to other ministries. Eight senior officials in the Ministry of Public Service, including the permanent secretary, were charged in connection with a scandal involving payments to 2,605 ghost pensioners that amounted to the equivalent of $ 60 m. The case continued, the accused having been released after paying a bond of slightly less than $ 20,000. Cuts in aid by donors, following the scandal in the prime minister's office, were estimated by the World Bank at $ 300 m.

Prime Minister Mbabazi and ministers Sam Kutesa and Hilary Onek, who in 2011 had been accused by an independent youth MP of taking bribes from oil companies, were exonerated after a parliamentary investigation. Opposition members of the team disagreed, voicing doubts over the way the probe was conducted.

In the **UPDF**, new Internal Affairs Minister General Nyakairima, who had served for a decade as chief of the UPDF, was replaced by Land Forces Commander (and former head of police) Edward Katumba Wamala, now promoted to general. Inspector General of Police Lieutenant General Kale Kayihura was also promoted to general. Authority over the land forces was given to Brigadier David Muhoozi (no relation to Muhoozi Kainerugaba). The 10,000-strong Special Forces Command, well-equipped and well-paid, part of the 50,000-strong UPDF and their linchpin, continued to be headed by Brigadier Muhoozi Kainerugaba. From 19 to 25 May, Jinja hosted 1,290 participants in the Eastern Africa Standby Force (EASF) field training exercise 'Mashariki Salam 2013', which was aimed at establishing interoperability of the EASF components. In August, a 4% increase in UPDF monthly pay was announced, the lowest-paid rank receiving the equivalent of $ 120, the highest $ 620.

The amnesty clause in the **Amnesty** Act, which mainly contained provisions for resettlement and rehabilitation, had been deleted in May 2012. It was reinstated a year later, to be in force for two years, as an inducement to LRA fighters to surrender; it did not apply to LRA top leaders.

Strained relations between the government and the Kabaka of Buganda eased when a memorandum of understanding was signed on 2 August, on the eve of the 20th anniversary of the coronation of this **traditional leader**. It provided for the return of property taken over for administrative purposes when the 1962 independence constitution was abrogated in 1967 and also for the settlement of outstanding arrears. Courtiers nevertheless complained when the list of the traditional heads recognised by government was made available to Parliament in November, since it included two heads of territories once forced by the British to become part of the Buganda kingdom. In neighbouring Busoga, the position of Kyabazinga continued to be vacant. In the west, a visit planned in June by the Omusinga of Rwenzururu to Bundibugyo, where the Baamba ethnic group was not interested in this monarch, was halted by government. In December, UNESCO inscribed the Empaako tradition of the Batoro, Banyoro, Batuku, Batagwenda and Banyabindi of western Uganda – the giving of specific additional names to children in order to foster social ties – on the List of Intangible Cultural Heritage in Need of Urgent Safeguarding.

First Deputy Prime Minister and Minister for EAC Affairs Eriya **Kategaya**, a long-standing companion of Museveni, died on 2 March at the age of 67. General Mustafa **Adrisi**, Amin's vice-president in 1977–8 and later an NRM supporter, died on 28 July, aged 91. Renowned left-wing intellectual **Chango Macho** died on 15 October, aged 86. Sam **Njuba**, a former NRM minister who later joined the FDC and became its national chairman, died on 13 December, aged 72.

Foreign Affairs

From 14–17 May, Kampala hosted about 600 participants in the Commonwealth Local Government Conference, which concluded with the adoption of the 'Kampala Declaration on developmental local government' and the 'Munyonyo Statement on local government's role in the post-2015 development agenda'. A meeting of heads of state and government of the countries contributing troops to the AU Mission in Somalia (AMISOM) took place on 4 August. An extraordinary ICGLR summit dealing with the security situation in eastern DRC was held on 5 September. On 14 September, the COMESA High Level Infrastructure Investment Conference met to discuss "innovative means of infrastructure financing".

Ugandans won respect in **international organisations and fora**. In May, Winnie Byanyima, former MP and wife of Kizza Besigye, assumed office as executive director of Oxfam International in London. In August, former vice-president Speciosa Kazibwe was appointed by UN Secretary-General Ban Ki-moon as his Special Envoy for HIV/AIDS in Africa. Speaker of Parliament Kadaga was elected chairperson of the Commonwealth Women Parliamentarians at their annual conference in Johannesburg in September. Jotham Musinguzi, a distinguished advocate of reproductive health, was one of two recipients of the 2013 UN Population Award on 28 June. In May, the AU Executive Council, after the withdrawal of Cameroon, approved the candidature of Uganda for the presidency of the 69th session of the UN General Assembly starting in September 2014.

Throughout most of the year President Museveni chaired, concomitantly, the EAC, COMESA and the ICGLR. During his one-year tenure as chairperson of the **EAC**, he actively promoted the regional integration agenda. However, frictions emerged, with Tanzania deeming itself sidelined by closer cooperation between Kenya, Rwanda and Uganda. Their three presidents met for a first Tripartite Infrastructure Summit on 24–25 June in Entebbe, followed by meetings on 28 August in Mombasa (Kenya) and on 28 October in Kigali (Rwanda), where South Sudan joined. This so-called Coalition of the Willing aimed to "fast track regional development" through infrastructural, as well as political and economic, integration; Uganda was singled out as the penholder on railway development and political federation. Three Tanzanian citizens, considering the initiative to be in contravention of the EAC treaty, filed an application with the East African Court of Justice, which postponed a hearing to February 2014. During the 15th ordinary EAC summit on 30 November in Kampala, a protocol on the envisaged establishment of an East African Monetary Union was signed, and Museveni passed the chairmanship to Kenya's President Kenyatta. With regard to **COMESA**, Museveni was credited with pursuing integration efforts and paying attention to the interests of small traders. The next summit, when he was to hand over the chairmanship to DRC President Kabila, was postponed to 2014.

On 24 February in Addis Ababa (Ethiopia), Vice President Edward Ssekandi, on behalf of Uganda and of Museveni as **ICGLR** chairman, signed a Peace, Security and Cooperation Framework Agreement for the DRC and the region concluded by 11 Eastern and Southern African countries in response to the chronic violence plaguing eastern DRC. The UNSC on 28 March welcomed the adoption of the framework and the appointment of former Irish president Mary Robinson as the UN secretary-general's special envoy for the Great Lakes. However, Museveni's attempts, started in December 2012, to mediate between the Kinshasa government and the M23 mutineers had long proved futile. At the joint extraordinary summit of SADC and the ICGLR on the security situation in eastern DRC, held in Pretoria (South Africa) on 4 November, Museveni was nevertheless commended for facilitating the 'Kampala Dialogue', which resulted in the signing on 12 December in Nairobi of declarations by the DRC government and the ex-M23 regarding their respective commitments. The former rebels were entitled to amnesty except with regard to war crimes.

Several waves of fighting in eastern **DRC** once more led to an influx of refugees; the UNHCR had assisted about 50,000 by the end of October. Congolese refugees, the majority having arrived during the last three years, made up almost two-thirds of Uganda's entire refugee population. At year's end, the Congolese army, supported by South African helicopters of the UN intervention brigade, retook the town of Kamango after an attack by the Allied Democratic Forces, a Ugandan rebel movement turned Islamist and operating in eastern DRC.

Subsequent to a 29 July directive by Tanzania's President Kikwete, by the end of September about 4,800 Ugandans had been expelled from **Tanzania**. Most of them had migrated from Uganda to the Kagera region in the early 1960s.

Relations with **Sudan**, having long been strained, deteriorated further. On 5 January in Kampala, various political activists, including the National Umma Party and the Sudanese Communist Party, signed the 'New Dawn Charter', which called for a transition to a government of national unity. Khartoum reacted by complaining to the UNSC on 23 January.

In mid-December in **South Sudan**, former vice-president Machar staged a coup attempt against President Kiir. In view of the close geographical, political and economic connections between the two countries, Uganda immediately responded by sending soldiers. Their task was given as protecting and repatriating the numerous Ugandan traders. Several transporter plane flights from Juba to Entebbe were organised and a corridor between Juba and the border town of Nimule was protected by the UPDF. Fleeing the fighting in their country, South Sudanese took refuge in Uganda. By year's end they numbered more than 7,000.

In **Somalia**, AMISOM made military advances. Its strength as of 25 January was given as 17,709 total uniformed personnel. Uganda was the top troop-contributing country, with 6,223 soldiers, followed by Kenya (4,652), Burundi (4,432) and Djibouti (960). On 12 November, the UNSC authorised a mandate extension until 31 October 2014 and an increase in strength up to 22,126. Ugandan force commander Lieutenant General Andrew Gutti handed over to a Burundian of the same rank in mid-December. After allegations of theft of fuel and soldiers' food by commanders, corruption in the Ugandan contingent was investigated by the UPDF. The EU Somalia Training Mission which, together with the UPDF, instructed Somali recruits in Bihanga Military Training School in Kamwenge district, wound up in December; the training was to be continued in Somalia. Altogether, more than 3,600 Somali recruits had received training in Bihanga since April 2010.

Attempts to uproot what was left of the **LRA** in the CAR made some, though not decisive, progress. The CAR government was ousted on 24 March by a militia group, launching a reign of terror, and efforts to lay hands on LRA leader Joseph Kony were temporarily stalled. A reward of up to $ 5 m under the US War Crimes Rewards Programme for information leading to the arrest of Kony, his main aides and the leader of a Rwandan exile force, announced on 3 April, was not collected. But regional and international efforts continued, including the extension until May 2014 of the AU Peace and Security Council initiative on 17 June, and a meeting of the International Working Group on the LRA co-chaired by the EU and the US on 4 October in Brussels. Key elements of the AU Regional Cooperation Initiative against the LRA were put in place. As reported by the UN, "with training, planning and operational support from US military advisers, the Ugandan, South Sudanese and Congolese contingents" became operational. On 9 August, the AU Regional Task Force resumed action, launching 'Operation Monsoon'. The DRC had agreed to movements of the South Sudanese contingent on its territory, thus allowing cross-border operations. The Congolese Garamba National Park continued to provide a refuge for the LRA. By November, troop strength had reached 3,085 (two-thirds being UPDF soldiers) of the 5,000 authorised. The UNSC president, in Council statement 2013/18 on 25 November, encouraged donors "to increase funding for humanitarian and early recovery projects" outlined in the 2012 UN Regional Strategy to Address the Threat and Impact of the Activities of the LRA.

Ugandan cooperation with the US Department of Defence and the US Africa Command (**AFRICOM**) continued. In late January, a five-day workshop on transnational threats was conducted for officials from East African nations and organisations. The civil aviation authority and UPDF facilitated US airlift missions staged out of Entebbe. The Junior Staff College located in Jinja's Gaddafi Barracks was the venue in April for a two-week course for 55 officers being trained by the US Army in how to deal with civilians during military operations. A Civil-Military Operations (CMO) force had just been established as a chieftaincy within the UPDF. In Singo Peace Support Training Centre, UPDF units ready to be deployed in Somalia received training from Western instructors, including US Marines and Military Police. On 23 July, US Deputy Defence Secretary Ashton Carter, the highest-ranking Pentagon official ever to visit Uganda, came "to affirm the growing security partnership".

International campaigns over the issue of **homosexuality** in Uganda continued. Lesbian activist Kasha Jacqueline Nabagesera, who in 2011 had been honoured by AI, was presented in June with the Berlin Christopher Street Day award by German Cooperation Minister Dirk Niebel and in September received the Nuremberg human rights prize, including a € 15,000 donation. Covert financial support to local and regional initiatives included money made available in January by the Canadian Foreign Ministry. Other Ugandan human rights groups were said to feel uneasy about the uncontrolled and unaccountable financial support from abroad for LGBTI groups. After the passing of the Anti-Homosexuality Bill on 20 December international calls were promptly addressed to President Museveni not to sign the bill into law.

Socioeconomic Developments

An underlying problem of Uganda's economy was pointed out by the IMF in January, when it highlighted "the need for a more radical fight against corruption" whilst welcoming the government's intention "to strengthen public financial management in order to reinforce controls and increase transparency of public sector operations".

The macroeconomic performance continued to improve. In late November, Finance Minister Maria Kiwanuka in a letter of intent to the IMF was able to report that "growth has been stronger than expected". In the financial year 2012/13, real **GDP growth** reached 5.8%, 0.7 percentage points higher than had been projected. Core inflation stood at 7.2% in October; the medium-term goal to keep it at 5% appeared to be realistic. Headline inflation (including food crops, fuel and electricity) at 3.6% in June reached a low, but went up to 8% in October owing to a temporary food price shock caused by drought. The exchange rate of the Uganda shilling (UGX) against the dollar appreciated slightly.

Advice and monitoring being the aim of the **IMF**'s Policy Support Instrument (PSI), on 18 December it completed its first review under the new PSI, which it had approved on 28 June. It noted that growth was steadily recovering "from the 2011/12 low" and that inflation generally was on the decline. The monetary policy of the Bank of Uganda won applause for having been "appropriately tightened". Uganda's external accounts were deemed "sustainable" and international reserves equivalent to 3.9 months of imports were seen as "a welcome buffer". A warning was sounded that "spending pressures need to be resisted" and that "expenditure needs to adhere to the budget". "Progress on increasing tax revenues and reducing arrears" were singled out as "remaining challenges".

Earlier in the year, Museveni had launched **'Vision 2040'**, a plan for transformation "from a predominantly peasant society into a competitive upper middle-income country by 2040", intending to put into practice the tenet of "building an independent, integrated and self-sustaining national economy" of the 1985 NRM ten-point programme. On 18 April, Museveni predicted that Uganda "will become a lower middle-income country by 2017 and an upper middle-income country by 2032". Emphasis was put on the contribution of the private sector. Among the core projects were the roll-out of ICT, as well as of science and technology; one nuclear and several hydro-electric power plants were intended to be built.

In line with Vision 2040 was the theme 'The Journey Continues: Towards Socio-Economic Transformation for Uganda' for the **2013/14 budget**, presented by Finance Minister Kiwanuka on 13 June. Expenditure of UGX 13,169 bn (then about $ 5 bn) was projected, representing an increase of almost a fifth over the previously projected budget for 2012/13. As a result of cuts by donors over the fraud in the prime minister's office and other corruption scandals, an even larger part of the budget was to be financed from internal sources than for 2012/13 when 75% had been projected. Now, with UGX 10,509 bn (including taxes of UGX 8,486 bn and the issue of government securities worth UGX 1,040 bn), this rate reached about 80%. Donor financing of the remaining UGX 2,660 bn, equivalent to 20%, comprised project aid to the tune of UGX 2,447 bn and budget support of just UGX 213 bn. Kiwanuka saw the "need to examine non-traditional sources of financing in light of declining budget support". Planned expenditure again showed high priority being given to infrastructure development, particularly in transport and energy. To increase revenue, some VAT exemptions were to be scrapped, including on water supply. Excise duty on petrol and diesel, non-locally produced tobacco products and car licences fees was to be increased. A 10% duty on mobile money transaction fees was to be introduced. Parliament later accepted Kiwanuka's proposals, but scrapped the planned re-instatement of duty on paraffin.

Serious risks to long-term economic progress caused by deficiencies in **education** and **health** came out into the open in November. Service Delivery Indicators, based on a sample survey and presented by the World Bank, pointed towards significant knowledge gaps among teachers and health workers and found a high incidence of absenteeism among both. In public schools visited, 40% of classrooms had no teacher teaching in them. This also indicated poor remuneration of staff; after a three-week strike, the government promised in September that it would honour an earlier commitment to another step up in teachers' salaries.

On 23 May, the National Tripartite Charter on **Labour Relations** was signed by the government, the Federation of Uganda Employers and the two trade union confederations, the National Organisation of Trade Unions and the Central Organisation of Free Trade Unions. This aimed, *inter alia*, at the promotion of decent employment and productivity.

For lack of funds, the population and housing **census** which had been postponed to August 2013 was again deferred, now to August 2014. 'The State of Uganda Population Report 2013', launched on 31 October, already provided some dismal findings by pointing out that Uganda had "the world's youngest population" and also "one of the highest youth unemployment rates in Sub-Saharan Africa". The population was growing annually by 3.2%, and the fertility rate stood at 6.2 children; these factors converged to "bring a very high youth dependency ratio".

The government embarked on implementing its long-standing plan to set up an **oil** refinery, although on a smaller scale than it had originally wanted. Construction of the refinery involved the resettlement and compensation of several thousand villagers in 13 villages; the whole area covered 29 km^2. Beginning in mid-December, to protests by some of the people affected, compensation was paid to land and other property owners in Bunyoro.

Floods displaced more than 25,000 people in Kasese district in May, and **landslides** in the region of Mt Elgon occurred again. The national **land policy** formulated by the government after comprehensive stakeholder consultations was published in February. Land disputes were a common cause of conflict; the origin was often to be traced to colonial policy, which had in effect created "multiple and conflicting tenure rights and interests often overlapping over the same piece of land".

The 2013 TI **Corruption Perceptions Index** released in December ranked Uganda 140th out of 177 countries (compared with 130th in 2012, 143rd in 2011, and 127th in 2010). The EAC partner states Rwanda (49th), Tanzania (111th) and Kenya (136th) did better, Burundi (157th) worse.

Volker Weyel

VII. Southern Africa

The generally peaceful atmosphere (in the sense of an absence of any military clashes or civil wars) that had characterised large parts of the sub-region for more than a decade was interrupted and abruptly disturbed by new terrorist attacks by Renamo in Mozambique. Civil disobedience and unrest also increased in Angola. In contrast, elections in Zimbabwe and Madagascar contributed to a gradual transition towards less disputed (though not necessarily more legitimate) political rule, especially in Zimbabwe, while the pseudo-elections in Swaziland served as another mockery of democracy under the autocratic rule of King Mswati III.

The sub-region was spared from any major natural disasters, and economic growth regained momentum in several of the resource-rich states, although the socio-economic circumstances of large parts of the populations meant that they still faced challenges in securing their means for survival. After the elections in Madagascar, the country's temporary exclusion from SADC meetings came closer to an end. The sub-regional organisation continued to shelve the SADC Tribunal. SACU was showing signs of wear and tear, with South Africa suspected of looking for exit options, while the EPA negotiations were still not concluded.

At the end of the year, the world bade farewell and offered tributes to Nelson Mandela, who had been a personification like no other of the anti-colonial struggle of the people in the sub-region and the ability to seek reconciliation.

Elections, Democracy and Human Rights

During the year, the peoples of Zimbabwe (on 31 July), Swaziland (on 24 August and 20 September) and Madagascar (on 25 October and 25 December) had to vote for (or against) the policy makers in their countries. The circumstances of these elections showed that democracy and democratic practice are relative and at best contested notions that are implemented in very different ways. A national referendum on a draft constitution in **Zimbabwe**, held on 19 March, marked the prelude to subsequent steps initiated by President Robert Mugabe and his Zimbabwe African National Union (ZANU-PF) to retake full control of policy in the contested government. On 22 May, the new constitution replaced the transitional Lancaster House Constitution, which had been in place since 1979. The subsequent announcement of an early date for parliamentary and presidential elections came as a surprise to the two separate parties of the Movement for Democratic Change (MDC) in the Government of National Unity (GNU), which were operating under separate identities and leaders after an earlier split. The announcement was the result of some strategic manipulation by Mugabe and his ZANU-PF and was confirmed by the courts, despite interventions from the other parties. Despite some initial concerns, the SADC mediation team around South African President Jacob Zuma, as well as the SADC member states, ultimately backed the move. The aging president had once again outwitted his competitors to secure the upper hand in what was widely considered a dubious election. In the end, Mugabe and ZANU-PF emerged with a much stronger mandate and thereby clearly outmanoeuvred the opposition parties and their leaders by obtaining a result that bordered on a landslide victory and returning to rule with an absolute majority. Mugabe almost humiliated his strongest opponent, MDC leader Morgan Tsvangirai, taking over 60% of the votes in the presidential election against Tsvangirai's almost 34%. The latter seemed to have lost some of his earlier credibility, not least as a result of his life style in office as prime minister, which had been marred by scandals, sexual escapades and dubious financial transactions. Ultimately, the general expectation was that the ruling party's consolidated new power base might bring more stability to the divided country and more security and peace to its people, who had been engulfed in militant struggles and exposed to an oppressive regime bordering on terror since the turn of the century.

National elections in **Swaziland** held on 24 August (primary elections) and 20 September (secondary elections) were tantamount to a mockery of democracy under the autocratic rule of King Mswati III. There were no freely chosen candidates; all were pre-selected by local chiefs to rubber stamp the will of the king in the National Assembly and Senate. The appointment of the prime minister was also at the king's sole discretion. A dubiously composed electoral roll and strict repression of any political protest added to the overall picture of a monarchy based on ruthless disrespect for any degree of meaningful citizen participation in the country's political affairs.

Somewhat differently, in **Madagascar** the lengthy horse-trading between Malagasy competitors for the presidency and the SADC mediators overseeing the process created an environment that was generally accepted as able to secure a reasonably fair and impartial election of a legitimate president. In the end, the original main rivals were eliminated as candidates from the race. In total, 33 candidates stood in the first round of presidential elections on 25 October, supervised by SADC, the AU and the UN. A deeply divided result ultimately benefited the two main candidates, Jean Louis Robinson and Hery Rajaonarimampianina, who led the pack with 21% and almost 16% of the votes, respectively. They competed in a second round, which took place together with parliamentary elections on 20 December. The final results, not announced till early January 2014, gave the victory to Rajaonarimampianina, with 54% of the votes. With the endorsement of the SADC observer mission, this paved Madagascar's way back into SADC as a full member. In the general elections, the parties of the two previous presidents received the most votes: 17.3% (49 out of 151 seats) went to the party of Andry Rajoelina, and 10.8% (20 seats) to the Ravalomanana Movement.

The role of SADC as a sub-regional body setting and observing election standards remained somewhat dubious and forgiving. The criteria for recognising elections as in principle free and fair were and remained contested and civil society often felt that the officials representing the SADC member states were all too generous in their definitions. To a large extent, the dominant perspectives were rooted in the past and guided by a selective perception. The political tone was set almost paradigmatically at a meeting of the heads of political parties arising from **former liberation movements** of Southern Africa, who continued to have a great degree of influence and control over SADC matters. The meeting took place in Tshwane (Pretoria, South Africa) on 8 March, and South Africa's head of state and African National Congress (ANC) party president, Jacob Zuma, hosted the highest ranking leaders of ZANU-PF (head of state and party president Robert Mugabe), 'Chama Cha Mapinduzi' (CCM) of Tanzania (head of state and party chairman Jakaya Mrisho Kikwete), the South West African People's Organisation (SWAPO) of Namibia (prime minister and party vice-president Hage Geingob), Frelimo of Mozambique (party secretary-general Filipe Paunde, representing state and party president Armando Guebuza) and the 'Movimento Popular de Libertação de Angola' (MPLA) of Angola (party secretary-general Juliao Mateus Paulo, representing state and party president Jose

Eduardo dos Santos). According to the communiqué released, the meeting served "to strengthen and consolidate relations among sister parties and adopting further strategies towards the establishment of the historic heritage for the former liberation movements". In this spirit of solidarity, ZANU-PF was commended for its leadership and "for guiding the country towards elections". The meeting also appealed to SADC "to continue walking with them as they move forward", and the parties agreed to continue with plans to establish a joint political school in Tanzania. That the host Jacob Zuma so blatantly took sides with ZANU-PF seemed not to be considered as representing a conflict of interest in his role as SADC mediator for finding an amicable solution to the impasse in Zimbabwe.

Governments and higher-ranking state officials did not shy away from rather undemocratic practices in domestic affairs, which all too often lacked transparency and accountability. The track record with regard to **human and civil rights** varied considerably between countries. In Angola, political repression and an ever growing tendency to curb press freedom characterised the further deterioration of a political culture marred by growing protests and violent state responses. Political assassinations remained almost the order of the day amidst increasingly frequent demonstrations, mainly by the youth. As stated above, the Swazi monarchy was also at the forefront of violating citizens' fundamental rights by violently preventing any forms of public protest. South Africa's democracy was still battling to come to terms with the shocking evidence produced in connection with the Marikana massacre a year before, when police, in an act bordering on executions, killed 34 miners taking part in a wild cat strike. The country's democratic image was further dented by the adoption of the controversial Protection of State Information Bill, reminiscent of Apartheid legislation to curb any unwanted reporting by the media with the threat of drastic penalties, thereby putting at risk whistleblowers and journalists who revealed information in the public interest. Latent conflicts fuelled by political in-fighting and rivalry were simmering to some extent in Malawi and Zambia.

South African scandals and large-scale misappropriation of funds, as well as diverse forms of dubious favouritism, made headlines and kept the independent press rather busy. The so-called Guptagate disclosed that an economically influential Indian family had been granted permission to fly 200 wedding guests in to a strategically important and sensitive military airbase, in violation of all fundamental national security regulations. The case made headlines for weeks and centred on the question of who in the president's office was informed and had granted permission. President Zuma rapidly lost popularity. The fact that the crowd attending the funeral ceremony of former president Mandela booed him when he stood up to speak sent a clear signal to the world. The biggest international headlines, however, were made by the case of the blade running athlete Oscar Pistorius, who on the night of Valentine's Day killed his girlfriend with several shots through a locked bathroom door.

Corruption and undue privileges for political office holders were also a matter of public discussion in Namibia, which had a similar independent media landscape. Cases of alleged corruption, often involving the blackmailing or prosecution of political opponents, were the order of the day in Zambia. Political and civil rights seemed to regress under the aging President Sata, who continued to display occasional unstatesmanlike odd and erratic behaviour. Embezzlement on a massive scale remained an integral part of governance by the dos Santos family in Angola. In Malawi, President Joyce Banda was exposed to criticism that her anti-corruption campaigns lacked consistency and were mainly aimed at prosecuting political opponents in a way that smacked of double standards, given her own dubious involvement in a financial scandal popularly called Cashgate.

In view of the relatively high level of political stability in the sub-region, **military clashes** reported from Mozambique made headlines. New acts of terror by the Renamo opposition ended 20 years of relative peace and once again put the security of parts of the country's population at risk, while the presidential elections set for 2014 were already casting their shadow in terms of internal positioning and wrangling in the governing Frelimo party. In Angola, the low-level insurgency of rebels belonging to the Liberation Front for the Enclave of Cabinda (FLEC) continued in armed clashes, though with no spectacular battles, while speculation concerning the future of President dos Santos and his likely succession remained an issue in policy circles.

Despite the occasional disturbances, the overall relatively peaceful situation and stability in the countries of the sub-region seemed not to be at risk, while **elections in 2014** were looming in South Africa, Malawi, Mozambique and Namibia. Domestic politics ahead of these markers were influenced in South Africa by the establishment of two new parties, the Economic Freedom Fighters (EFF), led by the ousted former ANC Youth League leader Julius Malema, and Agang, founded by Ramphele Mamphela, a prominent intellectual, while the Congress of South African Trade Unions (COSATU), an important government ally in the Tripartite Alliance, was increasingly tested, after the Marikana massacre, by internal differences and power struggles. In contrast, the Namibian political scene remained quiet, as usual, with a low profile opposition, while the SWAPO-internal realignments to consolidate the changing of the political guard under the new team led by Prime Minister Hage Geingob continued. In Malawi, the disappointment over President Joyce Banda's ambiguous policy suggested that her initial popular support was waning. In Mozambique, the dominant Frelimo received a warning when, during the municipal elections in November, the opposition Mozambique Democratic Movement (MDM) snatched the majority in the three significant cities of Nampula, Quelimane and Beira, and made remarkable gains in Maputo and Martola. Meanwhile Frelimo had narrowed down to three the list of possible official presidential candidates to replace Armando Guebuza after his second term in office. The incumbent, meanwhile, was seeking to gain more control over the party, thereby indicating ambitions not to surrender any political influence after his replacement.

Despite some of the flaws summarised above, Southern Africa once again included top performing African states of the 52 ranked in the **Ibrahim Index** of African Governance for 2013, which was published in October. Rankings were based on a total of 94 indicators grouped in 14 sub-categories, under four main categories: safety and rule of law; participation and human rights; sustainable economic opportunity; and human development. With Mauritius (rank 1/overall score 82.9 out of 100)), Botswana (2/77.6), South Africa (5/71.3), Namibia (6/69.5) and Lesotho (9/61.9), half of the top ten countries were from the sub-region. Only Zimbabwe (47/35.4) remained in the bottom ten worst performers, with Angola (39/44.5) ranking more places up from the previous year than any other state, despite remaining the second-worst performer in the sub-region. The sub-region's other worst performing states were Madagascar (37/45.7) and Swaziland (26/50.8). The fact that the Swazi monarchy, despite its dismal human rights record and the lack of democracy in the country, achieved a medium score somewhere in the middle of all African countries might be a sobering indication of the state of governance on the continent. Zambia (12/59.6), Malawi (16/56.9) and Mozambique (20/54.8) completed the comparatively favourable ranking of the sub-region's states, showing how relative matters are. An **Afrobarometer survey** carried out in late 2012 was published in late 2013. People in 34 African countries were asked how free they were to say what they thought. A surprisingly high 33% in Mozambique said they were not free. This compared with only 7% in Tanzania, 13% in Malawi, and 16% in South Africa – and 53% in Zimbabwe and 57% in Swaziland.

Socioeconomic Developments

The sub-region recorded an uneven economic performance during the year, with an estimated average **economic growth** rate of 3%, brought down by the weak performance of South Africa, which was negatively affected by ongoing labour unrest and a weak global environment. Its growth rate, at 1.9%, was the lowest of all economies in the sub-region. The exchange rate of the South African rand (ZAR) fell dramatically, which had the positive side effect of boosting exports. This might offer some opportunities for a slight recovery to an estimated 2.7% in 2014. Madagascar was still feeling the shocks of the chaotic political situation and, with 2.7% growth, was the only other country that achieved below the aggregated average growth rate. The consolidated political stability might also contribute positively to higher growth rates to come. Mauritius (3.3%), Lesotho (3.4%) Swaziland (3.5%) Zimbabwe (3.7%) and Namibia (4.2%) were projected to achieve moderate growth rates. As a result of growing investment in infrastructure and extractive industries, the highest growth rates were recorded in Angola (5.1%), Botswana (5.4%), Malawi (5.0%), Mozambique (7.0%) and Zambia (6.5%), and these were projected by the African Economic Outlook 2014 to accelerate to 7%-9% in 2014.

Southern African countries scored differently in the TI **Corruption Perception Index** of 177 countries, released at the end of November. Botswana remained the top SADC state with a score of 64 at rank 34, followed by Mauritius (52/52), Lesotho (49/55), Namibia (48/57), South Africa (42/72), Swaziland (39/82), Zambia (38/83), Malawi (37/91), Mozambique (30/119), Madagascar (28/127), Angola (23/153) and Zimbabwe (21/157). The **Open Budget Score** of all countries surveyed in the region placed Zambia at the bottom, with a score of 4 (out of 100), in the group of countries that provided "scant or none" information to the public. Even Zimbabwe (20) and Angola (28), scored better and those ranked higher were Mozambique (47), Botswana (50), and Namibia (55), all clearly topped by South Africa (90).

On 18 March, the governments of Angola, Namibia and South Africa signed the **Benguela Current Convention**, which defined the boundaries of the marine ecosystem stretching from Port Elizabeth in South Africa to the Cabinda province in Angola. Considered as one of the richest ecosystems on earth, the estimated value of related goods and services was close to N$ 500 bn a year, including offshore oil and gas production, marine diamond mining, coastal tourism and commercial fishing and shipping. The convention established the Benguela Current Commission as a permanent inter-governmental organisation mandated to promote the long-term conservation, protection and rehabilitation of the marine ecosystem.

The Regional **Tourism** Organisation of Southern Africa (RETOSA), headquartered in South Africa, was reportedly at the brink of collapse over fundamental differences that erupted at a meeting of SADC ministers in charge of tourism on 29 November in Maputo. South Africa, supported by Mozambique, had proposed the closure of RETOSA, while Zimbabwe, supported by Angola and Namibia, argued against abandoning the organisation, which they considered an important tool for commercial tourism promotion and for regional integration. At the core of the dispute were practices of South African tourism enterprises, who marketed and cashed in on sites in other countries, such as the Victoria Falls, in local packages without any remuneration for Zambia or Zimbabwe. RETOSA had criticised this as commercially unfair and unethical marketing practice. A committee chaired by Zambia with Malawi, Zimbabwe, Namibia, Mozambique and South Africa as further members, was appointed to decide on the future of the organisation. The discussion testified to the sentiments in some SADC states concerning South Africa's hegemonic status and behaviour.

UNAIDS announced in a report released on 30 July that levels of **HIV/AIDS** infection in Southern Africa had fallen by about 30% during the previous decade. On the basis mainly of 2011 data, services to prevent mother-to-child transmission (PMTCT) had reached over 80% of the population in Botswana, Namibia, South Africa, Swaziland and Zambia. As a result, the number of newly infected children had declined by more than half. In contrast, PMTCT coverage was less than 25% in Angola. HIV treatment with antiretroviral therapy had achieved more than 80% coverage in Botswana, Namibia, Swaziland and Zambia, while it was less than 20% in Madagascar. Botswana and South Africa funded more than 75% of their HIV/AIDS expenditure, and Angola, Lesotho, Mauritius and Namibia more than half, from domestic public sources, thereby also considerably improving domestic investment into AIDS treatment.

Energy remained in short supply, constituting a risk to the sub-region's further development. The sub-region had suffered from a shortage of electricity since 2007 and it was expected that supply might meet demand again in 2014 at the earliest. An Energy Sector Plan aimed at a 70% increase in power generation at an investment cost of at least $ 170 bn over the next 15 years was part of the SADC Regional Infrastructure Development Master Plan (RIDMP) adopted at the SADC Summit in 2012. The establishment of a SADC Centre for Renewable Energy and Energy Efficiency was proposed at a meeting of the Southern African Power Pool in Gaborone (Botswana) to make more substantial use of solar energy, which was available in abundance but not yet systematically harnessed. No decision was taken as to where such a centre should be located.

The effects of **climate change** remained a source of concern. It is anticipated that the sub-region's agricultural sector, a primary source of income and employment for most of the rural population, will be massively affected and lead to increased migration to urban centres. Droughts and floods, as well as changes in the frequency and intensity of dry spells, had already become part of seasonal cycles and contributed to less food security. During the year, northern Namibia in particular, but also southern Angola and parts of Zambia were most affected by **drought**. Crop failure and death of livestock were the consequences and food insecurity required emergency relief measures. Dry conditions for two seasons also resulted in a lack of water and scarce pasture in parts of Botswana, Zimbabwe and South Africa, where hydrological conditions sometimes required water restrictions and rationing.

In terms of FDI, South Africa remained the most attractive country to investors from abroad, with the highest number of projects on the continent. Significantly, Mozambique and Zambia entered the top ten ranked African countries for FDI. South Africa was the third highest provider of FDI on the continent, according to the "Africa Attractiveness Survey" for 2013 published by international professional services providers Ernst & Young, considered among the more reputable firms in this business.

Sub-regional Organisations

During the year, **SADC** member states signed a total of 27 protocols, as well as a number of further declarations, charters, and memoranda of understanding on various issues. Most protocols, however, albeit ratified and brought into force, imposed no obligations but reiterated principles without provisions for enforcement. As an observer from the Harare-based 'Southern African News Feature' observed: "In cases where obligations are clear, they are not measurable, unrealistic and unattainable and do not have time frames."

This shed doubt on the political will to implement the regional integration agenda beyond tokenism or lip service.

A SADC Extraordinary Troika Summit of the **Organ on Politics, Defence and Security Cooperation**, which had Tanzania, South Africa and Namibia as member states, was hosted and chaired by Tanzania's President Jakaya Kikwete in Dar es Salaam on 11 January. It discussed developments in the DRC, Madagascar and Zimbabwe. On 9 March, another Troika Summit took place in Pretoria, which discussed further developments in Zimbabwe. Another meeting of the three countries, also attended by President Guebuza of Mozambique as chairperson of SADC, was held on 20 July, again in Pretoria. The Summit welcomed the elections set for 31 July in Zimbabwe, thereby endorsing the contested timeframe.

The **Regional Indicative Strategic Development Plan** (RISDP), approved in 2003, was discussed by researchers from the member states as part of a mid-term review at a regional consultative workshop on 9/10 May in Harare (Zimbabwe). It was concluded that some of the targets defined for the various sectors were overly ambitious. Slow domestication and weak implementation of protocols remained a concern and invited a re- think of the integration model, in particular with regard to the powers of the coordinating mechanism, the SADC secretariat and the responsibilities of the member states.

An **Extraordinary Summit** of SADC Heads of State and Government was held in Addis Ababa (Ethiopia) on 26 May. It welcomed the mandate for the deployment of the intervention brigade in the eastern DRC under the auspices of MONUSCO as adopted by UNSC resolution 2098 of 28 March. On Madagascar, the Summit reiterated its decision that President Rajoelina, former president Ratsiraka and former president Ravalomanana's wife should all withdraw their candidacy in the forthcoming elections "for the sake of peace and stability". The Summit also welcomed the mediation efforts of President Zuma of South Africa and the preparations for elections in Zimbabwe.

The **SADC Lawyers' Association** held its 14th annual general meeting on 2–3 August in Lilongwe (Malawi) with a particular thematic focus on constitution-making and constitutionalism in the SADC region. Participants observed the limitations on and interference with separation of powers in the community and stressed the need to uphold the rule of law in the sub-region. The official communiqué noted with concern that the **SADC Tribunal** remained suspended, which impacted negatively on the rights of SADC citizens. It strongly condemned the decision of the SADC Summit in 2012 to bar non-state actors from access to the Tribunal, since such limitations on the Tribunal's powers impacted negatively on human rights as well as on trends towards regional courts, the SADC integration agenda and investor confidence.

The ordinary annual **SADC Summit** took place on 16–17 August in Lilongwe. It elected the host's head of state Joyce Banda as SADC chairperson and Zimbabwe's re-elected President Robert Mugabe as deputy chairperson. Namibia's President Hifikepunye

Pohamba was elected as chairperson of the SADC Organ on Politics, Defence and Security Cooperation and Prime Minister Thomas Thabane from Lesotho as its deputy chairperson. The Summit welcomed the establishment of the Special Electoral Court in **Madagascar** and its subsequent withdrawal of nine presidential candidates, including the three identified already at the Extraordinary Summit in Addis Ababa on 26 May. The "free and peaceful harmonized elections" on 31 July in **Zimbabwe** were welcomed and President Mugabe was congratulated on his victory. The Summit reiterated its call for the lifting of all forms of sanctions and expressed its deep concern over the removal of the constitutionally elected government in Egypt. Stergomena Lawrence Tax from Tanzania was appointed as **SADC Executive Secretary**, the first woman to take this position. She replaced Tomaz Augusto Salomão. Discussions over the introduction of a single common currency for the sub-region, initially envisaged for 2018, remained inconclusive.

The Summit also reviewed the SADC **Regional Infrastructure Development Master Plan** (RIDMP) adopted in 2012 and "noted progress made in marketing of the infrastructure projects". But the implementation of the ambitious plan suffered a major setback after the failure of efforts to secure funds from external donors at a SADC Regional Infrastructure Investment Conference on 27 June in Maputo, where over 100 cross-border infrastructure projects in priority sectors were presented. Estimated to cost $ 500 bn, RIDPM was intended to improve the sub-region's road, rail and ports infrastructure, increase its power-generation capacity and strengthen its communication systems. Priorities also included improved access to and distribution of water. In the absence of any provision of funds from major Western donors and multilateral financial institutions, the outgoing SADC deputy executive secretary for regional integration declared at the beginning of September that development experts had questioned SADC's ability to handle such an ambitious project.

The 4th **SACU** Heads of State and Government Summit took place on 12 April in Gaborone. On 28 June, a SACU Council of Ministers' meeting was held in Windhoek (Namibia), where the new SACU headquarters were under construction. Speculation was rife throughout the year concerning the organisation's future. Internal tensions suggested that South Africa might want to end this costly arrangement, under which it paid some ZAR 18 bn-20 bn a year to the four other member countries (Botswana, Lesotho, Namibia and Swaziland; BLNS), which all depended on the transfers to beef up their annual budgets. On the other hand, the BLNS states viewed SACU as the free entry point for South African commodities into their economies, at times to the detriment of their own infant industries, which they could not protect from South African competition.

Another bone of contention was the Free Trade Agreement that South Africa had signed with the EU, which provided unrestricted access for EU commodities to the BLNS states through South Africa. This negatively impacted on the negotiations for an **EPA** with the SADC configuration (which, as a further complication, represented only half of SADC member states). Throughout the year, the negotiations stagnated, since countries such as Namibia felt disadvantaged by the suggested terms and conditions.

The sub-region also engaged in **military interventions**. In January, South Africa sent 200 soldiers to assist those already in place to train CAR forces. In March, the contingent of the South African National Defence Force clashed with Séléka rebels in an encounter that led to the loss of the lives of at least 13 South African soldiers, and provoked a highly controversial public debate in South Africa over the justification for sending the detachment. There was also speculation as to whether such interventions should be discussed at all in SADC and if so, to what end. At mid-year, a South African battalion, authorised by the UNSC along with troops from Tanzania and Malawi, was deployed as part of a neutral force to intervene in the eastern provinces of the DRC. In May, South Africa had suggested on the occasion of the 50th anniversary celebrations of the OAU/AU that an African Capacity for Immediate Response to Crises be created with 1,500 soldiers in combat units drawn from a contingent of 5,000 highly trained troops that could be mobilised within 14 days. Such initiatives might have documented the concern of the Southern African hegemon to provide more security within the continent and beyond the borders of the immediate neighbourhood.

Last but not least, a whole country, and with it the continent and the wider world was united in mourning the passing of an icon. The death of **Nelson Mandela** in early December was followed by several days of commemoration of the legacy of one of the greatest statesmen of the 20th century, admired for his perseverance, tolerance and ability to contribute to the birth of what had become known as the "rainbow nation". The several commemorative events and the long list of international celebrities and leading politicians who attended was evidence of the fact that a world leader and role model had been laid to his final rest in his Xhosa home village.

Henning Melber

Angola

The dominance of the ruling party continued, though speculation about the succession to long-term president, José Eduardo dos Santos, continued unabated. Opposition parties and youth protests were vocal in their criticism of the government's poor social track record and violence against opposition activists, but protests were met with violent repression and the country's human rights situation deteriorated markedly. Abroad, Angola positioned itself as a power-player within the CPLP, flexing its financial muscle against Portugal and Brazil, and diversified South-South economic partnerships. Despite further economic growth, the socio-economic conditions for the majority of the population remained dire, with a high cost of living, low salaries, and underfunded public services.

Domestic Politics

The ruling 'Movimento Popular de Libertação de Angola' (MPLA) and long-serving President José Eduardo dos Santos continued to dominate politics. Although opposition parties, such as the MPLA's former civil war antagonist, 'União Nacional pela Independência Total de Angola' (UNITA), and the newly-formed 'Convergência Ampla de Salvação de Angola – Coligação Eleitoral' (CASA-CE), generally improved their public profile by taking more decidedly oppositional positions, the **MPLA's dominance** in the

National Assembly prevented any opposition initiatives from coming to fruition. In June, UNITA's head of faction, Raul Danda, stated that his party had tried to submit a number of issues to parliament, which had "not been met with any acceptance" by the parliamentary leadership.

The question of the **succession to President dos Santos** continued to preoccupy the public debate within the ruling party and opposition formations alike. In May, one of his sons, José Filomeno 'Zénú' de Sousa dos Santos, was made 'interim' chairman of the board of the Angolan Sovereign Wealth Fund, 'Fundo Soberano de Desenvolvimento Económico de Angola' (FSDEA) after the previous chairman, Armando Manuel, was made minister of finance. This 'interim period' lasted until the end of the year, with the fund not making any publicly known investment "to promote the diversification of Angola's economy and generate revenues for future generations", as its statutes stipulated. Rather, as Angolan commenters pessimistically surmised, the FSDEA appeared to be a vehicle for Zénú to be gradually manoeuvred into position as his father's natural successor at the 2017 elections.

In August, independent news sources noted dos Santos' six-week absence from the country, with no previous communication or explanation from the Presidency or the executive. After public questioning by UNITA and CASA-CE, the Presidency said the president had been in Barcelona for a "private visit" and would return shortly, and called for a "march of support" on his return. The Spanish press, however, circulated rumours that dos Santos had sought medical treatment in a private clinic. In November, dos Santos spent several more weeks in Barcelona, to be treated, according to non-government sources, for "serious" renal problems. The same sources also alleged that all his children had travelled to Barcelona at the same time. On 2 December, Sindika Dokolo, husband of the president's daughter Isabel, stated on the margins of the 7th International Art Biennial in São Tomé and Príncipe that reports about the **President's ill health** were "completely unfounded" and that dos Santos had simply taken a few weeks of well-deserved holiday after his "hard work" preparing the 2014 budget, and that even the First Lady, Ana Paula dos Santos, had had a hard time persuading the president to take a few days off. Dokolo further revealed that dos Santos had seized the opportunity of his stay in Europe to visit the dentist, but that Angola was used to "misunderstandings and communication problems in the foreign press", which had led to the rumours.

Dokolo also used the press conference to say that tarnishing Angola's image with allegations of **corruption** was a "dishonest and counterproductive manipulation of the foreign media", claiming that the "Angolan model" of economic success would be "unanimously recognised in 20 years", after 'Forbes Magazine' published a critical story on the illicit sources of his wife Isabel's multibillion dollar wealth.

More importantly, dos Santos' prolonged, repeated absence was seen as a **tentative trial for the succession**, allowing his handpicked vice president, his nephew, Manuel Vicente, to take on a more visible public role. However, although according to the Constitution the vice president should stand in for the president if the latter were absent or incapacitated, observers said Vicente was only formally in charge, and reduced to administering the secondary, 'social' portfolios of health, culture, education and social security, while real power was wielded behind the scenes by dos Santos' formidable head of security, General Manuel Hélder Vieira Dias 'Kopelipa'. In this reading, mounting repression against opposition protests in parliament and in the streets was a test run for a 'coup' by members of the security apparatus bent on safeguarding their economic and political interests against the wishes of the various MPLA factions. Nonetheless, dos Santos eventually returned again in public, putting these rumours temporarily to rest.

To improve their chances of countering the MPLA's dominance, five **opposition parties** formed a common platform, the 'forum for the democratisation of Angola', in December, to coordinate their efforts in future local elections. Parliamentary opposition parties UNITA, CASA-CE, and the historic 'Frente Nacional de Libertação de Angola', as well as the 'Bloco Demacrático' (BD), a small opposition party without parliamentary representation, and the 'Partido Democrático para o Progresso – Aliança Nacional de Angola' (PDP-ANA), stated at the celebration of the 65th anniversary of the Universal Declaration of Human Rights on 10 December that the "systematic violation of human rights" endangered the development of democracy in Angola, and that the MPLA was fabricating a "constant state of siege" to further delay local elections. Indeed, after surprisingly strong showings by UNITA and CASA-CE in urban centres in the 2012 general elections, the Ministry of Territorial Administration delayed local elections again, to at least 2015, citing the lack of technical resources and a population census as reasons.

But opposition parties were also beset by **internal problems**. In September, UNITA's National Judicial Council opened an inquiry into corruption allegations against its increasingly popular and outspoken youth leader, Mfuka Muzemba. Muzemba, elected leader of UNITA's youth wing 'Juventude Unida Revolucionária de Angola' (JURA) in 2010 and a deputy in the National Assembly since 2012, was accused of using his position to endorse visa requests to Portugal in return for money, as well as "non-avowed commitments to Bento Kangamba" (the MPLA's 'entrepreneur of the youth'; see Foreign Affairs below) to prevent anti-government demonstrations. Despite Muzemba's vocal defence in the press and his protests at being 'judged' *in absentia*, he was suspended from party functions for two years. Commenters noted, however, that potential challengers to UNITA's president, Isaías Samakuva, had a tendency to be 'neutralised' by intrigues.

The regime's control of the public sphere outside of parliamentary politics became further entrenched. **Press freedom** deteriorated, with most print publications now controlled by one group close to the regime, after the independent weekly 'Angolense' was bought by hitherto unknown "powerful rich people" in February. In May, 'Rádio Despertar' and the last remaining independent weekly publication, 'Folha 8', were threatened with suspension by the authorities for "offences and slander against state institutions and office holders" and for "calling for public disorder". Journalist Domingos Cruz was tried for "inciting war and violence", but was finally acquitted in September for lack of an applicable law. In May, after the international advocacy organisation Reporters Without Borders ranked Angola the worst of all Lusophone countries for press freedom, residents of the provincial capital and former opposition bastion, Huambo, also declared in media interviews that anyone seen in public reading private weeklies considered slightly more independent than the state-controlled 'Jornal de Angola' had until recently risked arrest and police harassment.

Political repression continued, with the overall human rights situation deteriorating. Activists for greater autonomy in the diamond-producing provinces of Lunda-Norte and Lunda-Sul, jailed in 2012 under a law 'for state security' since abolished by the National Assembly, continued to languish in jail in dire conditions. In January, traditional leaders of the Lundas travelled to the capital, Luanda, to lodge a formal complaint about persistent human rights violations in the diamond-producing areas, demanding that the government investigate the situation. In July, Benedito Daniel, the leader of the parliamentary faction of the opposition 'Partido da Renovação Social' (PRS) said that, over the last ten years, 578 citizens had been assassinated, 1,275 had been injured under torture, and 227 had lost their agricultural land.

Independent and international media publicised cases of the torture of prisoners in Luanda's prisons, while female street vendors ('zungueiras') in the capital continued to accuse police agents of blackmail, intimidation, extortion and sexual assault. Forced evictions and demolitions of informal inner-city settlements also continued. Police broke up various smaller youth demonstrations, with organisers arrested ahead of the planned gatherings. During her visit in May, UN High Commissioner for Human Rights Navi Pillay stated that **restrictions on fundamental rights** such as freedom of expression and demonstration, the expulsion of citizens from their land and homes, and the violent repression of demonstrations by the police, persisted and she disclosed that she had been prevented from visiting political prisoners in the Lundas. Her closing statement also "urged" the authorities to reduce the "huge disparities that have developed between the richest and the poorest". The state-controlled newspaper 'Jornal de Angola' unsurprisingly published a very selective text of the speech under the title "human rights progress", while political activists criticised Pillay for not meeting with opposition parties, protesting that she had only seen what the Angolan government had been willing to show her.

Public protest demonstrations were met with the full force of the security services. On 23 November, a peaceful demonstration in central Luanda was brutally repressed by the authorities. Youth activists and opposition parties had called for a protest against the authorities after revelations that two civil society activists, Isaías Cassule and Alves Kamulingue, who had disappeared ahead of protests in 2012, had been killed by state security agents and thrown into the crocodile-infested Bengo River. However, on the morning of the planned protest, government security forces surrounded the headquarters of the largest opposition parties, and used tear gas to prevent protesters from gathering. Over 300 people were arrested, and at least three were killed, including Manuel Hilberto de Carvalho 'Ganga', a leader of the youth wing of CASA-CE. Heavily armed police also prevented any protest gatherings in the provinces, and blockaded UNITA headquarters in Bié, Bengo, Benguela, Cabinda, Cunene, Kuando Kubango and Namibe. On 25 November, a protest by street vendors against police harassment was violently broken up and, on 27 November, a funeral procession for Hilberto Ganga, the murdered activist, gathered over 1,000 people marching towards the Santa Ana cemetery. After a quiet start, the procession increasingly became a protest rally, which was stopped by armed police with tear gas and water cannon. International media attention on these events, however, was eclipsed by the information – not entirely accurate, as it turned out – that Angola had become the first country in the world to 'ban Islam', and that the government was engaged in the systematic destruction of mosques. In fact, a government **crackdown on 'illegal sects'**, which in the Angolan reading includes Islam, coincided with, and fed into, government paranoia about political unrest orchestrated "from abroad", and conveniently distracted international attention from the domestic repression of political dissent.

The government also extended its control to the ever more popular **evangelical churches**. In February, the authorities suspended the Brazilian, neo-Pentecostal Universal Church of the Kingdom of God ('Igreja Universal do Reino de Deus'; IURD) and six other evangelical churches for 60 days, after 16 people were killed in the IURD's New Year vigil in Luanda's cidadela stadium on 31 December 2012. Domestic observers criticised the suspension as inadequate, saying the church leadership should be held accountable for overcrowding the stadium. In April, the IURD resumed activities in Angola under the supervision of the authorities, while the other churches were banned, which effectively ensured IURD's monopoly in the prosperity gospel market; again, the proximity of President dos Santos to the IURD and the popularity in Angola of its television channel, TV Record, did not go unnoticed by Brazilian and Angolan commenters.

Finally, the low-level separatist insurgency in the oil-rich northern province of **Cabinda** continued, albeit without any changes to the situation. Exiled leader Henrique N'Zita Tiago repeatedly stated the readiness of the 'Frente para a Libertação da Enclave de Cabinda' (FLEC) to enter into a dialogue with the government over the status of the province, but his offer was met with a resounding silence. In parallel, António Luís Lopes, the military commander of one of the FLEC splinter groups still active in Cabinda's remote north-east, said the people of Cabinda would continue to fight for their "inalienable and indispensable right to independence", guaranteeing that with the union of the Cabindan people, victory was possible. While another Cabindan 'nationalist' denounced to Voice of America the existence of a "concentration camp" with over 4,000 detainees in northern Cabinda, civil society activists, especially of the Catholic Church, also complained of harassment, constant surveillance, and the 'gagging' of free speech. In practice, the government thus successfully continued its containment strategy of imposing a heavy military presence and tight security control in the province, together with increased budget spending, while excluding any dialogue on the root causes of the conflict.

Foreign Affairs

Lusophone special relations continued within the CPLP, and bilaterally. On his first return from Barcelona in August, President dos Santos stopped in Malabo (Equatorial Guinea) to attend a Gulf of Guinea summit and reconfirm Angola's support for Equatorial Guinea's long-standing application to join the CPLP.

However, bilateral relations with **Portugal** took a dive after dos Santos announced, in his state of the nation speech in October, the "end of the strategic partnership" between the two countries. There was in fact no such formal agreement. The previous years had seen exponential growth in Portuguese investment in Angola, and even more Portuguese economic migration to Angola, and Angolan investment in the Portuguese energy, banking, telecommunications and agricultural (vineyards) sectors. In fact, through the investment of state oil company Sonangol, Isabel dos Santos, and other Angolan regime figures, Angola was now controlling parts of Portugal's public debt, and in September, one of the MPLA's 'trusted entrepreneurs', António Mosquito, became the majority shareholder in the Portuguese construction company Soares da Costa. Far from heralding an end to this lucrative economic entanglement, dos Santos' statement was thus a well-calculated warning shot, after the Portuguese judiciary had opened a number of investigations into suspected money-laundering and embezzlement by leading figures in the Angolan regime, including the temporary freezing of € 11 m in shares owned by Vice President Manuel Vicente. Subsequently, the Portuguese government multiplied its diplomatic efforts to restore good relations with Portugal, although Portuguese Foreign Minister Rui Machete was severely chastised in the Portuguese press for apologising for the judicial inquiry to Angola. In November, however, the Office of the Public Prosecutor announced the archiving of the case against Manuel Vicente, and the public procurator charged with the case said this would allow for "meetings and bilateral summits to be realised without unfounded stigmas".

Commercial and diplomatic relations with Angola's other main Lusophone partner, **Brazil**, were also further strengthened. However, activist Rafael Marques accused Brazilian arms manufacturer Taurus of colluding with Angolan national police commander, Ambrósio de Lemos, to over-invoice an arms sale to the Angolan police. Furthermore, in October, the Brazilian judiciary issued an international arrest warrant for General Bento dos Santos 'Kangamba' for trafficking women and running an international prostitution ring. Kangamba had already escaped arrest in June, thanks to his diplomatic passport, when he was briefly detained in Monaco carrying about € 3 m in cash. Kangamba, now on Interpol's most wanted list, denied all accusations, but the Brazilian press revealed more and more sordid details of the affair and the arrest warrant was maintained. The authorities and the MPLA declined to comment. Kangamba, a nephew of dos Santos by marriage and member of the MPLA bench, had already served a prison sentence in Angola in the 1990s for profiteering. Widely known as the 'entrepreneur of youth' and owner and president of the popular Kabuscorp FC in Luanda, his financial largesse in support of 'youth events' was one of the regime's tools in its attempts to quell youth protests.

Also within the CPLP, Angola furthered its economic grip on its 'nineteenth province', **São Tomé e Príncipe**: in May, Isabel dos Santos' telecommunications company, UNITEL, successfully bid for the first private mobile network operating licence; in July, Santomean President Manuel Pinto da Costa gave assurances of full support for Angolan investors and entrepreneurs in his country during a visit to Luanda, and Angola's state oil company Sonangol expressed interest in upgrading and operating São Tomé's deep-water port. In addition, the ministers of finances of the two countries signed a financial cooperation agreement in December, which paved the way for a $ 180 m Angolan credit line "for development projects".

International bodies other than the 'CPLP club' were less important. Angola continued its rather lukewarm participation in **SADC**, as Trade Minister Rosa Pacavira ruled out joining the SADC free-trade zone "before 2014 or 2015", as "some adjustments", for example to customs tariffs, were still necessary. In parallel, Angola expressed scepticism at the idea of interference in its internal affairs by the SADC tribunal, which it saw as serving the interests of its great sub-regional rival, South Africa. Nonetheless, diplomatic efforts to rebrand dos Santos as the region's elder statesman and Angola as a force for peace continued through the regional bodies SADC, CEMAC, the AU, and the ICGRL.

In June, Médecins Sans Frontières reported the often violent expulsion from Angola, over a period of three weeks, of 52,231 DRC 'irregular migrants'. However, contrary to previous years, these mass expulsions were not reciprocated by the repatriation of Angolans from the **DRC**. On the contrary, the two countries signed a contract in August with a private operator for joint oil exploration in Angolan and DRC territorial waters off the mouth of the Congo River, thus resolving a long-standing source of diplomatic tension.

In October, Angolan soldiers allegedly 'invaded' a border region in the **Republic of Congo**, occupying five localities and a border post, and 'kidnapping' a number of Congolese soldiers. Angolan Foreign Minister George Chicoty denied the allegations, saying that, if anything had happened, the lack of visible border demarcation might have led to a misunderstanding. Congolese sources, however, rumoured that the invasion had been a demonstration of force after Congolese President Sassou Nguesso unsuccessfully made a pass at Angolan First Lady Ana Paula dos Santos during a summit in Brazzaville. After five days of negotiations, the "unhappy incident" was solved diplomatically, with Angolan soldiers freeing the Congolese and withdrawing across the border.

Further afield, **China** remained Angola's most important commercial partner, despite a 4.2% drop in trade, with imports from China estimated at $ 4 m and exports at $ 31.9 bn.

The strategic partnership was reinforced when the foreign ministers of the two countries met in September.

The **USA** celebrated 20 years of diplomatic relations with Angola, and in February and March AFRICOM delegations discussed in Luanda the possibilities of reinforcing military and security cooperation between the two countries, underlining Angola's "crucial role" in regional peacekeeping initiatives. Nonetheless, the Obama administration took a tougher stance against dos Santos' long rule; in May US Secretary of State John Kerry cancelled a scheduled meeting with Angolan Foreign Minister George Chicoty during the latter's visit to Washington, DC, allegedly due to "lack of progress" in the human rights situation and the conduct of the 2012 elections.

Relations with **France** remained tense, with sources inside French oil company Total claiming off the record that its expansion plans in Angola had been thwarted by the persistent political disharmony; other French investors complained of high entry barriers to the Angolan market and the "challenges" posed by the interpretation of the law on public investments and delays in issuing permits, licences and visas. In November, in the hope of improving the situation, Laurent Fabius made the first visit to Angola by a French foreign minister in ten years, accompanied by leaders of leading French companies such as Alstom, Bolloré, Airbus, and Véolia. Other European countries scrambling for a part in Angola's economic boom included **Belgium**, whose Princess Astrid headed an economic delegation to Luanda in October. In August, the **UK**'s Price Harry visited Angola and criticised the lack of progress in demining the country.

Angola also revived old alliances: close cooperation with **Cuba** continued in the education and health sectors. Agreements on culture, education and fishing were signed with **Russia** in September, while in February the largely state-owned Russian diamond company Alrosa discussed the creation of a consortium with Angolan state diamond company ENDIAMA. In addition, Angola signed a $ 1 bn deal in November with Russian arms manufacturer Rosboronexport to buy 18 used Su-30 fighter jets, as well as helicopters, artillery and tanks. In February, the defence ministers of Angola and **Serbia** signed an agreement for the construction of military installations and the training of officers.

On a much more relaxed note, in June the Angola pavilion, with photographs by the artist Edson Chagas, won the Golden Lion for best national participation at the **Venice Art Biennale**, the first time a sub-Saharan African country had won the prize.

Socioeconomic Developments

Despite opposition and civil society criticism, the **state budget** was passed in its entirety on 15 January with 156 votes for, 8 against, and 31 abstentions in the National Assembly. The budget increased by 50% over the previous year to $ 69 bn. It included for the first time, to the World Bank's great approval, parastatal operations carried out by state oil company Sonangol, and was praised by the government as its best ever, with a third of the budget marked for social spending. However, as noted by the BD opposition party, 17.6% of 'social spending' was earmarked for defence, security, and internal order, while only 13.8% was allocated to health and education. According to investigative journalist and activist Rafael Marques, State Intelligence and Security Services had a budget of $ 695 m, compared with the Ministry of Agriculture's $ 611 m and the External Intelligence Service's $ 340 m. Moreover, the $ 1.8 bn budget for the Presidency – much higher than the $ 1.5 bn for the Ministry of Health – included $ 69.7 m for presidential security and $ 150.2 m for the Presidential Guard, an indication that the president felt the need to increase his personal security and bankroll a parallel, much better-paid, personal army in times of peace. The BD further noted that 70% of oil revenues and 52.3% of total fiscal revenues were directly under dos Santos' control, with several "strategic funds" and "special funds" at his disposal and not under the purview of the government's budget audit and control mechanisms. The budget, they said, thus aimed at "the reproduction of poverty, the militarisation and concentration of power, and the favouring of certain sectors over social solidarity". The BD also observed that the Angolan FSDEA, created in October 2012 with a starting capital of $ 5 bn and sustained by revenues from the production of 100,000 b/d of crude oil, did not figure in the budget, raising further conjectures that state revenues would serve to enrich the dos Santos family to the detriment of the Angolan people.

The National Bank of Angola successfully combated inflation and the 'dollarisation' of the economy. In July, a new law came into effect forcing all foreign operators in the oil sector to pay for goods and services in the national currency, kwanza, and through domestic bank accounts. **Foreign exchange reserves** remained stable at $ 35 bn, or eight months' worth of imports, public debt was reported at a moderate 31% of GDP, and inflation fell again to a yearly average of 7.7%, the lowest rate in 22 years.

Despite economic diversification programmes and the launch of a new, simplified commercial licence in August, 97% of exports were still dependent on **oil production**. With annual oil revenues estimated at between $ 60 bn and $ 70 bn, these made up around 50% of GDP and 75% of government revenue. Production hovered between 1.74 m and 1.76 m b/d, the highest levels since 2010, and the start of the production of liquid natural gas at the Soyo LNG plant gave a further boost to hydrocarbons exploration, and helped the industry diversify its customer base to new Asian markets. Despite the still insular nature of the sector, which formally accounted for only 1% of jobs, the oil industry offered new opportunities for education and employment to a restricted, but growing number of Angolans; Total Angola reported in June that over half of its director positions were now held by Angolan nationals. State oil company **Sonangol**, voted Africa's second most important company by the magazine 'Jeune Afrique' in March, continued its expansion drive, investing in oil exploration in Venezuela, Iran and Algeria.

In May, a new banking code was introduced to improve transparency and governance in the booming **banking sector**. The new law included ownership disclosure, risk management and auditing requirements, though the presence of politically connected individuals on the boards and as majority shareholders in the largest banks raised some doubts about the enforceability of the regulations. Strong demand from India and China also increased demand to the Angolan **diamond industry**, which remained Africa's third-largest with an output of around 8 m carats. In January, De Beers announced promising diamond finds in its remaining unexplored Mulepe concession in Lucapa, and Escom mining said conditions were finally right to start explorations at its Luô concession. In November, Angolan diamond producer Catoca also signed an agreement to explore for diamonds in neighbouring Zimbabwe. However, the ill-treatment of workers and local residents continued: when workers at the Camuto project went on strike in June to demand a salary raise to cope with rising food costs in the Lundas, the authorities dispatched the Rapid Intervention Police to allow the company to recruit new workers in place of the striking staff. Generally, **workers' rights** made little progress. In July, the governor of Lunda Norte dismissed over 100 schoolteachers who had been on strike for two months over salary arrears and unpaid bonuses, saying the strike had been plotted by UNITA in anticipation of the 2017 elections, and in December, a strike at Luanda's water provider EPAL was 'resolved' by the arrest of strike leaders.

GDP growth was estimated at 6.2% by the IMF, but international ratings agencies and commercial banks pointed out the "elevated vulnerability" of the economy to external shocks, highlighting poor governance, succession risks and growing social tensions as further sources of insecurity. Indeed, despite continued economic growth, the Africa Progress Commission (APC), chaired by Kofi Annan, said in May that Angola was one of the African countries "where the **inequality** between natural resource endowment and social well-being was felt at its most powerful". Although Angola was again Africa's second-largest oil producer, infant mortality remained among the world's highest, at 161 per 1,000 new-borns per year. Furthermore, while per capita GDP grew to $ 3,890, more than 55% of citizens lived on less than $ 1.3 per day. Unemployment officially stood at 25%, and, as the APC report noted, "some of the country's poorest are forced to buy water, at high prices, from private suppliers" – through collusion between the companies of army generals and the public water distributor EPAL, as people commonly said in Luanda. A social and economic report of the Catholic University's Centre of Scientific Study and Research also said the country was far from reaching its human development goals "because of corruption and the bad distribution of national revenues".

As an example of the government's setting of priorities, the Ministry of Social Assistance and Reinsertion officially declared in January that three municipalities in the drought-stricken southern province of Cunene were affected by **hunger** – a danger alerted to by local organisations and the Catholic Church since May 2012. The government then promised a swift response. In March, the EU contributed € 2 m to UNICEF to "complement" government activities with a nutrition programme, after an evaluation showed that over 550,000 children under the age of five were at risk of malnutrition in ten of the 18 provinces. The irony that the 2013 budget cut health and education expenditure to the benefit of defence and the Presidency was not lost on Angolan observers and in May the governor of Cunene said hunger had worsened. In June, FAO reported that Angola had reached its first MDG by halving hunger and malnutrition. While Angola's ambassador to FAO said this was a recognition of "the efforts of the Angolan government and President José Eduardo dos Santos", local NGOs in the neighbouring Namibe province appealed for urgent help for victims of drought and called the FAO statement an insult to Angolan victims of hunger. Finally, while the authorities were busy hosting the roller hockey world cup, UNICEF said in August that $ 14.3 m was needed to ensure food security and water for 1.8 m people. Despite some investments in agriculture, **dependency on food imports** continued. Thus, although agronomists underlined again the country's enormous agricultural potential, the Angolan sociologist Paulo de Carvalho observed that with imports 14 times higher than exports it was "not possible to think of a great future".

Road traffic mortality remained the world's third-highest, while bribe-taking by the traffic police remained rampant with drivers reporting paying 'fines' and 'tips' of up to $ 250 per trip from the capital to the southern coastal city of Lobito. Police Commander de Lemos appealed to road users to denounce these practices to help the corporation in its fight against corruption; nonetheless, the competitiveness of domestic food production remained somewhat limited due to such 'road taxes'.

The **health sector** also remained underfunded, with one medical doctor per 10,000 inhabitants, and 60% of these practitioners were concentrated in Luanda. Malaria remained the main cause of infant mortality; the country also registered cases of dengue fever, human trypanosomiasis (sleeping sickness) and cholera. In June, health authorities published a report claiming that around 300,00 people in Angola were living with **HIV/AIDS**, of whom 54,000 had followed antiretroviral (ARV) treatment programmes. NGOs said the actual number was much higher, though they admitted that the cultural stigma led to substantial underreporting of AIDS as the cause of death. The former UNAIDS representative to Angola accused the authorities of deliberately lying about the official 2% prevalence rate, saying that the real prevalence was much higher, and that 70% of people living with HIV/AIDS had no access to ARV treatment.

In the **education** sector, a middle-school student association in Luanda denounced the unsanitary state of school toilets, saying that overflowing faeces posed a serious health risk to pupils, and that children were often forced to clean school facilities. Similarly, the leader of the opposition party PRS, Eduardo Kwangana, said in January that, despite loudly proclaimed increases in social spending, the allocated budget never reached its destination and that the education system was designed "to keep children stupid". Thus, despite advances in primary enrolment, demand still outran supply in secondary and tertiary education.

Instead, the so-called "concrete policy" continued, with investment in physical infrastructure and prestige projects, without the necessary human and administrative resources to make them work. The model city of Kilamba, on the outskirts of Luanda, completed in 2012 year by Chinese construction companies, still awaited its residents, as the allocation of apartments was marred by delays, corruption and administrative incompetence on the part of Sonangol's subsidiary SONIP, which was charged with the marketing of the residences. The apartments, originally designed as **social housing** in partial fulfilment of the MPLA's 2008 and 2012 electoral promises, were initially offered at prices ranging from $ 60,000 to $ 125,000. Confusion and delays persisted until the end of the year, and the first lucky residents complained of the lack of water and electricity supplies, and inadequate transport to the city centre.

Luanda was again named the **world's most expensive capital** for expatriates by an international business consultancy. While some commenters rejoiced at this free publicity for the country, most deplored the fact that the cost of living remained extremely high, including for accommodation, food, transport and water, while the quality of services remained low. "The only thing cheap in Luanda are the salaries", said Angolan lawyer Ana Paula Godinho at a roundtable on the subject.

Jon Schubert

Botswana

Domestic politics was dominated by the political parties' primary elections in preparation for the 2014 general election. The country sustained its proactive foreign policy guided by its core values of democracy, good governance, the rule of law and respect for human rights. A key economic development was the successful relocation of the centralised diamond sales from London to Botswana's capital, Gaborone. Modest economic growth was recorded, despite an unstable global economic environment, although socio-economic disparities persisted.

Domestic Politics

As in previous voter registration exercises, the electoral authority did not succeed in registering the targeted number of voters, which may suggest that voter apathy had crept in. From 4 to 27 October, the Independent Electoral Commission conducted a general voter registration for the 2014 general election, registering 478,148 out of a possible 1,200,000 voters. The **Botswana Democratic Party** (BDP) held its 35th Congress in Maun on 5–7 July, when the party's central committee was elected. Particularly interesting was the contest for the position of party chairman between Minister of Education and Skills Development Pelonomi Venson Moitoi and Samson Guma Moyo MP, who had been the founding treasurer of the Botswana Movement for Democracy (BMD). Guma Moyo received 467 votes to Moitoi's 402, having pledged to bring back into the BDP most of the members who had left for the BMD. Mpho Balopi and Malebogo Kruger were elected secretary general and deputy secretary general, respectively. Long-time party treasurer and businessman Satar Dada retained this position, with Thapelo Olopeng, one of President Ian Khama's closest allies, as deputy treasurer. Surprisingly, Guma Moyo resigned as party chairman on 2 December following allegations that he had undermined Khama's authority and succession plan with the assistance of foreign elements. He dismissed allegations that he was harbouring intentions of becoming the country's vice president. Vice President Ponatshego Kedikilwe was appointed BDP chairman on 9 December.

The **BDP primary elections** were held on 9 and 30 November. The outcome was queried by a number of parliamentary and council hopefuls, in part because of issues relating to the electoral roll. A number of sitting MPs were defeated, including five senior ministers, three assistant ministers and the deputy speaker of the National Assembly. The senior ministers included Minister of Foreign Affairs and International Cooperation Phandu Skelemani and Minister of Defence, Justice and Security Ndelu Seretse (Ian Khama's cousin), who was considered a candidate for the vice presidency after October 2014. A number of BDP MPs who lost in the primaries indicated they might stand as independent candidates, citing irregularities in the organisation of party primaries. On 21 November, Khama suspended a BDP parliamentary aspirant, Chris Ntuba, for electoral fraud at the party office. The 'Botswana Guardian' reported on 6 December that Guma Moyo, Thapelo Olopeng and Mpho Balopi had manipulated "the voters roll in favour of some candidates ahead of party primary election" and linked this with Guma Moyo's resignation.

A **by-election** took place in the Letlhakeng West constituency on 6 April following the death of its BDP MP, Assistant Minister Maxwell Motowane, and were won by the BDP's Ngaka Ngaka. Another by-election was scheduled by the electoral authority for 23 November in Francistown West following the death of BDP MP Tshelang Masisi, but on 21 November the acting president, Ponatshego Kedikilwe, postponed the by-election to 25 January 2014 on public interest grounds. The opposition condemned this as abuse of office by the BDP, but a court dismissed their charges. The powerful BDP lawyer and chairman of the party's electoral board, Parks Tafa, had earlier suggested that the president had the authority to cancel a by-election order and issue a fresh one so as to allow the BDP candidate to submit his name. In some quarters the postponement of the by-election was perceived as a clear example of government control of the electoral authority. Others felt that the BDP was using public institutions to resolve its internal problems.

Members of the **opposition** coalition party, the Umbrella for Democratic Change (UDC) – the Botswana National Front (BNF), the BMD and the Botswana People's Party (BPP) – also held their congresses. The BMD held its 2nd elective National Congress on 9–12 May in Maun and retained as president Gomolemo Motswaledi, an interim secretary general of the UDC. The BNF held its 16th National Congress on 13–16 July in Ghanzi.

Duma Boko, an interim president of the UDC, was elected unopposed as BNF president. Boko declared at the congress that he had been offered P (pula) 40 m to become a member of the BDP, but the BDP rejected accusations of offering funds to possible members. The BNF also held its primary elections for constituencies allocated to it under the UDC, in preparation for the 2014 election. In May, the BPP held its elective congress in Themashangha. Interim UDC Chairman Motlatsi Molapisi retained the party presidency. The UDC allocated 27, 23 and 7 constituencies to the BNF, BMD and BPP, respectively, for the 2014 election. Meanwhile, the UDC suffered a setback in registering a logo that would combine the logos of the three members of the alliance because the use of the BNF logo was contested in court on the grounds that the BNF constitution bars it from joining another political party. The Botswana Congress Party (BCP) held its 6th elective congress on 13–16 July in Selibe-Phikwe; the party retained Dumelang Saleshando as party president and elected its first female national chairperson, Motsei Rapelana. It agreed on a controversial policy that gave priority to women, youth and people with disabilities as party candidates in the 2014 general election. The BCP primary elections were controversial in some constituencies and the BCP leader came under heavy criticism as some of his relatives were reported to be in business with members of the ruling party.

Corruption and maladministration remained a matter of public concern. The Directorate on Corruption and Economic Crime (DCEC) had in August in excess of 10,000 cases under investigation. One of these implicated senior government officials in a multi-million e-government project intended to raise funds to buy Botswana Telecommunications Corporation when it was privatised. The DCEC also investigated a Ministry of Education printing and photocopying project worth more than P 60 m. The secretary general of the Botswana Red Cross Society was suspended following an investigation into allegations of corruption. The case of Assistant Minister of Finance and Development Planning Vincent Seretse and his co-accused was yet to be concluded by the court, although Seretse continued to serve as an assistant minister. Also under investigation was the Morupule B Power Project, costed at $ 970 m, which was expected to generate 600 MW of electricity to alleviate the power deficit. The contract had been awarded to the China National Electric Equipment Corporation but had not been completed as agreed in October 2012. Power outages for extended hours had a major impact on the economy. The director general of the DCEC announced on 13 June the completion of its investigations regarding the award of the contract for a glass manufacturing project to Chinese Shanghai Fengyue Glass Company by the Botswana Development Corporation. The project, which had cost government more than P 500 m, was abandoned. A parliamentary select committee of inquiry into issues of maladministration regarding the parastatal Botswana Meat Commission (BMC) delivered its report on 12 November, which proposed that certain contracts and issues relating to the BMC be investigated by the DCEC. On 13 February, the minister of agriculture shared with Parliament the findings of a task force that had probed the BMC, which alleged that "poor financial management and oversight, lack of control and disregard of accounting policies" were contributing to problems in the beef industry. The BMC had recorded a loss of P 290.9 m in 2012. The minister did not take responsibility, however, nor did the president relieve him of his position.

The DCEC suffered setbacks in some **high profile cases**. Louis Garvas Nchindo, son of the former managing director of Debswana Diamond Company, and Joseph Matome, a former Debswana senior executive convicted earlier for misappropriating funds, won their appeal on 1 February. Nchindo committed suicide while the case was being tried. In April, the high court acquitted Moemedi Dijeng, the managing director of the cleaning and waste management company, Daisy Loo, and four Gaborone City Council employees on charges related to a P 21 m tender. Reports in the private media maintained that public funds had been used to build an airstrip on private land belonging to President Khama in Mosu Village. The government responded that the airstrip was being built on public land next to Khama's compound. The Office of the Ombudsman announced some preliminary investigations into the matter. The anti-corruption Act of 1994 was amended, and an **anti-corruption policy** was in preparation. Also related to corruption, the Public Procurement and Asset Disposal Act (Suspension and De-listing of Contractors Amendment Regulations) came into effect in March to address the challenge of non-performing contractors, and the Commonwealth Corruption Centre was opened on 27 February in Gaborone. At the launch, the director general of the DCEC declared that corruption as a major problem, although Botswana continued to rank as the least corrupt country in Africa.

Uneasy labour relations between the government and public sector unions, particularly the Botswana Federation of Public Sector Unions (BOFEPUSU), continued. In March, the Court of Appeal decided that the involvement of essential service workers in the 2011 public workers strike had been unlawful. In turn, BOFEPUSU issued a press statement on 14 March, questioning the independence of the judiciary and the appointment of some judges. This earned them a warning from the master and registrar of the High Court. On 20 March, the Court of Appeal also decided that the sacking of essential service workers was lawful, thus reversing a high court ruling. Subsequently, BOFEPUSU declared its support for parties and politicians that advocated workers' interests. Botswana had attracted criticism from the ILO for violating workers' rights.

Minority rights, especially in relation to the **Basarwa/San**, resurfaced. In January, Botswana pleaded with the UN Human Rights Council for assistance in protecting the rights of Basarwa, prison inmates, children and abused spouses. On 18 June, the high court decided in favour of the Basarwa of Ranyane settlement who were contesting their relocation by the government. Their British lawyer, Gordon Bennett, was declared a prohibited immigrant. In 2006, Bennett had successfully represented the Basarwa of the Central Kalahari Game Reserve when they challenged their relocation from the Reserve, but the government had only allowed the 189 litigants who had been party to the action to return. Basarwa who had not been applicants in the 2006 case took the government to court for the third time, but a high court judge dismissed their case in September. The leader of the BCP, Dumelang Saleshando, condemned the government's "determination to destroy Basarwa way of life by assimilating them into mainstream Tswana society", which he equated to "cultural genocide". The British NGO Survival International called for a boycott of Botswana's tourism industry. On 13 August, the minister of labour and home affairs stated that 406 foreigners had been declared prohibited immigrants over the past two years.

Foreign Policy

President **Khama travelled frequently**. He attended the 5th Tokyo International Conference on African Development in Japan on 30 May–2 June and the SADC Extraordinary Summit in Maputo (Mozambique) on 15 June. He visited South Sudan on 8–9 July and Lesotho on 17 July, attended the SADC summit in Lilongwe (Malawi) on 17–18 August and hosted the 4th SACU conference in Gaborone on 12 April, which discussed, among other things, the sharing of revenue. Khama participated in the first session of the Bi-National Commission between Botswana and South Africa on 18–21 November and attended celebrations for the 50th anniversary of Kenya's independence on 12 December. Minister of Foreign Affairs and International Cooperation Phandu Skelemani led a delegation to the 20th AU summit in Addis Ababa (Ethiopia) on 21–28 January and attended the Africa-France Summit on Peace and Security in Paris (France) on 5–7 December. Vice President Ponatshego Kedikilwe attended the 21st AU Summit on the occasion of the organisation's 50th anniversary on 25 May in Addis Ababa.

Several **high-ranking visitors** came to Botswana during the year. Malawi's President Joyce Banda visited on 24–26 March, to cement bilateral relations. Botswana offered a $ 10 m loan and donated 150 cattle. Other visitors included Minister-President of the Government of Flanders/Belgium Kris Peeters (5 April); Canadian Governor General David Johnston (17–20 May); President Salva Kirr Mayardit of South Sudan (24–26 June); Zimbabwean President Robert Mugabe (17 June); and Ugandan President Yoweri Museveni and Kenyan President Uhuru Kenyatta (6 November).

Botswana and **Kenya** evaded a diplomatic row over charges of crimes against humanity brought against Uhuru Kenyatta and his deputy, William Ruto, by the ICC. Botswana had suggested that Kenyatta would not be allowed into the country if he failed to cooperate with the ICC, a decision it withdrew on 15 March, after it emerged that Kenyatta was cooperating with the ICC, and on 31 March President Khama sent a congratulatory message to Kenyatta on his election as president of Kenya. In April, Botswana hosted a workshop on the ratification of the Kampala amendments to the Rome Statute of the **ICC**. Botswana ratified the amended statute, and urged state parties to support the ICC. Botswana was the only country that rejected a proposal by Uganda at the AU summit in May that charges against Kenyatta be withdrawn. Interestingly, after Kenyatta's visit in November, Botswana suggested an amendment to Article 63 of the Rome Statute, which was meant to protect African heads of state from facing trial at the ICC. The proposal, which was endorsed by the AU, was not supported by some international NGOs. In November, Botswana declared its intention of running for the presidency of the ICC's Assembly of States Parties in 2015 amidst AU criticisms of the ICC, for being biased against Africans.

On 25 March, President Khama announced the suspension of ties with **North Korea** in protest at its "dangerous actions and threats against other countries", and criticised it for conducting nuclear weapons tests – which had the potential to undermine peace and security. He also called on the UN to resolve the **Syrian crisis**, and intensify "efforts to end the suffering of the Syrian people at the hands of Assad's discredited regime". On 6 September, Botswana spoke in favour of regime change in Syria and criticised China and Russia for working against efforts to resolve the crisis. On 4 November, Botswana urged that the Assad regime be held accountable for its crimes.

Socioeconomic Developments

Modest economic growth was recorded despite a sluggish recovery in the global economy. GDP of 5.4% was projected. The **diamond market** showed signs of recovery, albeit still weak. A major achievement was the complete relocation of De Beers Diamond Trading Centre from London to Gaborone. The first sale by Diamond Trading Company Botswana (DTCB) was on 11 November. The Okavango Diamond Company, established to buy and sell up to 15% of Debswana's diamonds, held its first sale in October and sold P 343 m worth of diamonds. The government also reported the sale of diamonds worth P 900 m in September by Boteti Mining Company. A further 11 diamond cutting and polishing companies were registered, bringing the total to 27 by November. According to government reports, the sector was employing 3,651 workers by August. DTCB put diamond sales for the year at $ 770 m, in line with the country's local annual medium period target of $ 800 m.

The 2013/2014 **budget** demonstrated commitment to macro-economic stability. Revenues were put at P 44.02 bn and expenditure at P 43.23 bn, generating a surplus of P 779 m. The largest revenue sources were customs and excise at 31.1% (P 13.68 bn), minerals at 30.1% (P 13.25 bn) and non-mineral income tax at 20.4%. Foreign reserves amounted to P 67.6 bn by the end of December. Inflation was recorded at 5.8% and 4.1% in June and December, respectively, thus falling within the Bank of Botswana's 3%–6% medium target. The country retained a sovereign credit ranking according to Moody's and Standard and Poor's, with both agencies predicting a stable outlook. The IMF 2013 Article IV discussions underscored "the need to improve public sector efficiency and speed up reforms to promote economic diversification". The 2013/2014 World Economic Forum Global Competitiveness Report identified a poor work ethic as one of Botswana's major challenges and ranked the country 74th out of 148, a slight improvement from

79th out of 144 in 2012. The World Bank Doing Business Index placed Botswana 65th out of 185 countries.

The minister of finance and development planning described **poverty** as a key development obstacle that negatively impacted on Botswana's HDI status, which had improved from 0.587 in 2000 to 0.634 in 2011. Meanwhile, the government continued with its social safety net programmes for vulnerable groups, with 195,607 people supported at a cost of P 1.2 bn, according to a report on 4 November. It was further reported that a cabinet sub-committee for poverty eradication had registered about 15,000 recipients on the Poverty Eradication Programme. The Remote Area Development Programme recorded 1,055 recipients of poverty eradication projects by September, and 1,211 youth from remote areas registered with tertiary institutions through the Remote Area Development Programme's Affirmative Action, whilst 360 secured formal employment. President Khama also reported that the number of people who survived on less than $ 1 a day had fallen from 23.4% to 6.4% of the population between 2002/3 and 2009/10. The national poverty rate still stood at 21%, however. The national unemployment rate was estimated at 17.8%, with the youth most affected as 35% of the population were aged between 20 and 40.

The other key developmental challenge was **HIV/AIDS**. Preliminary results of the fourth Botswana Aids Impact Survey released in November recorded a 16.9% national HIV prevalence, a slight drop from 17.6% in 2008. On 4 November, Khama declared a 95% anti-retroviral 'uptake', and mother to child transmission was said to be 2% or below. In addition, slightly more than 89,000 safe male circumcisions had been carried out by August, out of a target of 385,000. The budget allocation for HIV/AIDS was P 1.2 bn. As part of government's commitment to contain HIV/AIDS, parliament ratified the revised National HIV and AIDS Policy in August. The policy reduced the age of consent for HIV testing from 21 to 16. An issue of concern, however, was that donor funding was waning.

David Sebudubudu & Keratilwe Bodilenyane

Lesotho

The coalition that had come to power after the election of March 2012, led by Tom Thabane of the All Basotho Congress (ABC), confirmed its position amidst unfavourable economic circumstances, while displaying an unexpected reformist streak in seeking to clamp down on human rights and other abuses by the police and in fighting corruption. However, the coalition between the ABC, the Lesotho Congress for Democracy (LCD) and the Basotho National Party (BNP) was to be rocked by charges of fraud being brought against Dr Timothy Thahane of the LCD, and his subsequent dismissal from his post as minister of energy, meteorology and water affairs. Although tensions were patched up by a cabinet reshuffle, fears that the coalition would prove unstable remained.

Domestic Politics

While there was considerable relief that the change in government that occurred after the March 2012 election had happened peacefully, there was also considerable uncertainty about how the new government under Tom Thabane would cope. Lesotho had never previously seen a **coalition government**, and there was concern as to whether what was essentially an alliance of convenience between the three parties would hang together. The Democratic Congress (DC) under former long serving Prime Minister Pakalitha Mosisili, with 48 seats in parliament, remained the largest party, but was faced by a majority patched together by the ABC (30 seats), LCD (26 seats) and BNP (5 seats), with 16 other seats split between nine parties. Lacking any significant ideological differences, the three parties had been brought together by their determination to wrest power from Mosisili, who had been in office for 14 years and had fallen out with the leaders of both the ABC and the LCD (Mothetjoa Metsing) when they had served under him. Given the fluidity of party structures and affiliations, Thabane had sought initially to achieve a careful balance of power between the coalescing parties, the ABC's 11 seats in **cabinet** being offset by the LCD's nine and the BNP's one. Furthermore, alongside Metsing being appointed deputy prime minister (as well as holding responsibility at the Ministry of Local Government and Chieftainship), Dr Leketekete Ketso of the LCD was appointed to the Ministry of Finance. For the moment, the government looked firm – yet it was widely acknowledged that, if future political differences were to lead to a rapprochement between either of the larger parties and the DC, Lesotho might see another change of government. Unsurprisingly, given the past history of military intervention in political affairs, Prime Minister Thabane also chose to double up as minister of defence, police and national security.

Governments in Lesotho, a country with little control over its own economic destiny and with the large majority of its citizens living in poverty and many lacking access to basic services such as sanitation and electricity, were always likely to run up against disappointed expectations. All parties had made the customary promises about promoting agriculture and industry and tackling poverty and unemployment, and Thabane had vowed to stuff his cabinet with technocrats in order to ensure implementation of his plans. Ultimately, however, he had been forced to appoint a bloated cabinet in order to achieve political balance, with concern for greater efficiency and service delivery taking second place. In any case, with Lesotho's economic prospects overwhelmingly dependent upon those of South Africa, and with the latter's economy also in the doldrums, the new government had little room for manoeuvre.

However, what the new government could do was to send out a strong message that it would clamp down on **corruption and waste**. Within a short space of time, responsibility for oversight of the Directorate on Criminal and Economic Offences (DCEO) had been transferred from direct control by government to control by parliament, a move presented as furthering its independence. A number of high profile actions followed. One was the seizure on 28 February of property from the home of Osman Moosa by the Lesotho Revenue Authority (LRA) because of his failure to pay tax owed as a result of a court order. Moosa had already been convicted of fraud but had recently been confirmed by the High Court as chairperson of the Private Sector Foundation of Lesotho. The LRA also seized control of the premises of his firm, Salkol Trading, an action which Moosa contested. Another move was a clampdown on maladministration of the government pension scheme. The minister of finance claimed in March that civil servants were receiving pensions for at least 6,300 dead people. Money stolen on pretence that claimants were still alive amounted to

M (maloti) 26.5 m, while theft of unclaimed pensions amounted to M 6.5 m. In August, ten persons including four Standard Bank officials were arraigned in court for the theft of M 18.5 m after transfers of money from dormant government accounts to various company and individual accounts between October 2011 and April 2012. The government also announced that it would be claiming major damages from Avis Fleet Services, responsible for running the government's vehicle pool, after a report by a World Bank consultant indicated irregularities in the award of a contract to the firm by the Department of Public Works in 2007. Avis Fleet Services was a subsidiary of Seahlolo Transport Logistics, which was reportedly one-third owned by Principal Secretary for Public Works Lebohang Phooko, and one-third by one of his relatives. In yet another case, Retselisitsoe Khetsi, a former principal secretary for home affairs, was charged with accepting a bribe for facilitating the award of a contract to Nikuv International Projects Ltd to produce Lesotho's new identification documents and electronic passports.

However, while all such moves were designed to rattle the cages of those feeding unjustly off official largesse, the case with most political implications was that concerning **Timothy Thahane**, a former minister of finance and one of the most influential and experienced members of cabinet. Thahane had, since assuming responsibility for energy and water affairs, facilitated the go-ahead of Phase II of the Lesotho Highlands Water Project, involving the construction of the Polihali Dam and gravity transfer tunnel to the Katse Reservoir, which would therefore have more water to transfer to South Africa via the 'Muela Hydropower Station in Lesotho. This would significantly increase Lesotho's electricity generating power, and there were strong hopes that this could be linked to a vast energy storage scheme at Kobong Ha Mallane on the banks of the Katse Reservoir. However, Eskom, South Africa's government-owned electricity supplier, decided that the Kobong scheme would be uneconomic (given other alternative supply possibilities), and in reality, Thahane had had little option but to go ahead with Phase II without it. Nonetheless, the decision seemed to have poisoned relations between the two major parties within the government, and the prime minister initially removed responsibility for water affairs from Thahane, before subsequently backing down and restoring it. However, on 4 November, Thahane found himself hauled in front of a magistrate to hear charges brought against him by the DCEO, which alleged that when he was minister of finance he had been party to defrauding the government of M 19 m in relation to various agricultural development projects. He was immediately dismissed from the cabinet in a move that rocked cabinet unity. Although his dismissal prompted a **cabinet re-shuffle** whereby Thabane sought to paper over party differences, some wondered whether the days of the coalition were numbered. Meanwhile, the political temperature had also been raised by the appearance in court of Monyane Moleleki, deputy leader of the DC, who was charged with fraud in a case relating to his earlier period in office as minister of natural resources.

Amidst its economic concerns, the government was faced by serious **disarray in the judiciary**, where conflict between Chief Justice Mahapela Lehohla and President of the

Court of Appeal Michael Radodibedi had severely impacted upon the administration of the courts, where the hearing of cases lagged seriously behind. In January, the prime minister had lamented that the system of law was also seriously undermined by widespread corruption among **police** and their excessive use of violence. Senior Inspector Lenkoane of the Lithoteng Police Station in Maseru warned the prime minister to be ready to compensate more victims of police torture, because he was going to intensify the torture of suspects. An official spokesperson distanced himself from these remarks, but civil rights organisations staged major protests and called for action to be taken against rogue police.

Foreign Affairs

Lesotho remained crucially dependent upon **foreign financial support**. In his budget, delivered on 22 February, Finance Minister Ketso indicated that 48% of project capital expenditure would be financed by donor grants (M 1,331 m) and donor loans (M 963 m). The largest recipient ministries would be: Energy, Meteorology and Energy Affairs (M 124 m); Public Works and Transport (M 351 m); Health and Social Welfare (M 429 m); Finance (M 428 m); and Education and Training (M 113 m). Significant donor funding included the 2007 Millennium Challenge Corporation grant of $ 363 m from the USA, provided for the health sector, sanitation, infrastructure projects, and climate change, although this was due to end in September.

Significant efforts were made to firm relationships with traditional **aid partners** such as the Irish and the British. The latter dispatched Prince Harry to the country to dispense royal charm and goodwill in February. A more unusual linkage was established by Prime Minister Mosisili's visit to Algeria and the Sahrawi Arab Democratic Republic in May, prior to his travelling to Japan to attend the 5th Tokyo International Conference on African Development on 1–3 June.

Dependent upon and surrounded by **South Africa** as it is, the country's most significant ties are with the neighbouring Republic. Although relations were ostensibly friendly and collaborative, there were continuing tensions. South Africa had tightened border controls in the lead-up to the 2010 soccer World Cup for security reasons, and these had never been adequately relaxed, resulting in massive congestion at the major crossing points, notably Maseru Bridge. Indeed, matters had been exacerbated by the South African Revenue Service's demand since November 2012 that importers and exporters declare their transactions electronically, ahead of their arrival. More worrying for Lesotho, along with Botswana, Namibia and Swaziland, was the strong possibility that South Africa would force a renegotiation of SACU. Its arrangements provided for major subsidies to their budgets (about a 70% budget subsidy in the case of Lesotho). With South Africa currently making payments to SACU of R (rand) 48 bn annually, while running up a budget deficit approaching R 150 bn, the Republic appeared increasingly keen to replace SACU with what it euphemistically termed a 'development community'.

Socio-Economic Developments

In presenting his budget, Dr Ketso sketched out worrying factors that made it unlikely that the government would achieve its goal of raising **economic growth** towards a sustainable level of 6% per annum. Lesotho expected its lowest income from SACU since 2008; the rand had dropped in value by nearly 10% over 2012, at a time when oil prices were expected to rise; and grain prices were rising, contributing to a higher rate of inflation (which Ketso estimated would rise to 6.9% in 2012/13). The growth rate for 2011/12 was estimated at 5.4%, but was expected to fall to 3.4% for 2012/13, in part because reduced rainfall levels had lowered domestic agricultural production.

The proposed **budget** for 2013/14, excluding principal repayments for the year, was set at M 14.6 bn (compared with M 13.9 bn in 2012–13), made up of M 9.7 bn recurrent and M 4.8 bn capital expenditure, an increase in the budget of 5.4%. Relating the budget to the government's National Strategic Development Plan 2012/13–2016/17, Ketso announced the introduction of a new Revenue Management System, and raised concerns about the high level of expenditure on the public service wage bill, which had reached nearly 50% of the recurrent budget. Even so, he announced a 6% rise in public service salaries. However, along with a host of measures to curb rising costs in government and improve fiscal management, he announced an increase in the old age pension from M 350 to M 450 per month, as well as similar improvements in other social benefits. Although this announcement was welcome, social benefits in Lesotho compared poorly with those in South Africa where, even so, recipients continued to struggle to make ends meet.

New **minimum wages**, involving rises of between 7% and 10% in the private sector were prescribed from 1 October, slightly above the inflation rate of 5.4%. However, even while lamenting financial constraints, the government found enough money to increase salaries substantially for politicians, senior civil servants, judges and parliamentarians. These were backdated to 1 April, and generally ranged between 21% and 35%. MPs were awarded an increase of 31.5%.

Roger Southall

Madagascar

This was a watershed year in Malagasy history. On 20 December, President Hery Martial Rakotoarimanana Rajaonarimampianina was elected. A first round of presidential elections took place under the auspices of SADC, the AU and the UN on 25 October. Former president Marc Ravalomanana and transitional president Andry Rajoelina were barred from running. With no candidates of national stature, the results were widely split between the 33 candidates. Rajaonarimampianina's victory came somewhat as a surprise to the international community but was rapidly embraced, while a long exasperated Malagasy populace accepted the results with relief. The Malagasy economy responded well. The IMF predicted real GDP growth of 2.6%.

Domestic Politics

After years of increasingly singular rule, President Rajoelina was weakened by the challenge of a **growing opposition** and the support of a shockingly small group of trusted advisors. His attempt to frame himself as a nationalist president in the face of Malagasy leaders asserting claims to power from abroad failed to mobilise the support he needed. The international community, including SADC, the EU, the AU, France, and the United States, were united in their calls for Rajoelina to join Marc Ravalomanana in declining to run in the elections scheduled for May. Civil society in Madagascar had long been weak, but individual leaders, such as Ntsoa Randriamifidimanana of the Association of Malagasy Employers (FIVMPAMA), began taking pivotal roles in mediating reforms. The relationship between the president and Prime Minister Jean Omer Beriziky was always poor but showed signs of souring further with accusations that presidential advisors and cabinet members were overstepping their authority in a variety of sectors, such as insurance and mining.

The **business sector** had played a critical role in shaping Malagasy politics for decades, but its power had been fully realised when Marc Ravalomanana, founder of the Tiko Group, became president in 2002. While Andry Rajoelina was Ravalomanana's nemesis, in many ways he followed in his footsteps. Rajoelina was founder of the successful printing company Injet and the Viva television and radio stations, and, like Ravalomanana, had been briefly mayor of the capital before taking power. With no elections left in a long electoral cycle, he was the sole opposition figure holding a major office and the only viable civilian leader to whom the military could hand power. Much of the bourgeoisie and new business class joined marginalised political networks and operators to openly question Ravalomanana. As a result, Rajoelina was a civilian candidate installed by the military but largely in the debt of social and business groups. For this reason, the loss of support from key business and military leaders proved a significant blow.

Early **contenders in the presidential race** included the President of the Special Delegation to the City of Antananarivo (an appointed mayor) and leading businessman Edgard Razafindravahy, Deputy Prime Minister for Development Hajo Andrianainarivelo, and Mamy Ravatomanga, head of the SODIAT Group, an industry leader in transportation food, hotels and travel, industrial oil and other sectors. It was not until March that Finance Minister Hery Rajaonarimampianina was considered a viable candidate. He was one of the president's few trusted advisors, and Rajoelina wavered as to whether to support him or Deputy Prime Minister for Development Hajo Andrianainarivelo. The latter was the first to declare his candidacy and his eagerness to distance himself from the ruling regime did not win him accolades from the president. Jean Luis Robinson, who had been health minister under Ravalomanana, followed suit days later, as did another Ravalomanana supporter, Benjamin Radavidson Andriamparany.

When Lalao Ravalomanana, wife of former president Marc Ravalomanana, declared her intention to run for president, President Rajoelina took this as a violation of the agreement that neither he nor Ravalomanana would run. He reasserted his own candidacy, throwing the race into disarray and the question to the courts. In Decision No. 05-CES/D of 28 May, the **Special Electoral Court** of the High Constitutional Court of Madagascar ruled that Rajoelina, Lalao Ravalomanana, and former president Didier Ratsiraka were all eligible to run and that the 24 July electoral date would stand. This decision was much criticised by both the international community and the Independent National Electoral Commission of Madagascar, and the former refused to fund the elections or consider them valid. A period of **legal-juridical crisis** ensued until Decision No. 11-CES/D of 21 August listed the final candidates and voided the eligibility of all three. The decision was largely derided in the Malagasy press and by Malagasy civil society as the result of an unwarranted intervention by the international community in domestic politics. The judgement nevertheless stood, and paved the way for a SADC-led **international observer mission**, international funding, and the elections of 25 October.

Rajoelina found it hard to resist making his mark on the electoral map. From 2004, Madagascar's primary level of administration had been **regions**, but the 2010 constitution reintroduced a secondary role for provinces while underscoring local government at the commune and *fokontany* (sub-commune) level. On 9 August, Rajoelina sacked seven of the 22 regional chiefs, who his council of ministers stated were addicted to illegal, arbitrary and abusive practices, but without specifying the offences. Many analysts saw this as retribution for the seven's support for opposition candidates and as an attempt to influence the elections. On 20 November, one month ahead of the second round of presidential and legislative elections, Rajoelina replaced ten regional chiefs. In their place, two trusted civil administrators were appointed for the regions of Sava and Antsiranana and Rajoelina turned for further leadership appointments to trusted factions in the often divided military. Three generals and five colonels were appointed to Anosy, Atsimo Andrefana, Atsima Atsinanana Vatovavy Fitovinany, Diana, Sofia, Ihorombe and Melaky. The strategic importance of these regions both in the elections and in the provision of critical mining and other high-rent resources should not be overlooked. At the time, there was concern that Rajoelina was preparing support for a coup d'état, should it become necessary.

The final **list of candidates** on 21 August made clear that none of the 33 who were standing was of sufficient national stature to dominate the elections. They could loosely be grouped into candidates close to Ravalomanana (such as Jean Luis Robinson and Benjamin Radavidson Andriamparany), candidates close to Rajoelina (Hery Rajaonarimampianina and Hajo Andrianainarivelo), former prime ministers and distant party heads (such as Camille Vital and Monja Roindefo), and perennial regional candidates (such as Roland Ratsiraka, Jean Lahinirik and Pierrot Rajaonarivelo). Fears began to mount that the **fracturing of the political space** could renew civil strife. Jean Louis Robinson won the highest percentage in the first round vote with 21%, and Hery Rajaonarimampianina came second with 15.9%. The fracturing proved a grave concern since Rajaonarimampianina faired well in the *ancien* province and opposition strongholds of Tulear, but not the capital, Antananarivo, while for Robinson the opposite was the case.

One of the seminal concerns in the race between Rajaonarimampianina and Robinson was that they were seen as proxies or, worse, **pawns of Rajoelina and Ravalomanna**, respectively. Each of the former presidents had become profoundly centralising as their influence waned and Rajaonarimampianina and Robinson were survivors within the presidential coteries. Many international leaders voiced concerns that a victory for Rajaonarimampianina would be a victory for Rajoelina and would represent a continuation of his regime. The specific concern was that Rajoelina would be appointed prime minister in a

Russia-like power play. **Legislative elections** were held on 25 December. Miaraka Amin'i Prezida Andry Rajoelina ('Together with Andry Rajoelina'), the coalition of the former president, won the largest bloc with 51 of the 147 seats in the National Assembly. Mouvance Ravalomanana came second with 18 seats, and a record 34 seats were won by independents. By year's end, it was clear that Rajaonarimampianina did not feel particularly beholden to Rajoelina and was ready to assert his own authority. While Rajoelina expected to be given the premiership, the new regime appeared to resist that, bringing the independents critically into play and delaying decisions about a premier for some time. Those close to the former president appeared to signal that Rajoelina would bow out of the race for prime minister rather than face embarrassment or cause political tensions.

Foreign Affairs

SADC, the AU, UN, EU, US, France and others close to the political negotiations in 2009–13 were cautious about naming specific markers to define an end to the crisis and the time for the resumption of **foreign aid**. Elections could not in themselves solve the governance challenges. Indicators for Madagascar had long pointed to a decline in governance standards, as reflected in the Mo Ibrahim meta-index. The primary question for the international community was: should foreign acceptance of the regime and the resumption of aid after the elections be used to help the restoration of governance? Or, should aid be given not as a reward for elections but only after outcomes of donor investment could be assured by an improvement in the quality of governance? During the period between the election rounds, it appeared the international community might not be united in their answer. This was a reason for concern because public opinion surveys pointed to the value placed by the populace on there being a single, clear international position.

The head of the SADC delegation, former Mozambican president Joaquim Chissano, had had a series of troubled meetings in Antananarivo, including a visit in August with Leonardo Simao of the SADC Mediation Board, Special Advisor to the Mediator Nuno Tomas, and John Tesha advising the Electoral Commission. They were intent on discouraging Rajoelina, Ravalomanana and Ratsiraka from standing for the presidency. Regarding the 25 October first round of elections, the SADC Observer Mission concluded in its 27 October report that, while there were some pertinent concerns raised by stakeholders, they were not of such a magnitude as to impact the outcome of what were otherwise free, fair and transparent elections. Chissano expressed further concern on 19 December, just before the second round of elections, that Rajoelina was deliberately flaunting electoral law and the SADC Roadmap to End the Crisis in Madagascar by campaigning for Rajaonarimampianina. Ibrahim Fall, head of the AU observer team, had similar reservations. After the second round of elections, the **response from the international community** was uniform and resolute with nearly all accepting the election results within days. SADC was first to congratulate Madagascar and the Independent National Electoral Commission on peaceful elections. This was a critical endorsement.

The French Ambassador, François Goldblatt, tweeted words of caution on 21 December but followed that tweet with a statement that the elections were a "culmination of the process of restoration of democracy as expected by the Malagasy". A US spokesperson commended the Malagasy electoral authorities and the UN and welcomed the new president as bringing a new opportunity. This was followed by an invitation from US President Barack Obama to President Rajaonarimampianina to visit the White House. A spokesperson for UN Secretary-General Bai Ki-moon reaffirmed the UN's commitment to support Madagascar and welcomed the opportunity the elections had brought for "genuine reconciliation" and "the deepening of democratic governance and economic recovery".

The **World Bank** signalled that it would start the process of normalising relations. The **EU**, as Madagascar's second largest donor, endorsed the elections in a 23 December statement, and EU Ambassador to Madagascar Leonidas Tezpsidis announced a commitment of € 455 m in aid between 2014 and 2020. The **US** welcomed the elections as an opportunity to re-engage with a new portfolio focusing on agriculture, environment, and global health. **France** had been the only major donor to continue granting significant aid and, by year's end, the French Embassy was signalling a desire to re-invigorate spending levels. Strategic donor plans in process, including the 2012 Interim Strategy Note of the World Bank, seemed to signal that the resumption of aid would be more demand-focussed than in the past and that direct government support, while it would be resumed, would be more cautious than before.

Socioeconomic Developments

According to the IMF, **GDP** rose by 1.9% in 2012 and was expected to rise by 2.6% in 2013 and 3.8% in 2014. Inflation stayed steady at 5.8% in 2012 and was estimated to be 6.7% in 2013. More than 92% of the population lived on under $ 2 per day, making Madagascar one of the poorest countries in the world. The tax rate as a percentage of commercial profits dropped steadily from a high of 47% in 2007 to 36%. Commercial profit taxes fell by two percentage points. In a country more than 95% dependent on value added and commercial taxes, this indicated a loss of both revenue and the capacity for revenue collection.

In mid-2013, the World Bank took stock of the **economic effects of the political crisis**, which took a heavy toll, especially on the most vulnerable people. The accumulated cost of the crisis since 2009 was estimated at above $ 8 bn, based on the assumption that average annual GDP growth would otherwise have been at 5%. As a result of the economic stagnation, combined with an average growth in population of over 3% a year, per capita income had fallen to the 2001 level and the proportion of people living below the poverty line had increased by an estimated 10%. The analysis predicted that the country would be unable to reach most of the MDGs, including those deemed potentially within reach in 2007 such as a reduction in child mortality, the expansion of primary education and the eradication of extreme poverty. Infrastructure had deteriorated and the ability to deal with external shocks was reduced.

Perhaps the most serious aspects of the socioeconomic crisis were the losses in the **health and education sectors**. Foreign aid in these areas actually increased during the crisis period, which should be viewed as largely a humanitarian response to state austerity measures. Public expenditure had fallen by over 20% since 2009, notably in education (14%) and health (23%). The net intake rate of school-aged children into grade one had fallen from 81% in 2008 to 77% in 2012, and private secondary school enrolment had dropped from 40% in 2008 to 36% in 2012, even as public schools fell into disarray. The number of grade school children not enrolled was estimated by the World Bank to be between 400,000 and 600,000. Dropouts before fifth grade had risen by an estimated 255,000 – less than half of students who enter school were now reaching grade five. A World Bank report on education concluded in September that financial considerations had had the greatest impact on primary school access and retention. Moreover, there were significant variations in the depth and nature of the impacts of the crisis between regions and socioeconomic levels. Equity in education had been significantly eroded.

A similar pattern was apparent in the **health sector**. Madagascar made international news in December with a reported 82 cases of bubonic plague. Each year, there had usually been between 300 and 600 known local cases of bubonic plague, which would be treated with antibiotics. But the inherent concern was that an increasing percentage of the population did not have regular access to health care so that treatable diseases could be addressed. According to a 2012–13 national household survey conducted by INSTAT, the Malagasy national statistics office, the incidences of disease had increased to an average of 11.1% of the population declaring a malady from 7.2% in a similar 2005 survey. Worse, the impact on the lowest quintile of the population was greater than on the upper quintiles, indicating an increase in vulnerability. Access to clinics was also a significant indicator, with local, particularly rural, hospitals significantly impacted by the economic downturn and the political uncertainty during 2009–13. There was a significant and growing divide along geographic and economic lines. The region with the lowest incidence of illness was Vakinankaratra with 8% of the population reporting ailments. The highest incidence was Vatovavy Fitovinany, at more than twice that level, with 16.7%. The lowest levels of disease were concentrated in the central highlands and the highest levels along the coast. The regional pattern was also consistent with the reasons given for not consulting a medical professional, with the worst impacted coastal regions seeing the greatest percentage of the population declaring their inability to pay for services. Worsening access along regional and economic lines was expected to be among the central issues addressed in new health and education planning.

Richard R. Marcus

Malawi

The massive abuse of public funds popularly called 'Cashgate' was the year's most dramatic story. This saga affected yet again the donor confidence that President Banda had tried to rebuild after the death of her predecessor, Bingu wa Mutharika, and it resulted in the suspension of aid and loans. The year also witnessed a lot of activity by political parties as they prepared for the first tripartite (presidential, parliamentary and local government) elections in 2014. The Malawi kwacha (K) fell in value by almost half during the first part of the year after it was floated on the market, resulting in rises in the price of commodities and in the general cost of living. This triggered various kinds of industrial action in both private and public sector organisations, aimed at pressuring employers to raise salaries.

Domestic Politics

It was a busy year for most political parties as the elections scheduled for 14 May 2014 drew closer. Various party **conventions** took place for the election of presidential candidates and party officials. In April, the Democratic Progressive Party (DPP) held its first-ever convention in Blantyre. Peter Mutharika won the party leadership, defeating Henry Chimunthu Banda. The Malawi Congress Party (MCP) held its convention in Lilongwe in

August. There were 12 contestants for the leadership, including John Tembo, the party's long-term president. A new era dawned when Lazarus Cakwera, a 58-year old politically inexperienced former Assemblies of God church president, was elected to lead the party. In his inaugural speech on 10 August, Chakwera pledged that the party would end its 20-year run in opposition by winning the 2014 elections. He stressed that his vision was to rebuild the party and make sure that it followed principles and policies that would give Malawians confidence. He also urged party followers to embrace democratic principles. By August, the ruling People's Party (PP) and the United Democratic Front (UDF) had also held their conventions.

Intra- and inter-party conflicts featured in the political arena. In the PP, Abida Sidik Mia, who had been the parliamentary candidate for a constituency in Nsanje, wanted to pull out of the electoral race due internal party conflicts. Similarly, in the MCP some officials resigned barely a week after the party convention because long-serving members of the party's National Executive Committee (NEC) had been excluded from the new NEC and replaced by new party members. On 13 January, supporters of the ruling PP and the opposition UDF clashed in a fracas that left several people injured after PP supporters were accused of removing UDF party flags from various strategic sites. There were similar tensions in Zomba on April 21, when supporters of both parties clashed and took down each other's flags. These fights erupted ahead of a planned whistle-stop tour by Atupele Muluzi, the UDF's presidential candidate, in the Eastern Region. In March, DPP supporters turned violent when their interim president, Peter Mutharika, and ten others were arrested following a Commission of Inquiry report that exposed attempts to circumvent constitutional order in the April 2012 power transition after the death of the late president Bingu wa Mutharika. Thousands of DPP supporters in Thyolo, Phalombe and Mulanje petitioned their district commission offices against the arrest of the DPP interim president and other party heavyweights. On 13 October, members of the DPP and the Alliance for Democracy (AFORD) clashed when AFORD supporters removed a DPP flag and assaulted its officials at a venue where DDP president Peter Mutharika was holding a rally.

Various laws were adopted during the year. In February, MPs unanimously approved the Gender Equality Bill, which among other things empowered women to choose whether to have a child or not, effectively a right to seek an abortion. On 22 May, Parliament passed the Accountants and Auditors Bill, which merged the Public Accountants Examination Council with the Malawi Accountancy Board to both avoid duplication of roles and strengthen administrative structures. On 23 May, Parliament also adopted the Local Government Elections Bill, aimed at facilitating harmonisation of the electoral laws for the 2014 tripartite elections. In December, the president assented into law the long-awaited Declaration of Assets, Liabilities and Business Interest Bill, which was expected to close loopholes that undermined asset declaration legislation. Among officials required to declare their assets under the new law were the state president, vice president, speakers of parliament and deputies, cabinet ministers, MPs, treasurers of political parties represented in parliament, and others. In August, President Joyce Banda declined to assent to the Land Bill, saying there was need for more consultation. This came after some organisations and individuals called on the president not to sign the bill since it disadvantaged women and the landless with regard to land ownership.

Corruption in the public sector was a major concern. Huge attention was given to the shooting of Budget Director in the Ministry of Finance Paul Mphwiyo by unknown assailants on the night of 14 September in Lilongwe. The murder was linked to his efforts to expose high-level officers who were abusing public funds and his closing of loopholes that gave opportunities for financial mismanagement in government. In October, extensive embezzlement at Capital Hill, the main government building, locally called 'Cashgate', made headlines. The total amount of money pilfered from the public purse reported in the months of September and October alone had hit a record K 1.2 bn. Early results of investigations revealed that suspicious transactions had been made and deleted from the government payment record, the Integrated Financial Management Information System (IFMIS). Theft of government money had been widely blamed on weak controls in the IFMIS, and government officials were caught with huge amounts of stolen money. For example, the principal accountant was caught with K 3 m in cash in the boot of his car as he left through the Capital Hill gate and a further $ 25,400 (K 10,160,000) was found in his house. The police also found K 7.8 m at the home of a female accounts assistant who worked in the office of the accountant general, and K 120 m was discovered in a male junior accountant's home. The Financial Intelligence Unit reported that about K 20 bn of stolen money was involved in this **looting scandal**, and reports of this massive theft by public servants drew criticism from various quarters.

President Banda reacted with a **cabinet reshuffle**, although this did not help much since only Minister of Finance Ken Lipenga and Minister of Justice Ralph Kasambara were dismissed. Five newcomers were appointed to the 32-member cabinet, including four non-MPs, among them Maxwell Mkwezalamba (as minister of finance), and former director of public prosecution Fahad Assan as minister of justice. These limited changed failed to impress observers.

Heads of government ministries where these thefts had taken place were, if anything, simply moved to other ministries. The president lost her remaining popularity as this seemed to prove that she was not serious about getting rid of 'thieves'. The government also introduced austerity measures aimed at minimising costs associated with external and internal travel for both the presidency and public servants, but this did not bar the presidency from extensive local travel. In May, the leader of the opposition parties in Parliament, John Tembo described it as morally wrong and unfair for the government to come up with austerity measures that were shouldered only by helpless Malawians while those in government lived a different life. Critics also said that government was trying to look innocent of the **plundering of public resources**, while pointers indicated that very senior government officials were among the culprits. By the end of the year, several prominent people had been linked to the scandal and held in police custody for questioning and further investigations. None of them were convicted, however, and they were released on bail. This further weakened confidence in the presidency, which was accused by donors, opposition parties and civil society for failing to take action to deal with the mess. Reports released by the Catholic Commission for Justice and Peace before the Public Accounts Committee alleged that Banda was at the centre of the scheme to siphon off public funds to finance her party's activities. Her failure to act despite promising the nation that she would not protect anyone involved in the scandal, no matter how senior s/he was in government and the party, was viewed as evidence of her involvement.

In May, President **Joyce Banda** was ranked as the most powerful woman in Africa and was 47th on a Forbes list of the 100 most powerful women in the world. In October, the president was also ranked 16th out of 52 African leaders in an Index on Leadership released by the Kenya-based Nation Media Group. The Mo Ibrahim Index on African Governance moved Malawi's ranking from 17th to 16th out of 52 countries, with improvements in safety and rule of law, and respect for human rights given as the main reasons.

Foreign Affairs

Malawi continued to enjoy good relations with other countries and international agencies, and received **international financial support**. In January, the World Bank released $ 695 m (K 238.3 bn) under its new Country Assistance Strategy for the next four years. According to a World Bank statement dated 29 January, the money was to support Malawi's effort to diversify the economy and make it more competitive and resistant to shocks. The World Bank also pumped in a further $ 50 m (about K 16.9 bn) in May. On 4 April, the US government committed $ 2.5 m in support of the preparations for the 2014 elections. On 17 May, the British Department for International Development provided an additional £ 16 m (about K 8.7 bn) for the health sector and to boost the country's foreign exchange (forex) reserves. On 16 September, Malawi and Germany signed a financial cooperation agreement worth € 12 m (about K 5.4 bn) to support the social cash transfer programme. Part of the grant was to be used to strengthen public-private partnerships for a reproductive health project being implemented through the Christian Health Association of Malawi. Both programmes were part of Germany's long-term support focused on improving basic health care. In August, the governments of Malawi and the USA signed an agreement to start rolling out the $ 350.7 m for the Millennium Challenge Corporation compact programme, under which the electricity infrastructure would be upgraded to revitalise Malawi's' energy sector so that it could cope with the increasing demand for power, which stood at 350 MW. These loans and agreements were suspended, however, pending the investigations into abuse of public funds in the Cashgate scandal. In December, the Norwegian government and the Flemish government in Belgium contributed K 2 bn and K 1.3 bn, respectively, to Malawi's health sector when donors under the Common

Approach to Budgetary Support resolved to delay budgetary support and funding to other sectors, again pending the Cashgate investigations. In April, the EU, later joined by Norway, threatened to put on hold K 9 bn in aid and budgetary support until weaknesses in the financial management system had been rectified. This jeopardised about K 6.5 bn in budget support that Norway was yet to release after already disbursing K 13.5 m.

In March, Malawi received a soft loan from diamond-rich **Botswana** of $ 10 m (about K 4 bn) to boost fuel reserves and for the agriculture and health sectors. The deal was signed during Banda's two-day state visit to Botswana, when the two governments also committed to sharing resources and expertise in a number of areas. In August, ten Malawians were awarded scholarships to study mining geology at the Botswana University of Science and Technology. However, relations between Malawi and its neighbouring countries were strained. Malawi and Tanzania were embroiled in a **border dispute** after Tanzania claimed part of Lake Malawi as its territory. Malawi insisted on its entitlement to the whole of the lake, apart from the south-eastern stretch which is part of Mozambique, while Tanzania claimed part of it under current international law. Malawi's argument was based on the Heligoland Treaty between Britain and Germany, signed on 1 July 1890, which mapped the boundary between the two countries along the Tanzanian shore. Malawi also protested against the deployment by Tanzania of two ships on the disputed part of the lake. The protest followed Malawi's concern over the involvement in the mediation process of a Tanzanian national who was working at the SADC secretariat. At one point, Malawi threatened to pull out of the mediation and take the matter to the International Court of Justice. The mediation team was chaired by Joaquim Chissano, former president of Mozambique. In early September, Malawi and Tanzania were given three weeks to analyse and respond to a report produced by the Forum of Former Heads of State and Government mediating in the Lake Malawi border dispute. On 12 September, Malawi and Tanzania exchanged documents on the margins of SADC.

On 10 August, Malawi hosted the **SADC** Heads of State and Government Summit in Lilongwe. Among the issues discussed were the status of finances, contributions from member states and HIV and AIDS projects. On 11 September, President Banda attended an extraordinary SADC Troika summit of SADC in Windhoek (Namibia), which discussed the volatile security situation in the DRC and the political situation in Madagascar. In August, she travelled to Zimbabwe to attend the 20th general assembly of the UN World Tourism Organization, which is responsible for the promotion of sustainable and universally accessible tourism. On 2 September, Banda received Rwanda's minister of foreign affairs in Blantyre, where they discussed how to strengthen mutual relations and enhance international cooperation. She then left for Austin, Texas, and Montgomery, Alabama, to deliver speeches ahead of the 68th UN General Assembly, scheduled to take place on 24–28 September in New York. On 9 December, the president attended the memorial service for the former South African president, Nelson Mandela, and delivered a speech at his burial ceremony on 15 December in Qunu, Mandela's ancestral home.

In June, president Banda entered into an agreement with the government of **South Korea** following a visit she made to that country in February to discuss the possibility of sending young Malawian men and women aged between 18 and 25 to work in factories and on farms on the Korean peninsula, due to lack of employment opportunities in Malawi. The plan to export about 100,000 young people as migrant workers was criticised by Malawian trade unions.

Socioeconomic Developments

The **cost of public utilities and services** continued to rise during the year. According to a Centre for Social Concern report, monthly expenditure on basic needs in the cities of Lilongwe, Blantyre, Zomba and Mzuzu increased by 1.3% to K 104,112 for a household of six people. In February, the Malawi Energy Regulatory Authority announced price increases for petrol, diesel and paraffin to K 704.30, K 683.60 and K 591.90 per litre, respectively. On 13 March, pump prices for petrol, diesel and paraffin rose again by an average of 2.2%. The Electricity Supply Corporation of Malawi (ESCOM) increased electricity charges by 40% in September. Between May 2012 and September 2013, ESCOM had increased power tariffs four times. In April, domestic water tariffs rose from K 720 to K 1,130 per 5,000 litres and commercial rates increased from K 2,540 to K 4,191 per 10,000 litres.

The year also witnessed **shortages of hospital drugs**. In January, public hospitals, especially district and referral centres had run out of 99% of essential medicines. On 4 February, doctors blamed the crisis on inadequate funding, long and bureaucratic procurement processes, the centralised nature of the health service and use of intermediaries to buy drugs. They described the country's situation as shameful because people were dying for lack of basic medicines. In a related development, it was reported that 30,000 cases of typhoid fever a month were recorded at the Queen Elizabeth Hospital in Blantyre, most of the victims being children. The total national **budget** for 2013/14, pegged at K 408 bn, was raised by 16% to K 475.8 bn during the fiscal year. The adjustment was attributed to pressure on some key expenditure lines during the first half of the financial year on account of the depreciation of the kwacha. These included procurement of drugs and high interest payments, with interest rates hovering at around 40%.

Dry spells affected some parts of Malawi, resulting in fears of hunger in Karonga, since the maize crops had wilted. On the other hand, from 10 to 16 February over 1,188 households in Chikhwawa were rendered homeless by **floods** following heavy rains. More than 900 houses were destroyed and 200 ha of crops were washed away. **Staple foods** and other basic commodities were scarce and rose in price. By February, maize was already in short supply due to increased demand from consumers. The Agricultural Development and Marketing Corporation started rationing maize by selling 10 kg per person instead of the normal 50 kg. On 26 March, it was reported that serious damage to the national maize reserves had occurred at the National Food Reserve Agency silos in Lilongwe: over 60,000 tonnes of the staple grain were destroyed by rain water following a leak. As a result, prices continued to increase. In March, prices of other commodities, including sugar, also soared by 15%. This was the second sugar price hike in four months following a 12% increase in November 2012 caused by the rising cost of fossil fuels and electricity.

Costs for **tobacco production** also rose. It was estimated that tobacco producers had lost about K 24.4 bn by mid-June due to the depreciation of the kwacha, which began in early April. During the year, Malawi produced a total of about 160 m kg of tobacco of all types, which was projected to bring in $ 362 m (about K 127 bn) in forex earnings, up from $ 79 m in 2012. Auction Holdings Ltd statistics indicated that, as of June, average burley prices had shot up to $ 2.29 per kg (from $ 2.18 in 2012), flue cured had fallen to $ 3.35 per kg (from $ 3.41), and dark fired rose had risen to $ 2.29 per kg (from $ 2.34). By end of June, the country had received $ 16.9 m from burley, $ 5.7 m from flue cured, and $ 0.4 m from dark fired tobacco.

The **local currency** (kwacha) appreciated significantly between April and August, mainly on account of improved tobacco proceeds and the clearance of the backlog of forex remittances. However, pressure continued to mount on the country's currency, as the lean period got into full swing, resulting in a fall in the trading value of the kwacha to K 405 to $ 1. As of October, Malawi's gross official **foreign reserves** stood at $ 442.6 m or 2.4 months of import cover. In September, foreign currency was still readily available on the market. According to the Reserve Bank of Malawi's (RBM) daily financial money market reports, total bank reserves stood at K 42.3 bn on 27 September, down from K 43.9 bn on 7 September. The average inter-bank lending rate rose from 18.2% to 20.4% in the same period, an indication that liquidity was worsening. The RBM official exchange rates report indicated that the kwacha had depreciated from 3 June to 30 September by 18% against the euro to K 518 to € 1, and by 20% against sterling, to K 619 to £ 1.

The year also saw **labour conflicts and other protests** in both the public and private sectors. On 12 February, civil servants marched to Capital Hill in Lilongwe, bringing work to a halt. They called for, among other things, the revision of allowances, including a 100% rise in local travel allowances and 25% for foreign travel to match the devaluation of the kwacha against the dollar. On 20 February, there were street demonstrations by primary school pupils in Blantyre and Lilongwe, calling for pay rises for teachers, in addition to strikes by other civil servants demanding a 67% salary rise. On the same day, the government brought in a 61% salary increase for the lowest paid civil servants and a 5% rise for the highest paid. In a related development, in October, hundreds of medical workers at Kamuzu Central Hospital in Lilongwe, which serves at least 5 m people in the Central and Northern regions, gave the government a 48-hour ultimatum to solve the drugs and medical supplies crisis that was rocking the hospital, or they would down tools. Reports revealed that over 40 people had died in a week from curable illnesses amidst the shortage of basic hospital requirements. In June, ESCOM employees gave their management a seven-day ultimatum to address their concerns over low salaries and poor working conditions or face a nationwide strike. The employees initially planned a sit-in, but management intervened and asked them to return to work with assurances that the company was looking into their concerns. The relationship between the ESCOM management and employees deteriorated further after the parastatal bought a fleet of new vehicles valued at K 1.4 bn. Similarly, support staff in the University of Malawi (UNIMA) went on strike in October to force the government to increase their benefits – an action that further affected an already disrupted university calendar. UNIMA lecturers were also set to join the industrial action following the government's failure to meet a commitment it had made to adjust their salaries by 25% from 1 July. On 18 January, the Consumers Association of Malawi led a successful and peaceful demonstration against the government and presented a seven-point petition against economic hardships to President Banda's administration. In the private sector, the Ministry of Labour intervened in a strike in May by Lilongwe shop workers who had staged a sit-in for better pay and conditions of service. The minimum wage was subsequently increased to K 18,600 per month. Similarly, hundreds of protesting workers downed tools on 24 June and blocked the entrance to Motal-Engil's Mkwinda Campsite in Neno, Chikhwawa, demanding that the Thai casual labourers recruited for road construction should be sent back to Thailand; they were seen as replacing Malawian casual labourers who had been fired to make way for them.

Tiyesere Mercy Chikapa-Jamali & Lewis B. Dzimbiri

Mauritius

The Mo Ibrahim Index of African Governance again ranked Mauritius as a top performer on the continent in terms of rule of law, personal security, accountability, persistence of democratic institutions, and sustainable economic opportunities. In the 'Democracy Index' by the Economist Intelligence Unit, Mauritius was ranked 18th out of 167 states, and was the only African country classified as a "full democracy". No spectacular events were recorded during the year.

Domestic Politics

Political stability prevailed, although the coalition government headed by Dr Navinchandra (Navind) Ramgoolam and composed of the Mauritius Labour Party (MLP) and the Mauritius Social Democratic Party (MSDP) had a majority of only five seats in parliament. Tactical manoeuvres were tried with the aim of splitting the opposition coalition of the Mauritius Militant Movement (MMM) and the Mauritius Socialist Movement (MSM) with Paul Raymond Bérenger as Leader of the Opposition, assisted by Sir Anerood Jugnauth, the former president of the republic, who had stepped down in 2012. Bérenger and Jugnauth intended to forge a viable opposition and go to the next polls with a reinvention of the alliance between the MMM and MSM that had been created in 2000. The weak government majority in parliament led to a **weak reform agenda**, but Ramgoolam, nevertheless, skilfully exploited various rifts in the opposition coalition. Observers expected that he would stay in power until 2015. He himself said he intended to go into the next elections without "crutches". While some observers believed that political support for Ramgoolam's MLP remained firm in rural areas due to a generally good performance, others maintained that the MLP, and Ramgoolam in particular, seemed out of touch with reality and everyday life. Although **parliamentary elections** were not due till 2015, there was speculation that Ramgoolam might be inclined to go for a snap election in 2014, as Paul Bérenger intimated in his New Year address to MMM activists.

The introduction of the numerical-digital **identity card**, which was launched in mid-year, gave rise to judicial and constitutional questions. The civil society initiative 'Platform No to ID' supported an appeal against the distribution of the identity card by civil rights activist Dr Maharaja Madhewoo, and collected 10,600 signatures and an association of social workers collected 70,000 signatures against it. They wanted the distribution of the card to be stopped on the grounds that it was unconstitutional, since finger prints and photographs of every person would be taken and digitally and stored. Pravind Jugnauth backed this protest as chairman of the MSM, indicating that he himself would take the government to the **Supreme Constitutional Court**. The grouping 'Rezistans ek Alternativ' opposed the implicit presumption of the law that everyone who objected to the new document would be treated as criminal and could be fined. Eventually, judge David Chan Kan Cheong rejected the demand for an injunction. Minister for Information Technology Tassraja Pilly Chedumbrum interpreted this decision as a blow to Pravind Jugnauth and assured the public that the digital information stored would be highly securitised; it would be handled exclusively by the 'Government Online Centre', and accessible only by judicial decision. A decision of the Supreme Constitutional Court was still pending at the end of the year.

Electoral reform, on the agenda for more than a decade, was still at the stage of preliminary consideration. On the occasion of the commemoration of the 113th birthday of Sir Seewosagur Ramgoolam, the founding father of Mauritius's independence in 1968, Prime Minister Navind Ramgoolam referred to the issue, indicating that the white paper on electoral reform was still in preparation. The communal election results of 2012 had created a tendency within the MLP to favour postponing this reform. In his New Year's address on 31 December 2013 Ramgoolam argued that electoral reform should contribute to reconciling the political elite and the people and not to dividing them. Another politically controversial issue of political was the envisaged introduction of electronic voting machines, which the government planned to install for the next general elections.

In a parliamentary debate in October, the Deputy Prime Minister and Minster of Finance Xavier-Luc Duval (MSDP) announced that the government envisaged a partial liberalisation of the **audiovisual media**, but only for channels that broadcast films, entertainment shows and sport.

Foreign Affairs

Mauritius considered itself to be not only a diplomatic and economic hub for SADC and COMESA, but also as a gateway to francophone Africa. In order to counterbalance the bias towards China in Mauritian outward-looking activity (Mauritius had in 2008 granted an economic free zone ('Tianli') to China near the capital, Port Louis), **India** (apart from having significant ethnic and family ties) was of particular importance in bilateral relations. Since 1983, the Comprehensive Double Taxation Avoidance Agreement and later Double Taxation Avoidance Convention had channelled Indian capital into financial markets through Mauritian offshore financial services. Due to Mauritius's close to zero capital gain taxes, these provisions caused concern to Indian and world public opinion, which labelled Mauritius a tax heaven and money laundering platform. In order to counteract this image, an Indian/Mauritius Joint Working Group on the double taxation issue met in order to close loopholes in legislation. A Limitation of Benefits amendment clause was introduced in order to strengthen standards of proof that companies had premises and were effectively managed on Mauritius, and other criteria. In addition, a Comprehensive Economic Partnership Agreement between India and Mauritius was under negotiation.

The **Chagos Archipelago** issue took a new turn as the UN tribunal on international maritime arbitration in The Hague challenged Britain's position on blocking the return of the island's exiled inhabitants. The unexpected ruling in January that the tribunal could hear the case was a challenge to the UK's unilateral declaration in 2009 of a marine protected area around the Chagos Islands. The Mauritius government alleged that the decision to establish a 545,000-square-mile marine reserve was made in defiance of assurances given at the time by the then British Prime Minister, Gordon Brown. Ramgoolam welcomed the fact that the UN tribunal would have the whole case before it when it next met. Never before had the UK had to explain why they had detached the Chagos Islands from Mauritius. Despite the Chagos conflict between Mauritius and the UK, bilateral relations remained stable.

On 28 September, Ramgoolam addressed the 68th UN General Assembly and sketched out Mauritius's international **diplomatic vision**. He said that sustainable development and climate change, a "resilience" concept between natural disasters and risks to societies and states that originated in human behaviour and activities were of global concern. **Interconnectivity** between economies in the globalized world needed a different vision of how they functioned, and Ramgoolam proposed that the global economy, which was "as weak as the weakest link in it", should alter the conventional concept of international divides.

Mauritius was chosen as one of ten countries to draft a road map for **African Development 'post-2015'** during a meeting of the AU on the margins of the UN General Assembly. According to Foreign Minister Arvin Boolell, Mauritius had been selected on the ground of its principles for effective governance: emphasizing sustainable development;

protection of social, economic and elementary human rights; and mobilizing financial resources for development.

Boolell signed an agreement with **China** that invited the Chinese authorities to participate in a public-private venture to create a regional airline for southern Africa. This initiative was originally launched by the Secretary-General of the IOC, Jean Claude de l'Estrac, in line with the idea of making Mauritius a regional hub and gateway for China's economic expansion on mainland Africa. Mauritius and the **Seychelles** signed a document for joint gas and oil exploration on the continental shelf between the two states. In October, President Ali Bongo Ondimba of **Gabon** visited Mauritius. Four agreements on diplomacy, agro-industries, food security and tourism were signed between the Ministers for Foreign Affairs, Arvin Boolell for Mauritius and Emmanuel Issoze NGondet for Gabon.

Socioeconomic Developments

In some respect the economy did better than the world average. In its Chapter IV Consultations report, the **IMF** stated, "The authorities maintained a stable macroeconomic environment in 2013, despite difficult external developments. The fiscal deficit rose in part because of spending in response to the March flash floods and larger than expected capital spending. Inflation fell to low levels."

According to **macroeconomic data**, GDP increased by 3.2%. Private consumption fell by 2.7%, and government expenditure grew by 1.7%. In line with world economic stagnation, gross fixed investment fell by 2.1%. The balance of trade remained stable: exports grew by 2.1% and imports by 0.6%, leaving a balance of trade deficit of 9.3% of GDP, or about 10 bn MUR (Mauritius rupees) (US-$ 1 ≈ 29.1 MUR). Agriculture recorded growth of 4.8% due to a good sugar cane harvest, followed by services (tourism and finance) with growth of 4.2%, and industry with growth of 0.2%. Government receipts were 21.2% of GDP and the public expenditure deficit was limited to 1.9% of GDP. The budget deficit was 3.7%. The public debt: GDP ratio was in the order of 54.8%, a slight fall in comparison with 2012. The unemployment rate hovered at 8.3%. Inflation peaked at 3.6%. At a meeting in October, the board of the Central Bank decided to leave its Libor-interest rate constant at 4.3%, having decreased it by 25 points at a meeting on June 17. This decision was in line with market expectations.

The trade deficit fell by 12% mainly due to a reduction in imports of capital goods and a good **sugar** export performance. Nevertheless, sugar producers feared that the agro-industrial basis of Mauritius sugar production would dwindle as a result of a massive increase in sugar production expected on the African mainland in the years to come: Ethiopia wanted to quadruple its output, Mozambique to double its output, and Sudan to increase production by 50%. With the two large producers India and Brazil maintaining their production levels, more sugar would enter the European market, which was itself shrinking as all major European sugar importers were reducing their intakes.

The IMF concluded that the **structural deficits** of the external current account remained a concern. To raise growth potential required the removal of infrastructural bottlenecks, a strong regulatory framework that encouraged private sector involvement, improved planning and implementation of the public investment programme, reform of the state-owned enterprises sector, a reduction in the cost of doing business, addressing the skills-mismatch and the further strengthening of educational outcomes, "as well as identifying and promoting new high value-added niche markets (such as health treatments, bunkering services etc.), where Mauritius could have competitive advantages".

The **budget** presented in parliament by the Vice-Prime Minister and Minister of Finance Xavier-Luc Duval on 7 November turned out to have a higher deficit than intended, at an effective 3.7% compared with the targeted 2.0%. The reasons given were a monsoon that caused expenditure on flood compensation at the beginning of the year and an increase in public sector of salaries during the year, as negotiated and agreed by the Public Revenue Board. This deficit put in jeopardy the long-term goal of reducing public debt to 50% of GDP by 2018, as stipulated in the Public Debt Management Act of 2008.

In principle, Duval considered his new 2014 budget as balanced, leaving the corporate and income tax on a flat rate basis of 15% and VAT unchanged at 15%. VAT remained the government's main source of income, contributing 86% of total revenues. **Subsidies** targeted productive growth poles, increased redistribution figures and augmented levies on specific items such as tobacco products and alcohol. Retirement and other pensions were increased by 3.3 MUR a month, and the poor were helped by the provision of pre-paid electricity meters and subsidized water tanks; tax allowances for housing schemes; and an increase in the provision of free elementary schooling from six to nine years for every child, thus abolishing the Certificate of Primary Education. Subsidies were also expected to encourage the creation of an ocean and green economy, aviation, bunkering and petroleum hubs for naval transport, and the Africa Expansion strategy (the last through support of 500 m MUR to a Mauritius-Africa-Fund). These activities were expected to create jobs. With these initiatives, Duval tried to counteract a sluggish Business Climate Index, which, at 85 points, had fallen to its lowest level since its introduction.

Despite repeated government declarations that it would diversify Mauritius's external industry and services links, about two-third of investments and exports, as well as earnings from tourists, still depended on the European market. This **EU dependency** made Mauritius vulnerable to the effects of crisis ridden Euro-markets. Nevertheless, tourism remained a pillar of the economy and the number of tourists increased in the first nine months of the year by 2.8%. The most significant growth was noted in FDI, which rose by 16% in the first six months, of which about one quarter originated from Asian sources.

Activity in the **free economic zone Jin-Fei** in the suburban area of Riche Terre, north of the capital Port Louis, which had started some years ago with extensive publicity, was limited. Only a metal working unit (Goldex) was operational, producing metal doors and windows for African mainland markets. In 2013, the Chinese contractor firm Cin-Jin announced the building of two hotels, a showroom complex, administrative buildings and a National Park in the Jin-Fei free economic zone.

Manufacturing employed 67,000 people in 2013, having steadily lost 20,000 posts over the previous decade. During the year, 22 industrial units ceased activity, with the loss of some 1,000 jobs. Structural and short-term changes in the manufacturing sector had knock-on effects, as textile and other industries operated with **migrant workers** (Chinese women, Bangladeshis, and others). In response to the contracting demand for labour, Minister of Labour Shakeel Mohamed ordered **deportations** of Bangladeshi workers to their country of origin. According to the MMM-MSM opposition coalition, the law provided the right to be heard by a judge before such a decision could be taken, but the minister ordered the deportations immediately after the workers' retrenchment from the factory, thereby breaching established norms of international labour law.

On 17 June, the IMF's **Africa Training Institute** became operative with financial help from the Australian Fund for International Development and funds from the Chinese authorities. Another international initiative, the **African Network for Good Governance**, was created by the International Finance Corporation, an affiliate of World Bank, in cooperation with African management and administration training institutes. This network fostered the exchange of know-how, information and training on governance and was related to the NEPAD Development Initiative.

During the celebration of 11 years of domestic independence of the island of **Rodrigues** on 12 October, Deputy Prime Minister Rashid Beebeejaun hailed the efforts that had been made towards the strengthening of resources by provision of wind-generated electricity and the construction of desalination units to treat water, one of the island's scarcest resources. A particular campaign to protect squid regenerated the stock and earned Rodrigues a reputation as an ecological island in favour of bio-diversity and natural resource conservation.

Klaus-Peter Treydte

Mozambique

The implication of having one of the world's largest gas fields was dawning on local elites and everyone wanted a share. After 20 years of peace, Renamo launched new attacks on road traffic and the army. Doctors went on strike. The gas field was not yet producing, but $ 624 m in capital gains taxes transformed relations with donors. Meanwhile, governing party Frelimo's main concerns were the succession and opposition successes in local elections.

Domestic Politics

Opposition party **Renamo** unexpectedly resumed **military action**, ending 20 years of peace. Renamo had signed a peace accord with the government in 1992 after a 15-year war and had stood in 1994 multi-party elections, becoming the main opposition party. But with the tacit acceptance of both the government and the international community, it retained small military bases and an armed militia called a "presidential guard". Renamo had held up approval of electoral legislation, demanding the politicisation of the electoral administration and an effective veto over election decisions. When legislation was passed at the last minute, despite Renamo objections, Renamo's leader, Alfonso Dhlakama, announced a boycott of elections, including not taking up Renamo posts on election commissions.

Renamo Secretary-General Manuel Bissopo said on 29 March that Renamo was prepared to go to war to prevent registration and elections. In the early morning of 3 April, the riot police (Força de Intervenção Rápida) raided Renamo party headquarters in Muxungué, Sofala province, and Gondola, Manica province. There were hundreds of men in each place, including some former guerrillas from the 1977–92 war. Renamo said that the gatherings were legal political meetings, just two of many being held by the party to mobilise against elections. The government called them military training camps. Two days later, Renamo guerrillas attacked a police post in Muxungué, killing four policemen, and the next days attacked traffic on the main north-south N1 road, killing three people.

Talks between the government and Renamo resumed on 2 May. The government delegation was headed by Agriculture Minister José Pacheco, a member of the Frelimo Political Commission. Renamo put four issues on the agenda: revision of the electoral law to give Renamo "parity"; reversal of the marginalisation of Renamo in the military; equitable distribution of wealth and greater participation by Renamo members in the economy; and reversal of the partyisation of the civil service. The second and third issues had long histories. When the peace accord was signed in 1992, Mozambique was a poor country with no mineral wealth; now with huge gas and coal reserves, there was much more money in circulation, and some elite Frelimo members had become relatively (and ostentatiously) wealthy. Frelimo membership seemed important for contracts, loans, promotions, etc., while known opposition members seemed to be excluded. Thus a key demand was for money, and for a higher status for Dhlakama and the Renamo military leadership. Speaking at a press conference on 10 April in Satunjira, Dhlakama said he had authorised the April attacks only because formers guerrillas said they would kill him if he did not. Local media unofficially confirmed this. Renamo generals felt they had not gained from 20 years of peace and wanted status and money.

Violence resumed on 24 May near Satunjira, when there was a shoot-out between the military and the Renamo presidential guard. On 17 June, Renamo attacked a military post and arms depot at Savana, along the main railway from the Tete coalmines to Beira port. Five government soldiers were killed and arms taken. On 19 June, Renamo announced it would cut road traffic on the main north-south N1 road, on the 100 km between Muxungué and the River Save. This was symbolically important because Renamo guerrillas had killed many people in that section of the road during the 1977–92 war. On 21 June, Renamo attacked road traffic, killing two people. The government reintroduced military convoys along that section of road, and there was a series of further ambushes over the rest of the month, as well as military confrontations near Gorongosa.

The number of incidents decreased and Renamo held a meeting with 300 party militants on 29–31 July in Satunjira. On the first day, Dhlakama made a very strong statement threatening to divide the country in half during the next week. After being contacted by ambassadors from the US and EU, he backed down. Renamo briefed the press that the ambassadors had promised that Frelimo would make concessions, but other sources denied this, and no concessions were offered at the next round of talks. **Fighting resumed** when Renamo attacked a police post in Muanza on 12 October, and there were gunfights between the two sides near Satunjira. On 21 October, the army occupied the Satunjira base. Dhlakama and Bissopo escaped, but Armindo Milaco, an MP and Renamo head of mobilisation, was killed. Dhlakama's whereabouts were not disclosed, but he apparently retreated to another former base in the dense forest further up the mountain. The army moved on to occupy the Renamo base at nearby Maringué, which had remained a Renamo military base since the end of the war in 1992 with the tacit acceptance of the government and local police.

Renamo stopped attending talks with the government and launched **more attacks** on the N1 south of Muxungué and around Gorongosa, and opened new fronts. Former guerrillas occupied a former base in northern Nampula province, and several times attacked the main road near Rapale, killing at least two people. Near the end of the year, guerrilla groups moved into Tete province near the border with Malawi, and into Homoine, Inhambane, which was the site of the worst Renamo massacre during the war. During the year, at least 60 people were killed and more than 300 injured in Renamo attacks and fighting between Renamo and the government.

The UN Special Rapporteur on extreme poverty and human rights, Magdalena Sepulveda, told a Maputo press conference on 16 April that during her visit she had witnessed very high standards of comfort in some areas of Maputo city, which contrasted dramatically with the harsh reality in larger areas of the capital. "If not addressed urgently, such marked **disparities and high levels of social exclusion** may pose a threat to social stability, as foreshadowed by protests in Maputo in recent years", she warned. In partial response, the government pushed the exchange rate with the South African rand below MZN (meticais) 3 to the rand in June, and kept it there for the rest of the year. Riots in the capital Maputo and the adjoining city of Matola in 2008 and 2010 had been partly over the cost of living, and most food and consumer goods in Maputo and Matola were imported from South Africa, so keeping the exchange rate overvalued kept the cost of living down in the capital. But it also meant that local producers could not compete with imported chickens, pigs, tomatoes and other fruit and vegetables. With the metical this low, South Africa goods were cheaper than local products even in places like Chimoio, more than 1,000 km from South Africa.

Demands to spread the wealth became more frequent. The Forum of Demobilised Soldiers had several confrontations with riot police as it attempted to demonstrate in front of the prime minister's office to push its claim for a much higher pension for all demobilised troops. Doctors went on strike in May, complaining that they were paid less than university professors and judges. The strike was mostly supported in Maputo and Nampula, and was abandoned by the doctors in June without gaining any concessions. Participants were penalised and leaders forced to retire. In November, hundreds of former secret police agents, as well as widows and children, demonstrated on 7 November in front of the office of President Armando Guebuza over what they said was the failure to pay their pensions.

There were also increasing reports of teachers and others being forced to donate to Frelimo, and of teachers linked to opposition parties being transferred to remote schools. The **Afrobarometer survey** carried out in late 2012 was published in late 2013. People in 34 African countries had been asked how free they were to say what they thought. A surprisingly high 33% in Mozambique said they were not free, compared with only 7% in Tanzania, 13% in Malawi, and 16% in South Africa – and 53% in Zimbabwe and 57% in Swaziland. Mozambicans were optimistic about the future but rated the government badly on job creation: 47% of Mozambicans felt the government was managing the economy well, but 60% said it was doing badly at improving the standard of living, 65% said it was doing badly at job creation and 63% said it was failing to narrow the gap between rich and poor. And 25% said their living conditions were good, 43% neither good nor bad, and 32% bad – but 68% expected them to improve in the next year.

In mid-2013, Guebuza moved to take tighter control of his party. Leaders of the youth organisation ('Organizacao da Juventude Mocambicana') and women's organisation ('Organizacao das Mulheres Mocambicanas') were replaced by **Guebuza loyalists**. Edson Macuacua, who had been marginalised as Frelimo party press spokesperson after the Frelimo Congress in 2012 when he was sharply criticised for his heavy-handed treatment of the media, was unexpectedly named Guebuza's press spokesman and began a campaign to improve the president's image. Rogério Sitoe, the respected editor of the state-owned daily 'Notícias', was dismissed in August. His replacement was an explicitly political appointment, Jaime Langa, who had no journalistic experience but was a Frelimo *vereador* (local minister) in Matola. Subsequently, the newspaper ran more articles praising Guebuza's achievements, and the main picture on the front page was usually of Guebuza. In September, Jeremias Langa was dismissed as editorial director of 'O Pais', the main independent daily newspaper, and director of information of STV, the main independent television station; both had come under pressure for being too critical of Frelimo.

Frelimo maintained its dominance in the 20 November **municipal elections**, winning the post of mayor and a majority in the municipal assembly in 49 of 53 municipalities. But the opposition Mozambique Democratic Movement (MDM) made its mark, winning three important cities – Nampula, Quelimane and Beira – and 30% of assembly seats nationally. In Maputo and Matola, the MDM won 40% and 42% of the vote, respectively, compared with Renamo's 14% and 9% in the previous local elections in 2008. Renamo boycotted the election but, despite threats, did not try to disrupt registration or the election. The results confirmed the MDM as the main opposition party. Turnout was 46%, the same as in 2008, but above the 28% of 2003. Registration from 25 May to 23 June hit 85% of the estimated number of voting age adults (who would be 18 years old on 20 November) in the 53 municipalities, which have about one quarter of the Mozambican population.

(Mozambique remains predominantly rural, and government structures in rural areas are appointed by central government.) The Constitutional Council threw out the results in one city, Gurué, because of corruption within the electoral administration, and forced a rerun, scheduled for 8 February 2014.

A short list of three **presidential candidates** for the national election due on 15 October 2014 was announced by the Frelimo Political Commission on 11 December. The final choice was to be made by a meeting of the party's Central Committee in 2014. The three candidates, all technicians from the centre and north and aged between 55 and 58, were: Agriculture Minister José Pacheco, a member of the Frelimo Political Commission and secretary of its Verification Committee; Prime Minister Alberto Vaquina, also a member of the Political Commission; and Defence Minister Filipe Nyusi, the only candidate to have a liberation war link, having attended the Frelimo school in Tunduru (Tanzania), before independence.

Foreign Affairs

A totally unexpected government-guaranteed $ 850 m European **bond issue** on 5 September raised funds for six coastal patrol boats and 24 tuna fishing boats for a new Mozambican government fishing company, Ematum (National Tuna Company), part-owned by the security services. Within Mozambique, there had been no internal discussion, no parliamentary approval, and even many ministers did not know about the bond issue or the new company. The bond was oversubscribed and increased, because it was government backed and at above-average interest rates. An IMF mission at the end of October was very angry with the bond issue and the final IMF statement was quite strong, saying the bond issue should "be included in the 2014 budget and transparently reflected in the fiscal accounts". Budget support donors were appalled, and several delayed disbursements. The government eventually agreed to include $ 350 m of the bond revenue, the amount allocated for military equipment, in the state budget.

The bond issue reflected a rapid change in **donor-government relations**. For more than two decades, Mozambique had been heavily donor dependent, which gave donors much more power than they had in many other African countries. Indeed, by 2009 the G-19 group of 19 budget support donors had become the main forum for dialogue on government policy. But at the same time, the very large investments in coal and gas were coming on stream, along with the realisation that within five years donor funds would be less important. The government began to resist what it saw as donor arrogance. A group of budget support donors had withheld aid for three months at the start of 2010 to put pressure on what they saw as 'governance' improvement. The government had resisted, and donors relented. Since then donors had reduced budget support and moved aid to support projects and individual ministries, where they felt they could wield more power. Foreign aid paid 51% of the state budget in 2010 but only 34% in 2013. On the other hand, donor support for civil society had increased, as had open support, especially from the USA, for openly anti-Frelimo groups. Donors again withheld budget support over Ematum, but the government made few concessions. This marked the **end of donor power**. The US Millennium Challenge Corporation (MCC) refused to grant a second aid package to Mozambique, surprising government ministers, who said they had expected a renewal. The MCC gave no reasons, but three factors seemed important: the Ematum bond further soured relations with the US, several MCC projects had not been completed on time, and Mozambique was refusing to agree to land privatisation, which had been a condition of the first compact. On 24 July, President Guebuza visited the Scottish oil city of Aberdeen, where he was trying to develop alternative **British support** for the oil and gas sector.

Guebuza completed his term as chair of **SADC** on 18 August and former finance minister Tomas Salomão stepped down as SADC executive secretary after two four-year terms. Mozambique turned down an opportunity to take the **AU** vice presidency from southern Africa for 2014 and thus become chair in 2015, giving the post to Zimbabwe which was next in line, so Robert Mugabe would be AU chair in 2015. The AU chair takes office in January, which is when the new Mozambican president, to be elected in October 2014, would be sworn in, and it seemed inappropriate for a new president to immediately become AU chair.

Relations with neighbouring **Malawi** had improved greatly since Joyce Banda became Malawi's president. In April, Guebuza visited Malawi and signed an agreement for a power interconnection to allow the sale of electricity to Malawi; the agreement had been blocked by the previous president, Bingu wa Mutharika.

Socioeconomic Developments

2013 saw the worst **floods** since 2000. In January, the Limpopo River flooded. The town of Chokwé was completely under water and the government provided humanitarian assistance to 172,000 people in 62 accommodation centres. There was also major damage to irrigation systems along the river. In September, the government admitted that of 285,000 people forced to move after the 2007 floods, the government had so far resettled only 163,000.

Minimum wages, negotiated annually, were announced in April, and remained unchanged at $ 83 per month in agriculture, $ 131 in manufacturing, and $ 90 in public administration. There had been large increases in 2011 and 2012.

In July and August, panic hit the suburbs of Matola and Maputo with people believing that there was a **crime** wave being committed by an organised group called G-20 (group of 20), which attacked with gratuitous violence, including using a hot clothes iron to burn people's arms. A photograph of a woman burned with an iron was circulated on mobile phones. Many people were afraid to sleep in their houses at night and many neighbourhoods set up community patrols and vigilante groups, who caught some thieves. The suburbs had high crime rates and were vulnerable because there were few lights and no police, and houses could be easily broken into. In fact, G-20 did not exist, no one ever complained to the police of being attacked with a hot iron, and the infamous photograph, taken from the Internet, was actually of a Brazilian woman who had been attacked by her ex-husband. The fact that the rumour was believed, and the resulting panic, indicated the widespread lack of confidence in the ability of the government and the police to protect people.

The wave of **kidnappings** for ransom continued, with 44 cases in 2013 – 31 in Maputo, nine in Matola, three in Beira and one in Nampula; there were 20 prosecutions of alleged kidnappers, leading to some convictions. Three policemen (including a member of the elite presidential guard) and three others were each sentenced to 16 years in jail for kidnapping six people in 2011 and 2012. It was revealed in court that ransoms of $ 165,000, $ 160,000, and $ 130,000 had been paid for three kidnap victims. The Confederation of Mozambican Business Associations referred in a statement on 7 November to "the climate of **tension and insecurity** generated by two phenomena that are happening at the same time – the attacks on civilian vehicles in the central zone, and the kidnappings in the major urban areas". Some Mozambicans of Asian origin and some Portuguese business people temporarily left the country, or at least sent their families away. At the peak of the crisis, in late October and early November, regular Council of Ministers meetings were cancelled.

ProSavana, one of Mozambique's largest development projects, became a hot potato. This joint Japanese-Brazilian programme in Nampula province, upper Zambézia, and western Niassa, initially based on a Japanese-funded programme in the Brazilian *cerrado* (savanna) in the 1970s, was opening up the area for very large corporate soya farms. ProSavana was very donor-driven and was specifically aimed at encouraging Brazilian companies to open giant farms in this area. However, objections from both local communities and the Mozambican Ministry of Agriculture led to major changes, including paying more attention to support for local farmers. On 8 August, Agriculture Minister José Pacheco attended a meeting between civil society representatives and stakeholders of Japan, Brazil and Mozambique, organised through two Mozambican peasant organisations. It revealed major divisions. On the one hand, the ProSavana office produced a draft plan saying that one of the highest priorities was to promote large-scale investment. On the other, National Director of Economy in the Ministry of Agriculture Raimundo Matule told the meeting that, while the target of the Brazilian *cerrado* programme was to promote big industrial agriculture, the target in Mozambique was to support tiny, small and medium farms.

Mozambique has exploitable **gas reserves** of more than 170 trillion ft^3 and more than $ 25 bn was being invested to construct liquefied natural gas production facilities, which could be second largest after Qatar. Exports would not begin until 2019 but large amounts of revenue were already coming in from capital gains tax on the sales of parts of the reserves by the original exploration companies, Anadarko of the US and ENI of Italy. Interest was largely from Asia, which wanted assured gas supplies, and parts continued to be sold to Chinese, Thai, Korean and Indian companies. The IMF estimated that capital gains tax payments amounted to $ 624 m, 4% of GDP. Production of small amounts of

crude oil began in an area linked to gas fields in Inhambane province; there was no evidence of oil anywhere else in Mozambique.

Mozambique has the fifth largest **coking coal reserves** in the world, and exports had begun. Two problems for the coal mining companies had been transport of the coal to seaports and the poor quality coal lying on top of the coking coal, which must be removed, but is not worth exporting. Up to an estimated 100 m tonnes of coal per year could be exported, but the only **railway** connection, the 578-km Sena line to Beira port, could only carry 6.5 m tonnes. This railway was being expanded and would carry 15 m tonnes a year from 2015. The Brazilian mining giant Vale was upgrading and constructing a 912-km railway line to Nacala port, the longest of the railway lines, including upgrading existing lines and adding 136 km of new railway in Malawi, It would open in late 2014 and would be able to carry 18 m tonnes a year by 2017. A third and totally new railway would follow the shortest route, 525 km, and take coal to a new offshore port at Macuze, just north of Quelimane. It had been the subject of controversy, because the Council of Ministers said the contract would go to the Frelimo-owned company SPI. Transport Minister Paulo Zucula went against this and put the contract out to tender, but this was cancelled by Prime Minister Alberto Vaquina. The prime minister of Thailand visited Mozambique in July and it was announced that the contract would be given, without tender, to Thai Moçambique Logistica, 60% owned by the Italian-Thai Development Company, 20% by the Mozambican state railway company CFM, and 20% by a new Zambezia Integrated Development Corridor company. Zucula was dismissed, and the contract was signed on 13 December. Construction would not start until 2016 and would take five years.

All of the Tete coalmines depend for their profitability on using the poorest quality thermal coal on site in coal-fired **power stations**. South Africa's Eskom had been the obvious customer for the electricity generated because it had been short of power in recent years, but had declined to buy any more electricity from Mozambique and was instead building two giant coal-fired power stations of its own, which when complete in 2018 would give South Africa surplus capacity. However, on 14 October Ncondezi Energy signed a 25-year 'non-binding' agreement with the state-owned Electricidade de Mozambique (EdM) to buy all the electricity from a 300 MW integrated thermal coal mine and power plant. Power generation should begin in 2017. It was announced in August that a 150 MW gas-fired power station, the largest thermal power station so far built in the country, would be installed at Ressano Garcia, on the border between Mozambique and South Africa, in a partnership between EdM (51%) and the South African Sasol New Energy (49%) It was estimated to cost $ 250 m and should come on stream in 2014. The gas would come from the Inhambane gas fields.

A Mozambican **anti-corruption** NGO, the Centre for Public Integrity (CIP), reported in November that, although Mozambique had been exporting natural gas by pipeline to South Africa since 2004, the revenue earned by the Mozambican state from this activity was insignificant. CIP calculated that gas worth more than $ 700 m crossed the border annually, but the Mozambican government's take was less than $ 10 m a year. Similarly, according to a study by CIP and the European Network on Debt and Development, published in December, Mozambique was deriving very little benefit from the mining of titanium-bearing heavy mineral sand deposits in the northern province of Nampula, thanks to the excessively favourable terms granted to the operator, the Irish company, Kenmare Resources. Kenmare's deal with the government included "contract secrecy, no corporate taxes for one part of the company group, and a halving of corporate taxes for ten years for the other part, no payment of value added tax for several goods, and no import or export taxes". Kenmare's only asset was the mine in Moma, which operated through a chain of eight companies, mostly registered in Mauritius and the British tax haven of Jersey. On 29 August, the director of the Central Office for the Fight against Corruption, Ana Maria Gemo, announced that it was investigating possible criminal practices at the Administrative Tribunal, the country's highest audit body. An audit showed $ 6 m in possible irregularities, including improper payments to suppliers and the hiring of Tribunal staff themselves as consultants. She also said that 599 cases against members of the public administration were processed by her office between January and June.

Macroeconomic data were generally favourable. Inflation was only 4.3%, compared with the 7.5% predicted. From January 2011, the Bank of Mozambique had cut the base rate – the rate at which the Bank lends to commercial banks, the 'Facilidade Permanente de Cedência' – 12 times, from 16.5% to 8.3% at the end of 2013. But the average rate for commercial bank loans remained a very high 20.3%. Mozambique's foreign debt reached $ 5.8 bn at the end of the year, which was 30% of GDP, according to Finance Minister Manuel Chang, and thus considered as sustainable. Most debt was long-term (20–50 years) with low interest rates. GDP growth was 7%. Agricultural production in the 2102/13 season was 2.2 m tonnes of cereals and 800,000 tonnes of tubers (cassava, sweet potato and potato).

The number of pupils per teacher in Mozambican **primary schools** had fallen considerably over the past four years – but classes remained overcrowded. Education Minister Augusto Jone said on 21 August that in in 2013 the ratio had fallen to 65 pupils to one teacher, from 76 to one in 2009.

LAM Mozambique Airlines Flight 470 crashed on 29 November into the Bwabwata National Park in Namibia en route from Maputo to Luanda (Angola), killing all 33 people on board. The **plane crash** was the airline's first fatal incident since 1970. Since 2011, all airlines certified in Mozambique had been banned from flying to Europe, and EU officials from flying in Mozambican planes, because of deficiencies, not in the airlines themselves, but in the regulatory agency, the Mozambican Civil Aviation Institute. **Wild animals** killed 59 people in the first five months of 2013; crocodiles continued to be the most deadly animals, killing 47. In addition, snakes killed six people, elephants three, and hippopotami three.

Joseph Hanlon

Namibia

2013 was a transitional year between the appointment of the future political leadership of the governing South West African People's Organisation (SWAPO) at the end of 2012 and the parliamentary and presidential elections at the end of 2014. The general macroeconomic performance remained stable while aggrandizement of the new elite and the lack of public services and delivery for many continued. A serious drought added to the misery.

Domestic Politics

During the year, the top brass of SWAPO, newly elected to take over political leadership in government after the parliamentary and presidential elections due to take place towards the end of 2014, became further strengthened. **Team Hage** (named after Prime Minister Hage Geingob, who was the party's presidential candidate) was able to expand its control over strategic positions in the party governance structure. President Pohamba also appointed several supporters of Geingob to higher-ranking positions in the public administration. The list of ten deputies appointed to the party secretariat at the end of May included only supporters of Team Hage. The party's founding president, Sam Nujoma, addressing a party rally in the first weekend of June, endorsed for the first time the result of the election held at the party congress in November 2012 and thereby signalled acceptance of Team Hage. The fact that this was considered an important message underlined the elder statesman's continuing relevance for daily politics.

This ended speculation concerning 'the old man's' preferences and corrected the impression created by the **Swapo Youth League**, who supported another candidate. In a statement on 29 May, the Youth League suggested that Nujoma agreed with them, and made a scathing attack on Geingob. The Youth League leaders were taken to task for this attack at the party's central committee meeting on 14 June. Several high-ranking party officials called for the leadership to be axed for misbehaviour at the forthcoming extra-ordinary congress, but Pohamba intervened by asking for an apology instead of taking disciplinary action. The apology was officially tendered and confirmed the political defeat of the Youth League, which had for some time been trying to gain more influence in the party.

Delegates at the extra-ordinary congress held on 22–24 June in Swakopmund amended the party constitution by stipulating, among other things, 50/50 representation of men and women in all party organs and structures. This **gender parity** was enthusiastically welcomed by female delegates but met with concern among men, and debates began as to how sure the predominantly male leadership would be of retaining their positions in office after the next elections.

On 18 January, Pohamba appointed the fourth **Delimitation Commission**, tasked with (re-)determining regional and constituency boundaries. Based on its recommendations, Pohamba announced on 8 August the creation of 14 new constituencies in nine regions. The Kavango region was split into Kavango East and Kavango West, increasing the number of regions to 14. The Karas Region was spelt in the vernacular as !Karas (later adjusted to //Karas), and the Caprivi Region was renamed Zambezi, giving rise to protests from some local inhabitants who considered the name change as a denial of their regional identity. Part of the region's population had previously sought greater autonomy from the rest of the Namibian state and territory, which had culminated in a failed violent secessionist uprising in August 1999, and the subsequent treason trial was still ongoing during 2013. Objections were also raised by some of the residents in Lüderitzbucht to the announced change in the name of both the constituency and the town to Naminüs. The change in the name of the town remained pending after it was established that this decision did not lie within the discretion of the president but rested with the town council as the local authority. On 3 September, a coalition of civil society agencies called for the release of the Delimitation Commission's report, which was not made public.

An **electoral law reform** process was initiated, with a Law Reform and Development Commission tasked to review electoral procedures. In early November, the commission reported back to the prime minister and the Electoral Commission of Namibia. The briefing was also attended by invited civil society organisations. The commission announced the tabling of four bills in parliament. Given the long-lasting legal contestations after the last parliamentary elections, preparations for the next elections were closely followed and remained a contentious issue.

In a speech on 27 November, Sam Nujoma gave a first taste of things to come in the forthcoming **election year**. He blamed civil servants for non-delivery, calling this an act of sabotage of government programmes and dubbing them "elements of Koevoet", a special army unit established by the South Africans to fight SWAPO but dissolved at Independence. At the party's politburo meeting in early December, Nujoma (using his entitlement to attend all party meetings as an honorary member), reportedly called for a national referendum to address the **land issue** but was informed that this would be unconstitutional.

The removal of the colonial **equestrian monument** in a surprise action on 25 December led to speculation that this was a prelude to government initiatives to establish its strength and appeal to anti-colonial sentiments. The statue was a prominent marker in Windhoek's memory landscape and a popular tourist attraction. Parts of the local German speaking community reacted with shock and dismay to its removal, which came as a surprise despite earlier discussions over the future of the highly symbolic monument, and led to widespread discussion and controversy.

The government continued to adopt a lenient stance on abuses of office by high-ranking civil servants and politicians involved in private businesses, which were tantamount to **embezzlement and corruption**. Large-scale transactions in the property market, mainly in Windhoek, as well as dubious practices in the awarding of tenders for public works, were indicative of a network of business interests benefitting from privileged information and preferential treatment. On 10 December, the Institute of Public Policy Research released a critical report on the lack of relevant anti-corruption legislation in non-compliance with the United Nations Convention Against Corruption, which had been signed by Namibia in 2003. TI's Corruption Perception Index released at the end of November ranked Namibia 57th (up one place from 58th in 2012) out of 177 countries. On 12 November, the auditor general disclosed that 11 ministries had failed during the past financial year to account for a total of N$ 15 m spent on travel and subsistence allowances.

The Reporters Without Borders Index on the state of **media freedom** released in November ranked Namibia 19th out of 179 countries, two places higher than in the 2011–12 index, and ahead of several Western democracies (Belgium, Canada and the USA). On 2 May, the UN Special Rapporteur on the Rights of the Indigenous People, James Anaya, published his report based on a fact-finding mission during September the year before. He maintained that, despite significant achievements in overcoming the destructive legacies of colonialism and apartheid, **indigenous groups**, particularly the San and the Himba, remained marginalised.

Foreign Affairs

Namibia's foreign policy had a relatively low profile during the year. It maintained an emphasis on good relations in the sub-region and the continent. On 6–7 November, President Jacob Zuma of **South Africa** made an official state visit, when he and President

Pohamba stressed the need for even closer cooperation and underlined the importance of the bi-lateral commission established the year before. Sub-divided into four sectoral committees, the commission had as one of its key functions the practical implementation of the 52 agreements and memoranda of understanding already entered into. A state visit by President Goodluck Jonathan of **Nigeria** announced for 9–10 May was cancelled one day ahead of his expected arrival; no official reason was given, but the cancellation was probably related to reported internal unrest in Nigeria.

Iran reactivated and intensified earlier relations with Namibia by re-opening an embassy after 15 years. Iranian Foreign Minister Ali Akbar Salehi visited Windhoek on 8–9 July for the opening ceremony and stressed Iran's interest in closer collaboration with Namibia as the continent's fourth largest exporter of non-fuel minerals. Namibia's Navy Commander Admiral Peter Villo headed a delegation of the Namibian Defence Force visiting Tehran on 10 October. He announced that the two countries planned to cooperate more closely on naval training and experience in manufacturing maritime facilities, given the common maritime threats.

Pohamba was appointed chairperson of the **SADC Organ for Security** at the SADC Summit on 18 August. On 10 September, the first Troika meeting to be held in Windhoek discussed the security situation in eastern DRC, and the political situation in Madagascar and Zimbabwe.

Speaking at the 68th UN General Assembly on 26 September, Pohamba focused on the MDGs. He used the opportunity to reiterate that the elections in **Zimbabwe** had been free, fair and credible and urged that Western countries should lift sanctions. Pohamba and Zuma had congratulated ZANU-PF and Robert Mugabe on their re-election at a time when no reports from election observers had yet been released.

Pohamba made a state visit to **Finland** on 13–14 November. Finland remained a donor country. During the year, its embassy in Windhoek was upgraded by the appointment of a new ambassador, the only one from a Nordic country. Pohamba then attended the **Commonwealth Heads of State summit** in Malaysia and made the first state visit to **Vietnam** by a Namibian president.

EU Commissioner for Trade Karel de Gucht visited on 16 June for further exchanges over the **EPA** with the prime minister and the minister for trade and industry. Despite increased pressure on Namibia to sign the Interim EPA, the government remained steadfast and refused to give in, since, in its view, the agreement would damage the country's economic interests by, among other things, preventing the implementation of an infant industry protection policy as a step towards industrialisation.

The 11th Conference of the Parties (COP11) to the **UN Convention to Combat Desertification** (UNCCD), which was attended by over 3,000 international delegates, took place over two weeks in Windhoek and ended on 28 September. Minister of Environment and Tourism Uahekua Herunga, who was the COP11 president, said the conference had strengthened the UNCCD as an agent of sustainable development. He presented the

"Namib Declaration on a stronger United Nations Convention to Combat Desertification for a land degradation neutral world", which called on stakeholders to commit themselves to enhanced sustainable land management and improved livelihoods at all levels.

Socio-Economic Developments

The latest **demographic statistics**, compiled during August 2011 by the Population and Housing Census, were released at the end of March. The total population was given as 2,113,077, showing an annual growth rate of 1.4% since 2001. Almost 52% were female, 56.5% were aged between 15 and 59 years, 23% between five and 14 years, 13% were younger than five years and 7% were 60 or older. 57% lived in rural areas (down from 67% in 2001); urbanisation had increased by 15% since 1991. More than half of the population lived either in traditional dwellings (38%) or in shacks (16%). The main language for almost half the population (49%) was Oshiwambo, followed by Nama/Damara (11.3%) and Afrikaans (10.4%), with only 3.4% of households having the official language English as a main language. The **labour force** was given as 847,415, with 312,503 (36.9%) unemployed. The Namibia Labour Force Survey 2012 was released in April and gave the number of unemployed as 238,174 or 27.4% out of an active work force of 868,268. Those registered as jobless were 56% of youths aged between 15 and 19, 49% of those in the age group 20–24, and only 13% of 50–54-year-olds. Most importantly, the figures confirmed the growing relevance of the younger segment in the population, which emerged as an increasingly strategic policy factor to reckon with since Independence.

On 5 March, Finance Minister Saara Kuugongelwa-Amadhila presented the **annual budget** for the 2013–14 financial year. Overall expenditure was expected to rise by 19% to N$ 47.6 bn (from N$ 39.9 bn in 2012), with a growth in current expenditure of 23% and capital expenditure estimated to increase by only 11%. This was a proportional decline from 6.3% to 6.1% of the total budget, representing a reduction of investment in and maintenance of infrastructure. The highest budget allocations were, as in previous years, to education (N$ 10.8 bn), followed by health and social services (N$ 5.3 bn), but defence (N$ 3.96 bn) and safety and security (N$ 3.8 bn) added up jointly to the second highest allocation. A major cost factor remained the bloated civil service, with an increase in personnel costs of over 230% since 2003–4 to N$ 17.5 bn, more than 40% of the total budget. Statutory expenditure, i.e. interest payments on public debts and loan guarantees for mainly state-owned enterprises rose to 4.7% of total expenditure. Revenue income was expected to increase by 8.2% to N$ 40.1 bn, leaving an anticipated deficit of N$ 7.5 bn or 6.4% of GDP. Additional borrowing increased debts to N$ 32.4 bn or 27.8% of GDP. The main source of anticipated income was once again from the SACU revenue pool and was expected to be N$ 14.7 bn or 37% of total revenue for the financial year, while taxes on income and profits of individuals and companies was estimated at 35% and value added tax at 21%. The tax threshold for individual income was raised from N$ 40,000 to

N$ 50,000 a year with an entry level set at 18% (down from 27%). All tax brackets were lowered except for the highest income segment, which remained at 37% on income above N$ 1.5 m a year. Corporation tax was reduced from 34% to 33%.

It was estimated that the combined tax relief increased **domestic spending** power by N$ 1.2 bn. According to the Namibian Consumer Price Index released on 12 November by the Namibian Statistics Agency, consumption patterns had changed considerably between 1993–94 and 2009–10: expenditure on alcoholic beverages had almost quadrupled, while spending on education and food had fallen substantially. Expenditure on communications (in particular mobile phones and internet) had increased dramatically, and spending on public utilities (water, electricity) as well as gas and fuel also absorbed a higher proportion of expenditure.

The annual **inflation** rate for 2012 was at 6.5%, according to a Bank of Namibia announcement in February. A prognosis released in August estimated that the rate for 2013 would be slightly above 6%. The economic growth rate for 2012 was 5%, with a forecast by the Bank of Namibia of 4.7% for 2013, while the IMF expected 4.2%. The GDP for 2012 was over US$ 12 bn. Given that the local Namibian Dollar (N$) was an internationally non-convertible currency and pegged to the South African Rand, the deteriorating **currency exchange rate** had massively contributed to rises in import prices. As from mid-year, the purchase price of the Euro had increased from 13 to 15 Rand and of the US$ from 9 to 11 Rand. While this suited export-oriented production, it had a negative effect on the rate of inflation by causing price increases, mainly for luxury consumer goods.

Mining activities benefitted from attractive world market prices for base metals and other minerals. North River Resources announced plans to re-open the lead and zinc mine near several uranium sites that had been closed in 1992, as the prices justified new production. Dundee Precious Metals confirmed that the sulphuric acid plant being built in Tsumeb with an investment of some N$ 3 bn was on track. Among the biggest capital projects in Namibian history, the new plant was expected to be operational towards the end of 2014. It was intended that the sulphuric acid generated would solve an environmental problem caused by the release of sulphur dioxide during the blister copper manufacturing process at the Tsumeb smelter; 90% of the expected production would be sold to Rössing Uranium. The multinational Anglo American announced for de Beers, the holding company for Namdeb, a 6% increase in its annual **diamond** production from 1,667,000 carats in 2012 to 1,762,000 carats in 2013.

Uranium production continued to be among the important income and employment generating activities, despite lower world market prices in the aftermath of Fukushima, in view of which initiatives towards improved institutionalisation and regulation took place. During March, a draft Nuclear Cycle Policy was finalised in cooperation with the Finnish Radiation and Nuclear Safety Authority, which was designed as a guiding document for exploration, mining, enrichment and nuclear power. It was expected to be finalised in 2014. The Namibian Uranium Association was established on 18 November as a kind of watchdog representing Namibian interests in the industry. It brought together stakeholders, experiencing common woes as a result of the low world market prices for uranium oxide, which rendered several big operations unprofitable. It emerged that, Rössing and Langer Heinrich, two of the biggest operations, had reduced production. The French Areva, which was developing its Trekkopje mine, and other investors had put large investments on hold. In contrast, construction at the Husab mine being developed by Swakop Uranium with Chinese investment to become the world's second largest mine, with full production after completion estimated at 6,800 tonnes a year, continued according to plan, but with complaints about the shortage of qualified workers and no secure long-term solution for water and energy supplies. Between 2007 and 2012 more than 30 companies from Australia, Canada, China and Russia had been engaged in uranium exploration activities, despite a moratorium on new prospecting licences. During the same period, annual uranium production had increased by almost 50% to about 4,500 tonnes a year. Other future mining sites included Valencia (developed by the Canadian Forsys Metals) and Etango (by the Australian Bannerman Resources). The OECD estimated future uranium production from new mining activities at 11,000 to 13,000 tonnes per annum, which would equal one-fifth to one-quarter of the current global supply from mining.

Namibia slipped 11 places in the **Ease of Doing Business** ranking from 87th to 98th out of 189 countries. Similarly, Namibia's ranking in the **Economic Freedom Report** 2013, based on 2011 data and compiled by the Fraser 80 Institute, deteriorated from 88th to 97th out of 152 countries. The ranking is based on five components. Namibia did well in two of them, namely Legal System and Property Rights (ranked 27th) and Regulation (50th), while falling behind in Size of Government (99th), Sound Money (referring to money supply and inflation, ranked 113th) and Freedom to Trade Internationally (117th). In the **Global Competitiveness Report** issued in September by the World Economic Forum for 2013–14, Namibia was among the top five performers in Africa and improved its ranking by two places to 90th of 148 countries.

Data presented in the UNDP's **Human Development Report** in 2013 disclosed socio-economic disparities. An annual average Gross National Income per capita of almost US$ 6,000 classified Namibia as a higher middle-income country. It ranked 101st out of 186 countries. The HDI, however, was at 0.608, which placed Namibia at 128th, i.e. 27 places lower. The discrepancy increased further with the Gini-coefficient. On a scale between 0 (absolute distributive equality among all persons) and 1 (where everything is allocated to one person only), Namibia, with .639, had the highest Gini-coefficient of all countries measured. The Inequality-adjusted HDI, which combined social inequality with the HDI ranking, was another 16 places lower, the third highest downward adjustment of all countries.

According to UNICEF figures released on World Toilet Day (19 November), 52% of the country's population had no access to proper **sanitation facilities**. This placed Namibia among the countries with the highest proportion of people in the world who had to defecate in the open, considered as one of the main causes of diarrhoea, which was the third most common cause of hospital attendance and the second highest cause of pediatric admissions in the country. A report issued on 18 November by the African Child Policy Forum, based on indicators from all available child-related indexes, ranked Namibia as 26th out of 52 African countries in terms of child-friendliness, defined as making the maximum effort to meet its obligations to respect, protect and fulfil the rights and **wellbeing of children**. This was a downgrade by 24 places compared with the 2008 index, the biggest decline among all countries on the continent. The main reasons given for the dramatic deterioration were reductions in government spending on sectors benefitting children, a fall in levels of performance concerning translation of resources into child wellbeing, and a poor record for access to international legal instruments and the domestication of child rights.

More positive were efforts to combat **HIV/AIDS**. Figures announced during World AIDS Day at the beginning of December showed that the HIV infection rate had fallen between 2001 and 2011 by 68% and AIDS-related deaths by 44%; 83% of HIV-positive mothers received antiretroviral treatment and mother-to-child transmission was reduced dramatically. However, there remained a surge in new infections in the 10–19 age group. On a visit in early December, UNDP Administrator Helen Clark attested that Namibia was making "good progress" in achieving the **MDGs**, though many of the defined targets remained unmet. UNICEF regional director Steven Allen, who visited at the same time, identified shortcomings in access to primary and secondary schooling, a dire need of qualified teachers and a lack of quality education.

A bad rainy season during the first months of the year led to the worst **drought** for 30 years. According to a report submitted to Cabinet in May, an estimated 330,900 people were directly affected by hunger and food insecurity, with a further 400,000 people estimated to be in medium-term need of food assistance. In response to reports that several people had died of starvation, Prime Minister Geingob stated in parliament in mid-October that malnourishment and hunger existed not only because of drought but as a daily feature of life for less well-off people.

Henning Melber

South Africa

The hype over the outcome of the ruling party's successful elective conference hosted in Mangaung in December 2012 soon dissipated in anticipation of the fifth national democratic election to be held in 2014, 20 years after the country's negotiated transition to democracy. Domestic affairs continued to be underpinned by issues of government transparency and accountability, and the oversight role of the National Parliament, as well as scandals and corruption cases related to state tenders, procurement of government contracts, and the use of state resources. On the international front, Africa and multilateralism remained the pivot of foreign policy making, albeit with sometimes limited coherence and success regarding Pretoria's global identity. In terms of socio-economic developments, poor economic growth and performance, exacerbated by strikes resulting in decreased productivity and industrial output, caused tensions between the state and its citizens. But the principal event impacting on the country was the death of President Mandela, South Africa's first democratically elected black president.

Domestic Affairs

In its annual **January 8 statement**, the ruling African National Congress (ANC) celebrated its 101st anniversary. The statement reflected on the party's 18 years in power and signified what was interpreted as its **pre-election manifesto** commitment to consolidating democracy and intensifying its programme of action in respect of economic transformation, equitable access to education and health, improvements in governance and the work of the legislature, ensuring peace and stability, and enhancing the country's international commitments. At the organisational level, the statement called for greater discipline amongst members to maintain core values, principles of unity and continuous collective leadership. This was seen as a response to what was becoming embedded factionalism in the party, the violent disruption of meetings and attacks on members, public spats and unauthorised public utterances, the use of money to buy members, gate-keeping and the manipulation of ANC processes for pre-determined outcomes. Linked to this was also the call for an organisational renewal based on the view that the party should not forget its overall objective of striving for a 'Better life for All' and the realisation of a mature National Democratic Society. In many ways, the January 8 statement brought to the fore the party's **internal challenges**, which informed the nature of the issues that underscored the discussions at the national elective conference in Mangaung.

On 14 February, President Zuma delivered the fourth and penultimate **State of the Nation Address** of his current administration. The theme of the speech, 'Socio-economic development through oversight and public participation', provoked mixed reactions from opposition parties, business groups and civil society organisations. It seemed that the speech reiterated issues and promises made in the 2012 State of the Nation Address. With broad statements alluding to the National Development Plan (NDP) as the roadmap for the country's 2030 vision to achieve the development priorities of the state, the speech was described in the widely read 'Mail and Guardian' (M&G) as barren of fresh ideas and lacking a comprehensive plan to address job creation. One of the common concerns highlighted by most commentators and opposition parties was a lack of substance and vision. Perhaps what frustrated most analysts was, as the M&G highlighted "the lack of time frames for some crucial projects and the failure to meet [and] implement deadlines", which forced the presidency to carry over announcements made a year or two ago. For others, such as certain unions affiliated to the Congress of South African Trade Unions (COSATU) and Business Unity South Africa (BUSA), there were positive aspects viewed as significant developments for the country, including the formation of an employment agency, the creation of a National Health Insurance (NHI) scheme, and the identification of education as an essential service. Responding to the debate that took place subsequently in the National Assembly, Zuma stuck to the script that South Africa was a better place in 2013 than it had been in 1994.

South Africa was shocked to learn that, in the early hours of 14 February, paralympic athlete, **Oscar Pistorius**, had fatally shot his girlfriend, Reeva Steenkaamp. The story not only caught South Africans off guard, but made international headlines because of Pistorius's reputation as a disabled athletic track star, as well as the fact that crime in South Africa was becoming pervasive and affecting all social classes. Following interrogation by the police, Pistorius was formally charged with Steenkamp's murder. He was granted bail of R (rand) 1 m and the case, originally set for the second half of the year, was postponed into 2014.

In March, the controversial **e-tolling system** took the spotlight again when the National Assembly passed the E-Toll Bill, officially known as the Transport Laws and Related Matters Amendment Bill. By adopting the Bill, the National Assembly essentially gave the South African National Roads Agency (Sanral) the green light to implement the e-tolls system in Gauteng Province. The measure was approved by 198 votes to 98 with two abstentions. The official opposition party, the Democratic Alliance (DA), strongly voiced its concern over the unaffordability of the tolls for already heavily burdened taxpayers, urged the government to seek alternative revenue collection mechanisms, and demanded a referendum for Gauteng. Opposition to the e-tolls was widespread. COSATU also lent its support to the protest campaign led by the Opposition to Urban Tolling Alliance (OUTA) and organised extensive protest actions against the tolls. OUTA pursued legal action in court to stop the government and Sanral from implementing the system. Although its court action had been dismissed in December 2012, the alliance was allowed to appeal the High Court's decision and took its case to the Supreme Court in January. The appeal was dismissed in October, although the judgement by the Supreme Court reversed an earlier order by the High Court that OUTA should pay its opponents' costs. The e-toll system was effectively operational as from midnight on 3 December.

In April, 'Eye Witness News' ran a story that the controversial Gupta family had used the Waterkloof Military air base in Pretoria, identified as one of the country's national key points, to land a private chartered flight with 200 passengers invited to attend a family wedding at Sun City. The story, which resulted in the so-called **Guptagate** affair, not only exposed the irregular procedures followed in gaining permission to land a private plane at the national base, but also included allegations that President Zuma could have been directly implicated by knowing about the lack of tight procedures and using his leverage to instruct officials to allow the plane to land. While Zuma protested his innocence, Chief of State Protocol Bruce Koloane was directly linked as the person who authorised the unlawful incident. Opposition parties took the opportunity to expose what they called undue power over state affairs wielded by the president's benefactors, and claimed that the incident had also exposed and threatened national security. A government investigation was initiated, from which a 30-page report was produced in May, which noted that the Indian High Commission, also caught up in the scandal, had not followed protocol and obtained diplomatic permission from the Department of International Relations and Cooperation (DIRCO) in respect of immigration requirements. In addition, the report also concluded that Koloane was under pressure from senior government officials to assist the Gupta family. In November, responding to questions in the National Assembly, Zuma denied all claims by the South African National Defence Force (SANDF) that he was involved, despite two military officers testifying that Koloane had indicated to them that the president was involved. The outcome of the investigation into Koloane resulted in his demotion in October to liaison officer in DIRCO.

Towards the end of October, expelled members from the ANC's military wing, the Umkonto We Sizwe, allegedly formed a political party called **South Africa First**. The formation of the party was in reaction to internal disputes emerging between the older leadership and younger Umkonto We Sizwe members over financial governance issues, as well as what the architects of SA First highlighted in its official statement – that the need had arisen to rescue South Africa's fledgling democracy from its tipping point. The party was perceived as bridging the divide between ordinary citizens and various civil society organisations that articulated common goals and pursued the same interest in upholding the Constitution. Following its fanfare launch, the party seemed to fade, with almost nothing heard of it in the run-up to the 2014 national elections.

On 25 April, the controversial amended **Protection of State Information Bill** (the Secrecy Bill) was adopted by the National Assembly by 189 votes to 74 with one abstention. Civil society groups such as the Right to Know campaign, which had been actively advocating for a complete overhaul of the provisions in the Bill, were not satisfied with the slight modifications made. One major concern that remained was the lack of protection for whistleblowers and journalists who revealed information as a matter of public interest. According to the new version of the Bill, journalists and whistleblowers could potentially be arrested for reporting information deemed classified by the government that exposed corruption, mismanagement or maladministration, despite the reporting of such information being in the public interest. On 10 September, Zuma refused to sign the amended Bill into law and returned it to Parliament for redrafting. He cited concerns related to Section 42, which dealt with failure to report possession of classified information, and Section 45, which addressed the proper classification of information, commenting that these sections lacked coherence and clarity and were therefore unconstitutional. The Right to Know campaign welcomed his decision, but still urged MPs and policy-makers to align the provisions to international standards on freedom of expression by including a public interest defence clause. On 12 November, Parliament adopted the revised Bill by 225 votes to 88. Again the Bill failed to take into account the concerns of civil society organisations and retained some of the draconian measures related to whistleblowers and the reporting of classified information. The Right to Know campaign described the revisions as farcical and vowed that it would continue its opposition. In December, red flags were raised by the media when it was believed that the Bill had been signed by President Zuma. Reports from Parliament quickly denied these claims and noted that the draft Bill had not been sent to the president for his signature. At the same time, the South African National Editors Forum (SANEF) had appealed to Zuma not to sign the revised Bill until the provisions in the proposed legislation were brought into line with the transparent governance enshrined in the Constitution.

Following the deaths of 44 mineworkers at Lonmin Mines in **Marikana**, North West Province, in August 2012, including 34 killed by police, President Zuma had set up the Marikana Commission of Inquiry, headed by retired Supreme Court of Appeal judge, Justice Ian Gordon Farlam, to investigate the circumstances leading to the deaths of the miners and the role played by the police. In the first four months of the year, the work of the Commission was obstructed by delays caused by the loss of vital documents (including video evidence), the deaths of witnesses, and an ongoing legal battle over state funding for lawyers representing the families of the miners killed, injured and arrested. In May, the Commission was adjourned until July. But lawyers representing the miners' families delayed the resumption of the Commission by requesting a postponement as they continued to battle with the state to cover the legal fees. The government opposed the funding application and the lawyers took their case to the North Gauteng High Court, which rejected the application in July, noting in its judgement that the right to state funding by the miners was not absolute. The Commission was further delayed to October when video evidence related to what happened on the day of the shooting could not be submitted on time. On 31 October, Zuma extended the term of the Commission to 30 April 2014. On 11 July, Julius Malema chose Marikana as the place to formally launch his newly formed party, the **Economic Freedom Fighters**, whose emblem was the wearing of a red beret.

At the end of May, **xenophobic attacks** on the homes and businesses of refugees, asylum-seekers and migrants erupted around Orange Farm, south of Johannesburg, the informal settlement of Sebokeng and Diepsloots. Many were displaced as a result of these attacks and approximately 60 foreign-owned shops were looted. The violence against the foreigners followed on the back of service delivery protests in the area, while residents saw it as competition for scarce resources, namely in respect of the allocation of Reconstruction and Development Programme houses. In June and September, similar attacks on Somali nationals in KwaZakhele and New Brighton in Port Elizabeth, in the Eastern Cape Province, left several shops looted and burnt. Due to the level of xenophobic violence, police relocated some foreign nationals to temporary shelters. The response by government was to downplay the fact that the attacks were xenophobic or motivated by intolerance. The xenophobic attacks that had occurred in 2008 remained an undercurrent in South African informal communities and townships and the Centre for Human Rights based at the University of Pretoria concluded that South Africans were becoming increasingly desensitised to attacks on foreigners. However, civil society groups such as People Against Suffering, Oppression and Poverty (PASSOP) had continued to increase their public awareness and education programmes around refugee rights and challenged the government for closing down three government Ayslum Reception Centres since 2011, despite the courts ordering the Department of Home Affairs to re-open the centres in the Eastern and Western Cape.

On 9 July, Zuma carried out the fourth **cabinet reshuffle** since his administration came to power in 2009. Tokyo Sexwale (Minister for Human Settlements), Dina Pule (Minister for Communications) and Richard Baloyi (Minister for Cooperative Governance and Traditional Affairs) were replaced by Connie September, Yunus Carrim and Lechesa Tsenoli, respectively. Ben Martins, who was minister of transport, and Dipuo Peters, who served as minister of energy, swapped portfolios. In assessing the factors behind the reshuffle, the 'City Press' newspaper asked whether performance or politics was the president's motive. In the case of Sexwale, politics appeared to be a critical factor in determining his fate. He had expressed strong opposition to Zuma's re-election as party president and was considered to be part of the 'Forces of Change' that sought to challenge the Zuma faction for leadership of the party, but at Mangaung he lost his bid to become deputy party president as well as his position on the party's National Executive Committee. Dina Pule, on the other hand, was punished for her behaviour and performance, having been accused of giving tenders to a boyfriend, meddling in tender processes, and interfering in the appointment of officials to the boards of state-owned enterprises; her dismissal from cabinet was welcomed by the media and political commentators. Unfortunately for Richard Baloyi, it would seem that he was a casualty of the mess surrounding the multi-million rand upgrade of the president's private residence in Nkandla.

Cases of **corruption and embezzlement** made headlines throughout the year. On 12 July, South African Revenue Service Commissioner Oupa Magashula resigned following allegations of misconduct. He was caught on tape in a conversation with a convicted drug dealer discussing the possibility of arranging jobs for pals. In a statement regarding the scandal, Minister of Finance Gordhan said that the integrity and ethical recruitment process of the Commission had to be preserved. In August, the Public Protector released the findings of her investigation into the role of the Independent Electoral Commission (IEC) chairperson, Pansy Tlakula, in securing a R 320 m lease for the IEC's head office in Centurion, Pretoria. The Public Protector found that Tlakula's role was irregular and violated procedural rules. According to the ruling, she had not only risked losing public confidence in the Commission, but had also threatened the institution's reputation as an impartial constitutional body. While opposition parties called for Tlakula's resignation, she remained adamant that she had not committed any wrongdoing.

By September, the rising **tensions within the labour movement** were manifest in a conflict between COSATU and one of its largest member unions, the National Union of Mineworkers of South Africa (NUMSA), when NUMSA went to the High Court seeking the reinstatement of COSATU general secretary, Zwelinzima Vavi. The COSATU leadership had suspended Vavi in July following a sex scandal involving a co-worker. But the scandal masked the inherent divisions emerging within COSATU, a partner in the ANC's tripartite alliance, especially between pro- and anti-Zuma factions. By October, NUMSA had declared its intention not to support the ANC in the 2014 national elections if the NDP was implemented as the electoral strategy, with NUMSA considering pulling out of COSATU and taking other smaller unions with it. In November, there was talk of NUMSA starting its own political party. NUMSA's belligerent stance was seen as a reaction to what some political observers noted as discontent with the Zuma administration and an anti-Zuma stance; Cedric Gina, a Zuma loyalist, resigned as president of NUMSA in December.

Chief Justice of the Constitutional Court, **Pius Langa**, passed away on 24 July at the age of 74 following a long illness. Justice Langa, who was appointed to the bench by Nelson Mandela in 1994, became the deputy justice of the court in 2001 and Chief Justice in 2005. On 5 December, former president **Nelson Mandela** passed away at his Houghton home in Johannesburg at the age of 95. Revered as the statesman who had led South Africa to a peaceful democratic dispensation, he had suffered since April from a recurring lung infection. Mandela's death was not without controversy. After he was admitted to the 1 Military Hospital in Pretoria on 8 June, Presidency spokesman Mac Maharaj issued a statement noting that Mandela was in a serious but stable condition. For weeks, the Presidency refused to disclose details of the former president's condition to the national and international media, whose reporters had camped outside the hospital. On 22 June, a local correspondent for CBS News reported that the ambulance transporting Mandela to hospital on 8 June had broken down, with adverse consequences for Mandela's fragile condition. While the Presidency confirmed that the ambulance's engine had failed, it emphasised that the incident had not compromised the former president's health. But on June 23, 'City Press' reported in its lead story that the ambulance ordeal had, in fact, led to Mandela having to be resuscitated while waiting for another ambulance from the hospital. While 'City Press' claimed it had several sources to verify that Mandela had to be revived, the sources could not provide details as to what had caused the situation. There was a public outcry that the privacy of Mandela's medical condition should be respected. After spending three months in hospital, he was released and taken back to his Houghton residence for home-based care. In the period between September and his death in early December, the top leadership of the ANC visited him several times, while the Presidency released vague public statements about his condition. The media frenzy continued, with reports speculating that tensions were emerging between Mandela's wife Graca Machel and the Mandela family.

The announcement of **Mandela's death** by President Zuma before midnight on 5 December caught the nation off guard, despite having being prepared for the inevitable through the preceding months. Fulfilling his desire as the country's first black democratically elected leader to advance a racially united South Africa, Mandela's passing away saw South Africans come together as a rainbow nation. A week-long period of mourning was declared with the national flag flying at half-mast. A public memorial service was held on 10 December, coinciding with UN Human Rights Day. Approximately 70 heads of state, more than 20 government representatives, and little over 30 former leaders attended the memorial service. The presidents of Cuba, India, Brazil and India, and the vice president of China were given the particular privilege of delivering eulogies during the service. President Obama also delivered a fitting tribute to the colossal politician, noting that the passing of Madiba had prompted in "each one of us a time for self reflection" to ask "How well have I applied his lessons in my own life?" The memorial service was marred by jeers from the crowd at President Zuma. As much as the ANC tried to control the situation, the incident revealed the president's failing popularity, which was perceived as an international embarrassment for the ANC leadership. Mandela was laid to rest at his ancestral home in Qunu in the Eastern Cape on 15 December, following three days of lying in state at the Union building, so that South Africans could pay their last respects to the 'father of the nation'.

Foreign Affairs

The government sent a delegation composed of President Zuma and a contingent of ministers and business leaders to the annual **World Economic Forum** in Davos (Switzerland) at the end of January. The meeting was significant as an opportunity to highlight the country's strengths as an investment destination and to allay investor fears in view of the ongoing labour disputes and socio-economic challenges. The strategic focus of the country's engagement at Davos was to showcase two plans seen as integral to the country's economic and industrial development, namely the NDP and the National Infrastructure Plan, which were identified as South Africa's long-term policy strategy.

South Africa's **military engagement in the CAR** took a bloody turn when 13 South African soldiers were killed in battles during 23–24 March in Bangui. This sparked mixed reactions in South Africa over the reasons why the soldiers were engaged there and the circumstances that had led to their deaths. The soldiers were part of a 400-man peacekeeping force deployed in January under a bilateral arrangement based on a memorandum of understanding signed with the Bozizé government in 2007 to maintain peace and stability. The soldiers were killed in a battle with Séléka rebels, who had seized control of the capital. Following the deaths of the soldiers, it emerged that the peacekeepers had few supplies and almost no intelligence regarding the local situation. Moreover, the formal explanation for the peacekeepers' presence was that they were to assist the Bozizé government with capacity building for its defence force and the planning and implementation of the disarmament, demobilisation and reintegration processes. But rumours surfaced that this was not in fact the case. One of the critical issues was why South Africa had sent troops to support a dictatorial government. Speculation was rife that there were other considerations at play, namely the protection of private mineral and natural resource interests. These included the oil company DIG Oil, which had prospecting rights in the south-eastern part of the country and which had Zuma's nephew as a board member. There were similar allegations regarding ANC business interests in the CAR. These speculations were rebutted by the Presidency and the party, but the debacle led to the DA asking Parliament in

April to investigate the deaths and determine whether Zuma had misled the legislature about the deployment. The defence minister downplayed the incident and, on 4 April, Zuma announced the withdrawal of South African troops from the CAR. While domestic criticisms increased, condemning the loss of life, the South African government maintained that it still had a role to play in the region's stability through ECCAS; the minister for international relations and cooperation was reported as saying, 'We cannot afford the luxury of saying Africa's problems are not our problems. It is also in our own national interest to have a stable, peaceful and developed Africa.' But South Africa's involvement in the CAR not only highlighted the extent of Pretoria's peacekeeping interventions in Africa, but also exposed the network of private material interests aligned to the ruling class in power there.

On 27 March, South Africa hosted the 5th Heads of State **BRICS Summit** in Durban, where it took over the Chair of the forum for a year. The Summit signified the completion of the first cycle of summits that began with Brazil in 2008. Assuming leadership of the BRICS Forum presented South Africa with an opportunity to showcase Africa as the central focus of its admission to the group. Entitled 'BRICS and Africa: Partnership for Development, Integration and Industrialisation', Pretoria also used the occasion to highlight that the Summit coincided with the 50th anniversary of the OAU/AU. The Zuma administration invited the chairperson of the AU, Dr Nkosana Dlamini-Zuma, as well as the head of the AU Commission, heads of state and government representing African Regional Economic Communities (RECs), and NEPAD representatives. The purpose of making Africa an integral part of the Summit was to spearhead and launch the BRICS Africa outreach platform. The initiative culminated in Zuma hosting a BRICS Leaders-Africa Dialogue Forum on the margins of the Summit under the theme 'Unlocking Africa's Potential: BRICS and Africa Cooperation on Infrastructure', to engage on measures to strengthen cooperation between the BRICS countries and the African continent to unlock its potential and promote regional integration through infrastructure development and industrialisation. This 'retreat' was also aimed at strengthening collaboration between the BRICS and the AU, NEPAD and the RECs in support of the implementation of projects under the Programme for Infrastructure Development in Africa as well as the AU/NEPAD Presidential Infrastructure Champion Initiative and the Regional Infrastructure Development Master Plans. Pretoria aimed to use the Summit to reshape funding for the continent through the BRICS by forging a new funding model for infrastructure development on the continent.

The Summit resulted in the **eThekwini Declaration**, which provided for cooperation in the following new areas: a BRICS public diplomacy forum; BRICS anti-corruption cooperation; BRICS state-owned companies and enterprises; national agencies responsible for drugs control; a BRICS virtual secretariat; a BRICS youth policy dialogue; tourism; energy; and sport and major sporting events. Some of the key outcomes from the Summit included: the leaders' decision that the establishment of the BRICS Development Bank be fast-tracked and that the initial capital contribution to the bank should be substantial and sufficient for the bank to be effective in financing infrastructure; the creation of a Contingent Reserve Arrangement of an initial $ 100 bn, which would help BRICS countries forestall short-term liquidity pressures and improve financial stability, thereby strengthening the global financial safety net and complementing existing international arrangements; the establishment of a BRICS Think Tanks Council and BRICS Business Council.

In addition, two agreements were initiated under the **BRICS interbank cooperation mechanism**: the BRICS Multilateral Infrastructure Co-Financing Agreement for Africa, which paved the way for the establishment of co-financing arrangements for infrastructure projects across the African continent; and the BRICS Multilateral Cooperation and Co-Financing Agreement for Sustainable Development, to explore the drawing up of bilateral agreements aimed at establishing cooperation and co-financing arrangements, specifically around sustainable development and green economy elements.

Critics, however, were less than flattering about Pretoria acting as an interlocutor between the **BRICS and Africa**, especially since two BRICS countries had formulated their own bilateral and regional arrangements with African governments through interstate fora, such as the India-Africa Forum Summit and the Forum on China-Africa Cooperation. The test for Pretoria would be to assess its achievements as chair of the forum and against a very broad action plan underpinned by meetings and consultations without any substantive outputs.

At the end of June, **President Obama** visited South Africa as part of a three-country African state trip. The purpose of the visit was to meet with leaders from business, government and civil society with a view to: reinforcing relations with Washington; expanding economic growth, investment, and trade relations; strengthening democratic institutions; and investing in the next generation of African leaders. For both Pretoria and Washington, the visit was seen as critical in identifying and reaffirming economic opportunities. This included focus on the 600 US companies that had invested in South Africa and the 150,000-plus jobs that these corporations had created, as well as on the need for more investment to enable more jobs and the continuing benefits under AGOA. The visit also underscored Pretoria's growing trade surplus with Washington. In certain media spaces, the visit was seen as Washington's attempt to reconnect with South Africa in response to China's increased engagement with Pretoria. But Obama's visit provoked anti-American sentiment. The Muslim Lawyers Association indicated that it would take the National Prosecuting Authority to court over its refusal to arrest the US president. In addition, the Association wanted South Africa to investigate Obama's drone policy. Meanwhile, the University of Johannesburg was caught in a battle with student movements over its decision to award Obama an honorary doctorate. A further dispute emerged between the DA-led government in the Western Cape and the national government over whether Obama should address Parliament or be awarded the freedom of the city of Cape Town. Despite these ructions, Obama's visit reinforced Washington's shared commitment with Pretoria to a reformed UNSC, the strengthening of the agreement on a rules-based, multilateral system that gave primacy to diplomacy and multilateral negotiations in the resolution of international disputes, and the need to work and cooperate with like-minded states on countering cyber-crime, ensuring the integrity of the non-proliferation regime, and fighting terrorism in all its manifestations. Perhaps what best characterised Obama's visit was his charismatic personality and constant referrals to the ideals of Nelson Mandela, which undoubtedly re-inspired the South African public about its own democratic principles.

In the run-up to the elections in **Zimbabwe** on 31 July, President Zuma, as the appointed SADC envoy, and through his special advisor, Lindiwe Zulu, undertook a set of scheduled meetings to mediate Zimbabwe's political transition. The discussions focused on an attempt to broker agreements on the future of the unity government and to set the date of the national elections. The dialogue also dealt with the implementation of reforms promised under the Global Political Agreement, which the Movement for Democratic Change partners had alleged the Zimbabwe African National Union-Patriotic Front (ZANU-PF) was refusing to implement. Moreover, it seemed that ZANU-PF was blocking the South African facilitation team from moving forward with its mandate. The 'M&G' reported in May that tensions had surfaced between Zuma and the top ZANU-PF leadership, who did not want the South African president to play a central role in Zimbabwe's election plan. In the same newspaper, a SADC representative revealed that the South Africans "had been told off the record that their presence was unnecessary and tantamount to interference in the running of government". South African efforts to hold meetings with ZANU-PF were continuously frustrated by the ruling party's unavailability. While Zuma sought to delicately defuse the impasse, Lindiwe Zulu had been more open about the failures of ZANU-PF to engage with the South African team. Her comments infuriated ZANU-PF and President Mugabe, and this led to a public attack on her by the 'The Herald' newspaper, which published an editorial calling on Zuma to "tether his terrier". Zulu was also criticised by Mugabe's spokesperson, George Charamba, who argued that she was not the appointed SADC envoy and so should not be making statements that amounted, in his opinion, to challenging the integrity of a sovereign country. Mugabe went a step further by calling Zulu a "street woman". In what was considered an appeasement strategy, Zuma's office issued a statement rebuking Zulu and asking her to refrain from making unauthorised and inaccurate public comments on developments in Zimbabwe. Zuma, in line with SADC, accepted the results of the elections of 31 July, despite Zimbabwean civil society organisations claiming that they were neither free nor fair and that the outcome had been manipulated. In congratulating Mugabe and ZANU-PF, Zuma's office said that he urged "all political parties in Zimbabwe to accept the outcome of the elections, as election observers reported it to be an expression of the will of the people". Critics and regional civil society bodies, who had lobbied the South African government to take a stronger stance and put pressure on the ZANU-PF leadership to respect the democratic process, were disappointed by the Zuma administration's response. In addition, it signalled what many interpreted as Pretoria's lack of political will to break ranks with the regional consensus and articulate an independent viewpoint in the interest of good governance, especially since Botswana had rejected SADC's endorsement of the electoral outcome.

In October, following the collapse of peace talks in Kampala regarding the conflict in the eastern part of the **DRC**, Pretoria was faced with a veiled threat from the M23 rebels that, for the situation to stabilise, it should remove its troops from the UN peacekeeping mission. South Africa had deployed more soldiers in April. Withdrawal was not an option that the Zuma administration would consider, given its close relationship with the Kabila government in Kinshasa. In November, Zuma made a state visit to the DRC and signed an agreement for the purchase of electricity from the Grand Inga hydroelectric dam by the South African electricity supplier, Eskom, thereby increasing Pretoria's economic footprint in the Great Lakes region. During the same trip, Zuma, who was accompanied by a contingent of ministers and business people, also sought to strengthen Pretoria's support for the Kabila government in neutralising the M23 rebels. Critics argued that South Africa's support for the UN mission was motivated by its economic interests in the DRC, but other commentators argued that South Africa was not a big economic player there. Be that as it may, in December the UN Force Intervention Brigade, in which South Africa, Tanzania and Malawi played a significant role, had not only successfully fought and pushed M23 rebels back from their strongholds, but also made further inroads by targeting rebels who were considered to be a threat to stability in the region.

Towards the end of the year, controversy arose when the Department of Trade and Industry gave notice that it would terminate several of its **bilateral investment treaties**, mainly those signed with European countries. This followed a multi-stakeholder review undertaken by the South African government between 2007 and 2010. The review concluded that the link between bilateral investment treaties and increased FDI was uncertain, and that the ambiguity inherent in many of the standard provisions of these agreements created uncertainty for both investors and governments. As a result, Pretoria decided to terminate its existing bilateral investment treaties and only to enter into new ones if there were compelling economic reasons to do so, and if the new deals clearly reduced the risks inherent in the earlier agreements. On 1 November, the Promotion and Protection of Investment Bill was published, with the aim of levelling the playing field in the protection of investor rights. South Africa's decision provoked intense criticism from its EU partners, who considered that Pretoria's action was biased and asked whether investors from the BRICS partners and other investment from the Global South were being treated in the same way.

Socio-Economic Developments

On 27 February, Finance Minister Pravin Gordhan delivered the 14th **budget speech** since the establishment of democracy in South Africa. In the run-up to the speech, speculation was rife as to whether the minister would introduce austerity measures in order to revitalise the country's lacklustre economic performance and control the rising levels of consumer debt and inflation. The minister adopted a cautious approach. The budget was intended to provide relief measures for South Africans. While taxes on alcohol and tobacco products rose, individual taxpayers enjoyed a welcomed respite with regard to personal income tax and VAT, which did not increase during the 2013/2014 financial year. However, this was offset by the cost of increased fuel levies (against the backdrop of rising global oil prices), which added to household expenses. While the DA, as the official opposition, recognised that the speech was broadly in line with the objectives of the NDP, it criticised the lack of substantive solutions that would roll-out significant structural reforms to the national economy aimed at higher growth rates. The business sector was divided in its reactions. BUSA welcomed the fact that the budget speech provided a roadmap for the implementation of the NDP. The South African Chamber of Commerce and Industry (SACCI), however, expressed disappointment that the national budget failed to outline plans to reduce South Africa's inflated public wages bill to sustainable levels. Neither did it outline the funding model for the proposed NHI scheme, bearing in mind that this would be linked to higher taxes, which was alarming since the tax base was already overstretched by providing most of the resources for the social welfare system. On the other hand, the SACCI welcomed the minister's announcement of the establishment of the Small Enterprise Financing Agency, which would reduce red tape for small, medium and micro enterprises seeking to expand their commercial interests in the domestic economy. Other positive outcomes from the speech were the incentive to attract FDI to the country's Special Economic Zones by promising to renegotiate tax incentives and considering an employment incentive programme.

Economic **growth** was slow but steady with performance reaching 3.8% in the last quarter of the year. This was considered to be reasonable quarter on quarter growth following the post-labour strike recovery period. Annual GDP increased by 1.9% compared with a 2.5% rise in 2012. The main contributors to the increase in economic activity were finance, real estate and business services, the wholesale, retail and motor trade, catering and accommodation, mining and quarrying, transport, storage and communications, and general government services, but the economy continued to suffer from the residual impact of difficulties in the eurozone, a major trading partner, and slower expansion in China and other major emerging markets, which affected exports and investment.

Labour unrest continued to affect the economy in key sectors such as gold mining, construction and car manufacturing, considered as critical to the country's industrial development. Strikes also put a damper on consumer and business confidence, pulling down consumption and investment, while overly-high wage settlements were seen as a key risk to inflation and growth prospects, according to a June report from the Reserve Bank. The strikes also led to a delay in the completion of a new 4,800-MW power plant, Medupi, now expected to come on line later in 2014, which should help to alleviate electricity shortages.

Demands for higher wages were considered a disincentive to recruitment. The overall **unemployment** rate hovered around 25% for the year. In October, the Youth Wage Subsidy Bill was passed, set to come into force in 2014, aimed at addressing burgeoning youth unemployment, which stood at around 50%, by providing tax breaks to companies that hired younger graduates. Part of the challenge in addressing unemployment was the need to invest more in human capital and skills training. In a Grant Thornton survey carried out in March, 83% of South African businesses reported a shortage of technical skills as a problem for recruitment. This was a serious issue for a country that needed to generate meaningful work and increase the value-added elements of its economy in a competitive global marketplace. Moreover, the **OECD**'s 2013 Economic Survey of South Africa highlighted the effect of weaknesses in the education system on deficits in South Africa's human resources. It suggested reforms, including better allocation of resources, improvements in teacher training and vocational education, and increased autonomy and accountability for senior teachers, and noted that government spending was not always matched by improvements on the ground.

On 23 October, Finance Minister Gordhan delivered his **medium term expenditure framework** budget speech, in which he recognised that excessive government expenditure had contributed to a sluggish economy. He noted that the country's debt would climb to 48% of GDP by March 2017. In addition, while trying to maintain spending limits and curb the wage bill to ensure that the budget deficit target was achieved, borrowing over the next three years was to increase, and Gordhan scaled down his economic growth forecast from 2.7% to 2.1%. Perhaps the most significant feature of his speech was his commitment to cut waste and extravagance in **government spending**. He announced a raft of measures that sought to reduce abuse of taxpayers' money, including: the termination of existing credit cards issued to government employees, with no new cards to be issued; new guidelines to control advertising costs, with officials urged to make better use of the Government Communication and Information System; cost limits on official cars, which would be standardised, and bulk purchasing to reduce costs; disallowing expenses claims for use of personal vehicles for official work and the hire of top-grade cars, except in special circumstances; rules for delegations travelling abroad, such as restricting first-class travel to ministers and directors general only, limiting the number of participants in delegations, requiring travel by direct routes only to cut stop-over expenses; ending the provision of hotel accommodation for ministers awaiting housing allocations and guidelines to limit the cost of refurbishments in ministers' homes; new restrictions on food, drink and entertainment, with entertainment allowances restricted to R 2,000 and no expenditure of public funds for alcohol, except in special circumstances; and steps to reduce office accommodation and government housing costs, and to slash electricity bills in state buildings. The **spending freeze** was welcomed by opposition parties and the business sector and civil society organisations, although some analysts questioned whether the move was part of a government election strategy. The question that remained was how far the government would go in ensuring the implementation of these measures after the 2014 national elections.

By year's end, South Africa had been dubbed the world's **social protest** capital. In the period between 1 April and 10 May, Gauteng province reported 540 social protests. In September, police reported that they had arrested more than 14,000 protestors over the previous four years. The nature of the protests was often linked to service delivery dissatisfaction and involved informal settlements, but the protests were also clearly becoming increasingly violent. Analysts suggested that this was part of the culture of protests that dated back to the anti-apartheid struggle, but many considered that the increased frequency and intensity of the protests reflected government failures, especially at local level, to satisfy the material needs of the poor and economically vulnerable in a society characterised by a widening inequality gap and rising poverty.

Sanusha Naidu

Swaziland

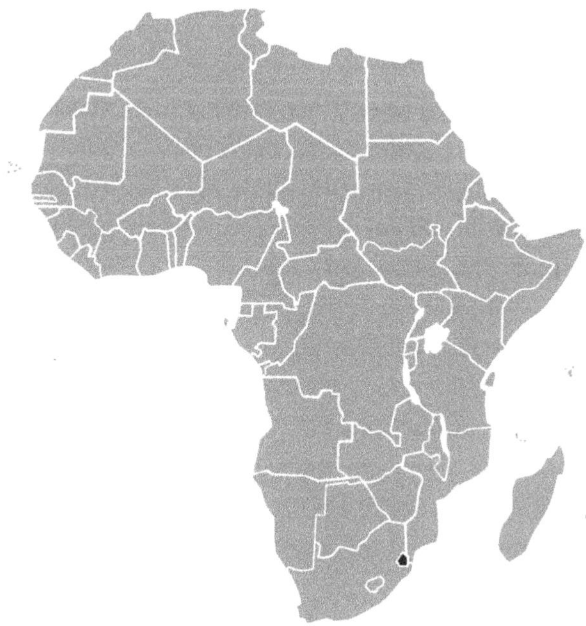

The political year was dominated by national elections to Parliament. The economic crisis eased slightly with a higher annual subvention from SACU. King Mswati III continued to occupy a fantasy economic space, spending millions in an attempt to complete an international airport. The king also announced that Swaziland would attain 'first-world status' in 2021.

Domestic Politics

The primary and secondary **national elections** took place on 24 August and 20 September respectively. Organised in line with the *tinkhundla* system of local governance, the country was divided into constituencies and each was presented with three candidates pre-selected by the local chiefs. The voters then elected one of the three to the national legislature. The result was inevitably a compliant body subordinate to the king. To further secure his control of Parliament, the king also nominated a bloc of MPs to both the upper and lower houses – ten of the 65 members of the National Assembly and 20 of the 30 members of the Senate (the remaining ten being selected by the National Assembly). In a break with tradition, amongst those nominated to the Senate were six members of the royal family. The king also selected the prime minister. In late September, he re-appointed for a third term the outgoing premier, Barnabas Dlamini, a hard-line anti-democrat and passionate monarchist. The only interesting successful candidate amongst the new MPs was the one-time trade union leader and opposition figure, Jan Sithole. While some saw this as a rare victory for the opposition, others interpreted it as a sign that Sithole had abandoned the oppositional role for a financially more secure future.

Protest actions by those advocating a boycott of the electoral process were heavily suppressed. Pro-democracy and anti-election activities were violently broken up by the police. Even church activities were targeted: in February, for example, a prayer meeting was disrupted by armed police. Many such interventions took place in the months leading up to the elections. With political parties banned, the trade union movement bore the brunt of police hostility. Despite the lack of democracy, the Swazi work force is highly organised and most union groupings adopt an anti-government stance. During pre-election voter registration, many groupings urged a boycott of the process, which caused several extensions of the deadline for registration. Ultimately, the Elections and Boundaries Commission (EBC) announced that, with just two days of registration still to go, only 344,679, or less than 58%, of an estimated 600,000 potential voters had signed up. The overall turnout on 30 June was finally 415,012 registered voters, including cases of multiple registration. The process was marred by budgetary constraints, since the EBC had to operate with an allocation by the government cut from E (emalangeni) 200 m to E 100 m.

The state continued its **crackdown on dissent**, with activists being arrested and often charged with sedition. In April, Maxwell Dlamini, secretary general of the Swaziland Youth Congress and possibly the regime's most hated opponent, was charged with sedition because he allegedly tried to organise a meeting to discuss the elections. Two weeks later, the veteran opposition figure and trade unionist Mario Masuku was placed under house arrest to prevent his attendance at a May Day rally. The government denied that they were against workers celebrating Workers Day but stated they would not allow the day to be celebrated under the banner of the new federation, the Trade Union Congress of Swaziland.

During the course of the year, civil society groups expressed concerns that Swaziland was becoming an increasingly militarised state. A complaint to this effect was made by the Open Society Initiative for South Africa (OSISA) at the African Commission on Human and People's Rights. OSISA argued that there were reliable reports of a **general militarisation** of the country through the deployment of the Swazi Army, police and correctional services to clamp down on any peaceful protest action by labour or civil society organisations. It was also reported that King Mswati had put aside E 13.1 bn for defence spending. The king was reportedly fearful of an Arab-Spring type uprising and purchased a huge stockpile of weaponry, as well as building a private underground bunker for his family. Others suggested that these weapons had actually been bought for onward sale to other countries such as Zimbabwe, which was affected by an arms embargo. The government also increased the size of the police force. Prime Minister Barnabas Dlamini stated in February that there was one police officer to every 700 people in Swaziland, but that the goal was one officer to every 200.

Violations of **human rights** increased over the year. According to a US State Department report, the main human rights abuses were police use of excessive force, including torture, beatings and unlawful killings; restrictions on freedoms of association, assembly, and speech; and discrimination against and abuse of women and children. The Swazi people were further victimised by the system as they needed authorisation from the police to receive treatment after police brutality. As a result, medics and NGOs were afraid to help the injured after suspected police violence.

Violence against women and children continued. Severe corporal punishment was carried out in schools, with reports of children having to be hospitalised, and there was even a case of death. Human rights organisations brought to light this excessive use of force. For instance, a 17-year-old female student was given 22 strokes of the cane by a male teacher because she continued to attend school although her unemployed parents had not paid fees. A ten-year-old girl at a primary school was blinded for life in one eye after a splinter from a teacher's stick struck it during the punishment of another pupil. Police refused to allow women of the Swaziland Rural Women's Assembly to march in protest against gender-based violence. However, the Assembly decided to defy the ban and undertook the march on 29 May. MPs were instructed not to get divorced during the next five years as this would embarrass King Mswati. Senate chief Gelane Zwane gave notice of this, making particular reference to females. While Swazi culture allowed marriages to be terminated, according to King Mswati only death could undo a traditional union.

There were many attempts to curtail communication and broadcasting of news, which impacted on **freedom of speech**. All broadcasting was state controlled and there was severe censorship of news and information. There were concerns that the eagerly awaited Swaziland Broadcasting Bill would not be enacted and that, even if it were, broadcasting would still be controlled by the king. The Bill would give the king the authority to take over broadcasting stations if there was a threatened public emergency. It would also allow the king to appoint someone to take over any or all broadcasting stations and control and direct them for as long as he considered it expedient. Journalists and print media were severely punished for criticising the courts and thereby showing disrespect. In April, Bheki Makhubu, editor of the 'Nation' magazine, was convicted of offending the court because he criticised the Swazi judiciary. He was fined $ 22,000 by the High Court with the alternative of serving two years in jail. According to the **Ibrahim Index** of African Governance, Swaziland ranked 47th out of 52 African nations for 'participant and human rights'.

Foreign Policy

Police stopped a panel discussion led by Jay Naidoo for causing anarchy and instability in the Kingdom. The meeting was to be a **Global Inquiry Panel** on trade union rights and democracy in Swaziland and was an initiative of the International Trade Union Confederation of Swaziland and South Africa's COSATU. It was to hear accounts in order to compile a report to be taken to the ILO for the Committee on the Application of International Standards. According to the police commissioner, the panel was part and parcel of a political agenda aimed at breaching the peace and causing anarchy and political instability.

Regional and international **election observers** criticised the process and credibility of the elections. The Commonwealth Observer Mission report called for the constitution to be reviewed and for King Mswati's influence in political affairs to be reduced. In addition to the Commonwealth's observations, the AU mission called for fundamental changes to ensure people had freedom of speech and of assembly. AfriMap, a group that monitors and promotes compliance by African states with the requirements of good governance, democracy, human rights and the rule of law, called the Kingdom an island of autocratic rule in the SADC. The SADC Electoral Observer Mission, headed by Namibia's Foreign Minister Netumbo Nandi-Ndaitwah, was markedly more generous. The 90 observers from nine SADC member states deployed in 24 observer teams in the four regions expressed concern over ten issues in total, but finally concluded that "although some of the concerns raised are pertinent, they are nevertheless not of such magnitude as to affect the overall electoral process".

Representatives of the People's United Democratic Movement entered into a strategic alliance with the Danish Red-Green Alliance facilitated by the Danish Institute for Parties and Democracy. The banned party's international secretary visited **Denmark** from 25 April to 2 May and outlined the political scenario at home. The party's president and organising secretary also observed municipal elections in Denmark at the end of November.

Socioeconomic Developments

Swaziland is part of the SACU and the Common Monetary Area. Its currency is pegged to the South African rand, and South Africa continued to be its largest trading partner. Subsistence agriculture employed 70% of the workforce. The soft-drink, textile, and cane sugar industries were the leading export earners and the largest private-sector manufacturers. Coal and diamonds were also exported. Political instability affected the **investment climate** and potential investors, particularly South African businesses, remained largely absent. In a survey, 60% of 400 South African firms declared that they would not mind trading with Swaziland, although only 27% of them did so.

An IMF report stated that **government spending** was out of control. Salaries for public servants remained one of the highest in SSA and amounted to about 15% of GDP. The Kingdom's budget deficit was at about 6% of GDP. A very large portion of the state budget went to the king and the royal family. It was reported that approximately $ 37 m a year went to 'royal emoluments', shared between the king's wives and children, his half-brothers and their mothers and other members of the royal family. The king had 13 palaces, a private jet and fleets of Mercedes and BMW cars. The country remained heavily reliant on foreign grants while the bulk of the country's wealth was reserved for the royal family. Excessive spending by the king continued to raise eyebrows. A E 2.2 m guard-house, connected to the royal bunker, had been budgeted to accommodate eight soldiers to guard the palace 24 hours a day. It was reported in March that the king – despite freezing the budget in October 2012 – had taken a 13% increase in royal spending for the financial year 2013/14. Three national security chiefs received bullet-proof cars at a cost of E 4 m. They were equipped with armoured passenger cabin, bullet resistant glass and an intercom system allowing communication with persons outside the vehicle without having to open doors or windows.

Sikhuphe Airport, a project to build an international airport in the wilderness that had been ongoing for ten years, made headlines throughout the year. Regarded as the king's vanity project, it had never been subjected to a needs analysis. The current airport in Matsapha processed about 70,000 passengers a year. Media reports estimated the cost of Sikhuphe at about $ 300 m so far. The government wanted to set up a national airline to use the airport.

The Swazi people continued to endure severe **food shortages**. A study assessing the economic impact of malnutrition in Africa indicated that Swaziland lost roughly 3.1% of its GDP due to the long term impacts of hunger. Around 270,000 adults, or more than 40% of workers, suffered from stunted growth. Cases of diarrhoea, anaemia, respiratory infections and other health problems related to hunger cost an estimated $ 6 m a year. It was also reported that starving people were being denied food by the government as punishment for the MPs who had passed a vote of no confidence against it. Despite these appalling conditions, it was reported that the government sold maize worth $ 3 m that had been donated by Japan to feed the Swazi people. Approximately 12,000 tonnes of maize was donated but sold through the national maize corporation for a total of E 24 m, which was deposited in a special account at the central bank. News of this scandal circulated worldwide. A press release was issued by government spokesman Percy Simelane to justify the sale. He claimed that the Japan International Cooperation Agency was aware of the arrangement, but this was not confirmed by Japan. Simelane further stated that "it was not the first time government had sold donated items: a consignment of fertilizer donated by the Japanese government had also been sold". About seven in ten of King Mswati's 1.3 m subjects lived in poverty on less than $ 2 a day.

John Daniel & Marisha Ramdeen

Zambia

President Michael Sata's cabinet faced important challenges throughout the year. Domestic politics saw six rounds of by-elections, which, apart from incurring significant financial costs, tipped the balance of power in favour of the ruling Patriotic Front (PF). At the end of the year, the PF held 51% of the seats in the National Assembly (10 more than in 2011), the Movement for Multiparty Democracy (MMD) held 27% (down 14 from 2011), and the United Party for National Development (UPND) held 20%. There were multiple changes in ministerial posts, with only six ministers remaining unchanged since 2011. The promised new constitution was postponed again. The fight against corruption intensified. The policy towards Chinese investment continued to be crucial. The economy performed well despite the rebasing of the kwacha. GDP and wages rose, but social unrest still escalated. Some donors pulled out of the country.

Domestic Politics

As in the past, **ministerial instability** continued. As early as February, the Minister of Foreign Affairs Given Lubinda was dismissed and replaced by his deputy, Effron Lungu; but after facing a disciplinary party committee, Lungu was suspended towards mid-year in the face of unclear accusations of betrayal and leaking information to anti-government media. He was succeeded by Wylbur Simuusa, the fourth to hold the post since 2011. Simuusa had till then been minister of lands, natural resources and environmental protection, and that post was given to Harry Kalaba, promoted from being deputy minister in the Office of the Vice President. President Sata also swore in a good number of **new deputy ministers**, not only from his own party but also as part of a strategic cooptation of opposition MPs. From the PF, he appointed Davies Mwango to the Office of the Vice President and Mwimba Malama to the Ministry of Transport, Works, Supply and Communications. From the UPND, Sata coopted Richwell Siamunene for the Ministry of Commerce, Trade and Industry, Chinga Miyutu for the Ministry of Youth and Sports, and Poniso Njeulu for the Ministry of Information and Broadcasting. Miyutu and Njeulu joined two other UPND MPs in the PF government, namely Greyford Monde (Agriculture and Livestock) and Richwell Siamunene (Commerce, Trade and Industry). This brought the number in the cabinet to 22 (president, vice president, and 20 ministers), and there were in addition 41 deputy ministers, at least one quarter of whom were from the opposition (MMD or UPND).

The 'election mood' continued with **six rounds of by-elections** held between February and November; they took place in 12 constituencies, spread across all provinces except Northern Province. The majority of these elections were caused either by floor crossing from the opposition to the ruling party (for example, six MMD MPs joined the PF), or by the court's decision to nullify seats in certain constituencies either on the grounds of malpractice or after declaring the 2011 elections unlawful (as was the case in Peatuke, Malambo and Mulobezi). At the end of the electoral year, the PF was the major winner, gaining six seats compared with three for the UPND and one for the MMD. The most **contested by-election** was held in Livingstone. It was seriously overshadowed by the mysterious death of the PF's Monze District Secretary Harrison Changa and violent clashes between the PF and the UPND, during which eight people were injured and a UPND vehicle was smashed. The election was postponed from 28 February to 14 March. Lawrence Evans (PF) took the parliamentary seat, beating his closest rival, Regina Musokotwan (UPND). The organisation of by-elections cost K (kwacha) 17 m up to June, way above of the K 5 m initially budgeted.

Infighting escalated within the ruling PF and two factions emerged, one led by Minister Geoffrey Bwalya Mwamba, who endorsed President Sata as the PF's sole candidate for the 2016 general elections, and the other led by Secretary General and Justice Minister Wynter Kabimba, who Geoffrey Bwalya Mwamba's supporters said was against Sata. Calls for Kabimba's resignation increased, backed by a petition signed by the majority of the ten provincial heads (Luapula, Northwestern and Western Province distanced themselves from the petition). At the same time, the opposition and the media pointed out that uncertainty about President Sata's health was one of the reasons why factionalism had escalated within the PF.

A very similar picture existed within the **major opposition party**, the MMD. Constant factionalism and defections since the party's foundation in 1991 had already led to the emergence of several off-shoots, including the current ruling PF. Removed from power in 2011 after 20 years of rule, the MMD soon faced leadership conflicts. The current party president Nevers Mumba, elected on 25 May 2012 in a landslide victory (870 votes to 422) over his closest rival, Felix Mutati, had failed to unify the party, despite the margin of votes, and was challenged from the onset, particularly after he expelled the national secretary, Richard Kachingwe. Kachingwe accused Mumba of having dual membership, as he was still the president of the Reform Party (RP) when he was elected president of the MMD. Kachingwe even appealed to the courts to remove Mumba from the party presidency, but without success. Until March, when the RP was finally dissolved, there were endless squabbles over whether Mumba was holding two party presidencies. In his own defence, Mumba insisted that the RP had ceased to exist in 2008 when he left it and that this had been communicated to the Registrar of Societies, who should have been held responsible for updating the records. It is worth nothing that the MMD is the third party headed by Nevers Mumba; in 1997, he had founded the National Citizens Coalition, which was disbanded because it failed to attract any electoral support.

New political parties also emerged. Former MMD minister of works and supply Mike Mulongoti launched the People's Party and the former MMD Lusaka province youth secretary, James Lukuku, founded the Republican Progressive Party. Peter Sinkamba, executive director of Citizens for a Better Environment, launched the Green Party on World Environment Day (5 June), former MMD defence minister George Mpombo formed the People's Democratic Party and finally, Daniel Pule, a Dunamis Church pastor, formed the United People's Jubilee Party. However, the Registrar of Societies refused to approve the name of Dan Pule's party, as it conflicted with the government's programme for the 2014 independence celebrations: the 50th Independence Jubilee.

Long gone was the PF's promise to deliver a **new constitution** within 90 days. The first draft had been released on 30 April 2012, put together by a 20-member technical committee appointed by Sata on the basis of the recommendations of previous review commissions. During the first half of 2013, this first draft underwent a public review throughout the country. On 31 October, the technical committee's spokesperson, Ernest Mwansa, announced that the final draft was ready to be printed and circulated, but the executive remained reluctant to make the document public. In early December, a consortium of civil society organisations, churches, student unions and political parties asked the government to release the final draft of the constitution immediately. Eventually, the anti-government 'Zambian Watchdog' and the 'Lusaka Times' released a copy, but scepticism remained as to whether the president would fulfil his promise and submit the constitution to a referendum. The official release of the constitution was still pending at the end of the year.

In the field of **political and civil rights**, the situation deteriorated under the PF government regarding respect for freedoms of speech, assembly and association. Instances of intimidation, harassment, direct and indirect censorship and unlawful detention of opposition politicians, journalists and civil society leaders were frequent. UPND president Hakainde Hichilema was arrested twice: for defamation of the president (17 January) and for advocating violence in Livingstone (26 February). MMD president Nevers Mumba was arrested for mismanagement of public funds (8 January) and for criticising President Sata on a 'Joy FM' radio programme (19 September). National Restoration Party leader Elias Chipimo was arrested and charged with unlawful assembly in Kitwe (2 May). On several occasions, opposition political parties were barred from holding rallies and were severely restricted in their ability to express alternative political views. Individual journalists and members of prominent civil society organisations (notably Brebner Changala of the 'Zambia Watchdog', Richard Sakala, editor of the 'Daily Nation', and McDonald Chipenzi, director of the Foundation for Democratic Process) were also arrested for presenting critical viewpoints to the public. With the help of China, the government set up a process of installing deep packet inspection (DPI) technology, which facilitated Internet surveillance and censorship. The government blocked direct Internet access to 'Zambian Watchdog' (www.zambianwatchdog.com) and also to news from **Barotseland** (including www.BarotsePost.com and www.RadioBarotseland.com), so they continued operating by using social media.

In the field of **human rights**, gay rights were on the 'hit list'. In April, a group of gay couples attempted to marry at the Lusaka Civic Centre but were stopped by the city council authorities. Later, human rights activist Paul Kasonkomona was arrested for supporting gay rights during a live interview on 'Muvi TV'. In November, a consortium comprising Civicus, Freedom House and 111 organisations from 46 countries called on the government to stop the implementation of the **Non-Governmental Organisation Act**, which had been approved by Rupiah Banda's executive in 2009 despite representations from civil society organisations and the PF, which was then in the opposition. The bill, which was considered unconstitutional and repressive by the NGO Coordinating Council, regulated the operation of thousands of civil society organisations in Zambia, granted sweeping powers to the executive to interfere in NGO operations and even to deregister organisations that were not acting 'in the public interest'. Towards the end of the year, the government backtracked slightly, and the opposition UPND was able to hold a rally in Mandevu, Lusaka, on the theme, 'no money, no jobs, and more suffering'. The Black Friday Campaigners and other civil society organisations organised a public assembly on 4 October to put pressure on government to release the draft of the constitution to the executive and the Zambian people simultaneously.

The **fight against corruption** took a prominent place, thanks to the actions of the Anti-Corruption Commission (ACC), which was created by the 2012 Anti-Corruption Act. As of 31 March, the ACC had investigated a total of 759 cases, though this included some cases carried over from 2012. Among the most publicised were those involving PF secretary general and Justice Minister Wynter Kabimba (accused of having received a bribe in exchange for a petrol/diesel contract awarded to Trafigura), Defence Minister Geoffrey Bwalya Mwamba (accused of having influenced the Zambia Electricity Supply Corporation to award his company a tender for telegraph poles), and former president Rupiah Banda (accused of several counts of corruption, including an oil deal), whose presidential immunity was lifted in March. As a result, Zambia improved its ranking (to 83rd out of 177 countries, with a score of 38) on the 2013 Corruption Perceptions Index.

Some **innovative policies** were introduced. In March, the PF government produced a simplified version of the budget, a 21-page 'Citizens' Budget'. This measure followed the publication of Zambia's low Open Budget Score (4 out of 100), which placed it in the group of countries that provide "scant or none" information to the public, below all other surveyed countries in southern Africa. In other innovative measures, the government set up a process to introduce biometric national registration cards embedded with security chips containing personal information about the holder.

Despite **media** harassment, the government issued broadcasting licences to three community radio stations ('Sun FM' in Ndola, 'KNC FM' in Kabwe and 'Kabang-abanga FM' in Solwezi) and a private TV station ('Chipata Television Station' in Eastern Province), and in September it launched newspapers in six local languages – 'Intanda', 'Ngoma', 'Tsopano', 'Lukanga', 'Liseli', and 'Imbila'.

Foreign Policy

Following established networks, PF secretary general and Justice Minister Wynter Kabimba spent a week in **Cuba** in February at the invitation of the central committee of the Cuban Communist Party. In March, Canada and Zambia signed the Foreign Investment Promotion and Protection Agreement, to protect Canadian investments in Zambia. According to the Canadian Foreign Affairs and International Trade Department, **Canadian mining investments** were worth over $ 6 bn, some 20% of all Canadian mining assets in Africa. The major ones included First Quantum Minerals (FQM) and Barrick Gold. In November, Mining Watch Canada launched a petition to stop a massive land grab by FQM in the Musele Kingdom in North Western Province. The expansion of FQM in these areas was controversial, and accompanied by a series of meetings with donors, local government and villagers in displacement zones.

April was the month of **China**. In his first trip abroad in almost half a year, President Sata travelled to China for a seven-day visit that coincided with the Boao Forum. Accompanied by five ministers and other high-ranking government officials, Sata spoke at the forum, and then continued with a state visit at the official invitation of China's new president, Xi Jingping. Zambia and China signed six bilateral agreements including: a loan from the China Development Bank Corporation for the construction of the

Mansa-Luwingu Road; a concessional loan from the Export and Import Bank of China for the Mbala-Nakonde Road; a framework agreement to promote small and medium enterprises in Zambia; an agreement for the funding of the Confucius Institute at the University of Zambia; and an agreement on cultural cooperation. Sata also commissioned the upgrading of Kenneth Kaunda International Airport in Lusaka to accommodate flights to China Jiangxi International. In April, the government introduced **Chinese as a foreign language** in selected secondary schools to address issues of communication related to the growing number of Chinese companies in Zambia. Sata also visited Japan to participate in the fifth Tokyo International Conference on African Development (TICAD V) on 1–3 June.

One of the major highlights of the year was the General Assembly of the UN World Tourism Organisation (**UNWTO**), which was held at Victoria Falls on 24–29 August. Co-hosted with Zimbabwe, the event attracted a lot of international attention and boosted the local economy in Southern Province. It attracted nearly 2,000 delegates, including foreign ministers, full delegates from UNWTO member states, delegates from countries worldwide, and a record 900 media delegates. President Sata, Foreign Affairs Minister Wylbur Simuusa, and Commerce Minister Emmanuel Chenda participated in the 68th Session of the UN General Assembly on 23 September in New York.

In November, Sata called for the establishment of more permanent missions in Zambia to strengthen **bilateral relations** with other countries. Receiving accreditation letters from 11 diplomatic representatives (Namibia, Mozambique, Russia, Switzerland, Poland, Philippines, Sri Lanka, Seychelles, the Netherlands, Côte d'Ivoire and Nepal), he identified Switzerland, Poland, Philippines, Sri Lanka, Seychelles, the Netherlands, Côte d'Ivoire and Nepal as countries with which to strengthen existing bilateral relations. The Netherlands had closed its embassy at the end of June and its interests in Zambia were thereafter represented at its embassy in Harare. The closure was related to an earlier decision to limit the number of development partners; the bilateral relationship between Zambia and the Netherlands would be predominantly economic. On the other hand, Sata announced that the government would open an embassy in Poland to strengthen bilateral relations.

Already a matter of routine, **Sata's embarrassing statements** caused opposition leaders, journalists and prominent public figures to criticise the head of state's sense of occasion at both the national and international level. In May, Sata criticised diplomats with an EU delegation who were holding a closed-door meeting with opposition leaders, saying that such acts were intrusive. In the same month, Sata was booed at an AU meeting after inappropriate comments about bald people, equating them with the disabled. It is worth noting that Sata attacked members of his own cabinet and Nevers Mumba for adopting a shaven hair style. At the same meeting, Sata surprised everyone by opposing regulations for the ICC, to which Zambia was a party, saying that the West should "try their relatives whose jurisdiction are they under". In October, Sata reversed his position on a maize deal with President Mugabe, under which he had promised 150,000 tonnes of maize valued at nearly $ 25 m to be delivered to **Zimbabwe** with no questions on payment asked in view of the country's severe food shortage situation, which Mugabe had called the "worst in living memory". There was another awkward moment in December, when Sata asked the ILO office in Zambia to create jobs in the country.

Socioeconomic Developments

GDP grew by 6%, below the 7% growth reached in 2012 due to a decline in copper prices. Zambian copper, the main export, accounted for 70% of African copper production and at least 60% of the country's total exports, its heavy reliance making it vulnerable to price variations. The global level of metal prices, as measured by the World Bank Metal Price Index, had fallen by 25% from the post-crisis highs and fell 6% from 2012. Consequently, in Zambia, the prices of copper fell by 14% from mid-February to mid-June (making a total of 27.5% since the post-crisis peak in 2011).

Despite being endowed with abundant water resources, mineral wealth and climatic conditions favourable for agriculture, Zambia continued to suffer from high **poverty** rates and unemployment (14%). The World Bank estimated that around 60% of Zambians were living below the national poverty line and 42% in extreme poverty. External debt increased to over $ 3 bn and two international credit agencies adjusted their sovereign credits towards the end of the year: Standard and Poor's lowered its economic outlook from 'Stable' to 'Negative' and Fitch downgraded theirs from B+ to B with a stable outlook. The national **budget deficit** was expected to reach 8.5% of GDP (the highest in years), against a target of 4.5%.

On 1 January, the Bank of Zambia rebased the **kwacha**, chopping off three zeroes. The new kwacha (KMW) circulated side-by-side with the old kwacha (ZMK) until 30 June. In March, the National Assembly debated a proposal to amend the Bank of Zambia Act so that it could more efficiently promote the operation of the **foreign exchange** system, as well as regulate and monitor: foreign exchange in-and outflows and amounts remitted; imports and exports of goods and other in- and outflows; international transactions in services; international transfers to or from non-residents; profits or dividends received in respect of investments abroad; borrowings and trade credits from nonresidents; investments in the form of equity and debt securities abroad; receipts of both principal and interest on loans to non-residents; and international money transfers into and out of Zambia.

In October, the government increased the **salaries** of the about 240,000 civil servants. Most received increases of 40%–50%, but rises ranged from 4% to 200%, with the highest increases given to the lowest-paid general workers, whose basic salaries increased to about K 3,000. However, some professional categories received the lowest increase and the strongest protests came from the **health sector**. In October, nurses, midwives and pharmacists throughout the country went on strike after being awarded only a 4% pay rise. The strike affected institutions in Western, Southern, Copperbelt, Eastern and Lusaka Provinces, including Zambia's largest hospital, the University Teaching Hospital, and central hospitals in Ndola and Kitwe. The government said it had actively negotiated with 12 unions representing nurses and allied workers, and the Zambia Union of Nurses Organisation explained that corrections would be made to the anomalies, but the strike continued for six days. The fact that the government had increased MPs' salaries for the third time since assuming power added to the sense of injustice. MPs's salaries had risen by a total of over 150% since the PF took over. In the mining sector, miners at Kansanshi Copper and Gold Mine (FQM) agreed to future salary increases of 10% in 2014, 8% in 2015, and 7% in 2016.

Unemployment remained an issue and employment creation was one of the most prominent promises of the PF, which had guaranteed to deliver more jobs and money to the people when it took office. Official figures indicated that the government had created 316,089 jobs (directly and indirectly) since assuming power. The government stance on maize meal alternated between liberalisation and protectionism. President Sata threatened to revoke the licences of millers who charged more than K 50 per 25 kg bag of breakfast meal. Nevertheless, the **cost of living rose** due to the government's removal of fuel and maize subsidies in May and also because of inflation in the prices of food and utilities towards the end of the year. The government increased fuel prices by over 21% (petrol 21.4%, diesel 21.5%, and kerosene 32.6%), making Zambian fuel prices the highest in the region. Amidst protests from civil society organisations, farmers and students, who expressed their displeasure on what they called 'Black Friday', Parliament voted against the reinstatement of subsidies on fuel and maize in July. Opponents, with the opposition MMD and UPND parties in the lead, pointed out that the removal of subsidies went against the PF's campaign promise of "more money in your pockets" and would affect the majority of Zambians, given the high levels of poverty and unemployment, but the cuts remained.

The **World Bank** approved a partnership strategy for Zambia for the period 2013–16, aimed at helping Zambia to reach its Vision 2030 of becoming a prosperous middle-income country. The partnership targets challenging policy fields and goals, poverty reduction, infrastructural development, anchoring inflation, increasing employment and the quality of governance being among the most important goals for the next three years. The **IMF** concluded another of its missions, but aimed to start talks about a new loan programme for Zambia in January 2014, due to the government's high spending, including on public wage increases and by-elections.

The country ranked 163th out of 187 on the **HDI**, which placed it directly in the group of countries with 'low human development'. Although the last year saw a small recovery, Zambia was still below the values it achieved during the 1990s and the HDI average for SSA in 2012 (0.448 compared with 0.475). Yet, according to the UN's second **World**

Happiness Report, Zambia still figured as the 91st happiest country in the world and the 5th happiest country in SSA.

As Zambia celebrated 49 years of independence, one of the main symbols of national pride, the 'Chipolopolo Boys' (a nickname for the national **football** team) became the first defending champion to be eliminated in the first round of the Africa Cup of Nations in 21 years and failed to qualify for the 2014 FIFA World Cup.

Edalina Rodrigues Sanches

Zimbabwe

The year saw the end of the Government of National Unity (GNU). A new constitution came into existence. The first half of the year was dominated by a controversial election, which was resoundingly won by the Zimbabwe African National Union-Patriotic Front (ZANU-PF). The second half saw Zimbabwe drifting back into economic problems. There were no significant shifts in international relations or socio-economic developments.

Domestic Politics

After months of wrangling and brinkmanship, on 17 January ZANU-PF and the two factions of the Movement for Democratic Change (MDC) finally agreed on a **draft constitution**, paving the way for the much-awaited referendum. President Robert Mugabe called this "the end of a marathon exercise", while MDC-T leader Morgan Tsvangirai labelled it "a defining moment for the country". The government had **funding problems** for both the election and the referendum. On 30 January, it was reported that principals in the GNU had tasked Justice and Legal Affairs Minister Patrick Chinamasa and Finance Minister Tendai Biti with sourcing money for the referendum and general elections from donors. About $ 85 m was needed for the referendum, while elections required $ 107 m. The Zimbabwe Electoral Commission (ZEC) had budgeted $ 220 m for the two events.

The reduction in the budget was a result of the abandonment of the delimitation exercise. On 11 March, Tendai Biti announced that Zimbabwe had issued a bond to raise funds for the referendum.

The **referendum** on the new constitution was held on 19 March, with all three GNU parties uncharacteristically on the same side, urging a 'yes' vote. The National Constitutional Assembly, which had unsuccessfully sought to delay the referendum, campaigned against the constitution, claiming it was not democratic and people-driven. There were concerns about the financing of the referendum. When the results were declared, the ZEC announced that the new constitution had been approved by an overwhelming majority of 3 m votes. Nearly 95% of those who participated had voted 'yes'. One of the key provisions of the new constitution was the limiting future presidents to two five-year terms. It also increased the number of legislators from 210 to 270, with 60 seats reserved for women.

On 22 May, Mugabe signed the **new constitution** into law, replacing the 1979 Lancaster House Constitution. This unleashed a wave of speculation and debate on the **election date**, which ZANU-PF wanted to be early. The new constitution required that a 30-day mandatory voter registration period be scheduled from the day the new constitution was published, while 56 days would be needed from the day the election date was decreed to the polling date. This meant ZANU-PF's target of holding the election when the GNU's term expired on 29 June would not be possible. This gave rise to debates, accusations and counteraccusations, with ZANU-PF insisting the 29 June date was feasible and some critics and experts maintaining the latest the election could be held was 31 October. ZANU-PF's insistence on an early date fuelled speculation, ranging from charges that ZANU-PF had a strategy to take advantage of the MDCs' lack of preparedness to suspicions that there were plots to rig the poll. ZANU-PF's desire for an early election date might have been driven by reports that the MDC-T was losing support. In a Freedom House-commissioned poll released in February, the Mass Public Opinion Institute reported that ZANU-PF support stood at 31%, up from 17% in 2010, with support for the MDC dropping from 38% in 2010 to 20%. On 4 May, the MDC-T rubbished the opinion poll, claiming the party would pick up 75% of the vote.

On 31 May, a landmark **Constitutional Court ruling** delivered by Chief Justice Godfrey Chidyausiku compelled President Mugabe to announce an election date by July 31. The person behind the court application was Jealousy Mawarire, whom the MDC-T claimed was a ZANU-PF stooge. In compliance with the court ruling, in a Government Gazette on 12 June, Mugabe unilaterally declared 31 July as the date for the harmonised national election, which immediately set him at loggerheads with Prime Minister Morgan Tsvangirai. On 13 June, an Extraordinary Government Gazette stated that the nomination court would sit on 28 June. Predictably, these unilaterally fixed dates became a source of tension and controversy among the GNU partners. Mugabe claimed he had been forced to set the dates by a court ruling and joined Tsvangirai in approaching the courts to have the elections postponed. There was widespread scepticism of Mugabe's sincerity, with claims that he was half-hearted in what was seen as his tokenistic pursuit of the case. This was interpreted as a strategy to outwit the MDCs, which appeared to be confirmed when, during the hearing of the case, the justice minister's attorney announced that the minister was abandoning his application to have the election date extended to 14 August. Tsvangirai's lawyer told the court the elections should be conducted under new electoral laws that would have to be passed through parliament in line with provisions of the new constitution. On 4 July, the Constitutional Court rejected the appeal to delay the elections. The ruling declared that the elections would proceed on 31 July in line with Mugabe's proclamation. As expected, both MDC factions were unhappy with the ruling, while the state media and ZANU-PF apologists welcomed it and flaunted it as confirmation that the rule of law prevailed in Zimbabwe.

In the run-up to the election, there was speculation about whether the two MDCs would be entering into an **anti-Mugabe election coalition**. While Tsvangirai appeared eager to forge a united front, Welshman Ncube, leader of the MDC-N, was reported to have dismissed coalition talks. On 21 April, Ncube defended his party's position, saying that, if they did not make a stand, Zimbabwe would be replacing one dictator with another. In the end, Ncube entered into a pact with Dumiso Dabengwa's Zimbabwe African People's Union (ZAPU), while Tsvangirai forged an alliance with former finance minister Simba Makoni's Mavambo/Kusile/Dawn and ZANU Ndonga. On 23 July, Ncube said he was yet to be approached by Tsvangirai's MDC about an anti-Mugabe coalition. He dismissed Tsvangirai's suggestion that Ncube did not want an alliance, calling it "the politics of deception". Commentators attributed the failure to forge an alliance to the political egos of the key players.

The **election campaign** was predictably acrimonious, with the usual accusations of violence and rigging being made by the MDC-T and ZANU-PF responding with characteristic denials and counteraccusations. The largely peaceful pre-election period was occasionally marred by reports of politically motivated violence in some rural areas. According to monitors, there was less violence than 2008, but there were reports of intimidation by pro-ZANU-PF supporters, militia and security personnel in the countryside. **Nikuv International Projects** (NIP), a secretive Israel-based company, featured prominently in the MDC-T's campaigns and in general public speculation, with allegations that it might be the key player in ZANU-PF's strategy to rig the elections. NIP, which specialises in population registration and election systems, had previously been accused of manipulating elections in the region. It was alleged to be involved in managing the electoral roll in cahoots with the Central Intelligence Organisation with a view to rigging the election in ZANU-PF's favour. The ZEC was also caught up in the speculation and was repeatedly warned by Tsvangirai against being involved in attempts to rig the poll. Tsvangirai confidently declared that the scale of the MDC-T's victory would make any rigging irrelevant.

The election was peaceful. When the election results were announced, ZANU-PF claimed massive victories in both the presidential and parliamentary elections. In the **presidential poll**, Mugabe won 60.6% of the vote, with Tsvangirai coming a distant second with 33.7%; Ncube was third with 2.7%. There were two other candidates: Dumiso Dabengwa of ZAPU got 0.7% and little known Kisinoti Mukwazhe got 0.3%. About 2% of the ballots were spoilt. In the **parliamentary vote**, ZANU-PF took 160 seats and the MDC-T 49, while an independent candidate won the remaining seat. With the proportional representation seats reserved for women, the election resulted in the following distribution of seats in the National Assembly: ZANU-PF 197, MDC-T 70, MDC-N 2, Independent 1. In the Senate, ZANU-PF, MDC-T and MDC-N took 37, 21 and 2 seats, respectively.

This was yet another **controversial election**. The MDCs unsurprisingly rejected the results, claiming the election had been massively rigged. Describing the election as "a huge farce", Tsvangirai said the nation was in mourning over the results. He claimed that over a million voters had been turned away from the polling stations and promised to fight the results legally and diplomatically. While ZANU-PF, its apologists and the state media quickly pronounced the election both free and fair, there were unclear signals from the cherry-picked observers. Many endorsed the freeness of the poll, but there was no agreement on its fairness. The AU observer mission on 2 August cryptically pronounced the election free and fair "from the campaigning point of view", and declared the elections "free, honest and credible". Notably, the mission stated that there were irregularities, but added that they were not of such a scale as to affect the election outcome. SADC observers agreed that the elections were free but did not declare them fair. On 1 August, the Zimbabwe Election Support Network (ZESN) – by far the largest group of domestic monitors with some 7,000 people on the ground across the country – stated that the elections were "seriously compromised". Echoing Tsvangirai's assertions, the group claimed that some 1 m voters had been unable to cast their ballots. According to ZESN, potential voters were much more likely to have been turned away from polling stations in MDC-T urban strongholds than in ZANU-PF's rural strongholds. The group further alleged significant pre-election irregularities, claiming that 99.7% of rural voters were registered on the electoral roll in June compared with only 67.9% of urban voters. On 8 August, the ZEC admitted mistakes, saying that 305,000 voters had been turned away and 207,000 other voters had received help when they marked their ballots. But the commission stuck to its original statement that the election was free and fair.

In a **legal challenge**, on 9 August Tsvangirai asked the Constitutional Court to nullify the controversial elections, arguing that he could have won if all his supporters had been allowed to vote. On 13 August, the High Court heard petitions by Tsvangirai for the ZEC to release voting data and related material to help back his main legal challenge to the elections. On 16 August, however, Tsvangirai announced that he had withdrawn his court case challenging Mugabe's re-election. In an affidavit filed at the Constitutional Court,

Tsvangirai gave his reason for this as the ZEC's refusal to release the election material he wanted to use in the court case. However, the Constitutional Court pressed ahead with the case, declaring that a petition challenging a presidential election "cannot be terminated by a withdrawal". On 20 August, Chief Justice Godfrey Chidyausiku handed down the unanimous decision of the Constitutional Court dismissing Tsvangirai's election petition. On the same day, it was announced by High Court judge Chinembiri Bhunu that Tsvangirai might face contempt of court charges for "disparaging remarks" he had made about the judiciary. The electoral court ordered the attorney general to investigate charges of contempt of court against Tsvangirai's lawyers for submitting – as part of its petition claims – that court judges were under the influence of ZANU-PF. Mugabe was sworn in as president on 22 August. By the end of the year, the MDC-T had not conceded defeat, and still regarded Mugabe's presidency as illegitimate.

On 10 September, Mugabe appointed a slightly trimmed **cabinet** of 26 members, down from 33 in the GNU. Largely recycled, it was a combination of hardliners and moderates. Significantly, the indigenisation and mining portfolios previously held by hardliners went to moderates, with Francis Nhema taking over the indigenisation portfolio and Walter Chidhakwa being appointed mining minister. In what was widely interpreted as a demotion, Saviour Kasukuwere, the militant former indigenisation minister, was moved to environment and tourism, and Obert Mpofu was moved to transport and infrastructure development. The finance ministry went to former justice minister Patrick Chinamasa. Emerson Mnangagwa, seen as a possible successor to Mugabe, was transferred from defence to justice. Another possible successor, Joice Mujuru, retained the vice presidency. Jonathan Moyo returned to the Ministry of Information.

The remaining year was dominated by the controversy surrounding the election and a return to intra-party politics. In November, it was reported that **factional fighting** had resurfaced in ZANU-PF. The public mudslinging was ignited by contentious provincial elections, seen as crucial in the succession saga. Elections for provincial chairmen in Manicaland, Midlands and Mashonaland Central were marred by allegations of vote rigging. As expected, the conflicts were between the Mujuru and Mnangagwa factions. There were public disagreements over the Mashonaland provincial elections between presidential spokesperson George Charamba and ZANU-PF secretary for administration Didymus Mutasa, a known Mujuru loyalist. Jonathan Moyo waded into the fight, defending Charamba. Tension had been bubbling below the surface for a long time as the feuding factions continued positioning themselves to take over from Mugabe.

ZANU-PF held its **14th National People's Conference** in Chinhoyi on 12–14 December under the theme 'ZIMASSET: Growing the Economy for Empowerment and Employment'. Some 7,000 delegates attended. Factional fighting reportedly intensified. Mugabe denounced divisions in the ruling party as factions positioned themselves in the on-going battle for the succession. Mugabe said that ZANU-PF could not build a united party "when we divide people into camps of those who belong to so-and-so and those who belong to so-and-so". The conference resolutions were the usual patriotic statements and calls for improvements in areas such as agriculture, social services, poverty eradication, infrastructure and utilities. Unsurprisingly, the 'illegal sanctions' imposed by 'Western imperialist countries' featured prominently. Interestingly, the party acknowledged factionalism but blamed it on the Western forces that were seeking illegal regime change. The party resolved to guard against these "uncanny machinations by the Western imperialists through factionalism and other divisive stratagems as new regime change tools".

Foreign Affairs

Zimbabwe's relations with the majority of African and Asian countries and organisations continued to be friendly. Relations with Western countries, which had appeared to be thawing despite the persistent 'illegal' sanctions mantra, dramatically worsened as Western countries publicly condemned the controversial elections. **SADC** continued its active involvement in Zimbabwe. A SADC summit on Zimbabwe's upcoming elections and funding, scheduled for Maputo (Mozambique) on 9 June, was inexplicably cancelled. There were reports that Mugabe had indicated he could not go to Maputo as he had more pressing election-related constitutional matters to attend to. Mugabe's office was at pains to explain that the president was not contemptuous of SADC, nor was he resisting the regional bloc's facilitation. In the run-up to the elections, Mugabe had become hostile to the regional bloc and, in an apparent threat to pull Zimbabwe out of SADC, he said on 6 July that Zimbabwe was in SADC voluntarily and could walk out of the organisation if it decided "to do stupid things". He was unhappy with SADC's facilitation role.

In their final report, released on 2 September, the SADC observer mission concluded that the elections had been "free, peaceful and generally credible", but crucially admitted that some irregularities cast doubt on their fairness. Although this was not the ringing endorsement that ZANU-PF needed, state media and ZANU-PF apologists used the statement to their advantage. In contrast to the SADC observer mission's ambivalence, the **SADC Council of NGOs** concluded that the scope and extent of the impact of the observed anomalies on the outcome of elections constituted "serious electoral deficits". This mission concluded that the credibility, legitimacy and free and fair conduct of the elections, and their reliability as the true expression of the will of the people of Zimbabwe had been highly compromised. In stark opposition to this, the **SADC Parliamentary Forum** Election Observation Mission to the elections concluded that the elections were "on the whole, a credible reflection of the will of the people of Zimbabwe" and declared the elections to have been free and fair. At the **SADC Summit** in Lilongwe (Malawi) on 18 August, the Heads of States and Governments endorsed Mugabe's electoral victory and called for the West to lift all sanctions imposed on Zimbabwe, with Malawi's President Banda saying Zimbabweans had suffered enough.

Zimbabwe's **relations with South Africa** were mixed. At times there was evidence of testy relations between Mugabe and President Zuma. There was speculation that ZANU-PF would have liked Zuma to be defeated at the ANC's 53rd Annual Conference in Mangaung in December 2012 and that ZANU-PF was working with expelled former ANC youth leader Julius Malema to undermine Zuma. In what was interpreted as a thinly veiled attack on Zuma, Mugabe said on 20 July that African countries should not spread lies about Zimbabwe. This came after Zuma had criticised Zimbabwe's preparations for the elections, saying the process was "not looking good". Mugabe expressed his reservations on Zuma's facilitation role, and publicly attacked Zuma's special adviser, Lindiwe Zulu, urging Zuma to call her to order. Mugabe had earlier insulted Zulu, calling her a "streetwalker" and "stupid idiotic woman". This came after she had indicated that SADC was looking for a one-month delay in the elections. On 4 August, Zuma congratulated Mugabe on his re-election, urging all political parties to accept the outcome of the polls. Despite the occasional public spats, South Africa continued to help Zimbabwe. On 25 January, a South African court temporarily halted a delivery of helicopters to the Zimbabwean military after a challenge by human rights group AfriForum. The group had made the urgent request following reports of a donation of South Africa's retired Alouette fleet. AfriForum was against giving the equipment to a force that it argued was not neutral. The South African defence ministry had indicated that the aircraft would be used only for spare parts. On 15 April, Finance Minister Tendai Biti announced that South Africa had approved $ 100 m in budgetary support to Zimbabwe. The money would help fund the poll.

After what had appeared to be a softening of its critical stance, **Botswana** again broke ranks with the rest of SADC on Zimbabwe by publicly rejecting the results of the elections. On 5 August, it called for an independent audit of the disputed poll, saying the elections could not be considered acceptably free and fair. Even after the SADC leaders' endorsement of the poll, Botswana maintained that its position had not changed. In contrast, Zimbabwe's relations with **Malawi** remained cordial. Despite having been close to Malawian President Joyce Banda's late adversary, Mugabe invited Banda to open the Zimbabwe International Trade Fair on 26 May. President Michael Sata of **Zambia** remained a close ally of Mugabe and promised in May to send 150,000 tonnes of maize to help drought-stricken Zimbabwe. Mugabe saluted Sata, describing him as a "grand man".

Relations with the EU appeared to have improved marginally at the beginning of the year, but deteriorated after the elections. On 5 March, state media announced that Mugabe had declared that Zimbabwe would not invite Western observers for the constitutional referendum and general election. The official reason given for this was the Western 'illegal' sanctions. As expected, the decision inevitably triggered a dispute in the GNU. On 25 March, the EU suspended sanctions against 81 officials and eight companies in

Zimbabwe. According to the EU statement, this decision was based on the conclusion of a "peaceful, successful and credible" referendum. The bloc still maintained its sanctions against Mugabe, nine senior ZANU-PF people and two companies. Following the announcement of the election results, the EU said it was concerned about alleged irregularities and reports of incomplete participation, as well as the identified weaknesses in the electoral process and a lack of transparency. On 22 August, the EU announced it would review relations with Zimbabwe given its "serious concerns" about the conduct of the elections.

Zimbabwe's relations with Western countries did not improve, not helped by their reaction to the conduct and results of the disputed elections, which the West had not been allowed to monitor. In a statement on 3 August, the **USA** said that the balance of evidence indicated that the announcement of the results was the "culmination of a deeply flawed process", citing irregularities relating to the electoral roll, unequal access to state media, a partisan security sector, and failure to implement the political reforms mandated by the new constitution, the Global Policy Agreement, and SADC. Relations with the **UK** remained similarly tense. This was not helped when, on 3 August, the Foreign and Commonwealth Office expressed concerns about the conduct of the elections, indicating that they had not been free, fair and credible. On 4 August, **Australia** also raised doubts about the credibility of the election results, saying that the remaining sanctions on Zimbabwe would continue. On 3 August, **Canada** expressed serious concerns about the reported irregularities and lack of transparency in the democratic process, stating these called into question whether the results could credibly represent the will of the people. On 26 September, in his speech to the 68th UN General Assembly in New York, Mugabe berated the USA and the UK for imposing "illegal and filthy sanctions" on Zimbabwe. The US delegation walked out.

Good relations with traditional allies in the east continued. Among those invited to monitor the elections were Iran and **China**, who promptly endorsed the results as soon as they were announced. In May, the Ministry of Energy and Power Development announced that a major Chinese bank had agreed to finance construction of the Hwange thermal power station. However, it remained unclear which Chinese bank would provide the funding and what portion of the production costs would be covered. On 11 November, Finance Minister Chinamasa announced that China would lend Zimbabwe $ 320 m to pay for the expansion of the Kariba hydropower station. However, China did not seem too enthusiastic: in November, Chinamasa went to China looking for budgetary support but came back empty-handed. Later in the month, it was revealed that Zimbabwe was seeking a $ 10 bn bailout from China to kick-start the economy, and in the same month it was reported that officials from the government and the Reserve Bank of Zimbabwe (RBZ) were in China seeking to negotiate a $ 4 bn loan. By the end of the year, the loan and bailout had not materialised. On 10 August, the then deputy mining minister, Gift Chimanikire revealed that a deal had been struck between **Iran** and the Zimbabwe government that would see Zimbabwe exporting uranium to Iran. Zimbabwe dismissed the report, denying that there was ever such a deal. In July, Education and Sports Minister David Coltart announced he was vising **South Korea** for bilateral talks to get Korean maths and science teachers to teach in Zimbabwean schools. It was not clear what trajectory relations would take in post-GNU Zimbabwe.

Relations with multilateral financial institutions were mixed. In September, the **AfDB** said the IMF-supervised economic reform was indicative of the significant improvement in Zimbabwe's cooperation on economic policies and its commitment to address its arrear problems. Earlier in July, the bank had launched a $ 24 m capacity-building project for public finance and economic management as Zimbabwe stepped up efforts to tackle its $ 10.7 bn external debt. As at 31 December, overdue payments to the **IMF** amounted to $ 81.7 m of which $ 16.5 m were charges and interest. In July, the IMF concluded that Zimbabwe remained in debt distress, with total external debt estimated at 88% of GDP, of which 50% of GDP was in arrears. According to the IMF, the external arrears continued to stifle economic growth by limiting the country's access to new financing. The **World Bank**'s lending programme in Zimbabwe remained inactive due to arrears, with the bank's role limited to technical assistance and analytical work.

Socioeconomic Developments

The economy seemed to get into trouble after the election. However, on average there was no huge decline in stability and no sharp decline in **economic indicators**. RBZ figures showed that the all prices consumer price index fell marginally to 100.3%, down from 102.9% in 2012. The year-on-year price increase was 0.3%. According to Economist Intelligence Unit (EIU) estimates, the real GDP growth was 2.2%. The national budget unveiled in December revised growth forecasts down to 3.4% from an earlier 5.5% projection. The national budget was presented later than usual because the government was looking for budgetary support. The EIU put the nominal GDP at $ 2.5 bn, up from $ 2.3 bn in 2012. Manufacturing declined by 5.3%. The low growth was attributed to lack of investment and excessive imports. The current account balance was –$ 0.6 bn up from –$ 416 m in 2012, while total international reserves dropped from $ 576 m in 2012 to $ 437 m. In the budget statement, the finance minister put the external debt at more than $ 10 bn. The external debt stock dropped marginally from $ 7,388 m to $ 7,088 m. The stock of accumulated arrears accounted for $ 4.72 bn, making up 78% of total debt stock. On 30 January, Finance Minister Tendai Biti announced that the country had only $ 217 left in its public account the previous week, after paying civil servants. He explained that he was making this revelation to show that the country had no money to finance the election. On 11 March, Biti announced that Zimbabwe had raised $ 40 m from a special bond floated to the local unit of Old Mutual and the state pension fund to help finance the constitutional referendum. He said the one-year bond would attract an interest rate of 7%.

On 22 October, the cabinet adopted the Zimbabwe Agenda for Sustainable Socio-Economic Transformation (**ZimAsset**), a five-year development programme extracted from ZANU-PF's election manifesto, aimed at transforming the country's economic fortunes and increasing growth from 6.1% in 2014 to 9.9% by 2018. An important feature of the programme was the proposal to leverage the country's natural resources to source external capital. The economic road map would run from October 2013 to December 2018.

Zimbabwe performed poorly in a number of **international league tables**. It was ranked 173rd out of 185 economies in the annual Doing Business survey and was ranked 172nd in the UNDP's Human Development Report with an HDI of 0.397, putting the country in the low human development category. The country also fared badly on some **individual indicators**. The poverty headcount ratio was 72%; average life expectancy remained fairly low at 52.7 years; and gross national income per capita in PPP terms was $ 424. However, at 90.7%, Zimbabwe's literacy rate remained the highest in Africa and among the highest in the global South.

No major economic changes with implications for the humanitarian situation occurred during the first half of the year. In terms of **food security**, prolonged dry spells and erratic rainfall patterns affected agricultural production. According to the results of the Zimbabwe Vulnerability Committee Assessment (ZimVAC) appraisal, 25% of rural households were projected to be food insecure at the peak of the agricultural season. This was a 32% increase in food insecure people compared to the previous season and represented 2.2 m people at peak hunger season not being able to meet their annual food requirements. On 11 June, UN agencies reported that Zimbabwe would require at least $ 131 m in aid, the bulk for food assistance after a failed farming season left nearly 1.7 m people facing hunger.

Public health issues during the year included typhoid, diarrheal disease and suspected cholera outbreaks, as well as floods in 12 rural districts and six urban localities in six provinces. Typhoid cases carried over from 2012, together with high levels of diarrhoea within the first half of the year, pointing to inadequacies in the provision of water, sanitation and hygiene promotion services. According to the Ministry of Health and Child Welfare weekly report for the week ending 8 December, there were 85 cases of typhoid in the country. Malaria outbreaks left 370 people dead, with 428,320 others treated for the disease. The government embarked on a national programme that saw all children under the age of 15 receiving praziquantel and albendazole for treatment of intestinal worms and bilharzia. Progress was reported in the country's response to **HIV/AIDS**. According to the National AIDS Council, 15% of Zimbabweans were HIV-positive. The estimated adult HIV incidence (15–49 years) was 0.831. The estimated number of people living with HIV was 1,242,768, with 58,472 new infections. The estimated number of AIDS orphans was 941,024. The anti-retroviral treatment (ART) coverage was 86.1%.

Despite some improvements, the **education sector** continued to experience problems with staffing, equipment and funding, although some funding was provided by the Education Transition Fund, a mechanism to allow donors control over their funds. In 2013, $ 25 m was earmarked for the fund, up from $ 12 m in 2012. There are some 106,000 teachers in the country and about 30,000 more were required. Threats of strikes haunted the sector throughout the year. As early as January, the Zimbabwe Teachers' Association, the largest union of teachers, announced it had lined up annual general meetings at provincial level across the country to discuss, among other things, deteriorating conditions of service for members. The more combative Progressive Teacher's Union regularly threatened to take strike action. The state-controlled media was supportive of the unions' tough stance and threats, interpreting these as a condemnation of the MDCs, whose ministers were responsible for education (MDC-N) and finance (MDC-T) in the GNU.

In September, it was reported that the Bankers' Association of Zimbabwe had set aside $ 620 m to **finance agriculture**. Individual farmers and suppliers were free to access the funds. Earlier, CBZ Bank had secured $ 100 m from the African Export and Import Bank to support agriculture. On 2 October, Chinamasa announced $ 161 m support for agriculture. The facility would be for the government's input support programme targeting 1.6 m communal, old resettled, small-scale and A1 farmers. This brought the total support package for agriculture to nearly $ 1 bn.

The **indigenisation drive** continued to be a controversial and polarising issue, even within ZANU-PF. Before the election, there was public disagreement between the minister of youth development, indigenisation and empowerment and the RBZ governor over the indenisation of banks, with the former seemingly protecting the sector. On 11 January, Impala Platinum Holdings (Implats) subsidiary Zimplats agreed to sell a 51% stake in its platinum operations to indigenous entities in Zimbabwe for $ 971 m, bringing the company in line with the country's indigenisation plan.

On 19 December, Finance Minister Chinamasa presented the 2014 national **budget** amounting to $ 4.2 bn. Recurrent expenditure accounted for 73%. Notably, cumulative expenditure to November had amounted to $ 3.5 bn against a target of $ 3.4 bn, resulting in expenditure overrun of $ 130 m. Total revenue collections up to November amounted to $ 3.36 bn, against a target of $ 3.4 bn, resulting in a negative variance of $ 35 m. In an apparent response to widespread speculation about the return of the Zimbabwe dollar, Chinamasa reiterated that the economy would continue using the multiple currency regime.

Zimbabwe's controversial **Marange diamonds** were in the news for most of the year. In June, the mines and energy portfolio committee raised the alarm about the lack of accountability for the sale and smuggling of diamonds from Marange. This was costing the treasury hundreds of millions of dollars in lost revenue. On 17 September, in a move spearheaded by Belgium, the EU agreed to lift sanctions on the state-owned diamond-mining firm the Zimbabwe Mining Development Corporation (ZMDC). Belgium said lifting EU sanctions on ZMDC would increase Zimbabwe's tax revenues by $ 400 m a year. In December, it was reported that Zimbabwe was to auction 300,000 carats of diamonds in the EU. On 13 December, mining company DTZ-OZ GEO announced it had found conglomerate deposits capable of producing 2.5 m carats of top quality diamonds in the Chimanimani area.

Amin Y. Kamete

www.ingramcontent.com/pod-product-compliance
Lightning Source LLC
LaVergne TN
LVHW080114011026
849160LV00013B/1094
* 9 7 8 9 0 0 4 2 7 4 7 7 8 *